D0402992

ALSO BY ANN HAGEDORN

Beyond the River

Ransom

Wild Ride

SAVAGE PEACE

Hope and Fear in America, 1919

Ann Hagedorn

Simon & Schuster
NEW YORK · LONDON · TORONTO · SYDNEY

SIMON & SCHUSTER
Rockefeller Center
1230 Avenue of the Americas
New York, NY 10020

First Simon & Schuster hardcover edition April 2007

SIMON & SCHUSTER and colophon are trademarks
of Simon & Schuster, Inc.

For information about special discounts for bulk purchases,
please contact Simon & Schuster Special Sales at
1-800-456-6798 or business@simonandschuster.com

Designed by Paul Dippolito

Manufactured in the United States of America

1   3   5   7   9   10   8   6   4   2

Library of Congress Cataloging-in-Publication Data
Hagedorn, Ann.
Savage peace : hope and fear in America, 1919 / Ann Hagedorn.
p.   cm.
Includes bibliographical references and index.
1. United States—History—1919–1933.   2. Nineteen-nineteen, A.D.
3. United States—Social conditions—1918–1932.   4. United States—Politics and
government—1913–1921.   5. United States—Race relations—History—20th century.
6. World War, 1914–1918—Influence.   7. World War, 1914–1918—Social aspects—
United States.   8. World War, 1914–1918—Peace.   I. Title.
E766.H34   2007
973.91'3—dc22   2006051258
ISBN-13: 978-0-7432-4371-1
ISBN-10:   0-7432-4371-4

In memory of Dwight

and

To Elizabeth

Contents

PART III · SUMMER: PASSION

PART IV · AUTUMN: STRUGGLE

History is a record of the incessant struggle of humanity against ignorance and oppression.

—HELEN KELLER, 1918

SAVAGE PEACE

Armistice Day 1918

We are here to see, in short, that the very foundations of this war are swept away. Those foundations were the private choice of a small coterie of civil rulers and military staffs. Those foundations were the aggression of great Powers upon the small. Those foundations were the power of small bodies of men to wield their will and use mankind as pawns in a game. And nothing less than the emancipation of the world from these things will accomplish peace.

— WOODROW WILSON, JANUARY 1919

Somewhere beyond the mist and the misery on that November morning, six men met in a railcar to end a war. News of the truce moved through the trenches on the trembling lips of soldiers waiting for the screams of flying shells to cease before they believed what they were told. Some heard it first from their captains who distributed strips of paper that read: "Cease firing on all fronts. 11/11/11. Gen. John J. Pershing." Others would never know. They were the unlucky ones killed in the fragile hours before 11 A.M., before the fighting abruptly stopped. The silence, so unfamiliar, was almost as unsettling as the sounds, as if a giant hand suddenly lay across this land of rotting flesh to hush the din of battle. Silence. Prayers. Tears. Then came the roar of cheering and the popping of bonfires piled high with captured ammunition and anything that could burn. The madness was ending, or so it seemed. And fear was giving way to hope.

"One minute we was killing people," a soldier later said, "and then the world was at peace for the first time in four years. It seemed like five minutes of silence and then one of us said, 'Why don't we go home?' "

"I shall never forget the sensation," wrote an officer who climbed out of the trenches when he saw rockets signaling the cease-fire. Onto the open, unprotected ground, he walked toward the front lines of battle. The sun shining on his vulnerability, he moved tentatively, as if the earth beneath each foot might cave in. First he saw German helmets and caps vaulting into a distant haze and then beyond a ridge he saw German soldiers dancing a universal jig of joy. "We stood in a dazed silence unable to believe that at last the fighting was over."

It was at once a magnificent and a brutal day. After 1,563 days of war on the Western Front, no one, on the front lines or at home, would forget the moment news of peace entered their lives. Especially moved were those who carried in their hearts and minds the greatest hopes for what the end of the war could mean. In the parlors and factories and fields of their future lives, they would tell the stories of where they were and what they were doing on the day in 1918 when the Armistice came. They would talk of lost friends and of bold dreams, of expectations and of plans for the world they had risked their lives to save. "The nightmare is over," wrote the African-American leader W. E. B. Du Bois. "The world awakes. The long, horrible years of dreadful night are passed. Behold the sun!"

Sergeant Henry Lincoln Johnson, America's first soldier to win the Croix de Guerre, France's Medal of Honor, surely would not forget. His twenty-one wounds still stung with the memory of the battle for which he had won his medal. Sergeant Johnson was in the Vosges Mountains in France on November 11, very near the German border. Low on supplies, short on water and food, and exhausted, the men of Johnson's regiment, the 369th, were setting the American record for the most consecutive days under fire: 191 in all. Sharing blankets on that brisk morning—one for every four soldiers—they cheered upon hearing of the truce, some filling the gray, sober air with songs. They must have felt they had learned all that the universe could teach them about fighting, about brotherhood, about the will to survive. The 369th was the first black regiment to arrive on the Western Front and now it would soon be the first American division to cross the Rhine River into Germany. "They had achieved the impossible," wrote one of their commanders. "These men were going home as heroes."

Two thousand miles northeast of the Vosges Mountains on a vast frontier of tundra and fir in northern Russia, the moment that made the Western world hold its breath came and went unnoticed. Fifteen thousand Allied soldiers, including at least seven thousand Americans, were scattered across hundreds of miles radiating out from the port of Archangel on the Dvina River, twenty-six miles from the White Sea. On the morning of November 11, there was no cheering and there was no relief. Isolated by long delays in receiving mail and blocked from cable communications, the troops in Russia were not told about the Armistice, and even if they had known, there were no orders for the Allied North Russia Expeditionary Force to cease firing. While their compatriots in the west slipped into reveries of life back home and their families laid out plans for joyous homecomings, a contingent of American soldiers of the 339th Infantry was fighting its hardest battle yet. In temperatures hovering at 60 degrees below zero and in shoes that had worn through six weeks before, around the time the snow had begun to fall, they were trying to defend an American outpost two hundred miles from Archangel. They would remember the day for the battle they had fought and for the one hundred soldiers who would die in the four days that the battle lasted. On November 11, Sergeant Silver Parrish, of Bay City, Michigan, wrote in his diary, "We were atacked on our flank front and rear bye about 2500 of the enemy & their Big field Guns. We licked the [Bolsheviks] good & hard but lost 7 killed and 14 wounded."

The long, steady scream of flying shells would continue to split the Arctic stillness for many more months.

ဆ

In Paris, at exactly 11 A.M., guns boomed, bells rang, and American and French flags seemed to fall out of the sky, hanging from balconies, dangling out of windows, and waving from rooftops. Thousands of people shouted "Vive la Paix!" as they swarmed the Place de la Concorde and moved up the Champs-Elysées. On the balcony of the Paris Opera House, a chorus led a crowd of twenty thousand in singing "La Marseillaise." "The song bursting from that crowd was enough to stir the spirits of the heroic dead," wrote the American journalist Ray Stannard Baker, who was there in the throng. "Such a thrill comes not once in a hundred years."

News of the signing of the Armistice had traveled swiftly to America by transatlantic cable, arriving at the State Department at approximately 2:25 that morning. At 2:50 A.M. the government informed the press that the war would end at 6 A.M., Eastern Standard Time, and that the terms of the Armistice would be announced shortly thereafter. As early as 3 A.M. Americans awakened to the sounds of victory rippling through their streets, moving westward with the rising sun. They rolled out of bed to join the delirious throngs, grabbing wooden spoons from cupboards to bang on everything from tin pans to garbage cans, clanging bells as big as cows' heads, tying copper kettles and dishpans to the bumpers of every kind of vehicle, and moving their feet in rhythm with the chiming of church bells and the unrestrained cheering that only intensified in volume and energy as the day progressed.

The month of November had been unseasonably cold on the East Coast, so cold, in fact, that a mail carrier flying between New York and Washington earlier in the month encountered a blizzard, at seven thousand feet, for nearly forty miles. The snow was so thick, the pilot said, he could not see the wings of his machine and the flight so frigid that the government decided it must provide electrically heated clothing for the pilots of its new Air Mail Service. It had been a harsh autumn nationwide, but for more reasons than the weather. Death lists from the war competed with those from the raging epidemic known as the Spanish flu. In the last week of October, at the height of the second wave of the outbreak, more than five thousand people had died in New York City and three thousand in Philadelphia. The death toll nationwide for that month alone would be nearly twenty thousand. Military posts were especially hard hit. "We have been averaging 100 deaths per day," wrote a doctor in Surgical Ward No. 16 at Camp Devens, in Massachusetts, where seventeen thousand soldiers and staff had died by the end of October. Although the war always up-staged the flu in news coverage, the flu took a fearful toll on the nation. Even little girls jumped rope to the chant: "I once knew a bird and its name was Enza. I opened a window and in-flu-Enza."

Rumors of peace, debates over Prohibition and the recent elections, and, of course, baseball were all popular distractions from the anxieties and fears inherent to a season of darkness and death. Babe Ruth helped lead the Boston Red Sox to a World Series victory in October, and Ty Cobb had been the American League's leading batter for the 1918 season. The Re-publicans had just recaptured control of both the Senate and the House of Representatives, causing considerable consternation in the White House, where the Democratic president, Woodrow Wilson, believed a unified gov-ernment was essential to achieve his goal of reconstructing the world. The elections too had boosted the number of states prohibiting the legal sale and consumption of alcohol. Prohibition was now only one state away from becoming the Eighteenth Amendment to the Constitution—cause for some to applaud and others to shudder. After Germany and Austria, said the Anti-Saloon League, alcohol was *the* enemy—on whose head the forces of temperance heaped the blame for the rising number of labor dis-turbances; for fuel shortages, because breweries and saloons used more coal than all the nation's schools and churches combined; and for the scarcity of sugar. "Did Booze ever benefit you?" read one ad. "Did it ever add to the happiness of your family?"

Nothing, however, distracted the people from their woes as much as their hopes for peace. And so it was that on the morning after the election returns, on November 7, Americans had awakened to the news they most wanted to hear: that the Germans had signed the Armistice and by 2 P.M. the war would be over. Although the news was false, paperboys bellowed, "The Germans gave up!" as they peddled *Extra* editions with gripping dis-patches from London and Paris about the Armistice. The nation broke into frantic revelry, only to learn late that night and early the next morning that the war had not yet ended. On November 8, the *Washington Post* reported,

"No one can say now with any certainty when the Armistice will be signed or when the fighting will stop." Three days later, an anxious populace awakened to the same news—and again believed it. This time it was real.

November 11 was a mild, springlike day in most of the United States— so unusual that chilly autumn. Perhaps the millions of people celebrating the Armistice, their souls aflame with the passions of victory and hope, had the power nearly to change the season, the way an earthquake can reverse the flow of a river. From sunup to sunup, they opened windows and unfurled flags, stood on rooftops tossing the shredded pages of telephone books, built bonfires with anything made of wood that could be easily detached, and waded through ankle-deep confetti, waving newspapers with two-inch headlines that read:

"ARMISTICE SIGNED: THE GREATEST DAY IN THE HISTORY OF NATIONS HAS DAWNED"

Stunts and lunacy were abundant. In New Jersey, a soldier on leave climbed a five-story building in Jersey City and at the top of a flagpole on the roof, 125 feet from the ground, he lost his grip and fell to the street, landing, unharmed and still cheering, on the cloth top of an automobile moving slowly through the crowd. In Chicago, funeral corteges of black hearses paid a tribute to war's end, one with a band marching next to it playing Chopin's "Funeral March." In San Diego sailors sprinkled countless containers of talcum powder on the crowds, while ships rang their bells and factories tied their whistles open.

The ear-splitting, horn-blowing, flag-waving mayhem spurred immediate—and premature—repeals of health regulations that, because of the flu, had prohibited public gatherings in churches, schools, theaters, and saloons since late September. Although the danger had hardly passed and the end of the war would enable a resurgence, the illusion that the nation's two biggest killers, war and flu, were now dead ruled the day. Doors opened. Churches filled as quickly as bars. Streets throbbed with the beat of a public heart that had been broken and mended in turns, creating a mentality of victory and defeat, of heroes and enemies, of high aspirations for all that democracy could mean. They carried the flags and sang the songs, each step in rhythm with every patriotic tune ever written, expecting nothing less than heaven.

෨෬

The sun rose at 6:47 A.M. in Washington, D.C., on November 11, where President Woodrow Wilson was informed of the Armistice at breakfast, shortly after seven. He immediately gave orders for all government employees to take the day off, and, with a pencil, he wrote his announcement to the nation, to be sent to the press: "My fellow countrymen. The armistice was signed this morning. Everything for which America fought has been accomplished. It will now be our fortunate duty to assist by example, by sober, friendly counsel and by material aid in the establishment of just democracy throughout the world."

Six hours later, the president stood in the House of Representatives before both houses of Congress, the cabinet, the diplomatic corps, and the U.S. Supreme Court. It was there, nineteen months before, that Wilson had asked the nation to go to war. Looking out at the hastily convened session with the solemnity of a warrior beginning a battle rather than ending one, he announced that the aims and hopes of the enemies of militarism had been achieved. "Armed imperialism" he said, "is at an end." And then he slowly read the thirty-four terms of the Armistice. From the second stipulation onward the grand chamber, where applause was strictly forbidden while Congress was in session, nearly shook from the furor of clapping hands, standing exultations, and screeching cheers. At precisely 1:21 P.M., Wilson declared the official end of the war, barely completing the seven words "The war thus comes to an end" before the tumult of victory cut him off.

That evening, in a city wild with joy, President and Mrs. Wilson rode in an open auto up and down Pennsylvania Avenue through crowds so dense that the Secret Service could barely force a space for the car and so immersed in revelry that only on the couple's return trip, amid the flickering light of bonfires, did the crowd even notice the presence of their president. When they did, they brought the car to a standstill long enough for a soldier carrying an American flag to force his way to the back of the car and, reaching forward, to thrust the large flag above Wilson's head. Apparently unalarmed, the president stood up and saluted the soldier. Then for the next two blocks he continued to stand, waving his own small flag and bowing to the pulsing crowds.

Despite the delirium and the pomp, Wilson's November 11 was no less consumed with the sober questions that would shape the peace. Would he, the president of the United States, dare to travel to Europe for the peace conference, although no U.S. president had ever left the country while in office? The people of Europe demanded that he come—this man who seemed to be the voice of their own aspirations. Europe's ruling class, however, which scoffed at Wilson's League of Nations and his notion of permanent peace, preferred that he stay home. But if he chose not to go, what would the consequences be? Who could fight as well as he against the greed, distrust, and fear that could rise up and set the stage for new wars? And if he chose to go, what would it mean to leave his nation during the transition from war to peace, sure to be an unstable, disquieting time?

Perhaps the biggest question of all was whether Wilson could fulfill his promise to the people of his own nation who had believed his pledge in 1916 of keeping America out of the war and who now trusted his promise of an enduring peace based on justice, equality, and respect for the common man, not on imperialistic self-interest. Was it possible that this man who seemed unafraid to dream of a better world could bring the masses of humanity to share that dream?

"Wilson has yet to prove his greatness," Ray Stannard Baker wrote in his diary in Paris that November. "The fate of a drama lies in its last act, and Wilson is now coming to that. Can he dominate the seething mass of suspicion and disbelief? And when it comes to the crucial point, can we Americans trust ourselves? Do we really believe what Wilson preaches? Are we willing to make real sacrifices and take on responsibilities to bring about the new heaven and the new earth?"

ରର

On Armistice Day, Theodore Roosevelt checked into a New York City hospital with severe sciatica; Samuel Gompers, the president of the American Federation of Labor, was in Washington for the funeral of his daughter, a victim of the flu; John Edgar Hoover, a young lawyer in the Department of Justice, had planned to dine with the daughter of a prominent Washington attorney, but she did not keep the date; A. Mitchell Palmer, the War Department's alien property custodian, responsible for confiscating, managing, and sometimes selling assets owned by Germans in America, announced the upcoming sale of property valued at approximately $200 million, including $200,000 worth of tea and 346 pearls, three rubies, and two emeralds valued at $2.25 million; Douglas Fairbanks, the silent film star who had just raised $7 million in Liberty Bonds for the war effort, left the nation's capital on a coast-to-coast tour to raise $25 million more. And suffragist Alice Paul was quoted in newspapers about the upcoming battle in the Senate: "Before these hundred days remaining in this Congress have gone, the suffrage amendment shall have passed!"

The poet and journalist Carl Sandburg was writing news stories out of Stockholm, Sweden, where he had been interviewing a Russian source who worked for the Bolshevik leader V. I. Lenin. British aviator Captain John Alcock was a prisoner of war in Turkey beginning his thirteenth month in captivity and working on his plan to fly an airplane nonstop across the Atlantic once he was freed. And the popular American writer who used the pseudonym David Grayson was standing in the throng at the Opera House in Paris, taking notes for one of his next books.

In celebration of the Armistice, Albert Einstein, a young German physicist teaching in Berlin, wrote a joyful letter to his sister: "The great event has taken place! . . . That I could live to see this!" At the same time in London, an international committee of astronomers and physicists announced its ambitious plan to send two expeditions, one to South America and one to Africa, to test Einstein's general theory of relativity and to demonstrate through science the value of global cooperation. Weather permitting, they would observe an unusually long total eclipse of the sun on May 29 to determine whether the sun's gravity could bend the light of the stars, as Einstein's theories predicted. With war's end, scientists could now focus their attention on the revolutionary concepts that Einstein's papers, smuggled out of Germany across the battlefields of Europe to England, had expressed.

For Roger Baldwin, who had protested the war and refused to fight, the day was memorable for the obvious relief of war's end, and for more. A firm believer that physical force was not a method for achieving any goal—whether or not the battle was for a worthy cause—Baldwin, a Harvard graduate and an outspoken advocate of free speech, was serving a one-year sentence for violating the Selective Service Act. This was his thirty-second day in the Tombs which, true to its name, was New York City's dark, dungeon-like jailhouse. And on this day, two U.S. marshals escorted him out of the Tombs to a better facility in Newark, New Jersey, where he would remain for the rest of his sentence.

Baldwin was one of thousands of Americans in jail in November of 1918 for violating the 1917 Selective Service Act or for violating the Espionage Act of 1917 or its amended 1918 version, known also as the Sedition Act, which condemned dissenting voices that allegedly threatened the security of the nation at war. In October one man had been sentenced to six months in the workhouse for saying he preferred Germany's kaiser to President Wilson. Another was sentenced to ten years in prison for delivering speeches in which he called conscription unconstitutional. Yet another received a twenty-year sentence and a fine of $10,000 for telling a Liberty Bond salesman that not only did he not want to buy any bonds but he also hoped the "government would go to hell."

At the Tombs that day, Baldwin left behind several such convicts, including a twenty-one-year-old Russian girl, Mollie Steimer, recently sentenced to fifteen years in prison for violating the Sedition Act by distributing leaflets that opposed American intervention in Russia. Outspoken about her preference for prison over surrender of her beliefs, Steimer had been at the Tombs since late August, when she was arrested. This "slip of a girl," as Emma Goldman would later call her, was her own field of force, despite her tiny, unobtrusive stature and her young age. Stirring up heated debates about free speech, about the meaning of the espionage and sedition laws, and about the harshness of prison sentences, Steimer agitated government men like J. Edgar Hoover, for whom she would soon become a fixation.

From her jail cell, Steimer may have heard the excited multitudes on the streets of New York and the loud clanging and singing in celebration of the Armistice, or she may have learned of the Armistice from Harry Weinberger, her lawyer, who visited the Tombs upon hearing of his own great victory: that the U.S. Supreme Court had granted Steimer's bail and that of her co-defendants, three Russian immigrants given twenty-year sentences also because of the allegedly seditious leaflets. At their trial, Weinberger had described his young clients as "liberty-loving" with a dream of a better life for their people. To be pro-Russian, Weinberger had argued, was not to be pro-German. And to protest the U.S. invasion of a nation struggling for its own new day in a revolution that the defendants viewed as progress for their homeland was not a violation of a law enacted for the purposes of protecting the United States during a war with Germany. How could pro-Russian leaflets fluttering onto Broadway from the seventh-floor restroom window of the shirtwaist factory where Steimer worked profoundly damage the war effort against Germany? "Sad is the day when America becomes afraid of mere words that are spoken or printed," Weinberger wrote.

Now, with the news of the Armistice, Weinberger knew that his argument for bail was stronger than ever. Without a war, there was no security-related reason to continue the incarceration of Steimer and the three young men. After all, they had been convicted and held without bail on the premise that they were endangering the nation while it was at war with Germany. Now, with the war over, Weinberger planned to push again for their release. But the Supreme Court saved him the trouble. While the justices were sitting in Congress listening to their president define the terms of the Armistice, Weinberger received a letter from a Supreme Court clerk saying that the High Court had approved bail for his young clients. Filled with renewed hope that the convictions might be overturned, Weinberger immediately began the daunting task of raising bail funds, $40,000 in all.

At the Tombs that day, male prisoners were taken out of their cells into the prison yard and told to rejoice. Steimer remained in her cell, with its walls covered in newspaper clippings about people she admired, such as Eugene Debs and John Reed. "Peace has come," she said to her cell mate, Agnes Smedley, who was serving time for disseminating birth control information, "but not for us. Our struggle will be all the more bitter now."

ತಿಂ

In the woods outside a small town in northern Alabama, a black man died on Armistice Day, at the end of a rope hanging from a tree. His name was William Byrd, and late on the eve of the Armistice a mob of at least one hundred men had dragged him out of his jail cell, where that same night police had incarcerated him for allegedly killing a police officer. No one knew exactly how old he was but those who watched him die said he must have been young, as he was so very strong or perhaps he was very determined to live or both. Whatever the reason, it took the man "longer than most," they said, to die. In fact, he died around the time that the State Department received its momentous cable from Europe announcing the Armistice.

For his reported crime of "creating a disturbance in the lower section" of the town, Byrd was the fifty-first black man on record to be lynched that year—in addition to three black women. On the night of the 11th, the mob found yet another man they suspected of shooting the policeman and they hanged him too, though not from the same tree. Across the nation, there would be two more black women and eight more black men lynched before the year ended, bringing the total to sixty-four. In 1917, the tally had been forty-four, and in 1919, there would be many more. For black Americans, the weeping would not end on November 11.

Two hundred thousand African-American men had heeded Wilson's passionate call to join the crusade in Europe to make the world safe for democracy. Of those, 42,000 fought on the battlefields of France. "You have won the greatest battle in History and saved the most sacred cause, the liberty of the world," wrote Marshal Ferdinand Foch, the commander-in-chief of the Allied armies, in a letter to the all-black 369th Infantry. "Be proud of it. With immortal glory you have adorned your flags. Posterity will be indebted to you with gratitude." African-Americans who stayed home led a different campaign during the war years. They wanted Wilson to make their own country safe for democracy, and for African-Americans. They wanted their president to include America's black citizens in the dreams he so eloquently expressed.

And so on the "11/11/11" cease-fire, America's black leaders worked on their strategies for using the upcoming peace conference to bring world-wide attention to the acute race crisis in Wilson's own nation. W. E. B. Du Bois, the founder and president of the National Association for the Advancement of Colored People and editor of *The Crisis* magazine, attended an NAACP board meeting that day at which he read portions of his "Memorandum on the Future of Africa," discussed his plan for a Pan-African Congress in Paris, and supported a resolution to send twenty-five black representatives to the Paris Peace Conference.

William Monroe Trotter, the founder and editor of *The Guardian* newspaper in Boston, and the head of the National Equal Rights League, also announced a plan that day for his National Race Congress to convene in early December in Washington, D.C. This congress would select its own black delegation to promote a race agenda at the peace conference, which would include well-known African-Americans such as the exceptional businesswoman Madam C. J. Walker.

Trotter rarely missed a step in his quest to expose the hypocrisies that so impeded the progress and peace of his race. Loudly had he protested racist dramas on the Boston stage, the opening of the 1915 film *The Birth of a Nation*, racist policies in the offices of the Wilson administration, and nationwide indifference to the pandemic of lynching. In September of 1918, he had lost his wife, who was also his co-editor, to the flu. But, by the day of the Armistice, using work as an antidote to his grief, Trotter was focused on squaring Wilson's actions with his promises and words. For now, this meant demanding that the president appoint a black man to the American peace delegation, and that Wilson add a Fifteenth Point to his acclaimed Fourteen Points: "The elimination of civil, political, and judicial distinctions based on race or color in all nations for the new era of freedom everywhere."

The upcoming peace conference, where Wilson hoped to see the world reconfigured along the lines of global democracy, seemed an obvious venue for demands of racial justice and equality. Was this not the greatest opportunity to expose and overcome the injustices still oppressing his race? In his announcement on Armistice Day, Trotter wrote: "The earth and the heavens resound with the petitions of all races for freedom and democracy with the close of the World War. Every proscribed race and class is preparing to have its relief included in the world adjustment."

∞

Thirty-five miles northwest of Boston, on the afternoon of November 11, the merchants and residents of Ayer, Massachusetts, were preparing for what they knew the Armistice meant for them: a flood of soldiers engulfing their streets and stores, taverns and trolleys. More than 100,000 soldiers had been trained at Camp Devens, in the southwest corner of Ayer, and soon many more returning soldiers—the ones from New England, at least—would reenter America through that same camp. When the flow would begin and just how many there would be was not yet clear. To demobilize 300,000 soldiers each month was the government's hope at the moment, beginning with the sick and wounded. For Ayer now, its stores must be abundantly stocked; its boarding houses and hotels must prepare rooms for soldiers' families; and its police force must be bolstered, especially for traffic control. A series of patriotic parades must be planned, and health alerts must be posted. There was, after all, the danger of the flu traveling home with the soldiers, adding to Camp Devens's already huge toll of flu casualties. The mass of humanity would overrun Ayer, possibly even spilling into the outlying areas surrounding the ponds: Squannacook Pond, Robbins Pond, Long Pond, and Sandy Pond, the biggest of all.

Sandy Pond, only two and a half miles from Ayer, was where the well-heeled in the region owned summer homes. On Armistice Day, one of the few permanent residents, if not the only one, Mabel Emeline Puffer, was tending to the tasks of preparing her cottage for winter. She was assisted by her handyman, Arthur Garfield Hazzard, who had worked for the Puffer family for more than fifteen years. The shades on Puffer's Sandy Pond home were up. As her neighbors during the warmer months well knew, this meant that the stately, soft-spoken, white heiress was having tea with her African-American hired hand. What they spoke about on this particular day is not known but their conversation likely drifted some distance from such topics as the impact of returning soldiers on their town and the possibility that some soldiers might take the trolley out to view the beauty of their placid Sandy Pond. Their thoughts and feelings were not necessarily centered on the end of the war and what it might mean for the world outside Sandy Pond, for Americans of African descent, for hopeful returning soldiers of all races, for the U.S. president, and for all who dreamed of a just world. But for the news surrounding them on that day, their world was a tiny one, focused on each other and their own plans for a life together.

PART I

Winter: Jubilation and Hope

I learned by experience that democracy lives on the exercise and functioning of democracy. As a child learns and grows by doing, a people learn democracy by acting in democratic ways. I knew from the history of other countries that even the best democratic constitutions did not prevent dictatorships unless the people were trained in democracy and held themselves eternally vigilant and ready to oppose all infringements on liberty.

—HARRY WEINBERGER, MARCH 1919

We have learned during the war that the Constitution is a very elastic instrument and that the Federal Government can do anything that it wants to do which it considers for the good of the country. That it can say how much sugar we may put into our coffee, how much coal we may put on our fires, when we must go to bed and when we must get up. Then it is absurd to think if the Federal Government really wanted to put a stop to the shooting and hanging and burning alive of citizens of the United States by mobs that it could not find sufficient authority in the Constitution to do it.

—JAMES WELDON JOHNSON, DECEMBER 1918

CHAPTER 1

Gods of War and Peace

On December 4, 1918, three weeks after the Armistice, Woodrow Wilson boarded the USS *George Washington* bound for the Paris Peace Conference with the grand mission of cutting through the darkness at the center of the universe to release a light of peace. That morning, President Wilson departed Washington on a train bound for Hoboken, New Jersey, where the ship was docked and where more than a thousand men and women would join him for the voyage. The president's train, drawn by a flag-decked locomotive, was a special one, running as a second section of the regular Pennsylvania Railroad express between Washington and New York City and consisting of seven Pullman cars and two baggage coaches. The president and first lady traveled in the middle car, which was called the *Ideal*. In two other cars were the French and Italian ambassadors, the Belgian minister, and members of their families, traveling to France as guests by invitation of the president. Among others were the American ambassador to England and his wife; the president's private secretary, Joseph P. Tumulty; Mrs. Wilson's private secretary; the secretary of state and his wife; the president's private physician; a member of the American Peace Mission, Henry White; Secretary of War Newton D. Baker; and a scattering of White House staffers, Secret Service men, agents of the army and naval intelligence services, and State Department attachés. With the exception of Baker and Tumulty, all would accompany Wilson on his transatlantic voyage.

The special train arrived at the Hoboken pier at 7:20 A.M. on the shoreline tracks normally used for freight cars, allowing Wilson's middle car to pull right up to the entrance to Pier 4. Thousands of soldiers, policemen, and agents of military intelligence and the Secret Service surrounded the train as it stopped. A band played the national anthem. The president left the train, walked to the pier entrance, which was draped with palms and flags, took an elevator to the upper level, where a breeze fluttered hundreds of Allied banners, and then boarded the ship.

Reporters and photographers hovered nearby as did 325 Army Transport girls in their freshly pressed khakis. Ferryboats, tugs, and other small craft, though kept at a distance, moved onto the Hudson River as close to the spectacle as possible. Across the river in Manhattan at least ten thousand New Yorkers stood shoulder to shoulder, chests to backs, to bid farewell to the first president in U.S. history to travel beyond the shores of North America while in office. And on Staten Island, five hundred children waited, with restless anticipation, for the moment when the ship passed the Statue of Liberty, their cue for hoisting one thousand tiny flags into the air, waving them vigorously like wings in a flock of red, white, and blue birds.

Two by two, the passengers from the special train followed Wilson and boarded the 699-foot-long *George Washington,* a former German luxury liner selected to transport the president to France by the assistant secretary of the navy, Franklin Delano Roosevelt. They were followed by dozens more, including members of the American Peace Commission; experts in economics, cartography, the Balkans, Russia, Turkey, and Alsace-Lorraine; assistants to the experts; War Department personnel, such as the head of the Military Intelligence Division, Brigadier General Marlborough Churchill; George Creel, chairman of the Committee on Public Information; Red Cross nurses; and YMCA workers. Already on board were the crew of seventy-five officers and 1,049 men of the navy and Marine Corps, the chef of New York's Hotel Biltmore and his staff, six thousand sacks of mail, 3,500 tons of cargo, and hundreds of Christmas parcels for the soldiers still in France.

At 10:15 A.M. the *George Washington* steamed out of her berth, escorted down the harbor by five destroyers, joined at Staten Island by a dozen more and led by the super-dreadnought USS *Pennsylvania.* Zeppelins circled overhead and two army planes performed aerial feats, looping and swooping, while thousands of spectators gasped and cheered. As the destroyers thundered out the presidential salute of twenty-one guns and small craft blew continuous blasts of whistles and toots, the president and Mrs. Wilson stood on the bridge of their ship and waved. And, as the ship slowly moved out of the harbor, it passed within fifty yards of another transport whose decks were crowded with returning soldiers waving and cheering. On its ten-day voyage, Wilson's ark of experts would take the southern route through the Azores, avoiding storms further north. "I anticipate no trouble," the ship's commander told the press that day, "with the faintly possible exception of a stray floating mine which might be encountered these days anywhere in the Atlantic lanes."

The unprecedented voyage of the president across the Atlantic Ocean to Europe was risky indeed, but for more reasons than weather and mines. According to the politicians who disagreed with his decision to go—both Democrats and Republicans—Wilson was risking his presidency and jeopardizing the success of the peace talks. Some claimed that by attending the conference and sitting down with foreign secretaries and prime ministers to negotiate, he would diminish what was now a messianic image worldwide. Instead of the arbiter of the future of humankind, he would be just another negotiator. Distance and aloofness enhanced his power, they said.

On the morning of the departure, former president Teddy Roosevelt—Wilson's longtime nemesis—told the press from his hospital bed in New York, "President Wilson has not given the slightest explanation for his trip abroad." Other Republicans accused Wilson of betrayal for leaving the country and labeled him "un-American." How, they asked, could the president do his job if he were on the other side of the Atlantic? How could he make civil appointments, meet privately with legislators, speak to citizen groups, pardon offenders, or receive ambassadors, if he was occupying an office in Paris? How could he listen to the pulse of the nation from such a distance? And, they said, if he were compelled by necessity or worry to return home, it would take him nearly two weeks.

One Republican senator, Lawrence Sherman from Illinois, went so far as to introduce a resolution on December 3 calling upon the Senate to declare Wilson "out of office" if he dared to leave the country, which, of course, he was scheduled to do the next morning. In the hope of stripping the president of his power to perform the duties of his office while abroad, the senator claimed that the president's absence was a "palpable violation" of the Constitution. Wilson's absence when Congress was in session and when domestic conditions were insecure, as they were then in the months following the war, was an act of "legislative and executive sabotage against the Government," Sherman said. "The President of the United States is not its President in France; he is an alien there, a mere citizen of this Republic, shorn of all his sovereign powers."

Still others attacked Wilson's daring belief that his new League of Nations could be the "indispensable instrumentality" of world peace and justice and that it was an absolutely necessary component of the peace treaty. They feared his focus on a "peace without victory," as Wilson had said. Instead they favored a crushing victory, which meant harsh terms for Germany and which would reinvigorate the old order of military rivalries that had led to the Great War.

Republican senator Henry Cabot Lodge from Massachusetts was resolute in his own view that Wilson's vision of peace not only misrepresented the people of the United States but also endangered a speedy, effective peace. Lodge advocated the harshest possible terms for Germany. "The first and controlling purpose of the peace must be to put Germany in such a position that it will be physically impossible for her to break out again upon other nations with a war for world conquest," he wrote in a memo to Henry White, the only Republican in Wilson's peace mission. To Lodge, crippling Germany was the only way to prevent future wars.

Lodge was so eager for his point of view to be heard in Paris that the day before the voyage, he visited White while the diplomat was packing for the trip and expressed his concerns. Then a few hours before White boarded the special presidential train to Hoboken, Lodge delivered to him a nine-page memorandum outlining his views—and undermining his president. He asked White to secretly show the memo to French premier Georges Clemenceau and other European statesmen so that they would know, Lodge said, that Wilson's visions were not backed by the majority of Americans.

But none of this would deter Wilson. His potent purpose blinded him to the risks of going to France and blocked out the shouting naysayers. He was determined to create a new world order, one no longer based on force and fear, jealousy and self-interest, and the endless antagonisms threatening to erupt into wars. These were conflicts endemic to a system of powerful nations vying for more power, overpowering smaller nations in the quest for hegemony. Wilson's world would be based on cooperation through what he described as a "single overwhelming, powerful group of nations who shall be the trustee of the peace of the world." Nothing of this magnitude had ever been attempted before: a fantastic plan for world peace in the aftermath of an equally unparalleled war. If such a war could occur, why shouldn't there be a peace to prevent such a war from ever occurring again?

At sixty-three, in delicate health, Wilson, who had never lost an election, went to Paris because he believed he must personally present—and protect—his plan for world peace. He may have believed what he promoted: that nations, small and large, had a right to determine their own governments and policies; and that, if given a chance, the spirit of brotherhood could be just as powerful as military might, capable of mending a broken world and achieving a permanent peace. "To conquer with arms is to make only a temporary conquest," Wilson once said. "To conquer the world by earning its esteem is to make permanent conquest." Wilson also said that he felt responsible for the 110,051 American soldiers who had died in the war. Two days before his departure to France, he told Congress: "It is now my duty to play my full part in making good what they offered their life's blood to obtain."

In a groping world anxious to begin anew, Wilson's enthusiastic supporters far outnumbered his critics at this point simply because they wanted to believe what he said. They wanted to know that their sacrifices in wartime would result in a better world, that Wilson was indeed the alchemist of the world, capable of turning lead into gold. In France, they would hail him as "the Champion of the Rights of Man"; in Rome, the "God of Peace"; and in Milan "the Moses from Across the Atlantic" and the "Savior of Humanity." In Paris, where two million people would greet him, he was "Wilson the Just." The editor of the *London Daily News* wrote, "I know how grave things are, but I rely on the stiff jaw of one great man."

Early in the morning of December 4, on the ferry from Manhattan to Hoboken, a young man on Wilson's France-bound staff started up a conversation with a sweatshop worker. How many hours do you work? the staffer asked. The worker told him, "Fourteen." And then the worker said, "Do you see that boat?" pointing to the grand transport docked across the river in the Hoboken port. "There's a man aboard her [who] is going to Europe to change all that."

"For a brief interval, Wilson alone stood for mankind," H. G. Wells would later write.

CHAPTER 2

Spies Are Everywhere

Perhaps the most common myth about war is that it ends when the textbooks say it does, when the cease-fires begin and the documents are signed. Ostensibly, by the time the *George Washington* left New York harbor, the European war had ended and the American president was embarking on his dramatic experiment to end all wars. But a world accustomed to conflict cannot with a mere pen stroke shut down the machinery of war or change the mentality of measuring the world in Manichaean terms of good and evil.

In Europe, in the weeks after the Armistice, bombs exploded in train stations; railways were often too unsafe for Allied troops to use; local skirmishes abounded; two hundred prisoners of war were found dead at a Belgian rail station; and military intelligence officers reported a plague of distrust regarding the Armistice, with troops believing it to be a German ruse to demobilize the Allies. In northern Russia, American soldiers continued to fight in icy swamps and snowfields while influenza and pneumonia swept through the outposts. And in America, "the shadow war" was far from over. This was the war behind the war, in which a vast network of secret agents spied on American civilians in the name of national security, reporting on the private lives of men and women who behaved in a way that was thought to threaten America's ability to win the war.

In the days immediately following the Armistice, the U.S. government, most specifically the Justice Department, made it clear to every domestic spy, whether paid or volunteer, that the job of securing the nation against Prussian deceptions wasn't over. There would be no war's-end relaxation for those who protected the nation at home. Now the task was to stop the propagandists who favored leniency for Germany at the peace table and to keep a "vigilant watch over anarchists, plotters and aliens," as the Justice Department told the *Washington Post* on Armistice Day. Seth Wheeler, Jr., a volunteer spy in Albany, New York, told his local paper on November 18, "I'm as busy in my patriotic work as at any time since assuming the post."

Espionage was hardly new to America. By 1917, when America entered the war, the private investigation business was thriving, with thousands of agents at more than three hundred firms, such as Pinkerton's, and in the intelligence departments of numerous corporations. What happened to domestic intelligence during the war, however, was far more extensive: it was, in fact, revolutionary.

By the time of the signing of the Armistice, a massive, highly organized intelligence community had evolved in the United States, composed of agents from the Office of Naval Intelligence, the army's Military Intelligence Division (typically referred to as the MID), the Justice Department's Bureau of Investigation (the BI), the Treasury Department's Secret Service, the U.S. Postal Service, and other agencies, including the U.S. Railroad Administration and the U.S. Food Administration. In addition, police departments in big cities had their own intelligence forces that coordinated with the army's MID. Even the YMCA had a battalion of spies.

The largest of all such groups was the MID, whose manpower was far greater than the navy's intelligence force or the Secret Service. The MID was even larger, in 1917 and 1918, than the Bureau of Investigation, and by the end of the war it had become the main clearinghouse for other agencies' reports on civilians. The MID also worked with the State Department on the sensitive work of screening passports. Modeled after the British counterespionage system, it named its branches MI1 through MI8. Domestic spies worked out of MI4.

Even more vast in numbers, however, than any of the federal intelligence staffs was a mammoth web of patriotic organizations enlisting thousands of volunteer spies, all of whom reported their findings to Naval Intelligence, the MID, or the Bureau of Investigation. As one historian later wrote, by November of 1918, "the U.S. had fielded a corps of sleuths larger than any country had done in all of history." Among them were the Liberty League, the American Defense Society, the Home Defense League, the National Security League, the Anti–Yellow Dog League, the All-Allied Anti-German League, the Knights of Liberty, the Boy Spies of America, the American Anti-Anarchy Association, and the Sedition Slammers. The most powerful was the American Protective League, or APL, a clandestine "club" of volunteers that was a major force behind the shadow war.

The APL began in the early spring of 1917 in Chicago, where the large

German population was a matter of grave concern to advertising executive A.M. Briggs, who volunteered to help the regional office of the Justice Department investigate leads on German agents. President Wilson had just severed relations with Germany, war was imminent, and the Justice Department had only fifteen agents to cover all of Illinois, Wisconsin, and Minnesota. It also had no motor cars. Briggs first offered himself and several of his friends as drivers, chauffeuring the small squadron of federal agents. Then he organized a group of wealthy men to buy several dozen motor cars for the Justice Department. Finally, he went to Washington to seek permission to go one step further: to launch a covert volunteer force headquartered in the People's Gas Building in Chicago. Approval came swiftly. And after war was declared, the APL became an unofficial branch of the federal government whose agents routinely sent reports to the Justice Department, the MID, and Naval Intelligence. Soon it would move its headquarters to a four-story building on I Street in Washington.

In its manual, the APL described itself as "the largest company of detectives the world ever saw" and "the mysterious power behind our Government." Its letterhead carried the banner headline, "Organized with the Approval and Operating under the Direction of the United States Department of Justice, Bureau of Investigation." The Justice Department, however, never dared to boast publicly about its volunteer branches. Still, both the BI and the MID benefited hugely, not only by expanding their manpower but also by extending legal capabilities, sometimes using Leaguers for their dirty work. In one case in New Jersey, for example, an APL member was acquainted with the Justice Department's main suspect and while at the suspect's home pocketed a much needed document for evidence in an upcoming trial. Although judges could not allow evidence seized illegally by a federal official to be used in court, they could, as in this case, use evidence confiscated by a civilian. In another case, in Illinois, the MID called in APL members to obtain confessions from twenty-one black soldiers accused of assaulting a white woman. Fifteen confessed and were court-martialed.

Although the Justice Department did not authorize the volunteers to make arrests or carry weapons, some local police departments, welcoming the unpaid backup, did. Also, Leaguers, as they were called, carried badges, which looked official and proclaimed membership in the Secret

Service. This didn't exactly please the secretary of the treasury, who headed up the Secret Service, and who worried about how to control abuses and zealotry in such a vast volunteer force. Indeed, there was no central or official membership list. And there were plenty of instances of Leaguers overlapping efforts or stepping clumsily where they shouldn't. Two Leaguers might hide a taping device independently in different parts of the same person's house or even the wrong house. In one case, a New York member planted a dictograph in a female suspect's apartment and another Leaguer's amorous adventures with the suspect, not knowing she was a suspect, were recorded, thus making him a suspect. He later found a dictograph in his own apartment, placed by a fellow Leaguer. After all, anyone associating with a suspect became a suspect, both being potential enemies of the government.

"SPIES ARE EVERYWHERE," a *New York Tribune* headline read in the spring of 1917, referring to German spies. But it could easily also have described the corps of American spies organizing to counteract such a threat. Indeed, most factories and public utilities nationwide employed one or more APL members to identify workers the government considered troublemakers. Posing as anarchists or socialists at labor meetings, Leaguers sometimes worked as provocateurs to entrap labor activists. At theaters, the first performance of a production brought in Leaguers like fans seeking autographs, but instead they were asking for every male actor's draft card. If there was a problem, they would remove the suspect and escort him to the local police, despite the scheduled play or concert.

By the autumn of 1918, there were at least 300,000 APL spies hidden in the folds of American society, watching, trailing, and taping their bosses, colleagues, employees, neighbors, even the local butcher or their children's schoolteachers. "It is my plan to enroll the responsible heads of the most important banks, trust companies, steamship lines and stock exchange houses, together with the large insurance companies and real estate concerns," wrote a New York banker in charge of organizing the Manhattan branch of the APL.

Riding a tidal wave of intolerance, Leaguers listened for the telltale whispers of a treacherous enemy force that could be conspiring to destroy America. No matter where they were—amusement parks, theaters, saloons, private parties—they stopped every man of draft age and demanded to see his registration card. If he could not produce it, they called the local police to have him arrested, or, flashing their badges, they demanded the civilian come with them to be interrogated. Even a day at the beach could be disrupted by an APL slacker raid, in search of draft dodgers. One August night in 1918 at 10 P.M., at least seventy-five Leaguers stood at the end of each of four piers in Atlantic City, New Jersey. Thousands of men, women, and children were told they could not leave until the men showed their registration cards. The searches continued until 7 A.M. In the end, seven hundred men were apprehended, of which sixty were slackers—draft dodgers.

The initial purpose of this war behind the war was to stamp out perceived threats to the security of a nation at war—in other words to find and destroy German spy rings, to crush German businessmen sending funds to their homeland, and to identify German sympathizers. The 1910 census listed 8,282,618 Americans who had been born in Germany or who had at least one German-born parent. The government was thus confronted with an unprecedented and alarming challenge: how to detect the enemies at home. How many German citizens were acting as agents? How many were truly loyal to the American flag? How should the government define a threat? Who should be targeted? In a war that was unpopular on the day Congress declared it, critics of government policy became immediate targets and were labeled as unpatriotic, threats to national security, and worse still, potential German allies. But what indeed constituted a threat?

On the day after the declaration of war against Germany, President Wilson vaguely answered that question when he ordered all government agencies to authorize supervisors to dismiss employees for any "disloyal talk." Wilson knew about the APL and even told his attorney general that he believed such a volunteer force could be dangerous. But he did not try to stop it, because the government needed the manpower. Further, he bestowed censorship and propaganda powers on the new Committee on Public Information, which under the leadership of former journalist George Creel established propaganda as a powerful tool of the U.S. government for snuffing out criticism and critics—a tool the government would continue to use long after the end of the war. Creel's propaganda machine transformed a nation that had elected a president who campaigned on a platform of peace in 1916 to a nation beating the drums of war and ready to persecute and incarcerate anyone who resisted. To counteract criticism of government policy and to stimulate patriotic zeal, Creel employed numerous strategies, including the dispatching of at least 75,000 men— known as the Four-Minute Men—to movie theaters, churches, schools, and labor halls to give over 750,000 four-minute speeches that promoted the importance of the war and issued a warning about the threat of domestic sedition.

And even further, Wilson put into motion several new laws to assist the government in identifying and eliminating troublemakers. One was the Selective Service Act in 1917, which made it a crime to obstruct the draft. Another was the 1917 Espionage Act, which made it a crime to obstruct the war. And that made it a crime to criticize the war, to discourage enlistment, to encourage mutiny, and to impede in any way the government's campaign to build a military force. The Espionage Act also gave the postmaster general the right to censor what he might consider "seditious" magazines and newspapers and to impound the mail of unpatriotic organizations.

In 1918, Congress passed the Alien Act, which gave the government the right to deport aliens who were anarchists or who advocated the overthrow of the American government. And in 1918, after heated debates in Congress, Wilson signed an amended version of the Espionage Act, which vastly extended the already long arm of the law. Under the new iteration of the 1917 law, it was a crime not only to obstruct the draft but to attempt to obstruct it. It was a crime to block the sale of Liberty Bonds. It was a crime to disrupt the production of goods deemed necessary to the war effort. And it was a crime "to willfully utter, print, write or publish" any expression of disloyalty toward or criticism of the U.S. government, its Constitution, its flag, even its military uniforms. The law also added to the postmaster general's censorship powers by giving him the authority to identify "upon evidence satisfactory to him" which individuals were using the mails to promote seditious ideas in violation of the new act and then to allow him to halt their mail deliveries. The penalties were fines up to $10,000 and prison up to twenty years.

In the June 1918 issue of its newsletter, *The Spy Glass*, the American Protective League rejoiced in the new sedition law: "Signed by President Wilson on May 16 [1918], the amended espionage law opens a new chapter in the work of the American Protective League. For the first time we have an inclusive law under which to operate—a law broad enough in its scope and classifications to cover and define as serious crimes a multitude of offenses which were classed as minor by our peace-time code."

Others feared the new law, especially the ninth clause, in which the word "willfully," included in all other clauses of the law, was left out. "Whoever shall by word or act support or favor the cause of any country with which the United States is at war, or by word or act oppose the cause of the United States therein," it said in part. This meant that, unlike the other clauses, a person could be convicted without having to prove any disloyal intent. "Like murder or burglary, espionage and sedition are now positive crimes," so said the APL newsletter. "No one who commits them can plead innocent intent. . . . The amended law is a powerful weapon put into our hands."

What began as a wartime measure to protect Americans on their own soil and to outmaneuver German spies evolved into a homeland war waged against anyone who did not agree with what the government was doing, especially with regard to the war. The APL's profile of the enemy included anyone who happened on one occasion to put together one sentence indicating opposition to the war, without any intention to betray his or her nation and without an underlying scheme of working for the Germans. Too often these were innocent citizens practicing their democratic rights of protesting, speaking their minds, writing their hearts.

Socialists, anarchists, pacifists, labor activists, African-Americans, and foreigners were the usual and obvious targets. All who associated with them or happened to attend a meeting organized by such groups were automatically at risk.

Russians, as well as Germans, were high on the list of the suspicious. This was because intelligence operatives and officials were certain that Germany was behind the Russian Revolution. The new Bolshevik government had pulled Russia out of the war in March of 1918, causing German troops to withdraw from the east and strengthen their offensive against the Allies on the Western Front.

All labor organizers—especially members of the determined yet small Industrial Workers of the World, known as the IWW or the Wobblies— had been targets before the war and continued to be during the war. Indeed, the volunteer spy corps, which drew so heavily from the business community, used national security and the Espionage Act as reasons to break up labor meetings and to detain labor leaders. Before the war, labor had struggled for union recognition and a portion of Gilded Age profits, encountering stiff, sometimes deadly, resistance from businessmen and industrialists. During the war, the battle against labor took on a new form— "patriots" fighting against workers who might disrupt war production and therefore be part of an enemy plot. Now, after the war, workers would again be targeted, this time as Bolsheviks and Bolshevik sympathizers.

African-Americans were also deemed suspicious. Alienation and unrest in black communities must be the fault of outside agitators, said the government. Thus, the MID had a special section of spies devoted to "Negro Subversion." During the war, unrest was a sign that Germans had stirred up blacks; after the war, unrest was a manifestation of the covert action of the Bolsheviks plotting to use blacks to foment revolution in the United States. Black soldiers returning from Europe were especially worrisome. As Wilson told a fellow passenger on the *George Washington,* they could be the "greatest medium in conveying Bolshevism to America."

So focused had most Americans been on the war in Europe and on the flu epidemic at home that they hardly noticed the shadow war. Those who did were often indifferent to it. Others applauded its mission of sweeping the radical rubbish out of sight using whatever methods might work— prison, deportation, beatings, lynchings—constitutional or not. There were those, however, who did what they could to obstruct such a covert war, claiming it had gone beyond protecting domestic security by targeting innocent civilians. On Armistice Day, they were the ones who cheered for the end of two wars, or so they hoped.

A week after the Armistice, despite the Justice Department's November 11 statement in the *Washington Post* about ongoing domestic surveillance, the head of the MID, Marlborough Churchill, sent an internal memo to his intelligence officers instructing them to drop all investigations of civilians, to dismiss all volunteers, and to collect the identification cards and any other credentials distributed to civilian spies. "The emergency no longer exists," he wrote, and any "unfinished disloyalty" cases were to be turned over to the Department of Justice. The army's battle against subversive civilians was over, claimed Churchill, who then prepared to join Wilson in Paris as head of intelligence at the peace conference.

But more than memos and edicts would be needed to stop the hundreds of thousands of shadow warriors from continuing their war on those they viewed as America's domestic enemies. Most MID branches ignored

Churchill's edict. Some believed the German threat had not subsided. Others conjured new threats. Still others, consumed with self-importance, were unwilling to end what they had put so much energy and identity into creating. And then there was the fact that despite any internal memos, the government was telling the media that regardless of the impending peace, the nation must remain vigilant. "The need for the League is as great now as it has been in the past and I am entirely satisfied that the need for this organization will continue for some time to come, entirely without regard to the progress of peace negotiations," A. B. Bielaski, the chief of the Bureau of Investigation, told the press.

Even before Churchill's memo, the New York City division of the MID decided not to disband, thanks in part to the head of its propaganda section, Archibald E. Stevenson. The day after the Armistice, Stevenson turned in a staggering report outlining his perceptions of the latest dangers to national security, principally the spread of Bolshevism. The tone was urgent. All of Eastern Europe was soon to follow the path of the Bolsheviks, he wrote, as well as Italy and France. And the "congested and industrial districts" of the United States were especially at risk. Consider that there are four million people in New York alone, he wrote, who are either immigrants or children of immigrants, all vulnerable to the propaganda of Bolshevist infiltrators. In New York, he knew there were at least ten revolutionary meetings each week, perhaps fifteen. And the reports he received from agents and stenographers attending those meetings were proof enough for him that "without a question there is an organized conspiracy to overthrow the present form of the American government." His report was sent on to Washington, where the MID acting director, in Churchill's absence, encouraged Stevenson enthusiastically to continue his observations and studies—a decision the MID would one day regret.

At the same time, the Espionage Act was still alive and well in Washington. Immediately after the Armistice, the Justice Department and its U.S. attorneys in major cities announced that these wartime laws would stay in effect until the war was officially over. Effectively nothing would change until the peace negotiations ended and the U.S. had signed and ratified a treaty. More than just keeping the laws on the books, they claimed they would continue to utilize them to expose any un-American sentiment that might be expressed. "There are still many individuals who have to be watched and reported upon, and there will be no cessation of vigilance in that direction," an assistant U.S. attorney in Los Angeles told the press. "We want the loyal people of Los Angeles to still keep an eye on the violators of the Espionage Act and make reports to us when they see such infractions. Arrests will be made for violations of the war laws, just as they have been in the past."

This attitude became pervasive nationwide. When a New York member of the Socialist Party spoke his mind at a November 1918 meeting in Manhattan, an attending MID agent and stenographer reported every word. In the days ahead the speaker was arrested under the act, convicted, and sentenced to fifteen years in jail. The Washington office filed a statement on the case and commented that it was essential for the New York branch of the MID to proceed in its coverage of "radical" meetings, concluding that "the wheels of justice continue to turn in spite of the Armistice"—running into and over everyone who had, as the Sedition Act instructed, even the appearance of disloyalty. Among those caught in the wide net of domestic intelligence was Carl Sandburg.

A few weeks after the *George Washington* left New York harbor, the SS *Bergensfjord* from Stockholm, Sweden, pulled in. It was Christmas Day 1918. After leaving the *Bergensfjord*, Carl Sandburg had planned to catch a train to Cleveland, where he would drop off a bundle of papers to his editor, and, as soon as he could, take a train home to Chicago. Sandburg had been on assignment in Sweden since early October and he was a new father who had not yet seen his one-month-old daughter. He ached for the moment when he could open the door of his Chicago home and wrap himself in the harmonious, safe world of his family. But that was not going to happen anytime soon.

Waiting for Sandburg in New York was Captain John B. Trevor, the head of the New York branch of the MID. Although the United States had not been at war with any of the nations about which Sandburg had been writing, mainly Finland and Russia, or in which he had been living, Sweden, Trevor nonetheless arrested him the moment he stepped off the boat on charges of violating the 1917 wartime law known as the Trading with the Enemy Act. Government agents from the Secret Service, the army, and customs confiscated all written materials in Sandburg's baggage and on his person and sent them to be analyzed by government censors. And then they commenced to interrogate him. It was an irksome, frustrating process that would last for several days—as long as three hours one day—followed by weeks of negotiations in a tug-of-war over the allegations against him.

Since July of 1918, Sandburg, then forty years old, had worked for the Newspaper Enterprise Association, a Scripps news service that placed its stories in three hundred or more publications with a collective circulation of at least 4.5 million readers. Sandburg's assignment was to cover Eastern Europe for the NEA from Stockholm, which his editor, Sam Hughes, believed would be an excellent place to find fresh, important stories from Germany and Russia. Onward from the day in the summer of 1918 when he first got the assignment, however, Sandburg grappled with a suspicious government and annoying red tape. It was possible, he soon learned, that the State Department might not even grant him a passport.

The destination was problematic. All branches of intelligence were closely watching the flow of human traffic through Stockholm, where intrigue seemed to be on the rise and where spies from the Allied and Central Powers congregated. But Sandburg himself was also a problem. An avowed socialist, Sandburg was sympathetic to those caught in the web of the Espionage and Sedition Acts, and he had many friends, including the outspoken radicals John Reed and his wife, Louise Bryant, who supported the Russian Revolution. Well aware of his liabilities, he asked his book editor, Alfred Harcourt of the New York publishing house Henry Holt, in addition to the highly respected attorney Clarence Darrow and labor leader Samuel Gompers, to write strong letters noting his patriotism and his reputation for objective journalism. Not until late September was Sandburg approved for a passport, and finally on October 4 he left for Stockholm. There he wrote numerous stories, as well as poems, and garnered excellent journalistic sources, including a Russian man who had taught school in Chicago and now had high-level contacts in the Russian government.

That autumn, Sandburg's NEA editor Hughes began to suspect that misinformation abounded in the United States about the Bolsheviks. Believing that Americans deserved to know the truth, he wanted to publish an article or series about the Bolsheviks, one that informed the American public truthfully about Russia's new ruling party. Hughes relied heavily on Sandburg to gather as much Russian material as he could—photographs, films, pamphlets, anecdotes, newspaper clips, interviews—while in Stockholm. By the time Sandburg was packing to return to the United States, he had filled two trunks with Russian books, newspapers, and pamphlets for the NEA, which he sent by mail. Knowing it would take two months or longer for Hughes to get the trunks, he also carried plenty of material with him on board the *Bergensfjord*, including notebooks from his interviews with as many as two hundred people, clips about Russia and Germany from Scandinavian newspapers, files of the Soviet Izvestia Congress from June 1918, and a recent three-volume history of Russia. Tucked in the inner pocket of his coat, he transported, with great sensitivity to its historical and current value, a published English translation of V. I. Lenin's *A Letter to American Workingmen from the Socialist Soviet Republic of Russia* printed by the Socialist Publication Society. He also carried with him some money: 400 kronor from the Russian source who had taught school in Chicago, for his wife who was still in America; and two drafts of $5,000 each for the head of the Finnish Information Bureau in the United States. When he was arrested the money was seized.

Writing to Secretary of War Newton Baker, Hughes protested Sandburg's detention and the confiscation of his papers. These were the sources of a journalist on assignment. Besides, America was no longer at war, and Sweden had been neutral. Calling Sandburg's detention an unconscionable act of censorship, Hughes would fight it, he wrote. Baker wrote back that Sandburg was carrying "revolutionary literature" and the money was for Finn revolutionaries. Hughes then informed Baker that he believed the government was detaining Sandburg because he was a socialist. Hughes pointed out that the government incorrectly believed Sandburg to be a German. After all, the government had spelled his name "berg" instead of "burg" in its files on him. This caused the suspicion, Hughes believed. What they were doing was wrong and when it was over, Hughes told Baker that he would tell Sandburg to write—for publication—what he knew to be true and what he felt was right, despite any shadow of government censorship. "Isn't it fine for the government to treat such a man like a dog of a traitor?" Hughes wrote in his letter to Baker.

Sandburg tried to remain calm. "Busier than a cranberry merchant these days," he wrote to his wife on December 27. "American and British intelligence officers and an assistant district attorney spent three hours asking questions." No amount of reasoning, however, could explain to him why his notebooks and clips were such a threat.

In a letter to Hughes, Sandburg wrote, "Day by day the retention of the

Russian 'revolutionary literature,' which is NEA property and which was brought in under instructions, becomes more preposterous. Of the total of stuff printed in the Russian language probably less than a half can be construed as 'revolutionary.' Of this more than 75 per cent has already been printed in publications in the United States and is now in the public libraries or on sale nation-wide at newsstands."

CHAPTER 3

Christmas at Villa Lewaro

In the majestic halls of Villa Lewaro on Christmas Day, spies and censorship seemed a world away. Situated on the Hudson River, twenty miles north of Manhattan, this veritable palace, with its splendorous view of the New Jersey Palisades, its thirty-four rooms, its Italian Renaissance porticoes and balconies, its sweeping marble staircase, and its stunning sculptures and tapestries, was one of the homes owned by businesswoman Madam C. J. Walker. On this day Walker was hosting a holiday gala for thirty guests.

Some of Walker's guests had arrived the night before and others came throughout the day. Passing under the eight two-story-high Ionic columns, they entered the house and stepped into the main hall, walking around the Cartier sculpture of a jaguar attacking a rearing horse, and congregating in the vast dining room with its ceiling of painted mermaids and demons. As they listened to Christmas songs piped to all floors of the house from an organ in the music room, they shook hands, put faces to names, and settled in for the next twenty-four hours. Among them were painters and sculptors, ministers and soldiers, professors and poets. A well-known Washington sculptor, May Howard Jackson, was there with her husband, who headed the Math Department at Washington's oldest black public school. There were several "Harlem Hellfighters" from the 369th Regiment, including one who had won the coveted Croix de Guerre. Of particular interest was a guest who taught Spanish at Dunbar High School in D.C. Her name was Hallie Elvira Queen.

Queen held a bachelor's degree from Cornell University and a master's from Stanford. Fluent in Spanish, French, and German, she had worked as an interpreter during the war and had chaired Howard University's Red Cross chapter. Besides her current teaching job, there was one more impressive detail about her work life—one that was missing from her résumé and that few if any of Walker's guests could have known. Since 1917, Queen had been working for the army's Military Intelligence Division as a translator and an informant, assigned to carry out surveillance of blacks. Queen, the woman who would be helping Walker that night wrap and tag gifts for her guests, was a spy.

For months, Walker's closest friends had warned her that her strong stands on race issues and her association with outspoken black Americans such as William Monroe Trotter of Boston and Ida B. Wells-Barnett of Chicago, both crusaders against black oppression, might earn her a spy or two. The government was watching her, the friends cautioned, and probably had been for years. An absurd idea, she would say, and certainly unnecessary, especially now that the war was over. How could anyone question the activities and intent of someone with such a stellar record of contributing to the progress of her race? In the coming year, 1919, Madam Walker might even reach her goal of becoming America's first black millionaire. And to be sure, one of the motives in building such a showplace as Villa Lewaro, as she often noted in interviews and speeches, was to show "the business possibilities within the race, to point out to young Negroes what a lone woman accomplished and to inspire them to do big things."

Walker had certainly done big things against colossal odds. By 1918, most African-Americans had heard at least some part of Walker's remarkable story. Sarah Breedlove, as Walker was named at birth, was born on a Louisiana plantation where her parents, former slaves, were sharecroppers. At age six, she was orphaned and moved to Mississippi to live with her sister. When she was fourteen, she married. Three years later, she gave birth to a daughter. Her husband died when she was twenty and she moved to St. Louis. Walker's options as a single black woman raising a child were few. In fact, there were only two: fieldwork or housework. And so for the next fifteen years, she labored as a washerwoman. She also suffered from a scalp disease during that time, which caused her hair to break off and fall out. In an anxious dream, Walker later told writers, she came up with a concoction to save her hair and restore the health of her scalp. Though never intending to market it, she wanted to help other women who were similarly afflicted and so she began to sell her solution, advertising it with the message that the cure had come in a dream, as a message from God. The success of her business, however, came on the wings of her passionate conviction about what women wanted and needed most: to be attractive and to be financially independent. Madam Walker eventually employed a sales force of ten thousand black women, referred to as "hair culturists," and she expanded beyond hair care products into cosmetics. By the end of 1918, the earnings of the Madam C. J. Walker Manufacturing Company had jumped ahead of the previous year by $100,000 to nearly $276,000.

Walker stood out in a way that all highly successful people do, which meant, among other things, that she had her supporters and her critics. Some African-Americans diminished her success, saying that she had taken advantage of the insecurities of black women who wanted porcelain complexions and straight hair. Others found her lifestyle of elegance and frills too indulgent. Walker tried to sway her critics by showing how many black women and their families had benefited from her business. After all, she had fulfilled one very big dream: offering a black woman options beyond working on her knees on the floor of a white woman's kitchen or bending over rows of cotton twelve hours a day. Besides, she had announced publicly that, after her death, her villa on the Hudson River would be left to a cause beneficial to her race. Her generosity was obvious. She donated large sums of money to numerous black charities. She helped to purchase Frederick Douglass's house and preserve it as a museum. She funded scholarships for young black women. And she assisted the NAACP.

Still, she had critics in the government and, as her friends suspected, she also had her own government "shadows," ever curious about how she planned to use her money and her power in the black community. What were the causes she championed? Was she sympathetic to the Bolshevik Revolution? Did she have ties to the Socialist Party? Did she donate funds to either? What was her relationship with William Monroe Trotter and his National Equal Rights League, with W. E. B. Du Bois and the NAACP? How much money had she given to African nations, and why? And with whom might she be meeting on any given day in the Villa Lewaro library with its wall-to-wall shelves of Moroccan-leather-bound volumes?

Exactly how long the government had been watching Madam Walker was unclear, but the Military Intelligence Division began their file on her about two weeks before the Christmas gala. It was around that time that Madam Walker had attended Trotter's National Race Congress in Washington, which was planning to send a delegation to the Paris Peace Conference to champion the rights of Africans and African-Americans. Walker was selected unanimously as one of the delegates, with more votes than any other. She and Ida B. Wells-Barnett, the bold Chicagoan who had

drawn national attention to the issue of lynching nearly thirty years before, were the only women delegates. Walker was honored—not only to be
chosen to represent the National Equal Rights League but also to be in the
company of Wells-Barnett, who as long ago as the 1880s had refused to
leave a passenger train car designated for whites only. In fact, she had bit-
ten the hand of the conductor who had tried to force her to move, and
then sued the Chesapeake, Ohio, & Southwestern Railroad. And Walker
was determined to go to Paris. The job of the delegates was to lobby for
racial justice worldwide and to push for the independence of Germany's
four colonies in Africa, whose fate the peace conference would determine:
Togo, Cameroon, German East Africa, and German Southwest Africa. The
presence of such accomplished women as Wells-Barnett and Walker would
surely make a difference.

Indeed Walker believed, as Trotter, Du Bois, and Wells-Barnett all did,
that black Americans could have a significant impact on the peace talks.
And for Walker to represent her race at Paris was consistent with her work
over the years on projects involving race equality and self-determination in
Africa. She had supported schools in Africa and African students in
the United States, and at one point she even dreamed of building a voca-
tional school in Africa much like the Tuskegee Institute. For any African-
American to go to Paris did not seem like a militant idea to Madam Walker
or to anyone else who attended the meetings that week in Washington—
with the exception of one attendee, Major Walter H. Loving, a black
MID agent.

What placed Madam Walker firmly in the MID's Negro Subversion file
was likely Major Loving's report on Trotter's congress. Loving was not only
a black agent working for the MID; he was the man in charge of "Negro
surveillance." For the past year, he had had his own private office in Washington from which he ran a national, highly secretive MID program organized for spying on African-Americans. To do this, he had traveled
nationwide putting together a core of black volunteer spies. In his own
sleuthing ventures, he spied on field secretaries in the black YMCA and he
assessed the tone of editorials in black newspapers. Marlborough
Churchill, the MID head now in Paris with Wilson, believed that if black
Americans complained about lynching or any other serious issues of race
conditions in America in speeches, at rallies, or on editorial pages, they
were endangering the security of the nation. Thus, part of Loving's role in

protecting his nation was to meet with editors who were publishing articles with the "wrong tone" and to admonish them, threatening to throw their newspapers to the government censors. The *Chicago Defender* and the NAACP's magazine, *The Crisis*, were among his targets. Churchill once said of Loving that he was "one of the best types of white man's negro."

The Crisis had been operating under the scrutiny of Loving and the MID since May of 1918. So too had its highly esteemed editor, W. E. B. Du Bois, and potentially all the 32,000 NAACP members. Ironically, Major Joel E. Spingarn, the white chairman of the NAACP board, was also working for the Military Intelligence Division, which meant that he was spying on members of his own organization. Even more intriguing was the fact that Du Bois knew this and still agreed to work with Spingarn. Although Du Bois's cooperation might have appeared to be a betrayal of his organization and even his race, in fact his motives were quite the opposite. If domestic spies attended meetings, rallies, and speeches in black communities and listened in on private conversations, they would learn, Du Bois believed, the true reasons for the distrust, dissension, and despair among black Americans. They would see that the racial unrest so evident and so worrisome in America was not a result of outside agitators from Germany or Russia, but rather the consequence of severe injustices in America. They would report back to the government about the refusal of the Red Cross to employ black nurses; about blacks allowed only third-class accommodations on trains; about government bureaus refusing to hire black stenographers; about Jim Crow laws and discrimination in restaurants, theaters, and hotels; and about the slanted way the white press reported black news. They would surely learn of the problems in the very building in Washington that housed the MID, where five black typists worked on the sixth floor and yet were only allowed to use the restroom on the first floor. But the complaint that would far exceed all others, the one that spies would report from all sectors of black America, if they were in fact gathering accurate information, would be about lynching.

Shortly after agreeing to work with the MID in the spring of 1918, Du Bois and Spingarn organized a conference of thirty-two black editors and ten black leaders to discuss what was really happening in black America. Considering the ongoing surveillance, the conference would be "covered," Du Bois surmised, and the final report noting the ideas of the participants might thus gain some attention in Washington. "German propaganda among us is powerless, but the apparent indifference of our own Government may be dangerous," the editors concluded. "Federal intervention to suppress lynching is imperative," they said.

By the end of 1918, sixty-four African-Americans had been lynched in the United States by mobs and without trials—a figure that was up by almost 40 percent from the previous year. Five were women, two of whom were pregnant, five months and nine. Eleven were soldiers, on leave or returning home, still in full uniform. Thirteen were charged with assaulting white women. Other offenses included "creating a disturbance," "stealing hogs," "immorality," "suspicion of threatening a white man's life," "attempted murder," "robbing house and frightening women," and "resisting arrest." An ad in the December 1918 issue of The Crisis read: "If you believe that lynching should be stopped and that the democracy for which we have fought is to apply to all people, and particularly to a race of eleven million loyal Americans who unstintingly and unselfishly gave their young men, their money and their efforts to help America win the war, in spite of these terrible outrages, even while the war was in progress on their race, you can show your desire to help in no better way than by" donating money for the NAACP to lobby the government for federal laws to prosecute lynching.

Du Bois would be proven right in the end, as the MID was indeed collecting information that when examined would reveal the unconscionable conditions of blacks in America even as it catalogued and indexed details about every black publication, black leader, and black thinker. But what would the MID do with it?

Three days before Wilson left for Europe, Du Bois boarded the transport Orizaba at New York, also bound for Paris. On board were ninety-eight newspaper correspondents, photographers, and motion picture operators. All of them were white except the president of Tuskegee Institute, Robert Moton, his assistant, a New York Age reporter, and Du Bois, who had managed to obtain a passport as The Crisis editor. Du Bois had requested a passport for himself and five other black Americans, who were awaiting the State Department's approval. Besides pressing delegates at the peace table to address black oppression worldwide, Du Bois planned to do interviews and collect firsthand material for a history of black Americans in the war. And, to draw even more attention to the just claims of the black race, he was organizing a Pan-African Congress in Paris, which, among other things, would send petitions and resolutions to the peace conference urging decolonization of Africa. "It would be a calamity at the time of the transformation of the world," Du Bois wrote in a memo to Secretary of State Robert Lansing, "to have two hundred million human beings absolutely without a voice."

Madam Walker, William Monroe Trotter, and others agreed. As representatives of the National Equal Rights League, they eagerly sent in their own applications for passports, not knowing they would not receive a firm response until early February. Like Du Bois, who planned on African-American representation at the Pan-African Congress, Walker and the eight other NERL delegates were hopeful for approval. They were confident that they soon would be making history in Paris. For they would be the representatives of their people asking the peace conference to apply the ideal of self-determination to African nations, to shine a light on the hypocrisies that oppressed them, and to return the German colonies in Africa to native control. But also like Du Bois—who was shadowed even on his transatlantic trip—they were being watched.

Hallie Queen's relationship with the MID had begun in August of 1917 through a former professor of hers at Cornell University, Dr. J. W. Jenks. That summer she sent Dr. Jenks several detailed observations of African-Americans she had been watching and considered suspicious. With the first of what were effectively surveillance reports she sent a note to Jenks that read: "I am sending you the enclosures, not that I love my race any the less but that I love humanity more."

Dr. Jenks forwarded that note, several of her reports, and a recommendation to an official at the War College, which during the summer of 1917 was in charge of Military Intelligence. Jenks's own note gave Queen high praise: "As I told you she was earlier a pupil of mine and I think would be intelligent and faithful in undertaking any work. I shall myself be glad to help in this connection in any way that I can."

On August 23 the official interviewed Queen and wrote a detailed report about his impressions. He was especially pleased that she was fluent in four languages and he believed that she was clearly "in a position to hear and observe unrest among the colored people, particularly the more educated ones." Soon Queen was watching various individuals in Washington and sending handwritten reports from her apartment to the MID via Dr. Jenks, who during the war was assigned to work on the Aircraft Production

Board. She signed her letters "Holding myself at your service, I am Yours very truly, Hallie E. Queen."

On Christmas night, Madam Walker's chauffeur, Louis Tyler, drove Walker, Queen, and a few other guests into Manhattan to see a basketball game at the Manhattan Casino at 155th Street and Eighth Avenue. Here Madam Walker's daughter and the well-known black writer James Weldon Johnson had hosted a glittery send-off for the soldiers of the 369th Regiment earlier in 1918. So celebrated was Madam Walker that she was asked to start the game by throwing the ball from her box. She then received a standing ovation. That night she and Queen stayed in the city at the elegant townhouse belonging to Madam Walker's daughter.

Madam Walker apparently never knew about Queen's covert work during the war nor did she suspect Queen of spying on her during the Christmas holidays, which Queen may or may not have been doing. But in the months ahead, Walker would awaken to the government's suspicions about her. "Now they [soldiers] will soon be returning. To what? To submit to being strung up, riddled with bullets, burned at the stake?" she said to a white businessman in Manhattan who had called her "militant." "No! A thousand times No! And what good friend, even of humanity, would wish it so?"

A few days after Christmas, Madam Walker and Tyler drove through the first severe snowstorm of the season to the southern tip of Manhattan to Pier A to watch the return of three warships in the Atlantic Fleet. While tens of thousands of New Yorkers lined the Hudson River shoreline, from Battery Park all the way to 173rd Street, Madam Walker joined a small group invited by the mayor to view the spectacle from a police boat. The group included the New York police commissioner, the governor of British Columbia, newspaper tycoon William Randolph Hearst, and retail executive Rodman Wanamaker. Three out of the eleven ships were scheduled to dock that morning: the *Kansas* with 1,428 returning soldiers; the *North Carolina* with 1,288; and the *Georgia*, with 967. En route were the *Nieuw Amsterdam*, the *Pastores*, the *Powhatan*, the *Koningin der Nederlanden*, the *Bali*, the *Siboney* and the *Karesaspa*, carrying in all 16,375 men, all white. The approximately 40,000 black soldiers who had fought in the war, including the Harlem Hellfighters, would begin their journeys home in early 1919.

That same morning, while the sun slowly warmed up the chilly New

York air, the victims of America's last lynching of 1918 were buried in Alabama—two black men, ages fifteen and twenty, and two black women, ages sixteen and twenty. All four had been hanged in Mississippi from the girders of a bridge spanning the Chickasawhay River. They were suspected of murdering a local doctor whose actual murderer, a white man, would be found several days after the hangings. As the four victims stood on the bridge with the nooses around their necks, they begged the white men to set them free. Despite the severe beatings they had endured to force their confessions, they continued to profess their innocence. But this only agitated their killers. To stop the cries of innocence, one man repeatedly struck the older of the girls in the mouth with a wrench, hitting her enough times to knock out all her teeth. She was five months pregnant. The younger girl was also pregnant, due in two weeks. They hit her enough times in the back that she was nearly unconscious by the time the four were hanged. On the afternoon of the burials, the younger girl's mother believed that the baby in her daughter's womb was still alive. But no one knew how to save it and everyone was afraid to seek help outside the circle of friends who had come to mourn the dead that day.

CHAPTER 4

Women and Molasses

At 4 P.M. on January 1, a horse-drawn wagon pulled up on the sidewalk in front of the White House, directly in line with the main entrance. Two women in full-length white dresses solemnly and silently unloaded a stone urn filled with firewood. A line of women carrying purple, white, and gold banners then appeared. One of them threw lighted matches into the pile of kindling while another deposited a slip of paper with an excerpt from one of President Wilson's speeches on democracy delivered in Europe, this one at Manchester, England. "We will enter into no combinations of power which are not combinations of all of us," it read.

Then, every two hours throughout the New Year's night, a bell sounded from the upper balcony of the headquarters of the National Woman's Party a half block away, signaling a new group of women to march to the White House, tend the fire, wave the tricolored banners of their crusade, and throw another of Wilson's recent speeches into the flames. The demonstration had been planned by Alice Paul, the leader of the National Woman's Party. She called her exhibition "the watch fires of freedom." The fire, Paul told the press, was a token of women's indignation against President Wilson's claim to be the spokesman of the people of his nation and the leader of world democracy while half of his own people were disenfranchised.

One excerpt soon to be ashes was Wilson's toast at Buckingham Palace in December: "We have used great words, all of us. We have used the words 'right' and 'justice,' and now we are to prove whether or not we understand these words." Another was from his December 13 speech upon his arrival in France: "Public opinion strongly sustains all proposals for co-operation of self-governing peoples."

At each enactment of the ritual, one woman fed the fire with the paper scraps bearing Wilson's speeches while two others unfurled a banner that read:

PRESIDENT WILSON IS DECEIVING THE WORLD WHEN
HE APPEARS AS THE PROPHET OF DEMOCRACY.

PRESIDENT WILSON HAS OPPOSED THOSE WHO
DEMAND DEMOCRACY FOR THIS COUNTRY.

HE IS RESPONSIBLE FOR THE DISFRANCHISEMENT OF
MILLIONS OF AMERICANS.

WE IN AMERICA KNOW THIS.

THE WORLD WILL FIND HIM OUT.

Taunting Wilson as a hypocrite and using the White House as a battle-field were not new tactics for the thirty-four-year-old Alice Paul. Born a Quaker in New Jersey, Paul may have had a demure, prim appearance and often listened with hands calmly folded in her lap, but at heart she was a warrior. After graduating from Swarthmore College in Pennsylvania, Paul went to London, where she studied labor at the universities of London and Birmingham and, like her fellow reformers Jane Addams and Eleanor Roosevelt, she worked with women in the London slums—an experience that raised her consciousness about the importance of women's equality. In 1913, she returned to the United States and founded the National Woman's Party, thus beginning her campaign for suffrage. In the spring of 1917 Paul had attacked the president for sending soldiers to Europe to fight for democracy while at home denying women their right to vote as citizens of a democracy. Exercising her right to demonstrate many times over the next six months, the slight, frail-looking Paul led battalions of suffragists in front of the White House, all brandishing banners of protest. On October 20, 1917, Paul was arrested for picketing with a banner that carried Wilson's words from a 1917 poster soliciting funds for a Liberty Bond: "The time has come to conquer or submit. For us there can be but one choice. We have made it."

Sentenced to seven months in prison, Paul, already only ninety-five pounds, immediately commenced a hunger strike, refusing anything other than bread and water. This, she believed, could be the strongest weapon of all to draw the nation's attention to her cause. During the three weeks and one day that the hunger strike lasted, prison officials threatened to remove her to an insane asylum. Still, she would not give up. Fearing she would die, prison doctors funneled liquids into her stomach through tubes forced down her throat. After five weeks in prison she was set free. Five weeks after that, President Wilson, who ardently opposed what he viewed as Paul's militant party—his respect leaned toward the more moderate National American Woman Suffrage Association—showed that he was listening carefully to her most recent threat: that women would withhold their support for his war if their right to vote was not granted. In early January of 1918, Wilson, who had said from the start that suffrage was a state issue, announced his endorsement of what was called the Susan B. Anthony Amendment to the Constitution "as a war measure." Women's suffrage was essential now, he stressed, as "We have made partners of the women in this war. Shall we admit them only to a partnership of sacrifice and suffering and toil and not to a partnership of privilege and of right?" But Wilson, the suffragists claimed, did not press Congress to move ahead with the amendment. Wilson announced his support, they said, and wanted theirs, but he was not putting his words into motion. Thus, Paul and her compatriots blamed Wilson when in October of 1918 the Senate voted against the amendment's passage, just two votes short of the necessary two-thirds majority: fifty-four for and thirty against. Now, armed with unwavering determination, a growing constituency, and a savvy understanding of the endgame dynamics of party politics, Paul looked at 1919 as *the* year.

By dusk on New Year's night 1919, hundreds of spectators had gathered to watch the shooting flames of protest. Then suddenly out of the cluster a dozen or more soldiers and citizens darted, firmly grasping rocks and hammers. They charged upon the women's giant urn, smashing it and hurling the shards at the women. Knocking down the women who held banners, they screamed cheers for the president: "The world's leader of democracy." "The best friend the women of America ever had." Police arrived and drove the mob away, though not arresting anyone. The women then started a new fire in nearby Lafayette Park in another urn. And just as the flames once again lit up the faces of the crowd, six women were arrested: Mrs. Phoebe Munnecke of Detroit; Mary Dubrow of Passaic, New Jersey; Julia Emory of Baltimore; Mrs. Lawrence Lewis of Philadelphia; Mrs. Annie Arnell of Wilmington, Delaware; and Alice Paul. As they were taken away, other members of their party appeared with fresh kindling, piling it higher and higher in the urn. By dawn, the watch fires were still ablaze and eight more women had been arrested. Given the choice of a fine or incarceration, they chose a five-day jail term. The light of the flames, Paul had told the press earlier that day, "will act as a spotlight on President Wilson who, while attempting to secure the allegiance of the nations for self-government declares himself unable to win one despotic Senatorial vote for self-government in America." On the third day of the year, a Mrs. John Winters Brannan and Mrs. John Rogers, Jr., both members of the National Advisory Council of the National Woman's Party, spoke to a *New York Times* reporter. "Our Liberty bonfires are a symbol of our contempt for words unsupported by deeds. We will not sit in silence while the President presents himself to the people of Europe as the representative of a free people when the American people are not free and he is chiefly responsible for it," said Mrs. Brannan.

A few hours later, as women waving their banners of justice streamed toward the White House once again, Mrs. Brannan, of St. Paul, and Mrs. Rogers, of Boston, were arrested, followed by more than a dozen others. Soon, with Paul, they would formulate yet another plan: this time to tour the nation on a special train they would call the "Democracy Limited," taking their cause to the people. Thus would they pressure legislators who had blocked passage of the suffrage amendment. For three weeks, beginning early in February, the twenty-six women, all "convicts" now from the watch-fire incident, planned to travel to at least fifteen cities. "From Prison to People" would be their slogan.

On that same January 3, a missive, unknown to Paul and the other watch-fire women, landed on the desk of Senator George Moses of New Hampshire—one that would coincidentally bless their next venture. It was from former president Theodore Roosevelt, written from his home on Long Island, where he was recovering from a two-month bout of severe inflammatory rheumatism. Resting in the hospital from Armistice Day to Christmas Day, Roosevelt had immediately begun a daily regimen of work that included letter writing. In the letter to Senator Moses, Roosevelt said that women's right to vote was not in any way a "wildcat experiment" and must, without a doubt, be adopted: "You know how fond I am of [Henry] Cabot Lodge, and I think he has done wonderful work during the past three months in international matters. But it is a misfortune from the standpoint of the war and from the standpoint of party expediency that he [and other senators named] should have been so bitter about woman suffrage. I earnestly hope you can see your way clear to support the national amendment. It is coming anyhow and it ought to come."

Three days later, on January 6, at about 4 A.M., Roosevelt died. His physicians said the immediate cause of death was a clot of blood that had detached itself from a vein and entered the lungs. The clot was attributed to the poison in his blood from a fever he had contracted five years before during a trip to Brazil. The nation mourned, the world mourned, and everyone, from statesmen and financiers to chauffeurs and hunters, had something to say about Roosevelt's indomitable will, his strong intellect, and his marvelous store of energy. He was a man of action. He was a man of thought. He was a man who at any cost of personal popularity defended what he believed to be right. Roosevelt's life ended at the commencement of a year destined to be a crucible of change.

On the day of Roosevelt's funeral, Paul and her cohorts were released from jail and immediately began work on the details of their national tour. It would begin in Charleston, South Carolina, they decided, and after stops in Jacksonville, Knoxville, New Orleans, San Antonio, Los Angeles, San Francisco, Denver, Chicago, Milwaukee, Detroit, Syracuse, Boston, and Hartford, it would end in New York in March on the last day of the present Congress. A *New York Times* editorial writer who dubbed the tour the "Prison Special" said that the timing was good, as the nation was vulnerable "these days to flying squadrons of agitators." Look at Prohibition, he noted. Perhaps suffrage was next.

Unlike the slow-moving suffrage amendment, the new constitutional amendment for prohibition of the sale and consumption of alcohol nationwide was only days away from passing the test of ratification in thirty-six states. Michigan, on January 2, was the 16th state to ratify it, and Nebraska, on the 16th of January, brought the vote to the three-fourths majority necessary to pass it. "The rain of tears is over," Evangelist Billy Sunday told an audience that day in Virginia. "The slums will soon be a memory; we will turn our prisons into factories, our jails into storehouses and corn cribs, our men will walk upright. Now women will smile, children will laugh, hell will be for rent."

The news about Prohibition, for most Americans, brought with it a certain amount of shudders and sighs, confusion and panic. When must saloons and liquor stores stop selling alcohol? What about ancillary businesses, such as distillers? When would it no longer be legal to drink at home? And what about private clubs? Prohibition was indeed the talk of the nation in mid-January, except in Boston where the focus was not on liquor, but rather on molasses.

On January 15, some Bostonians heard a loud, muffled roar shortly after noon coming from the direction of the waterfront near Commercial Street. Next they felt the ground beneath them trembling. Windows shattered; horses screamed; the sky darkened. A wave of molasses twenty-five feet high and 160 feet wide was moving through the streets of Boston's industrial north at thirty-five miles per hour, crushing autos, trains, trestles, horses, dogs, rats, and every man, woman, and child who could not outrun its unstoppable assault. Sucking its victims into the smothering folds of its sticky mass, the molasses slammed up against buildings, crashed through alleys, and rolled into Boston harbor.

Without a second of warning, at 12:40 P.M., a tank holding 2.3 million tons of molasses had exploded. It was owned by Purity Distilling Company, a subsidiary of the United States Industrial Alcohol Company, which sold the molasses to rum makers. In just five minutes, the waterfront district was leveled and the streets were waist-deep in molasses. As in all disasters, the body count was uncertain for days. Exactly how many animals died was never known, though the corpses of ten horses and one cat were found. At least 150 people were hospitalized and twenty-one died, including a fireman.

No one knew the cause, and regiments of investigators would be testing theories for many months. One explosives inspector claimed that the tank did not explode. It disintegrated. A structural weakness in combination with the fermentation inside caused the walls to crack and the building to collapse with such force that it sounded like an explosion. The government accused the company of criminal negligence for operating an unsafe, poorly constructed tank that had not been properly maintained. The company countered with one explanation "beyond question": sabotage by "evilly disposed persons." The proof, the company said, was that anarchists had attached posters to the fences near the molasses tank. Worse still, scattered throughout the wreckage were little pink slips of paper bearing anti-government messages.

To bolster the notion of sabotage, the company pointed out that on the last day of December bombs in Philadelphia had destroyed the homes of the chief justice of the Pennsylvania Supreme Court, the city's acting superintendent of police, and the president of the Philadelphia Chamber of Commerce. In fact, on New Year's Day, newspapers nationwide quoted the Philadelphia police chief, who said he and others were certain this was the "start of terrorist plots planned to reach from one end of the country to the other." By the time both the criminal and civil cases in the great molasses disaster went to trial, there would be more such incidents, which any legal defense team could twist into a conspiracy theory to explain the exploding molasses tank. It was a defense that in other times might have been received publicly as a transparent, far-fetched excuse for disastrous corporate oversight. But in 1919, nothing seemed more plausible than to blame radicals, anarchists, socialists, or at least immigrants, for the madness and the mayhem in the helter-skelter aftermath of war.

CHAPTER 5

The List

On the morning of January 25, as men and women across America read the front pages of the nation's major newspapers, many were asking the same question. Even top-level officials in the Wilson administration joined the impatient chorus: Who in the world is Archibald Stevenson?

It was the end of a week of testimony in a Senate subcommittee that, since September, had been investigating charges by government officials, including A. Mitchell Palmer—soon to be the attorney general—against the United States Brewers' Association and the liquor industry for plotting to exert a pro-German influence on the press, the public, and politicians during the war. Headed by Senator Lee S. Overman, a Democrat from North Carolina, the committee had loosely interpreted its mission to mean an extensive, general probe into pro-German activities and propaganda. As such it had become the first congressional investigation of political activities and opinions of American citizens. That the Overman Committee might creep past the boundaries of its mandate was not surprising, considering Overman's work during the war as a secret informant for the Bureau of Investigation rooting out potentially disloyal individuals nationwide. In his numerous reports, Overman had alleged that Germans controlled all Jewish businesses in the United States and more recently that munitions plants owned by Germans and Austrians were supplying weapons to radicals nationwide.

Toward the end of January, the committee had stepped the furthest away thus far from its initial intent when it entered the wide-open frontier of fear: Bolsheviks in America. To people like Overman, who trafficked in fear and suspicion, it seemed a logical step. Overman claimed to have evidence of collusion between the Germans and the Bolsheviks, which if true would justify his committee's interest in Bolshevism and would create the necessary bridge between wartime threats to American security and those in the aftermath of war. This of course would keep the fear-mongering spirit alive long after the Armistice.

First, according to Overman, there was the Treaty of Brest-Litovsk in March of 1918 between Russia and Germany, which took Russia out of the war, thus freeing German troops to strengthen their attack against the Allies on the Western Front. Then, in October of 1918, George Creel's Committee on Public Information had published *The German-Bolshevik Conspiracy*, a compilation of supposedly genuine Russian documents smuggled out of Russia by Edgar Sisson, who was Creel's representative in Petrograd (St. Petersburg). The Sisson documents—whose authenticity would eventually be questioned—supposedly proved that Germany and Russia were working together, that Lenin and Leon Trotsky were German agents, and that the Russian Revolution was indeed a German takeover of Russia. The documents purported to show that the Revolution was financed in part by the German Imperial Bank.

Next, there was the issue of labor strikes. As with the conspiracy imagined in Boston after the molasses tank explosion and the concurrent Philadelphia bombings, any confluence of events created the fear of coordinated evil. Thus, it was relatively easy for Overman and others to connect the Bolshevik Revolution in Russia with domestic labor unrest in America, where there was now an average of at least two hundred strikes a month.

And then, adding to the already volatile mix, there was the indefatigable Archibald Stevenson. A New York lawyer who had spent months studying the relationships of pro-German Americans, pacifists, Bolshevists, and radicals, Stevenson carried a card in his wallet embossed with the seal of the War Department and signed by Marlborough Churchill. The card identified him as "Special Agent 650." Although his exact job was a bit vague, Stevenson worked in a propaganda division of the New York branch of the MID, where he was known for his belief that Bolsheviks were German operatives. This was a notion that had inspired his inflammatory memo in November of 1918 in which he alerted the federal government to a Bolshevik conspiracy to take over the United States. In early January, the Union League Club in New York City, which was then an establishment of wealthy, patriotic dollar-a-year volunteers fighting "disloyalty" much like the American Protective League, appointed Stevenson to head a committee to explore Bolshevism in New York. As a member of the Union League Club, Stevenson had started a new division within it known as the Propaganda League.

On the 22nd and 23rd of January, Stevenson traveled to Washington to attend the Overman Committee hearings, intending to share his views about the link between German sympathizers and radicals in America during the war, between Germans and Bolsheviks in general, and then the final link between Bolsheviks and postwar radicals in postwar America. He was certain, as he testified, that the same individuals who had opposed the war were now to be found in various radical organizations and that Bolshevism was the "gravest menace in the country today."

On the afternoon of the 23rd, Democratic senator William Henry King of Utah asked Stevenson a series of questions about the wartime activities of radicals who had opposed the war and had protested the enforcement of wartime laws, such as the Selective Service Act. In his answers, Stevenson warned about the "interlocking relation" among German sympathizers, pacifists, and radicals, and he expressed deep concern about university campuses as centers of dangerous propaganda.

"Have you discovered that in many universities there were professors who subscribed to these dangerous and anarchistic sentiments?" asked King.

"A very large number," Stevenson said.

"And participated in this class of revolutionary and Bolshevist meetings and organizations?" King asked.

"Quite a large number of them, mostly among professors of sociology, economics, and history," said Stevenson, with a professorial air of certainty.

"It seems to me," King continued, "that this is a good time for the States and those who control the universities to look into this matter."

Senator Knute Nelson, a Republican from Minnesota, then added, "I should like to get a list of these professors."

Stevenson, ever willing to fulfill his perceived duties of being a patriotic American while seeking national recognition for his hard work, responded, "I have a 'Who's Who' here that I have prepared, giving a brief biographic sketch of each."

Stevenson's list of nearly two hundred names was submitted to the committee, which during the next twenty-four hours eliminated 140 or so individuals who had ceased any demonstration of antiwar sentiments after April 1917, when the United States declared war on Germany. It was decided also to eliminate excessive biographical data and simply to include the person's name, title, and names of organizations that had propelled him or her onto the list. The list was then given to clamoring reporters, whose editors certainly saw the front-page value and decided that the source for the list, being a member of the Military Intelligence Division, and hence part of the army, was reliable. What a dazzling, irresistible story it was: a roster of un-American Americans suspiciously engaged during the war and thus important to expose now, especially in light of Stevenson's warning of the link among Germans, pacifists, and Bolsheviks, and the Bolshevik plot to take over America.

On Saturday morning, January 25, Jane Addams, the esteemed social reformer from Chicago who had founded Hull House settlement house, which served the neighborhood poor and which had, only weeks before, earned her recognition as one of the nation's most oustanding citizens, saw her name first on the list. Noted next to her name were these credentials: chairman, Woman's Peace Party; vice chairman, American Neutral Conference Committee; Executive Committee, American Union Against Militarism; Council of Fellowship of Reconciliation; American League to Limit Armaments. Addams was dedicating her life to serving the poor and to bringing about world peace. Wasn't this also what the president was doing in Europe: trying to establish a world league to end militarism?

Without warning, without a letter from a lawyer or a government agency, without any previous knowledge of the compilation of such a list, sixty-two Americans found their names on the Who's Who of subversion in America. There were some obvious choices, such as Roger Baldwin, in jail for violating the Selective Service Act; the socialist Eugene Debs, who was awaiting his prison sentence for violating the Espionage Act during a speech in Canton, Ohio, the previous August; Kate Richards O'Hare, a prominent socialist from Kansas and the mother of four children, who was now in prison for violating the Espionage Act; labor activist Elizabeth Gurley Flynn, under indictment for defying the Espionage Act; Scott Nearing, a former University of Pennsylvania professor whose trial was set for February for violating the Espionage Act by publishing an antiwar pamphlet entitled *The Great Madness*; Oswald Garrison Villard, the bold editor of *The Nation* magazine; and Charles Beard, the esteemed historian who, after teaching at Columbia University for thirteen years, resigned in 1917 to protest the dismissals of two professors for their pacifism.

There were others, including the well-known New York sociologist, nurse, and teacher Lillian Wald, who had founded the Henry Street Settlement and whom the *New York Times* would later name as one of the greatest living American women, Frederic C. Howe, commissioner of immigration at Ellis Island in New York, and the noted reformer David Starr Jordan, then chancellor of Stanford University. The former dean of Columbia University's law school was named, as were professors from other departments at Columbia and from Brown, Princeton, Harvard, Tufts, and Cornell universities, Swarthmore College, the University of Chicago, Haverford College, the University of Texas, Wellesley College, the University of California at Berkeley, Boston School of Theology, and the University of Colorado. Rabbis and ministers from New York, Seattle, and Chicago were included, and lawyers from everywhere.

The initial shock of those named on the front page of the *New York Times* quickly gave way to indignation, rage, and action. Charles Beard fired off a sizzling letter to Senator Overman in which he said "I am not and never have been" a pacifist and explained that he had not even belonged to "Mr. Wilson's sweet neutrality band," in 1916. Lindsay T. Damon, a professor at Brown, was especially piqued. How could he be accused of being unpatriotic and disloyal if he had taken a leave of absence from Brown to serve his government and indeed was working for the War Department? Four days after finding his name on the list, Damon sought a reprieve and a public apology from the committee, which responded by telling him that they did not consider him to be "un-American" and that they would enter that opinion onto the record. In his appearance before the committee, Damon was irate. "Can I make myself clear? I am boiling with indignation that Mr. Stevenson ever used my name at all." However, the committee refused to take his name off the list or clear him publicly.

Another professor, Frederick A. Bushee from the University of Colorado, sent a letter to the committee demanding a retraction of his name and professing his strong support of the war from the beginning. He was as radical as Woodrow Wilson himself, Bushee said, and the Senate had "no business to permit names to be printed as suspicious when they know no more about them than they do about me."

Gilbert E. Roe, a New York attorney who worked with the National Civil Liberties Bureau, had a different approach. He sent a strident letter to committee chairman Overman, attacking Stevenson for having ulterior motives in the selections on his list—a vengeful, calculated list, thought Roe. A close look at the names, wrote Roe, showed that some were indeed steadfast pacifists but then again many were not. Some had been earnest advocates of war with Germany even before Wilson was; some had opposed going to war with Germany at the time President Wilson did; and some had changed their minds when the president did. Attitude toward the war could not have been the reason for Stevenson's choices. What most of the people had in common, Roe suggested, was that they had spoken out or written articles exposing and opposing the tactics of the shadow war "whereby the homes of citizens have been unlawfully invaded and their persons and property seized without warrant or pretext of legal authority. The emissaries of the Military Intelligence Department again and again have invaded homes, arrested persons, held them incommunicado for days, seized and carried away property," wrote Roe. Who was Stevenson, anyhow? Roe asked, as if he had played out all the possible scenarios and now with a heavy sigh was throwing up his hands and asking the obvious question. What right did this man have to judge the activities of any private citizen and then, worse still, publicize what he suspected?

Secretary of War Newton Baker wanted to know the same thing. The list was an embarrassment to the military and to the MID, and he seemed as agitated as those named. The day after the release of the list, Baker sent a scalding order to the New York Bureau of the MID to shut down, permanently. He instructed all MID personnel never again to share information with senators, congressmen, congressional committees, and persons in official or private life in Washington or anywhere else, without obtaining official, written, signed permission from Baker himself. No MID agent could ever again testify before the Overman Committee or any other congressional hearing. He told the press in a written statement that the list included "names of people of great distinction, exalted purity of purpose, and lifelong devotion to the highest interest of America and of mankind." And he told the media that to his knowledge Stevenson had never been employed by or was an officer of the Military Intelligence Division.

Offended and incensed, Senator Overman leaked to a *New York Times* reporter a copy of a letter dated December 17, 1918, from the MID in New York to the director of military intelligence in Washington. The letter suggested that "Archibald Ewing Stevenson of the propaganda section" would be an informed witness for the investigation of German propaganda and its link to radicals in the United States. A copy of the letter was sent on to the Overman Committee. "This committee never heard of Mr. Stevenson until his name was called to the attention of the committee" by the War Department itself in the December memo, Overman told the *Times.* He then chastised Secretary of War Baker for not knowing his own staff and for being out of touch with the intelligence division of his own department.

Baker did not respond specifically to Overman. Instead, he sent out more orders, calling off the civilian watchdogs and ending the MID's use of volunteer spies, such as the American Protective Leaguers, who were to shut down operations officially on February 1.

But while Baker was trying to muzzle the MID and its apostles of surveillance, two things happened that would soon reverse his policy and remobilize the MID. First, in Seattle, more than 35,000 shipyard workers went on strike on January 21 and the city's Central Labor Council announced that all unions in Seattle would join in a general strike on February 6 to show solidarity. To many it meant that Bolshevists had struck the Pacific Northwest like lightning bolts, soon to cause the nation to burst into the flames of revolution. Then, Overman asked the Senate to officially extend and expand his congressional investigation beyond German propaganda to Bolshevik propaganda and its promulgators in the United States. As citizens of Seattle were stocking up on supplies and preparing for a long siege and businessmen were purchasing guns and taking out riot insurance, the U.S. Senate approved Overman's request. The hearings were scheduled to begin on February 11 and to last until March 20. To Overman's way of thinking, if the American public was not convinced by now that Bolshevism was the new enemy, the Seattle strike and the testimony in the upcoming hearings would complete the job.

Ironically, in the midst of the Stevenson mayhem, Baker's loud repudiation of the list and the MID's black eye may have helped one American—one socialist American, in fact. Carl Sandburg. The government's embarrassment may indeed have hastened Sandburg's settlement with federal agents and lawyers, which until the appearance of the list had seemed intransigent. Sandburg not only wanted his confiscated research materials back so that he could write about Russia, but he also was trying to avoid federal charges for bringing money into the country from allegedly suspicious sources. On the one hand, he held an honorable discharge from the U.S. Army from 1898 and he had witnesses, including Clarence Darrow, who would attest to his pro-Allies stance going into the war. On the other, Sandburg's great journalistic source in Stockholm, the former Chicago teacher known as Mike Berg, who had introduced himself to Sandburg as Michael Borodin, was actually named Mikhail Markovich Gruzenberg. And that was a problem. Like many immigrants, labor organizers, and socialists in America who hastened to assist Russia's new "workers' state," in the fall of 1918, Borodin had been working for Lenin in Stockholm with the mission to send information about the Revolution to America. The MID knew about Borodin. However, by late January the government did not need another scandal involving a highly respected American. What they wanted was to examine and censor Sandburg's materials.

On January 28, Sandburg signed an affidavit that relinquished "all of the books, pamphlets, newspaper clippings, magazines, manuscripts, and other similar material" that he had brought into the country to the U.S. attorney for the Southern District of New York, the MID, and the Bureau of Investigation, giving them permission to allow any other government agency free access. The materials would be returned to Sandburg if the U.S. attorney could establish that they did not violate the Espionage Act or any other law. It would take three months—as well as appeals from George Creel and Secretary of War Newton Baker—for Sandburg to retrieve his papers. Nothing was said about the two drafts of $5,000 Sandburg carried to America to deliver to the head of the Finnish Information Bureau and there was no subsequent record of their fate. In the weeks ahead, Sandburg would deliver the 400 kronor to Borodin's wife in Chicago.

The next day Sandburg prepared to leave New York and in a letter to his wife, Paula, in Chicago, he wrote, "Always I have loved watching storms. And this world storm with all its shadows and pain and hunger has its points—I'm for it—just as I have no criticism of all the waste and afterbirth gore that go with a child born."

CHAPTER 6

A Mere Slip of a Girl

To Harry Weinberger, defense attorney in New York City, Archibald Stevenson's list was a mere rumbling, a tiny jolt, warning him—and all others who opposed the shadow war—about the vast domestic intelligence network seething beneath the surface of postwar America. Well known after his eloquent defense in 1918 of the young Russian immigrant Mollie Steimer and her alleged co-conspirators, Weinberger despised the espionage and sedition laws and thus focused his legal brilliance on assisting their victims. How easily democracy could slip from the grasp of ordinary people! It was not for the love of money or fame that Harry Weinberger practiced law; it was for the love of democracy.

Weinberger was not an anarchist, as many of his clients were, nor was he a communist. He was never a member of the Industrial Workers of the World. He wasn't even a socialist. He was, however, a deep devotee of democracy and a fighter for liberty for all individuals, whether or not he believed what they believed. In 1919, he was also a pacifist, despite his combative nature and his boyhood dream of one day becoming a soldier.

When Weinberger was twelve years old, he had tried to enlist in the U.S. Army to fight in the Spanish-American War. The recruiting sergeant turned him down but Weinberger insisted. "Don't you need a drummer boy?" he asked. "Go back to school," the sergeant told him. The boy again asked if he could participate in some way. He would do anything to be part of the war, he said. Though small in stature, he was a fighter by nature, he assured the sergeant, who again scolded him. "Back to school," said the soldier, turning his back on the boy. By the time of the next war, Weinberger was as persistent as ever, but he was now a pacifist. "As far as war between nations was concerned my mind was made up: All war was wrong," he wrote. "War only settled which side was stronger."

When asked about this dramatic transformation, Weinberger always said that the origin of his beliefs could be simply explained: the study of history. As a young man, he had memorized great speeches such as Jesus's

Sermon on the Mount, quoting fervently its "Blessed are the Peacemakers." He knew by heart Mark Twain's famous antiwar passages in "The
Mysterious Stranger." And from the writings of Robert Ingersoll, a popular
late-nineteenth-century thinker, he memorized: "I would rather have been
a poor French peasant, and worn wooden shoes, and gone down to the
tongueless silence of the dreamless dust than to have been that imperial
impersonation of force and murder that covered Europe with blood and
tears known as Napoleon Bonaparte."

So too he had read three times or more all of Emerson's essays. He knew
the histories of Greece and Rome, of France and England, and especially of
America, which he loved. He sympathized with the heroes of revolutions
who overthrew despots and at least attempted to provide justice to every
man. And he admired Henry David Thoreau largely for his creed that
"that government is best which governs least."

Like so many men and women of his generation, Weinberger was also
strongly influenced by the social philosopher Henry George, author of the
best-selling book *Progress and Poverty*. Selling hundreds of thousands of
copies worldwide in the early 1880s, this book confronted the conundrum
of industrial America: deepening poverty amid advancing wealth. George,
a writer, printer, and owner of the *San Francisco Daily Post*, identified what
he believed to be the essential flaws of capitalism: that it could not thrive
without producing poverty, war, and social inequities. But unlike other
thinkers of his era, such as Karl Marx, who believed such flaws were endemic to capitalism and thus irreparable, George believed the system could
be fixed. And for this, perhaps, as well as his passionate belief in liberty and
justice, George won the admiration of his readers. From George, Weinberger learned to be a reformer rather than a radical, standing guard at the
gates of a democratic capitalism. From George he knew that if the civil liberties of ordinary people were infringed, then the people eventually would
rise up and perhaps even revolt to regain those rights.

For Weinberger, the best chapter of any book ever written was "The
Central Truth" in *Progress and Poverty*, in which George claims that unjust
and unequal distribution of wealth in America would eventually destroy
the self-evident truths—the guarantee of liberty and justice for all—that
are the soul and heart of the Declaration of Independence. Weinberger
even memorized one line, as he was wont to do: "Only in broken gleams

and partial light has the sun of Liberty yet beamed among men, but all progress hath she called forth."

Weinberger was the son of Jewish immigrants from Budapest, Hungary. Growing up in an Irish neighborhood along New York City's East River, he learned quickly how to fight, becoming in his own words, "a pugnacious little East Sider who fought for the love of fighting." After high school, he immediately went to work as a stenographer to pay for his night schooling in law at New York University. When he passed the bar in 1908 fewer than one out of ten lawyers in New York were college graduates. Only five feet four and a half inches, Weinberger was still a great fighter; but now his battlefield was the courtroom.

In his early years of practicing law, he was an active member of the Republican Party in New York, serving as captain of his election district, publicly debating Democrats and socialists, working briefly as an assistant to the New York attorney general, and planning to run for office. But because of Woodrow Wilson's strong stand in 1916 against the war and Weinberger's firm commitment to prevent wars, he switched parties. As a Democrat, he worked hard on Wilson's campaign. But early in 1917, the faint roar of the drums of war was growing stronger and Weinberger began to distrust Wilson. When America declared war on Germany, Weinberger remained true to his principles of pacifism and isolationism and left the Democratic Party—thus, as he later wrote, "wrecking my political career."

And so it was that Weinberger returned full-time to the courtroom, following in the tradition of the writers and thinkers he had so admired in his studies. Weinberger, in his own way, would become a significant entry in his nation's history. Tightly embracing the ideals of liberty and justice, he was committed to democracy and dedicated to fighting violations of individual rights as guaranteed by the Constitution and Bill of Rights. Although he believed there were moments when leaders could be given special powers to protect the security of their nation, Weinberger was adamant in his belief that even at such times, in a democratic nation, the liberties of speech and press and the right to petition the government and to assemble peaceably must never be outlawed. "If liberty of speech and press is not to be permitted because Americans may too easily be converted from democracy, then Americans cannot be too well grounded in their ideals, and cannot love liberty as much as we have been led to believe," he wrote.

He was also committed to the underdog, especially immigrants, whom he saw as the core of much of America's greatness. "It is the little men and women who carry on the ordinary work of civilization, and who love and transmit to their children the songs, the stories and the poetry of democracy and liberty, and who supply the backbone and support of democracy everywhere."

It wasn't surprising then that Weinberger not only disagreed with Wilson's decision to go to war but also objected vehemently to the new wartime laws: the Selective Service Act, the Espionage Act of 1917, and especially its amended 1918 version. No longer aspiring to any political post in 1917, Weinberger directed his passion to assisting individuals caught in the nasty web of such laws. For his personal motto, he adopted a phrase that he had seen written on the wall of a Texas jail where he had tried to gain the release of several Mexican revolutionists: "IT IS BETTER TO DIE ON FIGHTING FEET THAN TO LIVE ON YOUR KNEES." The pugnacious little East Sider was now in for some of the toughest fights of his life.

Because of his outspoken stand against the Great War, Weinberger lost friends, many actually, all of whom he referred to as "those who go with the wind and the tide." He also lost clients who worried about his reputation for speaking truth to power. Even those who did not abandon him during the war and postwar years sometimes distanced themselves out of fear of the people he represented and the things he said and did to give his clients a chance to walk in the sun of liberty, if only for a few miles.

Although never an anarchist, communist, or socialist, Weinberger spent time in all of those circles, not only defending the right to express such beliefs but also working with the organizations. Shortly after Wilson announced America's entry into the war, for example, Weinberger joined Emma Goldman and Alexander Berkman's No-Conscription League. In May of 1917, at one of their meetings, he spoke out against the newly enacted Selective Service Act, calling it unconstitutional for violating the Thirteenth Amendment, which prohibits involuntary servitude. In June both Goldman and Berkman were indicted for obstruction of that act and although they represented themselves in court, Weinberger worked for their release on bail, appealed their case, and argued it before the U.S. Supreme Court in December of 1918.

It was Goldman who first connected Weinberger to the case of Mollie

Steimer, Jacob Abrams, and four other young Russian immigrants. On the 1st of September, 1918, from her prison cell at the federal penitentiary in Jefferson City, Missouri, Goldman wrote a note to Weinberger, asking him to check out a new case. She was worried, she said, that a group of ardent young activists operating without the guidance of a caring legal adviser would say things they might later regret. "I see some more of our N.Y. boys are in trouble, Abrams & others," her note began.

On September 10, Weinberger wrote to the defendants, telling them that he would represent their interests when they entered their pleas. They agreed to work with him, thus beginning one of the most significant cases of Weinberger's career—a case that would claim his heart, mind, and soul for many months and would touch an assortment of Weinberger's notable contemporaries, such as J. Edgar Hoover, A. Mitchell Palmer, and Ray Stannard Baker. And, because of Weinberger's fighting spirit, the case of Mollie Steimer, Jacob Abrams, and their comrades would land on the desks of the great jurists Louis Brandeis and Oliver Wendell Holmes, Jr., at the U.S. Supreme Court. Their responses would eventually affect every American whose freedom of speech was thereafter challenged.

The case effectively began on the morning of August 23, 1918, shortly before eight o'clock, at the corner of Houston and Crosby Streets in New York. There a group of boys and men sat on fire hydrants, talking about this and that before beginning their workday at a nearby garment factory. Suddenly the air was filled with leaflets, fluttering to the ground from somewhere high above them, landing on their shoulders and their heads, on the sidewalk, in the gutter. Some leaflets were written in Yiddish. The workers quickly discarded those and then discovered several in English, parts of which they read out loud:

> "Our" President Wilson, with his beautiful phraseology, has hypnotized the people of America to such an extent that they do not see his hypocrisy. . . . His shameful, cowardly silence about the intervention in Russia reveals the hypocrisy of the plutocratic gang in Washington and vicinity. The President was afraid to announce to the American people the intervention in Russia. He is too much of a coward to come out openly and say: "We capitalistic nations cannot afford to have a proletarian republic in Russia." Instead he uttered beautiful phrases about Russia, which, as you see, he did

not mean, and secretly, cowardly, sent troops to crush the Russian
Revolution. . . . What have you to say about it? Will you allow the
Russian Revolution to be crushed? YOU: Yes, we mean YOU, the
people of America! The Russian Revolution calls to the workers of
the world for help. Workers of the World! Awake! Rise! Put down
your enemy and mine!

Five young men and one young woman, all Russian immigrants who
lived as a group in a small, bare apartment in the back of the third floor of
an East 104th Street building in Manhattan, had written the leaflets.
Then, with a small motor-driven press and a hand press—both found later
by government agents in the basement of 1582 Madison Avenue—they
had printed five thousand copies each, in Yiddish and in English, distributing at least nine thousand to working people at various meetings and out of
factory windows in New York's garment district.

Mollie Steimer was the one who threw the leaflets from the washroom
window on the top floor of the shirtwaist factory where she worked for $15
a week. The workmen who read them immediately informed the police.
The police then informed the New York City branch of military intelligence, which sent two agents to the factory. Scouring the building, they encountered a young Russian worker, Hyman Rosansky, who confessed he
was part of the group distributing the leaflets and he named his comrades:
Mollie Steimer, Jacob Abrams, Hyman Lachowsky, Samuel Lipman, and
Jacob Schwartz. Steimer and Lachowsky, who had handed out most of the
leaflets, and Lipman, who had written the English leaflet, were quickly arrested and taken into custody. Detectives followed Abrams—who had acquired the printing press—and Schwartz—who had written the Yiddish
circular—to their 104th Street apartment. Police raided it, confiscating
the leaflets and arresting Schwartz, Abrams, and three other young men
who came into the apartment during the raid.

When they arrived at the station, Schwartz was spitting blood, and at
least two of the others bore the evidence of beatings, from fists and blackjacks. During the interrogations that ensued, the beatings continued. Four
agents, each standing in a corner of a small room, told Lipman to take off
his glasses and began to beat him, throwing him back and forth among
them, striking him with blackjacks. Even after he lay on the floor unconscious, they continued hitting and kicking him. Abrams would testify later

at the trial that Schwartz, who suffered from two heart conditions, chronic endocarditis, which is an infection of the inner lining of the valves, and mitral stenosis, which is an obstruction of the mitral valve, was "lying on the floor covered with sweat and with his handkerchief full of blood." Lachowsky's face was bloody, his clothing blood-soaked, and clumps of hair missing later that night, according to the account of one of the other boys. "Our arrest was most terrible," Schwartz wrote from his jail cell. "While we were sitting there so worn, thin, pale-faced and bruised, the whole 'chariot wheel of Justice' rolled on to crush us."

Abrams, Steimer, Schwartz, Lachowsky, and Lipman were indicted on four counts that charged them with conspiring to violate the Espionage Act by publishing leaflets containing disloyal language against the government with the intention of inciting resistance to the war effort and crippling war production. Also indicted were Gabriel Prober, a friend of Abrams's who had been at Abrams's Upper West Side apartment when the police arrived, and Hyman Rosansky, who agreed to cooperate with the government. All were confined to the Tombs, New York City's jailhouse. Another young man, Boris Aurin, also at Abrams's apartment when the police arrived and brought into headquarters for questioning, was released for lack of evidence. Abrams was the oldest, at twenty-nine years old, and Steimer and Lipman, the youngest, were both twenty-one.

Seven weeks later, on October 14, the trial began at Foley Square, the location of Manhattan's federal courthouse. The presiding judge was Henry De Lamar Clayton, a Southern Democrat who had previously been a U.S. representative from Alabama for eighteen years. As the chairman of the House Judiciary Committee, he had introduced the Clayton Antitrust Act before his 1914 appointment to the federal bench in the Northern and Middle Districts of Alabama. Judge Clayton had never tried an Espionage Act case. Nor was the sixty-three-year-old jurist an expert on war legislation. At Foley Square, there were three such experts on the federal bench but because of an overcrowded docket in New York, Judge Clayton was called in from outside the district to take the case.

Coming from Alabama, Judge Clayton had little exposure to immigrant populations and in fact had shown a hint of prejudice by favoring English literacy tests for immigrants, which would keep many of them out of the workforce. In Alabama there were few Russians, Bolsheviks, socialists, or anarchists and there was little evidence of what was perhaps a New York watchdog style of criticizing the government. Adding to his particular state of mind, five months before he was given this case, his brother, a graduate of West Point and a colonel, had been killed in France. When the trial began Judge Clayton wore a gold service star in memory of his brother. At that moment, his tolerance for pacifists who took a stand against the war in Germany or against U.S. intervention in Russia was low.

The trial started quietly enough, without any news coverage. War news took precedence that October as it had for months. However, because of Weinberger's decision to call to the stand several prominent witnesses— such as George Creel, the head of the Committee on Public Information, and Raymond Robins, the head of the American Red Cross mission in Russia—and because of the spirited Mollie Steimer, the case soon would have staying power on the nation's front pages.

The prosecution's approach was fairly straightforward, setting out to prove that the defendants had written, printed, and disseminated seditious leaflets and that they did it with criminal intent to derail the war effort and to incite resistance to government policy. Thus they clearly violated the Espionage Act.

For the defense, Weinberger maintained that the Espionage Act was unconstitutional, that, even if it were constitutional, the defendants did not violate it, and that there was no criminal intent on the part of the defendants. There was never a single piece of evidence showing that anyone who had read the leaflets had actually tried to stop any war anywhere. Further, his clients were not pro-German, he pointed out. They were not protesting America's involvement in the war with Germany and they had not in any way obstructed it. In fact, after the United States had declared war on Germany, Abrams had offered to join a regiment of Russian immigrants to go to Russia to fight against Germany. What his clients did protest was U.S. military aggression against Russia, a nation with which the United States was not officially at war.

One of Weinberger's strategies was to show that the circulars in question were effectively true because revolutionary Russia, which President Wilson had applauded at first, had indeed been betrayed—and invaded— by the Allies. Toward this end Weinberger tried repeatedly to persuade Judge Clayton to allow into evidence President Wilson's 1917 telegram to the new Bolshevik regime in which he promised to give Russia aid and assured them of the sympathy of the American people. Weinberger also read parts of the president's own writings and speeches that were similar to his clients' allegedly treasonous circulars. All of the statements in the leaflets were true, he said, and even the president had at one time or another expressed similar, if not the same, sentiments about Russia.

To demonstrate how the nation had been lied to, Weinberger sought to expose the fraudulent Sisson documents. The Committee on Public Information, according to Weinberger, had designed the Sisson story deliberately to sway American opinion against the new Bolshevik regime, thus providing justification for military intervention against the Revolution and the new government. Weinberger was determined to show that without the awareness of the American public and without the vote of Congress, the president had sent American troops to Russia. Thus his clients' protests against a war with a nation with whom we were officially at peace were not wrong.

A large part of Weinberger's strategy was to call prominent Americans to the stand who had been in Russia and who could substantiate all that he was saying—such as Creel and Robins. When Robins testified, Weinberger asked: "Did you investigate the Sisson documents and did you reach the conclusion that they were false?

"Is it not true that the Soviet Government, before the ratification of the Brest-Litovsk treaty, asked you to bring about an understanding with the Allies to continue the war, on the part of the Soviets against Germany, on condition of material aid, and that was to consist of transportation, instructors for the army, materials, and food?

"Was not that put in the form of queries put forward by the Bolsheviki Government to the United States?

"As far as you know, was any answer ever made by the U.S. to the offer of co-operation by the Bolsheviki Government against the Germans?"

Claiming that the questions were irrelevant to the case before them, the judge told the witness not to answer. But nothing deterred Weinberger. His questions were a legal device, as he had worded them in such a way to expose facts he wanted the jury to hear. Next, he did what some defense attorneys would not have had the courage to do: he called each of his young clients to the witness stand.

Lipman testified that police had beaten him, kicked him, and dragged him around the floor by his hair. He said that he was a socialist, that he had composed the English circular, and that he had done so because he sympathized with the Russian Revolution and, in fact, celebrated it. "I was over-joyed by the idea that, for the first time in the history of the world, we have a government by the people, for the people, and from the people." Wilson had provoked him, he said, by saying to Congress, "I stretch out my hands to the Bolsheviks" and then sending a military expedition to Russia that ended up fighting the Bolsheviks. Lipman wanted simply to protest that hypocrisy.

Lachowsky admitted he had printed the circulars, denied he was pro-German, and described his mission as a protest against the intervention into Russia. Abrams confessed that he was an anarchist but insisted that he had no intention of imposing the doctrines of anarchy on anyone and that not believing in governments had nothing to do with the leaflets. On cross-examination he said he had tried to enlist in the American armed forces in order to go back to Russia to fight against Germany but he was refused. He also testified that he saw Lachowsky's bloody head and Schwartz with blood everywhere, and that he heard Lipman's moans and screams from another room.

Then came Mollie Steimer, whose maturity, audacity, obstinacy, and pure grit must have surprised everyone—even Weinberger, who repeatedly referred to her as "this little girl." Steimer, who five years before had come from the Ukraine to the United States, was indeed small in stature, being only four feet nine inches tall and weighing a mere ninety pounds. And with her short curly black hair and her full, round face, she looked even younger than she was. Yet, of all the defendants, she delivered what many considered to be the most compelling, and perhaps the most indignant, of the defense testimonies. "When you are taken and you know that you did something, then you are ready to pay the price, but when you are taken by lies and falsehood then you feel very indignant," Steimer told a journalist sixty-one years later.

Like her comrades, Steimer admitted that she had done what she was accused of doing. And like them, she claimed that under the right of free speech and a free press, she had not violated any law. Nor would she ac-knowledge the law under which she was charged, the law that her lawyer claimed to be unconstitutional. Unlike her comrades, however, she refused to take the oath before testifying and she would not rise when the judge en-tered the courtroom. As an avowed anarchist, she did not recognize the

U.S. system of law and thus she would not honor the judge. Even Weinberger was put to the test when he called her "Mollie" in his first question. She would not respond until he addressed her more respectfully as "Miss Steimer." She was tough, independent, and high-spirited.

On the stand she said that she had distributed the circulars "to show the hypocrisy of the government of the United States and the Allies, those who claimed that they were fighting for democracy, those who called themselves staunch sticklers for the right of self-determination of nations, and at the very same time interfered with the situation in Russia."

As if teaching a class, she turned to the courtroom and defined anarchism, explained why she chose to be an anarchist, and talked about her concepts for a more humane, egalitarian society. "While at present the people of the world are divided into various groups, calling themselves nations, while one nation defies another—in most cases considers the others as competitive—we, the workers of the world shall stretch out our hands toward each other with brotherly love. To the fulfillment of this idea I shall devote all my energy, and if necessary, render my life for it."

Her descriptions of her family's poverty and of her bleak days as a shirtwaist factory worker without any possibility for a meaningful future were poignant and unforgettable. The oldest of six children, she, her seventeen-year-old sister, her fourteen-year-old brother, and her father all worked in factories. Her father, she said, labored long hours at Standard Oil Company in a low-paying job in the town of Elizabethport, New Jersey. "How tired he usually comes home from work and how much so when the day's work lasted fourteen hours!" she said, speaking to the courtroom spectators as if on stage. "He would just have supper, glance at the newspaper and go to bed. Early in the morning, when all were yet asleep, father rose, took his little bundle and again went to the plant. In this manner of miserable existence the years rolled by. What did this hard laboring man get out of life? Nothing! Absolutely nothing, except suffering."

Steimer's defiance and unwavering confidence annoyed Judge Clayton. From the first time they had met, which was the day she was arraigned in his courtroom, they had been at odds. On that day, Steimer had implied that the indictments were really about the government trying to "stifle free speech." To that Judge Clayton offered a fiery response: "Freedom of speech is one thing and disloyalty is another. What you term free speech does not protect disloyalty. I am sorry for the people of New York that have to deal with individuals who have no more conception of what free government means than a Billy goat has of the gospel."

Throughout the trial he spoke to her in disapproving, condescending tones and challenged her ideals whenever possible. He even quizzed her on a personal level, agitating her about such topics as free love and polygamy. As an anarchist who did not believe in laws, did she believe in any of society's laws to protect public morality, such as marriage? he asked. She responded that she did not think such laws were successful in protecting public morality. And no, she did not believe in the necessity of a legal marriage.

"Now when a girl marries it is for the sake of getting out of the factory. It gives her a chance to get something to eat," she told the judge. "Then, because they do not really love each other, she and her husband soon grow tired of their marriage. What is the use of law combining them when their hearts are not combined any more?"

"When love grows cold you think that ends the marriage relation? Do you not believe that the marriage relation should be protected by law?" the judge asked.

"I believe," said Steimer, "that two people should combine when they love each other truly, and not because of any law."

Then was she a proponent of free love, and polygamy? Finally she told the judge firmly, "Well, I do not think that this has anything to do with this trial."

But the judge continued to impugn her, as if forcing a duel. Belief in polygamy, he told her, leaning down to face her squarely, was one of the grounds for denying citizenship to aliens and deporting them. She had already put herself in jeopardy by admitting she was an anarchist, he warned her. But the "little girl" never flinched and boldly continued to play the judge's sparring game. Perhaps she knew she couldn't be the victor, even if she won the battle. And indeed Steimer's quest was not to win the case but rather to create a dialogue to expose truths. Steimer was then as she would be for the rest of her life, "consumed with compassion to work for the good of the people," whatever the cost, as one New York journalist later described her.

In her testimony, Steimer confirmed the stories of her co-defendants about the brutality of police and detectives during the night of the arrests.

When she saw Schwartz after his interrogation, for example, he was "deathly pale," breathing heavily, and coughing up blood. The police denied inappropriate behavior against any of the defendants. Schwartz would never make it to court.

On the first day of jury selection, which was October 10, Schwartz had a fever of 103 degrees and was taken out of the prison to a bed at Bellevue, a New York hospital that was then crammed with flu victims and severely short-staffed. On the night of October 13, the thirty-two-year-old Schwartz died. The official cause listed on the death certificate was pneumonia. But Weinberger saw it differently: "His heart bled from the third degree, thus weakening him and he developed pneumonia which was the secondary and apparent cause of death."

In his closing argument, Weinberger's years of studying history and literature shone through his legal arguments. Like the great orators whose works Weinberger had memorized as a young man, he eloquently compared the young radicals on trial to historical figures who had risked speaking the truth and had stood up for their beliefs. "You may think that these defendants are unimportant. If you look back in history, that same feeling was always present in every trial where great men or great women were convicted."

Then he brought up examples of people who seemed unimportant during their lifetime but were later revered for their bravery. He began with Jesus, who was "against the government at that time, contrary to the opinions of the District Attorney of his days, contrary perhaps to the written opinions of the newspapers of his day, and he was crucified, and his thought, back in those days of Judea, has influenced the thought of the world." Next, he spoke of the soldier and teacher Socrates, who taught men to question authority and who was condemned to death by a jury and forced to drink hemlock. Socrates was ahead of his time, Weinberger said, and his opinion was different from that of the majority. He noted the great European philosopher Spinoza, who was stoned for his beliefs and later lauded. And he referred to the abolitionists, such as Elijah Lovejoy, the anti-slavery newspaper editor whose printing presses were thrown into the Mississippi River and who was shot for his belief that slavery must end.

He compared the ideals of his clients to those of great thinkers in history, such as Pierre-Joseph Proudhon in France and Ralph Waldo Emerson in America. "Whoso would be a man, must be a non-conformist," said

Weinberger, quoting Emerson. Piotr Alekseyevich Kropotkin, he said, fled
Russia because of his protests against the czar, lived in exile safely in England where he was never imprisoned for his beliefs and where he wrote
numerous books on anarchism and on the French Revolution—books
used in U.S. colleges as texts of authority. His clients also bravely stood up
for what they believed was right, standing with the Russians in their revolt
against despotism and with America against militarism, he said.

His defendants had the right to question and protest against an army
being sent to Russia. Only Congress can declare war, Weinberger said, and
then only can the president send an army to make war.

> You know that we did not know in this country that an army was
> being sent to Russia, and we found that an army was at Archangel,
> an American army, without Congress ever declaring war. What is
> it that makes the government try to shut the mouths of those who
> protest? What is it that makes the government bring an indict-
> ment, and four counts at that, against defendants who say it is
> wrong to send an army into Russia? Are we so poor, are we so weak,
> are we such cowards, that we fear the truth, or the questioning of
> truth?
>
> If our Government is true, if our Government is right in its in-
> vasion of Russia, let us have a fair discussion. You cannot answer a
> fact, gentlemen of the jury, by sending people to jail. You may seal
> the lips with death, but you cannot stop a man's idealism and mes-
> sage from continuing in the hearts of others. You may close their
> mouths but for every man and for every idealist that goes to jail,
> ten thousand more step forward.

The defendants, he said, told the truth about what they had done, admitted to the accusations of writing and distributing the pamphlets, and,
he said, they "had one big idea to carry to the Americans, a liberty-loving
people, calling to their attention what they thought was a wrongful act by
the President of the United States, without authority of Congress, sending
an army to invade a nation we were at peace with, calling to the American
public to protest."

On October 24, the jury declared four of the defendants guilty on all
four counts. Prober was acquitted on all counts. The next day, Steimer,

Abrams, Lipman, and Lachowsky appeared before the court to hear their sentences. Each was allowed to speak, which, with the utmost composure and confidence, they did. There was no breaking down, no shouting, no pleading.

"If it is really a crime to stand up for the people you love," Abrams told the jury, "if it is a crime to believe in ideals, if it is a crime to stand up for the thing that you yourself are standing up for—your country—I am proud to be a criminal."

"I am glad you got that out of your system," responded the judge.

"I do not ask for mercy," said Abrams.

"That makes my task somewhat easier," said the judge.

When it was Steimer's turn, the young girl looked out on the throng of spectators as if to find inspiration from the crowd that had gathered. But just as she was about to speak, the judge snapped, "You turn around and address the Court [the judge]. This is one time, Mollie, when you are brought in touch with a knowledge that there is some authority, even over an anarchistic woman."

She then spoke: "I do not believe in any authorities but what I do want to say is this, that though you have sent military troops to Russia to crush the Russian Revolution, though you may succeed in slaughtering hundreds of thousands of revolutionists, you will by no means succeed in subduing the revolutionary spirit. On the contrary, the more you will seek to suppress the truth, the sooner will the thought of truth and light enter the hearts of the workers and the sooner is the international social revolution bound to come."

The judge replied, "Very well, I must commend you for having the merit of brevity, and Shakespeare said that brevity is the soul of wit."

He then commenced with the sentences. Abrams, Lipman, and Lachowsky each got a $1,000 fine and twenty years in prison, to be served in the penitentiary of the state of Maryland. Steimer was fined $500 and sentenced to fifteen years at the Missouri State Penitentiary for women. Rosansky got a $1,000 fine but only three years in prison, as his confession led to the apprehension of the others.

The courtroom was brimming with spectators, many of whom ended up standing in the corridor straining to hear the sentences, and when they did, they seemed shocked. "Why they are just children!" one person said. Another said, "Twenty years in prison for calling President Wilson a 'hypocrite'?" And another replied, "Or twenty years in prison for being a Russian and believing in the new Russia?"

The defendants were sent back to the Tombs, where they had been since their arrests and would remain until Weinberger could gain their release on bail.

That night at the Parkview Palace, a meeting hall on Fifth Avenue at 110th Street, at least 1,200 people attended a memorial service for Jacob Schwartz—including several agents from the MID assigned to shadow Harry Weinberger and John Reed. Weinberger and Reed, both passionate speakers, were asked to deliver the first eulogies. And perhaps because Reed was in the midst of writing his book *Ten Days That Shook the World*, and because Weinberger, just hours before, had listened to one of the most severe sentences of his career as a defense attorney, they spoke with more than the usual fire. Weinberger, for example, said that Schwartz was a highly principled man, one of those individuals who "leave behind them a memory of idealism—a memory of having fought and worked for the betterment of their fellowmen everywhere."

Seventeen days later, the Armistice was signed and, on the same day, Weinberger won his battle to gain the young Russians' freedom from the Tombs, on bail, $10,000 each. Raising the money was a challenge but Weinberger was inspired by the hopeful news. Perhaps the U.S. Supreme Court would not only review his case but also reverse the convictions, thus freeing his clients. It was now, for Weinberger, more than a mere hope: it was a mission.

Donations for Weinberger's fund came from all over the city: large ones from wealthy sympathizers with addresses on Fifth Avenue and Riverside Drive and small ones from the Lower East Side, the South Bronx, and East Harlem. Raymond Robins and his sister-in-law sent $1,000 in Liberty Bonds. Lillian Wald sent $300 in Liberty Bonds. Frederick Blossom, a socialist and an advocate of birth control, donated $6,000, which he borrowed from a bank with interest. Some donors, jittery about associations with such high-profile radicals, asked Weinberger to respect their wish for anonymity. And most of them ironically used their Liberty Bonds to free the young rebels caught in the web of a law that punished allegedly unpatriotic behavior.

After three months behind bars, Abrams was the first to be released, on a deposit of $10,000 in Liberty Bonds, on November 16. Then on the 18th, another $10,000 in Liberty Bonds set free Mollie Steimer; on the 25th, another $10,000 from real estate and bonds funded Lipman's release. On the 27th, it was clear that Weinberger still did not have the next $10,000 for freeing Lachowsky, who was now in poor health. It was unclear whether Lachowsky had the flu but because of Schwartz's death, he refused to go to Bellevue and was weakening each day. Knowing this, Abrams volunteered to go back to jail so that Lachowsky could be released and treated as soon as possible. And this he did, for three days, when at last Weinberger came up with the money for Abrams's second release, another $10,000 in Liberty Bonds. Rosansky, who had informed on his comrades, was not a sympathetic cause for anyone except his wife. No money was raised for him and so he was transferred to the Maryland prison to begin serving his term.

On the day of Steimer's release, her cell mate, Agnes Smedley, looked out the cell window as she left the prison. Smedley would later write about Steimer, who had deeply impressed her, especially because of Steimer's compassion for female inmates who suffered from venereal disease or struggled with sick babies. "I watched her pass through the prison yard that day," Smedley wrote. "A marshal walked beside her, talking out of the corner of his mouth. He did not offer to carry her suitcase, heavy with books. Mollie did not listen to him. Her eyes were looking straight ahead into the distance."

Steimer spent Christmas Day of 1918 with her family, but without her father, who had died while she was at the Tombs, and without her brother Jack, who had also died that autumn of the flu. Although no longer behind bars, Steimer would never be totally free, as she and her co-defendants would be shadowed at all times by at least one government agent. C. J. Scully, M. J. Davis, and Frank Faulhaber, often the agents stalking Steimer, were even present on Steimer's first night of freedom at a Greenwich Village café where friends and supporters were eager to hear every detail of her life now as a celebrated criminal. According to one of the agent's reports, Steimer told her friends that her time in jail was beneficial because she had learned a lot and because "hereafter she will know how to act when necessary."

Steimer would not be able to walk to the mailbox or to a friend's apart-

ment without a government agent close behind her. One young special
assistant in the Justice Department who was only two years older than
Steimer and who was relatively new to the department was especially
interested in monitoring her activities, partly because of her possible ties to
a publication called *The Anarchist Soviet Bulletin*, which the assistant and
his superiors wished to destroy. Under the guidance of this ambitious
counter-radical specialist, whose name was John Edgar Hoover, spying on
Steimer would one day assume the character of a mission. And daring, as
always, Steimer would respond with an array of deceptions to fool and embarrass her stalkers—tempting them with suspicious-looking papers, later
found to be blank, or leading them on pointless chases around the city.
Nothing the government did seemed to frighten Steimer or deter her from
her quest to stop the U.S. invasion in Russia.

Perhaps Agnes Smedley, who spent so many days in jail with Steimer,
best described Steimer's point of view. "Mollie's reasoning is something like
this," Smedley would write in early 1920. "Under the Czar we knew there
was no hope; we did not delude ourselves into believing that he would
release those who worked against the system which he represented and
upheld. In America we have been carefully taught that we live in a democracy, and we are still waiting for some one to feed us democracy. While
waiting, we starve to death or are sent to prison where we get free food
for 15 or 20 years."

Although Weinberger seemed to appreciate Steimer's determination,
spunk, and certitude, he did have a problem with her cat-and-mouse game
with the government. One of the stipulations of his clients' releases on bail
in November was that he would be responsible for them, making sure they
did not get into trouble or flee before the appeal in the case had been decided. In other words, they were in Weinberger's custody. In the months
ahead, this would prove to be a trying task, especially regarding Steimer,
who would be arrested eight more times. The only good news for Weinberger regarding his young clients was that by early 1919 they were no
longer the only voices protesting America's military presence in Russia.
Soldiers were risking courts-martial by questioning their country's involvement in Russia. Soldiers' families, shocked to learn that the Armistice
did not end the fighting in Russia, were signing petitions and organizing protests. And a few politicians were beginning to pick at the edges of
issue. Leading the pack was a Republican senator from California, Hiram

Johnson, who, calling the U.S. intervention in Russia a "criminal policy," spoke for hours on the Senate floor on January 29:

> Why did we enter Russia? I answer, for no very good reason; and we have remained for no reason at all. And what is our policy toward Russia? I answer we have no policy. We have engaged in a miserable misadventure, stultifying our professions, and setting at naught our promises. We have punished no guilty; we have but brought misery and starvation and death to the innocent. We have garnered none of the fruits of the victory of war, but suffer the odium and infamy of undeclared warfare. We have sacrificed our own blood to no purpose, and into American homes have brought sorrow and anguish and suffering.
>
> Bring the American boys home from Russia.

CHAPTER 7

Polar Bears in Peril

So dark were the days in northern Russia by late January that daylight lasted only thirty minutes. American soldiers fighting on the frozen tundra far from the nearest city, Archangel, depended upon moonlight and the Northern Lights for most of each day, telling night from day only by reading the hands of a twenty-four-hour military clock. But the time of day was of small concern to the hollow-eyed men facing the fury of the Arctic cold and camping for weeks without shelter. Fires, which could signal the enemy, were forbidden and overcoats and blankets were their only protection from the killing temperatures. Food was scarce, as were all supplies. A shipment of four hundred rabbits from Australia arriving in January was the first meat for several months. And communications from home were severely delayed. "It is such a desolate position that we have [only now] received the tardy word that the Armistice has been signed three months ago," wrote Sergeant Gordon W. Smith, of the 339th Infantry, Company D, in a January diary entry dedicated to his wife.

Yet something even darker than the darkness of the days and nights gripped the soldiers with the merciless intensity of a new form of plague. It was called the "northern horrors." "All members of the gallant 339th are afflicted with it," wrote one soldier, who described it as a "state of melancholia" brought on by a combination of the delayed mail and isolation, the long, cheerless Arctic nights, the absence of amusements, the overwhelming number of soldiers on the opposing side, and the longing for home. "They have been shunted off into that God forsaken and lonesome land to fight an unknown foe for an unknown reason," a *Detroit Free Press* reporter wrote.

The mission of the Americans in northern Russia over the past six months had been vague. Roughly seven thousand American soldiers, many from Michigan, had departed the United States in August and September bound for the Russian ports of Murmansk and Archangel. At the same time, thousands more—two infantry regiments from the Philippines and one from California—were transferred to Siberia, where their official purpose was to guard the Allied stores at Vladivostok. In northern Russia, the Americans were also assigned to guard Allied war supplies stored many months before for czarist troops fighting the Germans. But the reality of the American mission in Russia was far more intense than guarding stores.

With the withdrawal of Soviet troops from the war in March of 1918, the Allies did fear that the new Bolshevik government would give or sell their supplies to the Germans. Moreover, they feared that a massive movement of German troops from the Eastern Front in Russia to the Western Front in Europe could mean victory for the Germans especially if, added to their force, they had in their possession the vast stores of Allied war matériel. But soon after arriving in Russia, the American soldiers found themselves not standing guard over the Allied stores but rather fighting under British command in a civil war between the Red Army of the Bolsheviks and the White Army of the opposition. The British and French troops were fighting against the Red Army to instigate the collapse of the Bolshevik government in the hope that new leadership would bring Russia back into the war on the side of the Allies.

When the Allies first called upon Wilson to send troops, he hesitated— torn between his obligations as the leader of an Allied nation and the principle of self-determination of nations, which he so ardently espoused. But despite his principles, Wilson finally succumbed to pressure from the French and the British, who had sent in their troops as early as March of 1918. There was pressure too from American banking interests. Overthrowing the Soviet government, after all, was important to bankers who had loaned at least $86 million to czarist Russia during the war and now feared that the Bolsheviks would default.

Perhaps Wilson did it for the sake of his beloved League of Nations, surmising that he must agree to help the French and the British in their Russian campaign in order to secure their cooperation in Paris. He did try to minimize the domestic impact of the deployment by issuing a directive: the American troops were only to guard the military stores. They were not, under any circumstances, to fight the Red Army. But, at the same time, he agreed to allow the American troops in northern Russia to be placed under the command of a British general, who ignored Wilson's directive.

By the time of the Armistice, there were at least thirteen thousand Allied troops stationed along the Murmansk Railroad and eleven thousand more encamped hundreds of miles from Archangel, not safeguarding Allied supplies but rather waiting for commands to continue with an offensive strategy. By Christmas, press dispatches were reporting details of skirmishes between American and Russian soldiers, the taking and retaking of towns, and all the gore of a full-fledged war. And by January of 1919, the Americans were not only entrenched in Russia's civil war, but, because of the weather and the solidly frozen harbors, they were trapped in the trenches for a long while.

By January, food, munitions, and blankets were in short supply. Frostbite and pneumonia were common as was severe rheumatism caused by wearing wet clothing in the frigid temperatures. Morale was low. The American soldiers resented taking orders from British commanders. After learning of the Armistice they questioned the purpose of their presence. Why was peace not for them when the rest of the world was rejoicing?

An entry in Sergeant Silver K. Parrish's diary spoke for the boys in Russia: "We took 16 enemy prisoners and killed 2—then we burned the village & my heart ached to have the women fall down at my feet & grab my legs and kiss my hand & beg me not to do it. But orders are orders." In his next entry, Parrish, who was from Bay City, Michigan, wrote: "I drew up a resolution to request reason why we are fighting [Bolsheviks] & why we haven't any Big Guns & why the English run us & why we haven't enough to eat & why our men can't get proper medical attention & some mail." By the time of his next entry, Parrish had learned what Mollie Steimer and Hiram Johnson already knew: how dangerous it was to protest U.S. policy in Russia. "Some one squealed on S.K.P. [Silver K. Parrish] & I was called up before the Colonel & he read the articles of War to me & sho[w]ed me where my offence was. Punishable by death. But I knew it any how."

Engaged in a campaign against a country that had not attacked America or any other Allied nation and against which America had not declared war, many soldiers wanted out. They feared that back home in America, where the public was cheering the return of hundreds of thousands of soldiers, they had been forgotten. On January 30, Sergeant Roger Sherman Clark, from Detroit, wrote to his wife in response to her mid-November letter, which he had just received and in which she had told him about the Armistice: "This last piece of news staggered me, truly, as I have builded great hopes upon [peace] panning out some day or other. I almost believe it will yet, if we continue patient and in good heart. Only let us all hope that Congress doesn't forget Russia in the next few months."

The first politician to publicly challenge the veiled invasion of Russia was Hiram Johnson, a former California governor and a U.S. senator since 1917. Johnson "discovered" the forgotten soldiers through his friend Raymond Robins, the fellow Californian who led the American Red Cross in Russia. One of California's most successful lawyers, Johnson was the son of a schoolteacher from Syracuse, New York, and the grandson of an abolitionist and lawyer who had helped to found the New York branch of the Republican Party. An isolationist first and foremost, and then a strong Republican, he was an outspoken opponent of all that Woodrow Wilson supported, including the League of Nations and especially Wilson's decision to send troops to Russia. Johnson was passionate about ending what he firmly believed to be an unwarranted, unjust, and undeclared war against Russia, a war initiated by a series of lies. "The first casualty when war comes, is truth," Johnson said often in the coming months.

It was on December 12, 1918, that Senator Johnson first focused national attention on the troops in Russia by submitting Senate Resolution No. 384. At the time most Americans believed that the November 11 cease-fire had silenced all battlefields. The only mention in the media of the continued fighting in Russia had been a *Detroit Free Press* editorial in early December written by a professor of Russian at the University of Michigan, C. L. Meader, who expressed his dismay that the end of the war with Germany did not logically result in the withdrawal of Allied troops from Russia. Was there a policy decision that he had missed? Did the Allied nations fear they would lose their vested interests and their loans to anarchists? Did the Allies want to destroy a nation whose legal and economic principles were not the same as theirs? Were the Allies conspiring to annihilate the world's first workers' state before it spread to other nations? Perhaps the American public had misunderstood what the Bolshevik government was, wrote Professor Meader—not a small group of men exercising oligarchic powers but rather a government of workers and peasants councils ("soviets") with the ultimate goal of democracy in its purest form.

In his December 12 resolution, Johnson asked the U.S. secretary of state to send to the Senate all data and documents that could explain to the Senate and to the American people why American soldiers were in

Russia. For the sake of the families who had not heard from their loved ones in Russia for months and months, he wanted to know how many were there, who was there, and exactly where they were. He asked also for casualty lists. And he noted that he knew how unpopular this subject would be. These days, he said, "it is a dangerous and delicate thing to speak of Russia or to inquire concerning our activities there."

Although he had no sympathies for the Bolshevists, Johnson knew, he said, "that a demand that American boys shall not be sacrificed to the rigors of a Russian winter and conflict with a desperate people will be termed a defense of international agitators and of the 'red flag.' During the war it became fashionable to call all who disagreed with any governmental policy pro-German. Now the fashion has changed: and any man who will not accept the wrongful edict of entrenched power is by that token a Bolsheviki."

In a December letter to one of his sons, Johnson wrote, "I have raised merry Cain with my Russian resolution. My difficulty is to avoid getting mixed with the Radicals, whom I detest, and all of whom are enthusiastic about my actions." In another letter to the son, on New Year's Eve, he wrote, "The Russian situation is a shame and a disgrace, giving the lie to all our professions of democracy."

By the time Johnson returned to the Senate floor on January 29 to deliver his "Bring American Boys Home from Russia" speech, a grassroots movement was noisily surfacing in Michigan. The mayor of Detroit dubbed the soldiers of the 339th "Detroit's Own" and assembled a delegation of their parents to travel with him to Lansing to lobby the governor to cable President Wilson to recall the troops. Families of Detroit's Own—also called the "Polar Bears"—started a petition drive. Several prominent Michigan men sent telegrams to the state's senators and congressmen asking that they press the War Department for news of the Michigan men at Archangel and most of all that they demand their withdrawal by January 15. It was then, they stressed, that the port of Archangel was expected to freeze, thus isolating the troops until spring, which could begin as late as June in northern Russia.

Further, a public debate had begun over the condition of the soldiers. Wounded soldiers who had left Russia on November 20 were arriving home with reports of hunger, disease, and depression. The snows had begun in September; the temperatures were plummeting; the Red Army outnumbered the Allies nearly ten to one; and soldiers were stricken with a numbness of limbs and spirit. Arriving in New York harbor on the ship *Adriatic,* twenty-four Michigan men of the 339th Regiment commended the comforts of their cabins, which they said were high luxury after the "murderous" conditions in northern Russia.

The War Department refuted such reports, telling the press that the boys were "well supplied with food, clothing and medical attention and not in any danger of being captured or wiped out by superior forces." The government did send out a casualty list, perhaps in response to Johnson's plea. By January 4, 132 soldiers stationed at Archangel since September had died: sixty-four killed in action, sixty-five died of diseases, three died accidentally, and sixteen were missing in action.

On January 29, Johnson stood before the Senate and slung satchels onto the floor filled with letters from mothers and fathers and wives of men in Russia pleading with the government to end the intervention. Drawing attention again to what he viewed as Wilson's hypocrisy of intervening in Russian affairs while preaching self-determination, he suggested, with more than a hint of sarcasm, that perhaps the public had misunderstood the concept of self-determination. Did it really mean "determination by ourselves of the kind of government others should have and then impressing that kind of government upon an unwilling and a rebellious people? With this possible explanation we may see with greater clarity the reason for our activities in Russia."

The way the United States and its allies had dealt with Russia thus far exhibited "the crassest stupidity," he said.

> In the name of protecting military supplies, which were offered to us again and again and again and which we could have had for the asking, we shot down Russian peasants and our boys are shot down by them. No sooner had we landed at Archangel than we shot the Soviet government there, and set up a government of our own. No sooner did we go into the interior than everywhere we found a local society we shot it to death and set up our own mode of government. Then we tell our people that we intend no interference with the internal or local affairs of Russia!
>
> How the iron must enter the souls of those who have relatives there; of the mothers and fathers and the wives of men who were

drafted to fight Germany and then when the war with Germany
was ended, were forced to fight a war with Russia.

In the days following his speech, the *Detroit News* asked its correspondent at the peace conference in Paris, Jay G. Hayden, to interview President Wilson about the plight of the Polar Bears. Why were they still in
Russia? Why were communications so severely delayed? When will they
return home? Wilson told Hayden that he was not ignoring the issue but
that "the whole Russian problem" was entangled in international diplomacy. He favored withdrawal but to retain "harmonious relations with the
Allies" he could not yet pull the troops out.

Hayden also interviewed other government officials. And in his February 4 article, he wrote, "The history of the Russian intervention revealed to
me by an American authority so high that it is beyond the possibility to
question its accuracy, shows the position of the troops to be the result of
one of the worst possible policy blunders of the war."

At a Detroit church, on the night of February 4, at least two thousand
friends and relatives of the soldiers in Russia organized Detroit's Own
Welfare Association and started a petition drive soon to result in 110,000
signatures calling for complete troop withdrawal and the end of U.S. intervention in Russia. The next day the Michigan Senate passed a resolution
demanding the same policy. Kalamazoo sent its own resolution. And in
Benton Harbor, hundreds of Republicans met in solidarity, all crying out
"Get Out of Russia!"

But just as the petition drives and demonstrations gained momentum,
the cause of the Polar Bears was dramatically upstaged by an event that
captivated and terrified the American public and the federal government.
On February 5, Seattle's mayor Ole Hanson telegraphed Secretary of War
Baker informing him that by the next morning the entire city of Seattle
would be shut down in the first general strike in U.S. history. Was this the
beginning of the much-feared revolution?

On the morning of February 6, the word "Bolshevik" was ringing in the
ears of most Americans when they heard the news that at 10 A.M. in Seattle sixty thousand workers from 110 unions, most wearing red, had left
their jobs. Strikers included recently returned soldiers who were trade
unionists and who, on that day, proudly wore their uniforms. Workers and
trade unionists across the country applauded the boldness of their brothers

while politicians and law enforcement officials saw the daunting specter of Bolshevism.

Was it possible that the power of the workers' folded arms could bring down the capitalist system? As journalist and activist Anna Louise Strong pointed out later, no one really knew precisely what would happen. It was "like pulling the trigger of a gun without knowing with what ammunition it was loaded." The government thought it was loaded with revolution, while labor leaders said it was loaded only with workers' rights. The strike, after all, was called to show solidarity for the 35,000 shipyard workers who had gone on strike earlier in the year refusing to load ammunition to be sent to the Russian battle zone. The workers, like many Americans, read Strong's provocative February 4 Seattle editorial, excerpted in the days ahead in newspapers on both coasts: "We are undertaking the most tremendous move ever made by labor in this country, a move that will lead—No One Knows Where! We do not need hysteria! We need the iron march of labor! Labor will feed the people . . . Labor will care for the babies and the sick . . . Labor will preserve order."

Indeed Seattle labor did just that: it organized in such a way to keep essential city services operating during the general strike. Meanwhile, the Seattle branch of the Military Intelligence Division, ordered to shut down two weeks before, reversed its direction without waiting for any new orders from Washington. Battalions of volunteers emerged from the shadows to help identify and track the "enemy." The Minute Men Division of the American Protective League, though supposedly defunct, was on the job. Agents who could speak Finnish, Russian, and Swedish were called to the city. The mayor, hell-bent on being known as the man who stopped *the* revolution, sought the aid of 950 sailors and marines, 2,400 special deputies—mainly students from the University of Washington—and six hundred extra volunteer cops to quell the revolt. And, secretly during the days before the strike, Justice Department agents had rounded up fifty-four "IWW troublemakers, bearded labor fanatics, and red flag supporters" and loaded them into two cars of a train bound for Ellis Island. The immediate idea behind the train, which the press dubbed the "Red Special," was to weaken the strike by removing potential leaders. But the long-term concept was deportation as the way to calm a nation stirred up by radical aliens and Bolshevik agitators.

The strike was over in five days. The very next day Mayor Hanson, having gained national notice, left on a lecture tour to warn the nation of the Bolshevik threat. On the other coast the second phase of the Overman Committee hearings began. This one was devoted to the investigation of Bolshevik propaganda and its promulgators. It would be in session when Hiram Johnson continued his crusade in mid-February. In fact, while Overman was lining up Americans who, having been in Russia during and after the Revolution, could testify to the cruelties and horrors of Bolshevism, piling up evidence to support strong opposition to Bolshevism, Senator Johnson was trying to persuade legislators to withdraw American troops from Russia. It was not an easy task.

At the Senate, on those days, a Republican from North Dakota refuted Johnson's views about the situation in Russia, mentioned the Seattle strike, and called attention to what some of Senator Overman's witnesses were revealing. Sending "an adequate force" of 250,000 or more to put an end to the rule of Lenin and Trotsky, he said, was a better plan than withdrawing American soldiers. A Republican from Illinois denounced the Bolshevists, noted also the threatening strike in Seattle, but then supported Johnson's resolution, using it as a platform to criticize Wilson's decision to send troops to begin with. When the vote finally came, it was a tie. The vice president, Thomas Marshall, broke the tie by voting against Johnson. In press interviews later, Johnson vowed to continue the fight until the day he could stand at the end of a gangplank and shake the hand of the first Polar Bear to return to Michigan.

In a letter to one of his sons, Johnson wrote, "The propaganda for exploiting Russia is overwhelming, and I presume I will break [illegible] butting my head against so much wealth and power. However, I was always a crank, and the big fight, when one feels right, against great odds, is after all the only fight worth while."

On the very day the Senate rejected Johnson's resolution, a delegation from Michigan consisting of three representatives from the Detroit's Own association arrived in Washington with their 110,000 signatures calling for the end of intervention in Russia. The next day, they met with Secretary of War Baker for one hour. The secretary made the following points (according to the *Detroit News*):

"That the fortunes of war made it necessary for American troops to be in Archangel;

"That the conditions under which [the troops] were living were typical war conditions and must be endured;

"That the troops had been well outfitted for the rigors of the Russian climate; that the food was probably 'monotonous' as it was Army ration food, yet it was a scientific ration meant to supply sufficient nourishment;

"That if the necessity arose the troops could be withdrawn from the port of Murmansk which did not freeze completely as Archangel [did];

"That the troops could be withdrawn only after the Allies entered a general agreement to do so and that would happen when 'their interests' were met."

The secretary agreed to take a list of the names of soldiers whose families had not heard from them and to investigate their status. When asked if the soldiers in the outposts south of Archangel were in danger of annihilation, he said as far as he knew, they were not.

The Michigan delegation felt that it had done the best it could. Still, the men were not exactly sure what was accomplished. The press tore into Baker for evading the issue but also said that the secretary was basically powerless because the British were in command of the American troops. "Mr. Baker and his associates should be brought up with a round turn," said the *Detroit News* editor. The only hope he said was the "rising disposition of the Senate to take a hand in the matter."

Two days later, on February 17, Secretary Baker sent an official letter to the chairman of the Military Affairs Committee in the Senate saying that the American soldiers in Russia were now closed in by the ice but would be withdrawn "at the earliest possible moment."

This was a great victory, said Senator William Borah of Idaho, who publicly commended Senator Johnson for first drawing attention to the cause. Johnson told the press, "We cannot make whole again the maimed nor bring back the dear ones who have been killed in defiance of the law and in violation of the constitution in this miserable misadventure in Russia, but thank God American boys who are yet alive are to be returned to us."

But what exactly was the earliest possible date for their return? The War Department had already made arrangements for the 1.8 million soldiers in France to arrive home within the next six months, transporting an average of 300,000 men across the Atlantic each month. And what of the boys in northern Russia?

"In the spring," said Baker, unable to be more specific.

The cheering was hardly earsplitting in Michigan where there was wisdom based on experience about how late spring could be. There was also the fear that all good news out of government can evoke: the fear that with time good news could easily change to bad news. Indeed, the only battalions returning to Michigan that spring would be the troops mustered out from the Western Front.

CHAPTER 8

Sergeant Henry Johnson

In New York harbor, during the first half of 1919, dozens of ships coming from France delivered thousands of soldiers who, leaning over guardrails, reached out for their homeland as if touching it as soon as possible might transport them, just as quickly, back to the world they had left behind. New York harbor was the place where prayers were answered as soldiers and their loved ones spotted each other across the slowly narrowing gap between ship and shore. It was there that the rolling wave of hope from the Western Front met the rising tide of fear and intolerance back home.

Early in the morning of February 12, the USS *Stockholm* and the USS *Regina* steered past the Statue of Liberty and into the harbor, bringing four thousand African-American troops from France. On board the *Stockholm* were the "Men of Bronze" of the storied 369th Regiment, also known as the "Black Rattlers" and "Harlem's Own." When the regiment left New York in December of 1917, there were fifty-six officers and two thousand troops. When it returned, there were twenty officers and 1,200 enlisted men. Among them was Sergeant Henry Lincoln Johnson, the first American soldier of any color to win the Croix de Guerre, France's highest military honor.

Five days later, at least seven thousand men and women, mostly African-American, crowded into a St. Louis coliseum to hear Sergeant Johnson, the man billed as the "mighty slayer of Germans," tell the stories that had put the medals on his chest and had brought acclaim to his regiment. "And now it becomes my great pleasure to introduce to you the principal speaker of the evening, Sergeant Johnson, the hero of heroes," announced St. Louis's mayor, Henry W. Kiel, as a band played "Hail the Conquering Hero" and the audience cheered and whistled.

The roar of the crowd rose to a deafening pitch as a black man leaning tentatively on crutches slowly emerged from the backstage darkness, paused at the center of the stage, and then took a deep breath, thus expanding his chest by several inches and causing a loud rattling sound as the rows of military medals pinned to his uniform rolled into one another. In the front row were at least a dozen local ministers who had pooled the resources of their churches to bring the hero of the moment to their town. But if they had looked closely at the man on the stage, they would have noticed that the uniform he wore was not that of an American soldier from the Great War. Instead it was an indescribable mix of styles that seemed to be one part band uniform and one part bellhop, embellished with dime store ribbons. His cap was that of a mail carrier. His gun came from an Atlanta pawnshop. And the medals included a homemade iron cross with the head of Woodrow Wilson in the middle, (pounded out by a blacksmith in Mobile, Alabama); a Knights Templar Ascalon commandery badge, which was a green Maltese cross edged in gold given to members of this Christian group whose ancestors had fought in the Crusades; and an iron shamrock against a backdrop of four pennies mounted on red, white, and blue ribbons.

The man under the spotlight raised his hands to silence the roaring crowd. And as the spectators waited in hushed anticipation for the moment the man would speak, Rev. George T. Marin suddenly marched to the stage. The footlights eerily lit up his face and flashed a long shadow upon the stage curtain, as he announced, "He shall not speak. He is not the man. He is a faker. Do your duty, gentlemen." Out of the audience, three men in police uniforms suddenly appeared. A confused crowd burst into nervous laughter as the police hustled the man off the stage, down the main aisle, out the wide double doors of the coliseum, and into a waiting patrol wagon. The band played a funeral dirge. The mayor and the organizing committee left with the dazed audience. No one got their money back. And everyone had to wait until they read the morning newspapers to learn what had just happened.

The man on the stage was Albert Parker, a con artist, mostly recently from Mobile, who after appearing as Sergeant Johnson in that city and Montgomery, in Cairo, Illinois, in Atlanta and other Georgia towns, and making reasonable money in doing so, was now attempting to fleece the good citizens of several Missouri towns. But the Reverend Marin happened to read the afternoon newspapers that day, which in many towns reported the exciting news from New York City where the real Henry Johnson was parading up Fifth Avenue through a mist of confetti with the 369th In-

fantry in celebration of their homecoming. The real Sergeant Henry Johnson was the "bright star of the Harlem parade," the *New York Age* reported.

Mayor Kiel got one part of it right: Sergeant Johnson was indeed the
hero of heroes and there would be more Johnson impersonators throughout the next year standing before more audiences craving the spectacle of
an African-American war hero. After all, Johnson's valor showed the
world that those who had claimed with utmost certainty before the war
that a black man could not fight successfully with combat troops—and
thus must be relegated to manual jobs—were shamefully wrong.

When America entered the war in April of 1917, there were 750,000
men in the army and National Guard, of whom about 20,000 were African-
Americans. More volunteered in the weeks to follow but at many recruiting stations they were rejected—that is, until after May 18, 1917, when the
Selective Service Act was passed, calling for all able-bodied American
men between the ages of twenty-one and thirty-one to register. By July, approximately 700,000 black Americans had registered for the draft, though
only 367,710 served and out of those only 11 percent fought at the front.
The rest were assigned to service, supply, and labor units. Among those
who fought, there were two all-black Army combat units, the 92nd and the
93rd Divisions. The 92nd was an all-draftee division and it served under
the American flag. The 93rd, which consisted of National Guard regiments out of New York (the 369th Infantry), Illinois (the 370th), Ohio,
Massachusetts, Maryland, and the District of Columbia (the 372nd), and
draftees from South Carolina (the 371st), served with the French. The
American-led 92nd was not lauded and in fact was belittled as cowardly
and immoral, while the French-led 93rd was highly acclaimed, decorated,
and celebrated. The French would long remember the contributions of the
black Americans on the battlefield and their unexpected gift to French
culture: American jazz music, which was introduced in dozens of French
towns by the 369th Infantry's Lieutenant James Reese Europe and his
band. After the war, to be a black American in France was an honor.

The men of the 369th, formerly the 15th Regiment of the New York
National Guard, were the first black soldiers to go into battle on the Western Front. By the time they had returned to New York harbor, the story of
their Sergeant Johnson, a soft-spoken Red Cap porter from Albany, just
five feet four inches tall, slaughtering Germans and saving the life of a fel-

low soldier from capture, had already achieved legendary status. It was a story that African-American audiences, like the one in St. Louis, longed to hear, perhaps to justify their wartime sacrifices, perhaps to calm their fears in the uncertain aftermath of such a war, or perhaps to assure them of the possibility that a black man could achieve greatness, despite humble origins and racial prejudice.

Here was a man born into poverty in Winston-Salem, North Carolina, in 1897, a time when there were at least two hundred lynchings a year in the South and when popular culture depicted blacks as the lowest order of humanity. At the age of six, Johnson, with his family, migrated north to Albany, where, as a teenager, he found work as a baggage handler for the New York Central Railroad at Union Station. He lived at 21 Monroe Street in a black and Italian neighborhood, attended church regularly, belonged to the Colored Benevolent Society, and loved to play the piano. On June 5, 1917, two months after America declared war on Germany, he volunteered for the armed services. In September he married the "girl next door," the daughter of the preacher who lived at 23 Monroe Street, and in December his all-black National Guard unit went overseas as the 369th U.S. Infantry.

The 369th had landed in Brest on January 1, 1918, and at first was assigned to menial labor, mostly loading and unloading ships, and digging ditches for latrines. Eager to give his men the chance to fight, the division's white colonel, William Hayward, arranged for his all-black battalion to train with the French army under the command of the 16th Division of the French Fourth Army. Together the black and white troops made it to the front by March. And by May, they were in the Argonne woods near the Belgian border. On the morning of May 14, Henry Johnson and Private Needham Roberts, from Trenton, New Jersey, were on sentry duty in a trench under a bridge over the Aisne River. German patrols were targeting the bridge for recapture.

Around 2 A.M. Roberts heard the snapping sound of a wire cutter. Sensing that Germans were trying to cut through the tangle of wire that protected the rear portion of their post, he slipped over to Johnson's side of their trench and whispered his suspicions. Roberts then fired into the wire. In return the Germans sent a shower of grenades, hitting both Americans. Roberts, though severely wounded and unable to move, hurled grenades back out into the darkness while a dazed Johnson got back on his feet and began firing his rifle into the rush of soldiers storming the trench. Johnson shot at the shadowy figures, spending three cartridges and then, with no time to reload, used his rifle to club the enemy soldiers, who were tumbling into the trench in a landslide of bodies and weapons. At one point, he looked over his shoulder and through a haze of smoke saw two Germans dragging away the wounded Roberts. But just as they lifted Roberts into the air, Johnson pulled out his bolo knife, let out a shrill scream, and threw his entire 140 pounds onto one of the Germans. He plunged his knife into the man's skull, taking advantage of the fact that night patrols, to assure silence, wore soft wool caps instead of steel helmets. The other man dropped Roberts and attacked Johnson, who stabbed his attacker while another German fired a Luger pistol at him, hitting Johnson several times. Johnson cried out in pain, fell to his hands and knees, and just as a German soldier was bending over to capture him, Johnson thrust his eight-inch knife into the belly of the German. Though exhausted from the struggle and the loss of blood from multiple wounds, the twenty-two-year-old soldier pelted the oncoming Germans with grenades until they retreated.

At dawn, a relief party found the two men. Roberts had passed out from pain and Johnson was barely conscious, fainting upon the sight of his fellow soldiers. Later that morning, the commander of the unit, Major Arthur Little, interviewed both men about the details of their battle. As his commander knelt at his bedside, the Red Cap porter from Albany smiled and whispered, "You all don't have to worry about me. Ah'm all right. Ah've been shot before!"

In the afternoon, Major Little and other soldiers explored the grounds to determine exactly what had happened to the enemy forces. They followed a trail at least half a mile long, littered with blood-soaked bandages, clots of blood, wire cutters, Lugers—and dead Germans. They determined that at least twenty-four Germans had attacked Johnson and Roberts, four of whom were killed. The rest had been severely wounded. When Major Little wrote up his report of the battle, he recommended both men for the coveted Croix de Guerre, and for Johnson, the added Gold Palm for having saved the life of a fellow soldier.

The next morning Colonel Hayward brought journalists to the camp, including well-known writers such as Irvin S. Cobb of the *Saturday Evening*

Post, Martin Green of the *New York Evening World,* and Lincoln Eyre of the *World.* Having just heard about the battle, they now wanted to read Little's report and to interview the heroes. A few days later "The Battle of Henry Johnson" appeared on the front page of the *World* in the morning, and by evening all the New York papers had picked up the story. "Every colored man and woman in the United States can be proud of what the two colored fighters have done in the service of their country, which has given them much but which still owes their race surer guarantees of justice," read the article, which ended with a promise: "To resolve that so long as Negro fighters face the enemy and thereafter so long as the Republic they have helped to defend endures, throughout the length and breadth of the United States, law, public condemnation and swift punishment for the guilty shall combine to make the lynching of a Negro an abhorred and obsolete crime." By the next day the Associated Press was spreading the story nationwide, describing Johnson as a "wildcat warrior" who, despite his small size, was "indestructible." "Our colored volunteers from Harlem had become, in a day, one of the famous fighting regiments of the World War," Major Little later wrote.

In Albany, the newspapers were brimming with Henry Johnson stories and his wife was beaming in the spotlight of her husband's fame. "He told me he'd make a name for himself," she told the the *Albany Times Union,* "and he surely has done it." Local songwriters wrote rags about him. Friends with whom he played what the papers called "African golf" or craps, were quoted. His favorite ditty was memorized: "She brought me coffee, And she brought me tea— She brought me everything 'Cept the jail house key." The post office was inundated with letters addressed to Henry at his hospital in France. And a letter from Sergeant Johnson was considered a new form of currency, at least in the black neighborhoods: "more acceptable than money at the gate of any colored outing," wrote the *Times Union.*

On the white side of town, the women of the United Service Alliance held an unprecedented reception for Johnson's wife, Edna, who was black. The *Times Union,* which rarely published good news about Albany's black residents, reprinted the stories from the nation's papers and even ran a sidebar, "The Negro Fighting Man." This listed all the great black soldiers throughout world history, up to Henry Johnson. And throughout all the neighborhoods of Albany for the remaining months of the war, signs on top of streetcars read "How many war stamps did you lick today? Henry Johnson licked a dozen Germans!"

Back in France, Johnson received his award and the citation from the French that read: "Johnson, Henry. Being on double sentry duty during the night and having been assaulted by a group composed of at least one dozen Germans, shot and disabled one of them and grievously wounded two others with his bolo. In spite of three wounds with pistol bullets and grenades at the beginning of the fight, this man ran to the assistance of his wounded comrade who was about to be carried away by the enemy, and continued to fight up to the retreat of the Germans. He has given a beautiful example of courage and activity."

Despite his wounds and his inability to fight, Johnson did not go home. Instead, he stayed with the 369th, on the recommendation of Colonel Hayward, who knew Johnson did not want to leave and who also recognized that Johnson's mere presence would boost the morale of the black troops. "He may be disabled," Hayward told the press, "but we will carry him on our roll as the Seventh Cavalry carried the horse that survived the Custer massacre. He can neither work nor fight, but his presence will be good for the morale of our troops."

Throughout that May, the 369th defended more than 20 percent of all territory held by American troops in the Champagne-Marne, in some of the heaviest continuous fighting in the war. The regiment went on to fight with the French army in the Battle of the Argonne and in the Vosges Mountains. On November 18, they led the French army to the Rhine, the first of the Allied troops to cross the river into Germany, where they planted the flag of the state of New York. "So close were we behind the enemy," Colonel Hayward later said, "that he was pulling up his pontoon bridges on the other side of the river."

The 369th Infantry fought a total of 191 days with only one week's rest. They were feared by the Germans, who called them *blutlustige schwartze Männer* (bloodthirsty black men), and revered by the French, who hailed them in town after town as heroes. The French called them *les enfants perdues* (Lost Children) because they were abandoned by their own nation. More than one hundred members of the regiment won the Croix de Guerre or the Médaille Militaire. And then they returned to the United States—where they won no military honors.

February 17, 1919, was a glorious day for African-Americans, at least in

Chicago and New York, where millions of people, white and black, celebrated the return of parts of the 369th and 370th Infantry Divisions. In
Chicago, 400,000 people lined the streets and cheered as the all-black
370th, known as the "Black Devils," paraded down Wabash Avenue to
Michigan Avenue. To show respect, businesses in the Loop closed for the
duration of the parade. Chicago newspapers ran glowing editorials noting
the war record of "the Race" and the exceptional behavior of these men
who, as the *Chicago Defender* commented, "went out to fight for the white
race." No soldiers had ended up in internment camps for disloyalty, the
Chicago American newspaper noted, and none of them "gave the government any trouble" during the war.

"Not only their own people but all of Chicago should go out to do them
honor as they have added a bright chapter to the history of Illinois at arms
and they deserve all of the honors that a grateful city and state can give
them," wrote the *Chicago American* newspaper.

In New York, more than two million spectators lined Fifth Avenue
from 23rd Street to the corner of 145th and Lenox Avenue in Harlem to
hail the 369th. The 1,300 soldiers must have believed their troubles were
over as they heard the sounds of adoration flinging out from sidewalks,
windows, fire escapes, and rooftops for seven miles up the island of Manhattan. Showers of candy and coins seemed to spill out of the cloudless sky,
and the rattlesnake emblem of the 369th was everywhere. Coiled and
ready to strike, the rattlesnake was depicted on "Welcome Home" banners
stretched across store windows and balconies, on lapel buttons, and on
shirtsleeves.

Leading the parade was Lieutenant Europe, the jazz band leader who
was as famous, if not more, for his work in Europe as Henry Johnson,
though for different reasons. Europe was a musician, composer, conductor,
arranger, and director, known before the war for, among other things,
breaking through racial barriers with his music and internationalizing the
jazz movement in America. In 1912, for instance, he brought his 150-piece
Clef Club Orchestra to Carnegie Hall, which for that night only suspended
its rules for segregated seating. The next year he created another orchestra
that included songwriters Eubie Blake and Noble Sissle and that performed
at Delmonico's and the Hotel Astor. He was the musical director for the
famed dance team of Vernon and Irene Castle. His saxophone arrange-

ments moved that instrument to a new level of respectability and popularity. And his experiments in syncopation and orchestral direction nurtured the Jazz Age. After enlisting in the army and passing the officer's exam, Europe was asked by his commander, Colonel Hayward, to create a military band as part of Hayward's combat unit. He could recruit them from anywhere, Hayward said, which Europe did, including finding his reed players mostly in Puerto Rico. The 369th Infantry Jazz Band, known as the "Hellfighters' Band" and consisting of as many as sixty-five players, became world-famous as "the musical sensation of the war," "the band that set all of France jazz mad," and "the band that put wine into jazz, setting France ablaze with its rollicking melodies." On this day, as they moved up Fifth Avenue, Lieutenant Europe and his band were playing only marching music. Among their instruments were five kettle drums presented to them by the French soldiers with whom they had fought and one drum left behind by the Germans in a skirmish in the Champagne.

Close behind Europe and his band was Sergeant Johnson, in a convertible, standing as often as he could and waving a handful of red lilies in response to the shouts of "Oh, you, Henry Johnson." Stationed at a review stand on the corner of 60th Street and Fifth Avenue were New York governor Al Smith and his wife; William Randolph Hearst and his wife; ex-Governor Charles S. Whitman; New York's mayor, John Francis Hylan; and, among other public figures, Madam Walker, who was hosting a two-week-long open house at Villa Lewaro for soldiers and their families. Mrs. Vincent Astor and a cluster of wealthy New York women flashed American flags from the windows of her mansion at 65th Street and Fifth Avenue. And at 70th and Fifth, Henry C. Frick waved and cheered from his own mansion. As the procession reached the northern border of Central Park and closer to Harlem, it seemed to move faster, and Lieutenant Europe directed a 123-person band to play "Here Comes My Daddy Now." In the days ahead it was as if Harlem had been reborn.

At the end of the march, special subway trains transported the soldiers with their band to an armory at 34th Street and Park Avenue for dinner and speeches and music. The armory was surrounded then by thousands more New Yorkers eagerly awaiting the soldiers, mostly women and girls hoping to break through the barriers of police more easily at the armory than at the parade. In the distance, Park Avenue residents would one day recall hearing the cheers and the unmistakable sounds of Europe's famed band playing "All of No Man's Land Is Ours." And this was followed by the song Europe so often would play in the weeks ahead:

> *How 'ya gonna keep 'em down on the farm*
> *After they've seen Paree?*
> *How 'ya gonna keep them away from Broadway,*
> *Jazzin' aroun', and paintin' the town?*
> *How 'ya gonna keep 'em away from harm?*
> *That's the mystery.*
> *They'll never want to see a rake or plow.*
> *And who the deuce can "parley vous" a cow?*
> *How 'ya gonna keep 'em down on the farm*
> *After they've seen Paree?*

"On the 17th of February, 1919, New York City knew no color line," Major Little later wrote. New York's black soldiers came home from France with one of the bravest records achieved by any combat unit in the war. And the parade that heralded the homecoming of the Men of Bronze was without a doubt the biggest celebration for black Americans since the Emancipation Proclamation had been issued fifty-six years before. A milestone in black history, the parade would one day be seen as the symbolic emergence of the "New Negro" movement in which African-Americans in solidarity stood strong against oppression, publicly addressing issues such as integration and equality, expressing themselves through literature and the arts in that part of the movement that would be known as the Harlem Renaissance.

As the victorious black soldiers marched up Fifth Avenue in an unstoppable stream of human emotion, there was no turning back. From that day onward, fueled by the ideals of a war to make the world safe for democracy and the sacrifices made for those ideals, empowered by their achievements and this unprecedented recognition, and angered by the injustices they had faced and would face again in their own nation, black America would never be the same.

It would not be long before Henry Johnson would break through the fragile barrier between the world his fleeting fame allowed him to temporarily enter and the reality of black America. The 369th was mustered out of service at Camp Upton on Long Island and on their last night there Sergeant Johnson knocked on the door of the cardboard and tarpaper shack where he knew Major Little was staying. Dragging his crippled foot, he entered. He wanted to personally bid farewell to his major, he told Little, who was moved by the visit. "What are you planning to do, Sgt.?" Little asked. Johnson, with his wide smile, answered, "Why, I'm goin' back to my job, of course."

After the New York parade, Johnson eagerly returned home to Albany, where he was greeted at the train station by hundreds of flag-fluttering fans, including his wife, the mayor, and the governor. The mayor announced that there would be a street named in his honor and that he would also be given a monetary award of some sort. But what Johnson really wanted, he could not have: his old job. Because of his disabling wounds, he could not persuade his former employer at the Albany Union Station to rehire him as a Red Cap. Nor could he work at any of his other previous jobs, in a coal yard or even as a soda mixer at the local pharmacy. And so the New York State Bank at Albany announced, on February 21, that it was accepting contributions for the Henry Johnson Home Fund of Albany. In the weeks ahead, Johnson left Albany again, dutifully answering his nation's call for help. He toured the nation with Colonel Hayward, beating the drum of patriotism to add to the coffers of the government with the sale of Liberty Bonds.

For a brief moment, Henry Johnson was the hope of his race, the symbol of its emerging strength, the proof of its greatness—a greatness that, because of men like Sergeant Johnson, had to be recognized. In popular demand for lectures and appearances, the real Henry Johnson, unlike the pretender Albert Parker, was raising money for his nation—not for himself. And there was no stage spectacle of a man expanding his chest to show off his medals, for Henry Johnson was a humble man. In one interview he said of his bravery, "There wasn't anything so fine about it. Just fought for my life. A rabbit would have done that."

Parker and Johnson, however, did have one thing in common: disaster in St. Louis. At the same coliseum where Parker had performed, the real Henry Johnson gave a speech while on the Liberty Loan fund-raising tour. He stood on stage with the St. Louis mayor, the president of the Board of Aldermen, two bishops, a decorated lieutenant, a U.S. senator, and a congressman. All paid fine tributes to the courage of black troops. Hundreds of people attended, including numerous white men and women, who filled the theater's box seats. When the mayor introduced "the real Henry Johnson of No Man's Land," the building seemed to shake from thunderous applause. Finally, Sergeant Johnson raised both arms, as his predecessor had done, to calm the crowd. Then he commenced to tell his story of the now legendary night in May of 1918 that had made him famous. He spoke of his buddy Private Roberts who had nearly died. And he spoke modestly, as he always did, about what he had done to save Roberts and to destroy the enemy. But then suddenly he made a sharp turn: he began to talk about the prejudice against black soldiers fostered by "white American soldiers." Such men would not recognize the bravery of America's black infantrymen when in fact the white men themselves showed cowardice in battle on occasions, which he could readily recall, he said. It was as if he had waved a hand grenade. One by one the people standing with him onstage moved away from him. He, like his impostor, was then escorted off the stage. At his hotel that night, he received handwritten threats slipped under his door that were dire enough to compel the real Henry Johnson to leave St. Louis the following night in disguise.

Ironically, Sergeant Johnson was not the performer or crowd-pleaser that his impostor had been. He was, in fact, authentic and honest. And as such he did not say what the people wanted to hear. So too he was not a great speaker. But because his heroism was unmatched and was gaining so very much attention nationwide, black America forgave him for such a flaw and black soldiers praised him for telling the truth about the prejudice they had suffered. James Weldon Johnson, in one of his columns, wrote that Sergeant Johnson knew well how to be a hero as "the greatest individual hero produced by the whole American army" and he did not fault him for what happened in St. Louis. But he was critical of Johnson for not knowing how to "remain a hero." Stay out of the spotlight, Johnson advised the hero. If he did not remove himself from the public eye soon, he warned, he would be dishonored by the prejudice that surrounded him. "Heroes enhance their value through mystery and distance. Familiarity is to a hero what daylight is to theatrical scenery. Not even Napoleon was a hero to his valet."

Whether or not Sergeant Johnson read the column, his name would soon disappear from the headlines. He would no longer tour the nation for his government nor would there be a street named after him—at least not during his lifetime. No local fund would ever be raised on his behalf, no government benefits, no job. And soon Sergeant Henry Johnson would fall into the abyss of forgotten heroes.

Most returning soldiers, as they sailed so triumphantly into New York harbor, longed for the comfort and familiarity of home, for life as it once was: the same trees in the yard, the same dog at the door, and the same job they had before the war. African-Americans, like Henry Johnson, ached for the same. But unlike white soldiers returning home, they hoped that winning the war would not mean a return to the status quo: not the same injustices, not the same inequalities, not the same oppression.

In welcoming home the returning black soldiers, Robert Abbott, editor of the black newspaper the *Chicago Defender,* wrote:

> In a few short weeks you will have been absorbed into the body politic and your experiences will have become a memory but rest assured that you will not be forgotten. We who remained at home expect much of you. The same fighting spirit which you displayed upon the battlefields of Europe is needed in the titanic struggle for survival through which we are passing in this country today.
>
> We are loath to believe that the spirit which "took no prisoners" will tamely and meekly submit to a program of lynching, burning and social ostracism as has obtained in the past. With your help and experience we shall look forward to a new tomorrow, not of subservience, not of meek and humble obeisance to any class, but with a determination to demand what is our due at all times and in all places.
>
> You left home to make the world a safer place for democracy and your work will have been in vain if it does not make your own land a safer place for you and yours. If you have been fighting for democracy, let it be a *real democracy,* a democracy in which the blacks can have equal hope, equal opportunities and equal rewards with the whites. Any other sort of democracy spells failure.

CHAPTER 9

Trotter and the Passports

Somewhere in the throng of the parade to Harlem that February morning was one of the boldest proponents of Abbott's vision of "real democracy": William Monroe Trotter. Two days before, on February 15, Trotter, the controversial African-American editor of the Boston weekly newspaper *The Guardian*, had left his hometown of Boston and his newspaper. Taking an indefinite leave of absence, he was now spending his days roaming the piers of New York in search of a berth on any vessel bound for Europe. His quest was to personally meet with and persuade the delegates at the Paris Peace Conference to address the issue of racial equality worldwide and thus to bring the attention of the world to the oppression of all people of African descent.

Why would Trotter suddenly drop everything in his life in Boston and move to a boarding house on the New York waterfront to accomplish such a feat? The answer was indeed as intriguing as his flight: the State Department had denied passports to African-Americans planning to travel to Paris, except for those who had already gone in early December, such as W. E. B. Du Bois. But Trotter was determined to go, any way that he could.

In a move that may have been the State Department's first official interference in African-American politics, none of the requests for passports submitted by African-Americans intending to go to France to promote racial equality was granted. This pile of denials included the eleven delegates selected in early December at Trotter's National Race Congress to represent the National Equal Rights League and the five individuals Du Bois had chosen to attend his Pan-African Congress in Paris. Among those on the list, besides Trotter, were Madam Walker; Ida B. Wells-Barnett; Perry Howard, the editor of the only black daily newspaper in America, the *Baltimore Herald*; and black ministers from Boston, Atlanta, Seattle, St. Louis, Kansas, and Mississippi.

They had applied for passports to represent their race at the peace conference, to walk proudly into the Hotel Crillon in Paris, where all the delegates stayed and worked, and where, as Du Bois astutely wrote in an editorial in *The Crisis,* "the destinies of mankind for a hundred years will be settled." There they would stress the importance of ending racial injustice worldwide and of liberating African and Caribbean colonies from European rule. Du Bois's plan, as he had revealed in another column of *The Crisis*—written *after* he had arrived in Paris—was to use his congress, ostensibly called to discuss the disposition of the former German colonies in Africa, as a way "to focus the attention of the peace delegates and the civilized world on the just claims of the Negro everywhere." With great expectation, people came from all over the world to plead the cause of peace, justice, and equality in their own nations. It was imperative that African-American leaders have a presence. The *New York Times,* echoing both Du Bois's call for the congress and Trotter's drive for black representation at the peace conference, wrote that the time had come "for the interests and welfare of the negro to become articulate instead of relying upon philanthropic efforts and that there can be no stable League of Nations unless the negro's interests are safeguarded."

The reasons they were denied the passports were at first less apparent. The State Department, when confronted, insisted that there was in fact no official policy to block African-Americans from traveling abroad. And African-Americans were not the only ones whose requests had been denied. Two suffragists, Miss Mildred Morris of Denver, Colorado, and Miss Clara Wold of Portland, Oregon, had had their passports canceled on February 1 because the State Department learned that they had participated in the demonstration on the White House lawn on New Year's Day. What if they were to wave banners and demonstrate for women's suffrage in Paris? The State Department did not want to risk that.

Most of the African-Americans on the list of denials had been MID targets in recent months, such as Madam Walker and Trotter and Wells-Barnett, and thus shadowed by one or more government agents. Any black man or woman who was eager to go to France to fight for race equality would likely have been outspoken enough during the previous months to have appeared suspicious to the government. In the government's lexicon for African-Americans, the words "outspoken" and "suspicious" were synonymous.

Du Bois, for example, who was under the watchful eye of at least one secret agent, was regarded by the MID as a suspicious American—a "rock the boat" type who "may attempt to introduce socialist tendencies at the Peace Conference," said MID reports. However, he was the only one who had obtained a passport—as a writer for *The Crisis*—out of the six who applied for them in November to attend his Pan-African Congress. "When I was suddenly informed of a chance to go to France as a newspaper correspondent, I did not talk—I went," he later said, "because I knew perfectly well that any movement to bring the attention of the world to the Negro problem would be stopped the moment the Great Powers heard of it."

Although in all probability his cooperation with the MID helped, Du Bois was no puppet for the Wilson administration. His grand plan was to use his congress as a platform from which to shine an immense spotlight on the issue of race oppression. Some government officials must have figured out that denying the passports might not only diminish the power of the congress, but also shut it down. The State Department told the media that the French government did not "consider this a favorable time" for black people to be holding such a conference. At exactly the same time, Du Bois sent out a press release stating that "Clemenceau permits Pan African Conference February 12, 13, 14. North, South America, West Indies, Africa, represented." When challenged, the State Department stuck with its earlier statement that the French government had told the United States that no such conference would be held. The passport applications would remain in the "denied" bin.

On February 20, the day after the Pan-African Congress opened, the State Department asked the French government whether it had granted permission for such a conference and if so, could the date be postponed so that a "limited number of Negro delegates from this [U.S.] government" could attend. Obviously, it was too late. Knowing that the Wilson administration had falsely claimed the French government's objection to the conference, James Weldon Johnson wrote in his *New York Age* column, "the colored people of the U.S. will wait with great interest for the details of the Congress and 'puzzled officials' of the State Department will continue to wonder how they ever got into such a hole."

So the congress went on. At least fifty-seven delegates attended, representing fifteen countries and colonies and 157 million black men and women worldwide in, among others, the British West Indies, Haiti, Portugal, and France. After three days of meeting, they produced resolutions about educational opportunity, land ownership, accessible health care, and decolonization, all to be submitted to the peace conference. Over a thousand copies of the resolutions were distributed. It was Du Bois's hope that he could personally address the delegates at the Paris Peace Conference. Instead he was told he would be talking about the resolutions to Wilson's trusted adviser Colonel Edward House, the courteous and cultured Texan who had been working with Wilson in an unofficial capacity since Wilson was governor of New Jersey. Du Bois had to be content to trust that House would present his race resolutions to the peace conference.

Back in the United States, Trotter knew little, if anything, about Du Bois's activities in Paris. So distrustful, though, of white men's promises, he would not have dropped his mission, even if he had known that Du Bois had spoken with Colonel House about the Pan-African Congress resolutions. Trotter, a steadfast advocate of the fundamental principles of freedom for all peoples, was single-minded in his belief that the peace conference was and must be about race, perhaps more than anything else. Never before had there been such an opportunity to reach so many leaders at one time in one place. To Trotter, racial inequality was the issue the world must face—now—if peaceful coexistence among different races and nationalities was ever to be achieved. Therefore, it was only logical that Trotter should meet with President Wilson himself. Not Colonel House. Not anyone but the president. And much like Wilson, he would face a multitude of challenges to realize his dream—a fact that would be abundantly evident as he embarked on his epic journey to get to Paris. His plan now was to find a job on a ship headed for France; for this he did not need a passport, but rather a more easily obtainable seaman's permit.

For Trotter, facing Wilson was hardly a dream—more like Act III of a Shakespearean drama. It had happened twice before, first in 1913, shortly after Wilson's first presidential election victory. Trotter had worked hard for Wilson, a candidate who had pledged his allegiance to the cause of racial justice. Before the election, in a letter seeking support from Trotter's onetime friend Bishop Alexander Walters in New Jersey, Wilson had said "The colored people of the U.S. have made extraordinary progress towards self-support and usefulness, and ought to be encouraged in every possible and proper way. My sympathy with them is of long standing and I want to assure you that should I become President of the United States they may count on me for absolute fair dealing of everything by which I could assist in advancing the interests of their race in the U.S."

Trotter believed in Wilson. He wrote supportive editorials and talked him up in Boston's black community, where Trotter had lived and worked for many years and was well known. A magna cum laude graduate of Harvard University—third in his class—Trotter was Harvard's first black member of Phi Beta Kappa. After Harvard, he worked as an insurance and mortgage broker in Boston and married a black woman from Boston, whom Du Bois had dated. In 1901 Trotter started *The Guardian*, a weekly newspaper known first for its disparaging critiques of Booker T. Washington and later for its bold protests against discrimination, segregation, and lynchings. Always serving as a watchdog for his race, Trotter, in his nonviolent campaigns, tried to awaken white Americans to their shameful injustices against African-Americans—all white Americans, including and especially Woodrow Wilson.

After the election, in his congratulatory note to Wilson, Trotter wrote, "as your inauguration approaches, the clouds are lowering and a feeling of foreboding is creeping over the colored people." Trotter was concerned that the House had passed a bill making interracial marriages a felony in the District of Columbia. It was a dangerous piece of legislation, promoted by the Democratic Party, Wilson's party. In his post-election letter to Wilson, Trotter noted this and placed the responsibility on Wilson's doorstep. But Wilson didn't respond. Trotter wrote him another letter, urging him to steer clear of appointing a white Southerner to be postmaster general. Wilson was considering Albert Burleson, a Texan, for the post. In this letter Trotter reminded Wilson of his support for him and his continued belief that Wilson could be "the inaugurator of a new era of equal rights for Colored Americans." But Wilson did appoint Burleson and four other white Southerners to cabinet posts. Trotter did not himself hope for an appointment in the Wilson administration but he wanted Wilson to seek his counsel on race policy, which could not have been further from Wilson's plans. In fact when the new postmaster general and two other appointees suggested that their offices in Washington should be segregated, Wilson approved. He even appointed a white man to the typically black appointment of U.S. minister to Haiti.

Disappointed, offended, and humiliated, the NAACP urged Trotter to do something about it. Thus Trotter collected twenty thousand signatures on a petition objecting to the segregation policies and, accompanied by Ida B. Wells-Barnett, delivered the petition and a statement of protest in person to Wilson, who, he informed the readers of *The Guardian*, "listened attentively, responded courteously and gave them thirty-five minutes of his time." Wilson promised Trotter that he would investigate the segregation issue. Six days later Trotter sent Wilson another letter and three weeks after that another, reminding him of his promise to explore the issue, all without response from Wilson. A year later, in 1914, after no changes in White House policy, Trotter pushed for another interview, at a time when Wilson was in mourning over his wife's recent death and under pressure regarding the war in Europe. Neither Wilson nor Trotter would forget their second meeting, which took place on November 12, 1914.

The segregation in government offices, Wilson explained to Trotter, was necessary because of friction between white and black workers. Segregation was not humiliating, Wilson told his critic. Rather it was "a benefit." Trotter listened and then responded in a way Wilson did not expect, especially perhaps from a black man: he argued. At one point, Wilson interrupted him saying, "Your manner offends me."

"In what way?" Trotter asked.

"Your tone, with its background of passion," Wilson said.

Trotter continued and Wilson broke in again. Trotter continued again: "Two years ago, you were regarded as a second Abraham Lincoln." Then he went on to tell Wilson that black leaders who had so strongly supported Wilson during the presidential election were viewed now as traitors. Wilson accused him of blackmail for saying such a thing. Then Wilson spoke of his burdens as president, which he described as "more than the human spirit could carry."

The two men wrangled, politely, for forty-five minutes or so, until Wilson called an end to the interview. Upon leaving, Trotter told reporters that the meeting was "entirely disappointing," and he quoted the president as saying things that showed the public for the first time that Wilson was aware of the segregation problem and approved of it. Wilson's chief of staff told Trotter that he had "violated every courtesy of the White House by quoting the President to the press." The *New York Times* carried the story on the front page, which evoked a flurry of letters to editors, to Wilson, and to Trotter, who was now instantly famous. Wilson was criticized for his attitude and Trotter was condemned for having the arrogance to dispute the president. Trotter was no longer a fan of Wilson. And Wilson had no interest in Trotter. In fact, he humiliated Trotter by "forgetting" his name. In the future when Trotter would again draw the president's attention, Wilson would refer to him as "Tucker."

The battle only intensified with time. When D. W. Griffith's ambitious film *The Birth of a Nation* came out in 1915, Wilson not only agreed to have a private showing at the White House but afterward expressed how fascinated he was by it. Trotter was appalled. The film even attributed three quotes to Wilson—for example, "The White men were roused by a mere instinct of self-preservation . . . until at last there had sprung into existence a great Ku Klux Klan, a veritable empire of the South to protect the Southern country." Trotter organized protests against the film. Wilson was advised to change his stand on the film and told his chief aide that he would like to "if there were some way in which I could do it without seeming to be trying to meet the agitation . . . stirred up by that unspeakable fellow Tucker." That Trotter now believed he could yet again meet with Wilson—this time in Paris—was bold.

In an era when most black Americans still feared the consequences of speaking their minds, Trotter's persistent, outspoken style was often viewed as militant, extreme, even frightening. In fact, according to some individuals, such as Madam Walker's personal advisers, Trotter alone provoked the passport fiasco. After all, Madam Walker, and others who were on the list of those denied, had associated with Trotter on a number of occasions. But Trotter, Du Bois, and Walker were more certain that the underlying cause was the government's fear not just of Trotter but of any African-American traveling to Paris. What if they revealed to the world the truth about race relations in the United States?

They didn't know how right they were. Major Loving, the black informer who had attended the organizational meeting of the National Race Congress in December 1918, wrote in his report to the MID that if passports were granted to Walker and others on his list, the records regarding the activities of each of them would have to be locked up to avoid embarrassment for having issued the passports. These people were "more or less agitators." After reading Loving's report, the acting head of the Bureau of Investigation then advised the State Department to deny the passports in order to stop African-Americans from bringing up "the negro question at the Peace Conference."

"I think your inclination not to grant passports is a wise one," Secretary of State Robert Lansing had written to the State Department, after the decision was made. Racial questions, he said, "ought not to be a subject to come before the Conference."

At the heart of it all was indeed fear—fear that people who cared so much about the rights of their race would speak the truth about conditions in America, about the lynchings, about biased media, about hateful policies of segregation, about sheer oppression in the land of the free. It was a fear that was powerful enough to distort reality, turning heroes into traitors. What an embarrassment this would be for Wilson, a leader who was crusading for self-determination of all peoples in all nations. How could Wilson hope to make progress on issues of world peace, if such hypocrisies in his own nation were unveiled?

From the day the Armistice was signed to the day of the parade to Harlem there had already been at least a dozen reported lynchings of black Americans. One was burned to death after hanging for many hours without dying. Another, a uniformed soldier, was killed in Georgia during the last weeks of December by a mob of fifty or more unmasked white men, who had dragged the man from a train, carried him to the woods, shot him to death, and then sliced his body into dozens of pieces. And as the soldiers marched up Fifth Avenue to Harlem, some spectators must have recalled that exactly one year before, in one of the most sadistic lynchings on record, a black man in Tennessee accused of killing two white men was tortured with a red-hot crowbar and then burned to death in front of a crowd of approximately two thousand men, women, and children, all inhaling the rancid smell of burning flesh and listening to his screams for mercy.

In the coming months, black soldiers would be popular targets for white mobs largely because of grandiose fears about their experiences under arms in France. Would the returning black soldiers focus their battlefield valor on challenging the world of segregation? Would African-Americans now be uppity and demanding? Had the fighting in France made them believe they were smarter than white people? Worst of all, would they now be shamelessly unabashed about conversing with and even possibly marrying white women? Was it true that black soldiers in France had been sleeping with white women? Such speculation led to numerous incidents in which black men in uniform were beaten by mobs with baseball bats and even assaulted for simply talking about their wartime service. In Kentucky, a discharged black soldier wearing his army uniform resisted arrest on charges of robbery, fled, and was captured by a mob of seventy-five men, who hanged him from the branch of a sycamore tree. In Georgia, a black soldier stepping off the train in his hometown was greeted by a small yet deadly white mob that demanded he take off his uniform, walk home in his underwear, and never again wear his decorated military attire. Proud of his service, the soldier, a few days later, appeared in town in his uniform. A mob executed him later that day.

Lynching was a powerful weapon of oppression that used the ammunition of fear to hold down an entire race. The South had been wielding it for decades. And now, as more soldiers, black and white, returned from Europe, what the NAACP called "the shame of America" would only worsen. The solution, Du Bois and James Weldon Johnson had both said, was federal legislation condemning lynching as a federal crime. And, as the government suspected, those African-Americans planning to travel to Paris intended to expose it all to the world as a way to force the government to act.

In a poem published in the *Chicago Defender* black writer Edna Perry Booth wrote:

> *Now the war's over, Uncle, what will you do?*
> *For the brave Colored laddies who fought hard for you?*
> *Will they still be abused as they used to be?*
> *Ere they joined in the fighting for Liberty?*
> *Will you soon be forgetting the lives they gave?*
> *That the Stars and Stripes might proudly wave?*
>
> *What will you do down in Dixie, pray,*
> *With the Jim-Crow cars and the pauper's pay.*
> *With the no-account schools and the no-vote towns,*
> *Where poverty reigns and misery frowns;*
> *What will you do with the lynching tree,*
> *That hellish thing that shames Dixie?*

Whether Trotter would make it to France or Du Bois's resolutions would be presented via Colonel House at the peace conference was not yet certain. With or without their successes, though, the world would soon know of the hypocrisies in America. Denying the passports and thus preventing African-American attendance in Paris could not suppress the passions of the people who had applied for them. In the days ahead Trotter would cable a petition to the peace conference urging the delegates once again to pay heed to African-Americans: "Fourteen million colored Americans, soldiers and civilians who helped win the war, petition peace conference in fulfillment of war promises of democracy for everyone to incorporate in League covenant following clause: Real democracy for world being avowed aim of nations establishing League of Nations, high contracting powers agree to grant their citizens respectfully full liberty, rights of democracy, protection of life without distinction based on race, color or previous condition."

By the time the cable arrived, however, the first draft of the Covenant of the League of Nations was complete and Wilson was on his way home to America.

CHAPTER 10

The Magisterial Wand

Just as Trotter was stepping onto a train in Boston on February 15 bound for New York City to begin his quest to travel to France, President Wilson was boarding the *George Washington* in France, bound for Boston. After eighty-four days away from his country, the American president was returning home, though to stay for only nine days. In that time, he intended to speak at the last session of the Sixty-fifth Congress, to sign the bills of the expiring Congress, to appoint a new attorney general, and even to unveil the first draft of the Covenant of the League of Nations—a major accomplishment in the first phase of the Paris Peace Conference. So too he would commence his campaign to win national approval of the realization of his dream: a global league to oversee a permanent peace. And, to the many Americans who still believed that the man who was the hope of the world was also omnipotent, there was the expectation that, brief though his visit may be, Wilson would wave his magisterial wand and solve the mounting domestic problems that now beset his nation.

This was the time of trains and ships, when travel slowed the pace of life and long hours, or days, between destinations deferred the demands of busy schedules. For Wilson to spend ten days suspended between Europe and America on the luxury liner in his quiet, spacious three-room suite was a gift from a generous god. In fact, his physician, Admiral Cary Grayson, would always believe that the respite on board the *Washington* was crucial to maintaining the president's fortitude while under the extreme strain of the struggles in Paris. It even may have prolonged his life, for despite his aura of power and intellectual stamina, the president was not a physically strong man. As the journalist Ray Stannard Baker once wrote, Wilson was "a 600 horse-power motor in a frail, light, delicate chassis." Beset with physical limitations, the president had suffered a series of minor strokes at the turn of the century that affected his right arm, a retinal hemorrhage in 1906 that left him partially blind in his left eye, extremely severe headaches, and chronic hypertension. By the time Wilson was elected president, Dr. Grayson, who then became his doctor, was unnerved by the number of medicines he was taking. And by the time he began his second presidential term, Wilson's kidneys were showing signs of malfunctioning. He was also a workaholic—an addiction well served by the peace conference but at war with his body.

Indeed, Wilson began the February voyage home in a state of extreme exhaustion. Fortunately, despite heavy fog off the coast of Newfoundland nearly forcing the ship aground, the trip was for the most part a relaxing one. The president spent his days with Edith, his second wife, reading, playing shuffleboard, and conversing with the relatively few passengers— typically about topics other than world peace, self-determination, and the partisan struggles of launching the League. On board this time were congressmen from Kansas, Ohio, and North Dakota; the American ambassador to Russia and his wife; Dr. Grayson, of course; Ray Stannard Baker; and Franklin D. Roosevelt. "This young assistant secretary of the Navy had great charm of presence and of manner" wrote Baker of Roosevelt. "He was enthusiastic and earnest, and a mine of information regarding ships and the sea."

Probably the passengers most keenly aware of the stresses of Wilson's life in Paris were Dr. Grayson, Mrs. Wilson, and Baker. All three understood that Wilson's mission to break down old-style diplomacy and replace it with democratic processes was a quest that could break down the president himself. Wilson had gone to Paris not only to negotiate the terms of peace with Germany but also to launch a new international organization that would secure a permanent peace. "It was inevitable that President Wilson should be forced at Paris to bear the brunt of the heavy fighting— fighting that would have worn out a stronger, more robust man than he," Baker wrote later that year.

Baker was a writer renowned for his groundbreaking magazine pieces, which, with the work of his former colleagues Ida Tarbell and Lincoln Steffens, had defined the journalistic skill known as muckraking. Now, at the peace conference the forty-nine-year-old journalist was working for Wilson as head of the Press Bureau which consisted of 150 American correspondents. He organized information coming out of the many meetings of the American Peace Commission, packaged it, and disseminated it to the press corps. As a veteran journalist, he was also keeping a detailed diary with his usual keen observations of the world around him. His office was at

No. 4 Place de la Concorde and he knew most of what occurred a few doors down the street at the Hôtel de Crillon, where the many members of the American Peace Commission lodged and worked. Baker was also privy to all the intrigue, struggle, and contention taking place two miles away at the Palais Murat, the eighteenth-century mansion where President Wilson lived and worked, and which was connected to the Hôtel de Crillon and to Baker by an extensive phone system and postal service.

Baker witnessed firsthand the reasons for Wilson's extreme exhaustion that February. He knew the daily and nightly tugs-of-war between Wilson and the other representatives of the Allied nations. He saw the fierce struggle between the vision of a peace based on principles promoted by the president of a nation that was thousands of miles from the battle-fields and the demands for a peace based on the special interests of the leaders of those nations devastated by the war and still fearful of their neighbor Germany. Wilson demanded a settlement based on the principles set out in the Armistice, which in turn were based on his Fourteen Points, while the others wanted material reimbursements and the assurance of a crippled Germany. "So many of the discussions," wrote Baker of the early days of the conference, "seemed to be mere jockeying for position among groups of clever diplomatic traders, and to have behind them no clearly held principles or objectives, let alone any that were inspired, as had been President Wilson's recent addresses, by a passion for the general good of mankind."

When the Armistice was signed, the Allies appeared to be unified in the hope and excitement of a new world order. But by the time the peace conference began on January 18, 1919, the ambitions and power mongering that had inspired the onset of the Great War itself were resurfacing. America's European Allies seemed to be reverting to the old world order, like wolves returning to their den, dragging with them carcasses to divide and pick apart. For them, to decide the peace meant to divide the spoils of war and to punish Germany so severely that there would never be a reason to fear German militarism again. But for Wilson, the only way to end war was to prevent war, "peace without victory"—in other words no single nation or group of nations should dominate because of winning the war.

Wilson had told the public many times that he believed that no one class or nationality was better than another. It was this perhaps that drew the masses to him. In Brest when the *George Washington* had docked in mid-December, acclaim turned to frenzy and the crowd roared its reverences until the voices gave out. In London, thousands of schoolgirls with baskets of flowers lined the streets scattering roses in Wilson's path, and a meeting run by Ramsay MacDonald and Philip Snowden—future leaders of England—endorsed Wilson's plan for a permanent peace. In Italy, where Wilson's picture hung on the walls of many houses, the press pondered whether the triumphs of the Caesars had inspired crowds so large as the ones greeting this American, who they believed would slay the dragons of their darkness.

But while Wilson was performing his role as the man who would be God and greeting the workingmen and women on the streets of Europe, he was denounced in the parlors of the ruling class—ridiculed actually for what they perceived as his naïveté. Indeed, Europe's rulers were plotting to undermine his cause. Georges Clemenceau, France's premier, was telling his advisers that the old system of alliances was the only way to safeguard the world. In England, Wilson's opponents, the ones staunchly supporting a punitive peace and strong reparations against Germany, had just won seats in Parliament. In Italy, Benito Mussolini, the Italian editor of the Milan *Il Popolo d'Italia*, echoing the ruling class, called Wilson "a dangerous radical." And Wilson's own loss of power in the 1918 Congressional elections diminished his stature among the leaders with whom he would be negotiating.

The negotiations took place at various palatial buildings in the vicinity of the Place de la Concorde, in particular the residences of the Big Four representatives of the Allied Powers. It was these four men on whom humanity was depending to reconstruct the world: David Lloyd George, the fifty-six-year-old prime minister of England, who was a liberal politically and an opportunist at heart; the fifty-nine-year-old Italian premier, Vittorio Emanuele Orlando, who was a liberal and a pragmatist; Clemenceau, the seventy-eight-year-old French premier, known as "the Tiger" and conservative to the core; and Wilson, a liberal politically and an idealist at heart. From the start, the three Europeans appeared to believe they could run roughshod over Wilson—perhaps mistaking his understated demeanor and rather fragile physique as a signal to do so. Americans were too innocent for international politics, after all, and Wilson must be simplistic and naïve to believe in a plan to end all wars. When asked by a journalist about Wilson's Fourteen Points, Clemenceau responded "Le bon Dieu n'avait que dix" ("God had only ten").

By the time Wilson docked in Boston on the 24th of February, the conference had considered such questions as what to do about Poland, about Russia, and about revision of the Armistice terms. But center stage in the early weeks had been two issues: what to do with the German colonies and whether to include the League as part of the peace treaty or work on it after the treaty was signed. The colonial powers wanted to annex the German colonies as spoils of war. Wilson wanted to present a new principle of world policy. The League of Nations, he proposed, would assign trustees or mandatories to the colonies temporarily while the inhabitants of the colonies prepared to take control of their own lands.

Wilson warned that if their first act in negotiating a peace settlement was to divide up the spoils of war, then the world would immediately lose faith in the conference. Besides, annexation was contrary to the principles outlined in the Armistice itself, said Wilson, who was flayed by the foreign press for his stand. In the end, Wilson won the battle, thus persuading the delegates to adopt the principle that all German colonies would be treated as wards of the new League of Nations.

Even the Republican delegate Henry White, whom Wilson's nemesis Henry Cabot Lodge had enlisted to help in undermining the president in Paris, agreed with Wilson's proposal and said as much in a February 10 letter to Lodge. "I cannot but feel from what I have already seen at the Conference of the tendency of every nation, excepting perhaps Great Britain, to grab all that it can get," White wrote, "that the only way to stop that tendency is the proposed mandate of the League of Nations, which while giving the government of colonies or backward countries into the charge under such mandate of a nation which would otherwise have annexed them, is the only way to stop the tendency to which I have referred."

Wilson's opponents claimed that his principled approach stymied the peace process and delayed the signing of a treaty that would block Germany from breaking out upon the world once again. Germany must be stopped from renewing its strength, they said, and thus a speedy treaty enforcing the punitive peace was imperative. This indeed was one reason his

adversaries in both Europe and America argued for postponing the formation of a League of Nations until after the peace treaty was signed. Settling
the military and naval terms, fixing reparations, and establishing boundaries would be difficult and time-consuming enough without the added
struggle of working out the details of the League.

Lodge, the Republican senator from Massachusetts, led the slowly
strengthening opposition to Wilson back home. Wilson and Lodge had
been bitter rivals for years. Now they were at the pinnacle of their political
careers and their enmity too was rising to its most intense level yet. The
quintessential realist, Lodge was now, after the November 1918 elections,
the Senate majority leader and the chairman of the Senate's Foreign Relations Committee. Lodge believed Wilson's "peace without victory" was
poppycock.

In these early days of the peace negotiations, Lodge's greatest concern
was that Wilson would place more importance on perfecting the League
proposal than on designing physical guarantees against a German military
remobilization, effectively that his idealism would endanger the world. In
the memo he had secretly given to Henry White before White's departure
to Paris, and which White never did deliver to Clemenceau or anyone
else at the conference, Lodge had written: "under no circumstances must
provisions for such a league be made a part of the peace treaty which con-
cludes the war with Germany. Any attempt to do this would not only
long delay the signature of the treaty of peace, which should not be unduly
postponed, but it would make the adoption of the treaty, unamended,
by the Senate of the United States and other ratifying bodies, extremely
doubtful."

Lodge believed that the League was not as simple as it sounded in
Wilson's lofty speeches. And he felt certain that the concept of the League
would break down when practicality and reality entered the discussion,
and thus the peace conference would last for a dangerously long time. Was
it even possible to convert Wilson's high aspirations for such a League into
law? Back in December, around the time Wilson had arrived in Europe,
Lodge decried the League in a speech to the Senate. It is easy, he said, "to
talk about a league of nations and the beauty and necessity of peace but the
hard practical demand is, are you ready to put your soldiers and your sailors
at the disposition of other nations?"

Lodge demanded definitions and facts. Would the League have a military force of its own or would the armies of its members be on call to be summoned by the authority of the League at any time? Was America willing to enter into "a permanent and indissoluble alliance?"

"The attempt to form a league of nations" he told the Senate, "and I mean an effective league, with power to enforce its decrees—no other is worth discussing—can tend at this moment only to embarrass the peace that we ought to make at once with Germany."

Lodge frequently quoted his friend Theodore Roosevelt these days, who in the last weeks of his life was outspoken against the League. As Roosevelt understood it, the League would require each member nation to fight battles in which it had no material interest and it was his experience with the American people that they "do not wish to go into an overseas war unless for a very great cause or where the issue is absolutely plain." There were others in the Senate who agreed.

But Wilson, demonstrating his dedication as well as his unbending nature, clung to his belief that creating a vehicle for lasting peace must be part of the treaty itself or it would not be a peace treaty at all. Only in a world secured against international aggression could peace be lasting. And for Wilson, the League was that security. Further, if the task of working it out were left for last, after the treaty was signed, the delegates would be eager to return home and the organization of the League could be postponed—perhaps never again approached.

"The constitution of that League of Nations and the clear definition of its objects must be a part, in a sense the most essential part, of the peace settlement itself," Wilson said in a speech in New York shortly before the end of the war. "It is not likely that it could be formed after the settlement. It is necessary to guarantee the peace: and the peace cannot be guaranteed as an afterthought."

On February 14, in Paris, after days and nights of working and reworking the structure of the League Covenant—effectively the constitution of the League—the conference delegates voted to approve the inclusion of the League in the peace treaty. That day in a room filled with dozens of men in three-buttoned cutaway coats, white vests, and pin-striped trousers, men who represented half the nations of the world—and one woman, Edith Wilson—the president read out loud the Covenant.

"A living thing is born," he said. "While it is elastic, while it is general in its terms, it is definite in one thing that we are called upon to make definite. It is a definite guaranty of peace. It is a definite guaranty by word against aggression."

Observing Wilson that day in Paris was the American journalist William Allen White, who wrote that Wilson's audience, which comprised the full peace conference, listened as if they were hearing a new declaration of independence. White called it a declaration of "international interdependence." This, said White, was the apex of Wilson's career. "Two or three hundred newspaper men, standing on their chairs and on the table, stood on tiptoes to see the President's face as he read the words before him; words of tremendous import, it seemed, for we were hearing, for the first time, the Covenant of the League of Nations as the President read it to the Peace Conference," White later wrote.

Now Wilson was coming home to gain approval from his own nation and to show the American public and the leaders of Congress what he had done at the peace conference to set his convictions into motion and to justify the war they had just endured. When the *Washington* docked in Boston on the 24th of February, a considerable crowd greeted the president. The first news he received was that he had a new grandson. And then he was told about the arrests the day before in New York of fourteen Spanish immigrants, all young men in their early twenties, who allegedly were conspiring to assassinate Wilson.

The government told the press that Secret Service agents had determined that the would-be assassins were Bolshevik sympathizers who had planned to throw a bomb at Wilson as he walked off the boat at Boston. The bomb was made in Philadelphia, the agents said, where two of the Spaniards had lived since their arrival in the United States only eighteen months before. This was also where the plot was allegedly hatched. No bomb had yet been found. Ten of the men were arrested at a Spanish club in New York City on Lexington Avenue at 108th Street, where agents confiscated many copies of *El Corsario*, a radical Spanish newspaper found in a pile of miscellaneous radical "paraphernalia," including IWW membership cards and flyers to aid "American political prisoners."

This was the second plot to kill the president that the government had revealed to the public in February. On the 12th, a man was arrested in

Cleveland who allegedly headed up a "band of Nihilists" who, while at Leavenworth Penitentiary in Kansas, had plotted to kill the president. The Secret Service revealed to the press that at Leavenworth the men, twenty in all, had drawn lots to determine who would be the assassin, and that they would kill the assassin if he did not follow through. The man who drew the killer ballot was Pietro Pierre, who was in jail for violating the Selective Service Act. Two of his Italian cell mates exposed the plot, which included a scheme to kill William G. McAdoo, former secretary of the treasury and son-in-law of President Wilson. From the moment Pierre left Leavenworth on October 14, 1918, the Secret Service was tailing him. The trail was long, from Kansas to Division Street in Chicago, then to Michigan, to Virginia, Minnesota, back to Michigan, and finally to Cleveland. In both Chicago and Cleveland Pierre had paid a visit to IWW headquarters. After his rearrest, the police raided IWW headquarters in both Chicago and Cleveland. Headlines then read: "I.W.W. in Plot to Kill Wilson."

The night of his safe landing in Boston, Wilson spoke at Mechanics Hall downtown, which was the unofficial beginning of his campaign to persuade America to accept the League. Baker wrote later that it was one of the finest speeches of Wilson's career. Wilson seemed unstoppable. He had effectively won the first two battles of the peace conference and the American public appeared to be enthusiastic about his League. But, because of the Republican majority in both the House and the Senate, to secure ratification would be a bigger battle than the peace conference itself.

Landing at Boston harbor first, before going to New York, the usual port of arrival, was part of Wilson's strategy to win that contest. Boston was home to Lodge, the man as determined to kill the League as Wilson was to create it. And the resounding crowd greeting Wilson in Boston made it politically difficult for Lodge to eviscerate the president, especially because the Massachusetts governor, Calvin Coolidge, though a Republican, asked Lodge to restrain from vitriol.

But Wilson's main plan for winning the upcoming battle was to avoid describing to the public the details of the League, thus speaking in exalted tones and keeping on the high ground of his ideals where his popularity dwelled. The public was uninformed about the practical workings of his idea, a situation that opened the door for Lodge's own strategy for crushing Wilson's dream: to inform the public about every complicated, contradictory, and imposing detail of it. Knowing what demands the League would require of Americans, such as protecting other nations from aggressors, Lodge believed the public would never allow its congressmen to support it. After all, the winds of war might have the effect, especially now, of bending Americans in the direction of isolationism.

CHAPTER 11

Blinders

On the 25th of February, the USS *George Washington* pulled into Pier 4 at Hoboken, New Jersey. On board were the Wilson entourage and 2,294 returning soldiers. Thus the homecoming was doubly festive, with a grand band from nearby Camp Merritt, a cheering throng of workers from the Red Cross, the Salvation Army, and the YMCA, and an abundance of cakes, coffee, cigarettes, and candies. In the rush of excitement, the president left a pair of tortoiseshell spectacles in his stateroom. The ship's chief water tender, L. O. Jones, was given the special mission of personally carrying the president's eyeglasses to Washington with the instructions: "The President appears to value these glasses highly, so take care of them. Wrap them first in cotton, then a layer of excelsior, and put a round turn and two half hitches of stout spun yarn, and I guess that will hold them all right until you get to the White House tomorrow forenoon."

By the time Wilson had been reunited with his spectacles on the 26th, he had signed a new revenue bill calling for Americans to pay a "victory tax" annually to meet the war debt, which the Treasury Department said would amount to $1.2 billion a year for twenty-five years. He had announced his support for licensing civilians to fly airplanes. And he had agreed to march in a parade the next day for three thousand returning soldiers in the District of Columbia. That night, he dined at the White House with the members of the Senate and House committees on foreign affairs with the explicit purpose of going over the draft of the League Covenant.

From Paris, Wilson had urged each of the invitees to hold back from any debates over the League until that night. Senator Borah refused to attend the dinner, announcing that there was nothing Wilson could do or say to convince him to favor the League. Senator Albert B. Fall, another opponent, also declined the invitation. And if Wilson didn't know it in Paris, he would find out now: the debate over the League had already begun.

Senator James Reed's stand on the issue of the League's violating the U.S. Constitution, for example, was already being contested by one of the

League's strongest Republican supporters, former U.S. president William Howard Taft. "Most of the men who are sitting up with the Constitution to defeat the League are men whom I would not trust overnight," Taft told the *New York Times* that February.

Although Lodge was angry at the president for landing in Boston harbor instead of New York, he nonetheless attended the dinner. In a letter to Henry White in Paris, shortly before Wilson's arrival in Boston, Lodge wrote, "I accepted the invitation to the dinner. I should not have thought to do otherwise. I also felt, as a gentleman and man of honor, that having accepted the invitation to dinner I should comply with his request not to discuss the terms of the League as set forth in the draft of the committee, until after the dinner. The President, however, does not seem to look at it in the same way, and is going to land in Boston, my own city, and there address a great mass meeting which is all arranged for while I am reduced to silence because I wish to observe what I think is required of an honorable man."

After dinner, Lodge escorted Mrs. Wilson from the table and the thirty-six guests adjourned to the East Room, where Wilson calmly responded to two hours of cross-examination about the Covenant. A major point of contention was the fact that so much time at the conference had been consumed by the League. Little progress on the terms of peace with Germany would not please the American public, which wanted the complete return of the soldiers as soon as possible. And that could not happen until Germany signed the treaty. At the close of the evening, the lines were clearly drawn. The guns were loaded. And each side was taking aim.

The next day Senator Philander Chase Knox, a Republican from Pennsylvania, called the League "a betrayal of the people." A few days after that, thirty-nine Republican senators and senators-elect—enough to block ratification—signed a resolution stating that it was the Senate's wish that only after the peace treaty was completed should the League be considered and that the draft of the Covenant, as Wilson had presented it that week, should be rejected. Shortly after midnight on March 3, Lodge read the resolution out loud to the Senate, knowing that the Senate's objections to the League would be on file in the *Congressional Record* and that it would be chronicled in the press.

Wilson fought back. On March 4, Wilson and Taft linked arms on the stage of the Metropolitan Opera in New York while Enrico Caruso sang

"The Star-Spangled Banner." Wilson told the approximately five thousand people in the audience that when the treaty was done the Covenant of the League would most definitely be part of it, for "you cannot dissect the Covenant from the Treaty without destroying the whole vital structure." Guided by the shining light of his idealism, Wilson could see only his own path to peace. Like all idealists, he adjusted his blinders and charged ahead.

But for America, the blinders were a problem. As the president of a country facing the aftermath of a world war—and of a flu pandemic—he should have had a broader vision. While Wilson was working on a scheme for the reconstruction of the world, America also needed a reconstruction plan. And although expectations for a better world were still high among his countrymen, the realities of war's aftermath were lowering the threshold of hope. Nine days of presidential incantations to make everything right were simply not enough.

Wilson's nation was tilting off balance, dizzy from the onslaught of so many unsettling events and demanding issues. For example, thousands upon thousands of returning soldiers needed jobs at a time when the government was canceling wartime contracts, which caused companies to reduce their workforces for peacetime markets and to shut down factories. Labor strikes were hitting industrial America daily, drawing attention to low wages and long hours, the diminishing numbers of jobs and the rising cost of living.

At the same time, there was the fast-spreading fear of Bolshevism. There was the menacing indifference of white America to the injustices in black America—all pressing insistently for solutions. There were the crusaders for civil liberties who wanted Wilson to grant amnesty to the thousands of Americans indicted for obstructing the laws of wartime America, such as the Espionage Act and the Selective Service Act. And there were the suffragists who continued to blame Wilson for their inability to persuade the Senate to pass their constitutional amendment—the most recent defeat occurring two weeks before his return from France—and who demonstrated their anger when sixty-five of them burned Wilson in effigy in front of the White House on February 9.

In addition, several congressmen were accusing Wilson's postmaster general, Albert Burleson, of stretching his authority for the purpose of muzzling the press. They loudly urged Wilson to repeal the rigorous mail censorship that had existed during the war. There was too much concern, they said, about suppressing dissidents and identifying new enemies and not enough about securing a scheme for reconstructing postwar America.

Even the flu was back, in a third wave. The first wave, in the spring of 1918, was mild in comparison with the overwhelming second wave, which struck in the autumn that year and evoked comparisons with the Black Death of the fourteenth century. There had been the false hope around the time of the Armistice that the epidemic was over, and in some cities health curfews had been canceled, lifting restrictions on large public gatherings for the Armistice Day celebrations. But the pandemic hardly ended in November 1918. In December, as contaminated soldiers returned to America in the cramped quarters of ships, the third wave began. By January, the gauze masks, the bans on public gatherings, the daily reports of casualties had returned as the westward-bound troopships brought home the soldiers and the disease. Whether the new wave would break the record for devastation and horror that the second wave had established, or constitute a less intense resurgence, no one knew. In the winter months, it did not look good. In the last week of January, for example, more than a thousand people died of flu and pneumonia in New York City, a tally increasing weekly. And on February 26, the transport *Leviathan* pushed off from Brest with thousands of soldiers, including some who were severely coughing as the ship left port. At least two hundred developed the flu on board and seventeen died at sea or after arriving at Hoboken.

The loose ends of wartime were dangling everywhere, demanding decisions and action. What, for example, should Wilson do about Daylight Savings Time? The government had established it during the war to save fuel. Now that the war was over, there was a movement to end it. While Wilson was back, a U.S. senator from Oklahoma, Thomas Pryor Gore, called for the repeal of the Daylight Savings Act in the form of a rider added to the Agricultural Appropriations bill. He claimed that the need for repeal was put forth by farmers, who believed that the law had damaged their livelihood. On Gore's side were the utility companies, which would lose money if Daylight Savings continued. One group claimed that the act had saved the nation at least $8 million in gas and electric lights and one million tons of coal, which translated into huge losses in profits for the utility companies.

Fighting the repeal and wanting to keep Daylight Savings were Senator

William Calder of New York, who had invented the concept; the acting mayor of New York City, Robert L. Moran; the Playground and Recreation Association of America, the U.S. National Lawn Tennis Association, golfers, baseball players, and sportsmen generally, who claimed that that extra hour of sunlight benefited them; the California State Fish Exchange; all labor organizations; and many merchants associations, which declared that their employees benefited because at the end of the day they had some daylight for playing sports. Although a war measure, Daylight Savings continued to save Americans money, so said those against repeal. That was a group that included the president, who believed that to lose it would be an "inconvenience and an economic loss." The burgeoning auto industry got into the act, opposing the repeal because the extra hour of sunlight meant that men could take their families for a drive after work and before night. (Not all cars had headlights yet.)

Editorials lambasted the farmers for being selfish when most of America wanted to keep the new system. The head of the National Daylight Savings Association said it wasn't really the farmers stirring up trouble. It was the large gas companies urging legislators to end a system that had saved consumers money but had hurt corporate profits. Farmers then spoke up and said that was right, that they really weren't concerned as much as the press had depicted them. They could use that first hour in the morning for general chores and save the real farm work for the hours after the sun came up. Just in case the repeal failed, one company claimed it was trying to design a wristwatch that half the year would speed up and the other half slow down so that the time changes in the spring and autumn would not affect the human rhythm as much as the critics claimed it did.

Far more pressing than the Daylight Savings question was the persistent problem of what to do about Russia and the Bolsheviks. Despite Secretary of War Baker's announcement on February 17 that the government intended to withdraw the American troops from Russia, the issue continued to trouble the friends and families of the Americans still there. There was no date set yet for their withdrawal and the news from Russia was disturbing. During Wilson's February visit home, one infantryman from Michigan's 339th who had returned to America from Archangel with severe arthritis spoke extensively to the press. He described coldness that pushed through him with the sharpness of knives and said that for weeks he had worn wet clothing in subzero temperatures. Having lost several frostbitten toes, he was now unable to walk. He said that the American soldiers wanted to come home. Some were even beginning to refuse to fight. They did not understand why they were there, he said.

At the Overman hearings in the Senate, which had resumed on February 11, the government was calling witnesses, all of them former or current government officials who described heinous scenes in which Bolsheviks committed unconscionable atrocities. The Bolsheviks had caused indescribable chaos in Russia, said the witnesses. One man who had spent time in Petrograd testified that many of Russia's misfortunes were due to the influx of Jewish agitators from New York's Lower East Side.

"How would you describe these Bolshevik forces so that the average man would understand them and their composition?" a senator asked one witness.

"Like a mob of Captain Kidds with the exception that they operated by land instead of on the water," the witness responded.

Another witness claimed with the utmost certainty that there were at least three million people in America, mostly of Russian origin, who were Bolshevik sympathizers, and among those, many were spies. And, he added, Wilson seemed to be doing nothing about it. Yet another described the free love policy in Russia: all girls and boys upon reaching the age of eighteen become property of the State and must register at the Bureau of Free Love, which orchestrates forced, arranged matches once a month out of which come children who will then be government property. "Everything that makes life decent and worth living is in jeopardy if this thing called Bolshevism is allowed to go ahead," testified a former U.S. Department of Commerce employee in Russia.

These stories were not corroborated by the Quakers and others who worked for social agencies that assisted the Russian people after the Revolution. Some journalists too decried the dark testimonies of the former consular officials and diplomats. Among them were Louise Bryant and her husband, John Reed. Bolshevism was not something they would recommend in America, unless of course the majority of Americans wanted it, but there was no reason to lie about what was happening in Russia. Bryant, who had written for the *Philadelphia Public Ledger* and for *Cosmopolitan* magazine, among other publications, said that the Russians she knew were excited about the experiment of Bolshevism and that they were fine idealists. She and others said that the Russians were not planning a takeover of

America, that in fact they didn't want our system of government. They did not wish, she said, "an East Side or a Fifth Avenue like there is in New York or a West End as in London."

When Reed was asked whether he was in favor of a revolution like Russia's for America, he said, "I have always advocated a Revolution in the United States." When asked the question a second time, he added, "Revolution does not necessarily mean a revolution by force. By revolution I mean profound social change."

Bessie Beatty, editor of *McCall's* magazine, said that she was in Russia from June 1917 through January 1918. Beatty was not in favor of Bolshevism in America but believed it would improve conditions in Russia.

"Miss Beatty, do I understand your position to be that the majority of the Russians want the Bolsheviki and that therefore they should be permitted to have it?" asked a senator.

"Yes, that is my position."

"We have had men of the highest character before this committee. Some of those men were in Russian jails and they testified that they saw men tortured and led forth to execution without the formality of trial and without knowledge of the charge against them. Do you discredit the testimony of those witnesses?"

"No I do not," she said.

"Are you directly or indirectly connected with Bolshevist propaganda in this country?"

"No I am not."

"Well, was it your purpose in appearing before this committee to defend and justify Bolshevism?"

"No. All I want is for the Allies to withdraw their troops from Russia and let the Russians work out their own problems without outside interference," said Beatty.

Journalist William Allen White also told the world that February to leave the Russians alone. "If the Bolsheviki had got something worth while to develop in the form of government they ought to have the opportunity to do it without interference. If they have not got anything, they'll go on the rocks soon enough."

And Ray Stannard Baker, who saw similarities between Wilson and Lenin—both embarking on bold experiments for which the world might not be ready—wrote in his journal that February: "Sometimes, as during the other evening when I talked with Raymond Robins about Russia, I find myself looking into a vast chasm of wonder, with the solid earth a-tremble under my feet. What if Lenin and those despised Bolsheviks had the creative secret of a new world, and we—we serious and important ones—were merely trying to patch the fragments of the old?"

Before leaving again for France, Wilson appointed a new attorney general, A. Mitchell Palmer, a Democrat from Pennsylvania who had strong aspirations to run in the 1920 presidential race. Palmer was a Quaker but his firmest convictions at the moment centered on Bolshevism and political ambition. Bolsheviks were fouling the air in America, Palmer claimed. The scent was the strongest in immigrant communities. And in the name of national security, as the new chief law officer of the Department of Justice, he would try to exterminate the Bolshevik menace—in a very big and memorable way.

Until March, Palmer had served his country as the alien property custodian, which meant that he was responsible for seizing, managing, and selling companies and personal property owned by Germans in America as a defense against the use of such assets to aid America's enemies. As recently as late January 1919, for example, Palmer had engaged the Anderson Galleries in New York to auction such items as an eight-piece set of Louis XVI furniture, a rosewood table of the Louis XV period, a set of six English eighteenth-century Chippendale chairs, and more, bringing in nearly $50,000. During the war his department had managed the seizure of nearly $1 billion in property and assets from forty thousand estates or trusts owned by Germans in America. This was an appointed position that came out of the wartime Trading with the Enemy Act of 1917 and the appointment, coming from Wilson in October 1917, was likely in return for Palmer's hard work in campaigning for Wilson. In 1912, Palmer had been the vice chairman of the Democratic National Committee, and after Wilson's victory he was offered the post of secretary of war. In a letter dated February 24, 1913, Palmer declined, saying that he was a Quaker and that the nation "requires not a man of peace for a war secretary, but one who can think war." He was then offered a judgeship in the U.S. Court of Claims, which he accepted and where he had remained for more than four years.

Wilson's latest plan for Palmer, however, seemed a bit shaky. In fact, the new Republican Congress would not confirm Wilson's appointment of Palmer as the new attorney general, amid accusations that the alien property custodian had used his post to facilitate the transfer of some valuable German properties to high-level Democrats. Some of his critics also complained that he had favored Democrats for jobs within his jurisdiction and for high salaries. Although Palmer's work had been appreciated as necessary and adequate during the war, it was now somewhat controversial. His admirers claimed he had captured the "German industrial army" in America. His foes called him the "official American pickpocket." He denied the charges and beseeched the Senate Judiciary Committee to commence, as it wished to do, a thorough investigation of his duties in his previous post. On March 4, Thomas W. Gregory, the attorney general since 1914, resigned and Palmer, though not confirmed, nonetheless assumed the post as an "incumbent de gracia," as the *Christian Science Monitor* called it. The debate over his confirmation would resume in June.

On March 5, a cool, misty day on the East Coast, the president, first lady, Ray Stannard Baker, and others returned to Boston harbor to sail back to France. At the Senate that morning the Agriculture Appropriations bill with the Daylight Savings rider was defeated, thus keeping Daylight Savings intact. Also in the morning, at a meeting of the Senate Judiciary Committee, Sergeant Henry Johnson urged legislators to "take care of the boys who did their bit in the war" by passing a bill that would give veterans preference in civil service appointments and promotions. The press that day was abuzz with a decision out of the U.S. Supreme Court in which Oliver Wendell Holmes, Jr., claimed that the constitutional right of freedom of speech could be abridged if there were circumstances, such as war, that represented a "clear and present danger" to the nation. And William Monroe Trotter, who had just obtained his seaman's permit under the name William Trotter, revealed to his friends a new plan: he would learn to cook and then find a job in the galley of a ship bound for France. Trotter was still so focused on getting to Paris, where he hoped he could bring world attention to "real democracy," that he had not even tried to arrange a meeting with Wilson during the president's nine-day visit home.

At Boston harbor, suffragists awaited the president's arrival. Disappointed that the Senate had still not adopted the suffrage amendment and that some of them had been denied visas to follow the president to France, they waved derisive banners with renewed vigor and vitriol: "Mr. President, How Long Must Women Wait for Suffrage?" and "An Autocrat at Home Is a Poor Champion of Democracy Abroad."

As the *George Washington* steered out of Boston harbor, its engines sputtered and roared as if venting the stress of its passengers from their days in America. The noise of frenzied schedules and weighty expectations would subside, for the moment, as the ship pushed ever so slowly out to sea, heaving its behemoth body onto the waves, adapting to the rhythms of the sea. On board, the pace of life would wind down and the process of breathing would seem to be tied to the pulsating sound of water splashing against the bow.

CHAPTER 12

Shuffleboard

Ray Stannard Baker would always remember the trip back to France that March, perhaps because of what occurred when he and the Wilsons returned to Paris. If indeed he could have foreseen the events soon to unfold for the president and himself, he would have cherished the serenity of the voyage all the more.

In his journal Baker described the trip as "quiet and simple with a small group and a friendly one. Coming out of strenuous days, controversies and great meetings, the President rested. . . . I wish many Americans who thought [Wilson] a cold, unamiable man, could have seen him."

On most days Wilson avoided discussions about the peace conference and told stories or talked about history, especially about the French and Lafayette. Wilson described what he considered the peculiarities of the French—on his mind for obvious reasons—and he talked about golf. Baker would remember luncheons beginning with the president's quiet grace in low tones and then "the meal itself passing off with the friendly give-and-take of any American family meal." He would also remember the president laughing more than usual. The Wilsons took frequent walks on the deck, attended the performances of the ship's orchestra, played shuffleboard once, and did a lot of reading. Mrs. Wilson and Dr. Grayson took turns reading books out loud to the president, such as A. G. Gardiner's sketches of public men entitled *Prophets, Priests and Kings* and Gardiner's *War Lords*.

In fact, one of Baker's most vivid memories of the trip was the day he walked down the stairs near the Wilsons' cabin and heard the physician reading to the president from a book that was very familiar to Baker. It was written by David Grayson—no relation to the doctor—an author who, since 1906, had written several very popular books: *Adventures in Contentment*, *Adventures in Friendship*, *The Friendly Road*, *Hempfield*, and most recently, in 1917, *Great Possessions*.

The books were first-person observations of life in the country written with such an earth-loving, humane spirit and with such depth that they touched Americans deeply and widely. To his readers, Grayson seemed one part Thoreau and one part Mark Twain as he told of wayside adventures with strangers he helped and from whom he gleaned life lessons. The stories were not about escaping from the world by living in the country, not about isolation and narrowness, but rather about expanding an understanding of life by watching nature, listening to country sounds, smelling the changing seasons, digging fingers into the soil and feeling the texture of the earth. Grayson's books were about sincerity, authenticity, and diligence. They were idealistic narratives about looking at the world through a lens of hope and benevolence and always traveling on a "friendly road."

"What I am seeking is something as simple and as quiet as the trees on the hills," Grayson wrote in *Adventures in Friendship*, "just to look out around me at the pleasant countryside, to enjoy a little of this passing show, to meet (and to help a little if I may) a few human beings, and thus to get more nearly into the sweet kernel of human life. My friend, you may or may not think this is a worthy object; if you do not, stop here, go no further with me; but if you do, why, we'll exchange great words on the road; we'll look up at the sky together; we'll see and hear the finest things in this world! We'll enjoy the sun."

By the time Baker heard the words of Grayson on the deck of the *Washington*, the author had become so popular that there were even Grayson clubs. Graysonians, as one Florida club called them, were people who were "fond of the open air," lived fully in the present, found fulfillment in observing the details of nature, and were willing to retrace their steps to help a stranger. There were also Grayson impostors, largely because the author led a rather mysterious life, not allowing photos or interviews. Who was David Grayson? A lawyer in Atlanta who happened to have the same name did not deny the claim to the famous books, when asked. Another man in the Midwest said he was the acclaimed author and lectured under the name. Yet another who was later exposed as a bigamist in Utah lived his double life as David Grayson and decided he might as well also claim to be the author.

From the moment Baker heard the admiral read, he recognized the author, the particular work, and perhaps even the chapter. To be sure, Baker was more knowledgeable about the works of Grayson than anyone else in the world. After all, Ray Stannard Baker *was* David Grayson.

At that time, Baker wasn't certain whether Wilson knew that he was Grayson, though recently he had been open about it to the press, if asked. Uncertain that his Grayson books would be a success and perhaps wanting the freedom of anonymity, Baker long ago had chosen to use the pen name for his country sketches. For years, many readers had assumed that John S. Phillips, Baker's former editor at McClure's magazine—where he had worked with Tarbell and Steffens—was the real David Grayson. Even their colleagues and friends had believed that, a situation causing awkward moments when both men were present at dinners and other social occasions. At the mention of a Grayson book or phrase, guests would hold back their smiles and send an all-knowing look to Phillips, while Baker or Phillips quickly changed the subject. And for years the only two people, outside of Baker's immediate family, who knew the author's true identity were Phillips and Walter Page at the great New York publishing house Doubleday, Page & Co. Eventually the increasing numbers of impostors and one very perceptive fan forced Baker to surface. The fan, David Gray, wrote him a letter and asked if Baker would be offended if Gray were to write under the pen name Ray Bakerson.

Baker had created the virtuous, noble Graysonian world as a counterpoint to the ignoble parts of society and human beings he had been exposing for years as a muckraking journalist. Born in Lansing, Michigan, in 1870 and a graduate of Michigan State College, Baker had championed the cause of the disenfranchised and the underdog from his earliest days as a cub reporter in Chicago writing for the Chicago News-Record, to his years with McClure's magazine in the late 1890s, and later at the American Magazine. In his articles Baker examined every aspect of urban life, covering labor issues, such as the famous Pullman strike in Chicago and the 1893 Washington march of jobless men known as Coxey's Army, and writing about race long before most white journalists were even thinking about it. For his 1908 book Following the Color Line, he spent months interviewing blacks and whites in urban and rural communities throughout America. In 1916, in a piece for the World's Work magazine entitled "Gathering Clouds Along the Color Line," he presciently damned the race situation in America saying it was "full of danger" and he identified what he believed was its most menacing aspect: "the contemptuous indifference of a large part of white America to what is going on in the depths of the volcano just below."

Devotion to his journalistic work often plunged Baker into dark, hopeless situations. Longing for a lighter side, he invented David Grayson. In the name of Grayson, Baker decided to uncover the nobility of humans, to show them in virtuous circumstances, and, using a rural setting, to exhibit a genuine, simple side of life.

Grayson was a nineteenth-century idealist in the way that Wilson was. Perhaps it was Baker's ideals as expressed in the character of Grayson that caused him to bond so strongly with Wilson, believing in him at times when others didn't. Both Baker, through the character of Grayson, and Wilson seemed to be asking the same question: what does it mean to be fully human? But there was one major difference between Baker and Wilson. Baker used Grayson to move beyond the disturbing settings and issues about which he had been writing for years, to travel out of darkness into a heavenly world of high ideals and hopeful visions. Wilson's journey was just the opposite. In December he had traveled to Paris under a halo of noble visions and then descended into the hellish struggle with the ignoble Realpolitik of the old world order—the self-serving politics that had caused the war to begin with. And now he was returning to Paris, to the struggle, to the abyss. That the president was connecting to Grayson now on the voyage back to France intrigued Baker. It was like sitting on a sunny beach in the moments before the crushing descent of a tidal wave.

Indeed, Baker sensed the troubles ahead. In Baker's opinion, the president had two problems in Paris: the inextricable clash between his principles and the self-interests of the other nations at the peace conference and his unwillingness to communicate to the public exactly what he was doing to create a permanent peace. With charisma and eloquence, Wilson had expressed his ideas and made his promises, inviting the public into his world of hope and peace. But as he toiled day and night at Paris to square his actions with his words, he did not share with the public his challenges, his decisions, or his step-by-step successes. As Baker once said, Wilson's speeches were filled with the words "I think," "I believe," and "I hope," but were missing the words "I did," "I went," and "I fought." Baker believed that without this sort of communication Wilson would be misunderstood.

Yes, Wilson was idolized worldwide and yes, the American public thus far had responded favorably to the concept of the League and to Wilson's recent speeches about the Covenant. But the movement to defeat him and the League was growing, both in Paris and in Washington. To crush it,

Wilson must let the public see more of his world. If the people better understood the process of peacemaking, they might be less vulnerable to Wilson's critics. Intelligent and determined publicity was the solution, in the view of Baker, who believed that "publicity is the life blood of democracy."

Wilson's job in Paris was overwhelming. Yet how many people really understood what he was doing on a daily basis? Wilson carried the same burdens as Lloyd George, Clemenceau, and Orlando in negotiating the terms of the treaty with Germany. In addition, he was shepherding his cherished League by chairing the League of Nations Commission, which met in the evening for many hours, often beyond midnight. He was also meeting with journalists, businessmen, labor representatives, and representatives of hundreds of nations seeking freedom, food, or simply to be heard. Ho Chi Minh would come to Paris to ask for the freedom of French Indochina. Mohandas Gandhi came to urge Wilson and the commissioners to relieve India from British rule. And T. E. Lawrence, the British soldier who had led the Arabs in revolt against the Turks and who, now known as "Lawrence of Arabia," was a British delegate at the peace conference, sought nationhood for the Arabs, who had believed that in return for fighting on the side of the British they would be granted independence.

Baker would remember one delegation in particular: two Polish peasants wearing black fur Cossack caps and red-embroidered homespun wool shirts accompanied by a Polish priest who, speaking French, served as their interpreter. They came from a small community of Poles in the mountains of northern Austria and had been told that in the treaty they were supposed to now be part of the new nation of Czecho-Slovaks. Someone in their mountain village had told them that the American president was in Paris and that he believed that people should have a right to choose their own form of government. Because they were Poles they did not want to be in the new nation. And so one of them decided he would represent his people and walk from Austria to Paris to confront the president. But on the way he got lost and eventually met up with the other man, a Polish sheepherder who also wanted "to be free" and so, knowing how to navigate with the stars, the shepherd guided them both a hundred or more miles into Warsaw. A patriotic Polish society heard of their story and helped them the rest of the way to Paris, where they were told they must go to the Hôtel de Crillon. There they were directed to the president's house across the street.

Watching them walk up the carpeted stairs to the president's study and smelling their thick wool garments, Baker would never forget their determination and courage as Wilson assured them he would do what he could. "Everyone who came to Paris upon any mission whatsoever aimed first of all at seeing the President," Baker later wrote.

On the voyage back to France, Baker tried to talk to Wilson about the issue of publicity, pressing upon him the need "for more and better." But Wilson seemed to fear it. From Baker's point of view, it wasn't that Wilson was afraid of revealing the truth about what was happening in Paris, but rather he was worried about the facts being twisted to the advantage of his enemies. "As a highly cultivated scholar," wrote Baker, "he disliked exaggeration and distrusted sensationalism." Wilson believed that the less said, the better. Report the results, not the process. Let the events of the day go out in the smallest possible capsule.

For Baker, this was unfortunate and frustrating. Baker's job, after all, as head of Wilson's press bureau, meant that he had to communicate the activities of Wilson and the American Peace Commission to about 150 American correspondents every day. He knew what Wilson was facing on a daily basis, the sometimes small yet significant accomplishments, but without the president's willingness to share all, he could not build an adequate bridge between Wilson's world and the public. Considering the Republican majority opposing the League in the Senate, Wilson's only hope was to force the majority to back down by persuading their constituents to speak out strongly in favor of the League. However, public opinion was, as Baker and Wilson well knew, more focused on domestic issues. This was Baker's challenge as Wilson's publicity man, made more difficult by Wilson's failure to give full disclosure of the process of making the peace.

Adding to the challenge was the fact that foreign affairs had never been the most popular subject for Americans. And, unlike Europeans, who had always been well versed in international issues, Americans had no tradition of European involvement and no incentive to be informed about events in Europe—with the exception, of course, of the war. At the same time, there was the obstacle of the technology. News traveled from Paris to America through a few overcrowded cables or on an overloaded wireless system with enormous tolls. Each day of the peace conference hundreds of committees met, representatives from scores of nations discussed their affairs, and Wilson often worked a sixteen-hour day. To cull the most important details out of all that happened on any given day, to shape them in such a way as to reveal Wilson's step-by-step progress at the conference, was Baker's urgent wish. The more Wilson balked, the more Baker pushed. "When people complain vaguely that they have not been given the 'facts,' it is this that they mean," Baker later wrote. "They want to *see* and *feel exactly* what happened."

The only stressful moments during the voyage back to France were these discussions between Wilson and Baker. Wilson was outraged at what he perceived as the French government's control of the press. It was a veritable propaganda machine designed to undermine Wilson's attempts to force Clemenceau to adhere to a less imperialist approach to international affairs. In fact, a French editor had leaked a memo to Wilson proving that Clemenceau was manipulating his nation's presses. The memo instructed certain newspapers to write about the growing opposition to Wilson in America, to emphasize the disorder and anarchy in Russia and the need for more Allied intervention in that country, and to write articles about Germany's ability to pay a large indemnity—all representing Clemenceau's positions.

Baker urged Wilson to combat such a propaganda campaign. He was certain that his president was not aware of the strength of the forces against him. And Baker's journalist friends in Paris, including William Allen White, Ida Tarbell, and Walter Lippmann, shared such concerns. They agreed that Wilson's principles, despite the passion and determination behind them, could not alone topple the habits of centuries. Men like Clemenceau were not going to surrender a tradition of armed alliances to an untested system of international cooperation.

Wilson was a distant, very private man who, as Baker noted in his journal, "lived the lonely life of the mind." He was not easy to reach, but on the March voyage back to France Baker felt closer than ever to him. Baker believed in Wilson and never doubted his sincerity. He admired the president's courage to unveil his dreams before the entire world. But he questioned whether a world clamoring to return to life as it was before the war was ready for such a daring experiment. The approval of the League Covenant in February was a positive step, indeed an achievement, but Baker was not confident that the path ahead was clear.

In his journal, he wrote:

I have often, at Paris, and here on this voyage where I have had moments to think, the terrible doubt as to whether the actual work of the Conference thus far is in any degree fulfilling the promise of Wilson's words. Wilson has phrased the hope of the world—the people come to power; he has spoken the great true word, but has he the genius to work it out? Has he the power? Above all, is the time ripe?

How make peace when there is so little to make it of—so little of human understanding, human sympathy, above all so little willingness to sacrifice immediate advantage for the future well-being of civilization? How make any real peace in such an atmosphere of suspicion, fear, greed, hatred, as that which now pervades Paris?

March 13 was the last night of a trip that had clearly invigorated everyone on board, as fresh air and light talk supplanted the stale and heavy struggles on both sides of the Atlantic. After a calm, leisurely dinner, just as the passengers were returning to their cabins, the crew gathered and sang "God Be with You Till We Meet Again." Then everyone, including Wilson, sang "Auld Lang Syne." "I wondered among what other people in the world there could develop just such relationships and such a spirit!" Baker wrote that night.

Wilson's ship docked at Brest at 8:30 A.M. It was met by local celebrities, who cheered and greeted the president and his party, all of whom were rushed off to a special train bound for Paris. The news from Paris was shocking, all the more so after the calm cruise across the Atlantic—a veritable tempest of bad news. During the president's absence, from February 14 to March 14, his opponents had gained considerable ground. Flinging rumors like thunderbolts, some newspapers were reporting that the League was dead and that a peace with Germany would be made very soon—one that would contain no reference to a League of Nations.

On his secret American telephone circuit, Wilson immediately called Baker. The reports must be denied, he told him, and Baker must publicly reconfirm that the League will be "an integral part of the general treaty of peace." Baker knew that the reassertion of the president's unalterable stand could create a standoff of such magnitude that the entire conference might fall apart. But he also knew it was necessary. It was one of Wilson's boldest moves. Instead of succumbing to the rumors and the news, Wilson firmly reasserted his stand, reannounced the previous action of the conference that had declared the League to be part of the treaty, and proceeded as if nothing adverse had happened at all. While the controversies raged in the columns of French newspapers, the delegates resumed work toward the various settlements that would comprise the treaty. Two days later, the committees were conferring and the heads of state were meeting. Even the newspapers were toning down the storm of sensational coverage. But, as Baker wrote in his journal early one March morning, "It was clear there was still lightning in the clouds."

CHAPTER 13

In Like a Lion

March 1919 was not the best of times for Harry Weinberger or Mollie Steimer or anyone trying to remove the government's wartime muzzle on free speech. Not only was the Espionage Act still on the books but its advocates, mindful of the mounting fear of Reds and revolution, agitated for a peacetime equivalent, only stronger. Senator Overman, the chairman of the subcommittee of the Committee on the Judiciary officially seeking the truth about Bolshevism in America, was of the belief that much of the opposition against the act was because of its name, not its content. The word "espionage" conjured unseemly images of spies and daggers when in fact this act was designed to "protect our national sovereignty and our established institutions," according to the committee's final report.

For supporters of the Espionage Act and its 1918 amended version, the Sedition Act, the month began with a powerful boost. On the 3rd and again on the 10th, the U.S. Supreme Court issued three opinions that firmly validated the Espionage Act and its power to punish outspoken critics of government policy. From the nation's highest court, there was not even a whisper of dissent questioning the constitutionality of a law that Weinberger and numerous others saw as having twisted the meaning of the Constitution, which was intended to protect the rights of unpopular minorities against the tyranny of the majority. The nine justices were unanimous in upholding the convictions in each of the cases, thus endorsing the government's use of the Espionage Act in restraining the rights of individuals to speak and associate freely and thus diminishing the power of those, like Weinberger, who adamantly opposed the law.

In 1918, there had been a total of 988 prosecutions under the Espionage Act; 492 were brought to some sort of conclusion. Of those, 72 were dismissed, 57 were acquitted, and 363 resulted in conviction. In 1919, the law had outlived any reason for it to exist, in Weinberger's opinion, and the 496 cases pending should be dropped. He believed that if such wartime laws were not repealed, their advocates would invent ways to make them relevant. Already, those lobbying for a peacetime equivalent were whispering in the ear of the new attorney general, A. Mitchell Palmer, who, it was rumored, was keenly listening.

The Supreme Court's rulings didn't surprise Weinberger, but in his hopeful way he had expected more—at least one dissenting opinion. His own belief that the individual is more important than the State was the antithesis of the message coming out of the Court, which was that the State comes first, before the individual, and as such the State, in the name of national security, can restrict such basic rights as freedom of speech. Clearly the March opinions did not bode well for Mollie Steimer and her immigrant comrades, whose case Weinberger would press upon the Supreme Court justices as an example of the State stripping individuals of their First Amendment protections, and thus jeopardizing the foundation of a true democracy. What he wanted now was to see a dialogue coming out of the Court. But without dissenting opinions, there was no discussion and without the Court's acknowledgment of a basis for such discourse, there was every reason to believe that the government would have free rein in its aggressive campaign against aliens and subversives.

In the first of the three cases that March, Charles T. Schenck, the general secretary of the Socialist Party in Philadelphia, had been sentenced to six months in prison for publishing and distributing fifteen thousand leaflets that opposed recruitment and claimed the draft was unconstitutional. He sent most of them to men who had just passed their physicals and whose names he found listed in newspapers. "Conscription was despotism in its worst form," the leaflet said, "and a monstrous wrong against humanity in the interest of Wall Street's chosen few." In the second case, Jacob Frohwerk, a Kansas City man, was condemned to a ten-year prison term for publishing articles in the Missouri publication *Staats Zeitung* that protested the war and called it "a monumental and inexcusable mistake" engineered "to protect some rich men's money."

The third case was by far the best known, as it concerned the most famous socialist in America, Eugene Debs. A presidential candidate four times, including the 1912 election, in which he won 6 percent of the vote—8 percent in Ohio—Debs, now sixty-four years old, had protested America's entry in the European war and had supported the Bolshevik government in Russia. His crime, for which he had been sentenced to ten years in prison, was his speech at Canton, Ohio, in June of 1918 in which he had denounced capitalist wars and military recruitment. Although the speech was mostly about socialism's progress and the reasons to join its ranks, Debs also assailed all wars, in which, he said, working-class men always bore the heaviest burden. The revised Espionage Act of 1918 was only a month old when the U.S. attorney for the northern district of Ohio sent stenographers to transcribe Debs's speech. The next day the eager prosecutor told his Washington superiors that he had a case. But the Justice Department didn't agree and would not prosecute. Nonetheless the federal prosecutor from Ohio pursued the case, eventually securing an indictment from a Cleveland grand jury and a conviction in a jury trial. Debs, in writing his appeal, claimed, among other things, that he had been wrongly tried on his "state of mind" and that the Espionage Act clearly violated the right of free speech.

All three of the opinions, though representing the entire Court, were written by Justice Oliver Wendell Holmes Jr. And in one of them, the Schenck opinion, Holmes established a powerful measure for free speech, known as the "clear and present danger" standard. Holmes, in the spring of 1919, believed that the true test for determining a violation of the espionage law was in the intent and the circumstances of the alleged crime. If in the act of speaking or circulating a leaflet there was an intent to prevent or obstruct the government's war effort, then the act was a crime. In the Schenck case, for example, whether there was proof that Schenck's leaflets had directly influenced young men to avoid the draft didn't really matter. What Schenck had done was tantamount to holding a "lighted match near a haystack." In ordinary times, he would have been within his rights, protected by the First Amendment, but war times were extraordinary times. War was the special circumstance. Holmes wrote:

> The character of every act depends upon the circumstances in which it is done. The most stringent protection of free speech would not protect a man in falsely shouting fire in a theatre and causing a panic. . . . The question in every case is whether the words used are used in such circumstances and are of such a nature as to create *a clear and present danger* that will bring about the substantive evils that Congress has a right [through legislation such as the Espionage Act] to prevent. It is a question of proximity and degree. . . .

Holmes was a Civil War veteran—wounded three times—who had given a good deal of his money to war bonds in 1917 and 1918. He was not a champion of dissent nor was he an advocate of socialism. And so it was not surprising that he had just sent a message to the nation that the highest court was united in its legal understanding of the dangers of open criticism of government policy during times when national security was at risk. At seventy-eight, Holmes was also one of the greatest legal minds of the era and his great mind was not at ease. "I greatly regretted having to write [the opinions] and (between ourselves) that the Government pressed them to a hearing," Holmes wrote in a mid-March letter to his friend Harold Laski. "The federal Judges seem to me (again between ourselves) to have got hysterical about the war. I should think the President when he gets through with his present amusements might do some pardoning."

Laski was a confidant of Holmes's. Although only twenty-four years old, he was a professor of history at Harvard, concurrently a student at Harvard Law School, a regular contributor to *The New Republic* magazine, and soon to write his first book on political theory. Holmes considered Laski, who was a socialist, to be one of the most learned men of his acquaintance. The mutual admiration and trust was exceptionally strong. Thus in another letter to Laski, Holmes confessed that the first of the three cases "wrapped itself around me like a snake in a deadly struggle to present the obviously proper in the forms of logic—the real substance being [this]: Damn your eyes—that's the way 'it's going to be.' "

In the aftermath of Holmes's March opinions, *The New Republic* published several articles and editorials discussing Holmes and his point of view, including one by the esteemed University of Chicago law professor Ernst Freund. Appalled by the Debs decision, Freund began his article by pointing out that Debs himself issued a statement saying that the Supreme Court had not at all addressed the real issue, which was the question of the constitutionality of the Espionage law. And because there was no evidence proving that Debs had obstructed recruitment during the war, which was the offense for which he was sentenced to ten years in prison, then Debs's violent attack on the war was "stretched to mean a form of obstruction." And what this meant was that the limitations of freedom of speech were dependent on judicial interpretation rather than upon the legislation and the law itself. Toward the end of the article Freund wrote that "A country can ill spare the men who when the waves of militant nationalism run high do not lose the courage of their convictions. . . . The peril resulting to the national cause from toleration of adverse opinion is largely imaginary; in any event it is slight as compared with the permanent danger of intolerance to free institutions."

In response to the Freund piece, Holmes wrote a letter to Herbert Croly, the editor of *The New Republic,* saying that he "hated to have to write the Debs case and still more, those of the other poor devils before us the same day and the week before. I could not see the wisdom of pressing the cases, especially when the fighting was over and I think it quite possible that if I had been on the jury I should have been for acquittal." After writing this letter, however, Holmes decided against sending it. Instead, he sent it to Laski, who wrote for *The New Republic* and knew Croly.

Freund's article was the first of several that sparked a discussion on free speech and inspired Holmes to rethink his position. Corresponding with and meeting with some of the finest legal thinkers of the era, Holmes would listen intently to those who believed that public criticism was a necessary part of formulating government policy and that unrestricted discussion was the path to truth and justice. Then, in the autumn months, Holmes would show his greatness in a way that would deeply affect all champions of free speech, especially Harry Weinberger.

But for now, in the stormy weeks before spring, Weinberger and his compatriots were dodging a flurry of disturbing news. On the same day that the Supreme Court issued the opinions in the Frohwerk and Debs cases, U.S. Postmaster General Albert Burleson announced that he "firmly believed" that radicals were building up a strong network in the United States with the sole intent to overthrow the government. His plan to combat such imminent disaster was to continue censoring the U.S. mails with the same authority and verve he had employed during the Great War. And he called upon Congress to assist him "and all Americans" by expanding the government's network of domestic surveillance.

Also on that day, March 10, Senator Overman's committee hearings came to an end—a relief to some people, like the receding waters of a foul-smelling flood. To others, it was a time for chest thumping. After all, the Overman boosters claimed that the investigation had proven what its creators expected it would. The testimony of more than two dozen witnesses, a third of which were ardent anti-Bolshevists, revealed that the greatest danger facing America in the spring of 1919 was Bolshevism. And when the committee's 1,200-page report rolled off the government's presses, wrapped in darkness and fear, it seemed more like an adventure story than the summary of a Senate subcommittee.

"Bolshevism" had become a generic term in America, "nothing more than a slogan of the elements of unrest and discontent," and "almost every dissatisfied element in the nation, from the radical anarchist to the theoretical idealist, has seized upon it as approaching something of a Utopian nature," the report began. "Parlor Bolshevists," meaning "well-disposed persons" who defend Bolshevism and the Revolution, "have been deceived into the belief that they are promoting a social welfare movement by advocating Bolshevism." And because of this the committee's quest was to expose Bolshevism for what it really was: a brutal dictatorial system in which atheism, free love, corruption, deception, hunger, and murder were common. "We must bring home to the people the truth that a compromise with Bolshevism is to barter away our inheritance," Overman said in the report.

Throughout the hearing, witnesses had described hair-raising accounts of life in Russia after the Revolution. Former East Side New York Jews were largely responsible for the Revolution, Russians were "madmen" and "beasts," and Bolshevism was the anti-Christ. But the hearings did not uncover much, if anything, about the extent of Bolshevik propaganda in the United States, and the report, entitled *Bolshevik Propaganda,* contained little evidence of the true impact of Bolshevism in America. Still, the committee was certain the nation was in danger. The Seattle strike proved that and so did the increasing number of labor strikes elsewhere. It was no coincidence that red flags were the symbols for the socialists, the Bolsheviks, and the Industrial Workers of the World. As the report noted, "The radical revolutionary elements in this country and the Bolshevik government of Russia have, therefore, found a common cause in support of which they can unite their forces. They are both fanning the flame of discontent and endeavoring to incite revolution." In this way, labor unrest in America was characterized as a Russian Bolshevist plot for world domination, enabling America to deny the conditions that had caused the unrest.

The committee believed it had proven that working-class Americans, in particular union members and labor organizers, were especially vulnerable to the ideals and propaganda of Russia's new workers' state and thus dangerous. More than eight thousand unions in the nation were falling under the influence of Bolshevism, so claimed the committee in its report, and there were special "recruiting stations" in twenty-three cities, including Detroit, Denver, Spokane, San Francisco, Kansas City, Seattle, New York, Toledo, Reading, Oakland, Minneapolis, and Omaha.

Equally vulnerable and suspicious were immigrants, in particular Italians, Hungarians, Austrians, Germans, Chinese, and Scandinavians. "There has appeared in this country a large group of persons who advocate the overthrow of all organized government, and especially the Government of the United States," the committee reported. "There are found among the leaders of this group many aliens who unhesitatingly abuse the hospitality which this country has extended to them. . . . The alien element in this country is the most susceptible and is the first to adopt violence as an effective weapon for supremacy."

And how could America protect itself against imminent revolution? Stronger, more restrictive laws to curb the actions of aliens and radicals. Laws to ease the work of a vast and reliable domestic surveillance network, essential for identifying suspicious radicals and immigrants. Laws to streamline deportation of such immigrants and radicals. Laws to expand the postmaster general's powers of censorship—for example, requiring foreign-language publications to apply for licenses to use the postal service. And a powerful replacement for the Espionage Act.

Then, beyond the laws, the report advocated that the Allied troops stay in Russia to fight the Bolsheviks in their homeland. In a newly revised version of historical rationale, the report said, "It is interesting to note that the combined military force at Archangel was landed at the solicitation and request of the established and de facto government of the northern provinces of Russia to aid that government in protecting its citizenship from the murder, cruelty, and confiscation of the approaching Red Army of the Bolshevik government."

For Hiram Johnson, who despised radicals but disagreed with U.S. intervention in Russia and thus appeared to be a pacifist and on the side of the Bolsheviks; for Mollie Steimer, who insisted on standing up for the Revolution and protesting U.S. policy in Russia; and for Harry Weinberger, who defended radicals, aliens, Bolshevik sympathizers, socialists, and pacifists for the love of free speech, March was simply not a good month. And it seemed to get only worse.

On the 12th, for example, a prosecutor in Queens, New York, trying the case of Edith Mortimer, charged with second-degree manslaughter for killing a pedestrian while driving, accused the defendant of being "a creator of Bolshevism." Mortimer's management of her big racing automobile on the afternoon of the accident was "with absolute disregard of the rights of any one else," he said. "She by her actions said, 'If you are in the way, get out. The law was made for you to obey, not for me.' It is this attitude on the part of persons like Miss Mortimer which creates Bolshevism."

At the Plaza Hotel that day, Dr. Richard Morse Hodge delivered a public lecture entitled "Patriotism." His main theme was that pacifism is one of the chief causes of war. Pacifists, he said, "betray our lack of unity to the common enemy and encourage him in his hope of conquest." "SAYS PACIFISM CAUSES WAR," the *New York Times* headline read.

And on that same day, New York City's Bomb Squad, with the aid of immigration officers and Secret Service agents, raided the Russian People's House, a meeting center for Russian immigrants located on East 15th Street in Manhattan. Police herded 164 men and women into four patrol wagons while agents searched for radical literature, seizing one small pile. To assure a peaceful surrender, police reserves from the Elizabeth Street station surrounded the four-story building. But there was no hint of resistance. Everyone went peaceably, especially the elderly. Several carried violin cases.

"Police Round Up 200 Bolsheviki in East Side Raid," read the *New York Times* headline on the morning of the 13th. The detainees were "representatives of the most radical type in this country," and "a quantity of anarchistic literature is said to have been confiscated, including copies of the 'Red Book' which is said to advocate the overthrow of existing order." The *Tribune* called the single pile of confiscated publications "a great mass of seditious literature." "It is probable," that paper said about the raid, "that those of known radical tendencies who cannot prove their citizenship will be sent to Ellis Island and will face deportation."

On the afternoon of the 13th, 160 of the detainees were released. Of the remaining four, three of the men were charged with possession of seditious literature that could instigate "the downfall of the U.S. government by force and violence." One was a twenty-two-year-old printer. Another was a twenty-four-year-old manager of a Russian paper called *Bread and Freedom*. And the other was the twenty-seven-year-old secretary of the Federation of the Union of Russian Workers, the group that was meeting on East 15th Street that night. The federation, which began in

1907, was largely a mutual aid society for lonely immigrants looking for companionship and networking for jobs. After the 1917 Revolution, its radical founders had returned to Russia.

Also detained but not charged was the irrepressible young anarchist Steimer, who was listed as now living at 237 East 10th Street. She was sent to Ellis Island. The day after the raid, Weinberger contacted Anthony Caminetti, the commissioner of immigration, in Washington, "on the long distance telephone," as he said in a March 15 note to Steimer. As it turned out, there was an outstanding warrant for Steimer's arrest that had nothing to do with the March raid but rather had been issued after her conviction in Federal District Court the previous October. The warrant had been written up to keep an eye on Steimer so that if she were netted in a raid such as this, she could be detained. "I am positive that you will be released on Monday [March 17]," Weinberger assured her, adding, "All your friends send you their best greetings."

During the next five days, Weinberger and Caminetti tried to reach an agreement about Steimer. There was no evidence to hold her regarding the recent raid but there was the issue of the outstanding warrant. On March 17, Weinberger sent Steimer the following note: "I telephoned Washington this morning, and they said they would send a telegram to Ellis Island ordering your release. I kept after them all day, but they did not get the telegram but I finally got one late tonight so that you will positively be released to-morrow, Tuesday morning."

In exchange for Steimer's release this time, the government upped the ante for Weinberger. From now on, when immigration authorities or federal agents wanted Steimer for questioning regarding an organization or an individual or whatever they wanted her for, Weinberger must bring her in. He agreed. Steimer was then released on Tuesday morning. Her military intelligence file noted that "after a hearing lasting several days at Ellis Island, Miss Stimer [sic] was turned loose, there being insufficient evidence to hold her." Her file at the Bureau of Investigation noted that there was no sample of her handwriting on record in their files, as there was at the MID.

The handwriting oversight seemed to reveal a shift in authority regarding her surveillance. Since the Seattle strike, the Bureau of Investigation, though still very low-profile, was slowly emerging as a strong force in the shadow war, and, with the help of the new attorney general, it would eventually surpass all other agencies, local and federal, in its campaign against radicals. Soon, a daring new mix of federal and local investigators and agents would be tailing Steimer and hundreds of other immigrants, union members, and socialists, filling folders and file drawers with the details of daily routines, dinners, meetings, and errands, especially to the post office. Although for a while it had appeared that in the postwar months the shadow war was winding down, "Red hunting" was now emerging as a popular new trend and a government obsession. The unprecedented Seattle strike, fulfilling the prophecy of the threat of revolution in America, followed by the embellished accusations and sensational testimony of witnesses at the Overman hearings, supplied the trusses and planks needed to build the bridge from wartime fears to postwar hysteria.

And in March one of the master engineers of such hysteria was back on the job: Archibald Stevenson. Despite Secretary Baker's abhorrence of Stevenson and the notorious list of suspicious Americans, and despite Baker's orders to Military Intelligence to dismiss the man who had caused the War Department such embarrassment, the great Red hunter was alive and well with an ambitious plan to launch a statewide investigation of radicals. After the Military Intelligence Division rejected his latest scheme, Stevenson beseeched the Union League Club in New York, which appointed him chairman of a committee to study radicals and Reds. Stevenson then wrote a report entitled *Bolshevism*. Sending it to New York's state legislature, he sought funding for an aggressive, massive hunt for Reds in New York City, where he was certain there were thousands of them plotting a revolution likely to begin in that very city. Concerned and responsive, the New York State Assembly authorized $30,000 on March 20 for the new Committee to Investigate Seditious Activities and named it the Lusk Committee after its appointed chairman, Senator Clayton R. Lusk. Unlike Overman's investigation, which was a series of Senate hearings, the Lusk Committee was the nation's first legislative body to actually hunt down the Red menace, using its own agents and conducting its own raids. And although Lusk was the chairman, and the New York attorney general was the chief counsel, the person who truly led the hunt appeared to be the committee's associate counsel, the indefatigable Stevenson.

The Lusk Committee's headquarters was at the Prince George Hotel in midtown Manhattan on Broadway. It employed no more than fifty people, half of whom were agents. But with the help of Lusk's brother, who was the former head of the American Protective League's New Jersey division—which was not defunct, despite public announcements to the contrary—the committee was able to enlist battalions of New Jersey vigilante volunteers to expand the investigative power of Stevenson's "army." Organizations such as the Confederation of Christian Men and Women of America and its branches in the five New York boroughs, and other patriotic leagues that had disbanded after the Armistice now revived with special "secret service" units to assist the Lusk Committee. The New York police department supplied ID cards, guns, press credentials, and other props to assist the committee's network of informants in their spying, their burglarizing and bugging of suspects' homes and offices, their infiltrating of organizations, their interrogating, and their raiding. So too the Bureau of Investigation, although a federal agency, was involved. In the end, it would be easier to wage a domestic war against radicals locally through grassroots hysteria than nationally, as it was always easier to pass state laws to restrict individual rights than federal laws.

The head of the Lusk Committee's investigative division was a former BI agent, Rayme W. Finch, who had worked with Stevenson back in the summer of 1918 when Stevenson and volunteers from the Union League Club raided Roger Baldwin's office at the National Civil Liberties Bureau. It was Finch who actually arrested Baldwin, a conscientious objector now in the sixth month of his one-year prison term and one of the founders of the National Civil Liberties Bureau, later known as the American Civil Liberties Union.

While there would always be some competition between the Lusk group and the Bureau of Investigation, there was mostly cooperation. The committee would obtain information from BI files in Washington on individuals it was watching in New York, and, based on that intelligence, it would obtain local warrants, conduct a raid, confiscate materials, and interrogate the individuals. It would then send the BI whatever information it gleaned from the raids and the detainees. The BI effectively used the Lusk Committee as an intelligence-gathering branch. The reciprocity was at first handled in a secretive manner but soon Stevenson would be quite open about the relationship. When, for example, one federal agent, who was assigned to tail Steimer, asked Stevenson for information regarding the Russian workers organization whose meetings she attended, Stevenson said that "the federal Bureau could have any and all information" in his possession. The Lusk Committee would help the Bureau of Investigation to become a far more powerful agency than it had been, and both would fan the mounting public fears of Bolshevism and Reds. As *The Nation* wrote, "The process of turning the thoughtful working people of the country into dangerous radicals and extreme direct actionists goes merrily on."

In March, bloody scenes of Bolsheviks slaughtering their enemies, roasting them in furnaces, and chopping them up with axes, as described by the Overman Committee's witnesses, were still fresh in the public mind as were the images of the close call in Seattle and the headlines about imminent revolution at home. There was even a new scare in Seattle: on March 15, government officials there announced they had uncovered a plot to attempt a revolution that would begin in the logging camps on May 1, which was International Labor Day. Adding to the fearsome mix, there were labor strikes worldwide and daily stories of upheavals and revolution from the Rhine to the Yellow River. The socialists had come to power in Germany. Hungary was in the midst of a communist revolution. In fact, one-sixth of the world's landmass had come under Soviet influence. The emir of Afghanistan had just been murdered, a nationalist movement was surfacing in India, and violent outbreaks were spreading throughout Central Asia and the Caucasus. All of this was intensified by the panic of newspapers and legislative bodies. The American public needed wise counsel and leadership. Could the nation for just one moment indulge in introspection and not fear?

The answer was no. Instead, the country got the action-packed, warlike agenda of the new guardians of its safety, such as Overman, Stevenson, and Palmer. The typical American, still driven by a war mentality, was not inclined to resist an invasion of secret agents or a call for more restrictive laws, or whatever else it took to win the new war, the one at home against the Red Menace. The Reds were an obstacle to the peace Americans so longed for. Reds disrupted the dream of normalcy. And so the war on the Reds was the path to peace. All it would take would be one shocking, violent act to transform tacit support into a hysterical mind-set unable or unwilling to distinguish governmental frothing from public policy based on factual evidence. And in a year of such pounding intensity, that too would happen, later in the spring.

CHAPTER 14

Out Like a Lion

On the first day of spring, after weeks of successive frosts killing every early flower that pushed through the hard, crusty earth, a blast of cold air swept up the East Coast. The process of spring was stymied yet again and much of the nation seemed stuck in winter. In New Jersey, despite the lingering cold, Japanese beetles were in the process of invading roughly ten thousand acres near Riverton, and the New Jersey Department of Agriculture was working with the U.S. Department of Agriculture to devise a massive counterattack against this small insect known to feed on the leaves of orchard trees and to have a special fondness for roses. The plan was to create a defensive system of rings or belts of poison, surrounding the acreage at risk: one belt immediately outside the infested area and others at intervals further back. The *New York Times* likened the scheme to "a system of trenches much like human warfare." The problem was that all vegetation in the vicinity of the belts would be poisoned. Alternatives were being considered.

In the morning hours, at the state courthouse on Foley Square in Manhattan, carpenters hastily nailed boards around the bottoms of witness stands, three feet up from the floor, in response to the order of a censor recently appointed by the district attorney's office. The censor had determined that the hemlines of female witnesses appeared to be rising and as such could inappropriately influence a jury. The new boards, soon dubbed "spite fences," would prevent any possible flashing of hosiery or leg.

A few blocks away that morning, members of the American Society of Civil Engineers were preparing for a long evening meeting that would focus on the proposed vehicular tunnel under the Hudson River at Canal Street from Manhattan to Jersey City. Although all members recognized the necessity of such a tunnel, especially since a recent ferry strike, and most had confidence in the plan recommended by General George W. Goethals, the consulting engineer for the New York State Bridge and Tunnel Commission, there was still a good deal of doubt about the project. Some engineers who had worked on a similar tunnel in Cleveland under Lake Erie had recently expressed their concerns that not all the potential trouble had been anticipated in the current design. "Leakage will most surely result if the structure is finally built," one engineer said at the last meeting. And then there was the issue of ventilation. "Can the tunnel be cleared of poisonous gases without running into prohibitive figures for the installation and maintenance of an adequate ventilation plant?" the engineers were asking.

And at noon, in New York, Daylight Savings advocates gathered for a luncheon at the Waldorf to celebrate the recent defeat, in early March, of the repeal. At that same hour, the clock at Grand Central Station tolled one time, having been set at the new time, in advance.

The next day, like most everyone else in America, Harry Weinberger set his clocks forward one hour, but unlike most, he spent much of the day working on the cause to gain amnesty for those men and women convicted of violating wartime laws, either in prison now or awaiting the outcome of their appeals. Friends and clients of Weinberger's, including Emma Goldman, had urged him to embark on a speaking tour to promote amnesty for all political prisoners, but Weinberger had declined. He hadn't the money for the tour nor could he spare the time away from his clients, some of whom needed him more than ever. On this day, he added his name, after Upton Sinclair's, to a petition seeking the pardon of Eugene Debs and all persons imprisoned for "honest expressions of opinions against America's cause in the war." Advocating Debs's release and pardon on the grounds of his advanced years, "high moral character and long years of devoted service to the cause of human freedom, not withstanding his violation of law," the petition would be cabled to President Wilson in Paris. Although Weinberger would certainly not surrender his passion for the case of his young Russian clients, the recent Supreme Court opinions reminded him that the only true remedy was a general amnesty for all political prisoners.

In Michigan, during these last days of March, there was a sense of longing that was not about the anticipation of spring and the burst of colors soon to brush across the landscape. It was about the Polar Bears and their expected return home "in spring," as the government had told them. But by the end of the month, the families and friends of the 339th Infantry had heard nothing about a date for the soldiers' return and few of them had heard anything from the soldiers themselves for weeks, even months.

In Archangel, on the 28th of March, Corporal Frank Douma, of Grand Rapids, wrote in his diary: "It is very very cold again. About 56 below. . . . Several bags of mail which we wrote more than a month ago were found in a horse stable here. A Russian driver had left them and forgotten them."

In Detroit, beginning in late March, journalist Glenn L. Shannon, who had served in the 339th and was home now because of injuries, wrote a grueling three-part series for the *Detroit Free Press* about his experiences in and around Archangel. Smartly written, the series was painful to read for anyone with a son or husband or brother still in Russia. The headlines read: "Straight from the Shoulder Account of the Conditions Our Boys Are Combating—Grim and Unvarnished Truth as Vouched for by a Michigan Newspaper Man Just Returned from Archangel." "Shannon says 339th infantry, U.S.A. suffered untold hardships." He also said that the Allied troops in northern Russia were "beating the Bolos," meaning the Bolsheviks.

Shannon's news that conditions were horrific yet the campaign was successful deepened the dread of the Michiganders. How could they continue to demand withdrawal of the 339th and an end to the intervention if the mission was indeed a success? They would be viewed as symphathetic to the enemy, even more than they were now, and there would be no end to the campaign until the Bolsheviks were completely vanquished.

Worse still, on the morning of March 28, the families of Detroit's Own learned, from the Detroit newspapers, that 1,600 sailors on four third-class cruisers had just set sail for Archangel along with an abundance of guns and ammunition, sheepskin-lined coats, sea boots, socks, and mittens. Navy officials told the press that it was a "secret operation" and that even they did not know what the government had ordered the expedition to do once it arrived in Archangel. "We do know that it is not going to bring the American fighting force at Archangel home," the officials noted.

On the afternoon of the 28th, hundreds of relatives and friends of men in the 339th crowded into a large conference room in the building that housed the *Detroit News*. The meeting was called by three soldiers who had left Archangel on December 27 because of injuries and who had recently arrived home. One of the three, Sergeant Theodore Kolbe, moved to the front of the room, where he rather nervously pulled a bulging notebook out of a canvas bag. The pages of the notebook were noticeably tattered and encrusted with dirt. But to Sergeant Kolbe's audience it was nothing less than gold, for in it seventy-five soldiers had written names and addresses of people to whom they most desired to give news of themselves, plus a message for each.

One by one Kolbe read the names and delivered the messages, sometimes adding a story or two if he knew the soldier. One wife was relieved to hear that although her husband had been wounded he was writing songs that the sergeant had heard, he said. In fact, Kolbe was of the belief that they were good enough to be hits in the States. Another soldier in the notebook was the champion middleweight in his region in Michigan and the sergeant told the soldier's brother that "during the daytime he guards Bolshevist prisoners and at night he is boxing." When Kolbe told a father that his son was "happy and hopeful of getting home soon," though he had been wounded since Kolbe last saw him, the father anxiously asked, "Is there any way we can find how serious it is?" Kolbe paused and then explained the difficulty in getting information out of Russia.

Most of the guests were invited because their names were on the lists in Kolbe's notebook. However, dozens more, hearing about Sergeant Kolbe and the gathering, which was announced in the *Detroit News* the day before, came in search of any news about the 339th. They brought photos of their loved ones hoping that one of the three soldiers might know something that would help them endure the long gaps between news. "The chief thing the boys worry about is that you may be worried," Kolbe told the group. "We didn't have any picnic out of war but after the first confusions, after arriving there, we did eventually get food and clothing and other necessities."

In a subsequent interview with a *News* reporter Sergeant Kolbe, who had taken bullets in his cheeks, teeth, and knees, was more candid. When he left Archangel, he said, the worst of the problems was morale because the soldiers "have no more conception of the purpose of their expedition against the Russians than have the people back in Michigan." One of the other two soldiers chimed in, "Contrary to all the bunk that we see in the newspapers sent down through London, the Russians in Archangel do not like the Allies nor did they welcome us in the first place. We didn't know why we were fighting up there and couldn't find out. To us up there, it seemed that Senator Hiram Johnson of California was the only man who seemed to have a vision that we were simply meddling with Russia's internal affairs."

In 1919, March came in like a lion, and went out like one too. The new attorney general, A. Mitchell Palmer, ended his first month in office with an announcement on March 28 that Congress must replace the Espionage Act with a peacetime equivalent. The law had proven essential in safeguarding the nation, and it would become inoperative the moment the peace treaty was signed, he said. In response to the Overman Committee's report and recommendations, he said, the Justice Department was studying the subject and would make its own recommendation to Congress for the passage of a law that "will give the Federal Government authority to proceed against those plotting against the Government." Palmer stressed the need to protect the government "against the same influences which operated in the last four years."

On the last day of the month, the opponents of Daylight Savings renewed their effort to repeal it. New tactics were called for. One was to bring God into the debate. In an editorial that day, one religious group wrote that "what is very serious indeed is the certainty that this iniquitous law will give deep displeasure to God." It was God who created the sun and it is the sun that "declares in the heavens that it is 12 o'clock noon." Thus for people to say it is 1 P.M. or any other time when according to God's will it is noon, "is complete blasphemy."

PART II

Spring: Fear

Here is April, and still the black shadows of war press onward. Clouds of battle smoke rise to meet a grey dawn and float above a sea of human blood. Far over the crest of a battered hill there lies a boy whose young face is turned toward the earth, and who has gone beyond the hoary grievance of man.

—SERGEANT GORDON W. SMITH,
339TH INFANTRY,160 MILES FROM
ARCHANGEL, RUSSIA, APRIL 1919

It is one of the phenomena of human nature that once an opinion gets a popular start and becomes rooted in the mind of the public at large it is next to impossible to uproot it or kill it off. It may be proved over and over again that the opinion is not entirely true, or even that it is entirely false; and the public at large will listen to the proof and go right on believing in the opinion as before.

—JAMES WELDON JOHNSON, MAY 1919

CHAPTER 15

Inner Light

In 1919, it seemed almost possible to chart the year by tracking the movement of ships across the Atlantic Ocean. The ship that brought President Wilson back to America in February crossed on the same days as the one that took seventy deported immigrants out of America. And when the president's ship sailed back to France, it passed two transports coming from France with thousands of American soldiers returning home. Shortly after the president arrived in Brest, W. E. B. Du Bois left Brest on his return voyage to America. The cruiser *Chattanooga* and the converted yacht *Yanta* crossed the Atlantic in the early days of spring, taking American soldiers to Archangel, moving eastward as the *Leviathan,* the largest transport then afloat, sailed westward with 12,059 American soldiers on board, the largest number of troops to come home on a single ship since the Armistice. In April, the USS *Princess Matoika* landed five thousand American troops in Charleston, South Carolina, and picked up 2,200 German prisoners of war to take them to Rotterdam. The USS *Agamemnon,* known as *Rolling Billy* for having withstood fierce North Atlantic gales in 1918, would cross the Atlantic, back and forth from France, nine times in 1919 to bring back 41,000 American soldiers.

On cruisers, giant transports, and yachts sailing the high seas in every season of the year, there were soldiers, statesmen, journalists, Red Cross workers, deported aliens, prisoners of war, crusaders of all sorts—and there were scientists.

In March and early April, two ships sailed into the Atlantic from Portugal bound for two separate destinations, the village of Sobral in northeast Brazil and the Isle of Príncipe in the Gulf of Guinea, off the coast of West Africa. Both shared the same purpose: to observe the total eclipse of the sun on May 29. The passengers, however, were hardly the usual eclipse chasers ready to pop champagne corks at the first sight of the sun's brilliant corona highlighting the far-off edges of the moon. Rather, they were British physicists and astronomers embarking on a mission to test a German physicist's concepts about the relationship of space, time, and matter. The physicist's name was Albert Einstein, and the concept the general theory of relativity.

This was a scientific expedition imbued with all the excitement and stirrings of venturing to the shores of the unknown with the hope of discovering something meaningful, something new, something that might even change the world, or at least perceptions of the world. It was all about the thrill of "seeing physical science on the march in a new direction," Arthur Stanley Eddington, the renowned astronomer on the Príncipe expedition, would later write. And as Eddington well knew, it was about even more. Because of its timing, its purpose, and its participants, this expedition was about demonstrating the value of international peace and cooperation: British scientists and British money dedicated to proving the findings of a scientist in Germany. It was about sailing far enough away from the shores of postwar strife and international differences that the drumbeat of nationalism could no longer be heard. What the peace conference in Paris was seeking, the Einstein-inspired expeditions might find. Rolling across the unpredictable seas of new thought, these ships and their passengers were destined for greatness.

Eclipses, whether solar or lunar, partial or total, have always been marvels of a sort, viewed throughout the ages as spectacles of horror and magnificence, once feared as supernatural omens and later used as ways to probe the mysteries of the universe. The total eclipse of the sun on May 29, 1919, would be a marvel of the most memorable sort. To begin with, solar eclipses occur less frequently than lunar eclipses—roughly every eighteen months—and their totality, that is the time when the moon is directly in front of the sun, is far shorter. The 1919 eclipse was exceptionally long compared to most solar eclipses—more than five minutes—and it was a rare event because late May is the time when the sun passes through the constellation of Taurus crossing what is known as the Hyades, a rich concentration of very bright stars. For the sun to be covered for so many minutes on this date was an extraordinary opportunity for the scientists. With a cluster of bright stars close to the sun during the totality, the scientists could better measure the distance between the stars and the sun, thus providing a unique opportunity to test Einstein's calculations regarding the relationships of matter, space, and time. Measuring the distance between the stars and the sun during the eclipse and then comparing the positions of the same stars later could prove, or strike down, Einstein's theory that a massive body such as the sun could actually bend light and thus warp the geometry of space and affect the progression of time.

Einstein's theory refuted Isaac Newton's belief that space was rigid and time was absolute. Newton had recognized the gravitational pull of large masses, but Einstein's degree of deflection was twice as large as Newton's, large enough to significantly affect space and time in the universe, making space and time relative to matter. Time, according to Newton, was an absolute property, measured at the same rate for everyone and for everything. But under Einstein's principle, a clock in close proximity to a large mass slows its measurement of time. And if the clock is moving through space at a high speed, time also moves more slowly. Time and space, according to Einstein, were dependent on the presence of massive bodies.

If Einstein was right, then Newton, whose definitions of an absolute universe had been the foundation for scientific inquiry for more than 250 years, was not. And if space was indeed flexible, there were endless possibilities for bodies orbiting the universe. Could it be true that the formulaic and absolutely knowable tenets of the world were about to change and that ours was a world of barely visible fields of force for which there were no formulas to predict behavior? What new ideas, questions, possibilities would be raised by a new physics? What was at stake was a new concept of the universe in which Einstein, moving beyond Newton, effectively said that the presence and distribution of matter could change the shape of space and alter time.

There had been other expeditions to study eclipses with the hope of testing the deflection of light but none had succeeded. In 1912, Argentine scientists in Brazil were rained out. In 1914, Gustav Krupp, the German arms manufacturer, funded a large expedition to the Crimea led by a German astronomer, Erwin Finlay Freundlich, who had worked closely with Einstein. But a week before the August 21 eclipse, World War I broke out. The German expedition shut down and some of its members made it out just in time to avoid arrest. Those who didn't, including Freundlich, were interned briefly in Russia. Although observers from neutral and Allied nations, including the United States, were allowed to stay, the weather was too cloudy for any useful photos. Because of the war, another chance to observe an eclipse, in 1916, was missed, this time in Venezuela. And because the U.S. team at the Crimea site could not bring home all its equipment—

due to the difficulty of getting home after war was declared—observations of the June 1918 eclipse were stymied.

The eclipse of May 1919 was so favorable that every astronomer and every eclipse chaser on every continent must have been aware of it. But at a time when a large portion of the planet's population was consumed with war and hatred, who would have dared to plan an expedition to observe an eclipse that might prove the theory of a German scientist? Not the Germans, rationing all resources for the war. Not the Russians, in the midst of civil war. Not the Americans, having just entered the European war. Not the French, filled with enough hatred for the Germans to create a light-bending force of their own. Not the Italians, Spaniards, or Portuguese.

The answer was the British scientific community, largely because of two individuals: Britain's astronomer royal, Sir Frank Watson Dyson; and Arthur Stanley Eddington, the Plumian Professor of Astronomy and Experimental Philosophy at the University of Cambridge, the most prestigious astronomy chair in England. Eddington was also the director of the Royal Observatory in Greenwich and the world's leading exponent of Einstein's general theory of relativity.

Eddington was passionate about the theory and Dyson deeply respected Eddington. In fact, Dyson had been Eddington's mentor. Although he was not as confident about the theory as Eddington was, Dyson recognized the importance of testing it and he identified the 1919 eclipse as the ideal test. To this end, in 1917 Dyson urged the Royal Society and the Royal Astronomical Society of London to appoint a committee to plan the expedition. Although the war cast a spell of skepticism on the Eddington-Dyson dream, the Joint Permanent Eclipse Committee proceeded. Dyson applied for grants to fund it. And he put Eddington in charge of the committee. Eddington had read Einstein's theory for the first time in 1916. Despite the cessation of communication between scientists in England and in Germany during the war, he had acquired a copy of Einstein's 1915 paper on the general theory of relativity from Willem deSitter, an astronomer in neutral Holland. Immediately upon reading it, Eddington was impressed with the theory and saw its significance. At a dinner, years later, a colleague of Eddington's would compliment him by saying, "You must be one of three persons in the world who understands general relativity." Eddington was silent. The colleague then hastened to add, "Don't be modest, Eddington." Eddington said, "On the contrary, I am trying to think who the third person is." Eddington was so dazzled by Einstein's work that in 1918 he published the first account of the theory in the English language, *Report on the Relativity Theory of Gravitation*. "One of the masterpieces of contemporary scientific literature," one reviewer wrote. And in the preface, Eddington wrote: "Whether the theory ultimately proves to be correct or not, it claims attention as being one of the most beautiful examples of the power of general mathematical reasoning."

Born on December 20, 1882, Eddington was 36 years old for most of 1919. A man of average height and quite physically fit, he was by then known for his prowess at cricket, at bicycling long distances, at mathematics, and at writing about science in an accessible way. He understood the difficulty of conveying profound thoughts in science and philosophy to the layman, who, he believed, had a right to know the sometimes abstruse discoveries of scientists and philosophers. He was a sensitive man, quiet almost to the point of shyness, and a lover of great literature, with a fondness for William Shakespeare, Charles Lamb, and William Blake. He was particularly inspired by Blake's vision: "To see a World in a Grain of Sand, And a Heaven in a Wild Flower, Hold Infinity in the palm of your hand, And Eternity in an hour." Eddington routinely worked the crossword puzzles in the London *Times*, *The New Statesman*, and *The Nation*, rarely taking more than five minutes per puzzle. And he was a devout scientist.

Eddington would one day be considered the greatest British astronomer of the first half of the twentieth century. Credited with laying foundations in cosmology and astrophysics, he would make a number of remarkable discoveries regarding the evolution and energy of stars—for example, that atomic energy was the source that could keep stars shining for such immensely long periods of time. On a visit to Tivoli Gardens in Copenhagen, Eddington once told a friend that it wasn't just the beauty of the gardens that attracted him, it was the amusement park, because the merry-go-rounds and the swings were practical applications of two of his favorite subjects, mathematical probabilities and gravitation. It wasn't surprising then that from the time he first read Einstein's theory, Eddington was nearly possessed by it. While the pervasive mentality of war that gripped the Allied nations and the hateful campaign against all that was German would have caused most people to drop a campaign promoting a German scientist, Eddington was not deterred. His devotion to science and his sense of Einstein's importance to the future of science drew him to the theory and to its creator. However, what most allowed Eddington to transcend the prevailing prejudices of his times was his religion.

Eddington was a Quaker. His parents were Quakers. His grandparents were Quakers. On his mother's side, his lineage extended to the founders of the first religious Society of Friends in seventeenth-century England. He was as deeply devoted to the values of his Quaker faith as he was to science, always seeking truth in both and exploring the ways each affected the other. "In science as in religion the truth shines ahead as a beacon showing us the path," he wrote in his book *Science and the Unseen World*. And in his pursuit of truth, he ventured beyond science and religion to what he called the realm of mysticism. "If I were to try to put into words the essential truth revealed in the mystic experience, it would be that our minds are not apart from the world; and the feelings we have of gladness and melancholy and our yet deeper feelings are not of ourselves alone, but are glimpses of a reality transcending the narrow limits of our particular consciousness—that the harmony and beauty of the face of Nature is, at root, one with the gladness that transfigures the face of man."

Eddington spent his life trying to relate his religious experience and his scientific work. The Einstein expedition was one time when both came together. As a scientist he was able to see the groundbreaking significance of proving the bending of light rays passing near the sun, and he could not resist the chance to explore a theory that might reveal a scintilla of truth in the universe. As a Quaker he was able to rise above the intolerance of the world around him. Eddington knew the dangers of jingoism in science and so for him, bringing Einstein onto the international stage was just as much about advancing internationalism in science as it was about space, matter, and time. For Eddington, it was about forcing humanity to fly above the clouds of war and hatred on the wings of scientific discovery. "The lines of latitude and longitude pay no regard to national boundaries," he wrote in 1916. "The pursuit of truth, whether in the minute structure of the atom or in the vast system of the stars, is a bond transcending human differences."

As a Quaker, Eddington believed in the existence of the divine in everyone. People must follow their Inner Light, the voice of God's Holy Spirit, which is within each person. He believed that hatred and violence only begat more hatred and violence. He did not believe in war. In the Great War, he was an avowed pacifist and believed in maintaining a relationship whenever possible with the people of the "enemy" nations. Humanizing the enemy would weaken the hatred that fueled the war. He was not pro-German, as he did not approve of German militarism, but he was sympathetic to the German people and believed that pacifism was the best strategy for confronting German militarism. To the Quakers, the true enemy was war itself and the misery that came out of it. At the beginning of the war, Eddington and the Quakers of Great Britain issued a public statement: "We find ourselves today in the midst of what may prove to be the fiercest conflict in the history of the human race. [We reaffirm that] the method of force is no solution of any question [and] that the fundamental unity of men in the family of God is the one enduring reality. Our duty is clear: to be courageous in the cause of love and in the hate of hate."

When Britain instituted conscription in March of 1916, Eddington, though prepared to declare himself a conscientious objector, was exempted automatically because his work as an astronomer was considered war work with potential military value. Over the next two years, Eddington advocated the release of Britain's pacifists, including the writer, mathematician, and social reformer Bertrand Russell, despite the fact that the stands and beliefs of his fellow Quakers were shunned by the majority of his countrymen as nothing less than treasonous. This did not stop him from protesting the harsh treatment of conscientious objectors, many of whom were Quakers interned in camps or prisons. Nor did he hesitate to support the Emergency Committee for the Assistance of Germans, Austrians, and Hungarians in Distress, which was organized to help enemy citizens detained in Britain after the war broke out.

In the spring of 1918, when the Allies appeared to be losing ground almost daily and casualty lists were higher than ever imagined, Britain, in desperate need of more troops, raised the draft age limit to thirty-five and canceled many exemptions, including Eddington's. Eddington immediately declared himself a conscientious objector. At his hearing he testified, "I cannot believe that God is calling me to go out to slaughter men," and he said he would continue to refuse to fight no matter what the risk in doing so. His stand stirred several Cambridge officials to beseech the British Home Office to defer him again because of his importance as one of Britain's preeminent scientists. If he had to resort to the status of being a conscientious objector, it would damage his reputation, as those who protested the war were viewed as vermin. And he would go to prison. In

response, the Home Office sent a letter to Eddington offering an exemption as long as he did not claim his religious objection to the war. All
Eddington had to do was to sign the exemption. But he would not.

The only exemption Eddington would sign was one in response to his
own request to be deferred as a conscientious objector. He would not sign a
deferment based on his post at Cambridge while fellow Quakers were interned at camps in northern England peeling potatoes all day or worse,
for objecting to the war. The Home Office was caught between deferring
him based on his religious beliefs, as he asked them to do, or rejecting his
application, which meant he would be sent to a camp. His colleagues at
Cambridge were vexed and concerned.

Knowing that Eddington would refuse to fight and thus was headed for
prison, Dyson intervened with a possible solution. He asked the government to defer Eddington for the purpose of organizing the eclipse expedition to Africa. If the government would exempt him with this stipulation, a
requirement of duty to the Crown, Eddington might not see the deferment
as a result of his privileged post, but rather an obligation to his nation.
Dyson, who commanded a good deal of respect in political as well as scientific circles, was certain that he could persuade the government to do this
and that Eddington would agree to it. In his presentation, he compared Eddington to Charles Darwin and other stellar British scientists. He talked
about the grant he had just received to study the May 1919 eclipse and said
that Eddington must be the one to make the observations. He did not tell
them that the exciting new theory that the eclipse might prove came out of
the mind of a scientist in Berlin. The government granted Eddington the
exemption to prepare for the expedition and to participate in it, if the war
was over by the date of the eclipse. If the war was not over by May of 1919,
and if he still refused to fight, then he would face the consequences of his
beliefs.

Eddington agreed to the plan though he continued his advocacy for
conscientious objectors and his own objections to the war—a stand Einstein in Berlin shared. For Einstein too was a pacifist. To discover a pacifist
in the German science community during the Great War was nothing less
than a miracle to Eddington, who wrote to deSitter in 1916, "I'm interested to hear that so fine a thinker as Einstein is anti-Prussian." But Einstein's pacifism was not a response to any political, religious, or intellectual
theory. It was for him a matter of instinct, he told a group of Americans

in Berlin after the war, "a feeling that possesses me because the murder of men is disgusting." It was based, he said, on his "deepest antipathy to every kind of cruelty and hatred." Einstein had been in Germany for only four months when the war began, having returned to his homeland in April of 1914 to teach at the University of Berlin, after years of study and work in Switzerland. By 1918, he was the director of the Kaiser Wilhelm Institute of Physics. And with a tight focus on his work, he rejected the Prussianism, militarism, and nationalism that brutally defined his country.

During the war, the German intellectual community was deeply offended that the world press had made all things German synonymous with barbarity so much so that leading intellectuals wrote, signed, and sent to the press "The Manifesto to the Civilized World," defending their nation and its culture in the face of Germany's "severe struggle for existence which has been forced upon her." Twenty-two of the ninety-three who signed it were scientists and doctors. Einstein refused to sign, and with several others who disagreed with the Manifesto of Ninety-three, as it was called, wrote a counter-declaration: "Never has any previous war caused so complete an interruption of that cooperation that exists between civilized nations. . . . educated men in all countries not only should, but absolutely must, exert all their influence to prevent the conditions of peace being the source of future wars."

After the Armistice, in the international community of science, Einstein would still feel the pinpricks of prejudice, scorned as a German during the war, and now as a Red or Bolshevist. Some even described his general relativity theory as "Bolshevism in physics." One astronomy professor at Columbia University, upon learning of Einstein and his theory, declared: "When is space curved? When do parallel lines meet? When is a circle not a circle? When are the three angles of a triangle not equal to two right angles? Why, when Bolshevism enters the world of science, of course."

As a pacifist, as a Jew, and as a suspected Red, Einstein represented the "other," for whom the postwar world was not a kind place. The prejudices that dominated both Britain and Germany intensified the challenges of putting together the eclipse expeditions, making the observation of the May 29 eclipse all the more remarkable. The extraordinary confluence of people and events surrounding the 1919 expeditions seemed almost miraculous. Here were two scientists, one in England and the other in Germany, unknown to each other, living in nations at war with each other.

However, both opposed the war and both were ardent advocates of internationalism in science at a time when opposition to nationalism was tantamount to siding with the enemy. Their beliefs allowed them to transcend the prejudices of their warring nations and to form a bond in the name of humanity. As a result, the scientist in Cambridge read the findings of the scientist in Berlin, and despite the damning of all things German he embraced the theory and promoted it. This happened at a time when Britain's astronomer royal (Dyson), the mentor of the British scientist and a man connected to high-level government officials, helpful for fund-raising, was aware of the importance of testing Einstein's theory. And it all happened at just the right moment in the vast history of the universe: before an eclipse that was ideal for testing the theory and that would not occur again for many years.

Fund-raising and basic preparations for the expeditions began in earnest during the autumn of 1917. Eddington, Dyson, and the Joint Permanent Eclipse Committee knew that the path of the totality of the eclipse, that is, where it would be the most complete—and where it would last the longest—was across the open seas of the South Atlantic. There would be few landfalls, including the Portuguese-owned Isle of Príncipe just north of the equator and 150 miles off the coast of Africa; the western shore of Lake Tanganyika in Africa; and northern Brazil. The committee chose two locations: Sobral, a small village in northern Brazil, and Príncipe. Dr. Andrew Crommelin, an astronomer at the Royal Greenwich Observatory, would lead the observation at Sobral along with C. Davidson, also of the Greenwich Observatory; Eddington would head up the African expedition with E. T. Cottingham, a British astronomer.

Challenges were numerous. Raising money for such an expedition while the war was on seemed almost impossible. Because of the demands of the war, it was difficult to line up transportation. The destinations were not on well-traveled routes and there were no ships to spare for undertakings unrelated to the war. The equipment must be exceptional because the test would require a level of precision on the cutting edge of what was possible at that time. There would be four or more long and heavy telescopes lying in a stable horizontal position with pivoting mirrors called coelostats. These would reflect the image of the stars into the telescope, moving to compensate for the rotation of the earth and keeping the eclipse in the center of the photographic plate. The equipment must be able to withstand the humidity and heat of equatorial weather. In fact, several brands of photographic plates would be purchased from different companies to assure that there would be enough with a composition that operated in the tropics. The observatories at Greenwich and Oxford would supply the telescopes and coelostats, and Cottingham would recondition the ones that needed work. While the war was on, however, such work could be done only with a special government certificate from the Ministry of Munitions, and eclipses were not a high priority.

Ships could not be confirmed until after the Armistice and even then a steamer to Príncipe was not assured. Much of the work on the telescopes and coelostats was on hold until then. However, Dyson did obtain a £1,000 grant, and on the day of the Armistice the Committee was confident enough to announce publicly its plans for the great expeditions: the scientists, crews, and instruments for both tests would leave together on one ship from England in mid-March, sailing to Portugal and then on to their separate destinations, to arrive at least a month in advance of the eclipse.

The night before setting sail from England, Eddington and the three other eclipse observers met with Dyson at his Greenwich study. They talked about the calculations for the deflection of light and described their visions and expectations for the May event. To communicate weather conditions and results as quickly as possible to Dyson, Eddington had developed a telegraphic code. Weather was the major worry and there was concern about the condition of the equipment. Not one to dwell on fears, Eddington spoke confidently about his belief that the deflection would match Einstein's prediction. Cottingham then asked, "What will it mean if we get double the Einstein deflection?"

"Then Eddington will go mad and you will have to come home alone!" Dyson said.

The next day, like explorers of centuries past, the eclipse observers set sail from Liverpool on the SS *Anselm*, arriving in Lisbon on March 14, which happened to be Albert Einstein's fortieth birthday. Two days later, the Sobral group left for Brazil, landing first in the town of Para, where they learned that preparations in Sobral were not yet completed and thus decided it was best to postpone their arrival at the site for another few weeks. They were also informed that there was a severe drought in northern Brazil and they were reminded that the war with Germany was still fresh in the minds of Brazilians. A local Para paper wrote: "Instead of trying to establish a German theory, the members of the expedition who are well acquainted with the heavens, should rather try to obtain rain for the country which has suffered from a long drought." A few days later it began to rain in northern Brazil.

For the next few weeks they explored hundreds of acres of Amazon rain forest, taking note of things they had never before seen, such as plants that snapped shut upon being touched and leaf-cutting ants that marched in masses of thousands with slivers of leaves on their backs, like a green field in motion. On April 29, they arrived in barren, dry Sobral. A friendly group of local authorities, including two men who spoke English and one who had studied agriculture in America, greeted them. Soon they learned that their quarters had access to a permanent water supply, a local meatpacker would give them ice when needed for developing photos, and that during their stay they would have access to an automobile, sent from Rio de Janeiro and the first that the citizens of Sobral had ever seen.

Back in Portugal, Eddington and Cottingham waited weeks for their steamer to Príncipe and were unable to leave until April 9, finally pulling into the dock on the Isle of Príncipe on April 23. Eddington described the island as "very charming" in a letter on the 29th and he was startled to see sugar bowls full to the brim, after years of war rations back home. He was also eager to hear about world affairs. "[I wonder] whether the peace had been signed," he wrote in one letter. The island was covered with thick forests and hordes of mosquitoes. Malaria was clearly a problem, making the use of quinine and mosquito netting a part of the men's daily regimen. Very quickly, they began to build waterproof shelters for their equipment, working with local laborers from a nearby plantation.

Now was the time to build structures, test equipment, run preliminary photos, and rehearse every remarkable moment of the 302-second drama that would play out on May 29—what Eddington would describe as "the most exciting event, I can recall, in my connection with astronomy." But soon after arriving at Sobral that April, Crommelin and his cohorts discovered a serious optical defect on the coelostat mirror for the biggest and the best of the telescopes. And on the Isle of Príncipe it began to rain. The locals said the rain would surely stop sometime in the next several weeks—perhaps by June.

CHAPTER 16

Make-Believe Riots
and Real Bombs

In the days before the April debut of the movie *Bolshevism on Trial* its promoters sent a flyer to the magazine *Moving Picture World* outlining a plan for movie houses to make the film an unforgettable sensation. Run an extra show every night and arrange a special showing for schoolchildren, the flyer said. But most important of all, do this: Secretly, on the night before the opening, hang red flags all over town. On lampposts. Over balconies. From windows. Hire soldiers or actors dressed like soldiers to march into town the next day with great fanfare to tear down the red flags. In the midst of the mayhem, send the staff out of the theater with a "flaming handbill" to distribute to a confused crowd now hopefully swarming on the streets. *Bolshevism on Trial* is not an argument for anarchy, the circular should say, but rather a strong statement against it. Be sure to have the plan and the leaflets ready for the grand opening of the movie or the scheme might fizzle, so warned the promoters. By doing this, "you will not only clean up but will profit by future business."

Mayhem, conflict, fear, disgust, shock. Any one of them could draw attention to the film and bring in the crowds. It had worked in 1915 for D. W. Griffith's controversial *The Birth of a Nation*. Why not in 1919 for *Bolshevism on Trial*? There were a few similarities between the two films. Both, for example, were adaptations of books by the same author, Thomas Dixon, best known for his 1905 book *The Clansman*, which was the basis for *The Birth of a Nation*. *Bolshevism on Trial* was adapted from Dixon's 1909 book *Comrades*.

Having bought more than five million copies of his numerous books, most Americans knew who Dixon was. His novels as well as his plays typically explored the social issues of the day, especially the color line, and through his plots and characters he offered his own solutions to some of America's deepest problems. A preacher and a lawyer, as well as a writer,

Dixon railed against racial equality, which he believed would lead to miscegenation and sin. Women's suffrage, he believed, would destroy the family and socialism was simply evil. Dixon's views were exactly opposite those of his contemporary Upton Sinclair, who, in his newest book, *Jimmie Higgins,* released in April 1919, protested U.S. intervention in Russia. In fact, Dixon appeared to be in the business of boosting the platforms of hatemongers, racists, and war hawks. His books, as well as the films that adapted them, were vicious attacks against the "other" in America: groups and individuals who racially or politically were outside mainstream white America. His book *The Fall of a Nation* denounced pacifists just as *The Clansman* attacked blacks and *Comrades* vilified socialists.

The Birth of a Nation and *Bolshevism on Trial* both had anti-radical themes. In the first, the radicals were overzealous, lascivious politicians favoring race equality. And in *Bolshevism on Trial* they were maniacal, lying socialists and communists aiming to deprive Americans of their freedoms. In the plots of the two films there were also some interesting parallels. In both, a brutish, lascivious man stalks and entraps an innocent woman. This happens twice, in fact, in *The Birth of a Nation,* in which the two iniquitous men are black and the two victimized women are white. In *Bolshevism on Trial* the aggressor is labeled a socialist who, using high ideals and seductive world visions, lures a wealthy socialite trying to reform capitalism into his scheme for a new world and then deceives her. The distressed damsels in both films are depicted as trying to escape from tragic fates: interracial marriage in *The Birth of a Nation* and socialism in *Bolshevism on Trial.* The heroes in both films come in the form of an organized, unstoppable invasion of white men—in white uniforms (U.S. Navy) in *Bolshevism on Trial* and in white sheets (the Klan) in *The Birth of a Nation.* They are too late in *The Birth of a Nation,* for one of the women is so frightened of a black man who tells her of his wish to marry her that she jumps off a cliff and dies. The second woman threatened with miscegenation is rescued by hundreds of Klansmen on their glorious white steeds at the end of the film. *Bolshevism on Trial* ends similarly.

Bolshevism on Trial begins with a scene where Norman Bradshaw, a captain in the Great War, is showing his father, a wealthy industrialist, a newspaper story with the headline "Society Girl Joins Reds." Barbara Alden, the society girl, is also Norman's favorite girl. And so he decides to attend a "Reds meeting" where she lectures on the virtues of world socialism. Norman, hoping to impress Barbara, goes to the meeting with news of his promotion to president of a new company. But instead *he* is swayed by *her* speech, which begins: "I have come tonight to tell you how to make the world better as there must be a way so that hardships and poverty shall disappear."

Led by the cunning agitator Herman Wolff, who, the audience soon learns, has a secret plan to spread Bolshevism worldwide, Barbara raises funds from her affluent acquaintances to buy Paradise Island off the coast of Florida. There they will create a collective colony—"a land of happiness and plenty," she tells them. They balk at first and then Norman stands up and says he's "in" and "it's a plan worth trying." Later that night, he asks for funds from his father, who is irate about his son's "naïveté" and "idealism" and thus, at the moment of his son's passionate departure, refuses to shake Norman's hand. After Norman leaves, the father says, "He'll get his island and a lesson along with it."

When the throng of believers—men in coats and ties and women in silk dresses and floppy hats under lace parasols—arrives at their new island utopia, "every heart beat with high resolve," as Dixon described the scene in *Comrades.* "The heaven of which they had dreamed was no longer a dream. They were walking its white, shining streets. Their souls were crying for joy in its dazzling court of honour. The old world, with its sin and shame, its crime and misery, its hunger and cold, its greed and lust, its cruelty and insanity, had passed away, and lo! All things were new. The very air was charged with faith and hope and love. A wave of religious ecstasy swept the crowd. They called each by their first names. Strong men embraced, crying 'Comrade!' through their tears."

Norman, who hoists the red flag, is soon elected "Chief Comrade." The first step is to find out what skills people have so that the work of organizing the colony can begin. Thus the "comrades" fill out forms about the jobs they want to do for the community. The majority say "assistant managers," and the rest offer their skills as models, actresses, social chairmen, musicians, and sports coaches. But who will cook, clean, and sew? Who will plow fields, dig sewers, weave cloth? Norman asks. No one volunteers.

As if buried under the weight of their tasks, they lose their enthusiasm, sink into a state of constant dissatisfaction, and then begin to turn on one another. For example, there's a strike in the kitchen where the workers complain that the others aren't working hard enough. Soon Norman is ousted. Comrade Wolff assumes the top post—a move he had planned covertly—and immediately he creates a police force, bans marriage, and declares women and children the property of the State. He then orders Norman to be locked up. This awakens Barbara from her idealistic stupor and she sees the horrible error she has made. "These poor deluded people will starve and die as they are in Russia," she says, with hands flung into the air in despair. At the same time, Wolff decides that because of his plan to take over the world and his new post as Chief Comrade, he needs a new, younger, prettier wife and so he chooses Barbara. "I will make you the consort of a great revolutionary leader . . . myself!" he tells her.

"But I have no interest in the Colony now—only to get away. You've broken my faith in human nature. I'd rather be dead than marry you," says Barbara.

"You will NEVER leave the island except as my consort."

Wolff then forces her to kiss him. Barbara struggles in vain to be free. Meanwhile, Norman's father has used his considerable influence and money to commandeer an entire navy fleet to rescue both his son and Barbara. When the navy commander apprehends Wolff, the audience learns that Herman Wolff's real name is *Androvitch*! "You have been under surveillance for more than a year," the officer tells Wolff. The camera then pans to the flagpole, where Norman is lowering the Red flag. In the last scene he hoists the American flag and everyone cheers.

Bolshevism on Trial received excellent reviews. "Powerful, well-knit with indubitably true and biting satire,' wrote Julian Johnson of *Photoplay* magazine. The film's ad copy called it "the timeliest picture ever filmed" and with or without a sordid scheme for selling it, which only a few theaters employed, *Bolshevism on Trial* was a box office winner.

With this and other movies and books, Bolshevism was invading American culture. More than a political system that had been adopted by the largest nation in the world, more than a strange new idea moving like a pandemic through the neighborhoods of America's immigrants and laboring class, Bolshevism was becoming a household word, a provocative catchall term that embraced everything mainstream America feared, including voices critical of the government. The American public was following the government's lead in believing that fundamental social reforms were not the solution to social inequalities and political unrest. The best way to soften the jolting impact of life in the stormy aftermath of the first

American muckraker Ray Stannard Baker, who served as head of the Press Bureau for the American Commission at the Paris Peace Conference, shown here with President Woodrow Wilson in Paris, 1919. (BROWN BROTHERS)

The streets of Boston in the aftermath of the January 15, 1919, explosion of a tank holding 2.3 million tons of fermenting molasses intended for use in the manufacture of munitions and alcoholic beverages; a viscous wave 25 feet high and 160 feet wide moved through the streets of Boston's industrial north. (BOSTON PUBLIC LIBRARY)

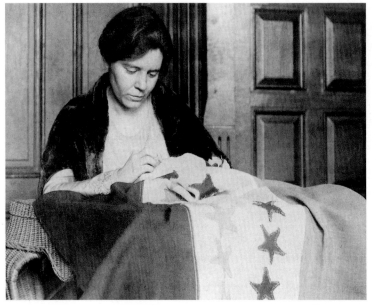

Alice Paul, who organized the "watchfires of freedom" demonstration for the cause of women's suffrage in January 1919, shown here sewing a star on the National Woman's Party flag to indicate that yet another state had ratified the 19th Amendment. (LIBRARY OF CONGRESS)

American journalist and poet Carl Sandburg at his desk in Chicago in 1918. (NATIONAL PARK SERVICE PHOTO)

Madam C. J. Walker, millionaire businesswoman, shown here at a meeting held at the Waldorf-Astoria Hotel, New York City, on January 17, 1919, to discuss plans for working with the Japanese in Paris to advocate racial justice at the Peace Conference. (A'LELIA BUNDLES, MADAM WALKER FAMILY COLLECTION)

William Monroe Trotter, founder in 1901 of *The Guardian,* an African-American newspaper in Boston. An outspoken journalist, he sought "real democracy" for African-Americans in Paris during the Peace Conference of 1919. (THE WILLIAM MONROE TROTTER INSTITUTE, UNIVERSITY OF MASSACHUSETTS)

W. E. B. Du Bois, considered the foremost African-American intellectual of the 20th century; editor of *The Crisis* magazine from 1910 to 1934 and head of the Pan-African Congress held in Paris in February 1919. (LIBRARY OF CONGRESS)

A political cartoon expressing the frustration of African-Americans in the aftermath of World War I and the hypocrisy of Woodrow Wilson's campaign to make the world "safe for democracy." (*NEW YORK AGE*, AUGUST 9, 1919)

The streets of New York City on February 17, 1919, when two million spectators lined Fifth Avenue from 53rd Street to the corner of 145th Street and Lenox Avenue in Harlem to hail the return of "Harlem's Own" 369th U.S. Infantry. (LIBRARY OF CONGRESS)

Sgt. Henry Johnson, the Pullman porter from Albany, New York, who fought in the 369th U.S. Infantry and was the first American soldier to earn the Croix de Guerre in World War I. (*ALBANY, NY, TIMES-UNION*)

Major Walter H. Loving, who served the U.S. War Department's Military Intelligence Division as head of a covert investigation of "negro subversion" from fall 1917 through August 1919. (HOWARD UNIVERSITY)

James Weldon Johnson, author, musician, and promoter of African-American literature and art; he wrote a *New York Age* column, "Views and Reviews," in 1919 and became executive secretary of the NAACP the following year. (LIBRARY OF CONGRESS)

The burning of the lynched African-American William Brown in Omaha, Nebraska, September 28, 1919. (BROWN BROTHERS)

An American soldier of Company I, 339th U.S. Infantry, known as the "Polar Bears," stationed in northern Russia; photo is dated February 17, 1919, when the temperature was fifty degrees below zero. (MICHIGAN'S OWN MILITARY AND SPACE MUSEUM)

global war was to identify an enemy, shift the blame for social ills to the enemy, and then focus the nation's resources on destroying the enemy—not to demobilize the bellicose war consciousness for the shift to peacetime, but to remobilize the public consciousness with a new war against a hidden enemy. Hence, Bolshevism was sweeping the nation like a hot wind. Whether a movie or book was for it or against it, the mere mention of it aroused curiosity and intrigue as well as hatred and fear. And hence it was marketable.

In April, *Bolshevism on Trial* was a popular movie and *Ten Days That Shook the World* became a successful book. John Reed's masterpiece of narrative journalism brought the Bolshevik Revolution to the reader with the intensity of a motion picture. Reed had witnessed what he believed to be a moment of destiny and he delivered every sight, sound, and smell of it to his readers. The American public nearly inhaled it, buying up thousands of copies in its first weeks after publication. So compelling was Reed's writing, so sharp were his observations, so passionate was his involvement in the story that his book cut through prejudices and differences, appealing to critics, to the ordinary reader, to those who saw the workers' state of Bolshevik Russia as a new way to run the world as well as to those who deeply feared it. Reaching out to what he hoped would be a more tolerant future, Reed wrote in his preface, "No matter what one thinks of Bolshevism, it is undeniable that the Russian Revolution is one of the great events of human history and the rise of the Bolsheviki a phenomenon of world-wide importance. In the struggle my sympathies were not neutral. But in telling the story of those great days I have tried to see events with the eye of a conscientious reporter, interested in setting down the truth."

Although the wave of books about the "Bolshevist menace" wouldn't crest until the following year, there would be more movies on the topic throughout 1919. Coming in early May was *The New Moon*, featuring the popular Norma Talmadge, who plays a Russian princess forced to separate from her fiancé, a Russian prince, during a Red Army attack on her palace. To save their lives, he impersonates a Red and she pretends to be a peasant. They are both caught, which is especially problematic for the princess because in the movie all women between twenty-three and thirty-two are property of the State. A nefarious Soviet leader wants her for his own but she refuses to be his. The prince rescues her and the Soviet leader commits suicide. Although not as popular as *Bolshevism on Trial*, *The New Moon* was successful enough to encourage more: *Red Viper, The Right to Happiness,* and even a heavy-handed comedy, *Bullin' the Bullsheviki.*

Such movies may have communicated the image the government itself wanted to project but the government was clearly not on board for the promotional tactic of make-believe riots in front of movie theaters. When the April column about promoting *Bolshevism on Trial* reached Secretary of Labor William Wilson, he was alarmed. The April 15 issue of *Moving Picture World* with its promotional suggestions had not escaped the scrutiny of the post office censors. The day after receiving it, the secretary told the press that never in his life had he seen such dangerous advice. "This publication proposes by deceptive methods of advertising to stir every community in the United States into riotous demonstrations for the purpose of making profits for the moving picture business and the owners of this particular photoplay." He also said he was appealing to Attorney General Palmer to take action "against moving pictures treating of Bolshevism and Socialism," although apparently the attorney general ignored the suggestion.

Secretary Wilson was jittery, and so were others in Washington. The passionate mix of the paranoia of Red baiters and the patriotism of returning soldiers made the threat of riots against pacifists, socialists, Bolshevists, Russian immigrants, and anyone else who seemed to represent the new enemy, all too possible. By April, the kindling was piled high on both sides. A make-believe riot, as Secretary Wilson feared, could be the spark.

Ironically, the government supplied some of that kindling with the help of the widely publicized testimonies at the Overman Committee hearings and the committee's inflammatory 1,200-page report that described Bolshevism as a "reign of terror" and warned of an imminent Bolshevist attempt to take over America. The Seattle mayor's nationwide speaking tour highlighting his bravery in the face of frightful revolution, meaning the Seattle general strike, added to the intensity of the times as did the rising number of labor strikes—more proof of the infiltration of Bolshevists—with 175 in March, 248 in April, 388 in May. And New York's highly publicized Lusk Committee, created in response to the dangers revealed by the Overman witnesses, contributed to the mood. There were also leaks to the press about imminent revolution, in letters and memos from Seattle Minute Men, former Bureau of Investigation agents, and American Protective League members. The movement to take over America was "well-financed and surprisingly well-organized" on the West Coast, wrote one former bureau agent who advocated "immediate action to curb the extreme radicals." A member of the Seattle Minute Men who said he had infiltrated the enemy forces called the Seattle strike "a revolution instigated and brought about by IWW's having joined hands with the bolsjeviki and all forms of radicals and having all become bed-fellows." After the revolution, the Bolsheviki would seize all land, factories, banks, media, private residences, and churches. And just as in *Bolshevism on Trial*, everyone would have to do some sort of basic labor, no matter what their station in life. There would be no more smooth hands.

At the same time, whistleblowers began to leak information about the inner workings of the government's tactics for surveillance and repression. One former member of the Seattle Minute Men, for example, spoke to a reporter for the *New York Tribune* about the group's elaborate spy network based on wartime Germany's domestic espionage system. Spies had infiltrated all meetings leading to the strike and had, in fact, planted a man on the inside of the main committee writing the constitution—a man who added wording that weakened the group's position. *The Nation* magazine, in its commentary about the *Tribune* article, drew even more attention to the hypocrisy: "If the government were not so busy at its own game of spying and Bolshevik-baiting we might suggest that this is one article of German make that might well be subject to permanent embargo. Used as a weapon of domestic terrorism it is bound to create an atmosphere of warfare and a bitter clash of loyalties in our own country, making enemies of mere dissenters."

The American Freedom Congress, the Workers Amnesty League, the National League for Release of Political Prisoners, and the American Freedom Convention, among numerous other groups, were crying out for amnesty for the hundreds of people in jail for opposing the war—whose release at this time was truly frightening to those who saw them as criminals and believed that, if released, such individuals would strengthen the forces of revolution.

The popularity of Eugene Debs, to whom President Wilson refused amnesty, was growing, despite and perhaps because of his new address, at the West Virginia penitentiary. Now truly a martyr to the cause of worldwide socialism and a working-class idol more than ever, Debs began his ten-year sentence on April 11. With a somber elegance of spirit and the appealing dignity that won him his following, he told the press, "During my incarceration my comrades will be true."

Adding to the irony, hypocrisy, confusion, and intensity of America's preoccupations with Bolshevism was corporate America's point of view that a new young nation such as Soviet Russia was a treasure trove of untapped markets. In a 1918 book about conditions in Russia, one New York journalist wrote that Russia was American capital's "greatest market in the future." And despite the rabid depictions of barbaric Bolsheviks that graced the nation's front pages, U.S. businessmen were bravely walking where few Americans dared to step—to the offices of the Soviet Bureau in New York City to meet with Soviet representatives and talk about trade.

The Soviet Bureau was Russia's unofficial embassy in the United States—unofficial because the State Department had not formally recognized the new Russian government. The unofficial Soviet ambassador was Ludwig C. A. K. Martens, whom Lenin appointed in early January 1919 to establish ties with American businesses. Martens also hoped to purchase much needed railroad supplies, medicine, shoes, clothing, food, and agricultural machinery for the new Bolshevik Russia. By April 1, he had a permanent staff of thirty with ten temporary assistants working in furnished offices at the World Tower Building at 110 West 40th Street in Manhattan. Among the directors of the bureau's departments were Russian immigrants who had graduated from Harvard, earned doctorates from Columbia, taught at the University of Chicago and at Princeton, and founded companies in the United States. The director of finances was a medical doctor, Julius Hammer, who also ran a successful pharmaceutical firm, Allied Drug and Chemical Company, and would soon be a member of the new Communist Party of America.

Exactly where Martens got his funding was a matter of intrigue. Especially curious was the Bureau of Investigation, which assigned agents to spy on the Soviet Bureau from the moment Martens announced his intentions in early January. One BI theory for the source of the funding was that it came from uncut diamonds smuggled into the United States. Such a possibility led to a customs shakedown of seamen aboard the USS *Stockholm*, during which one sailor bolted and was later caught and searched. In his trousers he had concealed envelopes, one of which contained $50,000 worth of diamonds. It was addressed to Martens. Another theory was that the wealthy Dr. Hammer was the major backer.

April was a busy month for the Soviet Bureau, which sent out informational letters to five thousand firms and press kits to more than two hundred trade papers. Martens's staff exchanged letters and conducted interviews with eager representatives of major U.S. companies, including Ford Motor Company, the meatpacking firms Armour and Swift, Marathon Tire and Rubber and Old Reliable Motor Truck, among others. The representative from Carolina Junk and Hide ended a letter to the bureau saying: "Assuring you of my deepest sympathy for bleeding Russia as well as bleeding humanity everywhere, and hoping that there are brighter days in store for the human race in every land in the near future, I remain faithfully yours."

On April 24 and 25, at the Sixth National Foreign Trade Convention in Chicago, two of Martens's directors set up temporary headquarters at the Hotel LaSalle and met with representatives of at least two dozen companies, including International Harvester; Marshall Field; Sears, Roebuck; and Calumet Baking Powder. And they arranged future meetings with some of Chicago's most prominent bankers and manufacturers, some of whom, by the end of the convention, had urged the two Russians to set up a branch of the Soviet Bureau in Chicago. Intelligence reports would later show that at least nine hundred American companies expressed interest in speaking with the bureau in the spring of 1919 and more than seven hundred offered to do business with it. Ford's representative sent out a press release that April saying that the company "considers their tractors suitable for Russian conditions, and that they are anxious to do business with Soviet Russia," and to "trade with [the Bolsheviks] on a regular basis." Soon Ford would sell 238 touring cars to Russia through an agent in Martens's office. In the years ahead Ford would conduct its business with the Bolsheviks through the Allied American Corporation of New York, a company established by Julius Hammer and his sons. By mid-May, the bureau would secure $300 million worth of contracts with U.S. companies. And according to Scotland Yard investigators at the time, by May, investment banking houses, including Morgan Guaranty Trust Company, were not only working with the Soviet Bureau but helping to fund it.

Throughout the spring, Martens continued his campaign for recognition by the State Department without success. Then at the end of April something happened that would make it nearly impossible for the government to recognize the new Russian regime, something that would raise the nation's level of intolerance higher than the box office totals of every anti-Bolshevik movie that year, something in New York, something frightening for both sides of the Bolshevism debate.

On April 30, at the New York City post office, Charles Kaplan, a night clerk, completed his shift in the parcel division. It was 2 A.M. and Kaplan, as usual, descended the grand stairs to Eighth Avenue, crossed the street to Penn Station, and took the subway north to his home in Harlem. On the seat next to him that morning was a copy of the April 29 *New York Times*, which caught his eye when he saw the word "Mail" in a headline. The story was about a bomb exploding at the Atlanta home of former U.S. senator Thomas W. Hardwick. The senator's maid had answered the front door, accepted the package, and was holding it when it exploded. She lost both hands. The parcel was described as small—about seven inches long, three inches wide, two inches deep—and was wrapped in light brown paper with a return address for Gimbel Brothers in New York. An almost identical package, with a bomb inside, had been found that same day at the Seattle post office, the article said. This one was addressed to Ole Hanson, Seattle's mayor. As the train pulled into the 110th Street station, Kaplan suddenly bolted out of his seat, ran up the stairs, out of the subway station, across the street, and down the stairs to the downtown subway platform, nearly holding his breath for all of the six minutes he had to wait for the next train back to Penn Station. Every second seemed like a day for the man who had just recalled that three days before he had lined up a dozen or more small brown-paper parcels on the insufficient postage shelf—all with the Gimbel Brothers return address.

The next morning, May 1, Kaplan found his own name prominently featured in the *New York Times*. The Harlem postal clerk had potentially saved the lives of the sixteen intended recipients of the packages, each of which did indeed contain a wooden tube filled with an acid detonator and a high explosive. That day, after the government sent an alert to all post offices nationwide, eighteen more Gimbel's packages were discovered containing eighteen more bombs. The targets included Senator Lee Overman; Postmaster General Burleson; Attorney General Palmer; Anthony Caminetti, the commissioner general of immigration; Secretary of Labor

Wilson; Justice Oliver Wendell Holmes, Jr.; John D. Rockefeller; and J. P. Morgan.

The total number of targets was now thirty-six. There were no suspects, but the image of the suspects was already painted for all Americans to behold: a band of murderous Bolsheviks. Headlines sizzled with the news that "Reds Planned May Day Murders." The "enmity of the radicals," the *New York Times* said, was to blame. Some newspapers cautioned people to call their local bomb squads before opening any box received in the mail. Others warned of the encroaching evil of anarchy. Still others urged the government to hang every bomb maker and deport every anarchist.

But there were some jagged-edged pieces that didn't fit so well into the picture: for example, why would a radical target Senator Hardwick, who was a solid supporter of Robert M. LaFollette, the Progressive senator from Wisconsin? Hardwick belonged to a newly formed group called the Committee of Forty-eight, which stood for civil rights for women and blacks, was pro-labor and antitrust, and advocated nationalization of railroads, public utilities, and natural resources. Among its members were the editor of *The New Republic*, Herbert Croly; Ohio State University historian Arthur M. Schlesinger, Sr.; and Frederic Howe, the commissioner of immigration at Ellis Island. Howe, also a target for the bomb packages, had nearly resigned from his post over the mistreatment of immigrants at Ellis Island and suggestions of a government policy of mass deportations. Several radical publications noted that there were people not targeted who would in fact be higher priorities for radicals. "They were addressed to all the people that a most ignorant and superficial outsider might think would be chosen by revolutionaries as the ones to get rid of," wrote the editors of *The Liberator*, considered to be a radical magazine. Hardwick was "nearly a radical himself," the editors said.

But hysteria, like a heavy fog, was blocking any vision of the truth. And so it was that two days after the opening of *Bolshevism on Trial*, the real riots began. On May Day, socialists, anarchists, labor leaders, and union workers paraded through the streets of several U.S. cities in celebration of workers' rights and in memory of those who had sacrificed their lives to improve conditions for the nation's working class. May Day, an American labor holiday, had been celebrated throughout the United States since the 1890s. But in 1919 in Boston, New York, and Cleveland, bands of vigilantes tried to stop the celebration. And riots ensued. In Boston, one union sponsored a May Day parade, during which bands of vigilantes attacked them and then moved on to the Boston Socialist Party headquarters. In New York, dozens of World War I soldiers raided the Russian People's House, gathered magazines and books, and set them on fire while forcing the immigrants meeting there to sing "The Star-Spangled Banner." In another part of town, hundreds of civilians crashed a reception of seven hundred guests at a socialist newspaper, smashed the furniture, and forced the attendees onto the street, beating seventeen with clubs. But Cleveland got the worst of it. On Superior and Euclid Avenues, fighting broke out between Red haters and socialists; citizens threw furniture out of the windows of the Socialist Party headquarters onto the sidewalks of Prospect Avenue; and ex-soldiers drove a tank into a parade of socialists at Cleveland Public Square. One person died and forty were injured in Cleveland that day. The radical press in Cleveland accused the Loyal American League of provoking the riots to make the radicals look bad. The Loyal American League said they were only defending "the Stars and Stripes."

The next day most of the nation's newspapers blamed the violence in all three cities on the "bomb-throwing radicals." Free speech was on the list of culprits. And editorial pages sizzled with pleas to the government to stop the madness before it got worse, even at the risk of violating the Bill of Rights. "Free speech has been carried to the point where it is an unrestrained menace," wrote the *Tribune* of Salt Lake City.

New York's Lusk Committee stepped up its schedule of investigations of radical organizations and called upon its "secret service force" to "sift the chaff from the wheat," as Senator Lusk put it. The committee decided also to come up with a plan to do something soon to show the world that it was not going to allow New York to surrender to the radical dreams of revolutionaries—something like a sensational raid on a radical organization. And how about the Soviet Bureau? The search warrant for such a raid could condemn the bureau for distributing subversive literature nationwide. And that became the plan.

The American Protective League, the Loyal American League, and other such groups raised their own pitch in an already screaming campaign to persuade Attorney General Palmer to reconnect government agencies with the battalions of volunteer spies on whom the government had relied during the war. One St. Louis APL veteran wrote to Palmer, "It has struck me from what I read in the papers in connection with these bomb fiends, Bolsheviki, IWW's and other fiends, who do not seem to want to conform to our government or any other organized government or respect our glorious 'Stars and Stripes,' that it might not be a bad, in fact might be a splendid idea to revive the 'American Protective League' to assist and help in running down these opponents of our government and institutions, and individuals who seem to prefer some kind of a rag, red or black, in place of 'Old Glory.' "

Thus far, Palmer had resisted. "It is encouraging to note that the Department of Justice has at least refused to cooperate with private organizations for espionage, and Attorney General Palmer deserves thanks for his statement that such espionage is 'entirely at variance with our theories of government,' " wrote *The Nation* in its April issue.

But it was now May, and America was off-balance and edgy, far more than at any time since the Armistice. On May 5, for example, at a Chicago amphitheater, a man was shot when he did not stand and remove his hat in response to a band playing "The Star-Spangled Banner." And when he fell, the crowd, which had gathered for a victory loan fund-raiser, clapped and cheered. The seeds of hysteria were sprouting. Any opportunist could now reap the harvest.

CHAPTER 17

It's in the Mail

By April of 1919, the National Association for the Advancement of Colored People and W. E. B. Du Bois had published 102 issues of the NAACP magazine, *The Crisis, A Record of the Darker Races,* never missing a month since its inception in November of 1910. How odd, its more than 100,000 subscribers must have thought, that by late April and early May, No. 103 had not yet arrived. Had the subscription expired? Was the May issue a special edition requiring more than the usual time to print? Was the NAACP skipping an issue for some reason? Could it possibly have gotten lost in the mail?

Indeed, something had happened at the post office. Approximately 100,000 copies of *The Crisis* were stacked in a back room at the main post office on West 33rd Street in New York City while censorship officials studied its pages to determine whether it was dangerous propaganda. The initial alert regarding the contents of the May edition came out of the little known division of the Justice Department called the Bureau of Translations and Radical Publications, which was based in New York City. The mission of the bureau's forty-five translators and analysts was to monitor the mails and censor any suspicious journals, magazines, or newspapers moving in or out of New York City. The head of the bureau was Robert A. Bowen, who after examining the most recent issue of *The Crisis,* found it objectionable. In fact, he believed it to be seditious. Despite the fact that the Armistice had been signed six months before, Bowen, using the authority of his post and the wartime censoring power of the Espionage Act, had the right to question the mailing privileges for publications that demonstrated "treason, insurrection, or forcible resistance to any law." And thus he stopped the delivery of *The Crisis.*

Bowen took a special interest in black publications, of which he routinely targeted at least eight in New York as "radical:" the *New York Age, New York Amsterdam News, Messenger, Negro World, Veteran, New York Independent, Crusader,* and *The Crisis. The Crisis* was frequently a borderline case, from Bowen's point of view. But that May there was no doubt in Bowen's mind that it had crossed the border into the "traitorous zone," as he described it. After advising the New York City postmaster to hold all copies of the magazine, he informed the U.S. postal solicitor, William H. Lamar, about what he believed to be the seditious contents. It was the postal solicitor's job to make the final decision about whether to censor a publication.

The writings of W. E. B. Du Bois were especially dangerous, Bowen pointed out, describing that month's work by the esteemed founder and editor of *The Crisis* as "insolently abusive of the country." Du Bois seemed to be issuing a "not too veiled threat" from black Americans to the rest of the nation, the anxious Bowen told Lamar. Whether thousands of African-Americans would read the most recent writings of Du Bois would depend on Lamar and his ruling. In late April, Lamar presented the question to his staff.

Du Bois was back from Paris where, as he described in his May editorial headlined "My Mission," he had persuaded the French government to allow him to conduct his Pan-African Congress. In fact, because of its success in Paris, it would now be a permanent body with an international quarterly entitled *Black Review.* "The world-fight for black rights is on!" was the last line of Du Bois's editorial. But it wasn't this line or the editorial that caused Bowen to gasp.

In Paris, Du Bois had also presented his resolutions of race equality worldwide to members of the American Peace Commission and he had conducted in-depth reporting on the experience of black American soldiers in France for a history that he planned to write. In the May issue his "Essay Toward a History of the Black Man in the Great War" exposed racism in official memos coming out of the U.S. military and proof of bias among the white officers who commanded the black troops—both highly volatile issues among American blacks, who had vehemently opposed a system in which black soldiers were subservient to white officers. And indeed it was this article that Du Bois himself told the *New York Tribune* he believed to be the reason for the government's censorship of the May issue.

But it wasn't this either that caused the Bureau of Translations director to panic. Nor was it the editorial that revealed the truth about the last of the lynchings of 1918, the ones in Mississippi around Christmas in which two young men and two young girls, both pregnant, were hanged on a bridge over the Chickasawhay River—an editorial that was almost too horrifying to read.

What struck Bowen, as if mugged in the dark alley of his own prejudice, was an editorial for which Du Bois would always be known and in which Du Bois, in his usual precise yet impassioned language, unveiled his vision of the black man's burden: the hypocrisy of America. On pages 13 and 14 of the May issue was Du Bois's "Returning Soldiers."

We are returning from war! "The Crisis" and tens of thousands of black men were drafted into a great struggle. For bleeding France and what she means and has meant and will mean to us and humanity and against the threat of German race arrogance, we fought gladly and to the last drop of blood; for America and her highest ideals, we fought in far-off hope; for the dominant southern oligarchy entrenched in Washington, we fought in bitter resignation. For the America that represents and gloats in lynching, disfranchisement, caste, brutality and devilish insult—for this, in the hateful upturning and mixing of things, we were forced by vindictive fate to fight, also.

But today we return! We return from slavery of uniform which the world's madness demanded us to don to the freedom of civil garb. We stand again to look America squarely in the face and call a spade a spade. We sing: This country of ours, despite all its better souls have done and dreamed, is yet a shameful land.

It lynches. And lynching is barbarism of a degree of contemptible nastiness unparalleled in human history. Yet for fifty years we have lynched two Negroes a week and we have kept this up right through the war.

It disfranchises its own citizens . . . It encourages ignorance . . . It steals from us . . . It insults us.

It has organized a nation-wide and latterly a worldwide propaganda of deliberate and continuous insult and defamation of black blood wherever found. It decrees that it shall not be possible in travel nor residence, work nor play, education nor instruction for a black man to exist without tacit or open acknowledgment of his inferiority to the dirtiest white dog. And it looks upon any attempt to question or even discuss this dogma as arrogance, unwarranted assumption and treason.

This is the country to which we Soldiers of Democracy return. This is the fatherland for which we fought! But it is our fatherland. It was right for us to fight. The faults of our country are our faults. Under similar circumstances, we would fight again. But by the God of Heaven, we are cowards and jackasses if now that that war is over, we do not marshal every ounce of our brain and brawn to fight a sterner, longer, more unbending battle against the forces of hell in our own land.

We return.

We return from fighting.

We return fighting.

Make way for Democracy! We saved it in France, and by the Great Jehovah, we will save it in the United States of America, or know the reason why.

It was these words that had frightened Bowen. Could this piece of writing possibly have come from the same man who had authored the editorial entitled "Close Ranks" in the July 1918 issue of *The Crisis*? "Let us not hesitate. Let us, while this war lasts, forget our special grievances and close our ranks shoulder to shoulder with our own white fellow citizens and the allied nations that are fighting for democracy. We make no ordinary sacrifice, but we make it gladly and willingly with our eyes lifted to the hills." From Du Bois's point of view, however, "Returning Soldiers" was not a deviation from any previous stand. If America were to wage another war, he would again call his people to defend their country. As he wrote, "Under similar circumstances, we would fight again." But now, his country owed its black soldiers the democracy they had fought for. And *this* is what struck Bowen, in a panicky moment, as untenable.

When the NAACP realized what had happened to the 100,000 copies of *The Crisis*, it enlisted its membership to help. Very quickly black Americans from women's clubs, business leagues, church groups, and trade unions sent a flurry of telegrams to the postmaster general's office protesting the censorship. Even four members of Congress lodged complaints.

While Lamar and his staff studied the issue, Bowen contacted the army's Military Intelligence Division, to harness the energy of yet another government agency for his urgent cause. General Marlborough Churchill, who had been back from Paris since April, carefully scrutinized Du Bois's piece. But what Bowen may not have known is that during the previous several months the MID had been conducting its own studies and its report "The Negro in the Army" effectively was in agreement with Du Bois. The MID's Negro Subversion division still had its agents spying on Du Bois and other black leaders, ever suspicious of Bolshevism infiltrating black communities. And the reports coming in were revealing that blacks in the army should be given greater opportunities for promotion, should be better treated by white officers, and should be acknowledged for their contributions.

Thus Du Bois's editorial did not shock General Churchill. He calmly informed Bowen that it was "of special interest" but not alarming enough to censor. Postal solicitor Lamar concurred. In Lamar's May 2 memo, he said that he and his staff had concluded that the editorial was "unquestionably violent" and that it was "extremely likely to excite a considerable amount of racial prejudice (if that has not already reached its maximum amongst the Negroes)." But they also believed that the underlying motivation of the writer was not to wage a war against the "constitutional authority of the U.S. government," but rather to protest and put an end to the "disagreeable and deplorable conditions" that his race was facing. The editorial therefore did not violate the Espionage Act. And the magazine was thus deemed "acceptable for mailing."

By the week of May 5, *The Crisis* subscribers received their May issue and for most, if not all, African-Americans who read it, Du Bois's editorial was hardly shocking. It described succinctly, accurately, and passionately what they knew in their minds and felt in their hearts to be true. Only white Americans would be shocked by Du Bois's comments. The reality was, as Ray Stannard Baker had pointed out in a 1916 magazine article, that white people didn't know or want to know the conditions in black America and such indifference to "what is going on in the depths of the volcano just below" was "appalling and dangerous." Baker had warned, "It must be sharply realized that injustice sooner or later brings its sure reward—and the more monstrous the injustice, the more terrible the consequences."

Soon, very soon, a New Negro would indeed marshal every ounce of brain and brawn to fight the "forces of hell" in his own "shameful land." The truth, whether white America would face it or bury it deeper, was that the war had transformed black America and from the month of May 1919 onward, it would be increasingly clear that there was no going back. In this year, three hundred years after the first slave came to America, the quest for equality was no less urgent than the cause of freedom during slavery days. Since the end of the Civil War, only fifty-four years before, progress had been far too slow for black America. And since the end of the Great War, change was urgent, as necessary for African-Americans as drawing breath.

On the night of May 5, at Carnegie Hall in New York, a notable gathering of educators, lawyers, legislators, judges, religious leaders, and a handful of covert government agents took their seats for the opening night of a two-day anti-lynching conference. Brought together by the NAACP, which had just celebrated its tenth anniversary, this was one of the most distinguished and influential groups that had ever met to discuss a strategy for abolishing lynching in America.

Ida B. Wells-Barnett had pioneered the anti-lynching movement in the 1890s after studying the lynchings of 728 black men and writing the first ever "inside story" of lynching, published in seven columns across the front page of the *New York Age* in June of 1892. Wells was driven to her bold crusade by the lynchings of three black grocers in Memphis that year, one of whom was a friend of hers. "This is what opened my eyes to what lynching really was," she wrote in her autobiography. "An excuse to get rid of Negroes who were acquiring wealth and property and thus keep the race terrorized and 'keep the nigger down.' . . . I found that in order to justify these horrible atrocities to the world, the Negro was being branded as a race of rapists, who were especially mad after white women. I found that white men who had created a race of mulattoes by raping and consorting with Negro women were still doing so wherever they could [and] these same white men lynched, burned, and tortured Negro men for doing the same thing with white women, even when the white women were willing victims."

By 1919, most Americans were indifferent to lynchings, believing that mob violence had nothing to do with them and thus was not their problem, or they simply accepted it, as they had for decades, believing that the victims must have gotten what they deserved. This New York gathering of men and women, black and white, on the other hand saw lynching as the current manifestation of the same evils that had sustained American slavery. To condone such barbarism and allow murders to go unpunished was—as Wells-Barnett had suggested to the world nearly thirty years before—tantamount to complicity in one of the greatest crimes against humanity.

At the conference, twenty-five states were represented, including Georgia, Mississippi, Alabama, and Tennessee. Among the speakers were the former governor of Alabama, a brigadier general of the 92nd Division, a well-known New York neurologist, and the NAACP's field secretary, writer James Weldon Johnson. Former New York governor Charles Evans Hughes gave the keynote speech. Hughes was a former associate justice of the U.S. Supreme Court who had quit the Court in 1916 to run against Wilson for president and who would one day be the Supreme Court's chief justice.

"Justice in America is not to be bought," began Hughes. "It is not necessary that any one should give his blood, either directly or vicariously, to obtain justice in this country. But to the black man, who in this crisis has proved his bravery, his honor and his loyalty to our institutions, we certainly owe the performance of this duty and we should let it be known from this time on that the black man shall have the rights guaranteed to him by the Constitution of the United States."

As long as black Americans are denied justice in the United States, said Hughes, "we can never properly appear as the exemplar of justice to the world. Little can be done in the cause of international justice unless nations establish, strongly and securely, the foundation of justice within their own borders."

The neurologist Dr. A. A. Brill had studied the psychology of lynchings, calling them "the most primitive sadistic outlet." The instincts aroused by lynching blacks can result in other crimes, as a lynching will evoke "the worst animal instincts in defective, perverse persons," he said. How else could one explain the grinning white mobs torturing their victims? No one, he said, who has ever participated in or witnessed a lynching can "remain a civilized person."

But perhaps James Weldon Johnson made the most astute observation when he said that the race problem in America had reached the point where the critical question was how to save "black men's bodies and white men's souls" and that the greatest challenge in reaching a resolution was to change public opinion. The American public was not against lynching. If it were, then lynching could not exist. While it was true that many Americans did not endorse lynching, they also did not condemn it. And when it happened, the citizens who abhorred it but did not try to stop it simply said "it was about the only thing that could be done under the circumstances."

Why this condoning attitude? asked Johnson. Because most Americans believed that the victims of lynchings were usually guilty of assaulting, usually raping, white women. These were the lynchings typically covered in the press. With headlines such as "Burly Black Brute," the press had "stamped upon the public mind" that each Negro who was lynched was a rapist. It is this problem, Johnson believed, that must be addressed and overcome to end lynchings.

During the conference, there was much discussion about the recent resurgence of the Ku Klux Klan. "THE KU KLUX ARE RIDING AGAIN! BACK TO LIFE AND VERY ACTIVE AFTER FORTY YEARS," a March editorial in *The Crisis* had proclaimed. Lynchings thus far in 1919 were recounted—for example, the three in one day in Montgomery, Alabama, earlier in the year, the January burning of a black man in Texas, and the March burning of a Florida black man accused of attacking a white woman. Especially disturbing were the rising numbers of beatings, tortures, hangings, and burnings of returning black soldiers. There was grief over the murder of Private William Little, the soldier whose body was found on April 3 on the outskirts of Blakely, Georgia, his hometown, where he was beaten to death while still in uniform. And what about Daniel Mack, a soldier from Sylvester, Georgia, who, one night in late April, was beaten almost to death by four armed men? Mack was taken from his jail cell, where he was serving time for allegedly knocking down a white man who had bumped into him.

The timing seemed to be right, remarked a few attendees. Southern states were represented at the conference. And at least one Southern newspaper was calling for federal legislation. In the aftermath of a recent torching of an accused murderer in Texas, the *Houston Post* had written an editorial that admitted failure on the part of states to end lynchings. "The failure has been shamefully complete, and when the Federal Government shall essay this task of suppressing anarchy and dealing with those who set at naught the laws of the country and set themselves up as judge, jury and executioner, no State which has a bloody record of mob law staining its escutcheon will have any right to protest." The *New York Times* called the *Houston Post* commentary "noteworthy," and added, "About its premises there can be no dispute."

As they faced a seemingly insurmountable task, these modern-day abolitionists must have felt much like their anti-slavery predecessors: they knew they were right. Armed with the faith that justice must one day prevail, they came out of the conference with three resolutions: one to secure federal legislation against lynching; the next, to organize in each state a committee to secure legislation against the practice of lynching; and the last, to raise funds for a nationwide advertising campaign against lynching to awaken the national conscience. Immediately, those attending the conference pledged funds totaling $9,300, of which $5,000 had been promised in advance from one exceptionally devoted donor, Madam C. J. Walker. Seriously ill, Walker had been unable to attend.

On Friday morning, May 9, at the headquarters of the Military Intelligence Division in Washington, General Churchill sent a memo to the army chief of staff along with recent reports that he believed, without a doubt, showed the need for better treatment of blacks in the army. In it he referred to the current "seriousness of the Negro question" nationwide. That afternoon, while Churchill's memo was circulating in the War Department, many miles away from Washington, in Pickens, Mississippi, a white mob strung up a decorated black soldier in full uniform for allegedly sending an insulting note to a white woman. Neither Churchill's memo nor Madam Walker's money could stop what was to come in the months ahead. In May, a series of events would be set into motion that would shake America into seeing just how "serious" "the Negro question" really was.

On May 10 in Charleston, South Carolina, as in many African-American communities that day, there was much talk about the tragic death the night before in Boston of a black hero, the great musician Lieutenant James Reese Europe. Perhaps Augustus Bonaparte was talking about it that Saturday night while he was getting his haircut—that is, until he looked out the barbershop window facing Charleston's King Street. And maybe S. M. Faress or H. B. Morris, who ran shooting galleries on King Street and on nearby Market Street, respectively, were talking about it when they saw out their windows what Bonaparte saw out his: a sudden stream of white men in blue jackets rushing down King Street. A closer look revealed sailors with guns, clubs, and ham-mers—some walking quickly, some riding in slow-moving cars. Then came the sounds of car doors slamming, glass breaking, and men screaming "Get a nigger."

They looted both shooting galleries. They wrecked the barbershop. They fired a shot through the door of the shop of a black shoemaker, hit-ting his thirteen-year-old assistant in the back. They dragged black passen-gers off trolley cars, beating some and shooting others. They even attacked a black hackman, William Randall, beat him, took his hack from him, and drove it down King Street.

Soon more blue jackets and packs of white civilians joined the mob, in-vading and occupying the black community. The police called in the marines; the sailors were herded onto trucks and escorted to the navy yard. By the early morning of May 11, the rioting that had begun around 8:30 the night before appeared to be under control. But it was not.

The *New Orleans Times-Picayune* would later write that the trouble began again at a downtown Charleston poolhall when a black man shot a white sailor. The *Memphis Commercial Appeal* said it began with a fight between a white sailor and a black man who had threatened to kill the sailor. The *New York Times* claimed that the shooting of a sailor by a Negro in a poolroom was the spark. The *Chicago Defender* said it all started at a King Street poolroom when a drunken white sailor, who had been insulting the proprietor and several black customers, pulled a gun from his pocket. He was then attacked and in the scuffle that ensued he was shot in the stomach.

The subsequent naval inquiry concluded that it was indeed the white sailor who started the episode. But the news of an accusation that a black man had shot a white sailor moved quickly through the community of sailors in Charleston that night and soon they were seeking revenge. Two black men died as a result of the rioting, including William Randall, the hackman. At least seventeen black men, seven sailors, and one white po-liceman were wounded. The bullet that hit the cobbler's young apprentice paralyzed him from the waist down.

Four days later, there were two more lynchings in America, one in Georgia and the other in Mississippi—both for alleged attempts to rape a white woman. There would be six more lynchings before May was over, making the total for the month eleven.

The Mississippi incident was in Vicksburg, where a twenty-three-year-old black man was covered with oil, set aflame, and hoisted to an elm tree. His name was Lloyd Clay and he was accused of entering the bedroom of a nineteen-year-old white girl who claimed he had attempted to violate her. After dogs and deputies chased him down, the girl visited Clay in jail, but she wasn't exactly sure that he was the man who had come into her room. Still, that night more than one thousand men and women broke into the jail and forced the jailers to give up Clay. As the flaming body was raised higher and higher on the tree, men, women, and children fired bullets into it, as if at a booth at a county fair. Two of the onlookers were accidentally hit, one fatally and one with a severe chin wound. In a few weeks, there would be wounds of a different nature, as it would be revealed that the young girl's visitor was a white man, one with whom she had been on intimate terms but did not want her parents to know.

The *Chicago Defender* wrote about the lynching of Lloyd Clay in its May 24 issue. "VICKSBURG, MISSISSIPPI DISGRACES CIVILIZATION WITH LYNCHING. Fiends and Perverts Feed Lloyd Clay to Leaping Flames. Usual Verdict, 'Parties Unknown.' " Evocative and haunting, the story beneath the headline began:

> What the best white citizens here termed the most glorious celebration held in this city for many years occurred Wednesday May 14th when innocent Lloyd Clay, age 23, was lynched and burned on the public highways by men, women and school children. Over 1,000 persons' voices rent the air with yells similar to that of cannibals when Clay was dragged down Farmer street to the "gallows tree." Clay made no outcry as his body bumped over rocks in the street and as knives and pistol shots perforated his naked form. He had been accused of entering the room of Miss Hattie Hudson, a white woman. Sheriff Scott stood idly by and puffed vigorously on a cigar as the bloodthirsty throng massacred their helpless victim. His mother requested that the charred body be given to her, but there was nothing left of it after the fire had parched it to a crisp and souvenirs were distributed to children, who yelled incessantly, "Mother, get me a piece of the nigger's finger."

With these horrible crimes screaming for justice, as had the hundreds before them, the wheels of the federal government slowly began to move. On May 24, Representative Leonidas Dyer of Missouri introduced a bill to the Sixty-sixth Congress that would make lynching a federal offense and would force the counties in which lynchings occurred to pay $5,000 to $10,000 to the victims' dependents. It was thought that House members from Pennsylvania, Massachusetts, New York, Illinois, and California would support it. And in the Senate Medill McCormick of Illinois, Hiram Johnson of California, and Henry Cabot Lodge of Massachusetts were supporters.

While the bill was being drafted, a hearse was carrying the body of Lieutenant Europe to Arlington National Cemetery. Europe was murdered during the intermission of a performance at Mechanics Hall in Boston on the night of May 9. Europe, who, seven years before, almost to the day in May, had conducted a 125-member orchestra—including forty-seven mandolins, eleven banjos, one saxophone, one tuba, thirteen cellos, two clarinets, one kettledrum, five trap drums, two double basses, and ten pianos—presenting the first jazz concert at Carnegie Hall. Europe, the quiet, bespectacled trombone player whose 369th Infantry band was so popular in France during the war, entertaining troops and dignitaries with its "wah-wah trumpets" and "setting France ablaze with its rollicking melodies," as the ads read. Europe, whose white commanding officer described him as "a most extraordinary man without qualification or limitation as to race, color, or any other element." Europe, who was born in Alabama, whose parents had both been musicians, and who, as a child, had studied the violin in Washington, D.C., with the assistant director of the Marine Corps Band. Europe, who was a brilliant star in the recent history of his race, who had survived the Great War and who was only thirty-nine years old. No, it could not be true.

The front pages of white and black newspapers on May 10 ran headlines "THE JAZZ KING IS DEAD" and told the grim story of his death. During the Boston performance, Europe, who was known as a perfectionist and a demanding leader, had told one of his drummers to "put more pep in the sticks." The drummer followed Europe to his dressing room during intermission, pulled out a knife, and slashed him in the neck, severing his jugular vein. Two hours later, Europe was dead.

Ironically, on the same newsstands that day was the latest edition of the

weekly *Chicago Defender*, prepared days before Europe's death. In it editor
Robert Abbott raved about Europe's recent performance in Chicago: "Europe and his band are demonstrating what our people can do in a field
where the results are bound to be of the greatest benefit. He has the white
man's ear because he is giving the white man something new. He is meeting
a popular demand and in catering to his love of syncopated music he is jazzing away the barriers of prejudice."

Showing just how popular Europe was, thousands of blacks and whites
marched from 131st Street in Harlem to 53rd Street in his funeral procession on May 14. It was the first public memorial service held for a black person in the city's history. Simultaneously, there were nationwide eulogies.
Especially powerful was that of Colonel Roscoe Conkling Simmons, a
renowned black orator who was also a columnist for the *Chicago Defender*
and a nephew of Booker T. Washington. Speaking at Tomlinson Hall in
downtown Indianapolis, Simmons said that Europe died at the hands of a
man he had befriended and helped in his life. "He died at the moment of
his greatest fame, when his own and all the world were eager to bestow
upon him the honors won through years of labor and sacrifice. He was
killed because one black man hated to take orders from a superior black
man. There is a lesson in this death for you and for me. It is that slavery dies
as hard within as from without, and that empty are our words about
progress until we can act as well as talk equality."

Dark clouds continued to gather over the black community in America. Conspicuously absent from New York's grand tribute to Europe in New
York and from the burial at Arlington Cemetery was one of Europe's
Harlem neighbors on 136th Street, and a close friend and fan, Madam C. J.
Walker. Too ill to attend the tribute of the burial, Madam Walker died exactly two weeks after Europe's murder, on May 25, at her Irvington estate,
Villa Lewaro. The woman who had caused a collective gasp of astonishment when she built her multimillion-dollar country estate in the very
white Westchester County had been struggling for weeks from the effects
of nephritis, an often irreversible inflammation of the kidneys. Reports of
her death met with utter disbelief causing further consternation in
America's black communities. Her last words, her doctor reported, were
"I want to live to help my race." At fifty-two, she felt that her work was
hardly complete. Having mingled with America's wealthiest and most

powerful individuals, she understood the challenges ahead. She also had hopeful visions.

This was the woman who told a *New York Times* reporter in 1918, "I am not a millionaire but I hope to be some day not because of the money, but because I could do so much more to help my race." In recent months her hopes had focused on the great potential in Paris for attention to race issues worldwide. Disappointed that the State Department had denied her passport request and determined to prevent the race issues from being buried in the denial and hyprocrisy of her times, she risked her reputation and even her business to associate with individuals considered to be radicals—such as the Reverend Adam Clayton Powell, Sr.; A. Philip Randolph, editor of the magazine *Messenger;* Marcus Garvey, editor of the *Negro World* newspaper; and her longtime friend William Monroe Trotter. With MID agents never far from her, she worked to create an independent black league—International League of Darker Peoples—which was to be a permanent organization for inspiring dialogue on race and peace. "If peace can be secured through a league of free nations," so read its declarations, "so can the hydra-headed monster—race prejudice—be destroyed by the darker peoples of the worlds . . . making common cause with each other in one great world body."

Her death was international news, though few reports focused on her vision of racial harmony. Hair treatments and her wealth dominated the stories. The Associated Press story, widely circulated, called her "the wealthiest negro woman in the United States, if not the entire world . . . credited with having amassed a fortune of more than $1,000,000 through the sale of a hair restorer." In the white press, the most thoughtful was the *New York Post,* which said that "Mrs. Walker demonstrated that [Negroes] may rise to the most distinctive heights of American achievement. Men who do nothing but sneer at what Coleridge-Taylor composed, Paul Laurence Dunbar wrote or Booker T. Washington built will be all respect when the Negroes have their full quota of millionaires." In her will, Madam Walker left thousands of dollars to dozens of black-based organizations, as well as a trust fund to help "members of my Race to acquire modern homes." And she willed her stunning monument, Villa Lewaro, to the NAACP "or such organization judged by the trustees to be 'doing the most for Racial uplift.' "

The memorial service on May 30 showed the vast sweep of Walker's life as attorneys, preachers, entertainers, politicians, activists, architects, composers, publishers, editors, jazz musicians, journalists, cosmetologists, and physicians assembled in the majestic halls of Villa Lewaro. Adam Clayton Powell read a eulogy which was followed by a composition written for the occasion by noted composer J. Rosamund Johnson. The minister of Baltimore's Bethel AME Church read the 23rd Psalm, Walker's favorite, and then recalled his last time with her, on Christmas Day 1918, when they read together out loud from the Book of Revelation. That day, he said, "She had had a premonition of an early death."

Missing from the high-profile roster of mourners was Walker's longtime friend William Monroe Trotter. By May 30, however, Trotter had been in Paris for nearly a month.

CHAPTER 18

Monsieur Trotter

The chief cook on the SS *Yarmouth* was more than pleased to hire "Will" as his new assistant, not just because Will could peel potatoes and cook but because he was also literate. Will knew how to write letters. And so it was that he not only got the job as second cook but also became the chief cook's unofficial secretary. For Will, this was convenient and some might say that it may even have been part of a plan devised by the very resourceful Will. In fact, it was possible that on that long trip across the Atlantic in the ship's galley every day, Will may have encouraged the cook to dictate letters to him—letters that would eventually have to be mailed at some port somewhere in France. For Will had only one thing on his mind: to somehow find his way to Paris.

When the small steamer reached its first French port, which was Le Havre, it did not immediately dock and the crew was ordered to stay on board. But the chief cook was so eager to get his letters in the mail that he asked his capable assistant to row ashore, mail the letters, and come back as quickly as possible. And so it was that Will concealed a small roll of money in his work clothes, rowed into the harbor, docked the dinghy, posted the letters, and never again saw the chief cook. After leaving his home in Boston, wandering the wharves of New York for nearly six weeks, obtaining a seaman's permit, disguising himself as a cook, and peeling potatoes on the transatlantic voyage, William Monroe Trotter had finally reached the shores of France.

The next day he purchased a change of clothes and booked passage on a train to Paris. And by May 7, months after the State Department had denied his request for a passport, Trotter was in Paris. This was the very day that Clemenceau was handing a draft of the peace treaty to the German delegates at Versailles—a draft *without* any statement about racial equality, without even a line from the proposal Trotter had sent to President Wilson in December and again in the new year, without a word from Du Bois's resolutions coming out of the Pan-African Congress, without even a mention of racial injustice or the problem of the color line and the need to address it in order to achieve world peace.

By the time Trotter finally got within walking distance of the great peace conference in Paris it was abundantly clear that the shaping and molding of the world was nearly complete. Who were the potters and what was the clay had already been decided. And no one in Trotter's race would be counted among the potters.

With the preliminary peace treaty in the hands of the German delegates, what could Trotter do for his race now? For most people, this would have been the end of the battle. But not for Will, who was never afraid of a fight. This was simply the beginning of a new phase. It was also perhaps one of the greatest stories of determination, persistence, and dedication to the cause of equality that year.

At 8 P.M. Paris time on May 11, Trotter sent a cablegram to his newspaper, *The Guardian* in Boston, which published it in the May 16 issue. "Arrived Paris Wednesday sent protest [to] Versailles. Campaign to Begin. TROTTER." "This trip," *The Guardian* noted, "is Mr. Trotter's greatest attempt and first great victory over President Wilson's autocratic ruling [of blocking the passports]. We will watch with care to see what will be said now."

During his first days in Paris, when he had no place to stay and little money, he found his way to the home of Mr. and Mrs. Thomas Kane, a black couple from Washington, D.C., living in Paris. A friend of Trotter's, a Mr. Clark, also from Washington, had told him to look them up if he ever got to Paris.

It was late in the night when the unshaven, disheveled black man arrived at the Kane home. Anxious and exhausted, he rang the doorbell repeatedly, while the Kanes' dog barked loudly on the other side of the door. When Mrs. Kane answered the door, she was already uncomfortable about who might be there. It was late and she did not know this man who told her his name was Mr. Clark. He had just arrived from Washington. Believing he must be an acquaintance of her husband's, she let him in, though reluctantly.

"He was absolutely like a tramp," she wrote in a letter to her sister-in-law in New York, "in rags, dirty, and in boots without soles." He told her he was hungry and tired. And so she warmed some food for him and told him he could stay the night. He then decided to tell her the truth: that he was not Mr. Clark. However, Mr. Clark assured him that Trotter could use his name in Paris if it would help him get established. He then told her his real name and his real purpose. He had come to Paris to see President Wilson and Clemenceau "to protest against the way colored people are treated in America."

The next day he met Kane and told him the story of his journey to Paris. He also asked if he could use Kane's name to cable the United States for money. He needed clothes and a place to live. But so fantastic was Trotter's story that Kane doubted it was true. He gave Trotter a cup of hot chocolate and asked him to come back later. Trotter left and did not return.

Trotter would continue to tell his story until he found someone who would listen and respond. And so, a few days later, he met a translator at a café, a man who was so taken by Trotter's persistence and pluck that he offered Trotter part of his office space in an impressive building on the Place de la Bourse, at the hub of the high-end business district of Paris. He helped Trotter get outfitted to give a better impression and he even shared his secretarial staff. Someone else whom Trotter met through the translator referred him to the Hôtel du Bon Pasteur on the Rue Ste.-Anne, where he found a room and where he immediately began churning out press releases and petitions, seeking an audience with the president through all sorts of indirect channels and telegraphing his protests against the preliminary peace treaty directly to Wilson, Clemenceau, Foch, Lloyd George, Orlando, and Baron Makino of Japan. "Being informed that the world peace treaty ignores the petitions for abolition of the undemocratic color discrimination . . ." his missives began.

After a week of this, he had not heard a single word from the recipients. And so, in his usual unrelenting way, he sent the same telegram in English and in French with a cover letter dated May 15 and a list of his credentials—Harvard University graduate, first black Phi Beta Kappa in America, editor of a major black newspaper in Boston—to every delegate at the peace conference and to several French newspapers. He beseeched the delegates to read his protest, hoping they would "be able to see the imperative need of recognizing this claim of democracy." He told them that he was now beginning his work "of letting the world know that the Negro race wants full liberty and equality of rights, as the fruit of the World War."

Every newspaper in Paris would soon be writing about the black man from America who said he represented all black Americans in claiming the fulfillment of the promises made by the Allies during the Great War. And many would give him space, from a few inches to an entire column, to state his cause and to express those grievances that President Wilson never wanted to be heard beyond the shores of his own nation. Within ten days of Trotter's arrival in Paris, a reporter from the newspaper *L'Avenir* dined with him and wrote about it, despite the language barrier. Trotter was still struggling with French and the reporter's English was not all that good, but they met without the translator, who usually accompanied Trotter now.

In the style of a social column, the reporter began his piece, "Monsieur William M. Trotter, mouthpiece of 14 millions of Negroes of the U.S. arrived in Paris the other day." Describing Trotter as a man with an "intelligent face, full of ardor," he chronicled Trotter's every move since his arrival in Paris and at the dinner that night. Trotter's meal consisted of escalope of veal with fried potatoes and café au lait. Between bites he talked about how much less democratic Wilson was at home than in Europe and about how urgent the "lamentable situation" in America was. "Assuredly," Trotter told the reporter, "there would be, if we do not obtain justice, a revolution of the Negroes of America and after that revolution, sir, then there will be peace."

In the article, which was published in the May 22 edition of *L'Avenir*, the reporter's response to this statement was glib: " 'Exactly,' I said to him, and then Monsieur lighted suddenly with a fire half mystical and said to me: 'This will be the peace of the world—the perpetual peace' with his bright eyes suddenly illumined with that profound light that the early Christians of the olden times must have had a very long time ago when they repeated with candor the phrase of the Apostle, quite new then: 'the Kingdom of God will reign again upon the Earth.' "

Another French publication, *Le Petit Journal*, talked of Trotter's persistence and his insistent petitions and pleas to the peace conference delegates. It told the story of Wilson's refusal to issue passports to black Americans. "Mr. Trotter alone sailed in disguise," the article said. And, "his protestation brings to light the inferior situation of the men of his race in the U.S. and the promises which were made to them during the war, promises which, he said, have not been kept."

And in late May a letter to the editor of the magazine *L'Intransigeant* described the new polished Trotter entering his office for a meeting wearing a black cutaway coat and trousers, a vest, patent-leather-tipped shoes, and white collar and black tie. As he sat down, the letter noted, he removed his derby hat, drew the gloves from his hands, laid his cane and black leather portfolio on the desk, shook hands, and greeted his guests. "This is the William Monroe Trotter of Paris," the article read.

The Wilson administration was not so impressed. The State Department had refused passports to the black delegates chosen in December of 1918 to represent Trotter's National Equal Rights League because the Wilson administration feared precisely what was happening now. Trotter even referred to himself publicly as NERL's elected delegate to Paris and thus was officially authorized to be there on behalf of his race, no matter what Wilson or the State Department might say or do. For Trotter to be in Paris and to be telling every French newspaper about shameful conditions in America, even saying there could be a revolution soon, was simply unconscionable and unbearable to the administration. Under no circumstances whatsoever would Wilson meet with Trotter. But Trotter would not accept Wilson's refusal "under any circumstances."

On the afternoon of May 30, President Wilson was at Suresnes outside Paris dedicating a new American cemetery. Thousands had gathered on this hot, sunny day, which was Memorial Day in America. A reverent crowd, consisting mostly of American soldiers and the families of deceased French soldiers, stood amid acacia groves on a hillside overlooking Paris. There were also diplomats and generals and statesmen, looking out upon the rows of American dead, and waiting for the American president to speak. Among the throng were Ray Stannard Baker and William Monroe Trotter.

Although weary from the daily battles in which his adversaries were lowering his high purposes for the treaty, Wilson proceeded to give a speech that Baker later described as having come out of "the volcanic depths of his being." With a powerful mix of grace and conviction, he spoke of the cause for which the soldiers had fought. Everyone there that day, he said, had a duty to see to it that such a cause was not betrayed. "They came to defeat forever the things for which the Central powers stood, the sort of power they meant to assert in the world, the arrogant, selfish dominance which they meant to establish; and they came, moreover, to see to it that there should never be a war like this again. It is for us, particularly for us who are civilians, to use our proper weapons of counsel and agreement to see to it that there never is such a war again."

Wilson's last words brought tears to his quiet, rapt audience: "I sent these lads over here to die. Shall I—can I—ever speak a word of counsel which is inconsistent with the assurances I gave them when they came over? Here stand I, consecrated in spirit to the men who were once my comrades and who are now gone, and who have left me under eternal bonds of fidelity."

Baker was moved tremendously by the speech. It came at a time when he could see only iniquities and deceptions at the peace conference and when he had wanted his president to fight even harder for what he believed the treaty must be. Wilson's words that day bolstered his own resolve and renewed his commitment. "I saw and felt a great soul struggling with the bleakest forces of his time," Baker wrote.

Trotter, however, heard only hypocrisy. In response, he sent this letter to President Wilson and also to every newspaper in Paris:

> Sir: Lawlessness and mob murder against citizens of color continue to take place in our country, the U.S.A. This was so while the world peace agreement was being written. Day before yesterday while the Entente Allies were waiting for the peace treaty to be signed by Germany, a man of color was taken by the mob from the courthouse itself in the State of Missouri and lynched in the courthouse yard after the court had decided that life imprisonment was the punishment due the victim.
>
> Yesterday here in France, in your Memorial Day address at the graves of American soldiers, you declared: "I stand consecrated to the lads sent here to die." Many of them were lads of color, gallant and loyal; fighting for France, for civilization and for world democracy. Will you, therefore, for their sakes and that they shall have not died in vain, grant to their kin and race at home protection of right and life in the world peace agreement? And will you not at once send a special message to Congress recommending that lynching be made a crime against the Federal Government?
>
> Yours, sir, for world democracy, William Trotter.

Back in America on May 30, a mob of unmasked white men in Arkansas abducted a black farm hand, Frank Livingston, from his home and burned him alive. Livingston, a soldier in the Great War, had gotten into an argument with a white farmer about some chickens. The farmer began shooting at Livingston. In self-defense, the black man grabbed an ax and struck the farmer, who died instantly. The farmer's wife then took the gun and shot at Livingston, who then killed her also with his ax. The idea of self-defense never registered with the mob, which, before thrusting Livingston onto a bonfire, tied him to a tree and stabbed him repeatedly with butcher knives and shards of glass from broken liquor bottles.

That day in New York, the play *The Noose* started its fifth week of performances. Set in Georgia, the play tells the story of a prominent lawyer who is absent from his home on Christmas Eve when his wife and their child return from a visit with his mother-in-law. The black handyman tells the wife that a "lynching bee" is taking place that night. She suddenly suspects that her husband might be part of it and she confronts him when he comes home. He admits to being a member of the lynching party. This provokes a fierce debate over the issue of lynchings. The wife soon learns that he was not only part of the mob but also had tied the noose. And she finds out that her husband's political connections, the ones backing him for his planned run for governor, are part of the same gang. She then gives him an ultimatum: either he condemns lynching or she and their child will leave. Taking such a stand will, of course, put an end to his gubernatorial campaign. He cannot give up the political opportunity and so the play ends with the wife and child leaving the house.

Reviewers commented that the play seemed contrived. It was their understanding that wives, mothers, daughters, and sisters did not condemn lynchings; rather they attended them. Besides, one critic wrote, "There are few, if any, cases on record in which happy couples have become separated because the husband was an acknowledged lyncher."

CHAPTER 19

302 Seconds in May

One afternoon in late May, on a small island in the equatorial Atlantic, an eerie half-light covered the landscape, silencing nature. Birds roosted. Flowers folded their petals. And people, in hushed awe, marveled at the spectacle above them where the vast energy of the sun, hidden behind a disk of darkness, was shooting flames a hundred thousand miles above its surface, as if struggling to escape the invasion of a devouring moon. At an encampment on a grassy plain in the northern reaches of the island, only the ticking of a metronome broke the silence, for 302 seconds.

It was May 29, the day of the total eclipse of the sun, a time of anxiety and portent since man had first experienced the phenomenon of moments of night in the midst of day. Perplexing monarchs and terrifying seers, solar eclipses had for centuries been signs of deadly things to come. Charlemagne died in the aftermath of a series of lunar and solar eclipses as did his son Louis, a month after a total solar eclipse on May 5 in the year 840. "These late eclipses in the Sun and Moon portend no good to us," wrote Shakespeare in *King Lear*. By the twentieth century, modern science, in the developed nations, had transformed the image of the phenomenon from the shadows of misfortune and doom to a thing of intrigue and even excitement. Indeed, for astronomers, an eclipse was a sign only of great opportunity.

Above the Isle of Príncipe, the moon would completely cover the surface of the sun for 302 seconds gauged by the sounds of a metronome. But whether the totality would be visible from Príncipe was in doubt, for the morning of May 29 began with the sounds of thunder and pounding rain— an ominous start for a day whose potential for greatness depended upon the weather.

Totality at Príncipe would begin at 2:15 P.M. and if, by then, the skies had cleared and the telescopes, mirrors, and cameras operated properly, Arthur Stanley Eddington and his fellow scientists would be able to prove whether or not the presence of the sun, the brightest star and the strongest gravitational mass known at that time, could have the effect of bending the light of other stars close to it. If the sun did in fact have this power, then, to the observers on earth, stars close to the sun would appear to have shifted from their positions when the power of the sun was absent; the closer to the sun, the greater the shift. If this were to be true, then Einstein's theory that matter could bend space and time, or space-time, as he called it, was right. And this would mean that the universe was not absolute, that it was far more vast than most people had ever imagined. Newton's three-dimensional world would be obsolete and Einstein's four-dimensional space-time would open up limitless possibilities for the future of science.

Eddington knew that the next opportunity to observe a total eclipse of the sun at a time when the sun was positioned so close to the Hyades cluster of bright stars, as it was now, would be 6,585 days, or eighteen years and ten days, from the 29th of May. This was why the British had sent two expeditions from London: one 3,473 miles to Príncipe and another 4,488 miles to the town of Sobral in northeastern Brazil. But on the morning of the 29th neither Príncipe nor Sobral looked very promising.

Since their arrival in late April, the Príncipe team had routinely coped with mosquitoes, monkeys, and rain. They hunted down monkeys that invaded their huts and scampered over every inch of their delicate, state-of-the-art telescope, which had a focal length of eleven feet and four inches. And they learned to develop photographs under tropical conditions, adjusting their machinery to the high temperatures and humidity. But despite all their methodical, disciplined preparations, a cloudy day—even a cloudy five minutes during totality—could ruin their quest. The weather had been rainy consistently since their arrival in April and despite assurances of local inhabitants that the daily pattern of rain would soon end, it didn't. In fact, as the month of May had progressed, the weather had worsened.

On the morning of the 29th, after the thunder subsided, rain continued to fall—in torrents. Only two hours before the metronome began its 302-second countdown did the rain stop. But clouds still covered the sky. It was not until 1:30 P.M., forty-five minutes before totality, that the sky delivered a sliver of the sun. By 2 P.M., a few tiny patches of clear sky burst forth, but the clouds never completely moved on. By 2:15, it looked as if this great adventure in time and space might never come to be.

Eddington persevered, as he was wont to do, his keen eyes and determined heart focused on the last-minute duties leading up to the very first second of totality. No veil of cloud would stop him now. In science, and in all of life, Eddington was steadfast, persisting in his beliefs, "whether it leads to the hill of vision or the tunnel of obscurity," as he wrote in one of his books. In his journal that day, he wrote, "There was nothing for it but to carry out the arranged programme in faith and hope for the best."

Once the eclipse began, Eddington did not watch it, though he did glance upward two times: once to be certain that it indeed had begun and again, 150 or so seconds into the process, to see how much cloud cover remained. He spent most of the crucial 302 seconds changing the sixteen photographic plates in rapid succession while his colleagues stabilized the telescope to avoid shaking. All that he needed to confirm the gravitational deflection of the starlight was one good plate with a clear depiction of the stars and a second plate to confirm the first. At the end of the totality he did not know whether the results would take him through the tunnel of obscurity or to the hill of vision. "The cloud has interfered very much with the star-images," he wrote in his journal. "The cloudy weather upset my plans. Everything shows that our arrangements were quite satisfactory, and with a little clearer weather we should have had splendid results."

Ten minutes after the sun had emerged from the shadow of the moon, the sky cleared. Every cloud disappeared. Eddington sent a telegraph to his close friend and associate Sir Frank Dyson, in London: "Through cloud. Hopeful." And then he and his crew set to work to develop the photographs. They would develop two each night until June 3, revealing the results of 12 plates. The other four would be taken back to England undeveloped because they were a brand that could not be developed in the heat of the equatorial climate.

Three thousand three hundred and nineteen miles west of Príncipe, on the other side of the Atlantic, in Sobral, Brazil, the day had begun with cloud cover, though, unlike Príncipe, the clouds had slowly cleared and the day had grown increasingly sunny. In their preparations, the scientists at Sobral had not worried about rain nor had they given much thought to cloud cover. Their concern had been the heat and its impact on their equipment, and the wind. Sudden gusts were common on the plain where they had set up their observation camp. Thus they had built windscreens. Fortunately, as the eclipse drew near, the patches of sun expanded in size and by the time the momentary night had begun, the sky around the sun was perfectly clear. Winds did not exceed five miles per hour throughout the totality.

In Brazil, the eclipse was a public event. Indeed, eclipse watchers came from everywhere, it seemed, including America, where the Carnegie Department of Terrestrial Magnetism had sent a team to observe the atmospheric electricity and, of course, the terrestrial magnetism of the eclipse. One observatory actually sold tickets to people who wanted access through a powerful telescope. But only the British scientists under the leadership of Dyson and Eddington saw it as a showdown between Newton and Einstein. And considering that the clouds began to break at exactly the right moment and that the sky was completely clear around the sun for four out of the five minutes of totality, Sobral appeared to be a successful observation. After the event, the lead scientists cabled Dyson confidently: "Eclipse splendid."

So eager was the Sobral team to view the results that they began to develop the plates that night. Early in the morning on the 30th, however, they were not so sanguine. Unlike the Príncipe results, all plates showed all identified stars, but the quality of the images in the first four plates was defective. The problem appeared to be the coelostat, a mirror attached to the large astrographic telescope. Instead of building a platform and mounting the telescope in such a way that it could rotate, scientists typically attached rotating mirrors to the telescopes to track the sun. The earlier problems with the mirrors, which the Sobral crew had discovered in April, had been corrected. But, as one of the Sobral men wrote in his journal on the 30th, at 3 A.M., the mirror had again caused problems: "It was found that there had been a serious change of focus, so that, while the stars were shown, the definition was spoilt. This change of focus can only be attributed to the unequal expansion of the mirror through the sun's heat. . . . It seems doubtful whether much can be got from these plates." Fortunately, at the last minute before leaving England, the Sobral team had added another telescope to their equipment, which might produce better results, though the plates would be developed in England.

Perhaps it was fortunate that the Príncipe team did not know what was happening at Sobral; nor did the Sobral scientists know of the clouds over Príncipe. During the six nights following the eclipse, the Príncipe team developed twelve of the photos, in chronological order. The early photos were all good of the sun, "showing a very remarkable prominence," Edding-

ton wrote in his journal. But the cloud cover had blocked out the star images. For days it looked as if the Príncipe observation was a failure. There
were five stars that the scientists had identified as necessary for conducting
their study. Photos of these same five stars had been taken in England in
January in order to compare their positions with the sun and without the
sun. By the fifth night of developing the plates, one or two of the stars
began to appear in the images, indicating that, with time, toward the end
of the totality, the cloud had lightened. And then finally on the fifth night,
June 2, images of all five stars appeared on two of the plates. One was faint
but the other was fairly good. Eddington and his crew measured the
stronger of the two images immediately, placing it in a micrometric measuring machine with the comparison photograph taken in January, film-to-
film, to ascertain the displacement, if any. Einstein's theoretical prediction
was 1.75 seconds of arc—each second of arc corresponding to about
1/1,500 of an inch. The result coming out of the machine at Príncipe that
night was 1.61 seconds of arc.

Eddington could not make a preliminary public announcement of the
results from Príncipe because all the material from Sobral, from Príncipe,
from the check plates needed to be compared and studied for possible errors. The plates would soon be subjected to myriad tests in laboratories
back in England for several months. But for now it appeared that indeed
Eddington would be returning to England with the potential proof of Einstein's theory.

In his journal, Eddington wrote that one of the plates "gave a result
agreeing with Einstein and I think I have got a little confirmation from a
second plate." In his understated way, though, Eddington was thrilled. In
fact, in later years he would refer to the discovery of that first plate, after
days of dismal results, as the greatest moment of his life.

Throughout the dramas at Príncipe and Sobral, Albert Einstein was in
Berlin, perhaps working in his stark attic study where the walls displayed
one picture only, a portrait of Isaac Newton, or perhaps thinking about his
upcoming wedding. That a man whom Einstein had never met had just
gathered the evidence that might confirm his relativity theory and thus up-
stage the man hanging on his wall was not yet known to Einstein. He was
aware of the expeditions to Sobral and Príncipe from his friends in Holland
who communicated with Eddington and Dyson. But he knew nothing of
what had happened on May 29 or what might be evident from the prelimi-

nary examinations of the photographs. By early June he had not heard even a hint of the results. In fact, on the very night that Eddington found the one good plate, Einstein had just returned from the registry office in Berlin, where he was married that day to Elsa Lowenthal, his first cousin. It would be months before Einstein heard any details about the eclipse. As late as September he would write to a colleague in Holland, "so far nothing precise has been published about the expedition's measurements so that even I know nothing about them."

Indeed, Einstein would not hear a word about the findings until late September. And the Royal Society and the Royal Astronomical Society, both in London, would not vote on the authenticity of the findings until November. But waiting for that day and for the most accurate, complete measurements of the plates was not a worry to Einstein, any more than it was to Eddington. Einstein had always been confident that his theory was correct. And Eddington, who would modestly never claim any credit for planning the expeditions, told at least one colleague in later years that in truth he had been so "fully convinced" of the truth of the theory that he had not seen the necessity of the expeditions specifically for that purpose. But the scientific community needed examples of phenomena in the universe that could not be explained by Newton's theories in order to accept and recognize Einstein's. Eddington had another motivation: using science to help unite a fractured world. His hope in leading the expeditions at that time in that year was to temper patriotic anger and to promote human progress through scientific cooperation. As he wrote in his book *Science and the Unseen World,* "I know of no better summary of the present scientific outlook as I conceive it than the statement of one of the greatest living mathematicians Hermann Weyl who wrote that modern science 'makes the world appear more and more as an open one, as a world not closed but pointing beyond itself.' "

Eddington was ever fascinated with large numbers. As a child he learned the 24 x 24 multiplication tables and began a project to count all the words in the Bible. Later, as a teacher and lecturer, he often used large numbers to make a point. Once in a lecture at Oxford he wrote the mass of the sun on the blackboard: 2,000,000,000,000,000,000,000,000,000 tons. And in a book, he began a chapter with the fact that there are 15,747,724,136,275,002,577,605,653,961,181,555,468,044,717,914,527, 116,709,366,231,425,076,185,631,031,296 protons in the universe and the same number of electrons. This became known as "Eddington's number" after his friend the renowned philosopher and mathematician Bertrand Russell publicly asked him if he had computed this himself and Eddington replied that indeed he had, on an Atlantic crossing. But the numbers for which he would achieve his greatest notoriety—marking a turning point in the history of science—were very small: 1.61, the measurement of the good plate at Príncipe, and 1.98, from the best plate at Sobral.

The results of the 1919 expeditions would be subjected to rigorous study and debate. For years to come, there would be questions of accuracy. But what was rarely argued was the power of internationalism in the scientific community. For above all perhaps, Eddington's expeditions proved that progress was possible, despite wars and the prejudices and hatreds that preceded and followed them.

Eddington, confident and brilliant, wrote a collection of quatrains about the great eclipse of 1919, in imitation of the twelfth-century Persian work the Rubáiyát of Omar Khayyám:

> Ah Moon of my Delight far on the wave,
> The Moon of Heaven has reached the Node again
> But clouds are massing in the gloomy sky
> O'er this same Island, where we laboured long—in vain?

> And this I know; whether Einstein is right
> Or all his theories are exploded quite,
> One glimpse of stars amid the Darkness caught
> Better than hours of toil by Candle-light

> Ah Friend! Could thou and I with Lloyds insure
> For Gold this sorry Coelostat so poor,
> Would we not shatter it to bits—and for
> The next Eclipse a trustier Clock procure

> The Clock no question makes of Fasts or Slows,
> But steadily and with a constant Rate it goes
> And Lo! The clouds are parting and the Sun
> A crescent glimmering on the screen—It shows!—It shows!!

Five Minutes, not a moment left to waste,
Five Minutes, for the picture to be traced—
The Stars are shining, and coronal light
Streams from the Orb of Darkness—Oh make haste!

For in and out, above, about, below
'Tis nothing but a magic Shadow show
Played in a Box, whose Candle is the Sun
Round which we phantom figures come and go

Oh leave the Wise our measures to collate
One thing at least is certain, LIGHT has WEIGHT
One thing is certain, and the rest debate—
Light-rays, when near the Sun, DO NOT GO STRAIGHT.

CHAPTER 20

What Happened on R Street

On the night of June 2, the moon was only a sliver in the clear skies above Washington, D.C. For the assistant secretary of the navy, Franklin Roosevelt, and his wife, Eleanor, the evening had begun with a dinner party on Capitol Hill. Four of their five children were away for the night in Hyde Park, New York, visiting Franklin's mother. The fifth, eleven-year-old James, was at home studying for his entrance exams to Groton, a private school. Staying with James was the Roosevelts' cook, Nora. Shortly before midnight, Franklin steered his Stutz into a rented parking garage several blocks from the Roosevelts' house on R Street. Located between Dupont and Sheridan Circles in the fashionable neighborhood of northwest Washington known as the West End, R Street, with its fine three- and four-story brick townhouses, was home to diplomats, congressmen, top-ranking officers in the army and navy, and high-society Washingtonians. The Roosevelts lived at 2131 R Street, across from the home of the new U.S. attorney general, A. Mitchell Palmer, at 2132.

As the young couple began walking toward their home, they heard a thunderous explosion. Franklin commented, in jest, that perhaps the souvenir shell he had brought home from Europe had fallen off the mantel. But then a cacophony of screams and sirens coming from the direction of their house turned their casual walk into a panic-driven run. The sidewalks of R Street, they soon discovered, were covered with leaves and tree branches, shattered glass, burnt scraps of wood, and parts of a human body: a leg on the street in front of their house and another leg near a neighbor's house. Pieces of bloody flesh lay upon the steps of their home. The smell of burning flesh and cordite filled the air. Then there was the sound of Nora crying. Between cries, she exclaimed that the world must be coming to an end. Roosevelt ran into his house and up the staircase, taking two steps at a time. What about James?

When the glass in the front bedroom window had shattered, James jumped out of bed and, though barefoot, ran across the glass-strewn floor to the window to see what had happened. It was there that his father found him. "I'll never forget how uncommonly unnerved Father was when he dashed upstairs and found me standing at the window in my pajamas," James wrote later. "He grabbed me in an embrace that almost cracked my ribs."

Out of the Roosevelts' windows was a scene that few politicians in Washington would ever witness. A bomb had exploded on the front steps of 2132 R Street, Attorney General Palmer's four-story townhouse. It had blown in the entire front of the house. Both sides of the double front door were dangling in pieces, their hinges still hot from the fiery blast. All eleven windows were gone. And debris was everywhere. While Eleanor took James back to bed, Franklin walked across the street to check on his neighbor and to invite the Palmers to his house for the night. But Mrs. Palmer and their daughter did not want to spend the night on R Street. Roosevelt thus drove the two of them to the home of friends several miles away. As Roosevelt was leaving, the attorney general said something to him that he never forgot: "Thank thee Franklin." At home later that night, Franklin told Eleanor, "I never knew before that Mitchell Palmer was a Quaker. He was 'theeing' and 'thouing' me all over the place."

In a June 3 letter to Franklin's mother, Eleanor wrote: "What a wonderful escape for the Palmers. If he had not gone to bed and had still been sitting in his sitting room in his usual chair he would have been blown to bits for there is nothing left of [his] chair."

The Palmers had retired earlier than usual that night, a decision that clearly saved their lives. Palmer told a *New York Times* reporter:

> I had been in the library on the first floor, and had just turned out the lights and gone upstairs with Mrs. Palmer to retire. I had reached the upper floor and undressed, but had not yet retired. I heard a crash downstairs as if something had been thrown against the front door. It was followed immediately by an explosion which blew in the front of the house. The door against which it was thrown leads into the library in which we had been sitting, and the part of the house blown in was in front of the library. The police and other agents who hurried to the residence to make an investigation found in the street in front of the house the limbs of a man who had been blown to pieces by the bomb. No papers were found

and no evidence has yet been uncovered to indicate his identity, and it is not yet known whether the limbs were those of the person who threw the bomb or of a passerby. I hope sincerely that they were not portions of the body of some innocent person passing the house. No one inside the house was injured by the explosion. It cracked the upper part of the first story of the house, blew in the front of the lower floor, broke windows, and knocked pictures from the walls. The damage done was chiefly downstairs.

And he told the *Washington Post*: "Had I remained at that window a few moments longer or had the explosion been timed a little earlier, I would certainly have been killed."

Throughout the neighborhood there was considerable damage. The front doors of the townhouses on both sides of the Palmers' were blown in. The facades with their intricate stonework and Juliet balconies were ruined. Part of a human body crashed into the front window of 2137 R Street, the home of the envoy extraordinary and minister plenipotentiary from Norway, shattered the glass, and then landed on the floor next to a cot where a baby was sleeping. Even in the next block, at 2201 R Street, the home of an Illinois congressman, every front window was smashed. In her June 3 letter, Eleanor Roosevelt described her own house: "The roof of our sun parlor and our front windows on the lower floor don't exist, all our front curtains and shades on all 3 floors were down, plaster fell promiscuously inside and out!"

By 1:30 A.M., on June 3, a Tuesday, police had failed to find the complete head of a man, though the parts of one man's head, or perhaps two, were everywhere, now neatly placed on a sheet of canvas in the Palmers' front yard beneath the shade trees still dripping with blood and fragments of human flesh. With the aid of twenty large searchlights, police had succeeded in finding other pieces of this gruesome puzzle, including what appeared to be the remnants of two left legs; the collar of a shirt, Arrow brand, size fifteen, bearing the mark of a Chinese laundry, and the monogram "KB"; a soft brown fedora from a Philadelphia haberdasher that appeared to be brand-new; shreds of brown socks and brown garters; tattered remnants of a black suit, with a green pin stripe, of an expensive grade of cloth—no label yet found—and also new; a small section of a rubber heel; the butt end of an automatic revolver; and the bottom and sides of one small suitcase made of cloth-mounted pasteboard with cheap brass clasps. "Of the 98-cent variety," police noted.

Scattered across R Street between the Roosevelts' and the Palmers' were about fifty or so leaflets, measuring six by ten inches, printed in black ink on pink paper and resembling those that had been found five months before in Boston around the site of the great molasses disaster. Under a pile of the pink leaflets was an Italian-English dictionary. Entitled "PLAIN WORDS," the flyers, in good English, effectively were declarations of class war and were signed "THE ANARCHIST FIGHTERS."

> Now that the great war, waged to replenish your purses and build a pedestal to your saints, is over, nothing better can you do to protect your stolen millions and your usurped fame, than to direct all the power of the murderous institutions you created for your exclusive defense, against the working multitudes rising to a more human conception of life. . . . Do you expect us to sit down and pray and cry? We know that all you do is for your defense as a class. We know also that the proletariat has the same right to protect itself. Since their press has been suffocated, their mouths muzzled, we mean to speak for them the voice of dynamite, through the mouths of guns. . . . We know how we stand with you and know how to take care of ourselves. Besides, you will never get all of us and we multiply nowadays. Just wait and resign yourselves to your fate, since privilege and riches have turned your heads. Long live social revolution! Down with tyranny!

On that Tuesday morning, by the time most of the residents of R Street would normally be going to work, police were confident that only one man had been blown apart in the explosion. Whether it was the bomber or a passerby, they could not comment—and they did not know—although they speculated that it was the bomber and that he had tripped on the front stoop while positioning the bomb, which then exploded prematurely.

By then, they did know that there had been explosions within the same hour in eight U.S. cities that night, killing two people. The home of the mayor of Cleveland had been dynamited as well as the residences of a municipal judge in Boston; a state legislator in Newtonville, Massachusetts; a silk manufacturer in Paterson, New Jersey; a federal judge and a police inspector in Pittsburgh; and a federal judge in New York City. In Philadelphia, the home of a prominent jeweler was targeted as well as a church, the Rectory of Our Lady of Victory. In New York, the bomb killed a night watchman who had been walking in front of the judge's four-story brownstone at 151 East 61st Street, where the bomb exploded in the vestibule and tore out the entire front of the first and second stories. The other death was the man whose body parts were scattered across the stoops and sidewalks of R Street.

The media consensus, as expressed on the front page of the *New York Times* on Tuesday, was that "the attempt to blow up his [Palmer's] house bore every evidence of having been the work of anarchists or Bolsheviki." An editorial in the *Washington Post* said "The first sample of Soviet government on R Street ought to be highly satisfactory to the American champions of the Bolsheviki." But the who, why, and how of what happened on R Street that Monday night would not be easy to establish. Suspects and motives abounded. All parts of government intelligence communities, from the Military Intelligence Division of the army to local police departments, pledged cooperation with the Department of Justice and the Bureau of Investigation to solve the mystery.

The initial "K.B." on the collar fragment alerted military intelligence operatives to a Cleveland anarchist, Karl Blum, for whom they had an outstanding warrant and who had been missing from the area since Memorial Day. Others in Cleveland, subsequently coming under investigation, included anarchist groups called the Double Trinity and the Group of Avengers. In Pittsburgh, local police investigators and army intelligence agents found the same type of pink leaflets as the ones scattered along R Street and they were particularly interested in a phrase that read "you have deported us." Knowing that most deportees from the United States at that time were Russians, they deduced Russian immigrants were the culprits. Thus they targeted the Union of Russian Workers, rounded up fifteen members, detained them for several days, and placed a covert MID agent in a cell with them. By the summer of 1919 the Union of Russian Workers was mostly a social club and educational center for young, unmarried Russian males, who had little if any interest in revolutionary activity. Once, indeed, it had been a meeting place for radical leaders but after the Revolution most of them had returned to Russia. Although the MID agent gained the trust of his cell mates, what he learned was not helpful. The

Russians knew nothing of the bombing and in fact they thought it was a rather stupid move on the part of anyone seeking change. Such violence would cause a reactionary response by the government, "a bommerang to the cause," so wrote the Pittsburgh intelligence agent in his June 12 report describing his conversations with the jailed Russians.

Radical leaders such as the journalist John Reed and Algernon Lee, the director of the Rand School of Social Science, a socialist school in New York City, agreed. They believed that no radical political group with any sense would have planned the bombings. The kind of social change envisioned by these radicals required the political mobilization of the vast majority of working men and women—not the acts of a small terrorist clique. From their point of view, the night of June 2 had to have been orchestrated by provocateurs who, according to Reed, were "interested in terrifying the ruling class into destroying the radical labor movement in this country." Lee believed that private detective agencies working for unofficial patriotic organizations volunteering to wage a war against radicals and immigrants were behind the bombings. They were all zealous nationalists, in Lee's opinion. They were people who wanted the American public to be afraid enough to demand that their government increase security measures and shut out foreigners. One government agent would eventually go so far as to say, years later, that he believed that the June 2 explosions were designed for the purpose of gaining national attention for the urgent need to enhance and revamp the government's intelligence capabilities. They might have been planned by some fringe group within the government, he suggested—a group wanting to incite Palmer to make drastic moves—or perhaps by one of those independent patriotic groups that had operated covertly during the war and believed themselves to be the nation's watchdogs and saviors. He was of the firm belief that foreign nationals were not the culprits. Even Palmer himself was suspicious to some observers; after all, he *had* retired early that night, breaking his usual routine.

Perhaps the soundest of the theories, and the one that would eventually be substantiated enough to be accepted by some local and national intelligence networks—though never officially confirmed—identified Italian anarchists as the perpetrators. There were clues pointing to Italian anarchists in nearly every location of the June 2 bombings, not just in Washington. The federal judge in New York who had been the target that day, for example, had sentenced two Italian anarchists accused of plotting to blow

up St. Patrick's Cathedral. In Washington, the revolver found at the scene
of the Palmer incident had been purchased by Luigi Calisieri at the Iver
Johnson Sporting Goods House in Boston. Washington agents dispatched
to Boston soon learned that Calisieri had been missing from Boston for several weeks. The motive seemed obvious. The Justice Department in March
had arrested Luigi Galleani, the leader of a group of fifty or sixty Italian anarchists, and was planning to deport him on June 24. The MID, the BI, and
the local authorities suspected that Galleani's followers had orchestrated
the June 2 bombings to protest his arrest and the prosecution of anarchist
leaders in general. In fact, BI agents had been tailing Galleanists since early
1918 as possible suspects in several explosions and bomb threats, including
most recently the mail bombs of late April and the January explosion of the
molasses tank in Boston.

On June 4, when the president was informed of the bombings, he sent a
cablegram to Palmer saying "My heartfelt congratulations on your escape. I
am deeply thankful that the miscreants failed in all their attempts." High up
in the Wilson administration, perhaps as high as the president himself, it
was well known that a rather small conspiracy of anarchists, the Galleanists,
who were no more than fifty strong, or perhaps another group of about the
same size, was likely behind the recent bombings. Even the president's doctor knew something of the motives for the latest violence. On June 4 in
Paris, Dr. Grayson wrote in his diary that the incidents were "apparently
being carried on in an effort to force the Government to stop its prosecution
of the anarchistic leaders and the IWW, who have tried to terrorize the
country." And, as early as June 7, the New York Times reported that the Justice Department had identified the man who blew himself up in Palmer's
front yard. He was, in fact, an Italian anarchist who belonged to a group
that was "well known to the Federal and local authorities," the Galleanists.

In short, three main theories would emerge from those days in early
June. First, American radicals and socialists would believe that the bombings were the work of agents provocateurs designed to bring on government repression of all groups seeking change in America. They would
continue to hammer away at the point that such individual acts of violence
and terror did not serve their aims or benefit their movement. In the second theory, the federal law enforcement agencies continued to build their
case identifying the Galleanists, the anarcho-terrorists whose motive was
retaliation for the prosecution of their leaders.

But before the case was resolved, the American public would be exposed to a third theory: that what happened on R Street on June 2 was one act of a far larger drama, a nationwide conspiracy of radicals to overthrow the U.S. government. In fact, the Justice Department, in sharing information about the culprits with the *New York Times* on June 6, actually for the first time linked the Italian anarchists to Bolshevism in America, saying that the Italians were "known to be sympathetic with the ideals of the Bolsheviki." Hence, the Palmer bombing, though clearly thought by most investigators to be an act of targeted retaliation by a specific group, became an expansive plot tied to the new enemy, Bolshevism. As one historian later wrote, "Despite strong suspicions that the bombings were the work of a small group of anarchists who were retaliating against government policies, Justice Department and Bureau officials sought to portray the attacks as the first step in a nationwide radical uprising."

There was no question that the bombings were real and terrifying for everyone in America, but those who had the strongest suspicions and the best access to information, those who were the closest to the truth, those who had the authority to quell the rising fears, did not do so. Instead, they allowed the scariest reel of all to run through the mind of every American, a narrative of death and destruction, a doomsday tale of a vast radical conspiracy, a story that would become more and more impossibly entangled with distortions and lies, forcing politicians and public officials to respond, encouraging opportunists to surface, and adding act after act to the dangerous play that in the end might hurt more individuals than the heinous schemes of the Italian anarchists. "I remember the morning after my house was blown up," Attorney General Palmer told a Senate committee. "I stood in the middle of the wreckage of my library with Congressmen and Senators, and without a dissenting voice they called upon me in strong terms to exercise all the power that was possible . . . to run to earth the criminals who were behind that kind of outrage."

The night of June 2 was the opening act in a sweeping drama of paranoid politics, extravagant patriotism, and spiraling fears that would one day be known as the Red Scare of 1919, not the Revolution of 1919.

CHAPTER 21

War of a Different Sort

A. Mitchell Palmer was a Quaker but all the "theeing and thouing" of the night of June 2 was not about returning to his Quaker roots and sensibilities. Rather it was about fear, which would soon be translated into a new war in America—a war against the "other." Reds. Radicals. Liberals. Labor Leaders. Union Men and Women. Anarchists. Socialists. Immigrants. Dissidents of every variety.

Before June of 1919, it might be argued that Palmer had not been demonstrably intolerant. And for a man in Palmer's post, which was effectively that of the nation's disciplinarian, to appear to be tolerant at a time when intolerance was in vogue was bold. But considering Palmer's plan to enter the 1920 presidential contest, any public display of tolerance would have to be short-lived. The May Day "riots" coupled with the June 2 bombings caused a sea change in public sentiment. Those events, the *New York Times* wrote in May, "convinced members of the House that the policy of tolerance which has marked the attitude of the Department of Justice must be dropped for one of vigorous prosecution if the Bolshevist movement is to be held in check."

Although in March Palmer had stated publicly that he was determined to replace the wartime Espionage Act so that the Justice Department would be armed with the legal power to "proceed against those plotting against the Government," he had also resisted extreme security measures in the face of such a threat. He had, for example, taken a stand against the American Protective League, rejecting the persistent pleas of businessmen and major APL contributors to reinstate its relationship with the Justice Department.

In March, Palmer told the press that espionage conducted by private individuals or organizations was "entirely at variance with our theories of government, and its operation in any community constitutes a grave menace." As if retaliating, APL members intensified their campaign to regain their wartime status as America's secret army of protectors. One tactic was to distribute widely the book that told their story, *The Web* by Emerson Hough. While the 511-page book appeared to be a tribute to an organization that once *was*, it was more a rallying cry for what again *could be*. Hough, the APL's official historian and a writer of western novels, advocated a new strategy for America that consisted of "selective immigration, deportation of un-Americans, and denaturalization of 'disloyal' citizens and anarchists. We must purify the source of America's population and keep it pure." Immigrants "form a body incompatible with the healthy growth of this country," wrote Hough. "It is time for another oath, sworn indeed for the protection of America."

In the spring, the APL's lobbying efforts appeared to be paying off when a resolution was introduced in the House to extend Congress's gratitude to "all members of the American Protective League for services rendered the Government during the war." At the same time, two senators wrote to Palmer recommending that he reinstate the services of two former Leaguers. Palmer declined. And he turned down a request from Ohio's Governor James M. Cox for the APL files in Washington about wartime German propaganda in the Ohio school system, showing how productive and useful the league had been and revealing the names of potential enemies in Ohio. In fact, Palmer told a Cleveland audience that the APL was unnecessary, that the U.S. Secret Service could do the job, and that APL reports on civilians "are not wanted." Although the *New York Times* chided Palmer for his stand, saying that the new attorney general was "perhaps a little hasty in telling the patriotic and defensive societies that their help in guarding the Republic is neither needed nor welcome," Palmer persisted.

During his first months in office, Palmer indeed appeared to be cautious. He reviewed wartime Espionage Act cases and urged attorneys general throughout the nation to review cases in their districts with the intent of dropping some. Although he did issue new indictments against several IWW members, he also ordered literally hundreds of suits to be dismissed. Out of the 239 individuals serving time under the Espionage Act, one hundred were granted clemency by President Wilson, at Palmer's behest. Further, in April, he granted the release from parole restrictions of more than ten thousand enemy aliens arrested during the war. For a while, he even considered amnesty for Eugene Debs, the famous socialist sentenced to ten years in prison for supposedly violating the Espionage Act.

Reexamining the issue of Debs that spring, Palmer requested that government officials in the case comment on the charges, the trial, and the severity of the sentence. Should Debs be pardoned? Should his sentence be commuted? The judge who presided over the trial said no to both. Others concurred with the judge, including the special assistant to Palmer's predecessor, who was known as an advocate for civil liberties. At the end of March when Debs's advocates' petitions had reached President Wilson in Paris, Palmer, at the request of Wilson, met with the president's secretary, Joseph Tumulty, to discuss the issue. Attached to Wilson's request was the damning comment that he doubted "the wisdom and public effect" of pardoning Debs. By that time Palmer had received unanimous feedback against clemency or commutation. Although Palmer had begun his examination of the case with the possible intent of freeing Debs, by the spring of 1919 Palmer's heightened awareness of the politically hot nature of the issue prompted him to tell Tumulty that it was "imperative" to deny amnesty to Debs.

The Debs case revealed how the politics of popular hostility toward radicals was gradually closing in on Palmer that spring. America had grown addicted to the war mentality. Palmer, looking at the cards in his hand, wanted to win the game of pleasing America. And when the Red Menace suddenly became real to him on the night of June 2, Palmer saw an opportunity as if the very light of the explosion had shown him the way. Winning the war on radicals would earn him the power and the position he so ambitiously sought. Red hunting could be the path to the White House.

In the aftermath of the June bombings, Secretary of War Newton Baker, as a fellow member of the Wilson cabinet, wrote a note to Palmer expressing shock and sympathy. In a June 9 response to Baker, Palmer wrote that he planned to use his post "as a means of putting an end forever to those lawless attempts to intimidate and injure, if not destroy, organized government in this country." His first moves were to appoint new people to the most powerful posts within his department and to ask Congress for a bigger budget.

For weeks Palmer had been planning to restructure the Justice Department and bring in new people. After June 2, he would be doing it under a very big national spotlight and choosing men whose attitudes he now shared. He appointed the former head of the Secret Service, William J. Flynn, to be the new director of the Bureau of Investigation. Flynn was the nation's "foremost expert on radicalism," Palmer boasted to the press, and "an anarchist chaser." Flynn's new assistant was Frank Burke, who had been the head of the Secret Service's New York office and of its Russian Division during the war. Palmer's own new assistant who would be in charge of the bureau's investigations was Francis P. Garvan, a former assistant district attorney in New York, Palmer's chief investigator in the Alien Property Bureau and his successor briefly as alien property custodian. And there was another appointment in the works, to be announced in the coming weeks: the director of Palmer's new unit in the bureau, the Radical Division. This new department, which would later be known as the General Intelligence Division, was assigned to compile facts and figures about radicals and coordinate such intelligence with that of other government agencies. With the right director, the new division could play a major role in fighting radicalism. Palmer already had someone in mind: a twenty-four-year-old lawyer in the Justice Department, J. Edgar Hoover.

On June 13, Palmer stood before the subcommittee of the House Committee on Appropriations, identified the bombings as "a combined and joint effort of the lawless classes of the population to injure, if not destroy, the Government," and asked for $500,000 to be added to his budget of $1.5 million and to be used specifically for investigating "ultraradicals or Bolshevists or class-war agitators." He told the committee, "We have received so many notices and got so much information that it has almost come to be accepted as a fact that on a certain day, which we have been advised of, there will be another . . . [attempt] to rise up and destroy the government in one fell swoop."

In substantiating the need for the $2 million budget, Garvan told the Senate subcommittee of the Committee on Appropriations that "the Russian Bolsheviki are pouring money in here at the rate of that much a month." Part of the proof, he said, was that since the Armistice there were now 450 radical publications in America, an increase of 150. Was there an organized effort to destroy the government in America? someone asked Garvan. "Certainly," he said. Adding to the aria of fear, Flynn declared that the bombings were "connected with Russian Bolshevism aided by Hun [German] money."

A week or so later, Garvan spoke to the same Senate subcommittee, this time confessing that he could not predict what the radicals might do or when: "It all depends on what breaks out in the country. Suppose a July

Fourth celebration broke out throughout the country. It all depends. You can not tell from day to day. . . . There is a great deal of talk to that effect."

The Republican Senate was not convinced. One senator asked Garvan, "Do you think if we increased this to $2,000,000 you could get one single bomb thrower? I do not mean in the papers; I mean actually get him?" Congress approved only an additional $100,000 for a total Justice Department budget of $1.6 million—and Palmer would return soon with a new request for funds based on confidential information about future bombings.

While Palmer and his assistants were sharing their fears with Congress, Marlborough Churchill, the head of the Military Intelligence Division of the U.S. Army, was standing before the Senate Military Affairs Committee seeking funds. Churchill also wanted money to prepare for what he argued was the imminent attempt by Reds to overthrow the U.S. government. To strengthen his argument he presented a map compiled by the head of the MID in New York, Captain John Trevor. A Harvard graduate, as was Churchill, and a New York attorney, Trevor, the man who had detained Sandburg back in December, was intensely eager to remobilize the intelligence force in New York. Certainly what was called his "zone map" would help fund the remobilization. The map pinpointed the typical meeting places of radicals in New York City. Over this, Trevor laid another map that showed the distribution of foreigners in New York, including those born in the United States with one or both parents of foreign origin. The collated color-coded maps then revealed zones of "trouble." The zone map helped earn the MID $400,000 from Congress to fight radicals.

On June 3, a *Washington Post* editorial called upon the APL to restore its network of volunteers to protect America against future bombings. Concurring with the *Post*, a professor from the University of Louisville sent an urgent letter to the attorney general asking that in light of the events of the past week, wouldn't it be "wise" to recall the APL "to assist your department in ferreting out this *new menace* that threatens the Peace and Security of our country?"

Palmer never gave the "APL official permission to resurrect its eager regiments of volunteer agents. He never ordered the APL to resume sending surveillance reports to the government, typically to the nearest branch of military intelligence or the local U.S. attorney's office. He didn't have to. The APL did it themselves. That June in Chicago, for example, an APL veteran offered his services and those of fifty-five operatives to the local MID office, whose director found it a "great pleasure" to receive such an offer and asked that the volunteers report to duty with a car for the next ten days when they would be called upon to report on radical meetings in the Chicago area. In Minneapolis, the former APL head used the old APL letterhead, which claimed government status for the group, to send information to the Justice Department regarding immigrant groups and their activities. And in New York City, APL members were finding plenty of opportunities to reconnect with the government, especially through the Lusk Committee. Helpful in restoring this bond was William McDermid, a former APL state inspector in New Jersey and the brother-in-law of New York state senator Clayton Lusk. McDermid was able to contact hundreds of APL veterans and enlist their aid for the Lusk Committee—mainly investigating, spying, and raiding.

On the 12th of June, after months of preparations and surveillance, a brigade of private detectives, volunteer investigators, and Red baiters—all in the name of the Lusk Committee—raided the Soviet Bureau, where Ludwig C. A. K. Martens had been trying to do business with American companies since January. In charge of the raid was the inexorable Archibald Stevenson, whom one editorial writer described as "the traducer of Miss Jane Addams and other reputable persons whom he gazetted in the public press as sympathizers with Germany [in January]."

Stevenson and the Lusk Committee claimed that Martens's bureau was the source of funding for the imminent revolution threatening New York. In the application for a search warrant, one of the investigators described the Soviet Bureau as a source of subversive literature distributed nationwide. Thus, on the afternoon of the 12th, at precisely 3:15 P.M., dozens of investigators, committee officials, and even one British Secret Service agent invaded the bureau, cutting phone lines, detaining all members of the staff, and taking everything out of the offices. Cash boxes, desks, briefcases, file cabinets, even photographs of staff members and their families were taken, although publications were the only items the search warrant authorized them to seize. Martens and his assistant were escorted to city hall under intense police guard and subjected to almost four hours of questioning during which they were not allowed to communicate with their lawyers. In the days that followed, Russia's commissar for foreign affairs issued a statement saying that he hoped that Russia would not "be compelled reluctantly to take reprisals against American citizens to be found on Russian territory." The acting secretary of state, W. B. Phillips, then cautioned the Bolshevik government about harming U.S. citizens. Such conduct would certainly cause "an overwhelming public sentiment of indignation against the authorities at Moscow."

In the aftermath of the raid, Martens would try to continue his quest to forge economic ties between the new Russian government and the United States. But most of his time was consumed with legal proceedings. So concerned were his new trading partners about the surveillance they would have to endure if they associated with the Soviet Bureau that they quickly vanished, with little collective memory of the few months in 1919 when they explored and indeed sought out the vast market potential of Russia.

The Lusk Committee refocused its lens of suspicion and its plans for future raids—this one only ten days later—on the Rand School of Social Science, believed to be the place where the revolution was being planned. Established in 1906 by the Socialist Party of America with funds bequeathed by the late abolitionist Carrie D. Rand, the school, located in lower Manhattan, had about six thousand students. Its director, the socialist Algernon Lee, had publicly called Stevenson "the greatest maker of bolsheviki in America." The Lusk Committee boasted that its June 21 raid was "the biggest raid of the kind in the history of the city." Among the raiders were forty or more APL members. In the days ahead the school's lawyer, S. John Block, told the New York Times that after what had happened in New York in the past week, it was possible, he firmly believed, "that people may be goaded to extreme action in this country by a disregard of their rights by those who are in power and who do not know how to exercise that power."

But who was listening to S. John Block? Certainly not Palmer's advisers, who were tightly focused on the concept of a revolution erupting in New York City on July 4. Bureau director Flynn called an urgent meeting of the police chiefs in major cities nationwide to alert them to the danger, which, like the June bombings, could be widespread. With the aid of Assistant Attorney General Garvan, Flynn devised a cooperative plan for federal, state, and local law enforcement agencies in New York to guard the city and to stop the revolution. At least eleven thousand policemen in New York would be mobilized for the twenty-four hours of Independence Day, to secure buildings, safeguard courthouses and judges, and watch prominent citizens. It wasn't clear exactly when the disaster would happen, though the Fourth of July seemed the most likely time. If not then, on some other day that summer, so said Palmer's prophets, Flynn and Garvan.

What was clear, though, was that the soldiers of one war were coming home—nearly two million by the end of June—but not to the land of peace and comfort that had consumed their wartime dreams. For now, at home, a war of a different sort was gearing up.

In those first six months of 1919, America the victor of the Great War had begun to see itself as America the victim of a dangerous conspiracy. The nation was not demobilizing for peace, but in fact preparing for the next heroic campaign. Fortunately, far above the swirl of paranoia, new and real heroes would emerge.

CHAPTER 22

Thrilling Feats

One June morning, as the sun rose over the banks of the Newfoundland coast casting ribbons of light across a small, rugged landing field near St. John's, Lieutenant Arthur Brown watched a large black cat amble under the wing of an airplane. It was the plane he was scheduled to fly that day, if and when the now gusting westerly winds lessened. As the cat turned around and retraced its steps, walking a second time under the same wing, Lieutenant Brown seemed troubled as if he feared the dire portent of its presence. But Brown's furrowed brow and sullen stare were not about black cats or bad luck. In fact, stowed away in a small cupboard at the tail of the plane were two more black cats nestled between bundles of white heather given to Brown by friends and colleagues for the journey ahead. What worried Brown was the 40 knot half-gale blowing straight out of the west. The uneven gusts had been strong enough to delay the flight that he, the navigator, and Captain John Alcock, the pilot, so long had planned: the first nonstop flight across the Atlantic.

The two men had arrived at St. John's by ship on the 13th of May. Another ship carrying their disassembled flying machine landed in Newfoundland on May 26. They had hoped to embark on their 1,980-mile crossing at the beginning of the full phase of the moon on Friday, the 13th of June. A coincidence of 13s caused quite a stir in the local and national media and among superstitious readers on both sides of the Atlantic. Alcock and Brown were either heavily cursed or charmed, so wrote several papers, considering the black cats on board and the uncanny list of 13s in their lives. Even the date that their plane arrived was a multiple of the number 13. Traveling with them from England were 13 mechanics to work on the plane, which was a Vimy bomber that happened to be the 13th of its type to be built by the Vickers company in Weybridge, England. The bomber had been completed on February 13 of 1919, and weighed about 13,000 pounds. And there was more. In 1913, the *Daily Mail*, a London newspaper, had announced its contest and handsome reward—now

£10,000 or $50,000—for the first nonstop flight across the Atlantic. In 1913 also, Captain Alcock had won his first flying competition. Add to this that during the war Alcock had spent 13 months as a prisoner of war in Turkey after being shot down after a bombing raid.

"Vimy Transocean Team Not Afraid of No. 13," a *New York Times* head-line read. The *Times* worked the angle, adding that the Vimy's wingspread was 67 feet—digits that added up to 13—and it carried 871 gallons of fuel, which was close to 67 times 13. Alcock's comment for the *Times* was, "If only we are lucky enough to get away by the full moon on the 13th." On the 14th, they were still on the ground.

Neither Alcock nor Brown relied on luck and neither feared the lack of it, although Alcock later admitted that the number 13 might be lucky for him and both used the word "lucky" when talking about their experiences in the Great War, especially about surviving many months as prisoners. Alcock also believed that he was lucky to catch what he called "the flying fever" during the first decade of the twentieth century. He once told a *New York Times* reporter that he intended to "keep on flying indefinitely" and that there was nothing in his life that he cared about as much as flying—a passion that began in his childhood.

As a teenager, Alcock, born in Manchester, England, in 1892, wanted to fly hot-air balloons and even designed several made of silk and bamboo. When he was eighteen he apprenticed to a French aviator, Maurice Ducrocq, studied aerodynamics, plane construction and design, and ex-perimented with gliders. By the time he was nineteen, Alcock was flying. Two years later he won second place in one of the more famous of the many flying competitions of the era, from London to Manchester.

Blond, six feet tall, and sturdy, Alcock was an affable, outgoing man who was also humble and unpretentious. He was well known in early avia-tor circles for his talents as a pilot and as a bold designer of planes. He was also notorious for his daring spontaneity. One night in 1913 while standing on the landing field of the Brooklands, the flying center outside London, Alcock commented to a friend about what a great night it was for flying, though for him most nights were good for flying. The friend agreed about that particular night and asked Alcock if he would take him for a spin. The spin turned out to be the first cross-country flight with a passenger at night.

During the war, Alcock joined the Royal Naval Air Service and was stationed in the east on Lemnos Island in the Aegean Sea, off the

Dardanelles. There, he designed the first successful triplane night-fighter and ran two bombing raids a month. During one raid, he dropped an entire ton of bombs—thirty-six in all—on the town of Adrianople, destroying a fort, an ammunition train, and at least three thousand houses. He was also the first of the Allied bombers to hit Constantinople (later known as Istanbul). He had recently gained the record for long-distance raids when, in October of 1917, on a return flight he lost an engine and was forced to land on the Sea of Marmara. Unable to find the patrol boat that was supposed to rescue him, he was captured and taken prisoner. After having flown one thousand hours before the war, 2,926 hours as an instructor in the early part of the war, and five hundred hours on the front, Alcock was grounded. He remained in captivity until November of 1918 after the signing of the Armistice. To endure, he spent all the time he could working on a plan to achieve what was then his dream: to fly across the Atlantic Ocean. After the war, Alcock took a job as a test pilot at Vickers Aircraft Company and persuaded his employers to enter one of their flying machines in the *Daily Mail*'s competition.

Arthur Brown was a reserved, quiet, and studious sort with prematurely graying hair, a wiry build, very blue eyes, and, like Alcock, quite handsome. He was an American citizen, born in 1886 in Scotland while his parents, then living in England, were on holiday in Glasgow. His grandfather had fought in the Union Army at Gettysburg and his great-great-grandmother had led a nurses corps during the Revolutionary War. His father, a mechanical engineer and an associate of the inventor of the automatic engine, George Westinghouse, moved the family to England from Pennsylvania to introduce the manufacture of Westinghouse engines. They settled in Manchester, where Brown spent much of his childhood, though he never knew Alcock. After working as an apprentice at the Westinghouse Electric and Manufacturing Company, Brown believed he was destined to be an engineer and by the time the war broke out in 1914 he had even been published in several engineering journals. Although an American citizen, Brown enlisted in September of 1914 in what was called the University and Public Schools Battalion. After serving in the trenches at Ypres and on the Somme, he transferred to the Royal Flying Corps, was shot down over Vendin la Vielle in France, recovered in England, then returned to the front, was shot down again and taken into captivity in Germany for fourteen months, followed by nine months in Switzerland. During his captivity, he studied aerial navigation.

When the wartime ban on aerial competition to cross the Atlantic was lifted, Brown hoped that one of the numerous firms preparing to compete would hire him. Despite his expertise in navigation, he now had a lame leg, which diminished his chances of finding a job flying. And then one day in the early spring of 1919 he went to Weybridge to the Vickers Company for a job interview. During Brown's interview, Captain Alcock, who had been with Vickers since his return to England, entered the room. It was then that Brown learned that Vickers was one of the companies planning to enter a plane in the transocean competition. Alcock was the chosen pilot. After a brief introduction, Brown revealed his ideas for the navigation of aircraft during long overseas flights—and all that he had analyzed so thoroughly while a prisoner of war. What an odd coincidence that each of the men had spent their time in captivity studying the challenges of a transatlantic flight and also that they had both grown up in Manchester, although they had never met. And so it was that Alcock then talked to Brown about coming to work for Vickers and about being his partner and aerial navigator in the transatlantic conquest. That was in late March.

On May 3, they set sail from Southampton on the *Mauretania* to Halifax, Nova Scotia, on to Port aux Basques, and then by way of the Reid Newfoundland Railway, they traveled to St. John's and checked into the Cochrane Hotel. Their Vickers flying machine, with its two Rolls-Royce aero engines and sturdy undercarriage, its many feet of hollow, seamless steel tubing, its eight tanks, its 166-foot wings, cockpit, throttles, control wheel, and leather cushions, was shipped in crates to St. John's ten days later.

In April, May, and June of 1919, the Cochrane was one of St. John's foremost hotels and surely the city's most famous. Operating for nearly fifty years on the corner of Cochrane and Gower Streets, the thirty-two-room Victorian Cochrane was the place where Guglielmo Marconi stayed when he sent the first transatlantic wireless message from Newfoundland's Signal Hill in 1901. In 1919, the Cochrane was effectively an international club for daring young aviators. What the Hotel Crillon was to the Paris peace treaty, the Cochrane was to the history of aviation. Despite Newfoundland's hilly, rough terrain, which was hardly suited for landing fields, the area surrounding St. John's was considered the ideal place for takeoffs as it was the easternmost reach of the North American continent. New-foundland to Ireland was the shortest distance between the two conti-nents.

By the time Alcock and Brown had arrived, the Cochrane was head-quarters for several teams of aviators entering the *Daily Mail* competition as well as newspaper reporters from America, Canada, Britain, Australia, France, and Italy covering what they hoped would be front-page stories about flying firsts. Shortly after their arrival, two more teams eager to win the *Daily Mail* prize checked in at the Cochrane.

So unusually busy were the skies over Newfoundland in May and June that a concerned citizen wrote this letter to the *St. John's Daily News*: "Sir—As one who protested against the bicycle nuisance twenty years ago, I desire to join in the present agitation to prevent motor cars from using the public roads, covering pedestrians with dust and interfering with their comfort generally and I also wish to voice a strong protest against airplanes being allowed to fly over the city of St. John's frightening our poultry and thereby interfering with the supply of eggs, so important during our present shortage of food. This nuisance is only just beginning and now is the time to stop it before the airplane becomes as great a pest as the bicycle and the dreadful motor car."

The bold men and their flying machines were indeed among the hottest news sensations of the year. In May, there had been three American teams at the Cochrane, all of which departed from Newfoundland on May 6 intending to be the first to fly the Atlantic. In his American naval sea-plane, the NC-4, American Lieutenant Commander Albert C. Read had achieved the honor on May 31, arriving in Plymouth, England, via stops at the Azores and Lisbon. And while Alcock and Brown were preparing for their attempt at what they hoped would be the next spectacular feat—a nonstop flight to Ireland—the great British dirigible R-34 was planning a June departure from England for an unprecedented round-trip voyage to America.

In the running for the *Daily Mail* prize for the first nonstop transatlantic flight were five teams altogether. Whether any of them succeeded, it was abundantly clear that someone soon was going to prove that it was possible to fly between the two continents nonstop within the time representing the limit of human endurance. The transatlantic airways were opening up and the talk at the Cochrane was that it would someday be possible, perhaps even in 1919, for airplanes to travel between England and America with passengers.

The force behind the prize was the *Daily Mail*'s editor, Lord Northcliffe, who in 1909 began to offer rewards for aviators achieving ever-increasing distances: £100 for the first nonstop flight of a quarter of a mile outward and back again and £1,000 for the first crossing of the English Channel, both achieved in 1909. In 1913, Lord Northcliffe announced that £10,000 would be given to the first to fly across the Atlantic within a time limit of seventy-two hours. During the war the paper stopped the competition, and after the war, when the *Daily Mail* resumed the contest, engine design had improved because of the war, enough to enable someone to actually achieve what Northcliffe had boldly dared. "Being myself a spectator of early attempts at flight, I realized that what was wanted was tangible encouragement; also that attention should be focused upon a science of such profound importance," Lord Northcliffe wrote in 1920. "The prizes given by my journals were devised, therefore, to these two ends—to encourage the flying man and to interest the public."

The first of the five *Daily Mail* contenders in Newfoundland took off from St. John's on May 18 in a single-engine biplane. Soon after takeoff, however, over the Grand Banks, the plane flew into dense fog, then heavy rain squalls, and a forceful north wind that forced the plane south of its course, which the team's navigator had mapped out above a steamship line. It also caused the plane to use far more fuel than anticipated for the early hours of the flight. The plane crash-landed not halfway across the Atlantic on the heaving waves of a storm at sea. A small cargo vessel traveling from Mexico to Perth happened to be nearby and to see the two men and their flying machine. At the Cochrane Hotel, where everyone was certain they had perished and where they had learned that King George V had already sent a message to the pilot's wife expressing his sadness at the news of the death of her husband, the news of the rescue of both pilot and navigator on May 15 was a relief. The next attempt from St. John's crashed on takeoff. Coming up in June would be Alcock and Brown.

Alcock and Brown's attempt was unique in several ways. For one, on board would be a mailbag containing three hundred private letters, each of which had a special stamp provided by the postal officials at St. John's. If the flight succeeded, this would be the first international airmail delivery.

Disregarding the shipping routes that others had followed, Brown mapped out a crow-line course from St. John's, aiming for the middle of Galway Bay in Ireland and landing very near to the town of Clifden. It was the nearest possible route to a straight line between St. John's and Galway Bay. Their plane, the Vickers Vimy, with its two 350 horsepower Eagle Mark VIII Rolls-Royce engines, had been designed during the war for long-range bombing; its purpose was to bomb Berlin. But the war ended before it could be used. It was thought that the Vickers Vimy had a range of 2,500 miles. Until the flight of Alcock and Brown, the stunning Vickers creation had received little or no attention.

While the crated Vickers Vimy sailed for Newfoundland in mid-May, Alcock and Brown spent their days looking for a stretch of land that would be suitable for takeoff and their evenings playing cards with the other competitors staying at the Cochrane. What they needed for a temporary airstrip was a level field measuring about one hundred yards wide and at the very least three hundred yards long. If they had to contend with strong winds, they would need to add two hundred yards to the length. In Newfoundland, finding such land was not an easy task, especially in the St. John's vicinity, where woods were common, soil was soft, and any cleared grounds were uneven, rolling, and dotted with boulders. The low supply and the high demand, considering the number of aviators currently in the St. John's area, made finding such fields very competitive. By the time Alcock and Brown began their search in mid-May much of the choice land had been claimed by competing fliers. And then the inevitable began to happen: owners of the few appealing plots began to ask for money for their use. Once when Alcock and Brown thought they had found an ideal place, the landowner demanded £5,000 plus an indemnity for any damage and the cost of preparing it.

When their plane arrived on the 26th, they had not yet found their aerodrome. Now, in addition to the land search, they began the stressful job of reassembling the plane, working twelve to fourteen hours a day with a team of mechanics and volunteers. So intense was the task that even newspaper reporters from the *Daily Mail*, the *New York Times*, and the *New York World* volunteered their labor. What was a standard Vickers Vimy bomber had to be altered for the journey. The bombs and bombing apparatus were taken out and replaced by extra gasoline tanks. The first of the tanks to be used and thus emptied was designed in the shape of a boat and could be used as a raft, in the event of a descent onto water. The cockpit was redesigned so that the pilot and navigator sat side by side rather than in a row, allowing the space behind the pilot's seat to be used for another tank. Tantamount to rebuilding a plane, the project attracted tourists who gathered by the dozens each day to watch and who became so curious and intrusive that the mechanics built an enclosure to protect the machine.

By the 6th of June, the Vickers Vimy was ready for testing and Alcock and Brown had finally reserved a suitable location for their aerodrome: a series of four fields near a place called Mundy's Pond. Although hilly in parts, the fields together provided about four hundred yards for takeoff. The price was high but after some negotiating, they got the land and they hired thirty workers to build a bump-free runway by blasting boulders, slicing off the tops of hills, and filling in the rugged dips. By then too, Lieutenant Brown had set up a receiving station on the roof of the Cochrane where he could practice sending and receiving wireless messages from the Vickers Vimy's new radio set.

On the 9th and 12th, pilot and navigator ran test flights. The machine was nearly ready except for the highly acclaimed wireless, which would not sputter a single sound. There were other snags, all of which prevented the planned takeoff on Friday the 13th. That night Alcock and Brown went to bed at 7 P.M. while the mechanics worked on the wireless and the rest of the plane all night long.

At 3:30 A.M. on the 14th, everyone met at the aerodrome. The plane and its crew were ready to go. The tanks were filled with 870 gallons of gasoline and forty gallons of oil. The food—a dozen sandwiches, chocolate bars, malted milk, two thermos flasks of coffee, a flask of brandy, bottles of water, and stores of emergency rations—was packed. The mascots—the two black cats, named Lucky Jim and Twinkletoe—were stowed away. In the cockpit was a small pocket flash lamp in case the cockpit lighting system gave out, a sextant clipped to the dashboard, a drift indicator under Brown's seat, a distance calculator on the side of the fuselage, charts on the floor of the cockpit, an electric flashlight, a pistol with red and white flares, and the battery for heating Alcock's and Brown's electric suits. In his wallet, Brown carried a tiny silk American flag, which his fiancée had given to him. And in Alcock's pocket was a silver kewpie doll from his girlfriend, who also gave him two yarn dolls, Ran-Tan-Tan and Olivette, that he hung by his seat in the cockpit. The only thing missing was a box of extra life-jackets that, sent by a U.S. company, had ended up by accident at the Bank of Montreal, which then stored the unopened box in its basement, mistaking it for office supplies.

At first light as Brown was staring at the black cat under the wing of his plane, the meteorological officer handed him the latest weather report: strong westerly wind. Conditions otherwise fairly favorable. As the morning progressed, the wind did not diminish. Neither did Alcock's and Brown's determination, despite the wind. "We had definitely decided to leave on the 14th, if given half a chance," Brown later wrote, "for at all costs we wanted to avoid a long period of hope deferred while awaiting ideal conditions."

At 2 P.M., seated under the wings of their plane, they ate lunch, still waiting for the hefty gusts to subside. Finally, two hours later, although nothing had changed, Alcock and Brown decided they must go. They donned their electrically heated clothing, their Burberry overalls, their helmets and their gloves, and climbed into the cockpit. There were few reporters and no tourists to watch their dramatic ascent, taking off against winds with gusts as strong as 35 knots on the still somewhat bumpy four-hundred-yard runway in an airplane that now, with an extra load of fuel, weighed close to five tons. With such high winds, no one believed the flight would begin that day.

Their meteorological expert had assured them that the wind would drop off to no more than 20 knots as soon as they were a hundred miles out to sea and then the weather would clear. Armed with that hope they pointed the plane westward and prepared to leave. The wind, coming out of the west, was too strong for the structure of their plane to permit them to take off to the east, as planned. Worse still, the plane, if pointed eastward, would face downhill—a daunting challenge with such high winds. For more than three hundred yards the plane lurched and wobbled, threatened every second by sudden upward gusts. Lifting off the ground at 4:17 P.M. they headed straight into the wind until they reached eight hundred feet and then turned toward the sea, reaching 1,200 feet by 4:28, at which time they left the coast of Newfoundland. Within the first few minutes of the flight, Brown spoke to Alcock about their bearings but Alcock heard only screeching vibrations. The communication gear built into their flight caps had failed, thus requiring pilot and navigator, from then on, to scribble notes to each other and converse through hand gestures. Better news came by the end of the first hour of their flight, when, just as their meteorologist had assured them, the winds calmed. The skies, however, were not clear. In fact, as the winds lessened, the haze thickened.

To navigate, Brown relied on measuring the angle of the sun or another heavenly body in relation to the horizon. Essential to the method was visibility. In the absence of a clearly defined horizon, Brown had a sextant that replaced the horizon with a bubble. But none of his equipment could serve as a surrogate sun or star. If neither was visible, he resorted to the method known as dead reckoning, calculating his position with compass bearings, speed and height of the plane, and wind velocity. If he couldn't use one or more of these, then, he would proceed along the course he had established from his most recent computation and simply hope, faithfully, for the best.

By 5:20, at 1,500 feet, the plane was immersed in heavy fog. Twenty minutes later, Brown wrote a note to Alcock saying "I can't get an obs. in this fog. Will estimate that same wind holds and work by dead reckoning." Shortly after six, they heard a loud noise that disturbed both men. Reminiscent of machine gun fire, the sound was the exhaust pipe breaking off. Now three cylinders of the engine were exhausting straight into the air. The uneven rattling sound grew louder, evening out to a constant roaring "thrum," as Brown called it, that would be with them throughout the rest of the trip. Accepting this, they focused on the more disturbing problem of visibility. Flying higher and higher, they searched for a clear patch of sky so that Brown could fix their position. At 5,200 feet, they still could not get above the clouds and could see nothing beyond the inside of the cockpit. "I waited impatiently for the first sight of the moon, the Pole Star and other old friends of every navigator," Brown later wrote. But by midnight, there had been no break in the fog. And Alcock later wrote, "For seven long hours we travelled thus, sighting neither sea nor sky."

Then at about half past midnight, at nearly six thousand feet, a tiny gap in the dense clouds appeared to the northeast and Brown spotted the star Vega, the moon, and the Pole Star, which is the end star in the tail of Ursa Minor, the Little Bear—all essential to finding his way. In the moonlight, Brown could see a cloud horizon and thus could establish a reading. They had flown 850 nautical miles in the past eight hours at an average speed of 106 knots. Brown's dead reckoning was slightly short of their position but only because he had built into his equation a calculation of diminishing winds, which, so distracted by other challenges, he had not realized had picked up again. Now knowing their position, they could descend several thousand feet, thus reducing the strain on the engines.

For the next hour and a half, they flew through an eerie haze of half-light that allowed them to see the shadows of their plane move across mounds of clouds beneath them. Something about the continuous roar of the engines, the inability to talk to each other, the indefinite nature of the fog that was alternately dense and light but always there, the necessity of sitting in a crammed cockpit for endless hours, the failed wireless radio, and the angle of occasional light slipping through the oddly shaped clouds surrounding them provoked an unsettling anxious feeling for both of them. Brown later called it an "aura of unreality." He would also later comment about his utter admiration for Alcock, who never complained once about the required permanent position of his feet on the rudder-bars and of his right hand on the joystick. Neither did Brown express any fears or discomfort to his stalwart partner, but by the tenth or eleventh hour in the air, he was conscious of the need to be as disciplined as was humanly possible. What was before them was a seemingly endless expanse of nothingness. Brown concentrated on his vision of the new dawn that surely they would witness in Ireland and he thought about the Irish coast, trying to envision what the first sight of land might look like. They had more than enough fuel and food; they appeared to be on course; and they were more than halfway to their destination. Now it was a matter of fortitude and focus and never allowing themselves to drift into fantasies of fear.

At 3:10 A.M., they were flying at about 3,500 feet when suddenly thick drifts of vapor enveloped the plane, so thick that they couldn't see the front of the fuselage or the far end of either wing. Their sense of the vertical and horizontal was suddenly askew. Pulling back the joystick, Alcock assumed they were nosing upward but at the same time the air-speed meter jammed and the instrument readings could not guide them to a safe horizontal forward movement. The plane "swung, flew amok, and began to perform circus tricks," Brown later wrote. But it was clear to both pilot and navigator that they were heading downward in a steep slant—a seemingly unstoppable nosedive. Both men prepared for the worst and loosened their safety belts. Then just as suddenly as the clouds had appeared, the air was clear and they found themselves to be a hundred feet above the surface of the sea. Alcock responded, centralized the joystick, and opened up the throttles. At fifty feet, they leveled out. So close were they to the water that they could hear the swooshing of waves breaking and swelling. And so dis-oriented were they that they were now heading back to America. Turning around, they proceeded eastward and once again entered a vast expanse of interminable clouds, though not as solid as what they had hit at 3 A.M. There would be other urgent moments. Trying to rise above the clouds, they would fly into rain, hail, and snow at 8,000 feet, requiring Brown to crawl onto the wings to scrape off the ice. And they would fly as high as 11,000 feet in search of even a pinpoint glimmer of the sun to allow Brown to fix their position. This happened at about 7:20 A.M., at which time they descended again.

At 8:15 A.M. they were 250 feet above the surface of the ocean. Brown was putting away the remains of food the two men had just shared when suddenly Alcock grabbed Brown's shoulder and moved his lips rapidly without the usual consideration of waiting to see if Brown had understood, as if he had forgotten that Brown could not hear him. Brown was alarmed until he saw what Alcock saw: specks of land ahead. These were the islands of Eeshal and Turbot. Ten minutes later, Alcock and Brown crossed the coast of Ireland. At 8:40 A.M., after sixteen hours and twenty-eight minutes in the air, flying at an average speed of over 2 miles a minute, they touched land near Clifden, as planned. And it would have been a smooth landing if they had not crashed into a bog, front end first, burying the nose, four propeller blades and lower wings in the ground as if staking a claim to their victory. Pilot and navigator scrambled quickly out of the cockpit grabbing instruments and the mailbag and the flare gun. Firmly on the ground at last, Brown shot off two white flares. Within minutes a group of men appeared from a nearby wireless station. "Anybody hurt?" asked one.

"No," said Brown. And then all the men helped Brown and Alcock to continue clearing the cockpit.

A few minutes later, one of them asked, "Where you from?"

"America," said Alcock, at which time one or more of them chuckled, thinking perhaps that if they didn't laugh a little they were not going along with the joke. They had no knowledge of the trip. The names Alcock and Brown meant nothing to them. But when Alcock showed them the mailbag with letters postmarked at St. John's, they sent out a loud burst of cheers and nearly knocked down Alcock and Brown in an effort to shake their hands.

In the coming days, Alcock and Brown would be hailed as international heroes, which shocked them no less than their 3 A.M. nosedive. "We had finished the job we wanted to do, and could not comprehend why it should lead to such fuss," Brown later wrote. "Now, however, I know that the crowds saw more clearly than I did, and that their cheers were not really for us personally, but for what they regarded as a manifestation of the spirit of Adventure, the true romance, the thrilling feat—call it what you will. For the moment this elusive ideal, which they so wanted and needed, was suggested to them by the first non-stop journey by air across the Atlantic, which we had been fortunate enough to make."

By the beginning of the summer of 1919, above the many ships crossing the Atlantic, there were now vessels in the air. An American flying boat, a British dirigible, and a British biplane had claimed three firsts: the first transatlantic crossing, the first nonstop transatlantic flight, and the first round-trip flight between the two continents. Technology was pushing mankind forward beyond the haze of war and its aftermath. "Even the worst pessimist of yesterday is perfectly willing today to theorize over the possibility of flying to the moon or to Mars or anywhere else," wrote the *New York Times* on June 16.

PART III

Summer: Passion

If we must die—let it not be like hogs
Hunted and penned in an inglorious spot,
While round us bark the mad and hungry dogs,
Making their mock at our accursed lot.
If we must die—oh, let us nobly die,
So that our precious blood may not be shed
In vain; then even the monsters we defy
Shall be constrained to honor us though dead!

—CLAUDE MCKAY JULY 1919

The expedition [to northern Russia] was nonsense from the
beginning and always seemed to me one of those sideshows born
of desperation and organized for the purpose of keeping up home
morale rather than because of any clear view of the military
situation.

—SECRETARY OF WAR NEWTON D. BAKER, 1929

CHAPTER 23

Missichusetts

In Concord, New Hampshire, on June 16, a man and a woman arrived to-gether in the lobby of the Phenix Hotel on Main Street. They asked for separate rooms and placed their signatures on the hotel register. Then, after depositing luggage in their respective rooms—his, room 55 in the south wing of the second floor, and hers, room 48 in the north wing, same floor—they met up again in the lobby and walked the three blocks to the state courthouse, where they applied for a marriage license. Again they signed their names, this time with birthdates, the day's date, their home-town of Ayer, Massachusetts, and their occupations: his, common laborer, and hers, elocutionist. A revealing, potentially damaging paper trail had begun for two people, one black and one white, who unknowingly were about to embark on a perilous crossing of the color line. The names on the registers were Mabel Emeline Puffer and Arthur Garfield Hazzard.

In New Hampshire, there was no law prohibiting interracial marriages. Nor had there been such a law in Massachusetts since 1843. The couple had come to Concord to be married because Mabel Puffer was a student of the new, forty-year-old religion of Christian Science, and Concord was the place where Mary Baker Eddy, the sect's founder, had died and was buried. Legally there was nothing to stop Mabel Puffer and Arthur Hazzard from marrying and in the name of humanity there was no reason to block the union. But there would be a legal delay. Under New Hampshire law, the couple would have to wait five days between applying for a marriage license and receiving one. And in those few days, out of a malevolent netherworld where fears and biases could easily crush the hopes of progress, reasons would surface.

Arthur Garfield Hazzard was thirty-eight years old when he arrived in Concord. A stout man, not quite five foot seven with black hair and dark eyes that some would say were black, Hazzard went by the nickname of "Honey." He was born in Lowell. His family had lived and worked in the area of Lowell and Ayer in Massachusetts for several generations. They had also owned considerable plots of land in the vicinity. Among blacks, Hazzard was considered a community leader and his reputation for reliability and honesty among the white citizens of Ayer was above reproach. Part of the community's acceptance of him emanated from the well-known fact that his father, William W. Hazzard, had fought in the Civil War, B Troop, 5th Massachusetts Cavalry. In fact, prominently placed on the wall of his mother's house was his father's honorable discharge—"enlisted December 30, 1863 and discharged in Texas on October 31, 1865"—framed and hanging above the divan. His father was also the reason, it was said, that his skin was far darker than the very light skin of his mother, whose grandmother had been white. In fact, the nickname Honey was based on the color of Hazzard's skin, described in one newspaper account as "dark honey."

When Hazzard was about eleven or twelve years old, he traveled with his mother, father and five brothers and sisters in a musical troupe known as the Happy Hazzards, which for a year or two in the 1890s gained a scrap of fame, mostly in Massachusetts and New York. There they performed in minstrel shows in theaters during the winter months and in the summers for groups of white people in white dresses and linen suits at picnics and religious revivals. But there was little money in the work and after the troupe disbanded, Arthur set about to learn just about every skill there was to know about maintaining houses and gardens. Now, though describing himself as a "common laborer," he was, in fact, a professional handyman who was never without work and whose robust tenor voice could be heard ringing out the songs of his youth as he trimmed hedges, watered gardens, built sheds, and tended to the needs of the rich folks of Ayer—especially the elite community that summered at nearby Sandy Pond.

Hazzard was not a reader nor was he a political sort. He had not been for or against the war, really, though he had not fought in it because he was blind in his right eye, from an accident that had happened, he would say, when he was too young to remember. He had known Mabel Puffer for nearly twenty-five years, but for most of those years he knew her only enough to acknowledge her presence with a nod or the tipping of his hat or simply his wide, inviting smile. Her father was one of his first employers and his job was to take care of the stately Puffer properties in Ayer as well as the country house on Sandy Pond. When her father died in 1916, Mabel Puffer, whose mother was deceased and who was her father's only child, inherited his estates, his bank accounts, and his handyman. And, in fact, during the past half year Hazzard had dropped his other jobs and was working exclusively for Mabel Puffer.

Mabel Emeline Puffer was named after her paternal grandmother, who was a devout Unitarian and a substantially wealthy woman, largely because of the land that had been passed on from generation to generation since the early eighteenth century. From the time Puffer was very young, her parents, in particular her father—who was her mother's second husband—took an interest in developing her mind. Indeed Mabel was a bright child but not an especially pretty one. Although slender by the summer of 1919 and described in newspapers as "handsome," she had tended toward an unattractive plumpness for most of her adult life. And whatever her weight, her slight chin seemed to slide into her neck giving a double-chin effect and accentuating the protrusion of a bulbous unflattering nose. Still, her thick, wavy ash-blond hair, which she typically stowed in a bun on the top of her head, and her sophisticated manner that revealed her background of wealth in the way she walked, in the slow meaningful way she talked, and in the way she could quote from books she had read and add a complementary detail to any conversation, gave her some appeal. Losing weight during the months since her February engagement to Hazzard enhanced the "handsome" appearance so described in the many news stories that would soon be written about her.

Puffer was a graduate of Emerson College of Oratory on Berkeley Street in downtown Boston. The school had been founded in 1880 by Charles Wesley Emerson, a Unitarian minister who believed that oratorical skills and the ability to communicate well were the keys to fulfilling one's potential, which was God's will. Around the turn of the century Emerson moved his faith to Christian Science, which was not an uncommon transition among Unitarians at that time and certainly not a dramatic deviation for a man who wrote in his college's manual that "the body was created that it might serve the soul." Too, Emerson invented a course called "Physical Culture." "We mean by this the development and refinement of the entire physical person through cultivating it to express the purposes and emotions of the soul." Required courses in the three-year degree program included such things as Voice Culture, Articulation and Inflection, Recitation, Philosophy of Expression, and Perfective Laws of Art in Oratory. In Puffer's senior year her marks ranged from 89 in a course called Evolution of Expression to 100 in Anatomy, mostly ranking in the high 90s for coursework in Law, Physical Culture, Gesture, Research, Voice, Vocal Physiology, and English Literature. Aiming for a career as an elocutionist or public reader, Puffer graduated with honors in 1893.

After Emerson, Puffer moved home to Ayer, where she worked for several years as she had intended, as a public reader. And she fell in love with a young man whom her father vehemently rejected as "not good enough." Devoted to her father, Puffer obeyed him when he demanded that she decline the marriage proposal and send away the man, whose name was Fred Gray. Around town the word was that Mabel Puffer's heart was broken. She must have been in her late twenties or early thirties. Soon thereafter Gray married a woman whom Puffer knew and together the couple bought a summer hotel in New Hampshire that later became a well-known destination among Puffer's class. After Gray's departure, Puffer brooded for a long while. Living with her parents in the house where she was raised, she immersed herself in the teachings of Mary Baker Eddy. Shortly after her father's death she moved for eighteen months or so to Hartford, Connecticut, to further her studies of Christian Science under the tutelage of a practitioner by the name of Catherine Hirsh. Upon her return to Ayer in early 1918 she moved out of the family home and into the far smaller country house at Sandy Pond. She withdrew from her only family members: a cousin in New Hampshire and a half-niece and two half-nephews, who were the children of a deceased half-sister, all living in Massachusetts. And she lost considerable weight. Now living a secluded life, with shades often drawn and rare appearances in town, Puffer became acquainted with Honey in a new, highly secretive way. She called him "Gar."

What Hazzard remembered best about the courtship were the long walks at night on roads around Sandy Pond, especially when the moon was full. It was unclear when the courtship had begun—possibly years before the deaths of Puffer's parents. "We used to talk about the moon and the stars and such things," he told a reporter later. "Or we would just stroll under the light of the moon in silence, holding hands. I sure did enjoy that but I didn't have the courage to propose." Puffer did, in February of 1919, and from then on the couple focused, secretly, on plans for a June wedding, which had always been Mabel Puffer's dream.

The night before their arrival in Concord, the full phase of the moon had begun. And so it was that every night that week they would stroll through the town, sometimes holding hands, under the light of the moon, and talk about similar nights on Sandy Pond. They spent their days together sitting in the lobby on a divan talking in whispered tones and exploring Concord's stores and streets, although they were forced to eat separately, she in the hotel and he at an eatery for Negroes in the town. They also worked on the arrangements for the upcoming Saturday morning wedding. Hazzard's sister and one of his brothers as well as his mother planned to attend the ceremony as witnesses. On Friday night there would be a party at the hotel for all who wished to attend the wedding, including Concord's mayor, Charles J. French, who agreed to marry them. Talking to the local press on the morning of the 18th, two days after the couple's arrival in town, the mayor said he would not hesitate to perform the ceremony. "In fact I would esteem it a unique experience to have the distinction of joining such a couple in the holy bonds of matrimony."

It was all so very smooth. The town seemed friendly. The mayor seemed pleased to marry them. Even the hotel seemed accommodating. And Puffer and Hazzard, feeling safe enough to remove the veil of secrecy that had concealed their relationship in Ayer, were floating on some distant cloud far from the realities of their 1919 world.

That they were marrying at a time when interracial unions of any sort were frowned upon in most parts of the country did not seem to deter them. Perhaps it didn't occur to them that the idea of a black handyman marrying his wealthy white female employer sounded an alarm loud enough to be heard from New Hampshire to Massachusetts and all the way to Mississippi or that black men in America had been murdered for even talking to white women or that every white racist in America viewed the mixing of white blood with Negro blood as nothing less than the work of Satan.

There had been twenty-eight lynchings so far that year nationwide and nearly one-half of them had involved some accusation that a black man had assaulted a white woman. In the month of June alone there would be ten lynchings: two in Mississippi, three in Alabama, two in Arkansas, one in Texas, and two in South Carolina. Five of those were provoked by allegations of assault or rape of a white woman. And two of *those* occurred during Puffer and Hazzard's five days in Concord.

The one in Texas took place on Tuesday, June 17, the day that Puffer
and Hazzard were planning their wedding ceremony and their reception
at the Phenix. It occurred in Longview, a rural cotton and lumbering community in northeast Texas. What happened was this: On June 16, a young
black man, Lemuel Walters, was discovered in the bedroom of a white
woman. He was thrown into the Longview jail without any formal charges.
The next day his body, after being handed over to a white mob by the white
sheriff, was found near the railroad tracks four miles south of Longview—
"shot to pieces." The *Chicago Defender* later reported that Walters "was
taken from the Longview jail by a crowd of white men when a prominent
white woman declared she loved him, and if she were in the North would
obtain a divorce and marry him."

Perhaps Puffer and Hazzard were just so secure after years of uninter-
rupted routines in the safety of isolated Sandy Pond that what they were
doing now together seemed normal. In Sandy Pond, a summer community
on a lake about two and a half miles from Ayer on the road to Lowell, the
idea of such a relationship was so unprecedented and so absurd that no one
ever suspected it. Perhaps Puffer and Hazzard mistook the silence for approval. Thus in New Hampshire they proceeded to reveal their private
lives, trusting that the world accepted them.

By Wednesday, the Ayer couple had been visible enough that they were
nearly celebrities in Concord. When they entered stores, onlookers stared
into display windows to catch a glimpse at the stately white woman and the
black man at her side. Some smiled and nodded. Others frowned, shook
their heads, and then shot arrows of disapproval, aiming at the very hearts
of the hopeful pair. Reporters from area newspapers were now well aware of
the "wealthy elocutionist from Ayer and her choreman," as one paper described them. And the story had reached the nearest big city, which was
Boston, where magazines and newspapers thought that the situation was
titillating enough to send reporters to Concord to check it out. On Thursday morning, the 19th of June, the *Boston Traveller* broke the story on page
two with the headline: "Will Marry Negro in 'Perfect Union': Rich Ayer
Society Woman Determined to Wed Servant Although Town Is Aflame
with Protest—Brooded Over Lost Love." The *Boston American* was next
and by the end of the day, the *Boston Evening Globe* had picked up the story
and placed it on the front page: "Hope to Prevent White Woman Wedding

Negro: Two Friends of Mabel E. Puffer Have Gone to Concord, N.H." Other papers followed the next morning.

In most of the stories, Puffer was described as a Unitarian who had become a Christian Scientist, which, the reporters claimed, accounted for her belief that, as she told them, "all is spirit" and mere differences of color or age were inconsequential in the pursuit of a "perfect spiritual union." One reporter dubbed the couple a "modern Othello and his Desdemona." All articles revealed that Puffer's commitment to Hazzard was firm as was his to her.

"I love Mr. Hazzard," Puffer told a reporter for the *Boston Evening Globe*. "And love doesn't stop at the color line."

"We have been in love for five years," Hazzard told the same reporter, who interviewed both of them in the hallway outside room 48, Puffer's room at the Phenix. The couple had been walking down the hallway when the reporter stopped them and asked if they would consent to an interview. They agreed and each time Puffer answered a question she looked lovingly toward Hazzard, who would nod and smile as she spoke. The reporter asked her at least twice whether she loved her fiancé and she responded "Yes, I certainly do love Mr. Hazzard and that's just why I am going to marry him."

"And I love *you*," Hazzard said, looking over the reporter's shoulder directly at Puffer.

To the reporter for the *Boston American*, Hazzard said, "I don't see what difference color makes in this marriage. We both got hearts and it's the heart that counts in marriage. I'm in this to stay and there isn't a derrick big enough to hoist me out of the matrimonial river."

By the time the *Boston Evening Globe* reporter interviewed him, Hazzard was beginning to respond defensively to questions, sensing that he was being singled out for doing something wrong. He began the *Globe* interview in the wake of an apparently tough exchange with the *Boston American*, whose reporter effectively crossed a line when he asked about Hazzard's new clothes for the wedding, especially his new suit.

"How about that new suit of yours? They say in Ayer she gave you $128 to buy your wedding clothes," the reporter said to Hazzard.

"No sir, I always have been a good dresser," Hazzard responded.

To the *Boston Evening Globe* reporter he said, "Now the story is this: get it straight. We did not elope. We did not run away. We came here because she is a Christian Scientist. . . . And I am not marrying her for her money, get that straight."

And when asked again about his wedding ensemble, he nearly shouted at the reporter: "Certainly not. I bought it myself like every man buys his wedding clothes. I never got money from her for this. . . . No money about this," and raising his voice, "WE WERE TALKING AND SHE SAID IT WOULD BE NICE FOR US TO GET MARRIED AND I SAID IT WOULD BE NICE TOO. SHE JUST TOOK A LIKING TO ME AND I TOOK A LIKING TO HER. I DON'T KNOW HOW MUCH SHE IS WORTH."

Back in Ayer, controversy had erupted and the town was "aflame with protest." The rumor was that Puffer, well known there, had eloped to Concord with a black man. Suddenly Puffer and her cottage at Sandy Pond were the main show for every gossip in both towns of Ayer and Lowell and all along the road between. She was eccentric, they said. She was a recluse. She was too thin. Rarely was food delivered to her cottage and thus she must be starving. Poor thing, she must be suicidal. THAT would explain the elopement. HE was her chore man, cut her grass, weeded her garden, ran her errands. SHE must be sick. Perhaps HE forced her to stay inside. Perhaps he had been living there secretly for years. Perhaps her father's death had been too much for her. And so on.

The reporters had come to Concord on Wednesday and so had two supposedly good friends of Mabel Puffer's. One was Catherine Hirsh—with whom the bride-to-be had lived at Harvard, Massachusetts, while studying Christian Science. Hirsh claimed years of friendship with Puffer, harkening back to their time together at Emerson. She was accompanied by Ayer attorney George L. Wilson, who was an Ayer selectman, and had looked after Puffer's legal affairs at least since the deaths of her parents. Their mission, as they told the press, was to stop the marriage by persuading Puffer to call it off. It was not about race, Wilson said. Like her father years before, Wilson as well as Hirsh said they were trying to stop Puffer because they deeply cared about her and believed that her choice for a mate was beneath her. In the end, she would not be happy, they were certain. Wilson told reporters that there was no legal way to block it. There were simply no grounds for canceling the marriage application. And although his first stop in the town had been to the police station, he assured the media that he did not want to resort to legal means to foil the marriage. Ending it must be her decision "somehow," he said. Toward that end, Hirsh and Wilson called upon Puffer in her hotel room shortly after their visit to the police. They then sought out Hazzard and arranged a meeting to be held early on Thursday the 19th in Puffer's hotel room.

That morning, Puffer, Hazzard, Wilson, and Hirsh—and the reporters who stood in the hallway and pressed glass tumblers against the hotel room door—gathered in room 48. During the meeting, one of the reporters wrote, Puffer talked directly to Hirsh about Christian Science, pointing out that it was a faith that taught "that materialism is nothing and it is the spirit always that matters." And thus she was right to marry the man she loved whether he was black or yellow or red. Another reporter commented: "After the conference ended, with Mrs. Hirsh making no effort to conceal her disappointment at the outcome, Puffer was asked if she really loved Hazzard and intended to marry him. And looking straight at Hirsh and Wilson, she said, "I do love him and I will marry him."

"REJECTS APPEAL NOT TO MARRY COLORED MAN," read the headline in the *Boston Evening Globe*.

That afternoon, on the 19th, with barely two days to go before the marriage license would be officially filed, Concord mayor Charles French was unexpectedly called out of town and thus could not perform the service on Saturday. Hazzard then sought out the city clerk, Henry E. Chamberlin, to replace the mayor. But Chamberlin, as the *Concord Evening Monitor* noted, had "passed part of his life in the South, and knows the feeling of the whites in that section toward the colored people," and that apparently was his reason for declining Hazzard's request. Scrambling for a replacement, Hazzard now asked Puffer to join him in the pursuit to find someone to marry them. Puffer suggested simply knocking on the doors of every parsonage in town, which they did, without much luck. Rev. Harold H. Niles, for instance, told the *Daily Patriot*, another local paper, that he "would have nothing to do with the ceremony." Rev. W. Judson Stetzer, whose name was all over the Friday morning papers as having consented, called the *Daily Patriot*, demanded a correction, and ranted about how he firmly believed "that the Legislature of this state should pass a law forbidding such marriages." The *Patriot*, in reporting the rejections, happened to inform the public that in Maryland performing a marriage ceremony for a white and black couple was a crime with a $500 fine. Others, including Rev. William Smith of the

Colored Church of the Holy Temple of Jesus Christ, said they were simply too busy to do it. Rev. John M. Stark, a white Presbyterian pastor, finally agreed to officiate.

Around the same time, it became clear that Wilson and Hirsh were not the only people trying to quash Puffer's dream. In town now were her only relatives—children of her deceased half-sister (her mother's daughter by a first marriage)—a half-niece from Swampscott, Massachusetts, and a half-nephew from Hollis, New Hampshire, neither of whom she had seen since her father's funeral. And with them was an attorney, who had filed a legal application in Ayer at the East Cambridge courthouse on Thursday to be the conservator of her estate, on the grounds that she was mentally incompetent, based upon the evidence that she was insane, based upon the decision she had made to marry "a Negro servant." The threesome had arrived in Concord on Thursday night, though Puffer and Hazzard were unaware of their presence.

First thing Friday morning, Puffer was told by the front desk at the Phenix that a letter had come to the hotel addressed to her. It was from Mrs. Josephine Quarles of Boston, who had read all about Puffer and her fiancé in the Boston newspapers and wanted to tell her: "I glory in your spunk. I married a colored man 25 years ago and he is the best man who ever walked." It was the first outside reassurance she had had during the entire week in Concord. Good things were happening, she must have thought as she emerged from the hotel to find a big surprise: Hazzard's family members waiting for her in his brother's seven-passenger touring car. For the next several hours, the couple rode through the countryside around Concord chatting excitedly with Honey's mother and siblings, sharing their decision of that morning to honeymoon at Lake Champlain and reading the Quarles letter out loud.

At the same time, however, Puffer's family members were brainstorming with the city clerk to figure out a legal reason *not* to issue the marriage license. As Puffer and Hazzard held hands in the back seat of his brother's car, a local citizen contacted a local judge asking how this "horrible event"—the marriage—could be stopped. The judge referred the citizen to the city clerk, who gave the citizen an application for a sanity investigation, and told the man that such a document had to be signed by family members. And, oh, by the way, the city clerk said, some of Puffer's relatives happened to have just left his office and were staying at the Phenix. The citizen contacted the relatives, who told him not to worry, as they had taken care of "the problem." Also while the hopeful couple was touring the environs, the chief of police from Ayer was driving to Concord. Not waiting for the governor of Massachusetts, Calvin Coolidge, to sign off on the extradition papers, which he never did, the police chief began his journey to New Hampshire, armed with an arrest warrant secured in the First District Court of Massachusetts charging the couple with the statutory crime of "lewd and lascivious cohabitation" and charging Hazzard with enticement. In the same envelope, he carried the committal papers against Puffer on the grounds of insanity, calling for a conservator to handle her estate.

By late afternoon, Puffer and Hazzard, their hearts still aglow and their minds blurred perhaps by the excitement of the upcoming event, knew about the efforts to stop them. But like stalked animals on the run, they did not stop to stare the enemy in the face nor did they protect themselves from potential harm. Around dusk, on Friday, Hazzard was in the local drugstore sipping on an ice cream soda waiting for Puffer to join him so they could celebrate the eve of their marriage and the end of the official five-day wait for the license, which they believed would be delivered to them in the hotel lobby at 9 A.M. the next day in time for the ceremony set for 10 A.M. A *Boston American* reporter spotted Hazzard and dashed to his side.

"So tell me how does the modern Othello and his Desdemona regard the opposition to their romance?" the reporter asked.

Hazzard responded: "They may think as they like. They can go as far as they like to try to stop our marriage but they can't separate two loving hearts that beat as one."

By then, the police chief from Ayer had arrived and had given the warrants to the local Concord police. Two hours later, Hazzard was on the steps of the hotel buying a newspaper to take to his sweetheart when a Sergeant Wallace approached and arrested him. Hazzard read the arrest warrant and said he did not understand the "enticement charge," but would not make a scene and was not a violent man. He did stress, though, that he believed this was "wrong to do." Ten minutes later, there was a knock at the door marked 48 in the Phenix Hotel. Thinking it was Hazzard bringing her the paper, in which there was an article about their impending marriage, Puffer opened the door. But it was not her Gar. Sergeant Wallace handed her the arrest warrant. She calmly read the warrant and looked up at him and said, "They'll have to prove that, won't they?"

Puffer was then escorted, without being allowed to pack her luggage, to the police chief's car, where Hazzard was waiting. Hazzard's mother, his brother, and his sister were in the lobby when Puffer was led out of the hotel. His mother ran after them screaming that there had to be extradition papers. Where were the extradition papers? They must be presented before there were any arrests. She received no answer from anyone and thus quickly jumped into the brother's touring car and motioned to her children to get in quickly, not bothering to return to their rooms, so that she could follow the police car back to Ayer. One local paper ended its coverage of the day with the scene of the two cars driving away and the words ". . . and Concord gazed after their departing dust with no regrets."

The next morning, Saturday, June 21, at nine, Mabel Emeline Puffer was in the detention pen in the basement of the Ayer city hall, where she had spent the night. She was conferring with her lawyer, George L. Wilson, who pledged "to fight to the last ditch" the charge that she was insane. One hour later, at the time, almost to the minute, that she and her Gar were to be married, she was arraigned with her fiancé on the charges of lewd cohabitation. William H. Lewis, Hazzard's attorney, hired only hours before the arraignment, argued that "Mr. Hazzard is an American citizen and is standing on the Bill of Rights. He is in a Massachusetts court, which has been established under the Bill of Rights. Massachusetts court shows no prejudice. Now what IS the case?"

Although Lewis did not represent Puffer, he appeared to be livid over the crusade to declare her insane. "No charge of insanity against this woman was ever made by anybody and I say now that the whole charge may be well described in the slang often heard at Camp Devens, 'It is pure camouflage' and I believe the court can see through it."

The headline in the *Boston Traveller* the next day read: "Miss Puffer Fights Charge of Insanity, True to Choreman." And William Monroe Trotter's newspaper, *The Guardian*, also in Boston, had this to say about the news of Puffer and Hazzard:

Perhaps there is a very small bit of silver in the lining of an ugly cloud over Ayer, a town which was in Massachusetts but which ought to be relegated into a diminutive state for which "Missichusetts" would be an appropriately dishonorable name. There will be a bright spot in the lining of the cloud if the lawlessness of Ayer opens to the eyes of the honest element of New England the fact that American mob violence is not caused by alleged crimes by Negroes and that the educated Christians, prosperous Caucasians are often the ringleaders of the mob.

Miss Puffer and Mr. Hazzard are the victims of one of the most brazen, insolent, wanton episodes of lawlessness that ever occurred. True it is that the Ayer mob did not go to the extreme of murder; but, as is publicly known, the gang was willing to go so far as the crime of kidnapping.

Arthur Hazzard (Negro) and Mabel Puffer (Caucasian) wanted to marry at a time when both were perfectly sane. No other person and no government has the right to prevent their carrying out their wishes. Massachusetts' legislature has not been guilty of giving statutory power—it has not the right—to frustrate the perfectly decent and moral attempt of the two clean-living sane adults. In view of this fact the lawbreakers proceeded to do much as what one of the "orderly" sort of Mississippi mobs might do.

Although Puffer and Hazzard's story was hardly over, their vision of a new life together began to slip from their grasp in a Massachusetts courtroom on June 21. It was the beginning of the summer of 1919—a summer that would be remembered for far more than the record high temperatures, or the two broken hearts at Sandy Pond.

CHAPTER 24

Paris

On the first day of summer in Paris, William Monroe Trotter was dining at the fashionable Chope de la Lorraine with editors of five French newspapers. The editor of *Du Pays*, who had printed five of Trotter's recent articles, was now pressing Trotter, who had quite a following in Paris, to do another. Could he write more about the segregation of the races in the American capital? Would he talk about President Wilson's refusal to issue passports to black Americans to attend the peace conference? In his columns, Trotter typically expressed his deep concern over the absence thus far of a clause in the peace treaty assuring full democracy for racial minorities, sometimes using examples of race discrimination in America as the reason for such a necessity. Indeed, from the pen of "William Trotter," as his byline read, the French were learning a good deal about life for "the darker races" in America. And at dinners such as this one, Trotter rarely held back any of his passion for the cause that had led him to Paris. But on this evening, he was distracted. He had just read the latest missive from Gilbert Close, President Wilson's secretary in Paris, in response to his own June 19 letter to Close. And he was not pleased.

The note from Close, as if produced from a mold, was like all others Trotter had received from the president while in Paris. It acknowledged receipt of his latest letter but nothing more. In Trotter's June 19 note to Wilson, which he also had sent to all of the French editors with whom he was now dining, Trotter had asked the president—possibly for the sixth time—to present to the principal negotiators at the peace conference the petitions of his National Equal Rights League. These were the petitions beseeching the president to acknowledge the importance of race equality: "Now that the war fought to democratize the world has been won and colored men have done their share in winning it, they should receive such equal rights as will be granted to the ethnic minorities in Austria."

Trotter's May 31 letter to the president had been widely published in the French press. This was the letter in which he had stressed the contradictions between the president's Memorial Day speech and recent news of yet another lynching of a black man in America, and in which he had beseeched the president to immediately recommend to Congress a federal anti-lynching law. The letter, however, had not aroused a response from the president. Nor had Trotter's June 12 request to meet with the president. After that one fizzled, Trotter, knowing that the peace conference was in its final days, anxiously experimented with a new tactic. On June 15, instead of writing to the president, he wrote directly to Wilson's secretary, Gilbert Close, who had been the point man for Trotter's deluge of requests and letters and petitions to Wilson.

"I desire to express to you my high appreciation for your prompt acknowledgement of the receipt of my letters and petitions to the president," the letter of the 15th began. Trotter went on to ask Close if he would be so kind as to ask Wilson whether he would meet with Trotter while they were both in Paris and that he, Trotter, needed to know soon. "My course in the immediate future depends upon his decision in this matter. Hence it is necessary for me to know his intention at once if possible. Or would it be in order for me to call and see you with regard to an appointment with the President? An early reply will be appreciated."

On the 17th of June, Close wrote to Trotter: "In reply to your note of June 15th, I regret to say that it is not possible for the President to arrange to give you an audience."

Trotter then returned to his usual tactic of writing directly to the president and sent the June 19 letter. His persistence, though unrecognized and publicly ignored at the peace conference, was highly visible and lauded in the French press, in which he had written numerous columns revealing the plight of the black man in America. As one French newspaperman put it in a letter to the *New York Age:* "Give credit to this man who came to Europe to fight for his people."

On the 25th of June, Trotter sent his last letter to Gilbert Close:

"Dear Sir: I thank you for your answer to my letter [June 12] asking whether the President would grant me an audience. I have your letter of the 21st instant saying that you will bring my letter of the 19th to the attention of the President as well as yours of the 24th stating the same as to my letter of the 21st.

"As the end is so near, will you do me the very great favor of informing the President that my mission makes it very important and necessary that I know whether he has, or whether he will present the petition of the National Equal Rights League to the Council of Four [Wilson, Clemenceau, Lloyd George, and Orlando] and ascertain the facts and let me know just as quickly as possible ere all is concluded. Again, thanking you I am Respectfully for the League, William Trotter, Secretary [of NERL]." He never received a response.

Neither Trotter's persistence about race in Paris nor Washington's concerns about domestic issues in postwar America could distract the president from his focus on the peace treaty and his League of Nations. Wilson would not respond to Trotter and he would not go home until the Germans signed the treaty.

Whether Germany would even sign the treaty was a question hovering over the peace conference from the moment the Germans had received the treaty on May 7. In a May 28 journal entry, Ray Stannard Baker wrote: "Everyone is now asking. Will the Germans sign? Up to noon every day I think they will; after lunch I am not sure; and just before going to bed I'm persuaded they will not. On the whole I think they will—with fingers crossed."

When the treaty was first printed, the president himself had confided to Baker that "If I were a German, I think I should never sign it." Baker had written in his diary in the first part of June that the treaty was "made by a group of nations suffering from shell shock." And in another entry: "I can see no real peace in it. They have tempered justice with no mercy."

If and when the Germans signed it they would be agreeing to pay billions in reparations; to hand over merchant ships and fishing vessels to the Allies as well as large quantities of coal from the Saar basin over the next ten years to France, Belgium, and Italy; to cede all their colonies in Africa and the Far East to the Allies to be administered as mandates under the League of Nations; to return Alsace-Lorraine to France, which had been Germany's since 1871, and which contained 72 percent of Germany's iron ore reserves; and to give up territory to Belgium, Denmark, and the new republic of Poland. The treaty gave the greater part of Germany's Togoland and Cameroon to France, with the remainder going to Britain. The Hapsburg empire was split into two separate states, Austria and Hungary. And the union of Austria and Germany was forbidden.

Upon learning the details of reparations against Germany, those who were informed about the signing of the Armistice must have recalled the ominous statement of a German delegate directed at France's Marshal Foch at the end of the railcar meeting: "The German nation, which for fifty months has defied a world of enemies, will preserve, in spirit of every kind of violence, its liberty and unity. A nation of seventy million suffers but does not die."

"Tres bien," Foch had said in response.

The last days in Paris that June were full of "the electricity of expectation," wrote Baker in his diary, "with the constantly growing assurance that Germany will sign." Indeed on June 28, at about 2 P.M. Paris time, generals and admirals in brilliant uniforms; dignitaries of all sorts with gold braids and medals draped over their shoulders; rank and royalty with jeweled headdresses and crimson sashes; weary, relieved delegates of the peace conference; and more than four hundred news correspondents climbed the grand marble staircases of Louis XIV's Palace of Versailles and walked the royal passageway to the Galerie des Glaces. It was in this giant hall, with its nearly six hundred mirrors, that Germany proclaimed its victory over France in January of 1871 after the Franco-Prussian War and thus began the German empire. Now, Germany would sign a treaty relinquishing all that had been gained in those nearly fifty years of empire building.

Over helmets with black manes, between the legs of Hussars, across the blues, browns, and yellows of antique rugs and tapestries, people strained to see the exact moment when pen touched paper. They glared at Germany's two representatives, Dr. Hermann Müller and Dr. Johannes Bell, as if hurling hate across the room was recompense for the grief of the past five years. Then, at 3:30 P.M., the Germans signed the Treaty of Versailles.

President Wilson was the first of the Allied delegates to sign the treaty, and by 3:45 the ceremony ended. The Paris Peace Conference had come to an official close. No one rose when the German delegates, blushed not with shame but with anger, walked slowly out of the nearly silent hall. But when President Wilson, accompanied by Clemenceau and Lloyd George, descended to the rear of the palace, a throng of hundreds of Frenchmen awaited them, screaming their relief: "Vive Clemenceau," "Vive Wilson," "Vive Lloyd George." In the background, guns boomed and low-flying airplanes roared in a paradoxical salute to peace.

Immediately after the signing, President Wilson cabled his aide Joseph Tumulty in Washington with the news:

The treaty of peace has been signed. If it is ratified and acted upon in full and sincere execution of its terms it will furnish the charter for a new order of affairs in the world. It is a severe treaty in the duties and penalties it imposes upon Germany, but it is severe only because great wrongs done by Germany are to be righted and repaired; it imposes nothing that Germany cannot do; and she can regain her rightful standing in the world by the prompt and honorable fulfillment of its terms. And it is much more than a treaty of peace with Germany. It liberates great peoples who have never before been able to find the way to liberty. It ends once for all, an old and intolerable order under which small groups of selfish men could use the people of great empires to serve their own ambition for power and dominion.

He also sent another memo to Tumulty—based on the advice of Colonel Edward House, who was responding to a strong persuasive suggestion from journalist Lincoln Steffens—to instruct Attorney General Palmer regarding amnesty. "It is my desire," wrote the president to Tumulty, "to grant complete amnesty and pardon to all American citizens in prison or under arrest on account of anything they have said in speech or in print concerning their personal opinions with regard to the activities of the Government of the U.S. during the period of the war. It seems to me that this would be not only a generous act but a just act to accompany the signing of the peace. I do not wish to include any who have been guilty of overt crimes, of course, but I think it would be a very serious mistake to detain anyone merely for the expression of opinion." Palmer cabled back immediately urging the president to wait until he had returned from Paris in July to make a final decision about "such an important issue." The president agreed.

Wilson left Paris on a train bound for Brest at 10 P.M. on the night of the 28th. Just before noon on June 29, he arrived on the docks at Brest. There, with flags waving and hands saluting, the mayor of Brest, French officials, American army officers stationed there, dozens of American soldiers, and crowds of Frenchmen bid farewell to the American president and his entourage, which included Mrs. Wilson, Ray Stannard Baker, and Dr. Grayson, as they boarded the *George Washington* for the trip home. Preceded by the battleship *Oklahoma* and flanked by American destroyers, the *George Washington* steamed slowly out to the open seas.

Trotter, who had watched the spectacle of the treaty signing from the palace gates, was deeply disappointed that Wilson had not met with him and that the great treaty did not contain a clause to address the issue of "full democracy" for racial minorities. And so, on the day that Wilson left Brest for America, Trotter prepared yet another letter. This time he wrote to Sir Eric Drummond, the secretary-general of the new League of Nations, saying: "Despite loyalty and sacrifice, is this 'Magna Charta of a new order of things' to contain no protection from the exclusion, the public segregations, the disfranchisement, from the rope and the faggot?"

Unknown to Trotter or to Wilson, back in America during the previous three days there had been three more lynchings of black Americans—two on the 26th of June and one on the 28th. All were monstrous. In one a black farm laborer in Arkansas refused to work for 35 cents a day in a cotton field, so the farm owner decided to force him to do the job, threatening him by accusing him of assaulting the farmer's daughter. He still refused and thus a mob took him to a bridge, stripped him naked, wrapped his neck in a rope, and placed hot irons on his body so that he would jump off the bridge and hang himself. The body was left hanging overnight with a sign nailed to the man's head reading: "This is how we treat lazy niggers."

Worse still—if that were possible—was the incident in Ellisville, Mississippi. There, a black man, John Hartfield, had allegedly assaulted a white woman and after being chased down and severely wounded, he "partially" confessed, or so it was reported. A mob then announced that for his crime Hartfield would be burned or hanged or both at the scene of the crime, near the Ellisville railroad tracks. Whether they would hang or burn him was a matter of contention among the mob's leaders. A "committee of citizens" publicized the event to occur at 5 P.M. on the 26th of June, advertising it in both the New Orleans, Louisiana, and Jackson, Mississippi, newspapers. "3,000 Will Burn Negro" read the two-inch banner headline in the New Orleans States. A column in the same paper ran the headline "Negro Jerky and Sullen as Burning Hour Nears." The front-page headline in the Jackson Daily News read: "John Hartfield Will Be Lynched by Ellisville Mob at 5 O'Clock This Afternoon." And the governor told the Jackson reporter that he was "powerless to prevent it. We have guns for state militia, but no men. It is impossible to send troops to the scene for the obvious reason that we have no troops." He added, "Excitement is at such a high pitch throughout South Mississippi that any attempt to interfere with the mob would doubtless result in the death of hundreds of persons . . . nobody can keep the inevitable from happening." Indecisive all the way to the hanging tree about whether to burn the man or hang him, the mob decided to do both. After burning him and then hanging him, they also shot him. The *New York Age* and *The Nation* called it "The Shame of America."

Back in Paris, the indefatigable Trotter sent one last petition on behalf of the National Equal Rights League to Drummond, the secretary-general of the League of Nations, asking one more time for clauses to be inserted into the League's covenant. And he took one last walk through his favorite parks, where there were three statues, one of General Dumas of Guadeloupe; one of his son, Dumas Père; and one of his grandson, Dumas Fils—all of whom shared an African ancestry. That a city such as Paris would grace its parks with the statues of three black men was to Trotter a most inspiring sight. Despite his disappointments with Wilson, he *had* made it to Paris and he *had* gained respect among Frenchmen for the cause to which he was so devoted. Although none of the Americans at the peace conference noted in their diaries the activities of Trotter during his two months in Paris—not Colonel House or Wilson or Ray Stannard Baker or Lincoln Steffens—and although he did not accomplish what he set out to do, Trotter, just for being there, had achieved something. On July 8, the very day that President Wilson would arrive in New York, Trotter left Paris for America on the ship *Espagne*. On board, he wrote a letter to a friend in which he said: "In the stern path of duty and with the help of God, I got to the seat of the World Peace Conference."

But the volcano, as Ray Stannard Baker in his 1916 article had called the conditions of black America, was about to erupt. By the end of June, freedom from oppression and injustice had become as important to African-Americans as drawing breath. There was no turning back.

CHAPTER 25

Independence Day 1919

Cornelius Vanderbilt, Andrew Carnegie, Henry C. Frick, and Vincent Astor, all residents of Fifth Avenue in New York, were given special guards. Men from the Secret Service and the Department of Justice were prepared. The New York State Guard was ready. The entire police force of the city of New York was called to duty, for three full days. And churches, the stock exchange and city hall were under surveillance. "Never before was the city better guarded," the *New York Times* reported.

On this the Fourth of July, the first day of the much heralded "reign of terror," America was well prepared for the possibility of violence. In Chicago, mounted police stood by industrial plants, stockyards, and public officials' homes, and Illinois reserve militiamen were stationed citywide. In Washington state, troops were called to Spokane to protect it against "radical outbreaks." In Pittsburgh, where police suspected that "radical agents" had possibly been stealing dynamite during the month of June, the state of Pennsylvania sent special troops to guard industrial plants. And in Boston, which was on high alert, two brothers—one sixteen years old and the other twenty—were arrested after a neighbor reported "mysterious activities" in a workshop at the rear of the boys' house. When police raided the home, they discovered that the young men had been making "bombs"—two- to three-inch gas pipes filled with black powder and with a fuse attached. The brothers told police they were making the devices for a big Independence Day celebration in their neighborhood. The boys were released later in the day.

On July 4, the nation waited for the bombs. "We have received so many notices and got so much information that it has almost come to be accepted as a fact that on a certain day in the future, which we have been advised of, there will be another serious and probably much larger effort of the same character which the wild fellows of this movement describe as a revolution, a proposition to use up and destroy the Government at one fell swoop," Attorney General Palmer had told the Senate in June. And

Bureau of Investigation chief William Flynn more then once had let it slip that the big day was July 4, although he later denied that he had designated a particular day. Whatever Flynn's memory of what he had uttered to the press, the Fourth of July was designated as the day when the carnage "might take place."

In the late days of June and the first three days of July, urgent meetings were called, and every law enforcement agency and bureau in the nation was alerted. On the Sunday before Independence Day (which fell on a Friday) Flynn and cohorts solidified the design for cooperation of federal, state, and municipal police authorities in "handling the possible outbreak by the 'red flag' elements of the population." And throughout that week before, at least half a dozen bills were discussed in Congress as part of a comprehensive program to curb Bolshevism and radicalism—one that the *Christian Science Monitor* called "a program of an extreme character." Central to the discussions was the big question of whether the current revolutionary propaganda circulating throughout the nation necessitated a law similar to if not the same as the Espionage Act. A Republican senator from South Dakota said he believed that this would be necessary in order to strengthen "the hands of the government in dealing with open disloyalty to the Constitution and the laws of the country." The bill that would soon be presented to the Senate would ban the red flag at all gatherings, prohibit under heavy penalty the distribution of anarchistic literature through the mails, and criminalize any expression of advocacy of revolution. The bill would also call for the deportation of any aliens violating any part of it. Further, a Democrat senator from Utah proposed that the penalty for sending bombs such as those mailed recently should be execution.

On Friday, the Fourth, temperatures in New York broke the record at 98 degrees. Despite the rays of burning sun, uniformed law enforcement officials patrolled the city and "inspected" the local "haunts" of at least twenty groups considered to be anarchistic and possibly dangerous. Buildings were searched and all reading materials found in them were seized. On the most wanted list of publications were the writings of Leon Trotsky and V. I. Lenin and any issues of the radical publication *The Anarchist Soviet Bulletin*. The occupants of the buildings were searched but no arrests were made. In other cities too there were raids without violence or resistance, and with few, if any, arrests.

The revolution didn't happen that day. The reign of terror did not begin. "Bomb 'Plot' Is a Fizzle" read one headline. The biggest news of July 4 seemed to be the record high temperatures in most of the nation: 100 in Boston, Philadelphia, and Washington, D.C. So hot was the day in Boston that people claimed they saw molasses from the January explosion bubbling up from the cracks in the sidewalks.

Generally, it was a sane, serene Fourth of July in all of America—except perhaps in Ohio. There, in Toledo, Americans unable yet to shift out of war mode got their pugilistic fix at the battle for the world heavyweight boxing title. What some people would henceforth call "The Slaughter of Toledo" took place at Bay View Park where, at the moment the fight began, the temperature was 110 degrees. At least fifty thousand spectators, soaking in sweat, sat in concentric circles around the sun-baked boxing ring where Jack Dempsey would try to wrest the world title from Jess Willard. Known as the "savior of the white race" for having smashed and battered big black Jack Johnson, Willard was confident he would keep his title. "Superior punching" would win him the title, he told a reporter on July 2. Dempsey was even more confident that Willard would lose the title.

Despite the blazing sun, or perhaps because of it, the audience was "electrified," as one newspaper put it. Jack Dempsey, whose real name was William Harrison Dempsey and who was born in Manassa, Colorado—the ninth of eleven children—was twenty-four years old, six foot one inch, weighed 187 pounds, and had won his five previous challenges in 1919, each time in the first round. As early as 1916, sportswriter Damon Runyon called him the "Manassa Mauler." Willard, a Kansan from Pottawatomie, was thirty-seven years old, six foot seven inches, 245 pounds, and had held the world heavyweight title since 1915. First into the ring, Dempsey, in his white shorts and tan body, radiated confidence and power. Willard wore black and was hardly as fit as he had been four years before when he had defeated Johnson.

The fight lasted nine minutes. Dempsey knocked down Willard seven times in the first round, leaving him hanging on the ropes. Dempsey broke Willard's jaw, knocked out four of his teeth, smashed his nose and cracked at least two ribs. At the start of the fourth round, Willard, eyes swollen shut, mouth bubbling with blood, body dripping with blood and sweat, sat down. Dempsey told the press he was horrified at what he had done to Willard: "I'll never fight again as long as I live. I'll never pull on another glove. I'm through with the game. My God, what a terrible sensation to hit a defenseless man. Even in the hour of my own success, I sympathize with him." But Dempsey was a warrior who would not stop fighting until he too was defeated. In later years, sportswriter Red Smith would describe Dempsey as "187 pounds of unbridled violence" and "the best of all pugilists."

In Detroit, where the temperature hit 101 at noon, another event far upstaged "The Slaughter of Toledo," the threat of terrorism, and even the heat of the day. The Polar Bears—nearly half of them anyhow—were home. And the entire state of Michigan, it seemed, had converged on the 982-acre island known as Belle Isle in the Detroit River for a day of celebrating.

By July 4, millions of soldiers had returned and thousands of cities, towns, and villages had welcomed them. Homecoming parades were so frequent that small businesses had formed for the planning of them. While the thrill of soldiers reuniting with their loved ones never waned, the celebrations had become predictable and mundane. The return of Detroit's Own from Arctic Russia, however, stood out. Trying to understand the difference, one *Detroit News* reporter wrote that perhaps it felt more dramatic because "no other unit came back bringing with it so strong a sense that it was returning from the dead." How odd it was, another reporter wrote, to be hailing the return of men who had been fighting an undeclared, effectively unconstitutional war, who should never have spent a day in northern Russia.

Of the seven thousand soldiers who had arrived in Archangel and Murmansk in September 1918, 4,500 were coming home. One hundred eighty-four would never return. Of those, 112 had been killed in action and 72 were dead from diseases. Sixty of those had died from the influenza. The rest would remain in Russia for several more months.

When in June the government informed the families of the 339th that most of the soldiers were no longer in Russia, some greeted the news with skepticism, especially because they did not know when exactly the troops would land in New York harbor. They did know that by June the ice of northern Russia had melted. The ports had opened. The railways were repaired. And, able to ride the rails to the port of Archangel, the 339th had shipped out in early June on the steamer *Czar*, arriving eight days later at Brest. From there they would soon sail for America. While in France, the men from Michigan stayed at an army debarkation camp at nearby Pontanezen and spent a good deal of time bathing, so wrote Jay Hayden, the *Detroit News* correspondent who had covered the story for months.

At Pontanezen too, Hayden interviewed soldiers about their nine months in Russia. It was cold. It was dirty. It was dangerous. The food was terrible. The rice and meal were usually moldy and the dried vegetables often spoiled. There was never fresh meat. The regiment remained on the front lines without a break but the worst part of it, they told Hayden, was not knowing why in fact they were there. They were first told they were guarding supplies and then they were sent to front lines of Russia's civil war for months, hundreds of miles from Archangel. The British, Hayden wrote, distributed leaflets saying that the purpose of the expedition was "the saving of the Russians from themselves." In the opinion of several soldiers who spoke freely and at length to Hayden, it was not "any of their business to attempt to tell the Russians what to do in their internal affairs."

From the moment the Polar Bears had arrived at Hoboken, New Jersey, on the morning of June 30, a misty disbelief seemed to envelop them. On both sides of the Hudson River that day, men, women, and children stood waiting, many having come as early as 2 A.M. And when the ship docked, some screamed the names of their loved ones, straining their necks and eyes for a glimpse of a familiar face. But others, as if unable to believe what was happening, stood in silence. So often during the past eight months had they believed that hunger, disease, or the Arctic cold had wiped out the 339th, that every one of the regiment had been massacred by the Bolsheviks, who they were told outnumbered the Americans forty to one, and that there would be no survivor to report who had died last. So often had they heard such dismal reports and so rarely had they received letters out of Russia that now it was hard to believe that the men about to disembark were in fact alive.

Among the quiet ones that day were the sister, brother, and mother of Private J. A. Brusseau. As they stood on the pier and watched as crewmen tossed the anchors into New York harbor, the mother gripped ever tighter the letter her son had sent to the *Detroit Free Press* and to her in May, appearing in the paper immediately after its arrival on June 10.

Dear Sir: Thinking perhaps you wouldn't mind having a little news from the far north for the people of Detroit, I consider it a pleasure to write you to tell you that at last the 339th is standing some show of getting out of the venerable country it has been in for such an un-predetermined period of time. . . . I know it's hard for the people of Detroit to get the real "dope" from Russia, but we can hope only for the luck of our letters getting through. We write what we think will pass censor, but whether it does or not is another question. . . . I have just come back to the railroad front after a three months' tramp through the jungles of forests and snow, with some experiences that are worthwhile knowing. I know well what it is to be rapidly freezing to death (or rather on the way there) to go hungry, tired and sleepy. To sleep in the snow is but a trifle as that is possibly better than mud and water. I know many other things, too, which I wouldn't dare mention here. Maybe it will be just as well to get in good old Detroit again. Now this time it's no rumor, no fooling—we are going home very very soon. It's honest to goodness true, take it from me. We should be home the beginning of July, sometime. I'll surely have heart disease all the way over. My heart is beating faster now than it has been.

When they finally arrived at Belle Isle on Independence Day, the men with "Russia" stenciled on their helmets, "NR" (Northern Russia) stitched on their sleeves, and white polar bears silk-screened on their armbands were all given flyers informing them of the many services, events, and speeches in their honor that day. Ask any of the Detroit's Own committeemen, the flyer said, "for anything in the world except a marriage license." There were baseball games, boat rides, swimming, and eating, mostly ice cream and chicken. The Belle Isle bathhouse passed out free swimming suits and the Detroit Yacht Club offered all services as it would to its members. There were seven band concerts throughout the day. A dance band played at one end of the island beginning at 2:30 P.M., continuing into the night. Politicians from thirty-seven cities attended. The 339th's Sergeant Theodore Kolbe, who had spoken so openly in December about conditions in Russia, was there, as he was now the deputy county treasurer in Detroit. And there were many speeches. "You fought under the greatest of all odds," said Detroit's mayor, James Couzens. "You fought doubts in your own hearts; doubts that Headquarters remembered your predicament, that the folks at home knew whether you still lived, that they had received your letters, that relief could ever reach you through the ice-locked sea."

California's Senator Hiram Johnson, the champion of their cause, came to Detroit on the train from Washington to greet the 339th. Upon his arrival at Michigan Central Station at 7:45 A.M. on the Fourth, he told the press that he came purely for "sentimental reasons" and without any intention of speaking about his latest cause, which, as an ardent isolationist, was to defeat the League of Nations and to flay Wilson's international policy any chance he could. Nor did he intend to discuss his opinions on the Paris Peace Conference, of which he was very critical, or the several thousand more American soldiers in Russia who were still fighting in Siberia and would not return until the spring of 1920, or his plans to run for president in 1920, of which he was very optimistic, or his views on Bolshevism, which he hated. He had no canned speech and he preferred eating breakfast to talking to the press, he told a *Detroit News* writer who asked him specifically about his opinion on the "bolshevik question." "The question of their [the 339th's] removal from Russia was purely American and had nothing else in it," said Johnson. "This country has nothing to fear from any idiotic, fantastic thing like Bolshevism."

Later in the day, however, at Belle Isle, after Mayor Couzens introduced Johnson as "the greatest possibility for the next President of the United States" and "the man who stood up so valiantly in the Senate to demand that the boys of the 339th be released from the terribly isolated country to which they had been sent without any explanation from their Government," Johnson, wiping sweat from his brow and rolling up the sleeves of his white shirt, spoke of more than the homecoming of the Polar Bears.

And now if this day has any lesson for any of us, for all whose hearts beat with Americanism, it means that you and I and all of us must solemnly dedicate ourselves on this happy homecoming day to the pledge that boys from America must not be embroiled in European troubles unless America's rights are invaded. We are facing today one of the greatest crises that ever came to this country. We are standing at the crossroads, and one leads to imperialistic control, and the other is the straight and narrow path of Americanism. As I think of the hardships you men suffered, and as I come face to face with you here I know that you will join me in consecrating ourselves to the aim that this nation shall be American and American alone.

On the Fourth of July, President Wilson gave his own speech to soldiers and sailors and seven French war brides on board the *George Washington*. This Fourth of July was the most important of all, he said, even more crucial than the very first one when the free nation of America was established with the intention of serving liberty for all mankind, within or outside its borders. Now, Americans had shown the world that they were true to their pledge "to be the servants of humanity and of free men everywhere, to tend to the troubles of other peoples whose freedoms were threatened. . . . My confident ambition for the United States is that she will know in the future how to make each Fourth of July as it comes grow more distinguished and more glorious than its predecessor by showing that she, at any rate, understands the laws of freedom by understanding the laws of service and that mankind may always confidently look to her as a friend, as a cooperator, as one who will stand shoulder to shoulder with free men everywhere in the world to assert the right. . . . This is the most tremendous Fourth of July that men ever imagined, for we have opened its franchises to all the world."

Neither Johnson nor Wilson mentioned the other reason for celebration that day, which surely affected every returning soldier. The flu epidemic was effectively over, although the government would not officially announce the end for several more months. In the first six months of 1919, in the third wave, approximately 190,000 men and women had died in America from the flu and its companion killer, pneumonia. Between September of 1918 and June of 1919—the second and third waves of the pandemic—the best estimate of deaths from flu and pneumonia, both civilian and military, had been 675,000 Americans. Even the worst effects of the war and the most difficult struggles of its aftermath could not compare with the devastation caused by the flu.

This group of returning soldiers would not face such threats, but, like all troops coming home, they would have to tackle the huge challenge of making a life in postwar America. Beyond the uplifting, reassuring, self-serving orations of Johnson and Wilson was the reality that the millions of troops arriving in New York harbor were causing shock waves as they returned to a nation that had not yet adjusted to peace—one whose munitions factories had not yet reconverted to peacetime production, whose laborers were underpaid, whose cost of living had reached an unprecedented high, and whose returning soldiers needed work. Never before had the nation experienced such a huge demobilization of soldiers. In the first three months after the close of the Civil War, 640,806 soldiers were mustered out of service as compared with 1,246,374 during the three months from November 11, 1918, to February 15, 1919. And the government did not have a well-conceived plan for adjusting to their return.

Indeed, for a while in demobilization camps discharges were delayed to prevent the overwhelming supply of labor from exceeding its already threatening levels. In March of 1919, *Life* magazine published a cartoon that showed Uncle Sam saying to a soldier "Nothing is too good for you, my boy! What would you like?" And the soldier responded, "A job."

The labor surplus added to race tensions and allowed employers to take advantage of the easily replaceable workers. Low wages and long hours— often twelve-hour workdays—and the quest for the right to organize to achieve better working conditions were all reasons for the rising number of labor strikes each month. In March there had been 175 strikes, in April 248, in May 388, in June 303, and now in July there would be 360. While the government blamed pro-German propaganda, the IWW, and the Bolsheviks for the worker unrest, the vise of low wages and rising living costs was tightening for American workers. In the previous five years food prices, for example, had risen more than 80 percent, clothing more than 100 percent, and furniture 125 percent. During the war, limited supplies of commodities had driven up the prices and because of the war people were willing to pay more. But now, manufacturers were not lowering prices. Some were even hoarding products to drive up the demand and thus maintain an excessively high price. The average American family was facing a cost of living that was 99 percent higher than it had been in 1914 when the war began. In May and June the soaring cost of living had caused such a stir that twenty-six Democratic members of Congress in conjunction with the Democratic Club of Massachusetts sent a cablegram to President Wilson in Paris urging him to come home: "The citizens of the United States want you home to help reduce the high cost of living, which we consider far more important than the League of Nations."

On Independence Day, the U.S. president was halfway between France and America, on his way home.

CHAPTER 26

The Narrow Path

On the 8th of July, the *George Washington* docked at New York harbor accompanied by the requisite dreadnoughts. It was greeted by great guns booming, dirigibles and airplanes crisscrossing the sky, and smaller boats tilting this way and that from the overwhelming crowds cheering, waving, and reaching out as if they had a chance to touch their president. "Honor to Woodrow Wilson, Peace Maker" read the banner stretched across the bow of one tugboat.

Although heralded as a grand homecoming, there was an aura of melancholy. Standing on the deck that day was Ray Stannard Baker, who tried in his later writings to grasp the bittersweet quality of Wilson's return:

> At the end of the war itself I was full of hope. The long struggle had at last been won; the terms of settlement [in the Armistice], including intelligent preliminary plans for a League of Nations, had been adopted by all of the belligerents. A great constructive transformation in world affairs seemed possible, even probable. During the long months at the Peace Conference these hopes, this faith, had gradually dwindled. There was a faint revival at the homecoming of the President. . . . It seemed momentarily possible that Woodrow Wilson's leadership might still prevail, that America by its own power and prestige might yet save the peace.

The treaty that was now signed and that Wilson carried with him in anticipation of America's approval was a great volume of 214 pages in two languages, English and French. Wrapped in the hopes and aspirations of a new world, it was also weighted down by greed, fear, vanity, and petty interests of the old world: the nations that had wrangled for six months to produce it. The president knew how deeply flawed it was and yet he seemed to believe that once the facts were presented to the U.S. Congress and to the

American public, the treaty would be accepted as the best possible settlement in the most complicated of worlds. He also knew that opposition had been growing since his trip home in February. Perhaps what he didn't know or refused to recognize was that in the six months since the peace talks had begun the American people weren't thinking about it much anymore. Many months had passed since their president had left for France and much had happened. Their thoughts had turned to jobs and prices and children and getting on with life. They were told that this treaty and this new League of Nations would obligate them to fight other countries' battles. It would take the men away again. It would disrupt lives. "The straight and narrow path of Americanism" of which Senator Johnson had spoken was more to the liking of most Americans, although Wilson would try to convince them otherwise.

Only two days after his return home, on July 10, the president presented the treaty to the U.S. Senate for ratification. He stood before them and admitted that it was not exactly as he would have wanted it to be. To accommodate the interests of all nations without making compromises was not possible, he told the senators. But he assured them that the League of Nations, whose Covenant was part of the treaty, was the "only hope for mankind." And he said: "We can only go forward, with lifted eyes and freshened spirit to follow the vision. It was of this that we dreamed at our birth. America shall in truth show the way. The light shines upon the path ahead, and nowhere else."

As those words wafted through the Senate chamber, that part of America excluded from the treaty and the Covenant of the League—the invisible men and women struggling to be seen and to be equal, the "volcano" as Baker had so astutely called it years before—was about to erupt once again, this time in Longview, Texas.

On July 5, the Saturday morning train through Longview brought, as was its routine, the latest edition of the popular black weekly the *Chicago Defender*. This particular issue would be of great interest to the one-third of the Longview population that was black, as it would give them new details about the heinous mid-June Longview lynching of Lemuel Walters. The article revealed that the statement of the white woman from Kilgore, Texas, who had professed her love for Walters and had told her white friends that if she lived up North she would get a divorce and marry him, was what had provoked his murder. The *Defender* claimed that Walters's only crime was this woman's love for him and her act of expressing it. The article described Walters's body riddled with bullets and thrown near the roadside. And it added the fact that underlying the incident was white anger at black people who had moved North during the past few years. Such migrations robbed the South of its cheap labor.

The *Defender*, which was founded in Chicago by its current editor, Robert Abbott, in 1905, had a considerable following in 1919 in East Texas and even a history. In previous years, black workers had read its ads about the need for labor up North and indeed had left the cotton fields of Texas for destinations such as Chicago. The migrations had infuriated white cotton growers, who depended on the cheap black labor to enhance their profit margins. Thus they associated their loss with the black weekly newspaper from Chicago. And in recent months articles had begun to appear again informing Southern blacks that there were places up North, especially in the Northwest, where laborers were wanted and would be safe. The May 24 issue stated that in the Northwest there was "the opportunity to secure labor surrounded by pleasant environment, carrying with it the security of your wives and families" and that this should appeal to "every man who is burdened down under the yoke of cast proscription and lynching, which have been the 'pastime' of the South."

In Longview, a town of 5,700 citizens, the readers of the *Chicago Defender* in 1919 consisted mostly of members of the Negro Business League. Organized by Dr. Calvin P. Davis, a local black physician, the league encouraged black cotton growers to bypass white middlemen and sell their cotton directly to buyers in Galveston, thus making more money. Working with Davis to improve conditions and wages of black workers was high school teacher Samuel Jones, described in the *Shreveport Times* as "well-educated and with a persuasive tongue." He was also the *Chicago Defender*'s agent in Longview.

During the weeks following Walters's lynching, Davis, Jones, and other members of the league had visited the county judge to talk about legal action against Walters's killers. Was there an investigation? they asked. Who were the chief suspects? Why were there no arrests? The judge cautioned them to keep quiet about it and also said he would mention their concerns to the district attorney, especially their suspicions that the police were delaying arrests until all evidence was destroyed and witness alibis were established. By July 5, there appeared to be no progress whatsoever in identifying the murderers of Lemuel Walters. No arrests. No investigation. Only silence.

Thus was the state of things in Longview on July 5 when the latest issue of the *Defender* arrived. Within hours of its circulation, white leaders and cotton growers were enraged. Especially offensive was the quote from the white woman expressing her love for a black man. She could not have said such a thing, said local whites. It must be a lie and the suspected fabricator must be Jones, the black man in Longview with the closest association with the *Defender*. To those who believed *that* lie, what happened next was only fitting.

On July 10, a Thursday, Jones was walking to his car, which was parked in downtown Longview, when he was approached by a group of white men led by the three brothers of the white woman quoted in the *Defender*. Two of them grabbed him by the arms and began to force him into their car. He refused to go. In response, one of the men struck him with a wrench. Another man hit him with the butt of a gun. Then one strike followed another until they tried to force a confession from Jones. He was the one who had written the *Defender* article, they wanted him to say. No, he was not, he kept repeating. And every time he said no, they beat him again. Finally, they let loose one last blow with a warning to leave town by midnight. Jones managed to crawl to Dr. Davis's office nearby and while Davis was treating him, a white mob was supposedly gathering to lynch Jones if he did not disappear as instructed. The mayor sent word to Davis and to Jones to leave as soon as possible but both refused. That night, the 10th, Davis went to city hall to seek help for the black community from law enforcement officials. As he entered, he was asked to take off his hat.

"Yes!" said Davis, with his hat still on. "That's all you all say to a colored man who comes to talk serious business to you: 'Take off your hat.' I am not going to do it. I want to know what protection we colored citizens are going to have tonight."

"You will have to take your chances," the mayor said.

Close to midnight, still on the night of the 10th, a mob had gathered and was moving through the back streets of Longview heading for Jones's house. When they arrived, they walked onto the back porch and demanded that Jones come out. When they heard nothing in response, they forced their way in. Davis was on the other side of the door and fired the first shot. Thus began the battle. Four white men died. A fifth man who had hidden under the house was dragged out and beaten by two black men. After retreating, some members of the white mob regrouped at the local fire station where they rang the alarm to call in more support. At least a thousand men answered the call to arms. At dawn, they broke into a hardware store and stole guns and ammunition. The now well-armed mob returned to Jones's house, which they found deserted. After drenching it in kerosene and setting it on fire, they moved on to Dr. Davis's office and burned it down, as well as a dance hall, a grocery store and meat market, the local drugstore, the lodge hall where the Negro Business League congregated, and two black residences. It was around this time that the police got involved. They arrested six members of the League for rioting, and formed posses to track down Jones and Davis, who were labeled the "ringleaders" in the local newspapers and who had disappeared. For one night Jones hid at the Longview home of a sympathetic white family, who then facilitated his escape to a town further north. Davis dressed in a soldier's uniform and then hopped a train on the outskirts of town. When he arrived at the station two hours in advance of the train of soldiers that he knew was coming, he bought popcorn and soft drinks and sang and danced, acting "in most approved 'darky' style," as *The Crisis* later wrote.

The police never found either of them. But in their hot pursuit that first night they paid a visit to Davis's sixty-year-old father-in-law, Marion Bush, who was not going to wait to find out whether the bloodhounds and shouting deputies wanted to take him into protective custody or arrest him. As he fled, running through a cornfield, one of the deputies shot and killed him.

Longview's mayor asked the governor to send the Texas Rangers or the National Guard or preferably both. While waiting for the hundred or so guardsmen and the eight Texas Rangers to arrive, local police ordered all undistributed issues of the July 5 *Chicago Defender* destroyed. On Saturday, after the guardsmen had arrived, a 10 P.M. curfew was put into place, groups of three or more people were prohibited from gathering on city streets, and all blacks and whites were ordered to turn over their guns. By Sunday 150 more guardsmen had arrived and the town and county were placed under martial law. Soon, seventeen white men were arrested for attempted murder and just as soon, each one was released on $1,000 bail. Nine white men were charged with arson, and also released on $1,000 bail. Twenty-one black men were arrested on charges of assault with attempt to murder, and sent for the rest of the month of July to Austin, for their own safety. And a local group consisting of bankers, merchants, lawyers, and farmers issued a statement that condemned both the white mob's burning of the houses and Jones's distribution of the *Chicago Defender.* "We will not permit the Negroes of this community and country to in any way interfere with our social affairs, or to write or circulate articles about the white people," the group told the *Shreveport Times.*

In Washington, a flurry of memos about Longview blew through the offices of congressmen, postal officials, the Justice Department, and the War Department. As incendiary as the May issue of *The Crisis* magazine was feared to be, the *Defender* was now the center of attention. Major Walter H. Loving, who watched over the Negro Subversion agents in the War Department, alerted those in the field to pay close attention to the responses of black communities to Longview and especially to be aware of the possibility of increased readership of the *Defender.* Congressman W. D. Upshaw of Georgia visited the offices of the postal solicitor, carrying a bundle of *Defenders* under his arm, and claiming that the weekly's role in exciting blacks should be a crime, though he did not know any law that could be applied to prosecuting the newspaper or its editor. "It may be that a remonstrance from the Government might 'slow up' the devilment a little," Upshaw wrote in a letter to the assistant postmaster general. A chorus of protest was growing ever louder and calling for the suppression of the supposedly inaccurate and explosive *Defender,* which was distorting life in the South. A senator from Louisiana joined in, as did the sheriff of Shreveport, which was sixty miles east of Longview, and the postmaster of Marshall, Texas, where there were two black colleges, Bishop and Wiley. Blacks were happy in Marshall, he said, and he wasn't able to stop the local agent from distributing the paper. So the contentment of the black man in the South would soon be ruined by the continued mailing of the *Defender.* When the *Defender* published reports of such condemnation of its pages, its critics became adamant about the government blocking the circulation to Southern destinations. The "decidedly rabid" attitude of the paper would likely incite more discontent and rioting in the South, the anti-*Defender* crusaders said, as they urged the Justice Department to investigate the paper and its writers and editors, and especially to determine just how much Bolshevist propaganda was influencing the paper's content. There was no mention of lynchings.

CHAPTER 27

Miss Puffer Insane?

Longview, Texas. Ellisville, Mississippi. Charleston, South Carolina. All were a long way from Massachusetts. But for Mabel Puffer and Arthur Hazzard, in the sizzling summer days following their hasty, high-profile exodus from New Hampshire and their return to Ayer, Massachusetts, such towns seemed all too close.

From the moment Puffer's relatives and their attorney had arrived in Concord to put a stop to the "insanity of such a marriage" to the day in mid-July when Mabel Puffer might be declared "insane," the names Puffer and Hazzard appeared in major newspapers nearly every day, often on the front page. Thus a frightened, bemused, cruel public watched as the courts eviscerated the couple's lives. There were no invitations for this lynching, as there had been in Ellisville, but there was daily attendance to the apparently entertaining event of the slow death of Puffer and Hazzard's relationship, conceived in innocence and aborted in shameful bigotry. "Ayer residents who enjoy a first rate legal battle are rubbing their hands in anticipation of developments," wrote the Boston Traveller. There was even audience participation.

Consider the deluge of letters sent to Puffer in her lonely cell, or "detention room" as the police called it, in the basement of the Ayer city hall, and to Hazzard, out on $300 bail, at his mother's home within view of the door to Puffer's cell and directly behind the police station. Numerous white men wrote to Puffer, proposing marriage to "save" her from "the Negro." Two or three black clergymen from Boston wrote with promises to marry her and her Negro fiancé. One offered shelter and help just in case the couple continued encountering difficulties. Hazzard received a letter from a white woman in Boston asking if she could meet him; perhaps she would be a better match in case the marriage to Puffer didn't work out. And one of his well-heeled employers—someone for whom he had beat rugs and chopped wood for nearly as long as for the Puffers—sent him a large bouquet of red roses, which he took to his mother and placed in a large vase on the center table of the their parlor. "I'd take them to Mabel if I could, only they won't let me," he told a reporter.

Both were targeted for hate mail. During the last week of June, Puffer received a letter, unsigned, with a Providence, Rhode Island, postmark, in which she was warned that if she did not break up with Hazzard, then the author of the letter, "aided by certain others," would "take matters into their own hands and see that Hazzard is dealt with in such a manner as to make the marriage impossible." There were other letters of this type bearing postmarks from Ayer, Boston, Lowell, and Swampscott, among other locales. Some were addressed also to the local police alerting them to the possibility of mob action against Hazzard.

At the same time, soldiers at nearby Camp Devens showed particular interest in both the wealthy society lady and her handyman. On the 24th of June, in YMCA Hut No. 21, they held a forensic event on the question: "Resolved, that marriage of white women with colored men should be forbidden by law." The discussion was led by the "secretary" or manager of the hut, who went to the court clerk's office that day to research the case and find information to back his argument. The following day small groups of soldiers could be seen in downtown Ayer asking people questions like: Just how strong is the local police force? Is there any tradition of state police bolstering local law enforcement if there's trouble? And how much interference would they encounter if they decided "to give Hazzard a taste of Southern persuasion." There was one group, about half a dozen, who came into town almost every day from then on. They told the townsfolk that they were "from the Southern regions of the nation." They were serious, they told the locals, and they wanted their presence to be known all around town, especially in the cell in the basement of the Ayer city hall and in the small house behind the police station. They were also looking for recruits for the "fun" they had in mind.

But they never had their fun—at least not in the way they had envisioned it. And while they did visit the courtroom on some days of the upcoming hearings and the trial, they eventually backed off from their bold flirtations with violence. Perhaps they were worried that Hazzard lived only fifteen feet from the back door of the police station. Perhaps in all their questioning, they had discovered that there were people in Ayer, some on the police force even, who had known Honey Hazzard for years, who were familiar with his habits of hard work, and who were not willing to watch him die at the end of a rope or amid the flames of a burning stake. Or perhaps they were just smart enough to realize that this black man would be destroyed by other means. This was a lynching of another sort— the Northern kind, they reckoned—and almost as good as what they could have done. It was all about using the law to scare the man away, destroying his reputation and his livelihood in the process. It was a legal lynching, so to speak. And in this case, it was a double one: the black man *and* his white fiancée.

"Miscegenation" was the technical word for interracial marriage and in America it had never been a very popular concept. The first colony to outlaw such unions was Virginia in 1691, ruling that any whites who married blacks, Native Americans, or mulattoes, would be forever banished. Then came Maryland the next year and, in 1705, Massachusetts, which was also one of the first to repeal the law, doing so in 1843. By 1919, forty-one out of the forty-eight states had at one time outlawed mixed race marriages, and thirty still had the law on the books. There had even been a push to make it a federal crime.

Indeed, U.S. Representative Seaborn Roddenbery, of Georgia, proposed to Congress on December 11, 1912, a constitutional amendment banning interracial marriage. "No more voracious parasite ever sucked at the heart of pure society, innocent girlhood, or Caucasian motherhood than the one which welcomes and recognizes the sacred ties of wedlock between Africa and America," he told his fellow congressmen. The proposed amendment provided that intermarriage "between Negroes or persons of color and Caucasians or any other character of persons within the U.S. or any territory under their jurisdiction, is forever prohibited; and the term 'negro or person of color,' as here employed, shall be held to mean any and all persons of African descent or having any trace of African or negro blood."

Opposition to Roddenbery's proposal was strong, especially among black Americans. This was not because they necessarily wanted to marry white men or white women. Rather, as W. E. B. Du Bois wrote in his opposition to it, it was because the amendment treated blackness as "a physical taint." He and others pointed out that such a law clearly banned black men from marrying white women yet at the same time, it gave white men who had sexual relationships with black women an excuse not to marry them. By making it illegal to legitimate such interracial sexual relationships, the law thus relegated black women in liaisons with white men to the position of mistresses. As Du Bois put it, the law would make "the colored girl absolutely helpless before the lust of white men." One letter written to Roddenbery suggested that "by all means let us have your resolution, but amend it so that if it is a crime for Negro men to marry white women legally in the north; it be a misdemeanor for white men to mate with Negro women illegally in the south."

There were other proposals before Congress that year regarding miscegenation, all quite obviously provoked by the lascivious behavior of Jack Johnson, the first black man to win the world's heavyweight boxing title. Johnson was outspoken about his preference for white women—and many of them. In fact he publicly denigrated black women, which thus made him unpopular with both races. In October of 1912, he was arrested and charged with the abduction of an eighteen-year-old white woman, Lucille Cameron, whom he said worked for him as a secretary at his nightclub, the Café de Champion. Cameron told police that "she loved Johnson and expected to become his wife." Police, her mother, and the public could not conceive of such "lunacy." Thus, Johnson was charged with violation of the White Slave Traffic Act of 1910, known as the Mann Act. At his trial, Cameron, who was held in jail and not allowed to communicate with Johnson, would not testify that Johnson was running a prostitution ring and that she was called to Chicago to be part of it. Prosecutors thus had to drop the charges, release Cameron, and dismiss the case against Johnson. Once released, Cameron did in fact marry Johnson. The governor of New York called the marriage "a blot on our civilization. Such desecration of the marriage tie should never be allowed." In the wake of this highly publicized case, Seaborn Roddenbery launched his 1912 crusade in Congress. That same year, the House did pass a law making racial intermarriage a felony in the District of Columbia.

Seven years later, not much had changed. In fact, it could be said that by the summer of 1919 as the "volcano" was about to erupt, the notion of a black man marrying a white woman, especially a wealthy white woman, might have been even more outrageous than it had been in 1912. When Puffer and Hazzard had first arrived in New Hampshire, they were not at all rejected. In fact, their candor, their friendliness, and their obvious affection for each other had seemed to grace them with that golden glow that humanity loves. Even the mayor had said that he would marry them. But when Puffer's relatives arrived to stop the marriage and the buzz of a scandal grew louder, the townsfolk, as if snapping out of a trance, suddenly looked at the mixed race couple as pariahs and at their dream as shameful. The popular current washed over the town, crushing Puffer and Hazzard's romance and sending both of them nearly into shock.

It was possible that Puffer and Hazzard's everyday life was so contained, so sheltered behind the Venetian blinds and in the perfect garden at the cottage on Sandy Pond that neither of them ever once connected their own hopeful plans with any of the prevailing prejudices that plagued America in the summer of 1919. And that on warm summer nights the sounds of bull frogs and crickets and the wind rustling across the tops of trees prevented them from hearing their neighbors' suspicious whispers. It was indeed probable that it had not occurred to either one that the very town they had both known for most of their lives could turn against them, that a city hall they might have passed thousands of times would hold one of them prisoner. That a vendor who for years had sold them newspapers would now avoid eye contact. And worst of all that their honesty and sanity, after years of building up strong reputations, could suddenly be questioned.

What did Mabel Puffer think about during those long isolated days in the basement of the city hall? Was she trying to place a calm, cool hand on the feverish present? Or was she anxiously bitter, comparing her situation to that of others and dwelling on the fact that there were white men, hardly as kind or as good as her Gar, who every day of the week married white women? And some of those white men married well-heeled white women like herself—for their money even!—but they were granted the privacy of such a decision. Did she wonder what her crime had been or why she was not allowed to see her fiancé? Did she even know of Hazzard's many attempts to send her notes and flowers and boxes of her favorite chocolates? Had she seen him standing on the stoop of his mother's house staring at the basement door of city hall waiting for it to open for her daily walk with the police matron who guarded her? And what should she do? Should she fake insanity to get the statutory charges dropped as she was told would happen if she was, in fact, declared insane? What could she do to be certain that Hazzard would be a free man? Did she know of the accusations against him, that he had stolen from her?

The challenge for the legal lynchers was that without the help of a federal law against miscegenation or such a law in either New Hampshire or Massachusetts, their case was weak. Hazzard's lawyer, William H. Lewis, who was black and who was a dynamic former assistant U.S. attorney in Boston, informed the Massachusetts judge early on that he was fighting mad about the fact that he was certain his client and his fiancée had not committed any crimes whatsoever. Rather, their accusers had. There had been no extradition papers and thus, Lewis said, those who presented the warrant in Concord and filed the charges contained in it had committed the crime of kidnapping. The statutory charge in the warrant should be dismissed, he said. And although Puffer was not his client, Lewis would help to prove that she was not insane for wanting to marry a black man. The actions against his client and his fiancée, he said, were blatant violations of the Bill of Rights. Lewis told the court that "Miss Puffer wasn't insane before she attempted to marry Mr. Hazzard. There was never any suspicion of misconduct between the two before her relatives learned that she proposed to marry a colored man. There is no law in this State that forbids a marriage between colored and white people. This is Massachusetts, not Mississippi. This is Ayer, not Atlanta. It makes no difference what Your Honor may think about a marriage of this kind, or what I may think about it. Justice must be done these two law-abiding people."

The opposing forces clearly needed a plan. Perhaps they could keep Puffer isolated, bring in alienists—the psychiatrists of the day—to examine her and then make a deal with her lawyer—and perhaps with her—that if she is to be declared insane the statutory charges against the couple will be dropped? Then, just to be sure that nothing would change before her half-nephew could get legal guardianship over his newly declared insane half-aunt and her estate—the earliest time would likely be September—find other charges against Hazzard, ones that would keep Puffer away from him. After all, between the release of charges and the legal establishment of Puffer's relative as her legal guardian, what was to stop the couple from running away to another state that did not have a five-day wait for a marriage license? Was this the strategy? It was clear that whatever the plan, it must induce Puffer to voluntarily reject Hazzard herself.

But by the end of the couple's first week back in Ayer, it was also clear that neither the daily advice of the police matron, who was apparently urging Puffer to end the relationship, nor the long days in the detention cell, nor the separation from Honey had succeeded in destroying Puffer's devotion to her fiancé. In an interview with a *Chicago Defender* reporter covering the story in late June—for an article that appeared in early July—Puffer had said firmly:

> It seems to me that the judge, lawyers and the people who have been writing letters to me need a little mental examination. I never knew there were so many queer folks in the world before. They are simply losing time trying to adjudge me insane for the purpose of separating me from Mr. Hazzard. . . .
>
> If some of these people who are trying to interfere with our marriage were as intelligent as Mr. Hazzard all of this trouble would not have happened. . . .
>
> They have done everything in their power to discourage him, but he is not made of the material that melts quickly after fire. Although his face is dark, the heart is white and spirit purer than the men of my race who are trying to intimidate him.

The court date for the hearing at which Puffer's sanity would be judged was July 11. During the two weeks preceding it, a flurry of events caused considerable confusion, for the townsfolk, for reporters, for anyone attempting to understand the drama. Nothing was as it appeared to be. Or was it?

For one thing, at a court hearing to judge Puffer's state of mind, she pulled off the opal engagement ring Hazzard had given her and told the judge that she would send it back to Hazzard, registered mail. At the end of the hearing, she embraced the half-niece who had stopped her marriage. Her lawyer told the press that the engagement was off and because there was no longer any need to protect her from Hazzard's influence, Puffer would be released from her cell at city hall. He said that she would be leaving town with a guardian for a few days and that she was planning to move to the Pacific Coast, perhaps California. He also said that there might not have to be an insanity hearing now, adding that Puffer had agreed to testify against Hazzard when he was tried for larceny.

Now that Hazzard was being accused of stealing Puffer's possessions and money, the police, armed with a search warrant, searched Hazzard's mother's house. Some reporters used the word "ransacked." And just as the police suspected, they found items that, as one paper put it, "had been removed from Puffer's house and 'taken' to his house." That was true. In fact, they were gifts from Puffer during the many months of their courtship. Around that time too, Puffer, in a conversation with her lawyer, said that two days before the wedding she had given Hazzard between $5,000 and $6,000 because he was soon to be the head of the household. She had also provided him the right to start a business at the front of one of her properties in town and to store tools and equipment in a nearby barn.

The quickly changing situation was baffling, at best. By July 5, when the *Chicago Defender* article came out, it looked like this: The couple is arrested on statutory charges of cohabitation. Hazzard is accused of enticement. Puffer's sanity is questioned, legally. They are taken out of state, although there are no extradition papers. Puffer arrives back in Ayer on the night of the 20th, is detained in her cell for days, is examined by physicians, and is told she will soon be examined again by alienists from Boston. On the 22nd, 23rd, and 24th, Puffer proclaims love for Hazzard, who on the 25th is suspected of larceny, so say all of the newspapers. On that same day Puffer gives up the ring and breaks the engagement and two days later she is released, at which time the *Chicago Defender* interviews her. Hazzard is arrested on the larceny charges on the day before she is released, gets out on bail, and goes to his brother's house to live temporarily, in Lowell. After the July 5 *Chicago Defender* article appears, Puffer is back in the detention hall until the July 11 insanity hearing, which has not been canceled, despite what her lawyer told the press.

After her brief release on June 27, Puffer was allowed to go only to the cottage at Sandy Pond and only with her shadow, the police matron, who reported that Puffer cried the entire time. By the time she returned to the detention hall, which she did without resistance, it must have been sadly obvious to her that what had begun as a struggle to be reunited with her fiancé and to reschedule a marriage had now escalated to a battle to avoid confinement in a prison or asylum and to prevent a tragic ending of some sort. Reports emerged that Mabel Puffer spent most of her time crying or staring silently at the walls of her cell.

After the alienists examined Mabel Puffer, they each reported to the court. One said: "Very talkative, but talks freely and apparently well oriented for time and place. She is contemplating marriage with an illiterate Negro of poor personal hygiene and appearance, and can see no difference between this man and the average run of man in any detail. She asserts that she will marry him at the first opportunity." The other, Dr. Frank S. Bulkeley, said, "She is as sane as we are."

Nevertheless, on the morning of July 11 in court, the judge declared Mabel Puffer insane. He then appointed her lawyer as her temporary guardian until her half-nephew could officially assume the post in September. And that afternoon, as her lawyer had promised, the statutory cohabitation charges against both Puffer and Hazzard as well as the charge of enticement against Hazzard were dropped. After the verdict, Puffer told the *Chicago Defender,* "It's too bad in this so-called free country that people can't marry whom they love."

In *The Guardian* on July 12 an editorial drew attention to the fact that Puffer was wrongfully snatched out of one state and into another without legal cause and then detained for no legal reason. "Anyone who wishes is at liberty to believe the physicians' statements that Miss Puffer is insane. We are equally at liberty to disbelieve the physicians' assertions. But even if it were true that the publicly ventilated persecution of Miss Puffer did mentally derange her, what decent motive could any one have in so extraordinarily secreting her?"

The next day the preliminary hearing in the larceny case against Hazzard began in district court. The all-white jury consisted of a farmer, a paper maker, a construction worker, and a leather cutter from Shirley, Massachusetts, and a car inspector, two store clerks, and a machinist from Ayer. Hazzard had pleaded not guilty to the charge of stealing a total of $6,000 in property, cash, and gifts from his fiancée, Puffer. The prosecution's star witness was expected to be Puffer, newspapers announced. And that was an invitation for what, by most accounts, was the biggest crowd ever to gather in that courtroom, increasing on the first day every hour until the throng spilled out into the halls and adjacent rooms on the first floor of the county courthouse.

Lovers testifying in court: one a Negro, and the other a white heiress. What a sensation! And what they heard—at least the ones who could hear—was even more entertaining than any of them could have imagined. Mabel Puffer testified that the man whom she was going to marry and who had received the gifts from her was not Arthur Hazzard. The man who had received the money and gifts was a man whom Puffer called Charles McKee. She had had no plans to marry a black man because Charles McKee, whom she believed Hazzard to be, she said, was a white man.

"Is McKee white or colored?" asked the prosecutor.

"White," said Puffer.

"Is Hazzard white or black?"

"Black."

"And you are positive that you gave the money to McKee?"

"Yes, I gave the money to the white man, not the black man."

Was her behavior that of a sane woman sharp enough to have spent the days and nights in her basement cell dreaming up a plan to outsmart her enemies and to release herself and Hazzard from the tightening legal noose? Did she only pretend to be crazy to conform to the plan of her foes, win their confidence, and then betray them in the end? Did she ignore and reject her lover, simply to end the nightmare for them both? Or had the stunning speed at which her life was changing pushed her into an unstoppable spin of insanity?

Puffer's story about the mystery man McKee had a dozen twists and turns that for the most part brought in Christian Science and metaphysics. It was odd, extraordinary. But it was a story she would stick to, consistently, for her long hours on the witness stand testifying supposedly against her former fiancé. Over and over she told the court that she had not given Hazzard the money he was accused of having deceptively taken from her. The deceiver was McKee. Thus, she fulfilled her agreement to testify against her former fiancée and yet she never once agreed that a man by the name of Arthur Garfield Hazzard ever received anything from her.

Other witnesses were called, including a local shopkeeper, a nurse who worked at a home near Puffer's, and Sandy Pond neighbors. All agreed that Puffer had begun to look sickly and wan in late winter when they also recalled seeing Hazzard enter the Sandy Pond cottage frequently. Their testimony was obviously meant to demonize Hazzard's character and intent. But had they asked Puffer why she was losing weight, they would have heard the obvious explanation: she wanted to look slim and sleek for her upcoming June wedding. Reporters too were called, mostly ones who had interviewed the couple during their days in Concord. Paul Harris Drake, a Boston newspaperman, talked about his conversations with Puffer in which she declared her love for Hazzard, and that on the way to Concord she had taken Gar to Hollis, New Hampshire, to meet her half-nephew. Puffer and Hazzard were respectful and polite to each other, he said. When Drake had asked if he could take their picture, Puffer asked Hazzard if he was comfortable with that and he said he was, but was she? And she said, there seemed to be "no good reason to keep their love a secret." When asked if she had ever mentioned the name McKee or had referred to Hazzard as McKee, Drake said no.

In his closing arguments, Hazzard's attorney, Lewis, said:

> These two people were acting within their rights before God and man. I characterize the action taken as an invasion of their personal liberties. I charge that the complaints against them were pure camouflage, brought for the sole purpose of breaking up and interrupting the marriage. And for what? The niece, who had not spoken to Miss Puffer for two years, not to be diverted from her right as a prospective heir-at-law was the cause, alerted after the introduction to the nephew. The ridiculous charge of enticing Miss Puffer away against Hazzard has been dismissed. The ridiculous charge, the slanderous charge, of cohabitation has been dismissed. These were purely fictitious charges, a malicious abuse of the process, a malicious interference with the contract entered into between Miss Puffer and Mr. Hazzard. If Miss Puffer gave her money to this man, she did it just as any woman gives to the man she loves. The harpies who never gave her the comfort of her society since April 1917 thought they would lose a little change so made these false, malicious and slanderous charges against this couple who openly and above board, honestly and decently went away to be married. They made these awful, scandalous, scurrilous charges to get her back and get their fingers on some filthy lucre.

The prosecutor countered simply: "It was the intention of Hazzard to milk her of all she had in the world. He realized that Miss Puffer was weak mentally and conceived the idea of getting her money, it being either his own idea or devised by other schemers."

On July 14, the judge presiding over the larceny hearing in district court found "probable cause" and set a county court date of September 2 for the grand jury to convene. The next day the attorney for Puffer's relatives sought an injunction to restrain Hazzard and any member of his family from disposing of the money, gifts, or property that he allegedly stole from Puffer. Under the injunction, Hazzard could not even pay his attorney. The

judge approved the injunction. At the same time, the Puffer relatives prepared to file a civil suit against the entire Hazzard family for conspiring to
commit the crimes of which they were confident Gar would be convicted.
The Hazzard family was working with Lewis and another attorney on
charges against the Puffer relatives and police officials on the grounds of
malicious prosecution and interference with a contract of marriage, among
other allegations. Hazzard alone was filing a countersuit for damages regarding the enticement and cohabitation charges. He would also claim
that his constitutional rights had been abused. And when the case was
heard by the grand jury—which convened in August, not September, and
failed to indict, Hazzard and Lewis would intensify the allegations in their
countersuit. At the same time, the half-nephew was filing papers to assume
legal guardianship of Mabel Puffer and her estate.

It had been only a month since the engaged couple sat on a divan in the
lobby of the Phenix Hotel talking in devoted whispers about how many
flower arrangements would be necessary to add a festive aura to the main
room of the lobby where both the wedding ceremony and the reception
would take place. How was it possible that now all of that was gone and
in its place was a legal tangle reaching Dickensian proportions? From the
Phenix Hotel to Bleak House in only a month. Whatever would be the
final cost of so much legal action to the state of Massachusetts, all in pursuit of justice and truth? And what of the truth? In the end, as in the beginning, there was really only one truth—and it didn't require evidence or
witnesses or trials to prove it. And that was that what Puffer and Hazzard
wished to do with their lives had been no one's business but their own.

CHAPTER 28

That Certain Point

The SS *Espagne* docked at Pier 57 in New York harbor early on the morning of July 15. One of the first passengers to disembark was William Monroe Trotter. And one of the first to recognize the now renowned African-American as he appeared at the top of the ship's ramp was a man who had been waiting for Trotter all morning long. Like the others crowding the pier that day, this man had been standing for many hours in anticipation of a ship that was now a day late. Watching closely for the moment Trotter came ashore, he appeared, like the others, to be awaiting the arrival of a close friend or a relative. And although he knew as much about the object of his attention as a friend might know, he was neither friend nor relative.

As Trotter walked down the ramp, he scanned the clusters of people on the pier in anticipation of spotting a few familiar faces. His newspaper in Boston, *The Guardian*, had posted a notice informing its readers about his departure from France and asking them to pray for his journey to be safe and swift. But because the ship was a day late, he wasn't expecting a welcoming committee. As he moved closer to the crowd, though, he recognized two ministers he knew from New York, a professor from his alma mater, Harvard, a colleague from *The Guardian*, and a journalist from the *Chicago Defender*. After the usual handshaking, hat tipping, and whispered greetings, these men escorted Trotter to a waiting taxi that whisked him away to a reception at 134th Street in Harlem, the home of the president of New York's black Civic League. As the cab drove away from the pier, the man who had been waiting the longest for Trotter but whom Trotter did not notice entered a cab parked directly behind Trotter's Harlem-bound cab. This man would never nod his head in approval or tip his hat at Trotter. In fact, Trotter would never make his acquaintance. For this man's job was to stay in Trotter's shadow and to send a full report of Trotter's first days back from France to the Negro Subversion division of Military Intelligence.

Despite Trotter's two months in Paris, Major Walter Loving never stopped gathering information about Trotter. Loving knew exactly what ship Trotter was on and when it had departed from Brest and when it would dock in New York. His agent followed Trotter to the address in Harlem and then waited outside until early evening, when the reception moved to a more public arena at the nearby A.M.E. Zion Church on West 137th Street. The next day, the agent sent a report to Loving, who then sent a memo to the director of military intelligence, Churchill, offering his boss an update on Trotter, who was now home. The memo began with news of the large reception and banquet held in Trotter's honor, which did not break up until 1:30 A.M. The agent had informed Loving that Trotter spoke that night about his experiences as a cook in getting to France on the SS *Yarmouth* and his exploits after his arrival in Paris. "But he has reserved the full story," the memo read, "until July 23rd [the lecture actually took place on the 27th] when he is to appear before a large public audience in New York. As the people know the method Mr. Trotter employed to get to France and have read the many cable reports in the daily press of his activities there, there is general anxiety to hear him speak and the meeting of July 23rd will no doubt be a monster affair. A full report of that meeting will be made." Sent on the 16th, the memo would arrive on Churchill's desk on the morning of July 19.

Trotter was a high-maintenance citizen from the government's point of view, with a set-in-stone profile: Militant. Unstoppable. Dangerous. Like a spark to tinder, Trotter was an agitator who had the capability to inflame the masses. His recent articles and perhaps the attention he received in France had raised the level of surveillance planned for his return, though the government had been tailing him for a long while. Trotter was the one, after all, who had so aggressively protested segregation of federal offices in the District of Columbia at the beginning of Wilson's first term; the one who could articulate the frustrations and angers of his race and who had the conduit to the public (his newspaper) to do so; and the one who had written in that newspaper, *The Guardian:* "Beyond a certain point the Negro will not show his back to his pursuers. He will turn and fight." *The Guardian* had published in its July 19 issue an article covering a fiery lecture by Boston's Rev. M. A. Shaw, who called attention to a recent lynching, in Laurel, Mississippi, in which a black woman was hanged, burned, and disemboweled for saying that if she could find the names of the men who had lynched her husband she would tell the sheriff. No black man or woman was safe anywhere in America, Shaw said, whether it was Boston Common or Mississippi. The headline read "Calls on Negroes to Kill Lynchers by Wholesale." Now, considering what had happened at Charleston in May and at Longview in June, what Trotter had done in Paris in May, June, and July, and what his newspaper was publishing in July, to trail Trotter had become a government imperative.

On the 19th when Churchill received Loving's latest memo, stamped "confidential," Loving was working on his last summary report to Churchill. This would be Loving's magnum opus, the culmination of one year of spying on African-Americans whose speeches, articles, and ideas Loving and his colleagues believed to be radical and incendiary. Loving as well as his agents had attended meetings of black organizations, scrutinized their publications, analyzed speeches, and made lists of the most suspicious black men and women. And they had done this to determine how deeply the Bolsheviks had penetrated the soul of black America. What were the exact sources of the revolutionary propaganda? Which organizations and individuals were most troubling? How were blacks being manipulated in the plans of the Bolsheviks? Were the Bolsheviks behind the riot at Charleston? What about Longview?

Loving's report would undoubtedly answer such questions but it appeared that his goal in writing it was a subtle yet very revealing variation on his assignment, perhaps reflecting the fact that he did not come up with the exact results the government had expected. The report, he noted in the preface, was not meant to describe the various organizations through which "radical sentiment has been diffused." It was not a summary of the many reports he had sent to the MID director over the past year. Loving's goal, he wrote, was to inform the government about "present conditions among the Negro population with regard to radical sentiment and propaganda." Although he would discuss certain organizations, publications, and individuals, this would not be the point of his report. He would simply use such facts to "throw light upon the causes underlying [the recent] outbreaks and point the way to some remedial action to relieve the growing tension between the races." He would show that there was in fact "radical sentiment among Negroes" and that it had intensified during the past four years. But his report would not confirm what the government suspected and perhaps even wanted to hear: that the causes for racial tensions were Bolshevists, socialists, and the Industrial Workers of the World.

In his report Loving did include commentary on Bolshevists, socialists, and the IWW and the fact that there were blacks involved with all three. And he would note the organizations that he believed encouraged radical notions among blacks: the League of Democracy, an organization of at least 150,000 black veterans of the recent war; the NAACP; Trotter's National Equal Rights League; A. Philip Randolph and Chandler Owen's National Association for the Promotion of Labor Unionism Among Negroes; and Marcus Garvey's Universal Negro Improvement Association—all of which Loving discussed. He identified four "black and radical" publications: *The Messenger*, a monthly edited by two black socialists, Owen and Randolph, and also the organ of their League of Democracy; *The Crusader*, a New York monthly edited by a West Indian, Cyril V. Briggs; *The Challenge*, a monthly, also out of New York; and *The Crisis*. And he included a section called "Individual Agitators and Propagandists," in which he devoted one full page to Trotter, calling him an "advanced radical" and noting that his influence had been "on the wane" until he figured out a clever way to get to France and then obtained endless publicity from the French press. But Loving made it clear that none of these groups or publications or individuals were *the* causes for the recent disturbances.

What "set the spark" that had released the pent up feelings of the masses, he wrote, was the awakened spirit of the black soldiers returning from France. After experiencing the free social intermingling in France, the discriminating restraints back home were "more galling" than ever before. While the soldiers were in France, Loving stressed, prejudice and discrimination were intensifying back in America to the extent that when the victorious soldiers went home, some of them, while wearing the uniform of their country, were burned and lynched. That the "bitter feeling of returning soldiers" would spread to the civilian black population was "but natural," he wrote.

Expending few words on Bolshevism and socialism, Loving moved from the shock of returning soldiers to the economic reasons for blacks' despair. He described the migrations of blacks coming up North from the South during the war to fill the jobs vacated by white enlisted men, how the white soldiers wanted their jobs back and resented black men making money, buying houses in white neighborhoods, and having good jobs. Misguided white workers had become so desperate and so angry and so filled with the prejudiced propaganda, Loving wrote, that they had thrown bombs into the homes that black men worked hard to purchase during the war. "The Negro has finally decided that he has endured all that he can endure. He has decided to strike back."

Of all parts of his report, Loving was the most strident in his discussion of segregation, which he called "a menace to public safety." This is the real danger, he wrote. When black and white families live in the same neighborhoods, Loving wrote, they know each other, become friendly, seek the same community benefits, fight for the same rights and privileges. But living in segregated communities, blacks and whites, through lack of knowledge, become suspicious of each other and fill in the blanks of the unknown with prejudice, fear, and then anger. The "black belts" in Washington, Philadelphia, Chicago, and New York, he wrote, are "a dangerous condition" that just by definition alone become war zones. Innocent whites fear stepping over the borderlines into them and innocent blacks fear leaving them. These "cities within cities" will nurture violence. Thus segregation must be stopped.

In these last weeks of July, Loving pulled together his perceptions of the black problem in America, culling from hundreds of pages of spy reports over the past year and creating a fifteen-page, single-spaced document that was more a warning than a report. In it, he cautioned his readers, who would include the director of military intelligence, the chief of staff of the War Department, and, he hoped, the president, that the situation was so dire that "The slightest occurrence may now light the magazine which has been formed by economic, psychic and social forces."

He concluded that it wasn't Bolshevism or socialism that was causing the problem. It was the simple, natural, logical fact that "as a whole, Negroes have resolved never again to submit to the treatment which they received in the past and any attempt to deny them such privileges and rights as they are entitled to, in common with other men, will be promptly resented. The above is a true statement of existing conditions, verified by personal observation and contact with Negroes of all classes."

Loving would complete his report by the first of August and submit it on August 6. Between the time he was writing it and the time his bosses read it, events moved swiftly onward.

As elsewhere in the nation, the month of July in Washington was the hottest on record. On July 19, it was 98 degrees. The heat was undoubtedly a factor in what happened that day—but hardly the cause. The reasons given would range from Bolshevik propaganda, always, to an insensitive Southern administration in the White House that had segregated federal office workers in 1913, to the impact of inflammatory headlines in newspapers sensationalizing a summer crime wave in the capital—in particular, stories of black men allegedly attempting to rape white women. On Saturday, July 19, the *Washington Post* ran a headline about one such case: "Negroes Attack Girl . . . White Men Vainly Pursue." The "attack," the story said, involved two black men who tried to seize the umbrella of a secretary walking home from work. When she resisted, they fled. In response, the chief of police issued the order that all men "found in isolated or suspicious parts of the city after nightfall" be held for questioning. Police brought in two suspects, but without evidence or witnesses, released them. The "attacked" girl turned out to be the wife of a man who worked in the aviation division of the Department of the Navy, and thus at least two hundred sailors and marines decided to find the two black men who had allegedly assaulted her, and to lynch them. They marched into the southwest section of town and stopped every black man—and woman—they met on the street, grabbing the victims' arms, slapping their faces, and sometimes punching them in the stomach or face. As they walked, civilians along the way joined their crusade for justice. Thus the throng of thugs and bigots grew, spreading through the streets like molten lava. But on Saturday night when the mob tried to break into a house into which a black man and his wife had fled out of fear, the local and military police intervened, dispersed the mob, and arrested two white navy men and eight black men, who were "held for investigation." Later that night police stopped three more black men in the neighborhood. One of them fired a gun, wounding a policeman.

On Sunday, the NAACP asked the secretary of the navy to restrain the white men who had started the attack. But he did not. And then that night what everyone from William Monroe Trotter in 1913 to Ray Stannard Baker in 1916 to W. E. B. Du Bois, James Weldon Johnson, the *Chicago Defender, The Crisis,* the *New York Age,* and even Major Loving all foretold, began to happen—an unstoppable rush of events marking the start of an unprecedented wave of black resistance in America.

On Pennsylvania Avenue, halfway between the Capitol and the White

House, a policeman arrested a young black man on a minor charge. A mob gathered while the police waited for the paddy wagon. They snatched the black man from the police, punched him, stoned him, and slashed him. When the police recovered him, they did not arrest a single white man. Minutes later down the street, white servicemen and black civilians attacked each other. Three black men were badly injured. By early Monday morning, scuffles seemed to be breaking out everywhere in the nation's capital. But the worst was yet to come.

That morning the *Washington Post* published articles on the violence of the previous weekend and included this paragraph: "It was learned that a mobilization of every available service man stationed in or near Washington or on leave here has been ordered for tomorrow evening near the Knights of Columbus hut on Pennsylvania Avenue between Seventh and Eighth Streets. The hour of assembly is 9 o'clock and the purpose is a 'clean up' that will cause the events of the last two evenings to pale into insignificance."

On Monday afternoon, in Congress, a Florida legislator argued that the cause of the "riots," as they were now termed, was that police had not been aggressive enough that summer in arresting black assailants of white women. He called for a congressional probe into the D.C. police passivity. At the same time, a New York congressman demanded that all servicemen in the region be restrained from joining the mobs. The secretary of war and the army chief of staff met to discuss a plan for using troops, if necessary, to quell what they expected would be more rioting. And blacks in Washington who read the "mobilization" story in the *Post* began to arm themselves. That night the rioting resumed and was far worse than the previous nights: four men killed, eleven seriously wounded. Of those fifteen, six were white policemen, one a white marine, three white civilians, and five black civilians.

On Tuesday, President Wilson met with the secretary of war, who then ordered the Washington police chief to request additional troops from Camp Meade, marines from Quantico, and sailors from two ships currently docked on the Potomac to help secure the nation's capital. For every D.C. cop there would now be two armed military men. By Tuesday night Wilson had authorized the mobilization of about two thousand federal troops. And the wartime volunteers in Washington, who called themselves the Home Defense League, were called to action.

The black community—as Loving and all well-informed blacks and whites well knew—would not passively stand by. On Tuesday, black leaders called for protection for black prisoners, whom they learned had been beaten upon arrest, some severely. They also visited city officials, asking why blacks carrying weapons had been arrested but the whites from whom they were trying to protect themselves had not been. And they demanded a congressional investigation of police "antagonism to Negroes." Black ministers sent out a call to all blacks to stay off the streets after dusk. And on Tuesday, at sunset, poolrooms and theaters and all gathering places were closed in black neighborhoods.

By Tuesday night, federal troops, including cavalry on horseback, and driving rain stopped the mobs from forming, though there were isolated incidents of violence in which one white member of the Home Defense League was killed and one black man fleeing from approaching officers was shot. The sound of the cavalry's galloping horses answering urgent calls and the sight of troops on street corners continued through Wednesday night. By Thursday the danger seemed to have passed, at least in Washington. The total casualties: six dead and at least one hundred wounded.

Then came an onslaught of meetings, strategies, and demands to prevent future mob violence in the nation's capital. The white solution was uniformly more security. If black insubordination was the cause, which many people believed, then suppression was the solution and fear of suppression through the presence of high-level security was an effective strategy. Local and federal law enforcement stressed the need for ongoing battalions of troops to police the city. It was imperative in a town that was also the nation's capital and thus a gathering place for international dignitaries and a hub of high-level meetings of worldwide significance to prevent "small causes" from throwing the city "into a state of lawlessness." The D.C. police chief and commissioner asked Congress for money to increase the number of policemen in the District and to raise their pay. Newspapers nationwide echoed their plea. As the *New York Globe* wrote on July 23, "There is nothing to be done but to quiet the rioters by force. We make no pretense nowadays of settling the race question; we simply keep it in abeyance."

From the white point of view, the riots were certainly a reason to maintain segregation in all cities in America. The overly confident, uppity black man who in Washington might now own his home and collect a high wage must be kept in his place and kept separate from his white counterpart. Only segregation would prevent such uprisings. The *Brooklyn Eagle* ran the headline "Race War in Washington Shows Black and White Equality Not Practical." Even the *New York Times* reported "the negroes, before the great war, were well behaved . . . even submissive" and nostalgically looked back on the prewar state of the nation's capital. "Bolshevist agitation has been extended among the Negroes," wrote the *Times*, "and it is bearing its natural and inevitable fruit."

Black leaders saw it differently, from whites and from each other. Some, such as Emmett Scott of Howard University in Washington, blamed the white mobs. And although they conceded that the black retaliation was abhorrent, in their opinion, it was natural, to be expected. It was necessary for survival. To stop it before it escalated and spread to other cities, interracial groups must be formed to create a riot-prevention strategy based on "mutual sharing of the rewards of American life, rather than on Negro subordination."

Others, such as Trotter, claimed that the only way to prevent riots was to end "the mobocratic lyncherized system" of segregation, discrimination, and prejudice in America. There would be violence until that was accomplished. The Wilson administration was in large part to blame for segregating federal workers, placing black workers under the supervision of white Southern bosses, sidestepping the urgent need for federal legislation against lynching, and not addressing Washington's postwar employment issues. For example, during the war the federal government added jobs that were filled largely with whites who abandoned private jobs to take them. Many of those private sector jobs were filled by blacks who had left federal jobs because of discrimination or had come up from the South because of job opportunities. The black skilled laborers in the private sector ended up making more money than the white government workers. Witnessing a rise in prosperity among blacks in Washington angered whites who had shifted from private to public work or had just returned from the war. Jealous and resentful, they wanted to put blacks in their place at a time when the black community was feeling more deserving of better treatment than ever before.

The NAACP favored an end to segregation and championed a federal law to criminalize the act of lynching, but in the aftermath of the Washington riot, it zeroed in on two issues: racial prejudice among the police, and irresponsibility on the part of the media. Du Bois was quoted in several newspapers as saying that it was clear that the Washington police did not try to stop the rioting until whites began to get hurt. James Weldon Johnson, of the NAACP staff and *New York Age* columnist, said that the riot would have ended on Saturday night, after the first outbreak, if the Washington police officers had had "the courage to enforce the law against the white man as well as against the colored." If black men felt unprotected by the law, then they would of course prepare to protect themselves, wrote Johnson.

On July 25, John R. Shillady, the NAACP's executive secretary, wrote a letter to A. Mitchell Palmer asking if the Justice Department was planning to take action against the *Washington Post* for publishing the "mobilization notice." Shillady, who was white—and whose work against racism would soon, in late August, result in a beating at the hands of a white mob in Texas—believed that that seemingly simple paragraph in the Saturday, July 19, *Post* had facilitated the mobilization of a white mob and had caused such fear and such anger among blacks already angry and afraid that it alone had incited the riot. Numerous black leaders agreed. Palmer said no.

On July 26, the Reverend J. G. Robinson of the African Methodist Episcopal Church in Chattanooga, Tennessee, sent a letter to President Wilson, published the next day in the Sunday *New York Times,* in which he reminded the president of his and other black Americans' loyalty during the recent war; pleaded for the president to support federal legislation to outlaw lynchings and to allow black men to serve on juries; and warned that before his people would submit themselves again to the injustices of white mobs, "the white men will have to kill more of them than the combined number of soldiers that were slain in the Great World War."

That Sunday was the day of Trotter's "monster affair" at the Palace Casino in New York City, which attracted an audience of more than three thousand men and women, mostly black. A long list of black speakers, including two ministers, two professors, one lawyer, and one doctor, preceded the guest of honor. Their master of ceremonies introduced them all by saying that they would, in their presentations, "assail every form of hypocrisy and injustice arrayed against the Race." So enthusiastic was the audience that they frequently cried out their endorsements of the sentiments of the speakers, and at times they rose up from their seats cheering the campaign to claim their rights and liberties as full-fledged Americans. Some screamed at the white reporters with words and phrases they wanted to see in the next day's papers. Write about the black man's gratitude toward France for its fair treatment of black soldiers! they shouted. Write about the shock of returning home to a lawless land! "Fiery Orators Condemn Unjust Treatment, Predicting a New Era," read the headline in the *Chicago Defender*.

Trotter's speech, which made it into Loving's final report—as Trotter's shadow loyally attended the lecture—began: "In the same week of my arrival home my heart is made to swell within me because the new spirit in my own race refused to be shot down in the capital of Lincoln [Washington, D.C.]. Unless the white American behaves, he will find that in teaching our boys to fight for him he was starting something that he will not be able to stop."

Trotter shared his story of finding his way to Paris as a cook's assistant and of getting his petition to the peace conference published in sixty-two daily newspapers worldwide. Although President Wilson would not meet with him, he told them, he did visit Wilson's Parisian residence and he left a missive for the president "representing the voice of 12 million colored people." The MID agent shadowing him reported: "Mr. Trotter was most enthusiastically applauded and $234.00 was collected to help him carry on his work."

CHAPTER 29

Weapons in Their Hats

In his stirring review of Carl Sandburg's book of poetry *Cornhuskers*, Chicago journalist Ben Hecht described the poet and fellow journalist as the "minstrel of our alleys." He said that Sandburg was always "looking at the world through his heart." Anyone who had read anything by Carl Sandburg would likely have agreed and if there had been any dispute it would be set aside after July of 1919. For that was the month that Sandburg spent nearly every day in the alleys and streets of Chicago's Black Belt, reporting and writing a series of articles for the *Chicago Daily News*—articles that hummed with the anxieties and hopes of an entire race. In July, Sandburg's heart must have ached.

After Sandburg's tussle with the government over the Espionage Act and his European reporting, he had resumed his work for the Newspaper Enterprise Association, commuting between the NEA in Cleveland and his home in Chicago. Utilizing his notebooks that government censors had finally released to him, he was able to write fresh, descriptive stories about the immediate aftermath of the war based on interviews and observations in Stockholm during November and December. "NEA Staff Correspondent Just Arrived from Northern Europe with Pictures and Documents Never Before Published," one NEA headline announced. Through his writings, Sandburg seemed to be sorting out what he referred to as the "waste and afterbirth gore" of the war, trying to shape a hopeful vision out of the struggles that now consumed his world.

But in May Sandburg and his bosses at the NEA hit an impasse. Although they thought him "a remarkable man," "a great writer," and "a fine, keen thinker," as one of his bosses wrote in his dismissal letter, the NEA and Sandburg were simply not "hitching well together." Implying repercussions from his scuffle with government agents and censors, his other editor wrote, "I don't believe you're as dangerous as some people would have us imagine and I know we are not as stodgy as some folks would have you think."

In his quest for another job, he wrote to the *Chicago Daily News*—where he had worked before the NEA—and offered to write two or three weekly articles about organized labor, returning soldiers and jobs, the strikes, steelworkers, and other postwar concerns. Eager to reinstate an excellent reporter who was now also a renowned, award-winning poet, the *Daily News* agreed and assigned him first to write about the American Federation of Labor. Toward the end of June, though, with instincts that would soon be proven nothing less than brilliant, his editors sent him to the Black Belt for a very big series—eighteen articles that Walter Lippmann would later write were "first hand" and "sympathetic." "They will move those who will allow themselves to be moved," wrote Lippmann.

Chicago's Black Belt consisted of an area roughly bounded by 26th Street to the north, 55th Street to the south, State Street to the west, and Lake Michigan to the east. During the five years since the beginning of the war, the population had more than doubled, from approximately 60,000 to 125,000. With that came a spurt of new black-owned businesses, churches, and weekly newspapers. Drugstores, tailors, fish markets, and bakeries rose up where there had been none before. The Olivet Baptist Church at South Park and East 31st Street boasted the largest membership of any Protestant church in the nation. And with the new Savings and Loan Association and four new banks, more and more black families owned their homes. But there were no new houses or tenements built to accommodate the nearly seventy thousand new residents. And so the Black Belt quickly became overcrowded. The overflowing population meant, as Sandburg soon learned, that six people lived where two people once had and that those blacks who could afford it were moving into white neighborhoods. Thus tension between blacks and whites in Chicago was growing. Add to this returning doughboys of both races battling for a limited number of jobs and it would seem that when Sandburg began his journey in early July of 1919, Chicago was drawing near that "certain point."

In his articles, Sandburg sought to depict the reality of black Chicago and so he focused on such critical issues as housing and real estate, the plight of women and children, jobs, returning soldiers, and lynchings. In one, he quoted from a recent survey that described a growing portion of the Black Belt as "a menace to health" and said it "constitutes kindling wood sufficient to keep Chicago in constant danger of disastrous conflagration." In another he showed that for those blacks who chose to step over the boundaries of the black district, there were dire consequences. White real estate brokers, Sandburg discovered, were persuading white owners to sell apartment buildings on streets where blacks, spilling out of the Black Belt, were now choosing to live. Sell them fast, they would say, before they are worthless, as the neighborhood will soon be black. The developers to whom the agents then sold the buildings charged the incoming black tenants rents that were far higher than before. Worse still, when blacks moved into their new homes in the partially white neighborhoods their reward for having escaped the ghetto was often a firebomb under a front stoop or through a kitchen window. Between February 5 and June 13 there had been eight such bombs thrown in the Black Belt.

Sandburg's reporting offered fresh perspectives on the reasons for the overpopulated Black Belt. The sweeping migration of blacks, up from the South during the war to fill jobs vacated by white servicemen, was an obvious feature of the story. Less obvious were the hundreds of black soldiers from Southern states who were mustered out in Chicago and—as Sandburg learned—were unable to afford to return home because the government had not given them stipends to do so. Or, as Sandburg also found, Southern soldiers discharged in Chicago sometimes had no desire to return to a culture where lynchings still occurred. Stories about the lynchings were widely publicized in the black weeklies and from the mouths of those who came up from the South and said they knew someone who knew someone else who had been killed by the wrath of a mob.

From his interviews, Sandburg picked up a version of the Vicksburg, Mississippi, lynching that would have surely discouraged a black man from returning to the South. Verified he said by the local NAACP office, though not reported in any newspaper as such, it went like this, as Sandburg reported it: "A colored man accused of an assault on a white woman was placed in a hole that came to his shoulders. Earth was tamped around his neck, only his head being left above ground. A steel cage five feet square then was put over the head of the victim and a bulldog was put inside the cage. Around the dog's head was tied a paper bag filled with red pepper to inflame his nostrils and eyes. The dog immediately lunged at the victim's head. Further details are too gruesome to print."

The lynchings were driving blacks out of the South. In fact, the minister of the Olivet Baptist Church, Dr. L. K. Williams, informed Sandburg that his membership was expanding not only because of returning soldiers but also because of the recent lynchings. Since the beginning of the year: three in Alabama, four in Arkansas, two in Florida, three in Georgia, four in Louisiana, seven in Mississippi, one in Missouri, two in North Carolina, one in South Carolina, and one in Texas. Dr. Williams said that eleven of his newest members had come up from Vicksburg in June.

The weeklies too played a role, Sandburg found, in influencing blacks to move to the North. Walking along State Street south of 31st Street, Sandburg would have passed what was effectively a black Newspaper Row, housing weeklies such as the *Chicago Defender, The Broad Ax, The Plaindealer, The Guide, The Advocate, The Whip,* and *The Messenger,* and monthlies such as *The Favorite, The Half Century,* and *The Crisis.* Advocating race pride and denouncing race prejudice while reporting on its daunting, often gruesome manifestations, these papers and their many columnists, their profiles of black businessmen and educators, their advertisements for events and products, opened doors that many of their readers never knew existed. And their circulation numbers were soaring, especially in the South. The *Defender* now had more than 100,000 subscribers in the Southern states, where the total number of subscribers of black weeklies, as Sandburg learned, was at least one million.

Major Joel Spingarn, who had for six years been the chairman of the NAACP, spoke with Sandburg for one of the articles in which the emphasis was on the importance of federal government involvement and national awareness to solve the race problem. "No city or state can solve it alone," wrote Sandburg. Spingarn was adamant about the need for federal legislation to ease the tensions. And he told Sandburg, "I have fought for my country two years as a major in the infantry and I wish to give it my mature judgment that no barbarities committed by the Prussians in Belgium will compare with the brutalities and atrocities committed on negroes in the south. And in effect, you may say that the negroes who come north have issued from a system of life and industry far worse than anything ever seen under Prussianism in its worse manifestations."

Sandburg interviewed black soldiers, storekeepers, ministers, mothers, leaders, and politicians. He described the homeless, the poor, the hungry, and the angry. He revealed the human cost of the scarcity of housing, dearth of jobs, rising cost of living, and growing prejudice in Chicago. He pointed out that these things affected white Chicago as well as the Black Belt. And he showed hope: On one of those hot July days Sandburg stood at the corner of South State and 34th Streets listening to Rev. W. C. Thompson of the Pentecostal Church of Christ. The reverend told his gathering of twenty or so men and women that he would speak and his singers would sing until the police forced them all to leave. "New things is comin' altogether diverse from what they has been," he began.

Spending weeks reporting on one topic, stepping beyond the dogma of comfortable opinion and moving as close to the truth as a white man in the Black Belt could get, gave Sandburg a sixth sense about his subject. He must have known that something dire was coming, though perhaps not as soon as July 27. Already an aura of sadness and anxiety hovered over Chicago in the aftermath of the crash of a giant Goodyear dirigible into the big skylight of the Illinois Trust and Savings Bank. It had happened on July 21, when the *Winged Foot Express*, which was ferrying passengers from Chicago's Grant Park to the White City Amusement Park, had caught fire 1,200 feet above the heart of Chicago's downtown. The mass of flaming wreckage hurtled into the bank, killing ten employees, two passengers, and a mechanic. For many Chicagoans, it was a portent of disaster.

On the afternoon of the 27th, a Sunday, Sandburg was working on what he believed to be the last piece of his series. Ironically, this one was about "constructive recommendations" to ease tensions between Chicago's blacks and whites. It was one of those sizzling hot Sundays in Chicago when it seemed that everyone was either in Lake Michigan, on the way to it, sitting on its beaches, or wishing to be there. By mid-afternoon the temperature had soared to 96 degrees, far exceeding the normal range of mid-80s. And then something happened.

It began at around 4 P.M. at a South Side beach that was located just over the railroad tracks between 25th and 29th Streets. The beach was not supervised nor was it publicly maintained but it was heavily used by both blacks and whites. And although there were no legal boundaries segregating the exact square footage of the beach and the lake where each race could safely sunbathe or swim, there was an imaginary line that extended from the beach clear out into the water, a line that neither race would dare to cross to the other side. Blacks were to stay in the northern part, which was nearest 25th Street, and whites, further south, at 29th Street. Located between these domains, however, was a small island behind the Keeley

Brewery and Consumers Ice, two businesses that ejected hot and cold discharges into the lake making that vicinity an uncomfortable place to swim. However, because of its privacy and neglect—no one wanted to swim near it—this place was the favored spot of five black teenage boys who had spent weeks building a raft that measured about fourteen by nine feet and that was tied now to what they called the "hot and cold"—their private oasis. None of them was a good swimmer and so they would routinely unhitch the raft and swim with it out into the lake, moving it through the water by kicking, taking turns diving under it, and moving it from one hitching post to another. On this day at about 2 P.M. they moved out from shore toward a marker they had identified as their goal. To get there required shifting slightly to the south, toward 29th Street.

Sometime during the mid-afternoon hours at the 29th Street beach, four black men and women walked across the sand toward the water, touching the fringes of the white sunbathers' beach towels and sharpening the edges of their intolerance. As the blacks neared the water, the whites began to yell at them and to throw rocks. The four blacks retreated. Minutes later more blacks arrived. They threw stones. The whites retaliated. And the race war that everyone sensed and feared had begun.

But the boys on their raft didn't know. As they pushed the raft further south, playing as boys do, they saw a tall white man, somewhere around 26th Street, throwing stones and rocks and pieces of brick at them. At first they thought it was a game and responded as if it were. He'd throw a rock, they'd duck under the water, they'd bob to the surface again and he'd throw another, and so on. But at some point, one of the boys, seventeen-year-old Eugene Williams, didn't duck at the right moment and was struck in the forehead by a rock. He didn't scream. He "just sort of relaxed" into the water, one of his companions, John Harris, said later. Harris dove to help him but the boy grabbed Harris's ankle, which scared Harris. "I shook away from him to come back up," Harris said, "and you could see the blood coming up, and the fellows were all excited." The man who threw the rock or brick let out an "Oh, my God," according to Harris, and then ran away from the beach.

Although an inexperienced swimmer, Harris was fueled by panic and swam as fast as he could back to the 25th Street beach to seek help. A life-guard there sent a boat to the spot where the blood had surfaced and the search for the body of Eugene Williams began. At the same time the boys

beckoned the black policeman at that beach to come with them to the
29th Street beach to search out the white man who had thrown the rock.
And indeed they could identify him, they told the white policeman on duty
at 29th Street, with the black policeman at their side. But the white policeman did nothing and he forbade the black policeman to detain the suspect.
The policemen then began to argue. And while the boys returned to their
beach to inform their people about what was happening on 29th Street,
the white policeman arrested a black man, based on a complaint from one
of the whites at the beach. When the paddy wagon pulled up to take the
black man away, the black crowd that now had gathered stormed the vehicle with rocks, stones, and bricks. And then a black man fired a revolver at
a crowd of black and white policemen, hitting a white officer. A black officer then returned fire, killing the black man who had fired the first shot.

Soon white gangs to the west, in the area around the stockyards and
packing plants, entered the fray. New black gangs formed to fight back. By
early in the morning of the 28th, twenty-seven blacks were beaten, seven
were stabbed, and four were shot. Four white men were beaten, five were
stabbed, and one was shot.

What made Sandburg's July 28 front-pager rise above others was that
he knew the terrain and the people; he knew where to go to get the story.
He was the only white reporter who relied on black sources for the details
and perhaps the only white reporter blacks trusted. He returned to Reverend Thompson, who said, for Sandburg's story that day, "To me and most
of my people this trouble came very suddenly. We did not expect an outbreak of violence." And Reverend Williams said: "It was but another expression of force to take away from the members of my race the right
granted to us by law. Let the best white and colored people come together
and form a program that will protect us all and save this city's fair name."
Another source from the series told Sandburg that the segregation line at
the bathing beach was drawn by the white police. There was no ordinance
or warrant or law and certainly no consultation with the black residents.
"They drew the color line and followed a policy precisely as the authorities
do in Georgia." Others noted that no one should be surprised that tensions
finally exploded over an imaginary line drawn on a beach and over the indifference of a white policeman to the death of a black child when prejudice in law enforcement and segregation were at the core of Chicago's
problems.

Unfortunately, Sandburg's perceptive coverage was offset by the kind of provocative, sensational story that most reporters would tell, even at Sandburg's own newspaper. Sharing the front page with Sandburg, for example, was a "Bulletin" warning Chicago that on the afternoon of the 28th, "300 Negroes were reported" to have gathered at South State and 35th Streets. Many were armed, it said, and "it is believed" that they would soon attack whites in the vicinity.

On Monday the 28th, in the afternoon, as whites and blacks returned home from work, the violence began again. The worst of it occurred at streetcar transit points, where white gangs were dragging blacks out of the streetcars and beating them. One white gang member was stabbed but not killed. Four blacks died from the beatings. That night large numbers of whites piled into cars and, speeding through black neighborhoods, fired rifles at random. In response, blacks stood on rooftops and fired at the cars. On the third day a streetcar strike forced most workers to walk to work, meaning that some blacks had to walk through long stretches of white districts. Two blacks walking through the Loop in downtown Chicago were killed by a white mob of soldiers and sailors. Another black man was killed in a West Side neighborhood that was mostly Italian. More were killed in battles with policemen. Four white men were shot by black men they had attacked. Homes of black families were burned to the ground.

On Tuesday, the 29th, Frederick Smith, a thirty-three-year-old black soldier, who had spent three years in the Canadian army fighting in Europe, returned home. He was aware that there had been race riots for the previous two days but wearing his Canadian uniform, which bore the stripes indicating his wounds, he was confident that no one would bother him. Besides, he couldn't wait for even one more day to come home. Gassed and shot several times, Smith was not a strong man and his fragility was evident by the slow, careful way he walked and by his very thin, nearly emaciated, physique. Still, as he was passing Harrison Street on South State Street a gang of white boys saw him as an easy target. All it took were two blows to the head to down the soldier. At the hospital, after he had regained consciousness, a *Daily Tribune* reporter interviewed him. "I don't see why they wanted to bother a fellow like me," he said. "I did all I could to help make this old country safe for just such men as these. I call this a pretty poor welcome home."

The injury tally on Monday had listed 229 people, two-thirds of whom were black; on Tuesday it was down to 139; and on Wednesday, 2 blacks and 2 whites were killed, 21 whites and 21 blacks were injured. Around 10 P.M. that night, after three and a half days of rioting, the mayor of Chicago, William Thompson, a Democrat, finally asked Illinois's governor, Frank Lowden, a Republican, to order the 6,200 infantrymen who had been waiting for days in local armories to join the Chicago police in an effort to end the violence. The difficult relationship between Lowden and Thompson, both presidential hopefuls for the 1920 race, had stalled the deployment of troops, despite the fatigue of the police force and the pressure on the mayor from local businessmen. On Wednesday, the situation was helped by the weather: it began to rain. By Friday the rioting had mostly stopped and by Saturday the troops left the city.

From the moment Eugene Williams died to the moment the last state infantryman went home, 38 men had died (15 white, 23 black), and 537 men, women, and children were injured, of whom 342 were black. At least 1,000 black Chicagoans were left homeless.

What stood out about the Chicago riot was that it was the first to occur in a Northern city during the summer of 1919. It lasted the longest. It was the bloodiest. And from what happened in Chicago, it was clear now that black Americans, beyond any doubt, would and could stand up against the intolerance, prejudice, and inequality that had kept them down for many years. W. E. B. Du Bois, in strong support of the choice of his people to resist the tyranny of oppression, wrote in his editorial in *The Crisis* about the Chicago riot: "Brothers we are on the Great Deep. We have cast off on the vast voyage which will lead to Freedom or Death."

What was also different about the Chicago riots were the organized gangs of white hoodlums who entered the fray on the second day, streaming out of the neighborhoods surrounding the stockyards and packing-houses where white poverty was as raw and wicked as it was a few blocks away in the slums of the Black Belt. This was an area, as Sandburg had reported in his series, where seven times as many babies died each year than in the neighborhood just one mile east. In the months ahead, the University of Chicago, utilizing the newest of disciplines, called sociology, would study the riots and especially the white gang phenomenon, raising the awareness of all American cities to the rise of city gangs. One such gang in Chicago, the Hamburgs, would one day gain greater fame than the violence it had helped to perpetuate that July, for one of its members was a teenager named Richard Daley, who would later become Chicago's mayor. Another gang, Ragan's Colts, attracted the attention of military intelligence agents. Secret agent August H. Loula reported that Ragan's Colts had been planning to burn down the entire Black Belt of Chicago but the gang was discouraged by the arrival of troops. Such plans would again be "underway, as soon as the watchfulness of the authorities is relaxed," wrote Loula in his August 4 memo. "Concealed weapons are reported to be carried in their hats in order to escape scrutiny and search by the police."

In the immediate aftermath, the press filled its front pages with mixed messages, unsubstantiated rumors, premature conclusions, and occasional wisdom. Radical propagandists, the black press, and Bolsheviks were the obvious culprits in some accounts. On July 28, one *New York Times* article bore the headline: "Reds Try to Stir Negroes to Revolt." Another *Times* story said: "The outbreak of race riots in Chicago, following so closely on those reported from Washington, shows clearly enough that the thing is not sporadic [but has] . . . intelligent direction and management . . . that the Bolshevist agitation has been extended among the Negroes." The *New York Tribune* of July 29 wrote that the violence in Chicago validated the fact that the "IWW and other agitators . . . financed from Russia . . . [were] spreading propaganda aimed to breed race hatred."

Others looked more deeply. The *New York Evening Post* wrote: "Why should we pay attention to dubious and obscure reasons when there is a glaring one in front of us? Treat [the Negro] well and we can laugh at tales of violent propaganda; treat him unjustly, and no propaganda will be needed to arouse him."

And the *Springfield Republican* wrote: "If there is the least danger of the Negro race being influenced by revolutionary propaganda against the existing institutions of the country, what is the best preventive measure that could be taken? The answer is so easy that no one really needs to be told. Stop the lynchings and burnings of Negroes!"

Still others proclaimed that Woodrow Wilson had heaved every black person in America into a dark abyss of unfulfilled promises. In a July 28th letter to Wilson, the president of the National Federation of Colored Organizations and Interests, based in Jersey City, New Jersey, wrote, "You yourself have taught us by your preachments during the world war that liberty and freedom are dearer than life itself; and by this doctrine we stand ready to live or die at home."

Sandburg, in both his early and later commentaries, blamed white poverty and lack of opportunity as well as white prejudice and black injustice. "On the one hand we have blind lawless government failing to function through policemen ignorant of Lincoln, the Civil War, the Emancipation Proclamation, and a theory sanctioned and baptized in a storm of red blood. And on the other hand we have a gaunt involuntary poverty from which issues the hoodlum."

Just as Sandburg in Chicago was completing his Black Belt series in the last days of July, Major Loving was preparing to turn over his *Final Report on Negro Subversion* to the government and to resign from his post as head of the Negro Subversion division of Military Intelligence. Despite an eagerness to finish the job, however, Loving took the time to add commentary about the Chicago race riot. He did not use it to bolster the government's theory that Bolshevism was at the heart of all racial instability. Instead, the recent race riots had persuaded him that it was segregation that was fostering race antagonisms and violence. Thus he added a new paragraph to his report: "As an example of the danger of segregation, I cite one incident of the Chicago riot. Fifteen white men in an automobile truck turned up State Street at 30th and began shooting right and left into the crowd of Negroes on the sidewalks. Before this truck reached 36th Street every man in it had been killed or wounded, the Negroes capturing the truck and taking the arms of the invaders. With this in mind, I wish to reiterate that in my opinion segregation is a public menace and should be discouraged."

In the end, Major Loving, after a year of intense spying on black Americans, came to a conclusion that was ironically in direct opposition to Wilsonian America. Although he confirmed that "radical" propaganda had a strong presence, on soapboxes in Harlem and every other Black Belt in America, at meeting halls, and in the columns of black newspapers, he concluded that it could only be effective if white America denied blacks the rights they deserved. "Defense of himself against German whites," wrote Loving of the black American, "was quickly shifted to defense of himself against American whites."

Loving turned in his report on August 6. On that very same day the *Chicago Tribune* ran two articles strongly favoring segregation as a solution to two social problems. The first told of a meeting of psychiatric experts who had decided that a farm colony must be created for the "segregation of misfits." The "subnormals" and "morons" in the city of Chicago must be taken out of the city to a farm and contained there in order to make Chicago safe for children. And the city must act quickly, said one doctor, because "Two weeks or a month from now the same public mind will be filled something else, unless this subject of morons is kept before the public eye. It has always been that way."

In the second article, Chicago's city council had come up with the "one real and permanent solution" to racial strife: segregation of the races, which it defined as "the establishment of residential racial zones for white people and colored people." In the considered resolution, the city council echoed almost the very words of Woodrow Wilson years before when confronted by William Monroe Trotter about segregation of federal government offices. "Whereas, the city council believes that many of the causes of friction can be removed by an intelligent and equitable separation of the races." There was no doubt, wrote the president of the Kenwood Property Owners' association, that the riots could be largely attributed to "the promiscuous scattering of Negroes throughout white residential sections of our city."

On the surface, segregation hardly seemed dangerous. It was the easy way out of the box, through a hole in the side. And it was a familiar solution, considered an acceptable practice for at least sixty years. In fact, a proposal later presented to the Senate Foreign Relations Committee and the House Committee on Foreign Affairs would take segregation to its ultimate extreme: to establish a "Negro State to be situated partly within the boundaries of the U.S. and partly in Mexico."

During August, Major Loving's report made the rounds in Washington, at least in the War Department. It was first read by Major J. E. Cutler, who at the same time had turned in his own report, *The Negro Situation*, specific to the military, based on interviews and observations of black returning soldiers. Cutler, who was white, noted in a memo to MID chief Marlborough Churchill that his black colleague Loving had "changed his viewpoint somewhat" over the past year but that he respected Loving and Loving's work—even the part about Loving's view that "agitation and the strongest pressure that the colored people can muster, short of actual hostilities, is now their only recourse." Cutler's cover memo plus his own report and Loving's moved up the line of command to General Churchill and then to the secretary of war. After reading both, Churchill sent a memo to the secretary of war in which he called the Cutler and Loving commentaries "important" because both men had devoted an entire year to studying blacks in America. Major Loving, General Churchill reminded the secretary, in a description he had used on other occasions, was "one of the best types of white man's Negro." And because of this, wrote Churchill, Loving's criticism of the government's "handling of the negro situation" has "important bearing on the seriousness of the situation."

But Loving's report apparently never made it beyond the desk of the secretary of war. There is no evidence that President Wilson ever read it. In fact, by the end of August the president had not yet given a public comment about the race riots. On August 29, the NAACP sent a well-publicized telegram to Wilson protesting the summer riots and the more recent incident of the brutal beating of NAACP secretary John Shillady in Texas on August 22. The telegram also noted that on the 28th of that month, Georgia had "tolerated" its eighth mob murder of a black man that year, showing an average of one a month. And it added that most of the lynchings had been followed by torchings of black homes, churches, and schools. The NAACP urged the president "in the interest of civilization" to ask Congress to investigate the failure of states to protect their citizens.

By the end of the month Major Loving had returned to the Philippines to his previous post as the conductor of the Constabulary Band. Although there were still some active agents sending reports to the MID about radical stirrings among black Americans—mostly monitoring Marcus Garvey or Jack Johnson—the Negro Subversion division, facing huge budgetary cuts, began to fade away. And so did the reforms that Major Loving had suggested. Regardless of its questionable tactics and the shadowing of unsuspecting civilians, the MID had attempted to understand the realities of race in America. There was even wisdom in it, as Loving noted that there was, in fact, Bolshevik propaganda everywhere in America in 1919, just as there was propaganda against Bolshevism. But *that* was not the problem and it should not be the central focus of the government's policy on race. The conditions that would make a class or race of people susceptible to propaganda of any sort were the problem. Segregation must end and now was the time to face it, or there could be years of race violence ahead. But that message had no lasting significance and fell like the leaves of autumn onto a rushing river.

At the end of August, the old myths surfaced in full force on the floor of the House of Representatives and on the front pages of every major newspaper. "Reds Incite Negro Rioters," the *Los Angeles Times* headline read. Representative James Francis Byrnes of South Carolina declared that a conspiracy between the IWW and the Bolsheviks was stirring up race hatred in the United States. He had the publications to prove it and he handed them over to the attorney general. Radical black leaders were urging their constituents to "resort to violence to secure privileges they believed themselves entitled to and the recent riots indicate that they are accepting this advice." An example of "this type of Negro leader," Byrnes said, was Du Bois, and he read out loud Du Bois's editorial from the May issue of *The Crisis*. "We return. We return from fighting. We return fighting," recited the South Carolina Democrat.

Representative Byrnes proclaimed that if the wording of that editorial was not a violation of the Espionage Act he could not conceive of language "sufficiently abusive to constitute a violation." Once again the image of the radical agitator or Bolshevik hard at work to destroy the nation blurred the real claims for equality, justice, and progress. Du Bois's editorial was not revolutionary. His language did not call for violent insurrection but rather for blacks to "fight" for democracy. Du Bois's words only appeared radical because America's practices lagged so very far behind its ideals.

In August, there had been a subtle changing of the guard in the government. In the battle to conquer America's internal enemies, the baton of domestic spying—on black as well as white Americans—was passing from the War Department to the Justice Department. Although the Military Intelligence Division would continue to scrutinize the military and would actually strengthen its surveillance of organized labor in the autumn of 1919, it would ease off of spying on African-Americans, and in all such matters it would take a back seat to the Justice Department's Bureau of Investigation. While both agencies as well as the Secret Service and the navy had dispatched agents to report on radical activities, and would continue to do so in the months and years ahead, the lead agency, the central clearinghouse for radical activity, the place where all other agencies would send the reports of their agents and their volunteer spies, would now shift to the emerging giant: the Bureau of Investigation.

Whatever might have seemed invasive or undemocratic under the supervision of the MID would soon look like mere practice for the big operation that was now taking shape. Indeed, on August 1, the new General Intelligence Division of the U.S. Justice Department opened its doors. And the first to enter was its newly appointed head, J. Edgar Hoover.

CHAPTER 30

King of the Index

The custom of kings, of feudal lords, and of governments, great and small, amassing information about people and property within their domains is timeless. In 1086, the new Norman king of England, William I, ordered a vast collection of details about English landholders, tenancies, inheritances, even an accounting of the number of oxen and swine on every acre of the English land he had conquered. Recorded in what was called the Domesday Book, the information empowered the new king to impose taxes, redistribute property, and administratively control his kingdom. For centuries—as far back in time as the fifteenth century B.C.—leaders have conducted such surveys to tax, to enlist military service, to consolidate, to protect, and to control tribes and nations. Only the methods and tools for inspecting, collecting, and assessing the information have changed with time.

In 1919, those tools were simple, especially compared with the advanced gadgetry and technology that would evolve in the years ahead. Telephones, cameras, dictographs, and wiretaps were state-of-the-art. Wiretapping was especially popular. In use by the federal government since the administration of Theodore Roosevelt, tapping phone lines was far more prevalent than the ordinary citizen might have imagined. In states where a court order was required to install it, local law enforcement or the Justice Department sometimes skipped over that step without pause, working directly with telephone companies and rarely worrying about privacy. In California, for example, there were cases in which the Justice Department had worked with the Pacific Telephone Company to attach a device that would tap lines to spy on labor organizers for the secretary of labor.

Another early twentieth-century trend was the use of the female undercover agent, popular during and after the war as an effective surveillance tool. Some were given high-level assignments. Hallie Queen, for example, who followed such notables as Madam C. J. Walker, had been one of the top agents in the Negro Subversion division of military intelligence. The field office of the MID in Washington had on its rolls a "Miss Anna W. Keichline of Bellafonte, Pa., an architect" who was sent to socialist gatherings to mingle and to probe. The Lusk Committee in New York had Agent 22, who was sent to work for Emma Goldman as her typist. Agent 22's real name was Margaret M. Scully and her real profession was acting. Unfortunately for the government, she was a better actress and spy than typist. Goldman fired her for incompetence. The American Protective League had enlisted women undercover agents early on. The Cleveland branch of the APL had an entire division of women spies who worked in airplane factories during the war trying to identify saboteurs. There was actually a debate within the APL leadership about women, some believing it was dangerous to employ them as spies and others lauding their talent for discretion, subtlety, and persistence. During that discussion, one APL leader sent out a memo saying: "Thousands of women are daily visiting cafes, hotels and other public places. . . . They could all be American spies! . . . Women are far more subtle than men, especially in such work as this. . . . If they are attractive they have little difficulty in getting what they go after. If I had one hundred smart women on my staff, I am willing to bet that I would get a tremendous volume of first-class information." By 1919 women had won respect as important tools of the nation's spy trade.

The age-old fine art of shadowing was a tool in itself. Trotter probably didn't spot his shadow on Pier 57 the day he returned from Paris nor did he see the agent slip into a cab behind his and follow him all the way to the homecoming reception in Harlem. The ability to rifle through file drawers without detection, carefully replacing documents after taking pictures of them, was a highly regarded method of information gathering. And among some spies, at least in the APL, burgling a house or office was the height of mastery. "It is supposed that breaking and entering a man's home or office place without warrant is burglary. Granted. But the League has done that thousands of times and has never been detected!" so boasted the APL's historian Emerson Hough in *The Web*.

The simplest of all tools, though, was perhaps the most powerful, or at least it had the potential for power in the hands of someone who knew exactly how to use it. And that was the index. With the use of an index the name of a specific individual on a card with twenty-five or more cross-references from other cards filed under more general and specific names and topics gave the user access to every possible detail about the person named on the card. Say, for example, the indexed individual frequented a restaurant where one night he sat next to and talked to a suspected radical. The individual also purchased a copy of the *New York Call,* a socialist newspaper, every week at the same newsstand; attended a street rally calling for amnesty for Eugene Debs; bought *Ten Days That Shook the World;* had a brother who taught at the Rand School; and met with Ludwig C. A. K. Martens, the unofficial Soviet ambassador who ran the Soviet Bureau and whose offices were raided by the Lusk Committee. This man's name would appear at least a dozen times in the index. It would pop up when a researcher looked under the name of the restaurant, of the suspected radical, of John Reed, Reed's book, the newspaper, the street rally, the date of the rally, other names of people who attended the rally, Debs, the Rand School, Martens, and the Soviet Bureau. With a series of "See" and "See Also" references, details in this man's life were easily accessible in the index. The flaw, of course, was that although the details might be accurate, the total picture might not depict the truth. But for organizing and accessing information, nothing was better. A well-honed index with many specific and general references was like a very detailed map, showing the exploratory and coincidental paths as well as the solid, well-traveled highways, all leading to the same destination.

After their June victory in the Senate, the suffragists were applauded not just for their persistence, devotion, and courage but also for their stunning card index. The *New York Times* even headlined an article "Triumph of the Index." Maude Younger, the "Keeper of the Suffrage Card Index," took the *Times* reporter to the pantry-sized room where the index drawers were kept and explained the "mysteries and purposes of the elaborate system of information." In the index, the victorious National Woman's Party organized the personal and professional details of the lives of every senator and representative in America. Based on years of astute observation of the politicians' comings and goings, the index contained no fewer than twenty-two cards per person. With this invaluable tool, the suffragists devised a winning strategy to lobby for the vote—tailor-made for each legislator. Exactly what time each congressman arrived at his office was noted. If he had coffee at a particular place, it was indexed. What was his favorite restaurant? What was the best time to corner him? In the morning in his office over coffee or at a restaurant over lunch? If he had a "financial backer," then the name of the backer was indexed. And if the backer was not yet pro-suffrage, a lobbyist would try to convert him or her with the intent of putting more pressure on the politicians he or she backed. Golf partners, exercise habits, church attendance, favorite magazines. Every detail was noted. If it was learned that a particular congressman had received very few letters about women's suffrage from his constituents, then that would be noted, and in the frequent assessment of cross-references in the file that detail would pop up. Soon letters would inundate his office. Each time one of the lobbyists visited a legislator, the cards would be updated if there was new information. The *Times* commented: "It worked."

Maude Younger didn't invent the index. Librarians had been using indexing systems to catalogue books and serials for many years. But in 1919 the index had not yet caught on outside the library world. The government and big business were just beginning to see how useful the librarian's way of organizing information could be. Every agency employed a system of organizing files. But thus far, the only person who had captured the power of the index for that timeless practice of observing and analyzing the populace had been Ralph H. Van Deman, the man known in government circles as the "father of Military Intelligence."

Van Deman preceded Marlborough Churchill as head of the MID and in fact was the person responsible for aggressively pushing the army and the War Department to create a separate division for intelligence, which they finally did in May of 1917. Van Deman was an astounding innovator in terms of government bureaucracy and funding, in addition to domestic surveillance. Within six weeks of winning his two-year battle to launch an intelligence unit, the army's most fervent advocate of a massive intelligence network in America persuaded Congress to increase the budget from the initial appropriation of $25,000 to $500,000, which, to avoid public scrutiny, he would spend through a system of confidential vouchers. A week later he arranged for another $100,000 from the quartermaster general to fund a small army of informants. That was July and by October Congress had given him another $500,000. That sum doubled the following year. He had the department, the funding, the informants. Now what he needed was an elaborate, efficient system of organizing the information contained in the bundles of reports that his agents sent into his office: an index. Eventually Van Deman would have an index of about 85,000 cards.

But in August of 1919, the crown was passed on to a new king of surveillance and indexing: J. Edgar Hoover.

Hoover was twenty-four years old when he began his new job as head of what was then called the Radical Division of the Justice Department's Bureau of Investigation, soon to be renamed the General Intelligence Division. His rise through the government bureaucracy had been nothing less than meteoric, enhanced by the fact that he was one of few men in his age group who was not in the military during the war years. When he was eighteen years old, he enrolled at George Washington University to study law and took a job as a messenger at the Library of Congress. His salary was $360 a year. Three years later, in 1916, at the age of twenty-one, he earned his bachelor of law degree and worked as a Library of Congress clerk. The next year he earned his master's degree in law and passed the District of Columbia bar. He also registered for the draft and, though fit, he did not serve. There were two reasons for this: he needed to financially support his parents because his father was ill, and his cousin, a former Justice Department attorney and now an associate justice of the District of Columbia Supreme Court, had found him a new job in the Justice Department that was draft-exempt. After four years at the library, he joined the Justice Department in July of 1917. It appears that at the start he was helping out with the overwhelming paperwork coming into the department regarding German aliens, referred to as "enemy aliens." Hoover's penchant for thoroughness and hard work—he very often worked overtime—along with the diminished competition in such civilian jobs for men his age, earned him two promotions very quickly. By December he was the head of the Enemy Alien Registration section. In this job, he summarized case files of interned aliens and those being considered for internment, and he fielded problems arising from the November 1917 law to register all German males in the United States. In an early 1918 memo to John Lord O'Brian, who was then the special assistant to the attorney general in charge of war-related prosecutions, Hoover wrote: "Attached hereto are the files on the case of Udo Rall, age, 24. An investigation conducted by the American Intelligence Bureau showed that Rall belittled the United States; talked against the War; spread pacifist propaganda and wrote against conscription. The United States Attorney recommends that Rall be interned for the duration of the war and the above facts are submitted to you for your consideration in acting upon his recommendation."

By March of 1918 he had his own secretary, Helen Gandy, who would stay with him for the rest of his working life. In April, when the Justice Department ordered that all German females register, Hoover assumed more responsibilities, and by summer he was promoted to the rank of attorney in the Justice Department. In that post, he evaluated legal cases of aliens applying for citizenship or resisting internment, he made decisions regarding the cases, and he wrote the official letters asking for the signature of his superiors. It seemed that nearly every month during 1918, Hoover's responsibilities as well as his authority in the Justice Department increased. By the time of the Armistice he was working on very complicated legal cases regarding aliens and keeping track of all registration statistics of enemy aliens, which he had done since the 1917 law was passed. After the Armistice he asked the head of the Justice Department if he could stay on permanently and O'Brian, Hoover's boss, took up his cause, speaking personally with the attorney general about Hoover's future.

Hoover's new job, for which he was paid $3,000 a year, was to run the new domestic intelligence network within the Justice Department. His mission was to gather and organize all information about radicals in America. To accomplish this, his department dispatched agents to collect information about radical organizations, publications, and individuals as well as events that radicals might be sponsoring or attending. It then organized the details of the reports of those agents as well as the agents in all other intelligence divisions of local, state, and federal agencies. The idea, according to the attorney general's annual report, was to allow the government to study the radical movement "from a more intelligent and broader viewpoint" and to amass the greatest amount of information about radicals to be found anywhere in America. It was an overwhelming task that would create a "virtual monopoly over information" and establish the foundation for the nation's future domestic intelligence network.

To meet the task, the division, in those beginning days, was equipped with thirty-five informants, some assigned generally to events and meetings and others working undercover on special duty. There were at least three black informants—Agent WW, whose name was William A. Bailey; Agent 800, who was James W. Jones; and Agent C-C, who worked undercover as the technical adviser for the Black Star Steamship Co. to keep a close eye on its owner Marcus Garvey. There were several women, including one assigned to replace Margaret Scully in the early autumn of 1919, and some special agents assigned to infiltrating unions, especially during strikes.

Hoover likely brought the idea of the card index to the Justice Department from his years of working at the Library of Congress, though some historians would later attribute it to Van Deman's index at the MID, from which Hoover gleaned a good deal of information. Whatever the source of Hoover's understanding of the power of the index, it would seem that the Information Age in the American government began in August of 1919. By the end of 1919, Hoover would have compiled an indexed system of 150,000 cards covering the activities of moderate radicals as well as anarchists. Within the next two years, it would expand to 450,000 cards. In an interdepartmental memo during his first months on the job, Hoover wrote: "At a moment's notice a card upon an individual, organization or a general society existing in any part of the country can be obtained and a brief resume found on the card requested."

As soon as an agent's report came into Hoover's office it was sent to a special "editorial room," where it was indexed and then filed. Hoover's staff was small: three assistants, five stenographers, seventeen clerks, four typists, and two messengers. Thirty-one people in all, for a very large task. Between mid-August of 1919 and mid-March of the following year, they would process 17,526 reports, 7,328 letters, 3,166 publications, 1,407 telegrams—indexing it all. This was efficiency of the highest order: an average of ninety-eight reports a day, forty-one letters, eighteen publications, and eight telegrams. All such inflowing information was divided into five categories. The first was individuals who had been in any way connected to what the government perceived as radical publications, organizations, or meetings. Their cards contained a name, address, nationality, a summary of suspicious activities, and a file number. Second were all organizations and their membership lists. Then came publications, which included all publishers, editors, description of content, circulation statistics, and locales. Next were cards on every state, major city, and foreign country and analysis of radical activity in each. And lastly were cards with descriptions of incidents such as protests, riots, or meetings. Then all cards were cross-referenced so that pulling up information on any individual or group was easily and quickly accomplished. This was the definition of power in government: organizing massive amounts of information and making it accessible. And Hoover was a brilliant pioneer. The flaw in the system, as in every such index, was that the facts being indexed were not verified for accuracy. An individual might be represented in Hoover's index based on something an agent picked up in a conversation or from a rumor or at a meeting run by people the government deemed as radical. Indeed, Hoover's operation would prove to be as treacherous as it was brilliant.

The first month on the new job must have been a bit disappointing, though, for the nation's new anti-radical warrior. In August, the attorney general and the Justice Department were far less rabid about the war on radicals—the raison d'être of Hoover's new division—than they had been during those disquieting days after the June bombings. For one thing, Palmer was proceeding more cautiously in the wake of the July 4 fizzle. None of Flynn's fearful forecasts had come true. There were also the criticisms earlier in the year regarding the "Red Special." This was the train speeding out of Seattle right before the general strike with fifty-four allegedly dangerous immigrant troublemakers huddling in two crowded cars that were guarded by fourteen heavily armed immigration officers. At Ellis Island, they were detained "incommunicado" for months. Many were later released for lack of evidence or after they renounced Bolshevik creeds. Only three were deported. The outcome whipped up some bad press, in which the government was lashed from both sides. Some papers used words like "extreme" and "too far." Others saw the scorecard of only three deportees out of dozens of detainees as humiliating and flaccid.

By August, although the season of Red hunting was far from over, other matters were higher on Palmer's list of priorities. He and his chief assistant, Francis P. Garvan, seemed to have established two top priorities: battling Palmer's opponents in Congress who were still trying to block his confirmation as attorney general and responding to extreme political pressure to attack the issue of the high cost of living. Illegal price fixing was possibly the major cause, and it was the attorney general's job to find and to prosecute the culprits.

On August 20, the Senate subcommittee investigating the accusations against Palmer, which had delayed his confirmation as attorney general, sent a favorable report to the Senate. Even the darkest of the accusations against him earlier in the summer seemed to have passed their review. The cabal of Palmer critics had been most suspicious and outspoken about the Chemical Foundation, an organization that Palmer, as alien property custodian, had formed to purchase more than 4,500 confiscated German dye patents and to protect the patents for the American dye industry. The foundation's board consisted of businessmen from whom Palmer had sought advice about the patents during the weeks leading up to the patent confiscations. And the president of the foundation's board was Francis P. Garvan. During the congressional debates over Palmer in June, Representative J. Hampton Moore, a Republican from Pennsylvania, complained that "A. Mitchell Palmer, Alien Property Custodian, having advised with these men up to the point where he seized these German patents by an Executive Order, obtained through himself, and conscious of their worth, looked about for a President for their corporation. With the approval of Attorney General Palmer, former Alien Property Custodian succeeded by Frank P. Garvan, they elected Frank P. Garvan as President and he is President today."

Now, two months later, it seemed that the case might soon be closed, and Palmer, after six months of mud slinging in the Senate, would finally be confirmed as the nation's chief law enforcer. On the day after the presentation of the Senate's report, however, Senator William Calder from New York called for a new committee to dig deeper into the machinations of Palmer's administration as alien property custodian. Now that the peace conference was over and the treaty signed, it was possible that some of the Germans whose industrial holdings and personal assets were confiscated by the Alien Property Bureau—totaling approximately $1 billion—would try to recover their property. In recent weeks, German newspapers had claimed that Palmer's wartime confiscation was proof of the reason America had entered the war. The *Deutsche Tageszeitung* called the seizures "The Deliberate Destruction of German Possessions in America." This was a problem, said Calder, as he suspected that some, if not many, of the assets were taken without proper legal authority. It could get very ugly, said the senator, especially considering the number of items seized and the subsequent sale of them. The United States did not want an attorney general who would soon be swept into such a nasty scandal. Also, Senator Calder said that he was bothered that Francis P. Garvan, who had been Palmer's chief investigator in the Alien Property Bureau, Palmer's successor as alien property custodian, and president of the foundation that Palmer had created, was now Palmer's assistant attorney general in charge of investigations.

Palmer fired back by accusing his accusers of collusion with Germans and by explaining that he had in fact opposed the sale of the patents to the Americans. Palmer also slipped one little detail about Calder into the hands of the press: Calder was planning to run in the 1920 election as the vice presidential candidate on the Republican ticket with Senator Hiram Johnson. This made Calder's attack on Palmer look more like political manipulation than ethical consideration. A week later, Palmer's appointment as attorney general was approved.

In the midst of this controversy, the indefatigable Palmer asked Congress for more money: $2.5 million to launch a crusade to lower the flagrantly high cost of living. Soaring inflation was one of the reasons for the extreme labor unrest and the general instability among the American public, Palmer recognized. And one of the main reasons for spiraling prices was that "unconscionable men," he said, were hoarding commodities and fixing prices. These were not just small businessmen but also large corporations such as the giant Chicago meatpacker Armour. There must be raids to confiscate the items and put them into the marketplace, thus lowering prices by increasing supply. Food was his main target. Every warehouse and cold storage house in America must be searched and if the hoarders refused to release the foodstuffs, the government would load the food onto railcars and distribute it nationwide. The hoarders would then be prosecuted. One million dollars alone, Palmer told Congress, would be needed to prosecute violators of the food and antitrust acts. He also wanted new laws that would criminalize the hoarding of such items as clothing and shoes. And in his ardent, focused way he called for an organized effort among American women to simplify their wearing apparel. Designers of women's clothes must lessen the number of style changes every year, so said the attorney general.

Perhaps it was Palmer's preoccupation with food hoarders and other such causes that inspired Hoover to add more to his mix of power than agents and an index. The cause of hunting down the Red Menace must not come to a halt. In August the Bureau of Investigation notified all agents to send reports about suspected radicals to Hoover's new division and they, in turn, called upon their old American Protective League volunteers to do the same. The Labor Department was asked to send Hoover its lists of aliens who might be labor agitators and thus possible candidates for deportation. But Hoover wanted more. At some point that August, as Hoover settled into his new job, he must have realized that to investigate and catalogue the activities of unknown, though potentially dangerous, Americans would not necessarily secure a position of power for him or serve his mission of excising the radical cancer spreading throughout America. This was especially true if those people or their organizations proved to be innocent. Both Hoover and the BI's Flynn—the man who had warned America about the threat of violence on the Fourth of July—knew that the cause needed high-profile threats to American security. And so it was that Hoover began to focus on people and organizations with names that had been in newspapers enough to make them recognizable to the American public, such as Emma Goldman, Ludwig Martens, the Union of Russian Workers, Mollie Steimer, and America's two new political parties, the Communist Party of America and the Communist Labor Party, both soon to be organized in Chicago. He also began a search for links between the most threatening high-profile events and issues in America and the Red Menace. For example, a late-August article in the *New York Times* about the race riots ended with this: "Agents of the Department of Justice are investigating. Facts thus far developed lead officials to believe that IWW and Soviet influence were at the bottom of the recent race riots in Washington and Chicago."

Soon Hoover would be able to detect a Red connection to just about every social issue of the day. And because of the celebrated stature of his targets, he would also have the publicity to draw every American's attention to the cause of "seeing Red" for many years to come. While thousands of his peers were returning from war, heroes in their hometowns and in their nation, Hoover was gearing up for battle, for a lifelong war against the Red-conspiring "other" in America, for his own campaign to be an American hero.

CHAPTER 31

"I'll Stay with You, Mary"

For some people A. Mitchell Palmer and J. Edgar Hoover were heroes, trying to save America from iniquitous forces; for others, *they* were the villains. Those who saw them as villains might have chosen Eugene Debs or William Monroe Trotter or Alice Paul for their heroes. Was an American hero someone who protested injustices, inequality, and prejudice? Or was it someone who protected the American public from the disruptions and confrontations of such dissenters and protesters? Was it the man who rounded up a mob to attack an alleged murderer? Or was it the man who took a bullet trying to stop him? Was it the worker who went on strike to improve wages and conditions? Or was it the manager who struggled to keep production moving during the strike? America's ideals of individualism and freedom sometimes confused the notions of villains and heroes. So often those Americans most feared in their own times for their willingness to oppose the popular current or stand up for the oppressed would become the heroes of the future, while those lauded as the heroes of the day might later be regarded as the most destructive people of their era.

Nineteen nineteen was a year of numerous heroes in America, including the hundreds of thousands of returning soldiers, the daring aviators, and the peacemakers in Paris. The press, always eager to boost circulation, grasped at heroes stories of every kind—for example, the participants in the nation's first transcontinental motor convoy, which arrived in San Francisco from Washington, D.C., on September 7 after traversing a very rugged 3,251 miles on often unpaved roads through twenty-two states. The purpose of the journey had been to test state-of-the-art military vehicles designed too late to be sent to Europe and to assess the capability of the U.S. Army to move across the country in the event of a national emergency. The convoy, which consisted of eighty-one motorized army vehicles, thirty-seven officers, and 258 enlisted men, simulated a security crisis in which an "Asiatic enemy" was invading the nation. Among the participants was young Lieutenant Colonel Dwight D. Eisenhower.

There were national heroes and local heroes; some who tried to be heroes and some who just happened to do something that people needed to perceive as heroic. It was as if the numbers of heroes emerging from a culture at any given time might be proportionate to the level of pain and struggle of its people.

In Chicago, for example, at the end of its tragic summer, three heroes emerged in just such a way, one woman and two seemingly little men whose very big sacrifices must have reminded the people of Chicago that there was still dignity and love in their world. One was William Fitch Tanner, a cashier in the Chicago offices of the Baltimore & Ohio Railroad. He was thirty-nine years old. His wife was thirty-eight. They lived on Linden Avenue in Winnetka, a north Chicago suburb. And they had three children. One Monday night, William's mother volunteered to stay with the children while the Tanners went to the cinema. To do so they would have to take the northbound train at Gage Street. To get to the northbound track they had to walk across the southbound track. When they arrived at the track they saw the flagman signal vehicle traffic to stop. But the Tanners thought that the southbound train seemed far enough away that they could easily cross with time to spare. And so they rushed across the track. Suddenly Mrs. Tanner stopped. "My foot's caught," she told her husband, trying to extricate her foot from between a board and a rail. He tried too and then hastily called the flagman, John Miller. Both men failed to free the foot. "My God man, it's hopeless," said Miller. "No, we must save her," Tanner said. As the train moved closer, the engineer saw them and threw on the emergency brakes. Both Miller and Tanner struggled to release Mrs. Tanner's foot until the engine was nearly upon them. Then, with the train only seconds away, Mrs. Tanner begged her husband to leave her and to save his own life. "I'll stay with you, Mary," he said and wrapped his arms around her. Miller was at the side of the track, still pulling at the board that was holding her foot when the train struck them, hurtling all three people fifty feet into the air. Miller, who was fifty-two years old, lived, but he fractured his right arm and his left leg was so severely crushed it was later amputated. Both Tanners died.

Chicagoans recognized all three as heroes: Miller for nearly sacrificing his life for two strangers; Mr. Tanner for staying with his wife; and Mrs. Tanner for begging her husband to save his own life. Benefits were held in Chicago for the six children affected by the accident—Miller's three and the Tanners' three. Contributors' names with the size of their donation were published in the local newspapers. Stories about the tragedy ran for weeks. "Chicago's imagination continues to be gripped and its purse strings loosened at the thought of the Hubbard Woods train tragedy in which William Fitch Tanner made the supreme sacrifice by dying with her before the train," wrote the *Chicago Daily Tribune*. Other cities, including New York, Kansas City, and Los Angeles, held benefits, as the words "I'll stay with you, Mary" echoed across America.

Around the same time, two heroes of a different sort surfaced. One was fictional; the other, very real. Both would be immortalized by Hollywood. The first appeared in the newsstands during August, in the cover story of a pulp magazine called *All-Story Weekly*. "The Curse of Capistrano," by Johnston McCulley, a former crime reporter, was the first of five episodes running between August 9 and September 6. The story's setting is Southern California in the early nineteenth century and its main character, a wealthy nobleman named Don Diego de la Vega. A seemingly quiet, genteel man, Don Diego has just returned to Los Angeles from his studies of art and science in Spain to find his town unjustly ruled by the cruel, corrupt, and oppressive command of Capitán Monastario. The task of overthrowing the capitán and his many troops is overwhelming and certainly not within the capability of the meek and awkward, though well-meaning, Don Diego. However, Don Diego has another side. His anger at the injustices that surround him drive him to adopt the secret identity of a masked vigilante who in the still of the night rides a black stallion named Tornado and who as a master swordsman duels villainous characters to right the wrongs of his world. His name is El Zorro, the "fox."

In New York, that same week in August, the story of another American hero debuted at the premiere of a film called *Deliverance*. Billed as "An Epoch-Making Three-Act Photo-Drama," the film opened at the Lyric Theatre on 42nd Street on the night of August 18. In seven reels, lasting one hour and fifteen minutes, it told the true story of a little girl named Helen Keller who, born in Tuscumbia, Alabama, was nineteen months old when she developed a fever so severe that she became deaf and blind. By the time she was five, she had not learned to talk and was so strong-willed and impetuous that she vented her frustration at not being able to express herself by behaving like an untamed animal. At age seven, her parents contacted Alexander Graham Bell, who worked with deaf children, and he connected the family to the Perkins Institute for the Blind in Watertown, Massachusetts. It was there that the impetuous child met a twenty-year-old teacher, Anne Sullivan, who taught the child to talk and brought alive what a film critic called "one of the most powerful minds of the times." In the second act, Helen Keller goes to Radcliffe College, "conquering her way into the kingdom of learning with tremendous strides against overpowering obstacles," as one reviewer wrote. The third act is in the present time: Helen Keller at age thirty-nine, dancing, enjoying classical music through vibrations, even beating time with an orchestra and laughing. And in that act Helen played herself, as did Anne Sullivan and Helen's mother, brother, and secretary. In the last scene, Helen rides a horse into the distance, as if, one reviewer said, "leading the multitudes into the true vision of life and Destiny."

Deliverance was the first feature film ever to show a disabled person in a positive light. Keller had worked with the screenwriter, written parts of it herself, acted in it, and partially produced it. And, despite a torrential rainstorm the night of its premiere, the theater was packed. Its many reviewers gushed with enthusiasm:

"A living, pulsing representation of the biggest battle a human soul ever fought and won. It is shot through with laughter and tears and it sends you away with a new desire for the things that count"—*New York Morning Sun.*

"Outdistanced all claims made for it"—*New York Evening World.*

"A succession of wonders"—*New York Times.*

"Cannot be praised too highly"—*New York Evening Sun.*

"A picture that will live long after photoplays of twenty years hence have passed and are forgotten"—*New York Evening Mail.*

And, from *Motion Picture News:* "Keller conquered her first night audience. Rounds of applause greeted each act as it ended."

One review from a Madison, Wisconsin, daily—and perhaps only one—pointed out Keller's ability to see the truths of her world, far beyond most fellow Americans who had two perfectly functioning eyes. Keller was a pacifist who had not only protested the war but had also stood up for workers' rights, women's suffrage, and civil liberties. She corresponded with Eugene Debs, who wrote to her from his prison cell, she was a member of the IWW, she would soon be one of the founders of the American Civil Liberties Union, she passionately loved democracy, and she would one day in the not so distant future occupy space in Hoover's files. The only truly blind persons in the world are the ones who do not see the truth, she would tell her audiences. The Madison reviewer wrote, "We wish every man, woman and child in Madison could go to The Fuller this week to witness this production. Take a day off from the grimaces and caprices of Charlie Chaplin and Mary Pickford and let Helen Keller make you see—SEE for one night. Helen Keller has consecrated her life to the great task of making a BLIND world SEE. And so much of the world is BLIND to the TRUTH in these days."

Keller had intended to sit in the audience at the premiere of *Deliverance*, and at the end to stand up and say a few words. But when she learned that the Actors Equity Association, the union organized in 1913 to arbitrate differences between actors and producer-managers, was on strike and that part of their protest was aimed at the Shuberts, who owned the Lyric Theatre where *Deliverance* was debuting, she didn't attend. She wouldn't cross a picket line and on Broadway that week nearly every theater had its line of picketers—except for one, the Lexington Theatre, on Lexington Avenue at East 50th, where the striking actors had put together a special show of music and skits to draw attention to their cause. It was there that Keller spent the evening of her film's premiere, in support of the striking actors whom she perceived as the heroes of the moment.

With Ethel Barrymore and her brother Lionel standing on the stage, hand in hand, bowing and smiling, the Lexington was filled. The audience loved the show so much they begged the performers to continue through the intermission. Thus, the Barrymores performed the second act of *Camille,* at the end of which Ethel stood center stage and breathlessly expressed her convictions: "I can't say anything but STICK, that's all. You stick, and I'll stick, and we can't lose. We'll win!"

What the actors wanted were four-week limits on unpaid rehearsals. Now, they had to rehearse for months without pay. They wanted half pay for the weeks following the limit. They wanted payment for extra matinees, and stipends for playing out of town. "Not More Pay, Just Fair Play," read the banners they waved in front of every theater on Broadway. When groups of chorus girls approached brokers and investors on Wall Street to solicit financial support for the strike and were asked how they could afford to be part of it, they said that it was just the same as rehearsing a play. They had lived without pay while doing rehearsals for as long as eight weeks and so how was this any different? In fact, they might be able to win the

Hiram Johnson, Republican Senator from California and first politician to publicly challenge the continued presence of U.S. troops in northern Russia after the Armistice.
(LIBRARY OF CONGRESS)

Harry Weinberger, New York City attorney known for his dedication to civil liberties. He represented radicals and immigrants such as Mollie Steimer and Jacob Abrams. (COLLECTION OF WARREN WEINBERGER)

Oliver Wendell Holmes, Jr., associate justice of the Supreme Court, renowned for his "clear and present danger" ruling of 1919 on the limitations of free speech, and for his dissent later that year in the Abrams case, considered a benchmark in modern free speech law. (LIBRARY OF CONGRESS)

Mollie Steimer, Russian immigrant sentenced to 15 years in prison for distributing leaflets to protest America's postwar intervention in northern Russia. (TAMIMENT LIBRARY, NEW YORK UNIVERSITY)

A young J. Edgar Hoover at his Department of Justice desk in the early 1920s. August 1, 1919, was Hoover's first day on the job as director of the General Intelligence Division of the Bureau of Investigation, now known as the FBI. (LIBRARY OF CONGRESS)

A. Mitchell Palmer,
attorney general in 1919.
(LIBRARY OF CONGRESS)

The façade of Palmer's house at 2132 R Street in Washington, D.C., after the June 2, 1919, bombing. (LIBRARY OF CONGRESS)

Albert Einstein with the acclaimed British astronomer Sir Arthur Stanley Eddington in the early 1930s. (SYNDICS OF CAMBRIDGE UNIVERSITY LIBRARY)

British pilot Sir John Alcock and American navigator Sir Arthur Brown, aviators who together made the first nonstop transatlantic flight in June 1919. (CYNTHIA LONG, ALCOCK AND BROWN VICKERS PLC COLLECTION)

Helen Keller on horseback in Beverly Hills, California, in August of 1919, the same month in which her movie *Deliverance* was released. (HELEN KELLER ARCHIVES, THE AMERICAN FOUNDATION FOR THE BLIND)

Scene from a play produced by the Actors' Equity Association after their walkout in August 1919, the first strike in the history of the American theater. (TAMIMENT LIBRARY, NEW YORK UNIVERSITY)

Judge Elbert H. Gary, chairman of United States Steel Corporation, speaking to steelworkers in Gary, Indiana, on September 19, 1919, three days before the nationwide steel strike. John A. Fitzpatrick, president of the Chicago Federation of Labor, is seen behind Gary. (BROWN BROTHERS)

battle and finally be paid for rehearsal time. It was a risk they were willing to take.

At the Lexington that night, W. C. Fields did what the critics called his "nightmare golf game act." Comedian, singer, and actor Eddie Cantor was there and so was Lillian Russell. Cantor got some laughs when he told the audience he would have complained about not being paid for the performance but he knew that that particular night he was getting the same pay as Ethel Barrymore: nothing. And so that was good enough for him. Comedian Ed Wynn, who had been legally enjoined from appearing on the stage at the Lexington Theatre, sat in the second-row aisle seat. Although he was told he could not do a performance as part of the show without violating the injunction, he told the audience what he would have said if he had been allowed to perform. Marie Dressler, a comedian of vaudeville and silent film, and Ethel Barrymore spoke up for the chorus girls. Five days after the strike had begun, they held meetings at the Hotel Astor with the dancers to bolster their courage to walk out, which they did, and to organize them into the Chorus Equity union. Dressler was its first president. When reporters asked Dressler why she was doing this, she said that she simply felt she belonged with the strikers. "I began in the chorus," Dressler told reporters, "and now I've got back with the chorus once more and I'm glad of it!"

The strike, which the New York Times called "one of the most remarkable situations ever known in the history of the American stage," had begun on the night of August 7 when a hundred or more actors in twelve Broadway shows walked out in the middle of their performances to protest the theater managers' refusal to negotiate with the Actors Equity Association. The first show to shut down was the Broadway hit Lightnin'. Thus the press called the strike's beginning "the night when lightnin' struck."

That night, when Ed Wynn, who was starring in Gaieties of 1919 at the Shubert Theatre, left the stage mid-performance, he met a crowd of theatergoers out on the street. After he explained to them why his fellow actors deserved better treatment, the crowd, in support of his cause, lifted him up and carried him down Broadway. As they walked, more protesters joined the throng. And soon reporters arrived. One asked Wynn why he was doing this. "I am striking for the privacy of my dressing-room," said Wynn.

"And what do you mean by that?" asked the reporter.

"I mean that my dressing-room is so full of people who come in to complain about the way they are treated by the managers that I never get five minutes to myself."

This was the first strike in the history of the American theater and before it was over, thirty days later, it would spread to eight cities, shut down thirty-seven plays, and prevent the openings of sixteen others. In the end, the actors got most of what they wanted in a five-year contract. And after it was over, Helen Keller could walk into the Lyric Theatre for the showing of her own movie.

During the days of the strike, Keller attended Equity gatherings and the Broadway shows Equity members produced to raise funds for the strike. She also wrote letters of support for their strike. "I congratulate you warmly upon the courage with which you are holding out in this great strike, and making your will felt," wrote Keller during the third week of the strike. "I rejoice that you have grown into a force to be reckoned with on the stage of life as well as on the boards."

There were other plays and movies that did not shut down that month. On Broadway, the *Ziegfeld Follies* remained open, as it was not tied to the organizations against which the Actors Equity was striking. At the movies, there was the latest anti-Bolshevik film, *The Red Viper*, in which a Lower East Side Russian immigrant who loves America and whose hero is Theodore Roosevelt falls in love with a Russian woman who has joined a Bolshevik group. The Bolsheviks plan to assassinate a federal judge who had sentenced one of them to die in the electric chair. The young woman is chosen to take a bomb to the judge's residence. Meanwhile, her lover, the hero of the drama, is hurt in a scuffle with the Reds. Still, injuries and all, he makes it to the judge's home before she does and stops her from planting the bomb. One of the Red "vipers" with whom she has been associating, the one who beat up her boyfriend, follows the boyfriend to the judge's home and shoots the judge. She is so revolted by the violence that she nurses the judge back to health. His kindness to her, despite what she had planned to do, inspires her to drop her Bolshevik ways and to marry the Russian hero, whose goal in life is to be like his hero, Teddy Roosevelt.

There was also Harry Houdini's latest film, *The Grim Game*, which also debuted during the strike in late August and was quite popular. This was the story of a man convicted of a murder he did not commit. He escaped from prison to find the real killers and to prove his innocence. In a mystery billed for its myriad "close calls," "real danger," and "endless heroism," the great escapist breaks out of chains several times. After his enemies leave him dangling upside-down in a straitjacket from the roof of a skyscraper, he frees himself fast enough to greet the villains at the end of their elevator ride down to street level. There is even a midair collision of two airplanes, from which "the heroic Houdini" escapes miraculously unharmed. Reviewers said the scene would live on forever in the memories of all Americans. During the filming, the collision, in fact, occurred by accident, and thus the producers decided to reshape the plot around the live footage. One plane was three thousand feet up circling above another, and Houdini, using a rope, was supposed to drop into the cockpit of the lower plane. But while he dangled from the rope and was within seconds of falling into the cockpit, the two planes collided, their propellers locked, and everyone plunged to the ground. "I was helpless but strangely unafraid," Houdini told reporters. "A lifetime passed in an instant. The crash will come. I shall be gone. But it is not all. There is another life. There must be!" Houdini's big secret was that he had been safely on the ground throughout the sequence. No one was killed. It was a very capable stuntman who was hanging from the rope. But the public believed Houdini's miracle story.

The crashing planes would not endure the test of time in the American memory, nor would *The Red Viper, Deliverance,* Equity's first strike, or indeed Helen Keller's ardent support of it. Houdini, the remarkable escape artist, would become a household name. And the deaf and blind girl who became a model for all women and men, disabled or not, would become an American legend. But the woman who wanted the rest of the world to *see* the truth as she saw it, the one who wrote in the *New York Call* that August, "We must fight for the deliverance of the oppressed, the beaten, the betrayed, the plundered," the one who was well represented in J. Edgar Hoover's mighty index, the one who had spent most of her adult life standing up for the oppressed, *that* Helen Keller would fade away with time. Instead, the fighter for the oppressed who would be featured in film over and over again was the fictional hero El Zorro.

And as for Zorro, Douglas Fairbanks, by most accounts, read the five episodes of "The Curse of Capistrano" on his honeymoon with Mary Pickford, and was dazzled by it. Fairbanks and Pickford were now partners with

Charlie Chaplin and D. W. Griffith in a new venture, United Artists, which they formed in February of 1919. Fairbanks saw the Zorro character as the hero in a historical setting that he had apparently been looking for. By the time the couple returned from their honeymoon, they had decided to adapt the story to film, a United Artists production of 1920 entitled *The Mark of Zorro.* "No force that tyranny could bring would dare oppose us—once united," said Zorro in rallying the caballeros to his cause. "Our country is out of joint. It is for us to fight for those held down and beaten, and us alone to set it right."

PART IV

Autumn: Struggle

The Washington riot gave me the thrill that comes once in a life time. I was alone when I read between the lines of the morning paper that at last our men had stood like men, struck back, were no longer dumb, driven cattle. When I could no longer read for my streaming tears, I stood up, alone in my room, held both hands high over my head and exclaimed a loud: "Oh, I thank God, thank God!" . . . I'm sure the editor will understand why I cannot sign my name.

—A SOUTHERN AFRICAN-AMERICAN
WOMAN IN A LETTER TO THE EDITOR
OF *THE CRISIS*, SEPTEMBER 1919

Intellectual darkness is essential to industrial slavery.

—EUGENE DEBS, SEPTEMBER 1919

CHAPTER 32

"*The Right to Happiness*"

Nineteen nineteen was a time in America when the pent-up hopes of a nation at war collided with the chaos of war's aftermath. It was a time when bombs exploded on porch steps and grown men threw sharp-edged rocks at little boys whose skin was a different color. And it was a time when working people, having experienced the highly organized, collective character of waging war, came to believe that through organized labor they could claim the power to achieve the happiness they felt they deserved after surviving such a war. It was a year when race riots erupted in twenty-six cities; labor strikes occurred at an average of ten a day; and always there was the looming terror of the new enemy, Bolshevism. It was indeed a year of struggle. An apocalyptic time, some would say. Others would say it was only a dark moment preceding a new day. For struggle can also be a sign of progress and the foundation on which all change must be built. Struggle is the cost of transforming dreams into reality. It *is* the way we progress.

By September, a nation still recovering from war and from a summer of racial violence plunged into a season consumed with labor struggle. So far there had been nearly two thousand labor strikes since January, some lasting only a few days and others as long as three months. From carpenters and machinists to streetcar conductors and suit makers, America's workers were asking for better conditions, higher wages, and the right to bargain collectively. In April even the telephone operators—referred to as "the telephone girls"—a seemingly tame group, had walked off their jobs in Boston and in almost every village and town across New England. On the second day of the strike, twelve thousand other telephone employees, considered company "insiders," joined the "girls" and on the third day, the federal government, which still held wartime controls over the phone companies, capitulated to the demands. Next up, for the autumn season: the Boston police, 350,000 steelworkers, and the coal miners.

No other year thus far had compared with 1919 in terms of the number of workers on strike. In New York alone since March, 75,000 garment workers had walked out, 15,000 streetcar men, 14,000 painters, 40,000 tobacco workers, and 20,000 harbor workers. And with the help of the timing of certain events, the high-profile lust of the Red hunters, and the sensational headlines, the critics of organized labor were able to generate strong suspicions among those predisposed to believe it that Bolshevism was behind it all. Although it was true that the membership of labor unions included Reds, the demands of the labor movement—effectively, inclusion in American democracy—did not emanate from the Red influence but rather from the conditions of the coal mines, the stockyards, the steel mills. Still, just as the Red hunters had dismissed the oppression of African-Americans as the most significant cause of racial disturbances—choosing to focus instead on Bolshevik "outside agitation"—many industrialists and those who identified with them also preferred to ignore the oppressive conditions of labor and to brand the struggle for workers' rights as a Bolshevik cause. By the winter of 1919, striking laborers would be labeled as radicals. America had been indulging in this self-deception for several years, but in 1919 it was rising to new heights of hysteria.

The Seattle general strike in February may have been the beginning of such fears that year. Adding piles of kindling to popping fires, the city of Winnipeg in Canada shut down in May when thirty thousand workers walked out on their jobs, giving credence in some circles to the notion that the Bolsheviks were practicing for something much bigger. Seattle and Winnipeg were simply rehearsals. Then came the prediction of a July 4 "reign of terror," which had included the threat of a nationwide strike to protest the imprisonment of radical labor agitator Thomas Mooney—a highly publicized forecast that bolstered the Independence Day hysteria, but never happened. Add to that the fact that throughout the summer the question of whether to maintain government control of the railroads or privatize the rails pitted organized labor, which favored nationalization, against corporate America, and allowed labor's critics once again to thrust the labor movement into the same box with the Bolsheviks. To nationalize transportation was perceived by some in America as consistent with the philosophies of Lenin and Trotsky, and thus a dangerous move.

More kindling arrived at the end of August in Chicago when radicals, including John Reed, former New York legislator Benjamin Gitlow, and Chicago millionaire William Lloyd participated in the formation of the Communist Labor Party. Its membership of ten thousand, primarily

English-speaking, pledged themselves to a manifesto that proposed "the organization of the workers as a class, the overthrow of capitalist rule and the conquest of political power by the workers." The next day, September 1, the Communist Party of America, whose sixty thousand members were mostly foreigners, was also formed. While the total membership of both parties represented only one-tenth of 1 percent of the nation's adult population, the parties launched dozens of new publications promulgating the communist philosophy in many languages—thus intensifying the threat of a workers' revolt and fattening Hoover's index of suspicious editors, writers, and subscribers.

As both communist parties supported the Russian Soviet "experiment" in workers' control, it became easier to link the actions and goals of the American radicals with those of the new Soviet state. And thus it became easier for the American public to believe that Bolshevik propaganda was the main factor behind the unrest in the nation, whether it was a race riot or a labor strike. By September, many Americans, if asked about the politics of organized labor, would say that to walk off the job, to picket, to protest was not only un-American but also part of a Bolshevik plot. And after the highly publicized walkouts in September, such a conspiracy would seem very real.

By 1919 there were effectively two parts to the labor movement. There was the more traditional American Federation of Labor, headed by Samuel Gompers, which was based on the premise that workers and a reasonable management could partner under the capitalist system. This part of the movement had supported the war and was composed largely of small craft unions populated by skilled white workers. The other, more radical wing, believed that no partnership between labor and capital was possible, that the drive for maximum profits would always occur to the detriment of working people. This faction did not support the war and focused its attention on building a labor movement large enough to challenge the capitalists for power, bringing in unskilled workers as well as women, blacks, and foreigners—groups often ignored by Gompers. This faction included socialists, communists, Wobblies, and anarcho-syndicalists, and it had won a stunning success in organizing Chicago's packinghouses during the war. By the fall of 1919 literally hundreds of thousands of workers were demanding that both parts of the labor movement—the traditional and the radical—assist them to establish union representation, get raises to offset the high cost of living, win fairer and safer working conditions, and claim a bit of the democracy the war had promised.

Gompers cautiously entered the labor struggles of 1919. He had actively supported Wilson in his 1912 campaign, had worked closely with industry leaders during the war to guarantee wartime production levels, and had sought political alliances to support his cause. An advocate of the theory of "industrial democracy," which aimed at reforming and taming capitalism—thus rendering radical alternatives unnecessary—Gompers backed President Wilson's plan for an autumn conference to devise various reforms that would humanize the prevailing industrial system. For many of America's most oppressed workers, however, especially in the steel mills and the coalfields, such a conference would be too little too late.

In his Labor Day address, on August 31, the president announced an October 6 conference to "discuss fundamental means of bettering the whole relationship of capital and labor, and putting the whole question of wages upon another footing." As he spoke, there were sixty-five strikes nationwide involving 300,000 people in twenty states. The real impetus behind his proposed conference, however, was the growing conflict between organized labor and management in the steel industry. During the week leading up to Wilson's announcement, a group of labor leaders had just received a response to their latest appeal for negotiations with the chairman of the United States Steel Corporation, Elbert H. Gary, the namesake of Gary, Indiana. Gary's resolute rejection and the leaders' disappointment would dramatically affect the lives of 350,000 workers nationwide.

The AFL had begun holding meetings to organize steel workers in September of 1918, under the supervision of the National Committee for Organizing Iron and Steel Workers headed by Gompers, John Fitzpatrick, who was the president of the Chicago Federation of Labor, and William Z. Foster, who had organized the meatpackers during the war and who would one day be the head of the new Communist Party of America. Self-taught, erudite, and passionate, Foster was an intellectual as well as an industrial worker in the tradition of Eugene Debs. By the end of the summer of 1919, Foster, Fitzpatrick, and Gompers had succeeded in signing up more than 100,000 workers in Cleveland, Chicago, Johnstown, Youngstown, Wheeling, Buffalo, and Pittsburgh, despite the resistance of the steel corporations and despite the violence—for example, gunmen hired by the steel trust murdered a young female organizer, Fannie Sellins, in West Natrona, Pennsylvania, on August 26. In the towns that steel companies virtually owned, organizing workers was a perilous pursuit. But enlisting them to the cause was not so difficult. Conditions alone were the motivation.

In 1919, the government calculated that the minimum income required for subsistence of a family of five in America was $1,575 a year and for what it termed "the comfort level," which was considered the American standard of living at the time, the minimum annual income was $2,024. In the steel industry, unskilled workers—nearly 50 percent of the workforce—made an average of $1,466 annually. Some earned a mere $1,000 a year. The typical workweek for the steel industry was about sixty-nine hours. Some men worked twelve-hour days; some eighteen; and some twenty-four hours. Many worked every day of the week. Living conditions were shocking. Census takers in a steel suburb of Pittsburgh called Bradford found two hundred families living in sixty-one houses. In one house there were thirty-five boarders. There three people occupied each bed, sleeping in eight-hour shifts. It was not unusual for a family of eight to share a two-room flat. A large percentage of the industry's unskilled labor force, which was mostly immigrant labor, lived without running water, without indoor plumbing of any sort. Several families used a single water pump and an open unsanitary drain in a shared courtyard or alley.

Perhaps one of the most startling details about U.S. Steel was that its financial surplus was huge. In 1918, for example, after paying out dividends of $96,382,027 and setting aside $274,277,835 for federal taxes to be paid in 1919, it had a surplus of $466,888,421, which was enough to have paid the company's entire wage and salary budget for that year twice and still leave a $14 million surplus. In 1919, it would be much the same. In July that year, the AFL's National Committee sent a letter to Judge Gary requesting a meeting to discuss the needs of the steelworkers. Gary, who had served two terms as a county judge in Illinois, was from that time forward referred to as Judge Gary, and from the day of the company's inception in 1901 until his death, he would rule. His stand against labor unions was firm and he was unbendable on the issue of long hours, which were a trademark of the steel industry at that time.

Among the demands expressed in the AFL's letter were: the right to collective bargaining—meaning union representation; an eight-hour workday; extra pay for overtime; one day out of seven without required work; the end of the twenty-four-hour shift; wage increases; and reinstatement of workers fired for union activities. The iron-willed Gary did not respond.

By August 20, to show their determination, union members had all signed a strike authorization, though no date was established to begin the strike. On the 26th, five union men—John Fitzpatrick, D. J. Davis, William Hannon, Edward J. Evans, and William Foster—tried to meet with Judge Gary in his office, urging him to take the demands seriously and to work with them on a resolution. An arbitration conference must be called, they insisted. Gary refused to meet but said he would read a letter from them. From the offices of U.S. Steel's Finance Committee at 71 Broadway in New York, Judge Gary immediately sent a response.

> We do not think you are authorized to represent the sentiment of a majority of the employees of the United States Steel Corporation and its subsidiaries. . . . As heretofore publicly stated and repeated, our Corporation and subsidiaries, although they do not combat labor unions as such, decline to discuss business with them. . . . In all decisions and acts of the Corporation and subsidiaries pertaining to employees and employment their interests are of highest importance. In wage rates, living and working conditions, conservation of life and health, care and comfort in times of sickness or old age, and providing facilities for the general welfare and happiness of employees and their families, the Corporation and subsidiaries have endeavored to occupy a leading and advanced position among employers.

Instantly upon receiving Gary's letter, the committee, all of whom were then staying at the National Hotel in Washington, D.C., sent another:

> You question the authority of our committee to represent the majority of your employees. The only way by which we can prove our authority is to put the strike vote into effect and we sincerely hope that you will not force a strike to prove this point. . . . We read with great care your statement as to the interest the Corporation takes in the lives and welfare of the employees and their families, and if that were true even in a minor degree, we would not be

pressing consideration, through a conference, of the terrible conditions that exist. The conditions of employment, the home life, the misery in the hovels of the steel workers is beyond description. You may not be aware that the standard of life of the average steel worker is below the pauper line, which means that charitable institutions furnish to the pauper a better home, more food, clothing, light and heat than many steel workers can bring into their lives upon the compensation received for putting forth their very best efforts in the steel industry. Surely this is a matter which might well be discussed in conference. . . . Surely reasonable men can find a common ground upon which we can all stand and prosper.

Wilson's speech and Labor Day came and went and so did every possibility of negotiation in the nation's largest industry. The local steel union shops were strongly pressuring the National Committee—Gompers, Fitzpatrick, and Foster, among others—to vote on a date for the strike to begin. On September 10, they did. Their "Call to Strike" read: "IRON AND STEEL WORKERS! A historic decision confronts us. If we will but stand together now like men our demands will soon be granted and a golden era of prosperity will open for us in the steel industry. But if we falter and fail to act this great effort will be lost, and we will sink back into a miserable hopeless serfdom. The welfare of our wives and children is at stake. Now is the time to insist upon our rights as human beings. STOP WORK SEPTEMBER 22."

The steelworkers' "Call to Strike" came on the first full day of another conflict that was drawing considerable attention. The day before the "Call," most of the Boston police force had walked off the job. That the nation's protectors were workers who sought to be part of the American Federation of Labor and were so often called upon to help suppress labor struggles must have seemed an odd concept to most Americans—and a frightening one. President Wilson called the strike "a crime against civilization." A policeman's loyalty must be to the state, not to his fellow workers. The obligation of a policeman was like that of a soldier, the president said. The press agreed. And that the first full day of the strike happened to be on the same day as the last stupendous parade to welcome home returning soldiers—this one in New York celebrating General Pershing's return—did not help the policemen's public image. The next day the front pages of many of the nation's newspapers carried the stories side by side: one about a parade celebrating the heroism of public service and the other about the public servants who had abandoned their posts.

The main issue behind the strike was that the Boston Social Club, which was the local policemen's organization, wanted to affiliate with the AFL, and it wanted the mayor and the police commissioner to reinstate nineteen officers who had been suspended from duty for organizing club members to join the AFL. City officials refused both demands. The policemen stopped work at 5:45 P.M. on the 9th. That night 1,117 out of the 1,544 Boston police were not on the street. Gangs of hoodlums smashed shop windows, looted displays, stoned trolley cars, and threw mud at the replacement policemen and the citizen volunteers patrolling the streets.

By the 10th, the city was in a panic. A volunteer police force supervised by the policemen who didn't strike tried to secure the town. Even the president of Harvard offered a thousand students to serve on the makeshift force. Citizens were ordered off the streets at night. City officials debated the next step. The mayor, a Democrat, wanted to settle the differences with the striking police, while the police commissioner, a Republican, did not. On the night of the 10th rioting broke out, during which three people were killed. The mayor sought help from the State Guard and after five thousand soldiers began patrolling the streets of Boston some peace was restored by Thursday. Still, with the mayor and police commissioner at odds, Massachusetts governor Calvin Coolidge decided to intervene and personally oversee the situation. At the same time, Samuel Gompers urged the police to stop the strike. When they agreed, he asked the mayor to reinstate them and to begin mediation.

Things might have been different for the Boston police if the press had presented the story a different way and if Washington had reacted more calmly. Not only were the police viewed as traitors to their duty as public servants but their short, three-day strike was depicted nationwide as a Bolshevik plot, continuing the Seattle strike and the May Day demonstrations. Quotes from local businessmen calling the strikers Bolshevists and deserters showed up everywhere. "Lenin and Trotsky are on their way," wrote the *Wall Street Journal* on its editorial page. And in Washington Red-hunting congressmen and bureaucrats painted a grim picture of a Soviet takeover in the making. There never was mediation. How could the city make a settlement with a group of people who might be in collusion with Bolsheviks?

In the end, the entire police force was fired and new police were recruited while the State Guard continued to patrol the streets for the next three months. One impact of the strike was to further associate organized labor with radicalism. Another was to heighten the national profile of Calvin Coolidge. It was Governor Coolidge who sent the devastating message to Gompers, under the bright beam of a national spotlight, that there would be no arbitration: "There is no right to strike against the public safety by anybody, anywhere, any time." Suddenly Coolidge, the man who took a stand against Bolshevism, was the hero of the moment. And while Calvin Coolidge became a household name, the striking 1,117 policemen also had a new image. They were now perceived as radical, suspicious, likely dangerous men linked to a plot to overthrow the government, and thus they were blacklisted.

The depiction of the police strike as Bolshevik-inspired set the stage for the steelworkers, though the stage would be far bigger and the drama would last far longer. Shortly after the September 10 "Call to Strike," Gompers urged President Wilson to ask Judge Gary to agree to mediation. Wilson asked, but Gary would not concede. The president then asked Gompers to put off the September 22 strike. Gompers passed the request to the heads of the organizing committee. By then, the pressure to strike from the local unions, the momentum of the workers to proceed on schedule, was like a fast-moving train. The leaders of the Youngstown workers, for example, during the week after the strike date was set, sent a telegram to the National Committee, in the tone of a warning. The AFL must stick to the September 22 date or "the men will strike regardless of any postponement and we will lose control of the situation." It was one of many such telegrams. There was no going back. The workers were unstoppable now. Fitzpatrick and Foster knew that. Believing that they would never again be able to create the momentum they now had among the workers and knowing how demoralized the workers would be if there were any delays, they declined Wilson's request. In a letter to Gompers, Fitzpatrick said that "It would be a thousand times better for the entire labor movement that we lose the strike and suffer complete defeat, than to attempt postponement now, except under a definite arrangement which would absolutely and positively guarantee the steelworkers substantial concessions.

If these things cannot be guaranteed, then, in our opinion, our only hope is to strike."

On September 22, 275,000 steelworkers across America walked off the job. By the 26th, this bold upsurge of the rank and file had swelled to more than 365,000, the biggest walkout ever. Hundreds of thousands of workingmen were struggling for some control over their lives, bravely taking a stand for a better life—the life they had imagined they could have in America. It began with the industry's largest corporation refusing to discuss the workers' demands and, by the end, would spread to every steel company, large and small, in the country. It included unskilled workers at a time when the national union organization, the AFL, represented skilled workers only. It crossed class lines and color lines. And it included immigrants from nearly fifty countries. It was daring and it was frightening. It was long, violent, and hugely significant for the future of labor. It was a struggle that more than a decade and a half later would lay the foundation for the first national union organization of unskilled laborers, the Committee, later, Congress, of Industrial Organizations, or the CIO.

But, as with the race riots, little of the public commentary focused on the truth. Once again Bolshevism became an easier enemy to target and to destroy than the dire conditions of life as a steelworker. Bolshevism was simpler to perceive as a problem than the convoluted politics and ethics of labor and capital. What the workers wanted was a better life. Communists had a presence in the labor community but, as Major Loving had stressed in his final report about race relations, Bolshevism was clearly not the enemy. It would have power only if the vile conditions did not improve.

Further, as in the black community, the war heightened passions and sharpened the moral issues. Many of these striking workers had risked their lives to make the world safe for democracy. Wasn't protesting in the cause of justice part of what democracy was about? While on the front lines in France, could they ever have imagined that their future bosses in America would refuse to talk to them about receiving a wage sufficient to feed their children? Never would it have occurred to them that the very same machine guns, perched on tripods, they had used in Europe would now be pointed at them as they stood outside their plants asking for what they felt they deserved. To steelworkers, the steel strike was not about Bolshevism, despite the screaming headlines. The steel strike was about fairness and about betrayal.

As the season progressed, Hollywood came out with its latest anti-Bolshevik film, which this time was also anti-Semitic. But in an intriguing twist, the movie was supportive of workers. *The Right to Happiness* was the story of an American millionaire living in Petrograd with his baby twin daughters when a pogrom occurs. In the chaos, one daughter disappears. The father returns to the United States with the other daughter. The lost daughter is taken in by a Jewish family, and raised as a "Red revolutionary." Years later, unaware of her true family history, she comes to America to organize workers at what turns out to be her father's factory. As the Red daughter, she inspires the workers to go on strike. During the walkout she is shot while protecting her twin sister from the ensuing violence. In the end, as the rebel daughter is dying in her father's arms, the father realizes that "workers are people too." In the last scene of the movie, the father cuts the workers' hours and raises their wages. The salvation of labor is thus portrayed as the work of a compassionate industrialist, awakened to the cause only after the unfortunate violent death of a loved one.

CHAPTER 33

Tugs-of-War and of the Heart

To be in Amherst again defined bliss for Ray Stannard Baker. So often during the strenuous months in Europe he had longed to ramble across his Massachusetts meadow, to pick the Belle of Georgia peaches and the Damson plums from his orchard, to check the productivity of his bees, or to immerse himself in the magic of his garden. "I have tried many things, and am happy only here," he wrote in his journal in early fall of 1919. "Of all that I have seen in these troubled months nothing satisfies, nothing comforts the spirit of man like this."

This was what had inspired Baker to write in the voice of David Grayson. But it was also what renewed him and gave him the fortitude to participate in the world beyond his Amherst garden. And with that strength came a sense of purpose that now he could not ignore. Despite the joy and the relief of being home, Baker would not allow himself to float on any sea of comfort, for he could not isolate himself from the struggles surrounding him, especially those of Woodrow Wilson and the League of Nations. "It seemed to me that the questions at issue were vital to the life of the world: that unless they were settled correctly there would soon be more dreadful wars, threatening the very existence of civilization," wrote Baker.

At the time of Wilson's return from Paris on July 8, his opponents in America appeared to have weakened since the spring months. Perhaps the strong gust of positive publicity following the signing of the treaty only a week or so before his return had capsized their plans to doom it. By early July, thirty-two state legislatures had publicly endorsed the treaty and at least thirty governors had spoken out in its favor. Newspaper and magazine editors and columnists were almost unanimously backing it. Even a group of prominent Republicans was firmly in support of the League.

But from that point onward, the winds of fortune began to blow in the other direction as Wilson's opponents regained their strength and added new recruits. On the surface, the battle had always appeared to be mostly a matter of partisan politics. The Republicans, especially senators, were offended when Wilson chose only one Republican for the American peace commission in Paris. And that Republican, Henry White, was a diplomat—not a senator. So too the Republican senator Henry Cabot Lodge, who had claimed at the beginning of the peace conference that Wilson himself did not represent the American people in Paris because he was a Democrat with a Republican Congress, bitterly opposed Wilson and the League and consistently scorned the president's ideals to the point of ridicule. Lodge never moved from his position that the president's ideas of collective security, of world peace, of organized international cooperation were naive. These were little more than the words of a gifted speaker and a persuasive, impractical idealist, said Lodge. The global system defined in the Covenant of the League that claimed an act of war against one member to be an act of war against all members was simply unrealistic, he said. And thus he urged the Senate not to ratify a treaty that brought with it such a system.

Just as stalwart were the extreme isolationists such as the Republican presidential hopeful Senator Hiram Johnson, who believed that the League's creeds of cooperation would entangle America again and again in overseas struggles. In the aftermath of war, as the longing for normalcy increased month by month, it was not all that difficult to drum up support for a jingoistic battle against a treaty and a new international organization that could lead the nation once again to wars abroad.

In the period after the signing of the treaty, Wilson's opponents had indeed acquired some unexpected allies. Beyond any partisan loyalties, there were now ethnic groups that were deeply disappointed with the results of the six months of negotiations in Paris—for example, Irish-Americans, whose homeland was still under British rule and now in fact in the midst of a civil war. The new world order Wilson had promised was a travesty, they said, as Wilson's compromises in Paris had resulted in nothing more than a rearrangement of the old order. Many felt that Wilson had betrayed his promises of the Fourteen Points, on which the Armistice had been based and which had been whittled away to a barely recognizable state in the final draft of the treaty.

Perhaps the strongest opposition surfaced out of what could be described as nothing less than the very core of American consciousness. While the concept of world peace and organized international cooperation was inspiring and laudable, the reality of it—just exactly how it would work—flew in the face of the American traits of individualism and independence. These opponents, though they respected the importance of international alliances, and thus were not isolationists, did not want America committed to the collective security of the world, nor did they want what they saw as an international agency controlling their nation's foreign policy. Under the terms of the Covenant, the League would determine matters of peace and war. America would be pulled into conflicts that would use its resources but would not necessarily serve its own vital interests. Under the League, nationalist aggressions would be stopped. But what if America deemed aggression appropriate? What if America's vision of the configuration of the globe differed from that of the many nations that would comprise the League?

Some would say that Wilson's dream began to shatter when it became clear that the League's covenant collided with the visions of numerous American politicians and businessmen for America's future. Could a nation that was emerging as a world power afford to endorse an agreement that might curtail that power? Especially daunting was Article 10 of the Covenant, which effectively guaranteed "the political independence and territorial integrity" of every nation that was a League member. This, said Wilson's opponents, "would be an attempt to preserve for all time, unchanged, the distribution of power and territory made in accordance with the views and exigencies of the Allies in this present juncture of affairs. . . . No generation can impose its will in regard to the growth of nations and the distribution of power upon succeeding generations."

To help shape such criticism and to provide the treaty's opponents with a sophisticated weapon to annihilate the treaty, Lodge and the Republican majority on the Senate Foreign Relations Committee created what were called the Fourteen Reservations—countering and mocking Wilson's Fourteen Points. Presented to the Senate in a report on September 10, the Reservations were devastating to the cause of the League. Reservation No. 2, for example, completely eviscerated collective security, the basic concept of the League, by demanding that America would not assume any obligations to "preserve the territorial integrity or political independence of another country" unless Congress passed an act or resolution to do so. In other words, the League would have no power over America to require its assistance in helping a nation preserve such independence. Worse still for

Wilson, the Preamble to the Reservations declared that America would not ratify the treaty until three of the four Allied Powers accepted the Reservations.

Wilson, however, refused to renegotiate the terms of the treaty or the Covenant, which the Fourteen Reservations would require. He would concede to any of the Reservations that clarified the purpose and workings of the League, but not to any that meant changes to its covenant and thus to the treaty itself. The reasons he gave publicly were that such changes would endanger the treaty, would embarrass the United States after it had played a major role in creating it, and would open the door for Germany to make new demands and campaign against the treaty's severe terms against it. In later years, though, some historians would say that perhaps Wilson had made so many compromises in Paris that he couldn't bear the thought of enduring such a process again. And so Wilson turned his attention away from the vexing senators and their threatening Reservations. He prepared to take his treaty and his League to the American people.

As the summer progressed, Baker saw that Wilson was losing ground in the battle. And by the end of August he was almost certain that there was enough doubt about the feasibility of the League and about the willingness of the nation to commit to ironclad oaths of collective global security to defeat Wilson's dream. Ratification of the treaty was about as likely to happen as American recognition of Soviet Russia. Baker knew that despite the cheering crowds at New York harbor on July 8, Wilson's spell over the American public was breaking. Their hopes and dreams had come home. To turn their focus to foreign policy and international peace was increasingly difficult.

With an aching heart, Baker heard the despair in the voice of Wilson's physician, who told him how he had warned the president that a prospective nationwide tour to appeal to the people—always successful for Wilson in previous times—was too strenuous for a man still recovering from the extreme fatigue of his labors in Paris. And when Baker heard Wilson's response, it seemed to him that a door had opened wide enough to see the future. As Baker later wrote, Wilson told his doctor that "his life did not matter if he could fire the people with the determination to support the new plans for world co-operation. I knew he meant exactly what he said." When Wilson left on the tour—to Ohio, Indiana, Missouri, Iowa, Nebraska, Minnesota, the Dakotas, the Pacific Northwest, major cities down the West Coast, Nevada, Utah, Wyoming Colorado, and Kansas—Baker could no longer find the magic at Amherst. The world beyond his garden tugged at his conscience. As a journalist who had been at the center of the peace talks and as close to Wilson as he could get for many months, and as a sensitive man who, despite his frustrations with Wilson and even resentments at times, wanted Wilson to realize his dream, Baker could not stand by. On the occasion of Wilson's departure, Baker wrote: "The sheer courage of the man! No doubt he saw the distracted world as clearly as I did, and he knew better than anyone else the power of the forces gathering to destroy all he had achieved at Paris, even to destroy him personally: and yet he continued to believe in the people. He still had faith that if he could get to them directly, they would listen to reason, and support him in his struggle. He had now no strong organization behind him: many of the leaders of his own party were lukewarm, if not opposed to him. He was setting out alone, risking his very life in a conclusive demonstration of his faith."

So it was that as Wilson set off on a journey across eight thousand miles of America in twenty-two days during which he would deliver forty speeches, Baker began to feel restless. When he learned that the British were insisting that their king bestow an honor on Lloyd George for his devoted service in Paris, Baker's restlessness turned to agitation. Why weren't Americans calling for such recognition of Wilson? How was it possible that the British were honoring Lloyd George, who had been one of his nation's most unpopular prime ministers, for his work at the peace conference, and yet in America, Wilson, who had been one of the nation's most popular presidents, was still hard at work trying to persuade the public of the value of what had happened at Paris. Finally, when Baker read in a New York newspaper that there was a petition circulating in New York calling for Wilson's impeachment "for high crimes," he packed his bags and took the night train to New York. The next morning he met with the managers of McClure's newspaper syndicate to pitch the concept for a series of articles about Wilson. He wanted to reveal exactly what Wilson had accomplished at the peace conference. The tug-of-war between Wilson and himself had been over the issue of what the public should know about the negotiations. Wilson was reluctant to reveal the inner workings of the peace talks, especially the battles among the Allied delegates. But the American public, Baker had pleaded, needed to know how their president was handling things, how he was trying to keep the Fourteen Points intact, and how he had accomplished a good deal despite the obstinacy and the deceptions of his Allies, particularly Clemenceau. Wilson would not allow such details to be released to the public. Now, while the president was on the road, Baker wanted American newspapers to tell the true story of what really had transpired in Paris. The *McClure's* managers, however, were hesitant and aloof.

"Are they ready?" asked one, referring to the articles. Baker had suggested a series of at least ten, possibly a dozen.

"No," Baker replied, "but I will have the first of them written by the time you can make arrangements with the publishers."

The managers then expressed their doubts about whether there was a market for such a series. Wasn't it too late? Wasn't the American public tired of international battles? No matter how revealing and fresh Baker's pieces might be, was there an audience? The public was "fed up with the Peace Conference," said one man. "They don't want to be bothered with the woes of Europe." There was simply too much indifference to launch such a lengthy series on a worn-out topic like the League of Nations and the treaty. But Baker persisted. The American people were so pumped full of propaganda about this and about that, they no longer knew the truth, he insisted. If they did, if they knew more of the drama of Wilson in Paris, it would renew their interest in the treaty and the League, Baker said. But Baker on that day could not convince them. And so, without the okay and without an advance from *McClure's*, Baker proceeded to write the series. When the syndicate tried to sell the first of the articles, the managers were surprised to find many newspapers interested. Publications in Brazil, Japan, and England as well as in America bought the articles.

Baker wrote the entire series in four weeks. In it he explained to the public the five decisive crises Wilson faced at the peace conference. He described scenes and confrontations that hadn't been reported during the six months of negotiations. And he showed how the president had been "fired at in front" and "sniped at from behind." Not only did *McClure's* discover there was a market for the articles, but Doubleday decided they were compelling enough to publish in book form. In the preface to *What Wilson Did at Paris*, as the series was titled when published by Doubleday, Baker wrote that his purpose was to offer the reader "glimpses of the President in action, describe the most important battles he fought in Paris, and the kind of foes he had to meet. The President himself can tell what he thinks and hopes—there is no man in the world today who is a greater master in the expression of ideas and ideals—but he has no genius for telling what he does. For this reason, Americans have not fully understood the real problems their President had to face at Paris, nor recognized the real victories he won." The book would be published in November.

During the four weeks that Baker sat at his typewriter trying to deepen America's understanding of its president in Paris, Wilson was on the road trying to clarify the League's purpose and to address his enemies' criticisms, which he believed had misled the public. History was calling the American people to a profound higher ground of world leadership and his critics were looking backward, causing a regression that would result in future wars and that would require years to reverse, he believed. American isolationism was and must be a thing of the past, he said in Des Moines, "because by the sheer genius of this people and the growth of our power we have become a determining factor in the history of mankind, and after you have become [that] you cannot remain isolated, whether you want to or not."

He talked about the Fourteen Reservations, especially No. 2, which he told his audience in Cheyenne was the same as agreeing to participate in the League only when it suited U.S. purposes. This, he said, undermined collective security, without which there would be no League. And in most of his speeches he warned that without the League, there would inevitably be more wars. Then referring to the children in the audience, he would add that not endorsing the League was "their death warrant."

Wilson began the tour in a weak and exhausted state that worsened with each day. Nervous strain caused such severe digestive problems that Dr. Grayson had to feed him predigested foods and nutritional liquids. Coughing spells, congestion, and extreme fatigue prevented Wilson from sleeping. In Montana he developed a throat infection and asthma. In Washington state, he had headaches that were so severe that when he stood up to speak he had double vision. In California, the cigarette smoke at a dinner caused more headaches. Yet he never complained, and when Dr. Grayson beseeched him to stop and rest, he would not. Then, in Pueblo, Colorado, on the return trip, the doctor noticed that the left side of Wilson's mouth had an irregular looseness and was dragging downward. Gravely concerned, Dr. Grayson and Mrs. Wilson canceled the rest of the trip and headed straight back to Washington. There, on October 2, Wilson suffered a severe stroke, which paralyzed his left side, although the press was not given that information. Grayson's medical bulletins described Wilson's collapse as "nervous exhaustion" or more technically "neurasthenia." And Grayson refused to comment when members of Congress and others asked him if it was in fact a stroke.

Perhaps, as Baker believed, Wilson was a man ahead of his time, whose quest for world peace in 1919 was about as practical as baying at the moon. Or perhaps Wilson was too late and America was already so deeply entrenched in its role as a world power that it would never be ready for peace as Wilson had envisioned it.

By October 1919, one thing was clear: the American public was more interested in the latest movie starring the year's biggest heartthrob, Wallace Reid, or the *Saturday Evening Post*'s latest episode in the life of the ever-popular fictional lawyer Ephraim Tutt, the Don Quixote of the legal world, or the upcoming World Series than in the concept of collective security or the challenge of global peace. There was a turning inward, which for the moment was impossible to reverse and which had been caused in part by the cacophony of voices raised against the president's vision of an enduring peace. America would no longer hear Wilson's call.

CHAPTER 34

Autumn Leaflets

One September evening just before six o'clock, Detectives Ford, Culhane, and Cavanagh of the New York City Bomb Squad were walking along Canal Street in lower Manhattan, likely at a relaxed gait after taking an early dinner near Centre Street. But as they headed west on Canal toward Lafayette Street, they were overwhelmed by a sudden shower of circulars. Landing on the windshields of passing cabs, on the heads and shoulders of pedestrians, and into the very hands of these three men, hundreds upon hundreds of leaflets fell from somewhere above. "Awake and change your old methods!" read the paper entitled "American Toilers—Where Is Your Freedom?" and signed by "A Group of Revolutionists." Another one, which was more prevalent, was entitled "Constitutional Day—What It Means to US-Workers!" and signed by "American Anarchist Federated Commune Soviets."

So dense was the deluge that its source was unclear. Moving to the other side of the street, Detective Walter Culhane was able to ascertain that a small human figure was flinging the flyers from the rooftop of a tenement at 245 Canal. Into the building ran the detectives and as they dashed up the stairs, they met a "black-eyed, demure looking girl" coming down just as fast. The detectives stopped her.

"What are you doing in this building?" asked Culhane.

"I am in the wrong house and was just leaving," she said.

"Are you the one throwing these circulars?"

"No," she said, not looking up as she continued her descent.

But then one of the other two detectives suddenly recognized the "girl anarchist" whose picture had been on front pages nationwide during the autumn of 1918 and again in March of 1919.

"Aren't you Mollie Steimer?" he asked, running back down the stairs.

"Yes," she said.

Before she reached the street, Detective Culhane arrested her on the charge of disorderly conduct. Throwing handbills from rooftops was considered a disturbance of the peace.

Steimer spent that night at the Tombs. It was the first time she had been arrested since March, when she was swept up in the raid of the Russian People's House, detained briefly at Ellis Island, and then released. This time, on the morning of September 18, Steimer was arraigned. However, as with all legal proceedings involving the young anarchist, the hearing was hardly routine. In the courtroom were two men, a New York state judge and an assistant district attorney, who both had received anti-Constitution circulars through the mail two days before. The circulars were similar to the ones now covering the sidewalks of Canal Street. Both men had tried to question Steimer at the station house upon her arrival the previous evening—but without results. Also at the hearing were the three Bomb Squad detectives who arrested her, the head of the Bomb Squad, and two federal agents (Mortimer J. Davis and Frank Faulhaber) from the Bureau of Investigation. Steimer appeared alone, without her lawyer, Harry Weinberger, and when asked how she pleaded, she said, "I do not desire to make any plea whatsoever. I want an adjournment but if you desire to go on with the case now, I am totally indifferent."

Bail was set for $500 and immediately after the formal hearing, Steimer was taken to an anteroom and questioned. In his report of the interrogation, agent Davis wrote that Steimer admitted to distributing the circulars at a building on the corner of 42nd Street and Sixth Avenue, a location she had selected, she said, because so many workers passed it daily. She wouldn't tell them where the circulars were printed or who else was involved in the operation, Davis wrote, adding that he and others in the room that day were convinced that the printers of these recent leaflets were likely the same people who had been tried the year before for violating the Sedition Act. Because of this, agent Davis suggested that Steimer be "well shadowed upon her release," and if the BI could not spare any agents at the moment, the police department must take care of it. Davis ended his report by saying that the hearing and the inquiry "consumed the entire morning."

Agent Faulhaber wrote in his report that Steimer, in the anteroom, confessed that she had thrown the circulars off the roof of the Canal Street tenement building and that she said, "I am responsible for that circular and

I stand by every line of it." Bomb Squad head Sergeant Gegan, in his report, noted that Steimer "would answer questions about herself but she would not answer any questions about other people connected with her." And Agent C. J. Scully, in his assessment of the other reports, wrote a few days after the hearing that "This woman is a menace to the community and . . . if possible, means should be devised whereby she be placed under a heavy bail bond. . . . She is of the type who have absolutely no respect for law and order. I, personally, have seen her openly defy the court and on several occasions refuse to leave her seat in the courtroom when a band outside was playing the national anthem." The next hearing in the case was set for September 25 and Steimer returned to the Tombs.

When Harry Weinberger heard the news that Mollie was in trouble again, he was in the midst of writing his brief for his appeal in the Abrams case to the U.S. Supreme Court. This was a fifty-one-page document and in it Weinberger repeated one of his arguments from the trial: that the defendants, Abrams, Steimer, Lipman, and Lachowsky, had not protested the war with Germany nor had they interfered with wartime production of machinery and weapons nor had they even tried to discourage conscription. Their focus, he wrote, was to stop American intervention in Soviet Russia. America was not officially at war with Russia nor was it legal for America to have sent troops there. It was this illegal war that the young people were protesting in the allegedly incendiary circulars, which got them into trouble in August of 1918. Weinberger stressed that his defendants did nothing more than criticize their government, and "the right to criticize is the foundation of our Government." Perhaps his strongest argument was that his clients had been charged with violating a law that, he argued, was itself a violation of the Constitution. The government, in Weinberger's opinion, did not have the right to restrict free speech at any time, even during war, for the sake of national security. If it could, then that freedom could "be taken away in peacetime on the same pretext." Moving to higher ground than his specific case, Weinberger stressed that for the nation this was a dangerous precedent. "Absolute freedom of speech is the only basis upon which the Government can stand and remain free."

On the 20th of September, Weinberger sent thirty copies of his brief to the clerk of the U.S. Supreme Court, posted bail for Steimer, and requested a postponement of her September 25 hearing. On that same day, the Bureau of Investigation was all abuzz about "Miss Stimer." Frank Burke, assistant BI director, sent a memo to the bureau's New York City office saying that Hoover's new division had learned that during the past three months Steimer had become very active in the Workers' Defense Union, which was closely affiliated with another radical group, the League for Amnesty for Political Prisoners, which was headed by a friend of Steimer's and a "well-known radical," Eleanor Fitzgerald. "It is the consensus of opinion of all officials, both Government [federal] and municipal that Mollie Steimer is a dangerous woman and that she should be deported immediately."

Weinberger too was pushing for the deportation of Steimer and all of her co-defendants. If he could not persuade the Supreme Court to reverse the convictions, then he would use the 1918 Alien Act to argue for the deportation of his clients to spare them twenty years in prison in the United States. To spend so many years incarcerated for distributing leaflets was a cruel fate. Besides, Weinberger knew that as soon as they served their time, the government would deport them. In August he had met with Palmer to urge him to drop the case and if not, then to deport them as soon as possible. As anarchist aliens, they were in violation of the 1918 law. Unless the government was intent on subjecting Weinberger's clients to unduly harsh punishments, then it seemed logical to deport them.

Weinberger also began a campaign to enlist the help and power of Ray Stannard Baker. First, he asked a friend, Mary Heaton Vorse, who knew Baker, to beseech him to try to persuade Palmer to give these young people a break. Then, on the same day that Weinberger sent his brief to the Supreme Court, he sent a copy of the brief to Baker with a cover letter in which he urged Baker to talk to President Wilson about the case. "With [Wilson's] expressed beliefs, especially at Paris, that the nation must stop and listen to the humblest member, I think there can be only one thing to do and that is to direct the Attorney General to confess error [in proceeding with the Abrams case]," Weinberger wrote.

Baker responded almost immediately. On September 23 he sent out two letters, one to Weinberger and one to the attorney general on behalf of Weinberger's clients. "I do not believe the doctrines which these young people preached," he wrote to Weinberger, "but I do agree with you in thinking that the punishment meted out to them was excessive and should be modified. This sort of treatment is no way of dealing with the problem involved in these cases. I sincerely hope you will be successful in your attempts to have the cases reconsidered and that these foolish young Russians may be allowed to return to their homes."

In his very diplomatic letter to the attorney general, Baker said that he believed the harsh sentences were a mistake because it made the defendants martyrs and helped to rally more radicals to their point of view. He said also that the case made the Justice Department look silly at a time when there were so many other crusades more worthy of the agency's focus. Baker seemed particularly appalled by the idea of sending a twenty-one-year-old woman to jail for fifteen years just for passing out leaflets. It "seems a kind of monstrosity," he wrote. "I do not know [the Russians] personally at all; I do not believe in their doctrines; I have no sympathy for their methods. But it seems to me that such a punishment for a group of foolish youths, scarcely more than of age (with one exception) for an act of political agitation which in peace times would have passed unnoticed, is excessive. . . . I believe that thousands of old-stock Americans like myself, to whom free speech is one of the most precious heritages of our institution, will feel just as I do about it."

A week later Palmer answered Baker in a brief note that said the case must be carried forward "to completion." It was not just about political agitation, not just about trying to interfere with the war, he said. It was also about a threat to overthrow America's form of government. It simply could not be dismissed.

Palmer wouldn't dare change the Justice Department's position in the Abrams case, especially considering the pressure he was facing by October. Using words like "lethargic" and "negligent," businessmen, legislators, and patriotic leagues were sending petitions to the government that derided the Justice Department for appearing to back off the war on radicals. Palmer, who was on the trail of food hoarders and conducting raids of sugar warehouses that month, was hardly passive. But still what impressive action was he taking against the rising threat of radicals? The petitions cited the evidence of such a threat: the formation of both the Communist Party of America and the Communist Labor Party, the nationwide steel strike, the bomb threats in Gary, Indiana, and other steel centers, the race riots, and the highly publicized exploits of anarchists like Steimer. What exactly was the Justice Department doing to prevent the overthrow of the government? Where *was* the attorney general?

In mid-October in the U.S. Senate, Miles Poindexter, a Republican from Washington who planned to run for president in 1920, accused the Wilson administration of being "soft on Bolshevism." The onslaught of labor strikes was based "on a desire to overthrow our Government, destroy all authority, and establish Communism." Pointing the finger at Palmer and Wilson, Poindexter lowered his voice and uttered a grave caveat: "Government will be overthrown when it ceases to defend itself." In a move that was more about political maneuvering than protecting the nation from revolutionaries, he introduced a resolution that required Palmer to tell the Senate about any legal proceedings the Justice Department was taking for the arrest, punishment, and even deportation of the people in the U.S. who were attempting "to bring about the forcible overthrow of the Government."

As naturally as a flower seeks the sun, a man seeking the presidency will turn his attention toward the resources he needs to succeed: public opinion, campaign funding, and legislative support. This was a motivating factor for Poindexter, the Republican, and also for Palmer, the Democrat—both presidential hopefuls. It was not surprising then that Palmer began to focus once again on radicals and the strategy of mass deportations. Considering that the government believed that close to 90 percent of suspected radicals in the U.S. were indeed aliens, Palmer closed in on immigrant radicals and used the Alien Act as his legal weapon.

The pressure on Palmer must have pleased Hoover, who was already on the task. In fact, he and his colleague William Flynn, the head of the BI, were as aggressive as the petitioners and congressmen in pressing Palmer to get tough on radicals. By October, using every resource ranging from military intelligence reports to Emma Goldman's mailing list to files of private detectives shadowing striking workers, Hoover had an index of 150,000 names. He also employed translators to read alien publications and to pluck names and incendiary quotes for his ever-fattening files.

Hoover saw the deportation crusade as a way to please his superiors and to get some press attention. Toward that end, in October, he presented the government's cases against the anarchists Emma Goldman and Alexander Berkman, both notorious among government officials and the American

public. The BI had started its files on Berkman and Goldman as early as
1916 when Berkman, who already had served fourteen years in prison for
having shot and wounded Henry Frick of the Carnegie Steel Company in
1892, started an anarchist publication called *Blast*. Goldman's association
with Berkman and her anti-government speeches gave her a file. And so
when the war began in the spring of 1917, the BI sent agents to infiltrate
their No-Conscription League and to report on their antiwar speeches. In
June of 1917, a month after Congress enacted the Selective Service Act,
both Goldman and Berkman were arrested for violating it and barely two
weeks later were sentenced to two years in prison and a $10,000 fine. On
the day of the sentences, the process began for the deportation of both as
soon as they had served their time in prison. Although the fate of Berkman
and Goldman was sealed long before the deportation hearings in October
of 1919, the ambitious new head of the Radical Division gave an impressive presentation, even tying both of them to the assassination of William
McKinley. Their writings and speeches had had a direct influence on the
assassin, Leon Czolgosz, Hoover claimed.

Hoover also took a keen interest in Mollie Steimer, whom he was certain knew exactly who had printed the *Soviet Anarchist Bulletin*, which
Hoover and other government officials had been targeting as dangerously
influential in recruiting Bolshevists. Steimer was a perfect target for
Hoover. Her name was frequently in the news. She was an alien. She was
an anarchist. Thus she must be deported—with great fanfare. And so by
early October, Hoover had put together a thick file on Steimer based on information from agents and reports coming in from local and federal agencies. Hoover's agent who used the name "Winslow" had her on his list of
most dangerous Bolshevists. "Lamb" knew of her activities in the Worker's
Defense Union. "Tucker" reported on the March raid during which
Steimer was detained at Ellis Island. BI report No. 38495 noted that she
had spent most of the summer in Stalton, New Jersey, with Jacob Abrams,
among others, at a "well-known community of anarchists" known as the
Ferrar Colony. Harry Weinberger had visited in June and Eleanor Fitzgerald was there quite often. Another file quoted verbatim the words of the
Canal Street leaflets and contained excerpts of affidavits from Culhane,
Cavanagh, Davis, Gegan, Ford, and others who attended the anteroom interrogation. It also contained a memo bemoaning the fact that the BI did

not have a sample of Steimer's handwriting—a detail noted several times in BI memos.

Hoover advised the immigration commissioner, Anthony Caminetti, that because Steimer was back in action and was clearly a dangerous alien, she must be deported. Thus on October 2, Caminetti approved a deportation warrant against Steimer with a $15,000 bail bond. The plan was to serve her with the warrant if she was not convicted on the disorderly conduct charge. The disorderly conduct hearing was set for October 7. If she was convicted, then they would wait until she served her prison sentence and then issue the deportation warrant. One way or another Hoover was determined to get Steimer off the streets. Soon she would be just another name in Hoover's index. That was the plan. But when the BI agents arrived in court that day accompanied by immigration officials who carried the deportation warrant, they learned that Weinberger had gotten a postponement of the hearings and that Steimer was still out on the $500 bond.

The more aggressive Hoover and the feds were, the bolder Steimer became. The more they wanted her, the more she taunted them. On October 10, for example, Steimer attended a trial in New York State Court involving anarchists the Lusk Committee had exposed. When the judge entered the court, everyone stood up, as they are supposed to do—everyone except Steimer. Steimer was escorted out of the courtroom and into the judge's chamber. After the judge found out who she was, he told her he would let her go so that she would not get another chance to look like a martyr and she would not be allowed in the courthouse except "as a prisoner."

Three days later, Steimer, accompanied by another woman and a man, dropped three envelopes into a mailbox at the corner of 17th Street and Broadway. As the three walked away, Steimer's shadows for the day from the Bomb Squad, Jerome Murphy and Louis Herman, approached the box and deposited some sort of marker that would allow them to later determine which letters were the suspicious three. Each of the envelopes, the Bomb Squad soon learned, contained an appeal to the steel strikers entitled "Arm Yourselves." They were addressed to Sergeant Gegan, the head of the Bomb Squad, to the assistant district attorney who was prosecuting Steimer's disorderly conduct case, and to the Lusk Committee's star witness, Archibald Stevenson. Steimer apparently had no idea she had been watched—not until five days later, on October 18, when she was arrested on charges of distributing seditious literature in violation of Section 118 of the Postal Laws. She returned yet again to the Tombs, and on the 20th of October she was arraigned. Bail was set at $5,000.

By the time Weinberger was standing before the justices of the U.S. Supreme Court on October 21 and 22, presenting his arguments in Case No. 316 on behalf of Steimer, Abrams, Luchowsky, and Lipman, the "girl anarchist" had racked up quite a list of illegal activities. She had allegedly violated the Sedition Act, for which she had been released on $10,000 bail, had been charged with disorderly conduct, for which a $500 bail bond had freed her, and now was being held for violating federal postal laws with a $5,000 bail bond pending. On top of that, Caminetti and Hoover had prepared the deportation warrant, just in case she found someone to put up the $5,000 bond and was out on the streets again. It required a $15,000 bail bond. The New York City Bomb Squad, the New York City Police Department, the Bureau of Investigation, the Military Intelligence Division of the Army, the Lusk Committee, the American Protective League, the U.S. Secret Service had all been involved at one point or another in the quest to silence Mollie Steimer. Certainly spending so much time and expending so many resources—local, state, and federal agents, prosecutors, judges, and officials—the Justice Department would be able to put a stop to the rebellious behavior of this now twenty-two-year-old "slip of a girl." Not necessarily.

On October 22, "the little Red," as one magazine called her, was sitting in her cell on an upper tier at the Tombs planning a ruse. After writing two encoded notes, she stuck one in her right stocking and the other under the collar of her blouse. One read: "EWOAE VAHOAOW TOAER OMOAST NESER POAYDAE ROAROFOAU OYOA." Soon two investigators from the Justice Department came to her cell. Steimer said nothing to them. Looking even smaller than her barely hundred-pound physique, she sat on the edge of her cot dangling her legs and avoiding eye contact with her visitors, as if she were a shy little girl. While they inspected her cell, Steimer mischievously removed the note in her stocking. Pretending to be secretive, she quickly moved her hands behind her back, where she tore up the note. The detectives pretended not to see the little pieces of paper falling on the floor behind and beneath the cot. They then asked her to move to a corner of the cell and face the wall, at which time they gathered the fragments of the note. Steimer then took the other note out of her blouse and began to eat it. Asked to spit it out, she obliged. When her visitors left they must have felt that they had accomplished far more than usual from such a routine inspection.

Later, they sent the shredded notes to police experts who discovered that by taking out all of the combinations "OA" and then reading the notes backward, they could see the message. The first, from her stocking, read "We have two more presents ready for you." The second one, using the same code, accused the police of brutality, likely based on Steimer's belief that her friend and co-defendant Jacob Schwartz had died as a result of rough treatment after his arrest in August of 1918.

On the 23rd, yet another drama unfolded. At her court hearing on the postal case, Weinberger persuaded the judge to apply the $10,000 bail from the 1918 case, which he had just appealed, to the current case. Thus, Mollie would be free to go. Attending the hearing, which began at 2 P.M., were Sergeant Gegan and BI agent Davis. Both men were stunned by the decision and caught without any way to stop Steimer from being free once again. Worried that she would prepare yet another handbill as soon as she could—an act they believed to be threatening and dangerous—they sent an urgent message to Ellis Island to deliver the deportation warrant before Steimer left the federal courthouse at Foley Square. They then tried to stall Steimer and Weinberger, who even asked them if they had any more warrants to serve on his client. An agent named Jones was on his way from Ellis Island carrying the much-desired warrant but didn't arrive soon enough. And so that evening, at about 7 P.M., three policemen and Jones stopped Steimer in front of her apartment and served her with the warrant calling for her deportation. She spent the night of the 23rd at the Tombs and the next morning was sent to Ellis Island. As she would say years later, "I never saw the streets of New York anymore."

The arrest clearly surprised Weinberger, who had walked out of Foley Square on the 23rd with a sense of accomplishment for having secured Steimer's release with the bond from a previous case—one of the few satisfying moments in the Abrams case, if not the only one. He had no idea there was a deportation warrant prepared for Steimer. On the morning of the 24th he typed a note to his client that read "My dear Miss Steimer, We tried to find out last night where you were but without avail. We finally located you at Ellis Island, and understand that you are held on Fifteen Thousand Dollars bail. I am taking this up in Washington to have the bail reduced, and will advise you further. If there is anything you need, advise me, and I will forward the message. Sincerely yours."

That same morning Steimer sent a handwritten note to Weinberger at his 261 Broadway office. At the time she didn't know whether Weinberger even knew where she was. Her note exuded a tone of anxiety and urgency, very different from her usual air of confidence and control. "Dear Sir, I wish to have a personal interview with you on very important matters. Would you please come down to the Island to see me as soon as possible?"

Steimer was the only female prisoner on Ellis Island and because of that she was segregated from the other prisoners. She was not allowed to converse with them at mealtime and she was kept in solitary confinement. Since her last visit to the island prison, in March, a new commissioner had been appointed, one who believed in rigid rules and who ordered the guards to carry nightsticks. After just a few hours, the isolation was unnerving for Steimer. By the end of the second day, Steimer and eight male prisoners started a hunger strike to protest the conditions. Considering that Steimer was already so thin, Weinberger urged the immigration commissioner to release Steimer from solitary confinement. When he refused, Weinberger gave his letter to the *New York Times* and the *New York Tribune*. "Miss Steimer weighs now about 75 pounds and this may mean death to her," he told the *New York World*. "And if it happens you and your department and the Secretary of Labor will have to share the responsibility." He told the *Times* that she was ill and suffering from a fever.

The hunger strike lasted four days. It was cut short by Steimer's conviction on the disorderly conduct charges resulting from throwing leaflets on Canal Street in September. By the last day of October, Steimer would be serving her first day of a six-month sentence at the workhouse on Blackwell's Island in the East River. Not long after her arrival, she sent a handwritten letter to Weinberger telling him to stop working on her behalf. "I have just received your letter from which I can see how much energy you are devoting for my release—I appreciate that very much; however, it is my sincere wish that you should abandon all your activities on the disorderly conduct charge," she wrote, adding that she believed that no sooner would she be out of jail than the government would find a way to throw her back in again. "I have therefore decided to remain in the Work House and by that I avoid much trouble for my people." She signed the letter, "Yours for a world without oppressors."

CHAPTER 35

Not Exactly Paradise

In 1919, even the weather in America was tumultuous. During three days of April, tornadoes struck Omaha, Nebraska, North Texas, southern Oklahoma, and parts of Arkansas, killing at least one hundred people. In June a tornado whipped through Fergus Falls, Minnesota, hurling seven train cars off their tracks and killing fifty-nine people. The day before that storm, New York City, rarely the victim of violent weather, was hit with fifty-mile-an-hour winds and torrential rains in an electrical storm considered to be one of the worst on record. Two months later, in August, after a summer of record-breaking heat, New York was battered again by a squall in which the waves were huge enough to tear away bathhouses and pavilions at Coney Island while the winds uprooted two hundred trees in Brooklyn, including the fifty victory trees planted after the Armistice in honor of the Brooklyn boys who died in the war.

During the first days of autumn, a ten-month-old baby girl, fastened by ropes to a water-soaked raft, floated ashore at Corpus Christi, Texas. She was alive, having survived one of the most deadly Gulf hurricanes in history. The press called the event a miracle. Texans hailed her survival as a sign that their luck had turned, although rescue workers continued to drag bodies out of the debris, piling them into temporary morgues. By the end of September, three hundred bodies had been found in the wreckage, including at least twenty soldiers of the Great War. That particular Gulf hurricane was the last episode of atmospheric violence in 1919 and as the fall season proceeded, the weather eased into a calmer pattern. However, storms of human protest continued to rage.

As if the summer race riots had started an unstoppable fire, race disturbances that autumn broke out in Nebraska, Arkansas, and Alabama. In Omaha an incident was sparked by a mob eager to lynch an incarcerated black man accused of raping a white girl. When the mayor of Omaha literally stood between the mob leaders and the jailed man, the mob decided first to lynch the mayor. As they were stringing him up on a trolley pole, policemen arrived and cut the rope. The mob swelled to thousands and with the mayor in the hospital suffering from severe injuries, it was the sheriff who now tried to stop them, with fire hoses. But the mob cut the hoses. When more police arrived, members of the mob shot at the policemen. They then advanced upon the jail, which was in the courthouse, and set it on fire. Firemen came. The mob cut their hoses too. And then more than a hundred prisoners were forced by flames and smoke to the roof of the courthouse where, to save themselves, they threw the black man off the roof into the throes of his rabid foes. When the mob then dispersed, the firemen put out the fire and saved the other prisoners. In desperation, the Omaha police called in troops from two nearby U.S. Army camps but the red tape—the governor was out of town and the War Department was slow to respond—delayed the troops' arrival. It took a personal call from a Nebraska senator to the secretary of war to get the soldiers moving out of Fort Omaha to the streets of the state capital. The Omaha mob shot the prisoner William Brown hundreds of times, set his body partially on fire, dragged him for hours through town at the end of a rope, and then dangled his charred torso from a trolley pole at a busy downtown corner for the first three hundred soldiers to see as they entered Omaha at midnight.

By the next day additional soldiers from Iowa, Kansas, and South Dakota boarded special army trains headed for Omaha. Major General Leonard Wood, a hero of the recent war, was put in command and he immediately set a series of orders into motion. Machine guns were posted in front of city hall, the courthouse, and at numerous street corners. Curfews were set. Crowds were not allowed to gather. Even the World Series scoreboards were taken down to prevent people from congregating to read them. Recognizing that sensational headlines about alleged black criminals had caused problems throughout the summer in Omaha and could incite more white mobs now, General Wood asked the local newspapers to censor themselves. And when he told outside newspapers the truth about what had happened, from his point of view—for example, that the girl who had accused Brown of raping her really wasn't sure about whether the rapist was black or white—he made sure that those newspapers were not sold in Omaha. From the viewpoint of The Crisis several weeks later, Brown and his accuser, who by most evidence was his lover, had been quarreling and to "get back at him" she claimed he had assaulted her. "It is said that at the time she was wearing a diamond ring given her by Brown," an editorial in *The Crisis* reported.

In those early days of autumn, NAACP officials, black and white, and other black leaders sent letters and telegrams to U.S. senators urging them to push hard for the passage of Senator Charles Curtis's resolution to recognize that the lynchings and riots were a national problem that must be investigated. The attempted lynching of Omaha's white mayor compelled James Weldon Johnson to write to Senator Curtis and point out that the racial violence was "reaching a stage in which the vengeance of the mob is not directed solely against the Negro." In one of his *New York Age* columns in late September, Johnson berated the solutions offered by some Southern whites. As an example, he quoted from a recent letter to the editor of the *Raleigh News & Observer* in which a white citizen of North Carolina suggested colonizing "the Negro in some other land" and then queried, "Will the Negro accept what we term as 'his place' or will he prefer to meet the same fate as the North American Indian?" Johnson answered with this: "It is time that the Southern whites understood that the Negro never intends to accept 'his place.' And as for going the way of the North American Indian, that worries the Negro about as little as does the final extinction of the light and heat of the sun."

NAACP secretary John Shillady wrote to A. Mitchell Palmer imploring him "urgently" to support the Curtis resolution. He also telegraphed a message to the recovering Omaha mayor that recognized his "courageous attempt to check mob violence." And, at the twelfth annual gathering of the National Equal Rights League in Washington, D.C., William Monroe Trotter sent a sardonic message to the president via his comments to the press about the current situation: "The new spirit among colored Americans of resisting attacks upon their lives is something for which President Wilson himself is chiefly responsible. His reiteration of noble sentiments and making our boys fight under their inspiration has given birth to a new spirit of manliness."

While the federal troops were still guarding the street corners and city buildings of Omaha, a startling rumor was spreading nationwide: black sharecroppers in Arkansas were organizing a revolt against white plantation owners. The truth would be twisted a thousand ways before the story of what was really happening was ever told. Black sharecroppers had organized the Progressive Farmers and Household Union of America, and the purpose of the group was to take a stand against plantation owners who were giving them low prices for their cotton and charging high prices for their supplies. Not an uprising, as some Arkansas whites were telling the press, but rather an organized, businesslike revolt against the tenant system that they believed was cheating them.

"The time is at hand that all men, all nations and tongues must receive a just reward," read one of the new union's leaflets. "This union wants to know why it is that the laborers cannot control their just earnings. . . . Remember the Holy Word, when the Almighty took John up on the mountain . . . and John said, 'I see all nations and tongues coming up before God.' Now we are a nation and a tongue. Why should we be cut off from fair play?"

The violence in Arkansas began on the morning of September 30 outside a black church in Hoop Spur. Located about three miles north of Elaine in the east-central part of Arkansas, Hoop Spur was just across the Mississippi River from the state of Mississippi. That morning a branch of the new union, which was based in Elaine, was meeting at the church to discuss the idea of whether to hire an attorney to represent their demands to the landowners, plantation managers, and merchants. They were not meeting to firm up plans to massacre whites in the region, as some newspapers later reported. Outside the church, a group of men, both white and black, had gathered who wanted to discourage blacks inside the church from joining the union. And to discourage them it was necessary to scare them. Who fired the first shot would be a matter of debate for years to come. The black men inside the church shot back at someone outside who had fired. And therein began a week of violence in Elaine and environs during which truckloads of white men came in from Mississippi and Tennessee to help their white brethren in Arkansas; during which five of them, including a soldier, were killed; and during which anywhere from twenty to eight hundred blacks were killed. In later years, it would be revealed that dozens, if not hundreds, of black sharecroppers were massacred at Elaine during that first week of October and many were thrown into the Mississippi River to destroy the evidence, just as the church at Hoop Spur was torched the day after the first shot was fired.

On October 3, while the U.S. Army was standing guard in Omaha and hundreds of "captured" Arkansas blacks were "herded" into makeshift stockades, a mob of twenty-five white men in Alabama showered gunfire down upon two deputies protecting two black prisoners in a car on the way to a state prison. Forcing the prisoners out of the car and into the nearby woods, they told them to run and then they perforated the prisoners' backs with bullets. One was a soldier who had fought in France.

On the very same day in Montgomery, a few white men sneaked into a hospital and murdered a black man suspected of having shot a policemen. And again, on the same day, a former soldier who was black, while walking along the main streets of Montgomery was attacked by a "band of white men." A week later, in Atlanta, the Ku Klux Klan, showing off the strength of its recent resurgence, filled the city newsstands with the first issue of its new newspaper, the *Searchlight*. With the help of its advertisers, which included Studebaker, Coca-Cola, and the Elgin Watch Company, it would soon be available in other U.S. cities and towns.

In October, the nation seemed to be sinking deeper and deeper into a quicksand of conflict and hatred. Instead of the calming words of peace and normalcy that so many Americans wanted to hear, the lexicon of war had returned to the headlines. Propaganda, prejudice, and fear mongering distorted the causes of legitimate struggles, making every problem appear to be instigated by foreigners or blacks or outside agitators who were all somehow connected to Bolshevism. It was abundantly clear that it was a dangerous time to stand up for one's beliefs. But, fortunately for the sake of democracy, some people did.

The industrial struggle of the steelworkers continued into October with outbreaks of violence as companies brought in black strikebreakers— approximately thirty thousand—pitting races and nationalities against one another, raising the tensions in an already scalding battle. In Donora, Pennsylvania, for example, two striking workers were killed when a riot broke out between immigrant strikers and black scabs. In early October, in Gary, Indiana, hundreds of special police and militiamen were brought in to quell a riot that became so bloody that the governor called for federal troops to occupy the city. Major General Leonard Wood, no longer on duty in Omaha and soon to announce his intention to run for U.S. president on the Republican ticket, then arrived with federal troops. While guarding the city, Wood asked the Army's military intelligence to investigate its streets and buildings in search of evidence of Bolshevik influence.

There were workers in every labor struggle that year who hoped for a revolution or dreamed of a workers' state. But most strikers simply wanted to be part of a union with enough power to negotiate effectively with management. Unfortunately for the steelworkers nationwide, the MID agents, in their probe in Gary, found evidence that exposed a few of the strikers who appeared to be plotting to bomb the offices and homes of prominent people in that town. With federal agents infiltrating every union branch and strike meeting, what happened at Gary could have been the result of planted evidence to enhance the image of dangerous radicals swirling around the strike, or it could have been real. Regardless of the truth, the discovery resulted in a full-scale government raid in Gary in which agents seized caches of circulars and books and arrested dozens of striking steelworkers. And then like a spreading fire, newspapers nationwide began to tie the ongoing story of the steel strike with the story of Bolshevism in America. Bolshevism was causing the strike and the strike was giving Bolshevism a platform. Thus, anyone who sympathized with the strikers was a security threat and a radical. Still, labor leaders who continued to support the workers voiced their support louder and more resolutely than ever. "We're going to take over the steel mills and run them for Uncle Sam," exclaimed Mary Harris Jones, the eighty-two-year-old labor organizer known as Mother Jones, at a meeting in Gary.

By late October when the United Mine Workers announced a call to strike, the image of workers standing up for their rights in America was enmeshed with radicalism and Bolshevism, violence and revolution. Such timing would hobble the coal miners and UMW president John L. Lewis, despite the fact that Lewis was a firm anti-communist. After negotiations with the coal operators broke down on October 21, Lewis ordered the strike to begin on the 1st of November. The conflict centered on the wartime contract between the government and the UMW in which workers would not receive wage increases because of the war. The wage freeze began in September 1917 and would last until the end of the war or April 1, 1920, whichever came first. After the Armistice, coal miners assumed the contract was over. But the coal companies would not concede because the war was not officially over—the United States had not yet ratified the peace treaty. The UMW wanted a six-hour day, a five-day week, and a 60 percent wage increase but the operators said there would be no negotiations over labor issues until April 1, 1920. With the cost of living rising and wages stuck at the September 1917 level, miners were threatening strikes with or without the UMW authorization, which they believed should have come months before.

In his announcement, Lewis assured the public that the mineworkers "have but one object in view and that is to obtain just recognition of their right to a fair wage and proper working conditions," he said. "No other issue is involved and there must be no attempt on the part of anyone to inject into the strike any extraneous purposes." But false propaganda immediately spewed out of the coal companies as their spokesmen informed the press that Lenin himself was behind the strike, and that in fact, the Soviet government was financing it. In addition, President Wilson, from his sickbed, said that a strike of coal miners just before the cold winter months was "a grave moral and legal wrong."

Three days before the starting date, A. Mitchell Palmer met with Wilson to discuss what to do. The next day, the attorney general obtained a temporary injunction blocking the involvement of any UMW leaders in the strike. This provoked Samuel Gompers, who had not been supportive of the strike, to publicly announce his endorsement of it. For the government to issue an injunction against labor was a betrayal, he said. Without their leaders, 394,000 coal miners walked out on Saturday morning, November 1.

The following Friday, November 7, three weeks after the Senate unanimously passed the Poindexter Resolution, which legitimized American fears of the Bolshevik terror, the Justice Department raided the Russian People's House on East 15th Street in New York—for the sixth time in less than a year. At least two hundred men and women were taken out of the building this time, some with their heads wrapped in bloodstained bandages, after being "badly beaten," as described in a New York Times editorial. Several were American citizens who were later released. Only thirty-nine out of the two hundred were held. Most were Russian workers who used the building as a social club, though the government identified it as the headquarters of the Union of Russian Workers, which the government considered a dangerous threat. This time, to prove their thesis, the raiders found "almost a ton" of radical literature, so said their reports, and they uncovered a large container marked "TNT" as well as small vials marked muriatic acid, sulfuric acid, ammonia hydrate, and glyercine sulphate—the ingredients for the manufacture of highly destructive bombs.

The next day the raids continued: seven hundred New York policemen arrested five hundred men and women after raiding at least seventy buildings in New York. And across the nation, in other cities, police stormed radical meeting places and organizations. A total of 246 aliens nationwide were detained and considered deportable. A week later the attorney general was able to answer the Poindexter Resolution with a full report of those brutal days in November and a letter that confirmed the radical danger in America. Also, for at least the third time, he called for new peacetime sedition laws to secure the nation from the threats of radicalism. Such a law would allow the Justice Department to extend its raids and investigations of radicalism beyond radical aliens to radical American citizens.

The autumn of 1919 was a cruel, unsettling time. Strikes. Riots. Violence. The president's massive stroke. The falling star of world peace. How was it possible to escape from such intensity, to feel safe again, to restore a glow of innocence? In October for many Americans, the answer was simple: baseball, specifically the World Series.

In 1919 the opponents were the Chicago White Sox and the Cincinnati Reds in their first World Series. The series opened at Redland Field in Cincinnati on October 1. The White Sox were the favored team, with betting odds of 8–5, until the Reds won the first game and then the odds preferred the Reds 7–10.

The Series was then played in a best-of-nine format. The Reds won the second game, 4–2. Game Three was played in Chicago and the Sox won 3–0. The Reds came back in Game Four, winning 2–0 and again in Game Five, with a score of 5–0. Back at Redland Field for the sixth game, the crowds swelled to more than 32,000 believing that the Reds, now with a 4–1 lead, could easily win the Series. But the Sox won both Game Six and Game Seven: 5–4 and 4–1. Going into Game Eight, the Reds were ahead four games to three.

Game Eight of the 1919 World Series was played in Chicago before an anxious crowd of nearly 33,000. It was a cloudy day with heavy winds, so strong that a flagpole nearly fell into the stands but not strong enough to stop the Reds from winning the game, 10–5. Cincinnatians were ecstatic and in the days of early October, the World Series had served its grand purpose as a great escape—a very important role in 1919. But in its aftermath, questions began to emerge. Some said there was something suspicious about the way Sox stellar pitcher Eddie Cicotte gave up a sequence of hits in the first game, during which he had slammed the lead-off hitter in the back with his second pitch. And in the second game Lefty Williams seemed to fall apart inexplicably in the fourth inning when he walked three and gave up just as many runs. In fact there were ten plays that Sox aficionados questioned, adding to the swell of rumors that had reached the press box and the offices of Sox owner Charles Comiskey even before the series began—rumors that the series was fixed.

At a time when sports gambling was not uncommon and games during the season were known sometimes to be fixed, it was not hard to imagine a fixed World Series. And consistent with what could almost be called a nationwide theme in America that autumn, there were labor issues in baseball. Owners of ball teams in effect owned their players, and the players, who were bought and sold like servants, had no rights whatsoever. If they thought their salaries were too low, they had no leverage for bargaining. If they asked for more and were told that their pay rate was fair from the point of view of the owners, then they had only one choice: play or quit. The World Series, the luminescent star of American sports, had never before been fixed. And the average American in the fall of a difficult year like 1919 wanted only to bask in the bright light of such a star. The biggest baseball news that season had been George Herman "Babe" Ruth, the Red Sox pitcher who had hit a record twenty-nine home runs. And soon his sale to the New York Yankees would distract sports fans from the dark prospect of a fixed Series. But the suspicions about the fix and certainly the causes underlying it were not going away. The following year, eight White Sox players would be indicted on charges of fixing the 1919 Series.

Fortunately, in the fall of 1919, there were also events that showed the brighter side of humanity. In October, for example, Andrew "Rube" Foster, one of the best black baseball pitchers of the early century, announced his plan to create an all-black baseball circuit. Comprised of Western clubs, which were the Chicago American Giants, Cuban Stars, Chicago Giants, Dayton Marcos, Detroit Stars, Indianapolis ABCs, Kansas City Monarchs, and St. Louis Giants, the new Negro National League would be owned and controlled by black businessmen, so wrote the *Chicago Defender*'s columnist Cary B. Lewis on October 4, thus putting the money from the games and the black players' work into the pockets of their own race. Further, Foster wanted to create for his race "a profession that would equal the earning capacity of other professions, and do something concrete for the loyalty of the race." The excitement seemed to leap off the page as Lewis informed his readers that the *Chicago Defender* "will have a sports writer in every city to report the games and this paper will have the biggest baseball column of them all." Indeed, the league, Foster hoped, would inspire more African-Americans to become baseball writers and umpires, in addition to showing off the greatness of black players. Ironically, just months earlier in Cairo, Georgia, on January 31, 1919, a player had been born who would effectively put an end to the new Negro Leagues. The grandson of a slave, his name was Jack Roosevelt Robinson, and in 1947 he would integrate major league baseball.

Toward the end of October, Norfolk, Virginia, was preparing for the installation of the nation's first dial telephones. The rotary machine was such a huge transition from the old crank phones and operator-dependent connections that local newspapers published detailed instructions about how to use them and what to expect. Readers were informed about the sound of a busy signal and about their new five-digit phone numbers. They were assured of the efficiency of the new system. Norfolk's city manager made the first call, after which *the Virginian-Pilot and the Norfolk Landmark* proudly reported, "Norfolk didn't believe the thing would work but it has."

And in October, American readers were introduced to a new writer named F. Scott Fitzgerald, whose short stories, such as "The Debutante," "The Cut-Glass Bowl," and "Head and Shoulders," had just begun to appear in the popular magazines *The Smart Set, Scribner's,* and *The Saturday Evening Post*—and whose work reflected a gradual turning inward of the American public. Only a few months before, in the spring, Fitzgerald had covered the walls of his New York apartment with 122 rejection slips. Then, during the summer, while Joseph Conrad's latest book, *The Arrow of Gold,* soared in sales and Booth Tarkington's *The Magnificent Ambersons* won the Pulitzer Prize for fiction, he moved home to St. Paul, Minnesota, to rewrite his rejected novel, which he called *The Romantic Egoist.* Fitzgerald resubmitted the book to Scribner's in the early fall under a new title, *This Side of Paradise,* and editor Max Perkins accepted it. This was a big risk for Scribner's, as it was unclear whether America was ready for Fitzgerald and his main character, Amory Blaine, whose attitude toward the recent war Fitzgerald described like this: "Beyond a sporting interest in the German dash for Paris the whole affair failed either to thrill or interest him." But in the spring of 1920, *This Side of Paradise* would be a runaway best-seller.

CHAPTER 36

Albert in Wonderland

While some Americans thirsted for escape, diversion, and stability that autumn, others sought meaning in the current suffering. They hungered for something to believe in again—something mystifying and far-flung, something that gleamed with a heavenly radiance, something that was important yet nearly impossible to describe and thus, in that way, magical.

On the afternoon of November 6, the Royal Astronomical Society and the Royal Society unwittingly delivered that something to America and to the world. At Burlington House in London, the fellows of both societies gathered to discuss the findings of the two eclipse expeditions the previous May. They eagerly took their seats in the crowded high-ceilinged hall to await the news of the studies of the expeditions' results. Would the royal astronomer announce that the photographic plates had confirmed Albert Einstein's general theory of relativity? Were the plates clear enough to make such a determination? Would the results unhinge the scientific community? Would scientists resist the new theory or would they embrace it?

The British philosopher and mathematician Alfred North Whitehead wrote that the atmosphere was so intense that day it could only be compared to a Greek drama. "We were the chorus commenting on the decree of destiny as disclosed in the development of a supreme incident. There was dramatic quality in the very staging—the traditional ceremonial, and in the background the picture of Newton to remind us that the greatest of scientific generalizations was now, after more than two centuries, to receive its first modification. Nor was the personal interest wanting: a great adventure in thought had at length come safe to shore."

The astronomer royal, Sir Frank Watson Dyson, officiated and spoke first. After a brief description of both expeditions, he concluded, "After a careful study of the plates I am prepared to say that they confirm Einstein's prediction. A very definite result has been obtained, that light is deflected in accordance with Einstein's law of gravitation."

Sir Arthur Stanley Eddington then talked of the scientific meaning of the results, which he said dealt with nothing less than the "fabric of the universe." And he described in detail the Príncipe expedition. He spoke of the challenges of cloudy weather. For those who had closely followed the expeditions, he revealed a very interesting fact. After the photographs from both expeditions were developed, it became clear that the cloud cover, which had been so troubling at Príncipe, was in fact a great blessing. At the other site, in Brazil, the heat of the sun had caused the pivoting mirrors on the telescopes to expand, thus causing a distortion of the image of the stars and ruining the accuracy of the photographic plates. If the sun had been shining at Príncipe, there might not have been reliable astrographic results from which to assess Einstein's theory.

And then the president of the Royal Society, Joseph J. Thomson, standing in front of the large portrait of Isaac Newton, addressed the keen audience, so eager to hear the official results. "If his theory is right, it makes us take an entirely new view of gravitation. If it is sustained that Einstein's reasoning holds good—and it has survived two very severe tests [which he names]—then it is the result of one of the highest achievements of human thought."

The general theory of relativity, said Thomson, was "not the discovery of an outlying island but of a whole continent of new scientific ideas." Then, taking a deep breath, lowering the tone of his voice, and looking straight into the eyes of the anxious crowd, he said, "It is the greatest discovery in connection with gravitation since Newton enunciated his principles."

On the night of November 6, Albert Einstein went to sleep unaware of what had just transpired in England. He had known since September about the results of the May expeditions. On the 27th of that month, Hendrik Lorentz, the well-known physicist and friend of Einstein's, had sent him a soon-to-be-famous telegram saying that "Eddington found star displacement at rim of sun, preliminary measurement between nine-tenths of a second and twice that value." Einstein then sent a postcard to his mother: "Joyous news today. Lorentz telegraphed that the English expeditions have actually demonstrated the deflection of light from the sun."

But he did not know about the details of the November 6 meeting nor could he have anticipated what the conclusions would mean in the world of 1919. For Einstein, it had been a strenuous year. He had divorced his first wife in February. He had married again in June. His mother was dying.

All the while his revolutionary theory, established in 1905 and refined in 1916, had been a source of controversy among the world's most prominent astronomers and physicists. And, after several attempts since 1905, it had finally been tested during the May eclipse.

On Friday morning, November 7, he awakened to a story in the London *Times* about the previous day's meeting with a headline that read: "REVO-LUTION IN SCIENCE. NEW THEORY OF THE UNIVERSE. NEW-TONIAN IDEAS OVERTHROWN." Einstein's life would never again be the same. Although hardly ordinary to begin with, he had nonetheless led a relatively private life, with his fame limited to scientific circles. But from now on, Einstein would be a public figure. He was suddenly the new shining star of humanity—that magical and inexplicable "something" that the world seemed to need at that moment. The news about Einstein soared beyond national boundaries, rising above the myopic notions of nationalism, and landed on the front pages of newspapers all over the world.

The November 7 *Times* article focused on the relativity theory, the eclipse observations, and the fellows' meeting more than the German scientist who had caused it all to happen. The November 8 *Times* wrote more about Einstein. Considering the fact that the treaty with Germany had been signed only five months before and wounds of the Great War had hardly healed, the issue of Einstein in Germany was still a sensitive one. Thus the article noted that he had taught in Zurich and in Prague as well as in Berlin and that he was one of the scientists in Germany who had protested the German manifesto of the men of science who supported Germany's right to go to war.

The news reached America on November 9 when the *New York Times* ran the Einstein story with the headlines "LIGHTS ALL ASKEW IN THE HEAVENS; Men of Science More or Less Agog over Results of Eclipse Observation." "EINSTEIN THEORY TRIUMPHS; Stars Not Where They Seemed or Were Calculated to Be, but Nobody Need Worry." "A BOOK FOR 12 WISE MEN; No More in All the World Could Comprehend It, Said Einstein when His Daring Publishers Accepted It." The theory of relativity shared the New York headlines that day with a story about a "World Outbreak Plotted by Reds" and "Lenin's Emissaries Sought to Start Rising All over Europe," plus the end of the United Mine Workers strike, more news about the Justice Department's recent raid on radicals, and the success of the test of the first rotary telephone in Virginia. The new theory of the universe was the biggest news, although few people understood what it meant.

That there were photographs taken of the total eclipse of the sun on May 29, which then allowed an observation of the impact of the sun on the position of the stars; that the photographs were studied over the summer and despite obstacles of bad weather and damaged equipment, there was enough evidence to show a deviation between the position of the stars when the sun—a huge mass of matter—was near and when it was not; that this deviation proved the deflection of light from the sun, which in turn verified the theory that matter bends light and space is curved; that that meant that Isaac Newton, who thought space was flat and absolute, was upstaged; and that this man Einstein must be brilliant because he figured this out and understood why it was important: these things could be understood by the thousands, albeit millions, who now had read about it. But who in fact understood the significance of this? Very few. As the *New York Times* wrote, only twelve men could possibly grasp it. "A Book for 12 Wise Men." Even the London *Times* confessed that it could not explain why it was important and what its impact on the world would be. "So far as we can follow it, the chief result appears to be that gravitation hitherto regarded as an absolute proposition becomes relative," wrote the London newspaper. "The simple majesty of the square of the distance has ceased to retain its isolated splendor as an expression of conformity between abstract thought and observation of the fabric of the universe."

Despite the remote, esoteric quality of it, there was an overwhelming sense that this was something positive, that in fact it must be progress and thus it must be celebrated. And all of the struggles and chaos of the previous months were suddenly wrapped up and tied together with a ribbon of hope that had slipped off everything, from Wilson to the World Series. Finally, here was an intriguing detail about life in the universe that could not be taken away, because no one fully understood it to begin with. And although some labeled it, in the hateful fashion of the year, "Bolshevism in physics" or simply made fun of it, nothing could dim its glow. And in a way it became the real articulation of international cooperation—not Wilson's League.

From that day forward for the rest of Enstein's life there would never be a year in which his name did not appear in the *New York Times*. Even the skeptical professor who wrote in the *Times* that after he heard about Einstein's theories he felt he had "been wandering with Alice in Wonderland and had tea with the Mad Hatter" could not knock Einstein from his perch so very high above the rest of the world. Besides, the professor may have been more astute than his column at first glance revealed. Wasn't it possible that Americans gave Einstein such instant celebrity status because his revolutionary universe was the bright new concept, the sort of wonderland they were seeking? Einstein's theory transcended earthbound troubles and was easier to accept than the Treaty of Versailles or the Covenant of the League of Nations or the notion of collective security. This was the type of progress that required no sacrifice on the part of any citizen. And the Mad Hatter? By November of 1919, it might have been more appealing to have tea with the Mad Hatter than, say, the attorney general or the president.

CHAPTER 37

Greatness

Across the Atlantic, on the 6th of November, another meeting of some importance convened at 1720 I Street in Washington, D.C. This was the home of U.S. Supreme Court Justice Oliver Wendell Holmes, Jr., and the meeting was in his study. What transpired, however, would never appear in any newspaper and in fact would never have been known to anyone had Justice Holmes not instructed his law clerk to leave the door slightly ajar between his study and the clerk's adjacent room. The clerk, Stanley Morrison, fresh out of Harvard Law School, told his friend Dean Acheson, who was Louis Brandeis's law clerk, what he overheard that morning: a judge being pressured but not succumbing. It would impress them both for the rest of their lives.

In November of 1919, Holmes was seventy-eight years old. Appointed by Theodore Roosevelt, he had served on the U.S. Supreme Court for seventeen years. His brethren that year were Justice William Rufus Day, also a Roosevelt appointee; the chief justice, Edward D. White, appointed by Grover Cleveland; Justice Joseph McKenna, appointed by William McKinley; Justices Mahlon Pitney and Willis Van Devanter, appointed by William Howard Taft; and Justices Louis Brandeis, James Clark McReynolds, and John Hessin Clarke, all Woodrow Wilson appointees. In Holmes's March opinions in the cases of Debs, Schenck, and Frohwork, the Court had affirmed three convictions under the Espionage Act. And in *Schenck*, the first of the three to be decided, he established what became known as the "clear and present danger" standard for free speech cases.

"The most stringent protection of free speech would not protect a man in falsely shouting fire in a theatre and causing panic," Holmes wrote in *Schenck*. Debs was convicted for obstructing conscription by giving speeches that expressed his opposition to the war. In October, a few days after Harry Weinberger had presented his argument against the harsh sentences in the Abrams case, Holmes wrote a letter to his good friend Harold Laski, which began, "I fear we have less freedom of speech here than they have in England." And when Justice Clarke—whom the chief justice had chosen to write the Court's opinion in the Abrams case—distributed to his colleagues what he had written, Holmes indicated he would be writing a dissenting opinion. Brandeis joined him in his dissent.

After Holmes's three opinions in March, often referred to as the Espionage Act trilogy, his intended dissent must have startled the other justices. Three of them—Justices Van Devanter, Pitney, and another whose name dropped out of the story as it was recalled in later years by friends of Morrison's—were worried enough that they visited Holmes in his study on the day he was to write the Abrams opinion. Fanny Holmes, the justice's wife, accompanied them. For the sake of the security of the nation, the justices said, he must sacrifice his own view. Mrs. Holmes agreed with them. They then beseeched him to hark back to his days as a soldier fighting against a common foe. Abrams, Steimer, Lachowsky, and Lipman were the enemy that must be reckoned with. Their severe sentences were deserved because of the threat to the nation their leaflets represented. It was a friendly attempt at persuasion. Holmes responded gently, yet firmly. He could not do as they wished.

Holmes had changed. Something had happened between March and November to cause him to rethink his position on free speech. When his guests left the study that November morning, he closed the door and began to write an opinion that would show just how much he had changed. Rarely, it seems, do individuals in positions of power have the courage to open their minds and face the possibility that they may have been wrong and thus must adjust their course of action. It wasn't that Holmes had been so wrong; he just hadn't gotten it exactly right. Realizing that he must modify his view and expand his definition of protected speech in America was a mark of Holmes's greatness.

The obvious explanation for the change was that Weinberger's brilliant presentation before the Supreme Court had influenced Holmes. The Founding Fathers clearly intended that "liberty of discussion" was a natural right, Weinberger had stressed. And this right could not be taken away, even, as Holmes had written in March, if the speech or circular contained wording that presented a "clear and present danger" of causing unlawful acts. The unlawful acts could be punished when they occurred, Weinberger said, but the speech could not be censored on the basis of the possibility that it might incite such acts. Speech must be "perfectly unrestrained," Weinberger argued.

Undoubtedly, the defense attorney's passionate presentation in October made an impression upon Holmes. But Weinberger was probably not the cause of the groundbreaking dissent that the justice would soon write. Indeed, Holmes had embarked on his intellectual odyssey many months before, almost immediately, in fact, after the March decisions. His remarkable change of attitude evolved out of a series of letters and meetings with astute legal scholars such as Judge Learned Hand of the U.S. Court of Appeals for the Second Circuit, New York, and Felix Frankfurter and Harold Laski. And it was the result of a lengthy reading list of books and articles such as one by University of Chicago law professor Ernst Freund in *The New Republic* magazine.

At this time in his long life, Holmes, with such stature and brilliance, had attracted what could be called an unofficial fan club in the form of a group of admirers who were at least forty years younger than he and who, representing various professions, shared an ardent interest in one of the biggest questions of the day: just where was the line to be drawn between the guarantee of free speech, as expressed in the First Amendment, and the government's right to suppress dissident speech? Herbert Croly, the editor of *The New Republic*, and the journalist Walter Lippmann were among Holmes's supporters, as were Frankfurter, who then taught at Harvard Law School, Laski, also teaching at Harvard, and the newest arrival to Holmes's circle, Zechariah Chafée, Jr.

During the summer of 1919, Holmes spent many days at his country house, which stood on a bluff overlooking the ocean at Beverly Farms, Massachusetts. There he immersed himself in legal and philosophical readings on the question of the limits of free speech. Among the articles that drew his attention was one in the June issue of the *Harvard Law Review*, which Laski, one of the *Review*'s editors at the time, had sent to him. Entitled "Freedom of Speech in War Time," it was written by a thirty-four-year-old assistant professor at Harvard Law School, Zechariah Chafée, Jr., who was from an old prominent Rhode Island family descended from the colonist Roger Williams. Laski had read the June article twice and as he told Holmes in a letter, "I'll go to the stake for every word." The article called for recognition of the fact that the First Amendment imposed limits on the government's power to gag the written and spoken expressions of dissidents.

Chafee, a graduate of Brown University and Harvard Law School, was also the author of an article entitled "Freedom of Speech," which Holmes likely had read in the November 1918 issue of *The New Republic*. In that one, he had advocated nearly absolute free speech, even in wartime. Free speech, Chafee believed, disseminated information and unless it caused a "direct and dangerous interference with the conduct" of war, then it must be allowed. If freedom of speech was censored in wartime, and if the war was unjust, then how could the people communicate to the government that they believed the war to be unjust? The First Amendment, he believed, was meant to protect the right to criticize the existing form of government, "the kind of criticism which George III's judges punished." Chafee wrote another piece for *The New Republic* in July of 1919 in which he said that "tolerance" was "the tradition handed down to us by Roger Williams and Thomas Jefferson."

The June article in *Harvard Law Review*, the one Laski had sent to Beverly Farms that summer, began:

> Never in the history of our country, since the Alien and Sedition Laws of 1798, has the meaning of free speech been the subject of such controversy as to-day. Over two hundred prosecutions and other judicial proceedings during the war, involving speeches, newspaper articles, pamphlets, and books, have been followed since the Armistice by a widespread legislative consideration of bills punishing the advocacy of extreme radicalism. It is becoming increasingly important to determine the true limits of freedom of expression, so that speakers and writers may know how much they can properly say and governments may be sure how much they can lawfully and wisely suppress.

And it ended:

> Those who gave their lives for freedom would be the last to thank us for throwing aside so lightly the great traditions of our race. Not satisfied to have justice and almost all the people with our cause, we insisted on an artificial unanimity of opinion behind the war.

Keen intellectual grasp of the President's aims by the nation at large was very difficult when the opponents of his idealism ranged unchecked, while the men who urged greater idealism went to prison. In our efforts to silence those who advocated peace without victory, we prevented at the very start that vigorous threshing out of fundamentals which might to-day have saved us from a victory without peace.

Whether Holmes read the article could never be absolutely proven, though Chafee was someone he would have respected for his post at Harvard and for his connection to *The New Republic* as well as his hard work on the issue of free speech. Considering also that Chafee, in this particular article, discussed at length the Espionage Act trilogy and was critical of Holmes, it seems hardly possible that Holmes did not read it. In late July Laski invited Holmes to tea at Cambridge, which was only a forty-five-minute train ride from Beverly Farms. He wanted Holmes to meet Professor Chafee. Holmes agreed. Felix Frankfurter had introduced Holmes to Laski in such a way, and Laski, the brilliant young English Jew who was an expert in church history, had a photographic memory, and read books as quickly as most people ate lunch, was to introduce Holmes to Chafee, another creative intellectual.

Although Holmes would never have attributed his sea change that summer directly to his readings or to his discussions with the young men in the upcoming generation of legal minds, he was undoubtedly moved by them. At the very least, they impressed upon him the continuing urgency of the issue—mainly its lack of resolution—and gave him ideas to consider in the task of reformulating the meaning of "clear and present danger" and of defining the limits, if any, of speech freedom in a democratic republic.

At the tea in Cambridge, Holmes expressed to Laski and Chafee his belief that the Espionage Act cases on which the court had decided in March should not have been brought to begin with and that if he had been a juror he would have voted to acquit Eugene Debs. But as a judge he must "allow a very wide latitude to Congressional discretion in the carrying on of the war." Now in the Abrams case, he had the opportunity to narrow that latitude by defining the great scope and strength of the First Amendment. In the previous cases, he had talked of the limits of free speech. Now he would talk of the protections of free speech, showing that he recognized the danger of what he had omitted in his previous rulings.

Holmes was not sympathetic to Abrams, Steimer, Lachowsky, and Lipman. He saw their circulars as trivial and almost silly, calling them "poor and puny anonymities." This was another case, like the others, that should not have happened. Their threat to America was insignificant. But his dissent in their favor, which was announced on November 10, was nonetheless stunning, groundbreaking, and hugely significant. And while he was heckled and ridiculed by some, especially in elite legal circles of Boston, many more applauded him. They claimed that his words would outlive the current hysteria.

Chafee compared Holmes to John Stuart Mill and John Milton. And those who had lived through 1919, those who knew how endangered the freedoms of their nation had become, and those who had watched people's lives destroyed for exercising such freedoms, must have nearly wept as they read the words of Holmes:

> When men have realized that time has upset many fighting faiths, they may come to believe even more than they believe the very foundations of their own conduct that the ultimate good desired is better reached by free trade in ideas—that the best test of truth is the power of the thought to get itself accepted in the competition of the market, and that truth is the only ground upon which their wishes safely can be carried out. That at any rate is the theory of our Constitution. It is an experiment, as all life is an experiment. Every year if not every day we have to wager our salvation upon some prophecy based upon imperfect knowledge. While that experiment is part of our system I think that we should be eternally vigilant against the attempts to check the expression of opinions that we loathe and believe to be fraught with death, unless they so imminently threaten immediate interference with the lawful and pressing purpose of the law that an immediate check is required to save the country. . . .
>
> I regret that I cannot put into more impressive words my belief that in their conviction upon this indictment the defendants were deprived of their rights under the Constitution of the United States.

One of Holmes's biographers later wrote that this dissenting opinion, which charted the legal course for free speech in America from then onward, became one of the "most-quoted justifications for freedom of expression in the English-speaking world." But when the news hit the papers on the 11th of November in 1919, the dissent in the case of Jacob Abrams was but a footnote. Justice Clarke's majority opinion was the focus of most of the coverage. The leaflets, wrote Clarke, were "clearly an appeal to the 'workers' to arise and put down by force the government of the United States." And, he said, the defendants had admitted in court that they were "anarchists" and "rebels."

The Court's vote was 7–2, with Holmes and Brandeis dissenting "in a few particulars." The *New York Times* headline read: "Upholds Sentence of Russian 'Reds'/Supreme Court Decides Against Four Who Threw Pamphlets from Rooftops." The *New York Tribune* noted, "Justice Holmes in his opinion said Congress could not forbid all efforts to change the mind of the country." Some papers emphasized that the Supreme Court had held that Congress did not exceed its authority in enacting the Espionage Law. "In making the decision," wrote the *New York Call*, "the court indicated a strong sentiment in favor of upholding the Department of Justice in its war against radicals."

Weinberger, though disappointed, was not surprised. He would now step up his campaign for his clients' deportations, thus sparing them many years in prison. It was his solemn task to inform his defendants that they had lost the case and that they had thirty days to prepare for their twenty years behind bars. Mollie Steimer was already in jail at the workhouse on Blackwell's Island, serving her six-month sentence for disorderly conduct. Hyman Lachowsky was in detention on Ellis Island, as he was one of the immigrants swept up in the Russian People's House raid a few days before. Jacob Abrams and Samuel Lipman were free and in New York, but not for long. They had no intention of serving time. After Weinberger contacted them, the two men jumped bail. Three days later, they were renting a room on Canal Street in New Orleans using the names "Mr. Stone" and "Mr. Green" and preparing to leave the United States on a steamer bound for Mexico.

CHAPTER 38

Armistice Day 1919

In November, the federal government announced that the flu pandemic was officially over, assuring Americans that they would not be suddenly surprised by a new wave, like the one that had hit during the early months of 1919. That month Austrian violinist and composer Fritz Kreisler ended his two-year exile—self-imposed because of anti-German sentiment in America—by playing his sensuous Viennese compositions to a grateful New York audience during the same week as violinist Yasha Heifetz graced New York with his own genius. The American Legion, founded in May in St. Louis, held its first national convention, in Minneapolis. The new Radio Corporation of America, established in October, created an American monopoly in radio by buying out—with the federal government's assistance—British Marconi, German Telefunken, and all French interests. And the most popular book in Norfolk, Virginia, was the newly released telephone directory.

In a landslide victory that November, the Republican governor of Massachusetts, Calvin Coolidge, was reelected. The *Wall Street Journal* announced that instead of backing Woodrow Wilson for a third presidential term, it was endorsing "that sterling defender of the ancient Anglo-Saxon tradition of liberty; that upholder of the constitutional guarantees of freedom; that passionate worshipper at the shrine of free speech, free press and assemblage" Attorney General A. Mitchell Palmer. Determined to vote in the 1920 presidential election, the women suffragists were on the road in the seventeen states that still had not ratified the Nineteenth Amendment. And prisoner No. 9653 at the federal penitentiary in Atlanta, Eugene Debs, was considering another run for the U.S. presidency. If he did, he would be the first inmate ever to pursue the presidency. Debs, whose sixty-fourth birthday was November 5, had served seven months of his ten-year sentence and while his health was weakening, his following was growing stronger by the day.

The steel strike trudged onward, though tainted and twisted by increasing violence and the strangling charge of Bolshevist intent. Because of the steel strike, said Senator Poindexter, "There is a real danger that the Government will fall." Searching for and hoping to eliminate the source of Bolshevik control over the strike, the Senate Committee on Education and Labor launched a probe into the causes of the strike and in the process uncovered many unknown details. In November, for example, among others testifying before the Senate was a nineteen-year-old black strikebreaker, Eugene Steward. He was one of two hundred men loaded into crowded railcars in Baltimore bound for Philadelphia where, they were told, they would be employed for $4 a day. When they arrived, armed guards unlocked the train doors and herded the men to the grounds of a steel company, where they were told to go to work. They were also told that the steelworkers at the plant were on strike. Steward refused to be a scab and when he was told he had no choice, he ran, climbed over a fence and was caught in a net like an animal. He tried again to flee, was captured again, and then he was jailed in a boat with dozens of others who had also refused to work as scabs. There he was told that the guards would shoot him if he tried to escape again. Still, finding a rope on board, he escaped again—this time successfully.

John L. Lewis ordered the end of the coal strike on November 11. "We are Americans, we cannot fight our government," he said, referring to the government's early November injunction. Considering the coming of winter and the dire need for coal, this appeared to be good news for most of the nation. However, the coal miners were hardly pleased and many refused to follow the order. Coal production levels were far below the demand as hundreds of industrial plants had either shut down or were preparing to do so. Still, at least for the moment, for most Americans, the end of the strike was something more to celebrate on the nation's second Armistice Day.

Across the nation on November 11 there were parades—endless numbers of parades—attended by a populace that had seen more parades in one year than their forebears had seen in their entire lives. In Washington, the occasion was marked by the regal visit of the Prince of Wales and the unusual presence of the U.S. president. The unsettling image of a frail Woodrow Wilson in a wheelchair, making his first public appearance since his October collapse, mirrored the sad reality that exactly one year had passed since the cessation of hostilities in Europe and still America had not yet ratified the treaty of peace. Nor had it endorsed the dream that had been Wilson's obsessive focus, the League of Nations. This was the man who only one year ago was building ladders to the stars. Now he was too weak to stay for the full Armistice Day program arranged in his honor. The ladders were falling. Only eight days remained before the Senate vote, and it was hard to imagine what could possibly happen to persuade the Senate to approve the Treaty of Versailles. If the United States did not ratify the treaty, then it would not be a member of the League of Nations.

Armistice Day 1919 stood out for another reason, for on that day there were two lynchings in America. A black man was burned to death in Magnolia, Arkansas, for allegedly attempting to assault a white woman. In the other, a white man, a former soldier and labor activist in Centralia, Washington, was tortured to the point of begging to be shot, which he was, but only after dying a slow death hanging from a railroad bridge. These were but two out of the ten lynchings known to have occurred in November.

At the beginning of the month, the NAACP released its report on lynchings for the period from January through October of 1919. Out of the total of sixty-three for the ten months, three were white, one was Mexican, and fifty-nine were black, of whom eleven had been burned alive at the stake. Georgia led the nation with seventeen, followed by Mississippi, which had ten. Tied for third place with eight each were Alabama and Louisiana. Besides those burned, twenty were shot to death, nineteen were hanged, two were beaten to death, one was cut to pieces, one was drowned, and nine died by unknown methods. The allegations that led to the sixty-three deaths included: insulting a white woman (five), attempting to pull a white person from a horse (one), altercation with a white man (one), talking about the Chicago race riot (one), result of race riot (one), not getting out of the way of an auto driven by a white man (one), insulting a white man (one), shooting a white man (six), misleading and lying to a white mob (one), boasting about killing a white man (one), being a local black leader (one), speaking out against lynchings (one), found under a bed in a white man's house (one), circulating supposedly incendiary literature (one), attempting to assault a white woman (sixteen), intimacy with a white woman (four), trouble between white and black cotton mill workers (one), murder (eighteen), and one case in which the provocation was unknown.

What happened in Centralia on Armistice Day deviated from the usual pattern of lynchings but it did emanate from the same dangerous mix of prejudice and fear. Centralia was located in lumber country about eighty-five miles south of Seattle. And being a small, very patriotic town, it had tried, through raids and intimidation, to discourage members of the anti-war IWW, who, active among the loggers, were attempting to establish a union hall. The orgy of hatred between the town and the Wobblies had been ongoing since 1914. In the autumn months rumors had spread that on Armistice Day the local members of the American Legion were planning to raid the new IWW hall. The Wobblies sought advice from a local lawyer, who told them to publicize their fears in leaflets because this might discourage the raid and violence. He also told them that legally they had a right to defend themselves if a raid occurred and if they were attacked first. Thus the Wobblies, sitting in the hall that day, as the ceremonial parade passed their doors, were armed, and when the expected raid occurred, two of them fired at the intruders, killing two Legionnaires. Wesley Everest, a Wobbly, shot and killed another intruder as he fled the hall. Running to the Skookumchuck River, Everest killed yet another of his enemies, a man who ordered him to surrender at gunpoint. Eventually Everest was cornered and taken to the local jail, which by now contained his fellow IWW members and their lawyer.

Then on the night of the 12th, an enraged mob removed Everest from jail and threw him into a limousine, where they castrated and beat him. "Shoot me, for God's sake, shoot me," he pleaded as they took him to a railroad bridge over the Chehalis River. Instead they hanged him three times; the rope wasn't long enough the first two times. Their victim still alive as he hung from the girders, they turned on the headlights of their cars, which shone on the body, and they shot at the dangling body until no sign of life remained. The mutilated body with its elongated neck was brought back to the jailhouse, where Everest's friends were instructed to bury him.

A week later Bureau of Investigation agent F. W. McIntosh sent a report stating that the townsfolk had attacked first and that the IWW members were defending themselves when they shot back. But the report, filed on November 20, never surfaced in any newspaper. The story that emerged from the Armistice Day tragedy, ever more referred to as the Centralia Massacre, was that once again the violence of the Wobblies and the horrifying reality of the Bolshevik menace had surfaced. McIntosh's report was followed by many others that added names to Hoover's index, mainly the names of people who contributed money to the defense fund for the jailed Wobblies.

Before the month was over, there would be six more lynchings in America—all of black men. In late November at a meeting at the Church of the Ascension in New York City, James Weldon Johnson, field secretary for the NAACP, burst forth with a solution: blacks had enough economic force that they could go on strike to protest lynchings in America. For blacks to go on strike would be shocking enough to draw attention to the issue. "If the negroes in a city like Jacksonville, Florida, for example, would get together," Johnson said, "they could do much to better their condition. For example, they could send a committee representing 10,000 negroes to the city government and tell them that if they did not receive protection they would not cook or work in any way. Such a course would be a method more effective than the shotgun."

And who was to blame for the ongoing crisis of lynchings in America? Johnson named Woodrow Wilson as the main culprit for never taking a strong position against lynching and never urging Congress for the sake of humanity to put an end to such brutality, so reminiscent of slavery days in America. "Coming from a Southern man, his protests would have carried great weight," said Johnson.

J. Edgar Hoover, who had a file on Johnson and who had assigned an agent to go to the Church of the Ascension, expressed his own concerns that month about African-Americans. Talking to Congress, Hoover said resolutely that "the present attitude of the Negro leaders" is largely due to "the identification of the Negro with such radical organizations as the I.W.W. and an outspoken advocacy of the Bolsheviki or Soviet doctrine." To prove his point, he called attention to a recently released Justice Department study of black newspapers and magazines, which began: "At this time there can no longer be any question of a well-concerted movement among a certain class of Negro leaders of thought and action to constitute themselves a determined and persistent source of a radical opposition to the Government and to the established rule of law and order." Based largely on the analyses coming out of the Bureau of Translation and its director, Robert Bowen, the report warned that black publications such as *The Crisis* and *The Negro World* revealed evidence of a new consciousness of race equality. "When it is borne in mind that this boast finds its most frequent expression in the pages of those journals whose editors are men of education, in at least one instance men holding degrees conferred by Harvard University, it may be seen that the boast is not to be dismissed lightly as the ignorant vaporing of untrained minds."

CHAPTER 39

Falling Ladders

Whatever James Weldon Johnson and J. Edgar Hoover were saying about African-Americans that November was far from the thoughts of Woodrow Wilson as he sat in his sickroom at the White House. Although he was physically weak and emotionally fragile, his mind was still sharp. And he was more rigid in his thinking than ever before. He spoke to few people and focused intently on one issue: the ratification of the Treaty of Versailles.

The battle over the treaty had narrowed to what Wilson called the "heart of the Covenant," Article 10. Although Senator Gilbert Hitchcock, a Democrat from Nebraska, had countered Lodge's reservations with five of the Democrats' own more moderate reservations, Lodge had prevailed. The choice before the U.S. senators was to approve the treaty without the Republicans' restrictions or the treaty with them or to reject the treaty altogether. Thus, as the day of the Senate vote drew near, it was abundantly clear that if Wilson was unwilling to accept Lodge's stipulations, which effectively nullified Article 10, then it was highly possible that the treaty would be defeated. For Wilson, forsaking Article 10 meant ruining the cornerstone of the League and betraying his promise to the American public, whose wishes he considered himself to be still representing. This he could not do.

And thus, on November 17, Wilson informed Senator Hitchcock of his decision to reject the version of the treaty that would include any of Lodge's changes. On the 19th, the Senate indeed voted to defeat the treaty with the Lodge reservations: 39 yeas and 55 nays. But then when the call came out for the vote on the treaty alone the vote came in at 53 nays and 38 yeas, falling far short of the two-thirds majority vote necessary for ratification.

For the next several months both political parties would struggle to come to a compromise solution, and in February the Senate would vote to reconsider the treaty. But what happened in November was effectively the end. Wilson would never move from his resolute position. And although many Democrats would defy his stand and vote in favor of the treaty with the Lodge reservations, the Senate vote in March would never reach the two-thirds majority needed to ratify the treaty.

Five days after the November vote, a new book appeared in bookstores and newsstands nationwide: *What Wilson Did at Paris.* For its author, Ray Stannard Baker, the publication was a bittersweet occasion. Critics hailed the book as a timely work and praised Baker for raising the curtain on the drama of the peace conference. By telling the stories of the crises Wilson had faced at Paris and by bringing alive such details as the president's dawn-to-midnight schedule of meetings with thousands of people, from kings and diplomats to sheepherders and fishermen, Baker, in his 113-page book, the critics wrote, skillfully revealed the dogged determination of the president to force upon the peace conference the ideals he had so strongly represented to the world. "A little book of great immediate and historic value," wrote the *New York Times* reviewer, and "a valuable aid for the proponents of the League."

But by the end of November Baker knew that despite the success of his book, despite the wide circulation of his autumn articles upon which the book was based and which had reached an audience of ten million American readers, despite the fact that the American public would now know far more than ever before about their president and what he had done in Paris, the drama was effectively over. "I had tried to help him with my little book—all to no purpose, as it seemed to me," he wrote in his journal.

The president whom Baker deeply respected was now a broken man whose own distorted judgments and perceptions of the real world would hinder, not help, the cause of ratifying the treaty and bringing America into the League. Wilson believed that the people were still cheering and worshipping him as they had on that December 4 morning, only one year ago, when he left for France the first time. Baker, however, understood that no matter what the public knew or didn't know at this point about their president, they were no longer behind him. Baker could see that Wilson lived in an unreal world. So unreal in fact that Wilson would try to turn the next presidential election into a single issue referendum: the treaty. And he would attempt to put himself in the running for a third term. But the harder Wilson pushed for success, the faster he seemed to sink into a quicksand of failure.

In the aftermath of the vote, letters inundated the White House. Some stood by Wilson; some were alarmed by the thought that America might not ratify the treaty of peace; and some bemoaned the Senate's disloyalty to the president's League. But many criticized Wilson's stubborn stand against the Lodge reservations and just as many denigrated the treaty for its deviation from the Fourteen Points. "Your acts will one day be judged by an all-seeing eye," wrote a man from Sandusky, Ohio. "Do not plead for justice and deny it at the same time. Do not cry liberty and in its name defend despotism."

Among his most resentful critics were African-Americans. In a letter dated November 25, William Monroe Trotter, who had in August publicly spoken out against the League, urged the president to use his power to end lynching and segregation in America. Showing his bitter disappointment in the League Covenant, he told the president in his letter that the racial inequities in America were the greatest "violation" of Wilson's idealism and thus, "Your League of Nations Covenant, void of measures or of declarations against these undemocratic conditions . . . deserved its fate."

Cruelty and indignation abounded in the coming weeks as the battle continued. Wilson's opponents even sent back to the White House the official copy of the treaty with the League Covenant, the one that Wilson had brought with him from France the previous February. It was an ugly gesture that Baker characterized as "the cruelest, most despicable act ever committed in American politics." How was it possible that a man once so revered was now so scorned?

For Baker, the publication of his new book in combination with the Senate's rejection set off a reel of painful memories. He recalled moments with an eager, hopeful Wilson on the deck of the USS *George Washington* on the first voyage back from France the previous February. The purpose of the trip had been to unveil to Congress the first draft of the League Covenant. It was a stormy voyage and one day Baker was walking on the deck just as the president was about to climb the stairs to the ship's bridge. The wind was so strong that it blew open the president's coat where, as Baker saw for a swift second, the Covenant itself was stuffed neatly inside Wilson's breast pocket. "It was the most cherished thing in his life," Baker wrote.

Baker also remembered the extremely violent weather the night before landing at Boston on that February trip. On the morning of their return, Baker learned that the ship was late and that it had lost its course during the night. The first person Baker met on the deck that morning who knew what had happened was a young man who was well informed about the ways of ships and sailing, Assistant Secretary of the Navy Franklin Roosevelt. What had happened in the night? Baker asked. Roosevelt told him that he believed that the ship had come very close to the rocks of Gloucester, narrowly escaping disaster.

And now ten months later, Baker could not block from his mind the image of Wilson with the precious document tucked in his breast pocket on the ship that stormy night. What if the boat had crashed into the rocks and the president had died that night? It was an uncanny thought, he well knew, silly and unprofessional—one that historians would not respect. But still, he could not stop wondering if such a tragedy had occurred, what would have happened to the treaty and the League? If the president had been a martyr for his cause, instead of an insistent and petulant crusader, would things have been different? In his diary Baker wrote, "But [Wilson] did not go down with the ship. He lived to struggle, and suffer, and fail. Few great Americans, I think, ever suffered more."

Even Wilson pondered the same possibility. Baker could barely listen the day that the president's physician told him that Wilson, in the aftermath of the Senate's rejection had said, "It would probably have been better if I had died last fall."

Baker was witnessing the slow, agonizing deaths of both a vision and its visionary. Among his most haunting and persistent memories of Wilson would always be a line from the president's speech in Omaha in August during the national tour: "I can predict with absolute certainty that within another generation there will be another world war if the nations of the world do not concert the method by which to prevent it."

CHAPTER 40

All Aboard

"Mr. Green" and "Mr. Stone" lasted no more than twenty-four hours. Within a day of their arrival in New Orleans, Bureau of Investigation agents picked up the scent of Abrams and Lipman and uncovered their scheme to hide in a steamer bound for Mexico. The agents tailed them from the morning of November 16 to the evening of December 1 when, hiding in the forward hold of the SS *Mexico,* they were arrested, taken to the city's parish prison, and held without bail.

December was a frantic time for Harry Weinberger. With the Justice Department moving in on alien radicals, defense attorneys like Weinberger were juggling appointments with prosecutors, judges, immigration officials, defense fund contributors, politically connected advocates, clients in jail, clients on the lam, clients at Ellis Island, and relatives of clients in prison. For example, during the same days that Abrams and Lipman were jumping bail and hiding out in New Orleans, Weinberger was placating one of the big contributors to Abrams's $10,000 bail bond. The man, Frederick Blossom, of New Jersey, had borrowed $6,000 with the understanding that the defense fund committee would pay the interest on the loan up to $30 a month. Five months later, he was now owed $150 in interest, yet had not received a cent from the committee. On December 2, he wrote: "I hope you will be able to get a quick response from the committee as the firm I borrowed from is pushing me to pay up this accumulation."

The Abrams case seemed at times all-consuming. Weinberger never complained about Abrams and Lipman trying to escape, although if they had succeeded, the $20,000 in bail bonds—held by the government as a guarantee against their escape—would have been forfeited. Once Abrams and Lipman were apprehended, there was still the matter of the bail. Although it would not be automatically forfeited, it would be yet another issue before the courts. The prosecutor would ask for forfeiture and a judge would make the final decision. In addition to that, Weinberger was tangled up in government red tape for three weeks in an effort to get Lipman and

Abrams back to New York. Among other complications, A. Mitchell Palmer insisted that Weinberger not only pay their train fare from New Orleans but also the round-trip tickets for their guards—a tab of $550.

Since the Supreme Court had handed down its decision in the Abrams case, Weinberger was busier than ever. Because the decision upheld the 1918 convictions, deportation was no longer a possibility until the Abrams defendants, now convicts, had served their prison sentences—that is, unless the government granted them amnesty. And so he launched a lively crusade to obtain amnesty for each of the four Russian clients. Ironically, to start such a campaign now was easier for Weinberger than it had been before the Supreme Court decision because of Holmes and his dissenting opinion. For a Supreme Court justice to have written that the Abrams case defendants had as much right to distribute their leaflets as the Founding Fathers had to issue the Constitution was a boost to Weinberger's cause and won him many new recruits eager to find a way to release these young convicts from the severity of two decades in prison. Among such compatriots were Professor Zechariah Chafee, Jr., at Harvard Law School, and several of Chafee's Harvard colleagues.

Chafee, along with eleven other lawyers and law professors who called themselves the National Popular Government League, would use the case in the coming months as a rapier to rip apart the government's assaults on civil liberties. They would even publish their *Report upon the Illegal Practices of the United States Department of Justice.* And because of this and other actions, Chafee would earn his own private file in Hoover's collection, bearing the heading "Attorney for Radical Organizations."

Chafee was one of the first to sign Weinberger's petitions for amnesty for each of his four clients. The very first to sign was Roscoe Pound, the dean of Harvard Law School. Other signatories were: Felix Frankfurter, the Harvard Law professor who would one day be a Supreme Court justice; Edward B. Adams, Harvard's law librarian; and Francis B. Sayre, the son-in-law of Woodrow Wilson, and a law professor at Harvard.

The petition for Abrams read as follows:

> We, the undersigned, respectfully endorse for Executive Clemency of Jacob Abrams. Our approval is based upon the following grounds:
>   First: We believe that the expression of opinion on the Russian

question by Jacob Abrams, was the honest expression of a Russian citizen on Russian intervention.

Second: That there was no intent to help Germany in the war.

Third: That there was no intent to hurt or hinder the United States in the prosecution of the war.

Fourth: That Jacob Abrams, being willing to be deported to Soviet Russia, the United States could in no way be injured by an amnesty at this time.

A similar recommendation was made by the signers for Lachowsky and Lipman, and they were willing to recommend amnesty for Mollie Steimer but she refused to sign an application. Steimer disapproved of the amnesty campaign because she felt that it was "extremely selfish"—as she said in a letter to Weinberger—to ask for amnesty for herself and her three friends when there were many other political prisoners in the United States who were not getting amnesty and who didn't have so many supporters. "The more I read the petition, the more opposed I am to it," she wrote, in the same letter.

Her greatest concerns at the moment were the conditions at the workhouse, which had provoked a riot recently; her family, from whom she had heard nothing for two weeks; and news of the world, which was prohibited in the workhouse. On December 6, she wrote a disquieting letter to Weinberger laden with urgency and stress. On the morning after the riot, she and four others had been "taken to the cooler," an isolated dark cell where prisoners were served only bread and water. The others were released two days later but she was forced to remain for nearly another day. Now her cell was locked all the time and, she told Weinberger, "no prisoner is subject to such severe punishment as I am. I am watched every step and for every turn, there is a penalty. If a girl could come over near my gate she is threatened with increasing her time! Please Weinberger find out how my mother is and send word to me immediately. I am anxious to know when we are to go to the federal prison. . . . I am intirely cutt off from the outside world."

At the time of her letter, Abrams and Lipman were in the New Orleans prison, which Lipman described as "filthy" in a letter to Weinberger. Hyman Lachowsky had been released from custody after the November 7 raid and was preparing to surrender within the thirty allotted days after the Supreme Court decision was filed. And so it was that Lachowsky submitted his letter of surrender on December 16. The writing was stunning and the content memorable to all who were working for justice in the Abrams case—the Harvard law professors, the many contributors to the defense funds, the two dissenting justices. Its message was timeless, as many of its readers knew.

> The United States Supreme Court has sent its Mandate to this Court affirming my conviction, and although out on bail, I herewith surrender myself to commence the service of 20 years in the U.S. Penitentiary at Atlanta, Ga., for expressing an opinion in a leaflet against American military intervention in Russia.
>
> If Dreyfus at Devil's Island was a shining disgrace before all the world, to France; if Robert Emmett's death on behalf of Irish freedom has been one of the blots on English history; so my imprisonment for the next twenty years will be a shining disgrace to America. When my country, Soviet Russia, takes her equal place among the Nations of the world, recognized by all the Nations of the world, Russia will demand my freedom.
>
> As an alien and as an Anarchist, I am willing to be deported to Soviet Russia, and have so stated at Immigration hearings, but if America wants to support me in jail for 20 years; if America wants that blot on her history, I am willing to be that sacrifice in the hope that by it, the true liberty-loving heart of America will awaken from its deadly sleep caused by the Espionage Law under which I was convicted.
>
> Hyman Lachowsky

After Lachowsky surrendered, he was incarcerated at the Tombs in New York. Two days later, on the 18th, Weinberger's $550 arrived in New Orleans, allowing Lipman and Abrams to begin their train trip back to New York. Although Lipman knew that he was simply moving from one jail to another, he was eager to return to New York, having learned that his wife, fellow anarchist Ethel Bernstein, was among a large group of Russian immigrants scheduled for deportation sometime very soon. Weinberger too hoped that Lipman and Bernstein could be reunited if only for a few minutes before the departure of what would be known as the first "Soviet Ark." He felt strongly enough about it to write to Attorney General Palmer on their behalf. "[Bernstein] is 21 years of age and is almost crazy with the idea of having to leave America without seeing Lipman who is being brought from New Orleans to New York," Weinberger wrote in his letter dated December 18. "If the story of Evangeline ever moved you in your school days; if the separation of lovers, one to Soviet Russia, and one to the United States Penitentiary, can move you, I believe you ought immediately to order Samuel Lipman deported with Ethel Bernstein. Will you wire me collect, your decision in the matter, and oblige."

By the 18th, an ancient, titanic army transport had quietly docked at a pier in South Brooklyn. Built in Ireland in 1890, the SS *Buford* had served in the Spanish-American War and in the Great War. During 1919, despite its age, it was one of those ships moving back and forth across the Atlantic—making four round-trips—between the United States and France to bring home thousands of American soldiers. Now, in one of its last missions, and certainly its most unusual, it would be the ship assigned to America's first mass deportation of political dissidents. By the 20th, New York, as the *Times* noted, had "more dangerous Reds, awaiting deportation or in custody pending legal proceedings than ever have been assembled here." BI director Flynn told the press that these deportees were "the brains of the ultra-radical movement." Adding to the intrigue and sensation were statements officials gave to the *New York Herald* calling the upcoming deportation "the beginning of an extremely rigorous policy against radicals. Another shipload is going out, perhaps this week, and a drive to cut down the Department of Justice's list of 60,000 radicals in the nation already has been started."

The exact day and time of departure was still a secret, though it appeared to be sometime around the 20th. Whenever the *Buford* set sail, it would be carrying 249 aliens, of whom 184 were members of the Union of Russian Workers, fifty-one were anarchists, and fourteen others were violators of immigration laws of some sort but not anarchists. Some of the Union of Russian Workers members still did not understand what they had done to deserve deportation. The Russian People's House, headquarters to the Russian union, was their social club, a mutual aid society. They belonged for no other reason than to connect with other Russian immigrants and, as many had testified, they were unaware of the wording in the union's charter, such as its commitment to "a Socialistic revolution by force." Joseph Polulech, for example, who had been in America for seven years, was taking a math class at the People's House on the night of the November 7 raid. He was arrested without a warrant, detained without counsel for six weeks, and, despite his pastor's testimony about his good character, immigration officials deemed him a threat because his name was on the Union of Russian Workers' membership list.

The best known of the *Buford*'s passengers were the now notorious anarchists Alexander Berkman and Emma Goldman. There were three women: Goldman, Ethel Bernstein, and Dora Lipkin, another anarchist. Also on board were two hundred soldiers, each carrying a rifle and two pistols. Their job was to prevent a mutiny and guard the "Reds," who would be confined to their staterooms at all times except for meals. The destination was as much a secret as their time of departure. A sealed envelope awaited the captain, not to be opened until the ship had left New York. In it were instructions to sail to Hango, Finland, first, and then take trains into Soviet Russia.

The ship left at 4:15 on the morning of the 21st. Because of the extreme secrecy, few people gathered on the New York dock that very cold December morning. There were army officers, some members of the U.S. House of Representatives' Immigration and Naturalization Committee, and three of the producers of the show: Flynn, Caminetti, and Hoover.

For Hoover, it was a glorious day. He was the one who had arranged the loan of the *Buford* from the army. He was taking the credit for the deportations of the only famous passengers, Goldman and Berkman. And he was the unofficial host of the send-off "party." Just in case those who had gathered at the pier didn't know it, he pointed out Goldman, calling her the "Red Queen of Anarchy," as she walked up the plank to the ship's deck. Even better for Hoover, this event would be the first step toward his own fame, for it would be Hoover's first-ever mention in major U.S. newspapers. The day before the ship's departure, the Justice Department released to the *Washington Post* Hoover's brief in the deportation hearing against Emma Goldman. The *Post*, which gave Hoover the title of "special assistant to Attorney General Palmer," ran the story on the front page on December 21. And on the day of the departure, a *New York Tribune* reporter asked Hoover for his own account of the "Buford story." The paper gave him plenty of space. Among the many things Hoover wanted to tell America, he said, was that "The Department of Justice is not through yet, by any means. Other 'Soviet Arks' will sail for Europe, just as often as it is necessary to rid the country of dangerous radicals." Hoover would also be given a good deal of space in the *Congressional Record* regarding the Buford deportation. A congressman from Colorado who had shared the pier with Hoover that morning described him for the *Record* as "that slender bundle of high-charged electric wire."

And there he stood two hours before dawn, on the stark, cold South Brooklyn pier—the stage for his opening performance. But so secretive was the *Buford*'s departure that despite the bright spotlight of the full moon and the powerful lines of the leading man reiterated later in the press, there was no audience. No relatives or friends attended. Few shared the stage with Hoover, who may not have even noticed how alone he was as the old transport sluggishly pushed away from the dock, separating the husbands and fathers, brothers and sons, daughters and lovers from their homes and families. Perhaps a man who mates with power forgets the pain and joy of such bonds.

Lipman was unable to see Bernstein before her deportation. Palmer never conceded to Weinberger's plea. Lipman and Abrams arrived in New York on the 22nd. Devastated, Lipman immediately cabled the following message to Bernstein c/o "Captain U.S. Transport Buford, Atlantic Ocean."

> I am going to the United States Penitentiary at Atlanta for twenty years for my opinions on Russian intervention, and you are being deported to Russia for yours. Though time and distance separate us, my love goes out to you over the waves. The humanity and heart of the world may yet demand that we be reunited by my deportation to Soviet Russia, where you are going. Love to all the comrades on board from myself, Abrams and Lachowsky.
> Reply care Harry Weinberger, prepaid.
> Samuel Lipman.

Weinberger paid for the cable and would have paid for a dozen more, so moved was he by the fact that Lipman and Bernstein might never see each other again. "They never had an opportunity to say good-by," Weinberger wrote to Chafee, as if in disbelief, adding that he felt that the cable Lipman had sent would go down in history as "a great heart message." For a man like Weinberger, who typically never gave up a cause, it was a helpless feeling to have been unable to arrange the reunion. Except for the amnesty campaign, there was nothing at the moment that Weinberger could do for Lipman, Lachowsky, or Abrams, who would spend Christmas at the Tombs and then, on the very next day, be moved to the federal penitentiary in Atlanta.

Although undoubtedly drained by the past few weeks of legal work and emotional duress, Weinberger now turned his attention to the woman in Cell 98 at the workhouse on Blackwell's Island. In the rush of things, Weinberger had not been able to respond to Mollie Steimer's letter of December 6 until now. But as he told her, he certainly had not forgotten her. With the Lipman drama so fresh in his mind, he assured Steimer that she would have the opportunity to embrace her mother, Rose, and her brothers and sisters before she had to leave New York for the federal prison in Missouri—a move that would not happen until she had served what would be a miserable six-month sentence at the workhouse. He told her about the other defendants and the plans to move them to Atlanta; about the *Buford* and the small Corona typewriters that some families gave to the deportees; and about a fountain pen that Rose had left in Weinberger's office for Mollie. He would bring the pen to her soon, he said, knowing that he would soon visit the workhouse on Mollie's behalf to ease the tensions between Mollie and Blackwell's superintendent.

During the last weeks of the year, Weinberger moved ahead with his campaign for the amnesty of all four of the *Abrams* case clients, despite Mollie's disapproval of asking for amnesty while other political prisoners did not get the same attention that she and Abrams, Lachowsky, and Lipman did. Weinberger again wrote to Ray Stannard Baker, urging him yet again to persuade President Wilson to pardon them. He enclosed copies of Lachowsky's powerful surrender statement as well as his own recent letter to Palmer pleading for the deportation of Lipman along with his wife on the *Buford*. He also went to court on the issue of Lipman's and Abrams's bail bonds; the judge ruled in his favor, allowing all of the generous men and women—including Frederick Blossom—who had funded the young men's bail bonds to get back their money by the end of the year. And he began yet another crusade: raising money for the immigrant women and children left without husbands and fathers when the *Buford* steamed out of New York harbor. On Christmas Eve, he received one of the first checks toward the cause: $500 from Ludwig C. A. K. Martens, the self-styled "ambassador"

from Soviet Russia. "Stark poverty and sorrow has visited these families by
the uncalled for hysteria of immigration officials and the Department of
Justice," Weinberger told the *New York Times*.

On Christmas morning, several hundred members of the League for
Amnesty for Political Prisoners, including Weinberger, gathered on West
11th Street in New York's Greenwich Village to walk up Fifth Avenue during the hour when most congregations were emerging from church. To
advertise their cause, some participants wore the gray clothing of convicts and jangled manacles as they walked. Despite the sloppy, ankle-deep
slush on the streets of Manhattan from days of intermittent snow, their
plan was to walk all the way to St. Patrick's Cathedral at 50th and Fifth,
stopping at the doorways of churches along the way to sing carols while
waving placards that conveyed messages such as "Ten Political Prisoners
Have Died for Their Opinions" and "Eighteen Bishops Helped Free English Conscientious Objectors." Other signs called attention to the uncon-
stitutionality of the Espionage Act and urged Christians to lobby their
legislators for the freedom of those imprisoned for violating that law. But
the procession abruptly ended when somewhere between 22nd and 23rd
Streets policemen arrived to stop it. The group, which called its protest
a "walk," had not obtained a permit for a full-fledged demonstration and
thus its members were in violation of the city laws. The wearing of prison
"costumes," police said, was another violation. The police grabbed the
signs, tore them up, and then commenced to arrest several of the marchers.
Because so many police had been sent out on special assignments to guard
the homes of the wealthy from possible Red attacks that day and members
of the city's Bomb Squad were assigned to watch buildings where radical
meetings might convene, law enforcement in New York was stretched that
Christmas Day and many citizens volunteered to assist the police. As the
Washington Post wrote, the holidays in New York that year were "a reminder
that even the spirit of Christmas has no influence on stopping the spirit
of anarchy."

CHAPTER 41

Boughs of Glory

On Christmas Day, despite the disappointments of the year that had just transpired, despite the collective anxiety that characterized the nation, despite the shattered dreams of peace that only a year before had appeared to be the blueprints for building a new world, despite the fears, despite the uncertainty, America nonetheless seemed to glitter with that irresistible tinsel magic that, if only for a day, could make the real world disappear.

The biggest gift of the season came from oil magnate John D. Rockefeller, who gave his nation $100 million: the largest single charitable donation thus far in U.S. history. Half of it would go to raise the salaries of college professors and half to combat disease through the improvement of medical education, public health administrations, and scientific research.

By Christmas Day the U.S. post office had far exceeded previous records for the number of packages mailed during the holiday season. And retailers were reporting unprecedented levels of holiday sales, especially in the nation's biggest cities, which were feeling the impact of the burgeoning class of the new-rich. By Christmas there were at least three thousand new millionaires in America, most of whom had hit the jackpot because of the war.

The "nation's new high-rollers are drunk with money this Christmas" and "flinging it around like rice at a wedding," wrote a Los Angeles columnist. Holiday prices were soaring—even higher than their already inflated pre-holiday levels. Because of such big spenders, in New York, a little silk purse could cost as much as $1,500, and $35,000 for a fur coat was not uncommon. "You have to go back to the days of Rome to find the equal of the debauch of money-letting to be found in the shops on Fifth Avenue this season," the columnist wrote.

The hottest gift of the season was a rectangular piece of wood measuring eighteen inches by twenty-four inches on which all the letters of the alphabet were painted in two rows—A through M and N through Z—positioned on top of another row with numbers 1 through 9 plus a zero.

Beneath the numbers was the word "Good bye" and in the upper left and right corners, respectively, were a brightly painted sunburst with the word "YES" next to it and a moon next to "NO." This board was usually sold with a small, pear-shaped piece of wood with three one-inch-high legs called a "planchette." The wooden board was sometimes called a "Talking Board" or "Spirit Board." One very successful manufacturer named it the Ouija Board. Two people sitting on opposite sides of the board would touch the planchette ever so lightly with their fingertips as spirits from "the other side" guided them to spell out messages. So possessed was the nation with death and grieving that nearly three million of these devices, or toys, as some claimed them to be, had sold by the beginning of the holiday season.

Books about the "other side" were equally popular—such as *Contact with the Other World: The Latest Evidence as to Communication with the Dead* by James H. Hyslop, Ph.D., LL.D.; *Spiritism and Religion: Can You Talk to the Dead? Including a Study of the Most Remarkable Cases of Spirit Control,* by Baron John Liljenerants; and the runaway best-seller *The Seven Purposes: An Experience in Psychic Phenomena* by Margaret Cameron, whose planchette was directed by "Frederick," a soldier in the Great War who had died in France and who "spoke" often about the war. Cameron told her readers of Frederick's warnings about a still greater conflict to come "when the evil forces that moved Germany must be fought with even more widely." His advice, she wrote, was: "Come, all ye who struggle and strive! Perceive once and forever the purpose of life. Join now the forces of construction, and bring to all men brotherhood. Forget the class and remember the man."

"The whole world is in a fury of mysticism," one reporter wrote, of the national pastime of trying to communicate with the dead. The "spook board," as some retailers called it, and the "other side" books were so popular that organized religion mobilized to try to stop the fad, especially during the holidays. In December the Catholic Church announced that "to attend any séances" or "to dabble in spiritualism" was unlawful under the decrees of the Church. "Even if all claims of the spiritualists were true, which they are not, no Christian is permitted, according to God's word in the Bible, to seek knowledge from the dead," said one New York priest. And thus, all Christians, Roman Catholic or not, were advised to rid their homes and purge their gift lists of the wicked Ouija.

For many Americans that year, despite Attorney General Palmer's crackdown on price fixers, the cost of everyday necessities was still so high that Christmas shopping was a luxury, if not an impossibility. "Nation's Newly-Rich Make Christmas an Orgy, as Cruel Prices Exclude the Poor" read a *Los Angeles Times* headline. No advice from the "other side" was focusing on the issue of poverty.

Indeed, Christmas 1919 was a cruel time for a large number of Americans. There were disabled soldiers unable to find work. There were perfectly fit soldiers who still needed jobs. There were workers on strike for better wages. The steel strike had just entered its eighth week on Christmas Day. And there were immigrants and African-Americans still living under the vicious tyranny of prejudice. Although no lynchings were reported for December 25, lynching No. 83 of the year occurred on the day before Christmas near Columbus, Georgia. And No. 84, the last one of the year—the hanging of a black soldier dressed in full uniform for the holidays—took place in North Carolina on the day after Christmas.

President Wilson spent Christmas Day in his sickroom at the White House where he and Mrs. Wilson exchanged gifts and had their holiday dinner. For the day, the medical restrictions on his diet were lifted. Secretary of State Lansing delivered the administration's holiday statement to the press:

> We have entered upon a new era of peace and of higher standards of international and national life. It is not a new era but the old era, which was ushered in by the birth of Jesus, perfected by his teachings and consecrated by his death, the old era, to which we return after a time of madness, of agony and of evil. Clothed in the ancient peace proclaimed over nineteen centuries ago on the hills of Bethlehem, the world, with conscience awakened by the fiery ordeal through which it has passed should find renewed hope that Christian principles will triumph and become the dominant force in the affairs of all men and all nations.

J. Edgar Hoover did not spend his holiday preparing for such a new era "of peace and of higher standards" or communicating with the dead. He worked every day that season on one project or another, including the first of many scrapbooks into which he would paste memorabilia such as the clips from his recent debut in the American press. With his twenty-fifth

birthday coming up on January 1, this was a time to look back on his accomplishments and to begin to chronicle them. Other tasks, though, were
more pressing. In December he had asked Robert Bowen at the Bureau of
Translations for a register of all wealthy people contributing to "the radical
movement." This was in response to Bowen's own firm belief—conveyed
to Hoover—that wealthy women in New York were financing radical publications. He was also in the process of acquiring a list compiled by New
York agent Mortimer J. Davis of prominent men and women nationwide
who were sponsoring radical organizations. Included on Davis's list were
Jane Addams, the social reformer, who had already made Archibald
Stevenson's earlier list of suspicious Americans and who would one day
win the Nobel Peace Prize; the highly respected University of Chicago professor of economics Thorstein Veblen; Hollywood's Charlie Chaplin; and
Eugene Debs's brilliant attorney, Clarence Darrow. Now Hoover was determined to put together his own list of wealthy radicals, those Americans
he was in the habit of calling "parlor Bolsheviks." A more urgent mission
for Hoover that Christmas, however, was a secret project that he shared
with his colleagues A. Mitchell Palmer and William Flynn—one that
would be unveiled on January 2.

For the U.S. attorney general, the Christmas rush that year wasn't about
gift giving but rather the frenzy of last-minute details for the big January 2
surprise: a series of raids unprecedented in scope and terror aimed at thousands upon thousands of alien radicals. It was his pledge to America to sustain an unflinching warfare against radicalism in America until every one
of the "criminals, mistaken idealists, and social bigots," as Palmer characterized them, were gone. And what was a better weapon than a massive
sweep of alien radicals followed by a flotilla of "Soviet Arks" just like the SS
Buford. In addition to cleansing America of its unsavory radical elements,
the raids were useful tactics for scaring radicals of all sorts—both aliens and
citizens—and for heightening the general public's awareness of the epidemic threat of the Red Menace. They also strengthened Palmer's lobby in
Congress for a new peacetime Sedition Act. Now, after the three big labor
strikes of the autumn, the successful small government raids of November,
the bloody Centralia tragedy, the consistent, incendiary headlines since
the Seattle general strike, and the loud publicity following the *Buford* deportations, the timing for the Justice Department's biggest of all offensives
in the war on radicals seemed perfect. The focus was the membership of

the Communist Party of America and the Communist Labor Party. In preparation, two days after Christmas, three thousand warrants were issued against members of either party.

On New Year's Eve, Palmer delivered a New Year's message to the nation vowing to prevent the "Red movement" from disturbing "our peace" in America. He would accomplish this great feat by "keeping up an aggressive, persistent warfare" against every Bolshevik and every Bolshevik sympathizer in America to preserve the gift of freedom. He called upon all newspapers, churches, schools, patriotic organizations, and labor unions to assist him by teaching the devious ways of the Red movement. Making his case, he said:

> Twenty million people in this country own Liberty bonds. These the Reds propose to take away. Nine million eight hundred and thirty thousand people in the U.S. own farms and 3.8 million more own homes, which they would forfeit. Eleven million people have savings accounts in savings banks and 18.6 million people have deposits in our national banks at which they aim. There are hundreds of thousands of churches and religious institutions all of which they would abolish. In other words, 110 million hardworking and saving Americans who own property, love liberty and worship God are asked to abandon all the ideals of religion, liberty and government which are the outcome of the struggles of their fathers and their own development and to place themselves, their homes, their families and their religious faith in the keeping and their property under the domination of a small group of Lenins and Trotskys. The [Red] movement will not be permitted to go far enough in this country to disturb our peace and well-being or create any widespread distrust of the people's Government. It will fall away before the light of popular knowledge and appreciation of its aims and purposes.

And so it was that America's new self-anointed prince of peace proceeded. On January 2, in thirty-three cities, in twenty-three states, in clubhouses, poolhalls, restaurants, bowling alleys, and even bedrooms, as many as six thousand aliens, suspected to be dangerous radicals, were swept into Palmer's net of security, in the name of peace. So huge were the raids that

the bureau's mere 579 agents could not handle the load and thus local police were called upon to assist, as were the ever-ready members of the
American Protective League. The exact number of arrests would never be
known.

Whatever the numbers, Palmer's raiders herded them into detention
centers, separating families, sometimes inflicting severe injuries, and holding them for days without access to counsel. A large percentage of the men
and women taken that day had nothing to do with Bolshevism, such as the
thirty-nine bakers in Lynn, Massachusetts, who had been meeting to organize a cooperative bakery in their town, and the woman arrested in her
bedroom in Boston who was an American citizen and had never expressed
the slightest interest in Bolshevism. Or the man in Newark, New Jersey,
who was arrested after asking what was happening and the one, also in
New Jersey, who simply "looked like a radical." Whether they were Bolsheviks or Bolshevik sympathizers, the treatment of the eight hundred men
and women apprehended in Detroit, a group consisting mostly of "ignorant
foreigners," was unconscionable. Kept in a windowless corridor for up to
five days, they slept on the bare floor, had nothing to eat for the first
twenty-four hours, and had access to only one toilet. And what about the
one, two, or possibly three thousand men and women arrested without
warrants?

Headlines shouting "All Aboard for the Next Soviet Ark" highlighted
articles hailing Palmer as America's new savior. The urgency of the moment pushed such things as constitutional rights deeply underground.
"There is no time to waste on hairsplitting over infringement of liberty,"
wrote the *Washington Post*. And from his now lauded position high above
America, Palmer promised exactly 2,720 deportations on a series of "Soviet Arks" in the coming year. It was what he had told the *New York Times*
in the days after the *Buford:* "a drive to cut down the Department of
Justice's list of 60,000 radicals in the nation."

Amid all the excitement that day, who would have guessed that out of
the thousands of people dragged from their homes, punched in the head or
face with fists or clubs, and held in illegal limbo for days, even weeks, the
government would be able to deport only 556 aliens, mostly for immigration violations that had nothing to do with Bolshevism or anarchism?

But then who would have thought that a year that had begun with the hope of peace coming on the wings of Woodrow Wilson's heavenly words would end with such an oppressive thud—a crash landing in a fog of hysteria and hate, blocking out that brilliant sun that W. E. B. Du Bois and so many others had beheld during those first wondrous moments after the signing of the Armistice.

More remarkable perhaps was the fact that a year that laid the groundwork for so many aspects of modern America—from the struggles for free speech and black equality to the establishment of a system of domestic intelligence—would quickly fall out of memory, tucked away between the "Great War" and the "Roaring Twenties," stuffed in historical files labeled "Woodrow Wilson" and the "Treaty of Versailles" with cross-references to "A. Mitchell Palmer" and "Bolshevism." Perhaps, like the president himself, the year was too complex to be understood in its own time. Its lessons and struggles were too intense to absorb for anyone living in the aftermath of both a war and a plague that had killed millions of people. Perhaps America was a nation in denial over what it had just endured. And thus, for many years, it dared not look back.

In late December, Sir John Alcock, the celebrated pilot of the first nonstop transatlantic flight the previous June, was flying alone from England to France in a Vickers hydroplane to attend an aviation exhibition in Paris. He planned to land on the Seine River, but very close to his destination he hit a heavy fog and, unable to sight the earth, flew too low. A wing of the plane smashed into the ground. The plane flipped over, pinning its pilot under the wreckage. Alcock died, at age twenty-six, in Rouen a few days before Christmas, having never regained consciousness. On Christmas Day, the front page of the London *Times* displayed a message from the Aero Club of America: "Please convey to Sir John Alcock's family our deepest condolences and express on behalf of the American aeronautical world our realization of the great and irreparable loss we have sustained."

From 1919, America would remember a few heroes and legends. But most of its true heroes that year would fade away, consumed, like Alcock and his own fame, in a fiery crash of time and lost dreams. Bold believers in "real democracy," champions of free speech, lovers of liberty, their early steps would lead to a place most of their contemporaries could not envision. Indeed, generations of Americans would be affected by the battles and passions of 1919. But in the midst of such tumult, few could grasp its significance. For America in 1919 was a nation immersed in struggle, a nation laboring to give birth to a better world in which the only true enemies would be prejudice, oppression, and fear. It was, as Carl Sandburg had so astutely understood it to be, a stormy, frightening time on the path hopefully to a more progressive future: "I have no criticism of all the waste and afterbirth gore that go with a child born."

EPILOGUE

Endings and Beginnings

Democracy is the manner of life of men who understand and love one another. We shall achieve democracy exactly in proportion to an understanding of our neighbors and our love for them. Democracy is now weak in America for we want of these qualities.

—RAY STANNARD BAKER, October 1919

On Election Day 1920, Woodrow Wilson tightly gripped his cane and tried repeatedly to climb the three small steps that Dr. Grayson had built for him for physical therapy at the White House. Wilson was not on the Democratic ticket that day. Nor was Attorney General A. Mitchell Palmer. The Democratic Party's choice for president was Ohio governor James M. Cox, who had what was considered an advantage that year: no close ties to the Wilson administration. For vice president, the Democrats chose the thirty-seven-year-old assistant secretary of the navy, Franklin D. Roosevelt, a fifth cousin of the recently deceased President Theodore Roosevelt.

California senator Hiram Johnson, Washington senator Miles Poindexter, Wisconsin senator Robert LaFollette, Columbia University president Nicholas Murray Butler, Illinois governor Frank Lowden, U.S. food administrator Herbert Hoover, General Leonard Wood, and Ohio senator Warren G. Harding competed for the Republican nomination. Governor Lowden, who had gained national fame during the 1919 Chicago race riots, and General Wood, who had won acclaim for administering martial law in the riot-stricken towns of Longview, Texas, and Omaha, Nebraska, were deadlocked in the race until the Ohio senator moved ahead and won the nomination. The Republicans' choice for vice president was Massachusetts governor Calvin Coolidge. Their platform focused on damning the League of Nations, lowering taxes, and tightening immigration laws. They pledged to bring a nation tired of idealism and instability back to "normalcy." Al Jolson sang for the campaign: "We need another Lincoln to do the nation's thinkin'."

The Socialist Party's candidate was Eugene Debs, who ran his presidential campaign from his prison cell at the Atlanta federal penitentiary. His platform included improved labor conditions and welfare legislation. Debs won 919,799 votes.

The winning ticket of Harding and Coolidge achieved 61 percent of the popular vote compared to the Democrats' 34 percent; and 404 electoral votes compared with the Democrats' 127.

Nearly 27 million Americans voted in the 1920 election, including women. The U.S. House of Representatives had passed the Susan B. Anthony Amendment in May of 1919 with a count of 304 legislators for and eighty-nine against; two weeks later so did the Senate, with a vote of thirty-six Republicans and twenty Democrats for it; and eight Republicans and seventeen Democrats against it. The senate victory came after four hours of debate during which senators fearful of such a change made every argument against the radical notion of women voting. Fear of the unknown, as one reporter described it, had been the greatest obstacle in the long, arduous journey to achieve women's suffrage. That June, acknowledging the struggle that precedes progress, Alice Paul told the press, "Freedom has come not as a gift but as a triumph." To reach their goal of voting in the 1920 presidential election, however, the suffragists had to persuade thirty-six states to ratify the amendment and so during the summer of 1919, members of the National Woman's Party, of which Paul was president, and the National American Woman Suffrage Association, whose president was Carrie Chapman Catt, hit the road in a nationwide campaign. In the summer of 1920, Tennessee became the thirty-sixth state, thus making it possible for women to vote in the 1920 presidential race.

At the Democratic National Convention in San Francisco in the summer of 1920, Attorney General Palmer had tried to win the nomination, standing firmly on the platform of an ongoing crusade "to tear out the radical seeds that have entangled American ideas in their poisonous theories." But by the summer of 1920, the American public was beginning to lose interest in Palmer's zealous hunt for the Red Menace and to shed its fears of an impending overthrow of the U.S. government. Fear mongering wasn't as easy as it had been in the stormy, threatening months of 1919. The number of labor strikes, for example, was diminishing considerably. In August 1919 there had been 373, and by December there were only forty-five. In early January of 1920, the steel strike, which at its peak included 350,000 workers nationwide, ended without gaining concessions and after losing $112 million in wages—and twenty lives. In 1920 it was clear that labor's leadership—the AFL, Samuel Gompers, John L. Lewis—would do their own Red hunting to purge their memberships of the radical element that had been so damaging to labor's image. Although anti-alien sentiments were still strong among most Americans, the specter of Bolshevism was not interrupting the average American's dreams. In fact, it didn't seem all that menacing, especially compared to the economic and emotional challenges of postwar and post-flu America. Getting a job, buying a car, and bringing a new generation into the world to clear the air of the miasma of death were the major concerns.

In February of 1920 the Justice Department did conduct another raid, which Hoover organized and in which twenty-nine members of an Italian anarchist group were detained in Paterson, New Jersey. But by the spring of 1920, there would be no more raids. Nor would there be any more mass deportations. The public was slipping from Palmer's anxious grasp and the Justice Department was facing criticism for its tactics in the January raids. In May of 1920, Zechariah Chafee, Felix Frankfurter, and ten other prominent lawyers and law professors, under the auspices of a group they called the National Popular Government League, published *To the American People. Report Upon the Illegal Practices of the United States Department of Justice,* which accused the bureau of conducting hundreds of arrests, searches, and seizures without warrants, thus violating the detainees' constitutional rights. Worse still, the government had imprisoned many of the aliens on exorbitant bails, the article said, and the Justice Department had denied them legal representation. Some detainees were even mistreated, possibly tortured, the article claimed. The work of Chafee's league and the widely publicized article provoked two congressional hearings—one in 1920 and the other in 1921—focusing on the accusations that the Justice Department's methods had been overzealous and potentially illegal.

After such attacks, Palmer made a few alterations in his story. The raids, he claimed, were his dutiful response to pressure from the Senate and a product of his loyalty to the American public. He had quickly answered the call of a hysterical populace. This hypocrisy damaged his image. Even more damning, however, was the second big revolution fizzle. That spring Palmer and his associates warned America that history might repeat itself on May Day 1920. In fact the demonstrations might be worse than those on May 1, 1919. This indeed might be the inception of the long-anticipated revolution. But there was no violence in America on May 1, 1920.

Palmer's credibility plummeted with the slashing speed of a guillotine's blade. By the time he stepped down from his post as the nation's fiftieth attorney general, on March 5, 1921, his political career was effectively over. During the next fifteen years he remained active in the Democratic Party but only in the capacity of helping with various campaigns such as Al Smith's presidential campaign in 1928 and Franklin Roosevelt's in 1932. In 1936, a week after his sixty-fourth birthday, Palmer died of complications after surgery to remove his appendix.

The Justice Department continued to investigate the bombing of Palmer's house throughout 1920. After the February raids in Paterson, Hoover himself went to Ellis Island to interrogate the leader of an Italian anarchist group in search of information about the June 2, 1919, bombing and the leaflets found at the sites. The man denied that his group, L'Era Nuova, had anything to do with the 1919 incidents. It was the Galleanists who had done it, he said. He also gave Hoover the name of an anarchist printer in Brooklyn who might have printed the flyers. Hoover sent agents to the shop who found the exact type used for the flyers found in front of Palmer's house and at other bomb targets. Two printers who were Galleanists were arrested and questioned on the fourteenth floor of the bureau's New York offices. One of them, Andrea Salsedo, confessed on May 2 to having printed the flyers and then jumped out the window— an apparent suicide, the government said, though his widow sued the government for wrongful death. Newspapers in New York and Boston ran stories saying that Salsedo had fingered the Galleanists for the June 1919 bombings. Although it was never absolutely confirmed, the government files reveal that there was some certainty that the man who blew himself up on Palmer's steps was Carlo Valdinocci, a Galleanist who was close to two members of the same anarchist group, Nicola Sacco and Bartolomeo Vanzetti.

"Anarchist chaser" William J. Flynn, the man Palmer praised as the nation's "greatest anarchist expert," resigned from his post as director of the Bureau of Investigation in September of 1921. Flynn was the first person to hold that title. He was succeeded by William J. Burns. Three years later, in 1924, J. Edgar Hoover took over the job, remaining in the post through the administrations of eight U.S. presidents, until the very day he died on May 2, 1972.

Under Hoover, the Bureau of Investigation became the Federal Bureau of Investigation in 1935. It gained the authority to carry guns and make arrests. And it carried on the tradition of a "shadow war" begun in 1917 to fight the German enemy within U.S. borders. By the 1920s, Hoover's bureau had consumed most of the domestic intelligence files, networks, and methods established in the Army's Military Intelligence Division by Ralph Van Deman and carried on briefly by Marlborough Churchill. The MID had ostensibly returned to its mission of investigating military personnel only, although some branches remained connected to their contacts in the

American Protective League. Except for spying on Marcus Garvey, the Negro Subversion division of the MID filed few reports from the early 1920s to the mid-1930s. In the late 1930s, however, it resumed its mission as it probed black unrest, A. Philip Randolph and the 1941 march on Washington, as well as the activities of the Communist Party of America in black communities.

The American Protective League survived all the official announcements of its termination in 1919 as well as Attorney General Palmer's unwillingness to reinstate officially its battalions of devoted agents for his war on radicals. Using names such as the Patriotic American League in Chicago and the Loyalty League in Cleveland, vestiges of the APL lived on. And considering the many APL reports informing the MID and the Justice Department in 1918 and 1919 about revolution brewing in America and about dangerous citizens lurking in the nation's immigrant communities, the idea that the nation needed to protect itself from its own civilians, in peacetime as well as war, became an established tenet. It was here to stay— as familiar and traditional as the flag itself. Thus, whether or not the APL ever again was given official recognition and authority, its eager volunteers were used periodically not only by state and city agencies to gather information about suspicious individuals and groups but also by a Justice Department that for many years did not have enough staff to conduct the numerous investigations it deemed necessary to maintain internal security. Even Palmer unofficially secured its aid for the early January 1920 raids. And between 1920 and 1924, the Ku Klux Klan added strength to its resurgence by recruiting members from the Southern branches of the APL and adopting techniques such as tapping phones and planting spies at meetings and in post offices.

In 1924, Hoover announced that he would not allow civilian volunteers to be part of domestic surveillance, a position he maintained even at the outbreak of World War II and officially throughout the rest of his career. Still, in the 1940s Hoover called upon the American public to spy on and send the government reports on "neighborhood subversives." This inspired a resurgence of "private intelligence units" that continued to operate in most American cities long after the end of the Second World War, through the second Red Scare of the 1950s, and into the 1960s, at least. Although Hoover never would give volunteer spies the official authority they so desired and although organizations such as the APL never again assumed the level of power they achieved during 1918 and 1919, the web had already been constructed. And like an old map stuffed in a drawer, it could be retrieved, dusted off, and used again by leaders uninformed about its precipitous past and disrespectful of the difference between democratic dissent and dangerous disloyalty. As the APL's official historian Emerson Hough wrote in *The Web*: "The A.P.L. had folded its unseen and unknown tents. It will bivouac elsewhere until another day of need may come."

                 ❖❖

Mollie Steimer, Jacob Abrams, Samuel Lipman, and Hyman Lachowsky spent 1920 in federal penitentiaries waiting for favorable news from their attorney, who fervently pressed forward with his campaign for their amnesty. Enlisting the aid of every contact he had ever known in government and every contact's contact, Harry Weinberger doggedly pursued the attorney general, the president, the president's secretary, and the U.S. pardon attorney, urging them all to see the case from his point of view. Why keep his young clients in prison for twenty years? Why not send them back to Russia? How could deporting them threaten or injure the nation? Even the law that they violated was soon to be repealed.

On his side were leftists and socialists as well as mainstream figures such as George Creel, the former head of Wilson's Committee on Public Information, and Ray Stannard Baker. "I shall be very glad indeed to sign the recommendations for amnesty. I sympathize with Justice Holmes' decision and believe these men [and woman] should be pardoned and allowed to return to Russia," wrote Baker in a March 23, 1920, letter. Weinberger again called upon Baker in September that year to put pressure on Palmer and yet again in February of 1921 to urge the president to pardon his clients before leaving the White House.

On February 8, 1921, although Wilson still refused to pardon them, he did authorize the commutation of their sentences to two and a half years. This meant that Steimer would be in prison for twenty-one more months and the others, who had started their terms earlier, for sixteen more months. Weinberger was told that the Wilson administration and specifically Palmer "would do nothing further in the matter." Still he pressed harder.

On March 1, Weinberger wrote to Baker asking if he would personally talk to Wilson about the matter in the last days of Wilson's presidency. "If [Wilson] leaves office without letting these four Russians go, he will come under the quotation from Emerson 'Your actions speak so loud, I can't hear the fine words you say,' " Weinberger wrote. "I hope you can put the pressure in the next day to save the situation."

But Wilson never moved on it. "I have all along believed that these poor people should be set free and allowed to return to Russia," wrote Baker to Weinberger on March 3. "I have said so where I thought it would help. I think the only thing now to do is to take it up with the new administration."

In March, Congress repealed the law that the Justice Department had used to prosecute Abrams, Steimer, Lipman, Lachowsky, and Schwartz as well as Eugene Debs and numerous others since its passage in May of 1918. This was the Sedition Act, which had extended the reach of the Espionage Act to include "disloyalty" in speech and writings. The Espionage Act would never be repealed and as of 2006, it was still on the books. Although Weinberger considered the Sedition Act to be unconstitutional and its repeal must have been good news for him as well as for the numerous lawyers who agreed with him, the *Abrams* case clients were not at all affected. And the new administration did not appear to be any more lenient toward political prisoners.

Disheartened and wearied by a series of disappointments, Weinberger was unable that spring to write his usual optimistic notes to his four young incarcerated clients. Still, he was unstoppable. By late spring and into the summer of 1921, he had managed to persuade everyone from President Warren Harding to J. Edgar Hoover that something must be done about Steimer, Abrams, Lipman, and Lachowsky. At one point President Harding actually agreed to pardon them but the pardon attorney, James A. Finch, protested. That October, Weinberger agreed to a deal that if he made all the arrangements for the four Russians to return to Russia and conducted all the negotiations with the Russian government to accept them, and if the government did not have to pay for their voyage, then their sentences would be commuted immediately after such plans were finalized.

Making the necessary contacts in Russia would not be easy. However, a surprising coincidence lessened Weinberger's task: Ethel Bernstein, Lipman's wife, worked at the Foreign Office in Moscow and knew how and with whom Weinberger needed to connect. Within a month, the Russian government cabled Weinberger with the information that the four young Russians would be admitted back into Russia if indeed the United States released them from jail. Weinberger then focused on raising funds for their passage, telling the funders that because of what they had endured he wanted to book them in second class instead of third. He also tried to arrange reunions between his clients and their family members before the deportation. He could not persuade the government, however, to allow Abrams and Lachowsky to leave Ellis Island with security escorts for a few hours to visit Abrams's sister and Lachowsky's mother, who were both too ill to attend the deportation farewell.

On November 23, the four young Russians boarded the SS *Estonia* bound for Latvia. At least sixty friends and family members gathered on the dock to send them off, including Mollie Steimer's mother and La-chowsky's bedridden mother, who was carried on a cot to see her son one more time. In saying goodbye to Weinberger, both Lipman and Abrams handed him notes of appreciation for all he had done for them. Lipman thanked him for his "laborious and continuous work" on their behalf and he wrote that he wished "for the day when you will be proud of your native country—but until then—do not give up."

In December, President Harding pardoned Eugene Debs, then sixty-six years old. On Christmas Day 1921, Debs was at home in Indiana where he would spend the last five years of his life writing articles, giving speeches, and trying to recover from the physical strain of his imprisonment. "Is it not strange that in this land of fabulous plenty there is still so much poverty, so many million of our people whose life consists of a long, hard, fierce struggle all the way from youth to age and at last death comes to the rescue and stills the aching heart and lulls that victim to dreamless sleep?" he asked an audience in Chicago in 1925. Debs died the following year. His home in Terre Haute was later designated a National Historic Landmark.

Mollie Steimer and her comrades were also back "home" in Russia by Christmas Day 1921, having arrived in Moscow on December 15. Steimer stayed in Russia until September of 1923 when she and her male compan-ion, Senya Fleshin, were expelled from Russia for providing food, clothing, and books for incarcerated anarchists and protesting the harsh conditions at the prisons and concentration camps. They continued their relief work for anarchists in Berlin and in Paris, living in one city or the other, depending on political circumstances, until December of 1941, when they moved to Mexico. There, Steimer was reunited with Abrams and his wife, who had lived in Mexico since 1926, when they edited a Yiddish newspaper in Mexico City. Steimer and Fleshin, a photographer, eventually ran a photographic studio called SEMO—for Senya and Mollie—in Cuernavaca, where they spent the rest of their lives together. The iron-willed, tenderhearted girl Emma Goldman once described as "fearfully set in her ways . . . a sort of Alexander Berkman in skirts" died in 1980 at age eighty-two in Cuernavaca. By then her fellow defendants in the Abrams case had all passed away.

Their exceptionally devoted and "liberty-loving" attorney, Harry Weinberger, continued to champion the cause of civil liberties, and then in the 1920s, expanded his practice to copyright law. He had a special interest in screenplays and the theater and represented playwrights, including Eugene O'Neill. Weinberger was one of the organizers of and the lawyer for the Provincetown Players, whose roster of writers and actors included O'Neill, Edna St. Vincent Millay, Djuna Barnes, and Paul Robeson. When O'Neill was sued for plagiarism for his play *Strange Interlude*, Weinberger represented him, won the $2.5 million case, and became well known for his phrase: "A sure sign of greatness, with success, in literature is that someone sues for plagiarism."

In 1941, he began writing his autobiography, which he called *The Fight*. But on Sunday, December 7th, that year, he put down his manuscript. So stunned was he by the injustice of the attack on Pearl Harbor that he not only suspended his writing but he also changed his stand on the issue of war. Until then Weinberger had been a pacifist who opposed conscription as well as an isolationist who contested the League of Nations. By 1942, he strongly agreed with U.S. entry into the Second World War.

Although he never completed his autobiography, Weinberger wrote an article that he called "A Rebel's Interrupted Autobiography: A Personal Document on the Impact of War on One Who Has Made a Lifelong Fight Against It." In it, he praised the courage of immigrants coming to America "with bare hands and stout hearts," giving the best of their sons and daughters, enriching American soil with their blood, making America the powerful nation it became. "It is the little men and women who carry on the ordinary work of civilization and who love and transmit to their children the songs, the stories and the poetry of democracy and liberty and who supply the backbone and support of democracy everywhere," Weinberger wrote. He talked about literature, about the law, about Henry George and other influences in his life. He talked of his cases and the causes at their core. He talked of war. And he talked of oppression. "My autobiography, interrupted by the bursting of bombs and the marching of invaders' hosts, can wait while I live the life of a rebel against oppression to the full," his last line read.

On the morning of March 6, 1944, Weinberger, at age fifty-eight, died of a heart attack at his Greenwich Village apartment. Headlines hailed him as a "copyright expert." And although the obituaries culled many details from his life, none revealed his extraordinary devotion to his clients, his depth of character, or his exceptional dignity. And none were so beautifully written as Jacob Abrams's farewell note to Weinberger in 1921:

"I know you to be a man first and the lawyer after. I also believe that you are a liberty loving man for you could not carry on your legal work in defending those that fight for it if it would be a matter of dollars and cents only. [I] hope that in the near future we will not need lawyers to defend the human rights."

☙❧

Lynching had existed in America since colonial times, but in the 1880s and 1890s white supremacists used it more than ever before and perhaps more sadistically than in the past to oppress and control African-Americans, especially in the South. Between 1889 and 1922 at least 3,500 men and women, mostly black, were lynched in America. Ninety-nine percent of the perpetrators were never punished. Ida B. Wells-Barnett headed up the first bold national crusade to stop it. The NAACP was organized in 1909 to bolster the cause. The 1919 Anti-Lynching Conference, with the help of W. E. B. Du Bois, James Weldon Johnson, and others, shone a national spotlight on the barbarity of the crime. And on January 26, 1922, the U.S. House of Representatives passed the first bill to make lynching a federal crime with a vote of 230–119. But lynching never became a federal crime.

Sixteen anti-lynching bills presented to the Senate between 1901 and 1920 never emerged from committee. In fact, the nearly two hundred anti-lynching bills introduced into Congress during the first half of the twentieth century all failed. Then, on February 7, 2005, the U.S. Senate issued a resolution apologizing to the victims of lynching and the descendants of the victims for its failure to enact anti-lynching legislation and for depriving the victims of "life, human dignity, and the constitutional protections accorded all citizens of the U.S." The resolution called attention to the history of lynching "to ensure that these tragedies will be neither forgotten nor repeated." On June 13, 2005, the Senate, perhaps blushed with shame, adopted the resolution.

In another belated recognition, Sergeant Henry Lincoln Johnson received a posthumous Purple Heart in 1997 from President Bill Clinton. Despite Johnson's heroism during the Great War and France's recognition of his bravery, he had never received a military award from his own country. In 1998, the New York National Guard filed an application for Johnson to receive the highest U.S. military award, the Congressional Medal of Honor. While evaluating Johnson's war record in consideration of the award, a military committee discovered Johnson's gravesite, which for seventy years had not been known. Johnson's death was in fact as much of a mystery as his postwar life.

In 1919, after Johnson helped raise funds for Liberty Bonds, he returned to Albany and to his family: Edna and their two-year-old son, Herman. There he tried to find work that would not require him to stand for any prolonged period of time. Despite his achievements and his fame, he could not find an employer who would accommodate his needs. The government did not assist him in his search for work nor did it provide him with any disability benefits. In 1923, he and Edna were divorced. With Herman, Edna moved to Kansas City to live with relatives. Without his family, without a job, and without relief from his pains, Sergeant Johnson, the pride of his race in 1918 and 1919, slipped into a valley of depression and alcoholism. He died alone and impoverished at the Albany Veterans Administration Hospital on July 2, 1929, at age thirty-two.

For many years, Henry Johnson's son believed that his father was buried in a pauper's cemetery in Albany. But in 2002, the military committee that was considering his nomination for the Medal of Honor discovered a newspaper clipping noting his burial at Arlington National Cemetery. Still, there was no grave at Arlington under the name Henry Lincoln Johnson. Probing further, committee members found the name William Henry Johnson in the cemetery files and checking the original paperwork for this man, they learned that back in 1919 there had been a clerical error. And so it was that in 2002 New York governor George Pataki honored New York's and the nation's hero at his Arlington gravesite, giving him full military honors. In 2003, Johnson was given the Distinguished Service Cross. In 2004, Albany renamed a post office facility the U.S. Postal Service Henry Johnson Annex, adding to other recent local honors such as a bust of Johnson in the city's Washington Park and a major Albany thoroughfare renamed after him. By 2006, the campaign for him to receive the coveted Medal of Honor was not yet successful.

The fates of Mabel Puffer and Arthur Hazzard were no less difficult to uncover. Litigation continued for two more years. The grand jury did not find enough evidence to indict Hazzard on the charge of larceny. Still, Puffer's half-nephew, who became her permanent legal guardian, sued Hazzard and his family in an attempt to reclaim the gifts and money Puffer had given him. Hazzard filed a countersuit against Puffer's relatives and their lawyers, which a judge dismissed. And then he filed a suit against Puffer alone, alleging breach of promise to marry him. Eventually he dropped the suit. In 1921 a judge ordered Hazzard to return the gifts he had received from Mabel Puffer during their courtship, including $3,200 plus interest, which was the total amount that she had given him over the years. Puffer and Hazzard were never reunited. In fact they may never have seen each other again after 1921. She was committed to the Worcester Mental Hospital, while her guardian handled the issues of reclaiming her property from her fiancé. Puffer died of heart failure in 1937 in Worcester. Hazzard lived with his mother in their house behind the Ayer police station until at least 1930 when he was forty-nine years old, according to census records. In the 1930s, Hazzard seems to have disappeared, and thus far there is no trace of a record of his death. The legal lynching of the Puffer and Hazzard relationship was forever buried in the files of insanity cases in the commonwealth of Massachusetts.

ରଙ୍କ

In the 1920s William Monroe Trotter continued his boisterous and bold attacks against race discrimination, segregation, and lynching. Turning his back on the Democrats in 1920, he campaigned for a U.S. senator from his home state of Ohio, Warren Harding, whom he hoped would be far more receptive to race issues than Woodrow Wilson had been. President

Harding soon knew the name Trotter and the causes he so tirelessly pursued. So did Harding's successors. In 1926, Trotter carried petitions to President Calvin Coolidge with 25,000 signatures calling for an end to the segregation of federal offices in Washington—a system Wilson had put into place. When traffic caused him to be late for the meeting with Coolidge and a presidential staffer was critical, Trotter said, "Why, the President is Republican. The Negro has been waiting 50 years on the Republican Party; it won't hurt the President to wait a few minutes on the Negro." The meeting with Coolidge lasted twelve minutes and the president told Trotter that the federal buildings were in the process of being integrated. In 1933, Trotter was back again in the capital with the same request, this time seeking the attention of President Franklin Roosevelt for the cause of desegregating U.S. government offices.

Despite a rushing stream of disappointments, Trotter never quit the fight for "real democracy." During the remaining years of his life, his fierce adherence to integration led him to battles not only with resistant whites but also skeptical blacks who worried that integration could lead to loss of racial identity. His persistence seemed only to fuel his reputation as a militant and zealot. And while his work was a harbinger of the 1960s civil rights movement in America, he would never know the impact of his commitment and sacrifice. The tragedy of Trotter's life was that he would die "without much assurance that his dedication had been worth it," his biographer later wrote.

In the 1930s, Trotter struggled financially to keep his newspaper and his causes alive. He lived in an apartment in Boston with Mrs. Mary Gibson, the woman who in 1919 had taught him to cook so that he might find a job on a ship bound for France. On the night of April 6, 1934, unable to sleep, Trotter went up to the roof of the apartment building. Recently he had been agitated and nervous, often pacing back and forth in his office and at home. That night he paced across the flat roof, returned to his room again to try to sleep, and then went back to the roof. Early the next morning Mrs. Gibson's son heard an odd sound and, seeing that Trotter was not in his room, looked for him on the roof. Peering over the front edge, he saw Trotter lying motionless on the ground below. The great guardian of justice died on the way to the hospital. It was his sixty-second birthday. Whether Trotter fell or jumped, no one would ever know. In 1969, Boston's first officially desegregated public school was named the William Monroe Trotter

School. And seven years later Trotter's home on Sawyer Street, where he had lived for many years, was designated a National Historic Landmark. "We have come to protest forever against being proscribed or shut off in any caste from equal rights with other citizens and shall remain on the firing line at any and all times in defence of such rights," so wrote Trotter in the first issue of *The Guardian* in 1901. The last issue of *The Guardian* was April 20, 1957.

In the years following 1919, *The Crisis* pushed hard for anti-lynching legislation. And it became a virtual bulletin board for the budding cultural movement known as the Harlem Renaissance. Like a poem with orchestral sweep, the Harlem Renaissance was an expression of black liberation coming from the many voices of poets, playwrights, novelists, songwriters, musicians, painters, and sculptors. One part literary movement and one part social revolt, it was an outpouring of talent that awakened all of America willing to listen to the richness of the African-American heritage. Emerging out of the spirit and struggle of 1919, the "New Negro," as black writer Alain Locke called the metamorphosis of his race in the 1920s, raised the consciousness of African-Americans to a new level of self-awareness and pride.

The 1920s would be as much about Langston Hughes and the New Negro as it would be about F. Scott Fitzgerald and the Jazz Age. And much of the Harlem Renaissance talent would grace the pages of *The Crisis*, whose editor, W. E. B. Du Bois, was considered the patriarch of the movement. Claude McKay, Zora Neale Hurston, Arna Bontemps, Jean Toomer, Gwendolyn Bennett, Countee Cullen, and Langston Hughes, among many others, proclaimed their rightful place among the nation's most talented writers.

The organized black resistance to white mobs in 1919, the anti-lynching campaigns, and the emergence of the New Negro and the Harlem Renaissance laid the foundation for the civil rights movement forty years later, which would give birth to the world for which African-Americans of 1919 had struggled.

∞

For the United States, the Great War did not officially end until October 1921, when the Senate passed a bill officially declaring that America was no longer at war with Germany, Austria, or Hungary. The United States never ratified the Treaty of Versailles nor did it ever become a member of the League of Nations.

Sixty-three countries belonged to the League at its peak, including France and Great Britain, both of which joined at the start and stuck with it until the end. A succession of events in the 1930s, such as Italy's attack against Ethiopia, showed how weak the League was in the face of flagrant violations of its peace-directed Covenant. In 1933 Germany, under Nazi leadership, withdrew its membership, followed by Japan, Italy, and more than a dozen nations. Nearly extinct by 1940 and clearly unable to stop World War II, the League dissolved at the end of the war. Although it was never strong enough to prevent war or to fulfill Wilson's mission of collective security, the lessons of the League helped to shape the next attempt at international cooperation, the United Nations.

In 1920 the winner of the coveted Nobel Peace Prize was Woodrow Wilson. The next year Wilson returned to private law practice in Washington, but he spent most of his time at home on S Street in his library. Neither the three steps that Grayson had built for him nor any other therapy or treatment could restore the president's health. He was nearly blind, partially paralyzed, and sadly bitter.

On the night of November 10, 1923, the eve of Armistice Day, Wilson delivered a speech from his home to the American public using the new national medium, the radio. It would be the last time the American nation as a whole would hear the eloquent words of the man so many of them had once idolized. He began:

> The anniversary of Armistice Day should stir us to great exaltation of spirit because of the proud recollection that it was our day, a day above those early days of that never-to-be forgotten November which lifted the world to the high levels of vision and achievement upon which the great war for democracy and right was fought and won; although the stimulating memories of that happy time of triumph are forever marred and embittered for us by the shameful fact that when the victory was won, be it remembered—chiefly by the indomitable spirit and ungrudging sacrifices of our incomparable soldiers—we turned our backs on our associates and refused to bear any responsible part in the administration of peace, or the

firm and permanent establishment of the results of the war—won at so terrible a cost of life and treasure—and withdrew into a sullen and selfish isolation which is deeply ignoble, manifestly cowardly and dishonorable.

His last lines were:

The only way in which we can worthily give proof of our appreciation of the high significance of Armistice Day is by resolving to put self-interest away and once more formulate and act on the highest ideals and purposes of international policy. Thus, and only thus, can we return to the true traditions of America.

The next day, at least twenty thousand people gathered outside his window to show their appreciation and admiration. He spoke briefly to them on his front steps. Three months later, on February 3, 1924, Woodrow Wilson died at home.

The visitation was at the house on S Street, where the body lay in the large room at the front. The service was held at the Chapel of the National Cathedral in Washington. "It was the most notable gathering of Americans I had ever seen on any one occasion," wrote Ray Stannard Baker in his journal.

After the funeral, Baker found himself repeating a passage he had recently read and committed to memory from Dostoyevsky's *The Brothers Karamazov:* "The just man passeth away, but his light remaineth: and it is after the saviour's death that men are mostly saved. Mankind will reject and kill their prophets, but will love their martyrs and honor those whom they have done to death."

Baker had spent a good deal of time with Wilson in recent years. In fact, he had lived with the Wilsons for their last two months in the White House and had moved with them to S Street, where Baker had his own study for the purpose of writing his next book. The president had decided in December of 1920 to allow Baker to read through all his papers from the conference, many of which were secret documents and confidential memos. It was an invitation that Baker never anticipated. In Baker's book *What Wilson Did at Paris,* he had been so honest in his criticism of the president's unwillingness to reveal the inner workings of the conference that he believed the president might be offended and even shun him. The "supreme failure of the Conference was the complicated failure in publicity," Baker had written. But to Baker's surprise, Wilson actually respected him for his candor and even suggested that Baker write a book that would reveal the secret machinations of those crucial months in Paris. The result was Baker's 1922 three-volume work entitled *Woodrow Wilson and the World Settlement—A History of the Peace Conference.*

Despite its ponderous title, the work had a vast audience, some of whom hailed it as an excellent accomplishment, while others skewered Baker, labeling him an apologist for Wilson. Indeed, the book stirred a rather heated debate between those who believed Wilson had known about the secret wartime treaties among the Allies regarding colonies and territories, believed the peace conference was a farce, and thought Wilson was a liar; and those, like Baker, who believed that Wilson had ignored the treaties and had in turn naively trusted the Allies to set aside such old agreements. Baker defended Wilson, saying that the president had assumed that after the terms of the Armistice were agreed upon, then the secret aims of wartime would be set aside for the higher purposes of peace and a new world order. He pointed out that Lloyd George had given a speech in January of 1918 in which he disavowed "the imperialistic aims of the Allies as disclosed in certain of the secret treaties." Baker compared the situation to the San Francisco earthquake, which he had covered as a journalist. After such disasters and shocks as earthquakes and wars, "men remembered themselves again," as Baker put it, and were lifted to a higher plane. He went so far as to say that Wilson did not even read the secret treaties. For the rest of Baker's life he would be enmeshed in one controversy or another regarding Wilson's character and his work at the peace conference, especially the matter of the secret treaties. Although it was a hugely complicated issue that historians would continue to debate, Baker would always believe that Wilson, though a difficult, stubborn man, had tried his best to push his ideals at the peace conference. But his critics could see only the ashes of a dream torched by Wilson himself, who lacked the courage to stand up to the old despotic ways that had caused the war and who was unwilling to give up America's own imperialistic aims. Perhaps in the pursuit of truth, Baker was derailed by hope.

While that pot was still simmering, Baker began his next project, which was a multivolume set of the president's public papers. Then in the midst of that immense task came another: the biography of Woodrow Wilson. Baker had explained his vision for such a work to the president in a letter in 1923 and again in 1924 but the president never responded—at least not directly to Baker. Always torn between his journalistic side and the creative life he expressed through the works of David Grayson, Baker decided in the summer of 1924 that he must choose one or the other. Although his journal revealed that he chose David Grayson over Ray Stannard Baker, he was still not at ease with his decision. By January of 1925 he in fact had changed his mind. It was then that Mrs. Wilson shared with him a letter the president had dictated to her nine days before his death, a missive to Baker that read: "Every time you disclose your mind to me you increase my admiration and affection for you. I always dislike to make, even intimate, a promise until I have at least taken some steps to facilitate my keeping it. I am glad to promise you that with regard to my personal correspondence and other similar papers I shall regard you as my preferred creditor, and shall expect to afford you the first—and if necessary exclusive—access to those papers. I would rather have your interpretation of them than that of anybody I know."

Baker proposed a four-volume work on the life of Wilson, and eventually wrote eight volumes entitled *Woodrow Wilson: Life and Letters*. The first volume appeared in 1927 and the last in 1939. In 1940, Baker won the Pulitzer Prize for biography for the last two volumes of the series. He then embarked on his own story, publishing the first volume of his autobiography in 1941. Before he completed the second volume in 1945, Baker worked as a consultant to Darryl Zanuck for the $5.2 million film *Wilson,* which debuted in August 1944.

David Grayson too was prolific. Despite Baker's twenty-year immersion in the life of Woodrow Wilson, Grayson wrote *Adventures in Solitude* in 1931, *The Countryman's Year* in 1936, and *Under My Elm* in 1942, as well as numerous essays for *Reader's Digest.* One side of Baker marched forward with the fast rhythm of every devoted journalist while the other side wanted to stop the march of progress and ponder the meaning of life. In *Under My Elm,* Grayson wrote: "I have been where there was too much talk, too many *things,* food more than I needed, amusement keyed too high; where speed and not beauty seemed the test of life; and I come home again to my own calm hills, my own town, to the beautiful quiet of my own thoughts. If only people would be still for a little and look at the world before they drown everything in torrents of talk!"

Springtime would always be a celebration for Baker. Even from his sickbed after suffering a heart attack in the spring of 1946, he watched his bees and his budding trees from an open window. By July he was outside again. On July 8 he wrote in his journal, "Walking out this morning into the clear still sunshine, I had a great thought. It has been with me all day, blessing what I have seen and done, restoring my soul, giving me new courage and strength . . ." He never completed the sentence and never revealed what the thought was. The next entry in his diary was written by another hand, on July 12: "Dear Ray died at 3:30 this morning after a severe heart attack."

Baker's last published work was the second volume of his autobiography, entitled *American Chronicle.* It covered the period from his years as a muckraking journalist to the completion of his eight volumes on the life of Wilson. And he ended it in a way that effectively showed a union of the voices of Baker and Grayson. With a touch of Baker, he wrote in the last paragraph that his greatest satisfaction in the late years of his life was to know that his writings about Wilson had advanced an understanding of the man, thus allowing Wilson to be recognized for the "pre-eminent man that he was." And then with a touch of Grayson, he ended the book with a poem that reflected his now deep understanding of all truth seekers who boldly pursue a cause:

> *Curious, in time, I stand, noting the efforts of heroes:*
> *Is the deferment long? Bitter the slander, poverty, death?*
> *Lies the seed unreck'd for centuries in the ground?*
> *Lo! To God's due occasion,*
> *Uprising in the night, it sprouts, blooms,*
> *And fills the earth with use and beauty.*

Note on Sources

In the midst of writing a nonfiction book, the task of compiling source notes seems very appealing and quite simple. It will come at the end like a reward for completing the writing, which is a far more complicated undertaking than any compilation of citations. Then one day the manuscript is complete, except for the source notes and the acknowledgments. And, suddenly the patina is tarnished. Source notes in reality are grueling.

Shortly after the publication of my third book, I had lunch at the Century Club in New York with Arthur Schlesinger, Jr., to discuss *Savage Peace*. Toward the end of the luncheon, we began to talk about source notes and particularly those in my third book, which was about the controversial antebellum social movement known popularly as the Underground Railroad. The source notes in that book gave me an opportunity to reveal my careful process of scrutinizing the credibility of the sources I used—mostly court records and memoirs from before the Civil War. Skepticism is essential when studying a movement steeped in apocryphal stories. As we were leaving Arthur complimented me on my source notes, which he had read and which he said were excellent. I was honored. When I began the *Savage Peace* notes, I sent Arthur a brief missive informing him that I had decided he would be my inspiration for getting through the notes this time: indeed, my muse. Thank you, Arthur.

In these notes, I have cited the secondary and primary sources, matching sources with topics mentioned in the text as well as with direct quotations. To further assist the reader, I've included in this introductory essay brief discussions of sources for the main narrative strands of the book. And for clarity in the body of the notes, I've inserted brief summaries of sources for subjects such as Carl Sandburg, the Chicago race riots, the steelworker strike, the American Protective League, the case of Mabel Puffer and Arthur Hazzard, and the nonstop transatlantic flight of Alcock and Brown. I have also provided explanations of some sources that could be confusing, such as the files of the Military Intelligence Division's Negro Subversion unit and the Bureau of Investigation files.

I always prefer primary sources in my research, for obvious reasons. And during the research for *Savage Peace* I fortunately found a wealth of court records, letters, memos, diaries, declassified government documents, leaflets, public papers, and contemporary newspaper accounts. Fortunately too I discovered some excellent secondary sources—all noted below—without which I would have spent a decade at least researching the book's various themes. I have carefully interwoven details from these excellent works with the facts I culled from the primary sources to try to bring alive the year 1919.

For the parts of the book about Harry Weinberger, Mollie Steimer, and the *Abrams* case, I relied on various sources, often letters from the Harry Weinberger Papers at Yale University's Sterling Library, Manuscript Group 553, mostly from Box 2, though a few of the letters used in this book were found in Boxes 1 and 3; Weinberger's "A Rebel's Interrupted Autobiography," in *American Journal of Economics and Sociology,* October 1942; the excellent book about the *Abrams* case by Richard Polenberg, *Fighting Faiths;* the Bureau of Investigation files at the National Archives, Record Group 65, filed under several numbers but in this book I used mostly OG362977 for Steimer and for Weinberger OG382544, OG154434, and OG355441; the Abrams trial transcript, United States versus Gabriel Prober, Jacob Abrams, Jacob Schwartz, Samuel Lipman, Hyman Rozansky, Hyman Lachowsky, and Mollie Steimer, alias Mollie Stimer, alias Mollie Stein, Record Group 21, U.S. District Court for the Southern District of New York, Criminal Case Files, Archives Box 83, Docket Number: C15–23 (the case file is physically located in Lee's Summit, Missouri, but can be retrieved via National Archives and Record Administration at 201 Varick Street in NYC); the *Abrams v. U.S. file,* 250 U.S. 616 (1919), Docket 316, Argued, October 21, 1919, Decided November 10, 1919; the 1918 pamphlet published by Political Prisoners Defense and Relief Committee entitled *Sentenced to Twenty Years Prison;* Zechariah Chafee, Jr.'s, article "A Contemporary State Trial—The United States Versus Jacob Abrams et al.," in *Harvard Law Review,* April 1920; and newspaper articles, mostly from the *New York Tribune,* the *New York Times,* and several from the *New York Evening World,* the *New York Herald,* the *New York Call,* and *The Nation* magazine. Only a small percentage of Weinberger's letters regarding Abrams and Steimer and their relationship with the U.S. government are used in this book. The letters as a whole are fascinating—worthy of reading in their entirety. They reveal Weinberger's fund-raising efforts; his networking among highly placed government officials to make his case as visible as possible; his kind, consistent correspondence with his clients in jail; his dedication to the cause of justice for his clients; among other details. Weinberger would be an excellent subject for a biography, in fact. I culled details of Steimer's life from *Fighters for Anarchism: Mollie Steimer and Senya Fleshin,* edited by Abe Bluestein, and from Agnes Smedley's description of Steimer in her series "Cell Mates" written for the *New York Call's* Sunday magazine, February 15 through March 14, 1920, as well as the sources noted above.

For the chapters in this book about domestic surveillance, the Negro Subversion division agents, the American Protective League, censorship and monitoring of publications, government raids to purge the nation of radicals, and events such as labor strikes that were affected by such surveillance, I turned often to the excellent research of Roy Talbert, Jr., *Negative Intelligence: The Army and the American Left, 1917–1941*, Regin Schmidt, *Red Scare, FBI and the Origins of Anti-communism in the United States*, Theodore Kornweibel, Jr., *Seeing Red: Federal Campaigns Against Black Militancy, 1919–1955*, Joan M. Jensen, *The Price of Vigilance*, and Robert K. Murray, *Red Scare: A Study in National Hysteria, 1919–1920*. (*The Price of Vigilance* is thus far the only in-depth examination of the APL). As often as possible I culled from MID and BI agents' reports, the official memos of the War Department, the post office, the Justice Department, the MID, and the BI, to be found mostly in the National Archives.

Perhaps the most exciting and yet sometimes most confusing part of the research for this book was the exploration of declassified government records, some fortunately available on microfilm and thus obtainable on interlibrary loan, and others on file in College Park, Maryland, at the National Archives. The College Park facility is a simple, ordinary building housing an extraordinary collection of primary sources. There I used documents from Record Group 28, which contains the old U.S. post office records, useful in studying the effect of the Espionage Act and the Sedition Act on surveillance of magazines, newspapers, and the mails in general; Record Group 165, which contains the War Department files including the Military Intelligence Division records; and Record Group 65, which designates the old FBI files, then, of course, the BI files. The files that I used in RG65 were what are called OG files, Old German. For the years 1916 to 1922, the FBI, or rather the BI, records are divided into three categories: the Miscellaneous File, which are straight numbers (1–42,975), the Mexican File (border unrest and the Mexican Revolution investigations), and the Old German file, which includes items relating to World War I, the Red Scare of 1919, surveillance of suspected radicals, and questions about publications and organizations considered potentially dangerous to national security. In the notes, these are referred to as the OG files. Mollie Steimer, for example, has a file in the Miscellaneous File and also in the OG. I culled mostly from the OG file 362977 for the Steimer story. (Steimer—"Stimer" in the government files—also has a file in MID but it appears that all of her files eventually ended up at the BI in the above file.) I also used RG60, the Department of Justice files, in particular the Glasser file, which contains files on the race riots of 1919.

In RG165, I focused on file No. 10218, which is the vast record of the Negro Subversion division of the MID. Those particular files regarding surveillance of African-Americans are also available on microfilm on Reels 19, 20, and 21 of a twenty-five-reel set edited by Theodore Kornweibel, Jr., and covering all agencies and their surveillance of African-Americans from 1917 through 1925. The cite is: *Federal Surveillance of Afro-Americans (1917–1925): The First World War, the Red Scare, and the Garvey Movement,* ed. Theodore Kornweibel, Jr., and guide compiled by Martin Schlipper. Kornweibel's introduction to this microfilm project is especially helpful in explaining the exact location of documents pertaining to the government surveillance of African-Americans during the years 1917–1925 as well as the relationship between the MID and the BI at that time, and the history of the MID. Also very helpful was the following thirty-four-reel collection, which provides a very large portion of RG165: Randolph Boehm, ed., *U.S. Military Intelligence Reports: Surveillance of Radicals in the United States, 1917–1941.* For example, Mollie Steimer's earlier files are on Reel 12 of this collection, revealing some details that are not in OG362977, though some of the files in this grouping were clearly moved to the BI after J. Edgar Hoover began his work as director of the new BI General Intelligence Division in August of 1919. The six reels of RG165 that pertain to the Negro Subversion division of the MID are not in the Boehm collection—only in the Kornweibel collection. Thus, the combination of these two sets provides superb access to primary sources on the MID in general and surveillance of African-Americans in particular. Also useful and available on microfilm is the *Correspondence of the Military Intelligence Division Relating to "Negro Subversion," 1917–41.* This consists of six reels and has a helpful introduction that includes a clear history of the MID and its record keeping. I also used the following: U.S. Military Intelligence, *Weekly Summaries (1917–1927),* which is a reprint of a series of secret documents prepared by the MID in the designated years. There is also an FBI file on the APL—1,400 pages in seven volumes—accessible through the Freedom of Information Act.

For the Alexander Mitchell Palmer Papers, I relied on information gleaned from the Palmer Papers at the Manuscript Division of the Library of Congress, 1910–1923; the Woodrow Wilson Papers at LC; the Ray Stannard Baker Papers at LC; the Weinberger papers at Yale; and various secondary sources, including the works mentioned above by Talbert, Schmidt, Polenberg, Jensen, Murray, and, of course, Stanley Coben's biography, *A. Mitchell Palmer: Politician* (New York: Columbia University Press, 1983). Details about Palmer's nomination and the controversy surrounding his confirmation as attorney general are from contemporary newspaper accounts and from *Hearings Before the U.S. Senate Committee on the Judiciary,* 66th Cong., 1st Sess., on June 4, 13, 20 and July 24, 25 (Washington: Government Printing Office, 1973) and August 8, 1919 (Washington: Government Printing Office, 1971).

I culled the details about J. Edgar Hoover and his early years with the Justice Department from the excellent research of John Fox, the FBI historian, which he sent to me; the BI files, RG65 at the National Archives; and several biographies, including Richard Gid Powers, *Secrecy and Power: The Life of J. Edgar Hoover,* and Curt Gentry, *J. Edgar Hoover: The Man and the Secrets.*

Biographical information on Sergeant Henry Johnson came from an interview with his son, Herman Johnson, who was a Tuskegee Airman, in Kansas City on May 9, 2003; Arthur Little, *From Harlem to the Rhine: The Story of New York's Colored Volunteers;* Victor J. DiSanto, "Henry Johnson's Paradox: A Soldier's Story," in *Afro-Americans in New York Life and History;* the *Albany Times Union* stories, May 21–23, 1918; Gail Buckley, *American Patriots: The Story of Blacks in the Military from the Revolution to Desert Storm; Chicago Defender,* February 22, 1919, 1; Colonel Theodore Roosevelt, "America's Heroes of the Great War," *American Magazine,* August 14, 1927; Benjamin Griffith Brawley, *Negro Builders and Heroes;* and from the Albany, New York, Veterans of Foreign Wars; and National Archives, RG65, BI Files, OG265935.

For the details throughout the book about Ray Stannard Baker, I have relied on the second volume of Baker's autobiography, *American Chronicle;* Robert Bannister's excellent biography *Ray Stannard Baker: The Mind and Thought of a Progressive;* my interview with Robert Bannister in Bryn Mawr, Pennsylvania, in October of 2002; Baker's article in the June 1916 edition of *The World's Work* magazine, "Gathering Clouds Along the Color Line"; two of his books, *What Wilson Did at Paris* (1919), and *Following the Color Line: An Account of Negro Citizenship in the American Democracy* (1908); and entries from his notebook or diary entries, which are available in the Ray Stannard Baker Papers in the Manuscript Division of the Library of Congress (Series II, Notebooks 21–26). And for the details about David Grayson, I have relied on my own readings of the works of David Grayson; the writings of Robert Bannister, especially his Baker biography; Walter A. Dyer, *David Grayson: Adventurer;* Frank Prentice Rand, *The Story of David Grayson;* Winifred K. Rugg, "Ray Stannard Baker and David Grayson," *Boston Evening Transcript,* December 31, 1932; and "Chronicle and Comment: David Grayson," *Bookman,* March 1916. The Bannister biography includes an excellent bibliography of the works of Baker, and the Library of Congress Manuscript Division has a bibliography compiled by Baker's daughter, Mrs. Rachel Baker Napier.

For the Polar Bears, I used the vast collection of primary sources at Michigan's Own Military and Space Museum in Frankenmuth, Michigan; the letters of Senator Hiram Johnson and the diaries of Frank Douma, Silver Parrish, and Roger Sherman Clark, among others, at the Bentley Historical Library at the University of Michigan; Henry Coke Lower's biography of Hiram Johnson, *A Bloc of One: The Political Career of Hiram W. Johnson;* George F. Kennan's *Soviet-American Relations, 1917–1920,* Vol. 2, *The Decision to Intervene,* U.S. Department of State, *Papers Re-*

lating to the Foreign Relations of the United States: 1919, Russia (Washington: 1937), available at the Library of Congress; Roger Crownover's "Stranded in Russia," in *Michigan History Magazine*, Jan.–Feb. 1999; newspaper articles in the *Detroit Free Press* and the *Detroit News*; U.S. Army, American Expeditionary Forces, North Russia, Microfilm, 2 reels (National Archives and Records Service, General Services Administration, 1973); Harry Costello's *Why Did We Go to Russia?*; E. M. Halliday's *The Ignorant Armies*; and National Archives Record Group 395, which consists of the files of the U.S. Army regarding its overseas operations for the years 1898 to 1942, including eleven reels of records relating to the activities of the American Expeditionary Forces in Russia, 1918–1920.

Information about William Monroe Trotter came largely out of his newspaper, *The Guardian,* on microfilm at the Boston University Library; the biography written by Stephen R. Fox, *The Guardian of Boston;* the *Boston Globe* and the *New York Times* for the appropriate dates; several dissertations, but most significantly, Ruth Worthy, "A Negro in Our History: William Monroe Trotter, 1872–1934" (MA thesis, Columbia University, 1952); Nicholas Patler, *Jim Crow and the Wilson Administration: Protesting Federal Segregation in the Early Twentieth Century;* the Schomburg Collection at the Harlem branch of the New York Public Library; Trotter papers at Howard University and at Boston University; and obituaries of Trotter found in the *New York Age, The Guardian, The Afro-American,* the *Pittsburgh Courier,* and the *Philadelphia Tribune.* For an excellent list of dissertations and unpublished monographs about Trotter, see pages 290–99 of Stephen R. Fox's source notes in his Trotter biography.

I found the information about Eddington, Einstein, and the expedition of 1919 to observe the total eclipse of the sun on May 29 from numerous sources: Arthur Stanley Eddington's books and articles, including *Space, Time and Gravitation: An Outline of the General Relativity Theory,* and *Science and the Unseen World;* Allie Vibert Douglas's *The Life of Arthur Stanley Eddington;* Subrahmanyan Chandrasekhar's *Eddington: The Most Distinguished Astrophysicist of His Time;* Matthew Stanley's article "An Expedition to Heal the Wounds of War: the 1919 Eclipse and Eddington as Quaker Adventurer"; Thomas Levenson's *Einstein in Berlin;* Philipp Frank's *Einstein: His Life and Times;* Ronald W. Clark's *Einstein: The Life and Times;* Alfred North Whitehead's *Science and the Modern World* (New York: Macmillan, 1947); various issues of the journal *Observatory,* published by the Royal Greenwich Observatory, Cambridge University, and available from Cambridge University Library in the Royal Greenwich Observatory Archives; from a 1999 article *Einstein* by James Gleick, whose observations confirmed my decision to include the eclipse and Einstein in this book—"Humanity was standing on a brink, ready to see something new," wrote Gleick. The article can be found online at www.around.com/einstein.html; and from the many sources brought together for the inspiring exhibit on Einstein at the American Museum of Natural History in New York, which I visited four times in November 2002.

Throughout the book, I used quotes and information from weather reports to events coverage out of the following publications: *New York Times, New York World, New York Tribune, Washington Post, Boston Globe, Boston Post, Boston Sunday Globe, Boston Evening Globe, Turner Public Spirit, Boston American, Boston Traveller, Albany Times Union, St. Louis Argus, Los Angeles Times, Wall Street Journal, Cincinnati Enquirer, Detroit Free Press, Detroit News, Christian Science Monitor, New York Call, New York Age, Chicago Defender, The Crisis, The Guardian, Chicago Tribune, Chicago Daily News, Kansas City Star, Shreveport Times, Colbert County Reporter, Florence Herald, Florence Times, Washington Star, Worcester Evening Gazette, The News and Courier* (Charleston, S.C.), *Scientific American, The Nation, The Liberator, The New Republic, Harvard Law Review, Akron Law Review, The Forum, McClure's, American Magazine, Observatory, Military History Magazine, Michigan History Magazine, The Saturday Evening Post, Outlook, Everybody's, The World's Work, Isis, Collier's, American Journal of Economics and Sociology,* and *Journal of Modern History.*

At the Manuscript Division of the Library of Congress, I used the Woodrow Wilson Papers, the Ray Stannard Baker Papers (Series II, Notebooks 21–26), and the Alexander Mitchell Palmer Papers; at Yale University's Sterling Library, the Harry Weinberger Papers; at the Schomburg Library (Harlem branch of the New York Public Library), reels of the *New York Age, The Crisis,* and various files on Trotter, Pan-African congresses, lynching, and W. E. B. Du Bois; at the National Archives in College Park, Maryland, as noted above, I read through reels of files of the Bureau of Investigation, the post office, the Military Intelligence Division of the War Department, and the Department of Justice (mainly the attorney general's annual reports); and at New York University's Tamiment Library I listened to an interview of Mollie Steimer taped on January 27, 1980, in Cuernavaca, Mexico.

I also accessed books and manuscripts from the following libraries, historical societies, and archives: New York Public Library, Research Branch on 42nd Street; Princeton University Library; Harlan Hatcher Graduate Library, University of Michigan; Woodrow Wilson Presidential Library in Staunton, Virginia; Swarthmore College Library in Bryn Mawr, Pennsylvania; Chicago Public Library; Northwestern University Library; Boston University Library; Boston Public Library; Ayer (Massachusetts) Public Library; Concord (New Hampshire) Historical Society; Jones Library, Amherst, Massachusetts; Alice Paul Center for Research on Women and Gender in Philadelphia; Norfolk Public Library; New

Hampshire State Library; Tuck Library at the New Hampshire Historical Society; New York University Law Library; New York University Bobst Library; University of Michigan Law Library; Ann Arbor Public Library; court archives for the U.S. District Court for the Southern District of New York, accessed at 201 Varick Street, Manhattan; the American War Library in Gardena, California; New York State Library at Albany; New Hampshire State Library; Cambridge University Library in England; and the American Museum of Natural History in New York City.

Sources for the photos are the following: Library of Congress; Tamiment Library, New York University; Helen Keller Archives, American Foundation for the Blind in New York City; Carl Sandburg Home National Historic Site, Flat Rock, North Carolina; *Albany Times Union* in Albany, New York; Brown Brothers, Sterling, Pennsylvania; William Monroe Trotter Institute, University of Massachusetts; Boston Public Library; Stanley Bozick, Michigan's Own Military and Space Museum; A'Lelia Bundles in Washington, D.C.; Cynthia Long, Toronto, Canada; Warren Weinberger, San Diego, California; Cambridge University Library, Cambridge, England; Howard University; and the *Chicago Defender*.

The chapter by chapter citations follow.

Notes

PROLOGUE: ARMISTICE DAY 1918

Page

1 "We are here": *The Nation*, May 24, 1919, 848.

3 six men met in railcar: Marshal Ferdinand Foch, Admiral Rosslyn Wemyss, Matthias Erzberger, Count Alfred von Oberndorff, General Detlev von Winterfeldt, and Captain Ernst Vanselow: Ferdinand Foch and Thomas Bentley Mott, *The Memoirs of Marshal Foch* (New York: Doubleday, Doran, 1931), 477.

3 Some heard it first: McKinley Wooden, PBS film, *Lost Peace 1919*, a co-production of WGBH Boston and the BBC, 1998; viewed at the New York Public Library, Fifth Ave. and 42nd St.

3 captured ammunition: Diary of Army Sergeant Tom Brady, in *A Prose Anthology of the First World War*, selected and edited by Robert Hull (Brookfield, CT: Millbrook, 1993), 57.

3 "One minute we": Wooden, *Lost Peace 1919*.

3 "I shall never forget": Captain Chester D. Heywood, *Negro Combat Troops in the World War* (Worcester, MA: Commonwealth, 1928), 231–39.

3 "The nightmare is over": W. E. B. Du Bois, editorial, *The Crisis*, December 1918, 59.

4 Sergeant Henry Lincoln Johnson: Arthur W. Little, *From Harlem to the Rhine: The Story of New York's Colored Volunteers* (New York: Covici Friede, 1936), Chapters 30, 42, 43.

4 "They had achieved": Ibid., 350.

4 Armistice Day in northern Russia: Various sources, Sergeant Gordon W. Smith, "The Forgotten Regiment," as related to Odessa Ruth Smith, *Detroit Free Press*, May 25, 1930; Harry J. Costello, *Why Did We Go to Russia?* (Detroit: H. J. Costello, 1920); and the diaries of Corporal Frank W. Douma, Corporal James B. Smidley, and Sergeant Silver Parrish, available at the Bentley Historical Library, University of Michigan.

4 "We were atacked": Diary of Sergeant Silver Parrish, November 11, 1918, Bentley Historical Library, University of Michigan.

5 "The song bursting": Ray Stannard Baker, *American Chronicle* (New York: Stratford Press, 1945), 368.

5 News of the signing: November 12 front-page stories in the *Los Angeles Times, Washington Post, New York Times, Cincinnati Enquirer,* and articles in *McClure's* and *Collier's* during November 1918.

5 mail carrier: *Cincinnati Enquirer*, November 6, 1919, 1.

5 second wave of the outbreak: Alfred W. Crosby, *America's Forgotten Pandemic: The Influenza of 1918* (Cambridge: Cambridge University Press, 1989), 60–61.

6 "We have been": September 29, 1918, letter written by a doctor stationed at Camp Devens, Massachusetts, in a collection of medical papers given to the Department of Epidemiology at the University of Michigan in 1959; former department chairman Victor Hawthorne gave his permission to use a quote from the letter for this book.

6 "I once knew": Crosby, *America's Forgotten Pandemic*, 125.

6 "Did Booze ever": *Cincinnati Enquirer*, November 1, 1918, 7–8.

6 "the Germans gave up!": *Cincinnati Enquirer*, November 8, 1918, 1; *Washington Post*, November 8, 1918, 1.

7 "No one can say": *Washington Post*, November 8, 1918, 2.

7 November 11 was a mild, springlike day: *Cincinnati Enquirer, November 12, 1918*, 14; *Washington Post*, November 12, 1918, 11.

7 "ARMISTICE SIGNED": *Los Angeles Times*, November 12, 1918, 1; *New York Times*, November 12, 1918, 1; *Washington Post*, November 12, 1918, 1.

7 In New Jersey: *New York Times*, November 12, 1918, 1.

7 In Chicago and San Diego: *Los Angeles Times*, November 12, 1918, 2.

7 repeals of health regulations: *Cincinnati Enquirer*, November 12, 1918, 1; *Washington Post*, November 6, 1918, 1.

8 "My fellow countrymen": *New York Times*, November 12, 1918, 1.

8 "Armed imperialism": Ibid.

8 President and Mrs. Wilson: *Cincinnati Enquirer*, November 12, 1918, 2.

9 dare to travel to Europe: *Washington Post*, November 13, 16, 1918, 1; *New York Times*, November 13, 14, 1918, 1; *Los Angeles Times*, November, 12, 1918, 1; *The Nation*, November 23, 1918.

9 no U.S. president had left the country while in office: August Heckscher, *Woodrow Wilson: A Biography* (New York: Collier Books, 495). Note that Theodore Roosevelt did travel to Panama in 1906, which, as of May 1904, was owned by the U.S.

9 "Wilson has yet": Ray Stannard Baker, *American Chronicle*, 364.

9 Theodore Roosevelt checked into a New York City hospital: Patricia O'Toole, *When Trumpets Call: Theodore Roosevelt After the White House* (New York: Simon & Schuster, 2005), 400.

9 Samuel Gompers: *Washington Post*, November 11, 1918, 20.

9 John Edgar Hoover: Anthony Summers, *Official and Confidential: The Secret Life of J. Edgar Hoover* (New York: G. P. Putnam's Sons, 1993), 31–32. The author says that his source for the details of Hoover's courtship of a woman named Alice was Helen Gandy, Hoover's secretary of fifty-three years, whom, Summers notes in his book, he interviewed before her death in 1988. Although Gandy did not reveal Alice's last name, Summers writes that "there is no reason, though, to doubt the story. Gandy talked about aspects of that evening in 1918 with two FBI officials, and she was a firsthand witness to Edgar's humiliation" (page 32).

9 A. Mitchell Palmer: *New York Times*, November 10, 1918, 25; details of the actual sale, one part in late 1918 and the other in January 1919, in *New York Times*, January 28, 1919, 7.

10 "Before these hundred": *New York Times,* November 11, 1918, 20.

10 Carl Sandburg: Penelope Niven, *Carl Sandburg: A Biography* (New York: Charles Scribner's Sons, 1991), 316–17.

10 British aviator Captain John Alcock: Sir John Alcock and Sir Arthur Whitten Brown, *Our Transatlantic Flight* (London: William Kimmer, 1969), 26.

10 the popular American writer: Ray Stannard Baker, *American Chronicle,* 368.

10 "The great event": Thomas Levenson, *Einstein in Berlin* (New York: Bantam 2003), 197. And see my Note on Sources for more details on sources for the expeditions to Sobral, Brazil, and the Isle of Príncipe to observe the May 29, 1919, eclipse.

10 Roger Baldwin: Robert C. Cottrell, *Roger Nash Baldwin and the American Civil Liberties Union* (New York: Columbia University Press, 2000)), 93–94; Richard Polenberg, *Fighting Faiths: The Abrams Case, the Supreme Court, and Free Speech* (New York: Penguin, 1989), 85.

10 the Tombs: Jeremiah A. O'Leary and Michael A. Kelly, *My Political Trial and Experiences* (New York: Jefferson, 1919), 163–66.

11 In October one man had been sentenced: Examples taken from *The Nation,* November 21, 1918.

11 "slip of a girl": Emma Goldman, *Living My Life* (New York: Dover, 1970; originally published by Alfred A. Knopf, 1931, 702.

11 For Steimer and Weinberger, see the sources mentioned in Note on Sources.

12 "Sad is the day": Letter from Harry Weinberger to Hon. F. H. La Guardia, then president of the Board of Alderman in New York City, April 16, 1919.

12 "Peace has come": From the series "Cell Mates" written by Agnes Smedley in *The Call,* Sunday Supplement to the *New York Call,* February 15, 1920, to March 14, 1920, and here taken from Eileen Barrett and Mary Cullinan, eds. *American Women Writers* (New York: St. Martin's, 1993), 362.

12 Alabama lynching: *New York Age,* November 16, 1918, 1; *Florence Herald,* November 14, 1918, 5; *Florence Times,* November 14, 1918, 4; *Culbert County Reporter,* November 14, 1918, 1.

13 lynchings: NAACP, *The Fight Against Lynching: The Anti-Lynching Work of the NAACP for the Year 1918* (New York: NAACP, 1919), 19; *The Crisis,* February 1920, 183–86.

13 Two hundred thousand African-American men: David Levering Lewis, *W. E. B. Du Bois: The Fight for Equality and the American Century, 1919–1963,* Vol. 1 (New York: Henry Holt, 1993), 563.

13 "You have won": Little, *From Harlem to the Rhine,* 324.

13 "Memorandum on the Future of Africa": Lewis, *W. E. B. Du Bois,* 561–62.

13 William Monroe Trotter: Stephen R. Fox, *The Guardian of Boston: William Monroe Trotter* (New York: Atheneum, 1971), 222–23.

14 "The elimination of civil": Ibid., 223.

14 "The earth and the heavens". Ibid.

14 To demobilize 300,000 soldiers: *Washington Post,* November 16, 1918, 1.

PART I: WINTER: JUBILATION AND HOPE

Page

17 "We have learned": *New York Age,* December 21, 1918, 4.

17 "I learned by experience": Harry Weinberger, "A Rebel's Interrupted Autobiography," *American Journal of Economics and Sociology* (October 1942), 115.

CHAPTER 1: GODS OF WAR AND PEACE

Page

19 passenger list on train and ship: *New York Times,* December 4, 5, 1918, 1.

20 Franklin Delano Roosevelt: James Roosevelt and Sidney Shalett, *Affectionately, F.D.R.: A Son's Story of a Lonely Man* (New York: Harcourt, Brace, 1959), 79.

20 the *George Washington* steamed out of her berth: *New York Times,* December 5, 1918, 2.

20 "I anticipate no trouble": *New York Times,* December 5, 1918, 1.

21 "President Wilson has not given": *New York Times,* December 4, 1918, 13.

21 "out of office" and the objections of Lawrence Sherman: *New York Times,* December 4, 1918, 1–2.

21 "indispensable instrumentality": Ibid.

22 "peace without victory": Ibid.

22 Henry Cabot Lodge: *Congressional Record,* March 23, 1918.

22 "The first and controlling": Memo written by Henry Cabot Lodge to Henry White on December 2, 1918, in Allan Nevins, *Henry White: Thirty Years of American Diplomacy* (New York: Harper & Brothers, 1930), 353; also in the Henry White Papers at the Manuscript Division of the Library of Congress.

22 a nine-page memorandum: White Papers; Nevins, *Henry White,* 352.

22 "single overwhelming": Arthur S. Link, ed., *The Papers of Woodrow Wilson* (Princeton: Princeton University Press, 1990), Vol. 5, 294–302.

23 "To conquer with arms": Ray Stannard Baker, *Woodrow Wilson: Life and Letters,* Vol. 8, *Armistice, March 1–November 11, 1918* (New York: Doubleday, Doran, 1939), 582.

23 110,051 American soldiers: *New York Times,* December 3, 1918, 1.

23 "It is now my duty": Ibid.

23 "God of Peace": Thomas J. Knock, *To End All Wars: Woodrow Wilson and the Quest for a New World Order* (New York: Oxford University Press, 1992), 195.

23 "I know how": Ray Stannard Baker, *American Chronicle,* 373.

23 Early in the morning: Diary of Raymond B. Fosdick, December 14, 1918, from Arthur S. Link et al., *The Papers of Woodrow Wilson,* Vol. 53 (Princeton, New Jersey: Princeton University Press, 1990), 384–85; John A. Thompson, *Woodrow Wilson: Profiles in Power* (London: Pearson Education, 2002), 188–89.

23 "For a brief interval": H. G. Wells, *The Shape of Things to Come* (London: Corgi, 1933), 96.

CHAPTER 2: SPIES ARE EVERYWHERE

Page

24 in the weeks after the Armistice: *Military Intelligence, Weekly Summaries, November 2, 1918–February 1, 1919*, Richard C. Challenger, introduction (New York: Garland, 1978), Vol. 6, 207–9.

24 "vigilant watch": *Washington Post*, November 11, 1918, 2.

24 "I'm as busy": *Albany Times Union*, November 18, 1918, 4.

25 Military Intelligence Division: Roy Talbert, Jr., *Negative Intelligence: The Army and the American Left, 1917–1941* (Jackson: University Press of Mississippi, 1991), 55–73.

25 "The U.S. had fielded": Joan M. Jensen, *The Price of Vigilance* (Morristown, NJ: General Learning Press, 1975), 234.

25 American Protective League: Ibid., 24–26; and from the APL itself in its own historical account, Emerson Hough, *The Web: A Revelation of Patriotism: The Story of the American Protective League* (Chicago: Reilly & Lee, 1919). See, regarding the APL after the war, Jensen, *The Price of Vigilance*, 91.

26 "The largest company of detectives": Hough *The Web*, 13.

26 letterhead: Ibid., 12.; Jensen, *The Price of Vigilance*, 89.

26 In one case in New Jersey: Jensen, ibid.

27 Leaguers overlapping efforts: Hough, *The Web*, 167–75.

27 "SPIES ARE EVERYWHERE": Jensen, *The Price of Vigilance*, 78.

27 "It is my plan": Letter, Richard Levering, New York City, to A. B. Bielaski, Chief of the Department of Justice, May 21, 1917, BI files, RG65, OG2910 at the National Archives.

28 One August night: Hough, *The Web*, 216.

28 Americans who had been born in Germany: U.S. Census report for 1910.

28 "disloyal talk": Talbert, *Negative Intelligence*, 66; Harry N. Scheiber, *The Wilson Administration and Civil Liberties, 1917–1919* (Ithaca: Cornell University Press, 1960), 13–28.

28 Wilson knew about the APL: Talbert, *Negative Intelligence*, 66–67.

28 George Creel: Scheiber, *The Wilson Administration and Civil Liberties*, 13–28.

29 Espionage Act: Richard Polenberg, *Fighting Faiths: The Abrams Case, the Supreme Court, and Free Speech* (New York: Penguin, 1989), 34.

29 "to willfully utter": Ibid.

29 "Upon evidence satisfactory": Ibid.

29 "Signed by President Wilson": Hough, *The Web*, 505.

30 "Whoever shall by word or act": Ibid., 506.

30 "Like murder or burglary": Ibid., 508.

31 "greatest medium": A'Lelia Bundles, *On Her Own Ground: The Life and Times of Madam C. J. Walker* (New York: Scribner, 2001), 256; Theodore Kornweibel, Jr., *Seeing Red: Federal Campaigns Against Black Militancy, 1919–1925* (Bloomington: Indiana University Press, 1999), 37.

31 "The emergency no longer exists": Talbert, *Negative Intelligence*, 137.

32 "The need for": *Washington Post*, November 10, 1918, 18.

32 staggering report: Randolph Boehm, ed., *U.S. Military Intelligence Reports: Surveillance of Radicals in the United States, 1917–1941* (Frederick, MD: University Publications of America, 1984), November 12, 1918, Reel 12, 1004–1007; Talbert, *Negative Intelligence*, 141.

32 "There are still many": *Los Angeles Times*, November 14, 1918, 2.

33 " 'the wheels of justice' ": *Negative Intelligence*, 144.

33 Carl Sandburg: Nivens, *Carl Sandburg*, 322–30; Talbert, *Negative Intelligence*, 144; Herbert Mitgang, *Dangerous Dossiers: Exposing the Secret War Against America's Greatest Authors* (New York: Primus, 1996), 870–89; papers of the New York Branch of Military Intelligence. Also see Natalie Robins, "The Defiling of American Writers," *The Nation*, October 10, 1987, 367.

35 "Isn't it fine": Niven, *Carl Sandburg*, 323.

35 "Busier than a cranberry merchant": Letter, Carl Sandburg to Paula Sandburg, December 27, 1918, in Herbert Mitgang, ed., *The Letters of Carl Sandburg*, (New York: Harcourt, Brace & World, 1968), 145.

35 "Day by day": Letter, Carl Sandburg to his editor, Sam T. Hughes, January 17, 1919, in ibid., 149.

CHAPTER 3: CHRISTMAS AT VILLA LEWARO

Page

37 Villa Lewaro is a National Historic Landmark located on North Broadway in Irvington on Hudson, New York. The majority of the details of Villa Lewaro and Walker's life are taken from the excellent biography by Walker's great-great-granddaughter, A'Lelia Bundles, *On Her Own Ground*.

37 Some of Walker's guests: Ibid., 234–35.

37 Hallie Elvira Queen: Hallie Elvira Queen file in the National Archives, RG165, Military Intelligence Division records, Negro Subversion division, File 10218, declassified, March 26, 1986.

38 "the business possibilities within": Bundles, *On Her Own Ground*, 235.

40 Major Walter H. Loving: Kornweibel, *Seeing Red*, 79–80; Talbert, *Negative Intelligence*, 117; Bundles, *On Her Own Ground*, 255.

41 "One of the best types": Memo dated August 20, 1919, Negro Subversion microfilms, Reel 5, 1026.

41 About surveillance of NAACP: Talbert, *Negative Intelligence*, 113–34.

41 five black typists: Talbert, *Negative Intelligence*, 129.

41 "German propaganda": Negro Subversion microfilms, Reel 2, 622–24.

42 "creating a disturbance": *The Crisis*, December 1918.

42 "If you believe": Ibid.

42 *Orizaba*: *Chicago Defender*, December 7, 1918, 1; *The Crisis*, January 1919; *New York Times*, December 2, 1918, 2.

43 "It would be a calamity": Bundles, *On Her Own Ground*, 252; David Levering Lewis, *W. E. B. Du Bois* (Markham, Ontario: Fitzhenry & Whiteside, 1993), 698.

43 "I am sending you": Hallie Queen MID file, undated letter to Dr. Jenks preceding her official interview on August 23, 1917.

43 "As I told you": Ibid., note from Jenks to Herbert Parson at the U.S. War College, August 13, 1917.

43 "in a position": Ibid, August 23, 1917, interview, 1.

44 "Holding myself at your service": Ibid., Queen's handwritten reports.

44 On Christmas night: Bundles, *On Her Own Ground*, 248.

44 "Now they [soldiers] will soon be returning": Ibid., 242.

44 A few days after Christmas: Ibid., 248.

44 three warships: *Washington Post*, December 31, 1918, 3.

45 last lynching of 1918: *The Crisis*, May 1919, 24–25, 37.

CHAPTER 4: WOMEN AND MOLASSES

Page

46 "We will enter": Inez Haynes Irwin, *Up Hill with Banners Flying: The Story of the Woman's Party* (Penobscot, ME: Traversity Press, 1964), 402.

46 "the watch fires of freedom": Ibid.

46 "We have used great words": Ibid.

46 "Public opinion strongly": Ibid.

47 "PRESIDENT WILSON IS": Ibid.

47 Alice Paul: Ibid.; *New York Times Magazine*, May 23, 1919.

47 "The time has come": Irwin, *Up Hill with Banners Flying*, 255.

48 "as a war measure": Alexander Keyssar, *The Right to Vote: The Contested History of Democracy in the United States* (New York: Basic, 2001), 216.

48 "The world's leader": *New York Times*, January 2, 1919, 2.

48 six women were arrested: *New York Times*, January 8, 1919, 9; and for further arrests and the burning of Wilson in effigy, see *New York Times* coverage February 9–16, 1919.

49 "will act as a spotlight": *New York Times*, January 2, 1919, 2.

49 "Our Liberty bonfires": *New York Times*, January 4, 1919, 12.

49 "Democracy Limited": *New York Times*, January 27, 1919, 13.

49 "From Prison to People": Ibid.

49 "You know how fond": *Detroit Free Press*, January 10, 1919, 1.

50 "Roosevelt died": *New York Times*, January 7, 1919, 1; O'Toole, *When Trumpets Call*, 404.

50 the "Prison Special": *New York Times*, January 27, 1919, 13.

50 "The rain of tears": *Boston Globe*, January 17, 1919, 1.

51 The company countered: Stephen Puleo, *Dark Tide: The Great Boston Molasses Flood of 1919* (Boston: Beacon, 2003), 131.

51 little pink slips: Ibid., 172.

52 "start of terrorist plots": *New York Times*, January 1, 1919, 13; *Los Angeles Times*, January 1, 1919, 1.

CHAPTER 5: THE LIST

Page

53 the first congressional investigation: Regin Schmidt, *Red Scare, FBI and the Origins of Anticommunism in the United States* (Denmark: Museum Tusculanum Press, University of Copenhagen, 2000), 140.

53 In his numerous reports: Ibid., 141; from BI files, RG65, OG190822, National Archives.

54 The Sisson documents: Schmidt, *Red Scare,* 137; George F. Kennan, "The Sisson Documents," *Journal of Modern History* (June 1956), 130–54.

54 Archibald Stevenson: Schmidt, 138–39; Robert K. Murray, *Red Scare: A Study in National Hysteria, 1919–1920* (New York: McGraw-Hill, 1964), 98–99; Talbert, *Negative Intelligence,* 26, 141–46.

54 "Special Agent 650": Talbert, *Negative Intelligence,* 146.

55 Overman Committee: BI Files, RG65, OG341494.

55 "gravest menace": Talbert, *Negative Intelligence,* 146–47; Schmidt, *Red Scare,* 139.

55 "interlocking relation": Talbert, *Negative Intelligence,* 146.

55 "Have you discovered": *New York Times,* January 25, 1919, 1, 4.

56 On Saturday morning: Ibid.

57 and whom the *New York Times: New York Times,* January 20, 1922.

57 "I am not and never have been": *New York Times,* January 26, 1919, 1.

57 "Can I make myself clear?": Talbert, *Negative Intelligence,* 148.

57 "no business to permit": *New York Times,* February 1, 1919, 4.

57 Gilbert E. Roe: Ibid.

58 "whereby the homes": Ibid.

58 The list was an embarrassment: Talbert, *Negative Intelligence,* 148.

58 "names of people": *New York Times,* January 28, 1919, 1.

58 "This committee never heard": *New York Times,* January 29, 1919, 6.

59 Baker did not respond: Talbert, *Negative Intelligence,* 148–49.

60 "all of the books": Mitgang, *The Letters of Carl Sandburg,* 147–49; Niven, *Carl Sandburg,* 326.

60 "Always I have loved": Niven, *Carl Sandburg,* 328; Letter, Carl Sandburg to Paula Sandburg, January 30, 1919.

CHAPTER 6: A MERE SLIP OF A GIRL

Page

61 "Go back to school": Harry Weinberger, "A Rebel's Interrupted Autobiography," 114.

61 the study of history: Ibid.

62 "I would rather have been": Ibid.

62 *Progress and Poverty:* Henry George, *Progress and Poverty* (New York: Robert Schalkenbach Foundation, 1946); Polenberg, *Fighting Faiths,* 77–78.

62 "Only in broken gleams": Weinberger, "A Rebel's Interrupted Autobiography," 114.

63 "a pugnacious little East Sider": Ibid., 113.

63 In his early years: Polenberg, *Fighting Faiths,* 77.

63 "wrecking my political career": Weinberger, "A Rebel's Interrupted Autobiography," 115.

63 "If liberty of speech": Ibid., 116.

64 "It is the little men": Ibid.

64 "IT IS BETTER TO DIE": Ibid., 122.

64 "those who go with the wind": Ibid., 119.

65 "I see some more": Letter, Emma Goldman to Harry Weinberger, September 1, 1918, Box 28, Weinberger Papers, Yale University, Sterling Library.

65 Weinberger wrote to the defendants: Letter, Harry Weinberger to Abrams and others, September 10, 1918, Box 2, Weinberger Papers, Yale University, Sterling Library.

65 leaflets: BI Files, RG65, OG362977, National Archives.

66 treatment of defendants: Ibid. and Polenberg, *Fighting Faiths,* 88–95.

67 "lying on the floor": Polenberg, *Fighting Faiths,* 88–95.

67 "our arrest was most terrible": Political Prisoners Defense and Relief Committee, *Sentenced to Twenty Years Prison* (New York, 1918), 15.

67 the trial began: The best sources on the trial and the sources for the quoted testimony: United States versus Gabriel Prober, Jacob Abrams, Jacob Schwartz, Samuel Lipman, Hyman Rozansky, Hyman Lachowsky, and Mollie Steimer, alias Mollie Stimer, alias Mollie Stein, trial transcript, Record Group 21, U.S. District Court for the Southern District of New York, Criminal Case Files, Archives Box 83, Docket Number: C15-23 (the case file is physically located in Lee's Summit, Missouri but can be retrieved via National Archives and Record Administration at 201 Varick Street in NYC in three days). *New York Times* and *New York Tribune* daily coverage from October 14, 1918, to October 26, 1918; Polenberg, *Fighting Faiths,* 82–147; Political Prisoners Defense and Relief Committee, *Sentenced to Twenty Years Prison* (New York, 1918); Zechariah Chafee, Jr., "A Contemporary State Trial," *Harvard Law Review* 33 (April 1920); Abrams v. U.S. file, 250 U.S. 616 (1919).

67 Henry De Lamar Clayton: Chafee, "A Contemporary State Trial"; Polenberg, *Fighting Faiths,* 100–101; *New York Times* and *New York Tribune* coverage.

68 spirited Mollie Steimer: For more sources on Steimer, see the Note on Sources. Some sources say that Steimer was the oldest of five children and some say six. Six children is from *Fighters for Anarchism* (page 4). Also there is a discrepancy regarding her wages because until just a month or so before her arrest her wages were $10 a week; at the time of her arrest, she appears to have been paid $15 a week. The quote "When you are taken" is from a tape-recorded interview with Steimer in Mexico in 1980, Oral History of the American Left Collection (Series IV, Filmmakers' Tapes and Transcripts: Anarchism in America, Interviews, prod. Steven Fischler and Joel Sucher), Tamiment Library at New York University, New York.

68 The prosecution's approach: Polenberg, *Fighting Faiths,* 275.

68 Abrams had offered to join a regiment: Letter, Harry Weinberger to A. Mitchell Palmer, Box 2, Folder 12, Weinberger Papers, Yale University, Sterling Library.

71 "Freedom of speech": *New York Times,* September 13, 1918, 1.

72 "consumed with compassion": Journalist Paul Berman, 1980, Oral History of the

American Left (Series IV, Filmmaker Tapes and Transcripts: Anarchism in America, Interviews). Tamiment Library, New York University.

73 "His heart bled": Weinberger as quoted in Political Prisoners Defense and Relief Committee, *Sentenced to Twenty Years,* 15.

75 corridor comments: *The Liberator,* December, 1918, 16–20.

76 "leave behind them": Polenberg, *Fighting Faiths,* 92.

76 Raising the money: Letters, Harry Weinberger to Lillian Wald and Frederick Blossom, Box 2, Weinberger Papers, Yale University, Sterling Library; About the bail bonds: Ibid.; Polenberg, *Fighting Faiths,* 151.

77 "I watched her:" Eileen Barrett and Mary Cullinan, eds., *American Women Writers: Diverse Voices in Prose since 1845,* 363 (based on Agnes Smedley's "Cell Mates" series in *New York Call,* February 15–March 14, 1920).

77 shadowed at all times: U.S. Military Intelligence Reports, *Surveillance of Radicals in the U.S., 1917–1941,* Reel 33, November 19, 1918; BI Files, RG65, OG362977; Polenberg, *Fighting Faiths,* 153, 387.

77 "hereafter she will know": BI files, RG65, OG362977.

78 John Edgar Hoover: Polenberg, *Fighting Faiths,* 184; Curt Gentry, *J. Edgar Hoover: The Man and the Secrets* (New York: W. W. Norton, 2001), 72–74.

78 "Mollie's reasoning": Barrett and Cullinan, eds., *American Women Writers,* 363–64.

79 "criminal policy": Hiram Johnson, January 9, 1919, speech to the U.S. Senate, "Bring American Boys Home from Russia," *Congressional Record,* January 29, 1919.

CHAPTER 7: POLAR BEARS IN PERIL

Page

80 "It is such a desolate": Diary of Sergeant Gordon W. Smith, Michigan's Own Military and Space Museum, Frankenmuth, Michigan.

80 "northern horrors": *Detroit Free Press,* April 16, 1919, Sunday Feature Section, 1; also in Roger Crownover, "Stranded in Russia," *Michigan History Magazine,* (Jan.–Feb. 1999), 37.

80 "They have been shunted": *Detroit Free Press,* April 16, 1919, 1.

82 "We took 16 enemy": Diary of Sergeant Silver K. Parrish, of Bay City, Michigan, Bentley Historical Library, University of Michigan.

82 "This last piece of news": Correspondence of Sergeant Roger Sherman Clark, August 1918–July 1919; includes essay about the reasons for bad morale.

83 Johnson "discovered": Richard Coke Lower, *A Bloc of One: The Political Career of Hiram W. Johnson* (Palo Alto: Stanford University Press, 1993), 120.

83 Senate Resolution No. 384: *Congressional Record,* December 12, 1918.

83 *Detroit Free Press* editorial: C. L. Meader, *Detroit Free Press,* December 8, 1918, 16.

84 "It is a dangerous": *Congressional Record,* December 12, 1918.

84 "a demand that American boys": Ibid.

84 "I have raised merry Cain": Letter to son Arch on December 29, 1918; Letters of Hiram Johnson, University of Michigan, Bentley Historical Library.

84 "The Russian situation": Letter to son Jack, December 31, 1918; at Bentley Historical Library.

84 Wounded soldiers: *Detroit News*, December 27, 1918, p. 1; *Detroit Free Press*, January 1, 1919, 1.

85 "well supplied with food": *Detroit Free Press*, December 31, 1918, 4.

85 "determination by ourselves": *Congressional Record*, January 29, 1919.

85 "the crassest stupidity": Ibid.

86 "the whole Russian problem": *Detroit News*, February 4, 1919, 1.

86 "The history of the Russian intervention": Ibid.

86 on the night of February 4: *Detroit News*, February 5, 1919, 1; *Detroit News*, February 6, 1919, 1.

86 petition drive: The petition with names, addresses, signature, and date of signing is available at Michigan's Own Military and Space Museum.

86 On February 5: Talbert, *Negative Intelligence*, 159.

87 "like pulling the trigger": Anna Louise Strong, *I Change Worlds: The Remaking of an American* (New York: Garden City Publishing, 1937), 72.

87 "We are undertaking": Ibid., 79.

87 the Seattle branch of the Military Intelligence Division: Jensen, *The Price of Vigilance*, 258–59; Talbert, *Negative Intelligence*, 159–61.

87 The mayor, hell-bent: Murray, *Red Scare*, 63.

87 "IWW troublemakers": *Chicago Tribune*, February 10, 1919, 1.

87 "Red Special": Murray, *Red Scare*, 194–95; Jensen, *The Price of Vigilance*, 259.

87 The very next day: Murray, *Red Scare*, 66.

88 At the Senate: *Congressional Record*, February 10, 13, 14, 1919.

88 Johnson vowed: *Detroit News*, February 15, 1919, 2.

88 "The propaganda for": Letters of Hiram Johnson, February 14, 1919.

88 On the very day: *Detroit News*, February 15, 1919, 1.

88 "That the fortunes of war": *Detroit News*, February 16, 1919, 1.

89 "Mr. Baker and his associates": Ibid., 12.

89 "at the earliest possible moment": *Detroit News*, February 18, 1919, 1.

89 "We cannot make": Ibid.

89 an average of 300,000 men: *New York Times*, January 28, 1919, 6.

90 "In the spring": *Detroit News*, February 8, 1919, 1.

CHAPTER 8: SERGEANT HENRY JOHNSON

Page

91 St. Louis coliseum: *Chicago Defender*, February 22, 1919, 3, 11; James Weldon Johnson, "Views and Reviews," *New York Age*, March 29, 1919; BI Agent C. K. Berge in reports filed February 28, 1919, and March 26, 1919, in BI Files, RG65, OG265935, at the National Archives; BI Agent G. C. Outlaw in reports filed March 3, 1919, and March 12, 1919.

92 "He shall not speak": *New York Age*, March 29, 1919, 1.

93 African-Americans in the war: Gail Buckley, *American Patriots: The Story of Blacks in the Military from the Revolution to Desert Storm* (New York: Random House, 2001), 167.

95 "You all don't have to worry": Little, *From Harlem to the Rhine*, 198.

96 "Every colored man and woman in the United States": *The World*, May 22, 1918, 1. Also in the *New York Tribune*, May 23, 1918, 1, and in the *Albany Times Union*, May 23, 1918, 1.

96 "To resolve that": *Albany Times Union*, May 23, 1918, 1.

96 "Our colored volunteers": Little, *From Harlem to the Rhine*, 201.

96 In Albany the newspapers: *Albany Times Union*, May 21, 1918, 1.

96 "The Negro Fighting Man": *Albany Times Union*, May 23, 1918, 1.

97 "How many war stamps": *New York Age*, March 1, 1919, 2.

97 "Johnson, Henry": Little, *From Harlem to the Rhine*, 36.

97 "He may be disabled": *New York Times*, February 13, 1919, 1.

97 the 369th defended more than 20 percent: Buckley, *American Patriots*, 206.

97 "So close were we": *New York Times*, February 13, 1919, 1.

98 "went out to fight": *Chicago Defender*, February 22, 1919, 1.

98 "gave the government": *Chicago American*, February 22, 1919, 1.

98 "Not only their own people": Ibid.

98 parade to Harlem: *New York Times*, February 18, 1919, 1; *New York Age*, February 22, 1919, 1; *Chicago Defender*, February 22, 1919, 1; *Washington Post*, February 18, 1919, 1; Buckley, *American Patriots*; Bundles, *On Her Own Ground*.

99 "the musical sensation": *Chicago Defender*, April 19 and April 26, 1919.

99 "the band that set all of France": *St. Louis Dispatch*, June 10, 1918, 1.

99 "the band that put wine": *Boston Globe*, May 15, 1919, 1.

100 "On the 17th of February": Little, *From Harlem to the Rhine*, 361.

100 The 369th was mustered out: Ibid., 367–68.

101 "What are you planning": Little, *From Harlem to the Rhine*, 367.

101 Johnson eagerly returned home: *New York Age*, March 1, 1919, 2.

101 "There wasn't anything so fine": Ibid.

101 disaster in St. Louis: Ibid.; BI Reports: *St. Louis Argus*, April 4, 1919.

102 James Weldon Johnson: *New York Age*, April 12, 1919.

103 "In a few short weeks": Robert Abbott, *Chicago Defender*, editorial, February 22, 1919.

CHAPTER 9: TROTTER AND THE PASSPORTS

Page

104 passports: *New York Age*, December 21, 1918, 4; Bundles, *On Her Own Ground*, 263–65; Fox, *The Guardian of Boston*, 224–25; BI files, RG65, OG336880, for memos regarding passports.

104 first official interference: Kornweibel, *Seeing Red*, 15; honorably credited by Bundles, *On Her Own Ground*, 264.

105 "the destinies of mankind": *The Crisis*, December 1918, 60–61.

105 "to focus the attention": *The Crisis*, March 1919, 224–25.

105 "for the interests": *New York Times*, February 16, 1919, Section 2, 1.

105 Two suffragists: *New York Times*, February 2, 1919, 11.

105 "rock the boat": BI Files, RG65, OG17011, December 3, 1918.

106 "When I was suddenly": *The Crisis*, May 1919, 7–9.

106 State Department and Pan-African Congress: *New York Age*, February 8, 1919, 1; *New York Age*, February 15, 1919, 1; *New York Times*, February 1, 1919, 1; *New York Times*, February 13, 1919, 1; *Guardian*, February 1919 issues; Bundles, *On Her Own Ground*, 263–64; Fox, *The Guardian of Boston*, 224–25.

106 "the colored people": *New York Age*, March 1, 1919, 1.

107 Du Bois and Colonel House: *The Crisis*, April 1919, 271–74.

107 "The colored people of the U.S.": Alexander Walters, *My Life and Work* (New York: Fleming H. Revell, 1917), 195.

108 "as your inauguration": Fox, *The Guardian of Boston*, 169.

108 "the inaugurator of a": Ibid.

109 "listened attentively": *The Guardian*, November 15, 1913, 1.

109 in 1914: Fox, *The Guardian of Boston*, 179.

109 "a benefit": Ibid., 180–81.

109 "entirely disappointing": Ibid.

109 "violated every courtesy": Ibid., 182.

109 The *New York Times* carried the story: *New York Times*, November 13, 1914, 1.

110 "if there were some way": Fox, *The Guardian of Boston*, 189.

110 "more or less agitators" and "the negro question": Ibid.; BI Files, RG65, OG336880, National Archives; Bundles, *On Her Own Ground*, 264; also discussion of this in Kornweibel, *Seeing Red*, 15.

110 "I think your inclination": Bundles, 252.

112 "Now the war's over": Edna Perry Booth, *Chicago Defender*, April 12, 1919.

113 "Fourteen million": Dr. Charles Wesley, president, Wilberforce University, "Trotter Pioneered in Drive for Negro Voice," *Chicago Defender*, October 9, 1943, 1.

CHAPTER 10: THE MAGISTERIAL WAND

Page

114 Wilson's health: Ray Stannard Baker, *American Chronicle*, 386; diary of Ray Stannard Baker, November 5, 1919, Baker Papers, Manuscript Division, Library of Congress; Dr. Bert E. Park, "Woodrow Wilson's Stroke of October 2nd, 1919," in Appendix of Link, *The Papers of Woodrow Wilson*, Vol. 62, 639–43; Cary T. Grayson, *Woodrow Wilson: An Intimate Memoir* (New York: Holt, Rinehart & Winston, 1960), 2–3; Ray Stannard Baker, *What Wilson Did at Paris* (Doubleday, Page, 1919), 4.

114 "a 600 horse-power": Diary of Ray Stannard Baker, November 5, 1919, Baker Papers, Manuscript Division, Library of Congress.

115 "This young assistant": Ray Stannard Baker, *American Chronicle*, 384, 470.

115 "It was inevitable": Ray Stannard Baker, *What Wilson Did at Paris*, 4.

115 head of the Press Bureau: Ray Stannard Baker, *American Chronicle*, 375; *New York Times*, January 15, 1919, 2.

116 "So many of the discussions": Ray Stannard Baker, *American Chronicle*, 377.

117 "a dangerous radical": George Seldes, *Witness to a Century: Encounters with the Noted, the Notorious and the Three SOBs* (Boston: G. K. Hall, 1988), 107.

118 "Le bon Dieu n'avait que dix": Ibid., 108 (translation "The good Lord had only ten").

118 By the time Wilson docked in Boston: Ray Stannard Baker, *What Wilson Did at Paris*, 34.

118 Wilson warned: Ibid., 32–33.

118 "I cannot but feel": Nevins, *Henry White*, 374–75.

119 "under no circumstances": William C. Widenor, *Henry Cabot Lodge and the Search for an American Foreign Policy* (Berkeley: University of California Press, 1980), 298.

119 "to talk about": *Congressional Record*, February 28, 1918, 728.

120 "The attempt to form": Ibid.; Widenor, *Henry Cabot Lodge*, 298.

120 "go into an overseas war": Stout, Ralph, ed., Roosevelt in the *Kansas City Star: War Time Editorials by Theodore Roosevelt*. Boston: Houghton, Mifflin, 1921, 294.

120 "The constitution of that": Ray Stannard Baker, *What Wilson Did at Paris*, 40.

121 "A living thing is born": Nevins, *Henry White*, 380.

121 "international interdependence": William Allen White, *Woodrow Wilson: The Man, His Times and His Task* (Boston: Houghton Mifflin, 1924), 407–8.

121 conspiring to assassinate Wilson: *New York Times*, February 13, 1919, 1; *New York Times*, February 24, 1919, 1–2.

121 walked off the boat at Boston: Widenor, *Henry Cabot Lodge*, 305–8.

122 "band of Nihilists": *New York Times*, February 13, 1919, 1.

122 "I.W.W. in Plot": Ibid.

122 Lodge's own strategy: Widenor, *Henry Cabot Lodge*, 313.

CHAPTER 11: BLINDERS

Page

124 "The President appears": *New York Times*, February 26, 1919, 5.

124 "victory tax": Ibid., 4.

124 dined at the White House: Nevins, *Henry White*, 385, 390, 392–93.

125 "Most of the men": *New York Times*, February 19, 1919, 1.

125 "I accepted the invitation" Nevins, *Henry White*, 390.

125 After dinner: Ibid., 390, 392, 393.

125 "a betrayal of the people": *Congressional Record*, February 28, 1919.

126 "you cannot dissect": Nevins, *Henry White*, 394.

127 Even the flu was back: Crosby, *America's Forgotten Pandemic*, 184.

127 Gore called for the repeal of the Daylight Savings Act: *New York Times*, February 21, 1919, 5.

127 controversy over Daylight Savings: *New York Times*, February 22, 1919, 8; *New York Times*, February 23, 1919, 28; *New York Times*, February 25, 1919, 12; *New York Times*, February 27, 1919, 17; *New York Times*, March 2, 1919, 5; editorial, "Farmers

Want Old Time," *New York Times*, February 2, 1919, Section 3, 3; *Scientific American*, March 8, 1919, 220; *Scientific American*, March 29, 1919, 315.

128 "inconvenience and an economic loss": Wilson's lengthy commentary on the subject in the *New York Times*, July 13, 1919, 1.

128 one infantryman from Michigan's 339th: John Przybylski report, Company M, 339th Infantry, *Detroit Free Press*, February 23, 1919, 1, 4.

129 At the Overman hearings: *New York Times*, February 12, 1919, 1; *New York Times*, February 14, 1919, 4.

129 "How would you describe": *New York Times*, February 14, 1919, 4.

129 Another witness claimed: *New York Times*, February 15, 1919, 16.

129 "Everything that makes life": Ibid.

129 Louise Bryant and her husband, John Reed: *New York Times*, February 21, 1919, 5; *New York Times*, February 22, 1919, 1, 5.

130 "an East Side": *New York Times*, February 22, 1919, 5.

130 "I have always": Robert A. Rosenstone, *Romantic Revolutionary: A Biography of John Reed* (Cambridge: Harvard University Press, 1990), 344.

130 Bessie Beatty: *New York Times*, March 6, 1919, 4.

130 "If the Bolsheviki": *New York Times*, February 9, 1919, 1, 5.

130 "Sometimes, as during": Baker, *American Chronicle*, 388.

131 a new attorney general: *New York Times*, February 28, 1919, 4.

131 "requires not a man of peace": Letter, A. Mitchell Palmer to Woodrow Wilson, February 24, 1913, in Stanley Coben, *A. Mitchell Palmer: Politician* (New York: Columbia University Press, 1963), 70–71.

132 "German industrial army" and "official American pickpocket": *Boston Daily Globe*, June 21, 1919, 5.

132 "incumbent de gracia": *Christian Science Monitor*, June 8, 1919, 1.

132 "take care of the boys": *New York Times*, March 6, 1919, 7.

132 At Boston harbor: *Boston Globe*, March 6, 1919, 1.

132 "Mr. President, How Long": *New York Times*, March 5, 1919, 3.

CHAPTER 12: SHUFFLEBOARD

Page

134 "quiet and simple": Ray Stannard Baker, *American Chronicle*, 388.

134 "the meal itself": Ibid., 389.

134 *Prophets, Priests and Kings*: Ibid.

135 "What I am seeking": Walter A. Dyer, *David Grayson: Adventurer* (New York: Doubleday, 1928), 21.

135 "fond of the open air": C. D. Morley, "The Graysonians," *Book News Monthly* (February 1916), 258.

135 A lawyer in Atlanta: Dyer, *David Grayson*, 14; *New York Sun*, April 15, 1916, 1.

136 For years, many readers: Dyer, *David Grayson*, 13–14.

136 "full of danger": Ray Stannard Baker, "Gathering Clouds Along the Color Line," *World's Work*, Vol. 32 (June 1916), 236.

137 "I think," "I believe," and "I hope": Ray Stannard Baker, *What Wilson Did at Paris*, 14.

138 "publicity is the life blood of democracy": Ray Stannard Baker, *American Chronicle*, 387.

138 two Polish peasants: Ray Stannard Baker, *What Wilson Did at Paris*, 6–8.

139 "Everyone who came to Paris": Ibid., 6.

139 "for more and better": Ray Stannard Baker, *American Chronicle*, 387.

139 "As a highly": Ray Stannard Baker, *What Wilson Did at Paris*, 15.

140 "When people complain": Ibid., 15.

140 Wilson was outraged: Ray Stannard Baker, *American Chronicle*, 387.

140 And Baker's journalist friends in Paris: Ibid., 391.

140 "lived the lonely life": Ibid., 386.

141 "I have often": Ibid., 388.

141 March 13 was the last night: Ibid., 389.

141 "I wondered among": Ibid.

141 "an integral part": Ibid., 392.

142 "It was clear": Ibid., 393.

CHAPTER 13: IN LIKE A LION

Page

143 "our national sovereignty": "Bolshevik Propaganda," U.S. Congress, Senate Report on Hearings Before a Subcommittee of the Committee on the Judiciary, 65th Congress, 2nd and 3rd Sessions, Washington, 1919, 22. (Also in RG65 at the National Archives, BI files, OG 341494.)

143 Espionage Act statistics: Report of the U.S. Attorney General, 1918, 17, 20–23, 47–57.

143 in Weinberger's opinion: Weinberger, "A Rebel's Interrupted Autobiography"; Polenberg, *Fighting Faiths*, 75–81.

144 Charles T. Schenck: Sheldon Novick, *Honorable Justice: The Life and Times of Oliver Wendell Holmes* (Boston: Little, Brown, 1989), 326–28.

144 "Conscription was despotism": Leaflet, "Long Live the Constitution of the United States," reproduced in the BI Files, RG65, OG362977, and in U.S. Supreme Court files for the *Abrams* case.

144 "a monumental": Novick, *Honorable Justice*, 326–28.

145 All three of the opinions: *Schenck v. U.S.* 249 U.S. 47, 39 Supp. Ct. Rep. 247 (1919); *Frohwerk v. U.S.* 249 U.S. 204, 39 Supp. Ct. Rep. 247 (1919); *Debs v. U.S.* 249 U.S. 211, 39 Supp. Ct. Rep. 252 (1919).

145 "lighted match": Liva Baker, *The Justice from Beacon Hill: The Life and Times of Oliver Wendell Holmes* (New York: HarperCollins, 1991), 523.

145 "The character of every act": Ibid., 523–24.

146 "I greatly regretted": Mark DeWolfe Howe, ed., *Holmes-Laski Letters: The Correspondence of Mr. Justice Holmes and Harold J. Laski, 1916–1935* (Cambridge: Harvard University Press, 1953), 190.

146 Laski: Novick, *Honorable Justice*, 320.

146 "wrapped itself around": Howe, *Holmes-Laski Letters*, 139.

146 "stretched to mean": Ernst Freund, "Debs Case and Freedom of Speech," *New Republic*, May 3, 1919; Liva Baker, *The Justice from Beacon Hill*, 527.

147 a letter to Herbert Croly: Liva Baker, *The Justice from Beacon Hill*, 528; Howe, *Holmes-Laski Letters*, Letter written to Croly on May 12, 1919.

147 "firmly believed": *New York Times*, March 10, 1919, 1. For a glimpse of the Senate debate over censorship and the crusade led by Senator Borah, who believed Burleson's censorship powers were too broad, see *New York Times*, February 9, 1919, 1.

148 "Bolshevism": *Bolshevik Propaganda*, 3.

150 "a creator of Bolshevism": *New York Times*, March 13, 1919, 2.

150 Dr. Richard Morse Hodge: *New York Times*, March 14, 1919, 6.

150 raided the Russian People's House: Todd J. Pfannestiel, *Rethinking the Red Scare: The Lusk Committee and New York's Crusade Against Radicalism, 1919–1923* (New York: Routledge, 2003), 16; *New York Tribune*, March 13, 1919, 1; *New York Tribune*, March 14, 1919, 1.

150 "Police Round Up": *New York Times*, March 13, 1919, 1.

150 "A great mass": *New York Tribune*, March 13, 1919, 1.

150 "It is probable": *New York Tribune*, March 14, 1919, 1.

150 "the downfall of the U.S. government": Ibid.

151 "on the long distance telephone": Harry Weinberger, letters to Mollie Steimer, March 15, 1919, March 17, 1919, Weinberger Papers, Box 2, Yale University, Sterling Library.

151 "I am positive": Harry Weinberger, letter to Mollie Steimer, March 17, 1919.

151 "I telephoned Washington": Ibid.

151 "after a hearing": Boehm, Randolph, ed., U.S. Military Intelligence Reports. Surveillance of Radicals in the United States, 1917–1941. (Frederick, MD: University Microfilms of America) 1984. Reel 12.

152 Lusk Committee: Pfannestiel, *Rethinking the Red Scare*, 19–24; Polenberg, *Fighting Faiths*, 168–73; Murray, *Red Scare*; Schmidt, *Red Scare*; and see BI Files, RG65, OG185161, OG208369, OG350625.

153 "the federal Bureau": Schmidt, *Red Scare*, 124.

154 "The process of turning": *The Nation*, editorial, "Danger Ahead," February 8, 1919.

CHAPTER 14: OUT LIKE A LION

Page

155 "a system of trenches": *New York Times*, March 26, 1919, 4.

155 "spite fences": *New York Times*, March 13, 1919, 4.

155 tunnel under the Hudson River: *Scientific American*, April 5, 1919, 337, 353; *Scientific American*, March 8, 1919, 222.

156 "Leakage will most": *Scientific American*, March 8, 1919, 222.

156 "Can the tunnel": Ibid., April 5, 1919, 337.

156 "honest expressions": *Detroit Free Press*, March 24, 1919, 1.

157 "It is very very cold": Diary of Corporal Frank Douma, of Grand Rapids, Michigan, Bentley Historical Library, University of Michigan.

157 Glenn L. Shannon: *Detroit Free Press,* March 30, 1919, April 6, 1919, April 13, 1919.

157 1,600 sailors: *Detroit Free Press,* March 28, 1919, 1; March 29, 1919, 1; March 30, 1919, 1.

157 "We do know": *Detroit Free Press,* March 30, 1919, 1.

157 On the afternoon of the 28th: *Detroit News,* March 29, 1919, 1.

158 "have no more": Ibid.

158 "Contrary to all": Ibid.

159 "will give the Federal Government": *New York Times,* March 29, 1919, 9.

159 "what is very serious": *Christian Science Monitor,* March 31, 1919, 16; and same group represented in letters in *Scientific American,* October 18, 1919, 389.

PART II: SPRING: FEAR

Page

161 "Here is April": Diary, Sergeant Gordon W. Smith, April 1919, Bentley Historical Library, University of Michigan.

161 "It is one of": James Weldon Johnson, column, *New York Age,* May 10, 1919.

CHAPTER 15: INNER LIGHT

Page

164 "seeing physical science": Allie Vibert Douglas, *The Life of Arthur Stanley Eddington* (London: Thomas Nelson & Sons, 1957), 52.

165 other expeditions to study eclipses: Peter Coles, *Einstein and the Total Eclipse* (London: Icon, 1999), 44–45.

166 Willem deSitter: Matthew Stanley, "An Expedition to Heal the Wounds of War," *Isis* (Winter 2003), 68.

166 "You must be one": Subrahmanyan Chandrasekhar, *Eddington: The Most Distinguished Astrophysicist of His Time* (Cambridge: Cambridge University Press, 1983), 30.

167 "One of the masterpieces": Douglas, *The Life of Arthur Stanley Eddington,* 39.

167 Eddington: Ibid., 51.

167 "To see a World": Ibid., 131.

167 crossword puzzles: Chandrasekhar, *Eddington,* 6.

168 "In science as in religion": Arthur Stanley Eddington, *Science and the Unseen World: Swarthmore Lecture, 1929* (London: George Allen & Unwin, 1930), 16.

168 "If I were to try": A. H. Batten, "A Most Rare Vision, Eddington's Thinking on the Relation Between Science and Religion," *R.A.S. Quarterly Journal,* Vol. 35 (September 1994), 252.

168 "The lines of latitude": *Observatory,* June 1916, 271.

169 "We find ourselves": Stanley, "An Expedition to Heal the Wounds of War," 61.

169 Eddington and Britain's pacifists: Ibid., 71; Chandrasekhar, *Eddington,* 25.

169 "I cannot believe": Levenson, *Einstein in Berlin,* 212.

169 conscientious objector: Douglas, *The Life of Arthur Stanley Eddington*, 39; Stanley, "An Expedition to Heal the Wounds of War," 73; Levenson, *Einstein in Berlin*, 212–13; Chandrasekhar, *Eddington*, 25.

170 "I'm interested to hear": Stanley, "An Expedition to Heal the Wounds of War," 69.

171 "a feeling that": Philipp Frank, *Einstein: His Life and Times* (New York: Alfred A. Knopf, 1947), 154.

171 "The Manifesto to the Civilized World": Stanley, "An Expedition to Heal the Wounds of War," 61; Corey Powell, *God in the Equation: How Einstein Transformed Religion* (New York: Simon & Schuster, 2002), 63–64.

171 "Never has any previous war": Stanley, "An Expedition to Heal the Wounds of War," 62.

171 "Bolshevism in physics": Frank, *Einstein*, 160; *New York Times*, November 16, 1919, 12.

171 "When is space curved?": Frank, *Einstein*, 143.

172 Fund-raising and basic preparations: Eddington, *Space, Time and Gravitation: An Outline of the General Relativity Theory* (Cambridge: Cambridge University Press, 1920), 114; Stanley, "An Expedition to Heal the Wounds of War," 73.

173 "What will it mean": Douglas, *The Life of Arthur Stanley Eddington*, 40.

173 "Instead of trying": Frank, *Einstein*, 138.

174 automobile, sent from Rio: A. C. D. Crommelin, "The Eclipse Expedition to Sobral," *Observatory* (October 1919), Vol. 42, 368–71.

174 "very charming": Stanley, "An Expedition to Heal the Wounds of War," 75.

174 "the most exciting event": Chandrasekhar, *Eddington*, 24.

CHAPTER 16: MAKE-BELIEVE RIOTS AND REAL BOMBS

Page

175 "you will not only clean up": *Moving Picture World*, April 15, 1919.

175 *The Birth of a Nation* and *Bolshevism on Trial:* Comments are based on a viewing of both movies by the author.

178 "Powerful, well-knit": Julian Johnson, "Review of Bolshevism on Trial," *Photoplay*, April 30, 1919, and in introductory material written by Anthony Slide in the Blackhawk Films video. (Full quote: "powerful, well-knit, indubitably true and biting satire.")

178 "the timeliest picture ever filmed": Ibid.

179 *Ten Days That Shook the World:* Newspapers of the day; Rosenstone, *Romantic Revolutionary*, 339; John Reed, *Ten Days That Shook the World* (Franklin, TN: Tantalion, 2002), editor's introduction.

179 "No matter what": John Reed, *Ten Days That Shook the World* (New York: Modern Library, 1935), Reed's preface, xii.

180 "This publication proposes": *New York Times*, April 19, 1919, 4.

180 Minute Men: Schmidt, *Red Scare*, 126–35; Jensen, *The Price of Vigilance*, 125–29; William Preston, Jr., *Aliens and Dissenters: Federal Suppression of Radicals, 1903–1933*, 2nd ed. (Urbana: University of Illinois Press, 1994), 155–56.

181 "well-financed and surprisingly well-organized": Agents' reports in BI Files, RG65, OG91928, National Archives.

181 "a revolution instigated": Ibid.

181 Spies had infiltrated: Editorial, *The Nation*, April 5, 1919.

181 "If the government were not": *The Nation*, April 5, 1919.

182 "During my incarceration": *Detroit Free Press*, April 12, 1919, 1.

182 "greatest market": "Pfannestiel, *Rethinking the Red Scare*, 45.

182 The Soviet Bureau: Ibid., 37–61; also see Murray, *Red Scare*; Schmidt, *Red Scare*; Talbert, *Negative Intelligence*.

182 $50,000 worth of diamonds: Pfannestiel, *Rethinking the Red Scare*, 42.

183 "Assuring you of my": Ibid., 56.

183 Marshall Field, etc.: For a list of companies that attempted to do business with the Soviet Bureau see, Pfannestiel, *Rethinking the Red Scare*, Appendix 1.

183 "considers their tractors": Ibid., 61.

183 Julius Hammer: Ibid.

183 And according to Scotland Yard: Ibid., 62.

184 Charles Kaplan: *New York Times*, April 29, 1919, April 30, 1919, May 1, 1919, May 2, 1919; Murray, *Red Scare*; Talbert, *Negative Intelligence*; Schmidt: *Red Scare*; Boehm, ed., U.S. Military Intelligence Reports, Reel 12.

185 "Reds Planned May Day Murders": Murray, *Red Scare*, 71.

185 "enmity of the radicals": Ibid.

185 hang every bomb maker: Ibid., 72.

185 Committee of Forty-eight: Talbert, *Negative Intelligence*, 186.

185 "They were addressed": Editorial, *The Liberator*, July 1919.

186 But Cleveland got the worst of it: Pfannestiel, *Rethinking the Red Scare*, 32; Jensen, *The Price of Vigilance*, 270.

186 "bomb-throwing radicals": Pfannestiel, *Rethinking the Red Scare*, 32.

186 "Free speech has been": Ibid., as quoted from *Salt Lake City Tribune*.

186 "secret service force": Ibid., 33.

186 a sensational raid: Ibid., 64.

187 "It has struck me": Jensen, *The Price of Vigilance*, 270.

187 "It is encouraging": *The Nation*, April 1919.

187 On May 5 Chicago shooting: *Washington Post*, May 7, 1919, 2.

CHAPTER 17: IT'S IN THE MAIL

Page

188 100,000 copies of *The Crisis*: *New York Tribune*, May 2, 1919, 7.

188 Robert A. Bowen: Kornweibel, *Seeing Red*, 56–58; Schmidt, *Red Scare*, 91–94, 164, 182–83; BI Files, RG65, OG387162; Post Office Files, RG28, File 47732, National Archives.

188 "treason, insurrection": Kornweibel, *Seeing Red*, 57.

189 "traitorous zone": Ibid.

189 "insolently abusive": Ibid.

189 "not too veiled threat": Ibid.

189 "The world-fight": "My Mission," editorial, *The Crisis,* May 1919.

191 flurry of telegrams: Post Office Files, RG28, File 47732, National Archives.

192 "of special interest": Kornweibel, *Seeing Red,* 58.

192 "unquestionably violent": Ibid., 57.

192 "what is going on": Baker, "Gathering Clouds Along the Color Line," 232–36.

192 "It must be sharply": Ibid.

193 anti-lynching conference: James Weldon Johnson, "The Fight on Lynching," *New York Age,* May 10, 1919; *New York Age,* May 3, 1919, 1; *Chicago Defender,* May 24, 1919, 1; *The Crisis,* May and June 1919; *New York Times,* May 6, 1919, 15.

193 "This is what": Ida B. Wells, *Crusade for Justice: The Autobiography of Ida B. Wells,* ed. Alfreda M. Duster (Chicago: University of Chicago Press, 1970), 64, 71.

194 "Justice in America": Bundles, *On Her Own Ground,* 271.

194 "the most primitive": *New York Age,* May 3, 1919, 1.

195 "black men's bodies": Speech made by James Weldon Johnson as reported in the sources noted above for the May anti-lynching conference and repeated in his column in the *New York Age,* May 10, 1919.

195 "THE KU KLUX ARE": *The Crisis,* March 1919.

195 Daniel Mack: *New York Age,* May 3, 1919.

195 "The failure has been": *New York Times,* March 9, 1919, Section 3, 1.

196 "noteworthy": Ibid.

196 "seriousness of the Negro question": Talbert, *Negative Intelligence,* 129.

196 On May 10 in Charleston: William M. Tuttle, Jr., *Race Riot: Chicago in the Red Summer of 1919* (New York: Atheneum, 1970), 23–25; Lee E. Williams II, "The Charleston, South Carolina, Riot of 1919," *Southern Miscellany,* 151–76; *Charleston News and Courier,* May 11, 12, 16, 1919; Arthur I. Waskow, *From Race Riot to Sit-In, 1919 and 1960's* (Garden City: Doubleday, 1966); proceedings of a court of inquiry convened at the Navy Yard, Charleston, South Carolina, May 27 to June 19, 1919, RG125, National Archives.

197 They looted both shooting galleries: Williams, "The Charleston, South Carolina, Riot of 1919," 157–58; Charleston newspapers.

197 The subsequent naval inquiry: Record of court of inquiry proceedings, 268–69.

197 news of an accusation: Williams, "The Charleston, South Carolina, Riot of 1919," 163.

197 At least seventeen: Ibid., 163–64.

198 "VICKSBURG, MISSISSIPPI": *Chicago Defender,* May 24, 1919.

199 "wah-wah trumpets": *Chicago Defender,* April 12, 19, and 26, 1919 (advertisements). "Setting France Ablaze": Ibid.

199 "a most extraordinary man": Buckley, *American Patriots,* 191–92; *New York Evening Post,* May 3, 1912.

200 "Europe and his band": *Chicago Defender,* May 10, 1919, 1.

200 "He died": Ibid.

200 "I want to live": Bundles, *On Her Own Ground,* 273.

201 "I am not": Ibid., 234.

201 "If peace can be": Ibid.

201 "the wealthiest negro woman": Ibid, 276.

201 "Mrs. Walker demonstrated": Ibid., 277.

201 "members of my Race": Ibid., 270.

202 memorial service: Ibid., 275.

202 "She had had a premonition": Bundles, *On Her Own Ground*, 275.

CHAPTER 18: MONSIEUR TROTTER

See Note on Sources for sources used for Trotter portions of the book. The story of Trotter in Paris: from articles written throughout his stay in Paris in *The Guardian; New York Age; The Crisis;* Fox, *The Guardian of Boston,* and for the letters between Trotter and Wilson, Trotter and Close, Trotter and House, Wilson Papers, Manuscript Division, Library of Congress.

Page

203 Le Havre: *Chicago Defender,* 1943.

204 "Arrived Paris Wednesday" and "This trip": *The Guardian,* May 16, 1919, 1.

204 Mr. and Mrs. Kane: *New York Age,* June 28, 1919, 2.

204 "He was absolutely like a tramp": Ibid.

205 translator at a café: Letter, G. W. Baker to the editor of *New York Age,* published September 16, 1919; Fox, *The Guardian of Boston,* 227.

205 "Being informed that": *Chicago Defender,* October 9, 1943, 1; Wilson Papers, Library of Congress.

205 "be able to see": *Chicago Defender,* October 9, 1943.

206 "Monsieur William M. Trotter": *L'Avenir,* May 22, 1919, translated by Mrs. Lillian L. Feurtado for *The Guardian,* December 13, 1919, 2.

206 *Le Petit Journal: Chicago Defender,* October 9, 1943, 1; "The Parisian Trotter," *The Guardian,* July 19, 1919, 1.

206 *L'Intransigeant:* Ibid.

207 "under any circumstances": *The Guardian,* June 14, 1919, 4; *Chicago Defender,* October 9, 1943.

207 "out of the volcanic": Ray Stannard, Baker, *American Chronicle,* 437.

207 "They came to defeat": Ibid., 436–37; Woodrow Wilson, Ray Stannard Baker, and William E. Todd, eds., *Public Papers of Woodrow Wilson: War and Peace, Presidential Messages, Addresses and Public Papers, 1917–1924* (New York: Harper & Brothers, 1927), Vol. 1, 502.

208 "I saw and felt": Ray Stannard, Baker, *American Chronicle,* 438.

208 "Sir: Lawlessness and mob murder": *New York Age,* September 16, 1919, 4.

208 Frank Livingston: *Chicago Defender,* June 1, 1919, 1.

209 *The Noose: New York Age,* April 26, 1919, 8.

209 "There are few": Ibid.

CHAPTER 19: 302 SECONDS IN MAY

Page

211 The Príncipe team had routinely coped: Stanley, "An Expedition to Heal the Wounds of War," 75.

211 equipment: Eddington, *Space, Time and Gravitation*, 12.

211 On the morning of the 29th: Stanley, "An Expedition to Heal the Wounds of War," 75.

212 "whether it leads": Eddington, *Science and the Unseen World*, xvi.

212 "There was nothing for it": Eddington, *Space, Time and Gravitation*, 14.

212 May 29, the day of the total eclipse: Note that the official time of totality on record for the May 29, 1919, total eclipse of the sun is six minutes and fifty-one seconds, which occurred at various locations along the 240 miles of totality but mostly over water. In Brazil and Príncipe, totality was 302 seconds.

212 "The cloud has interfered": Eddington, *Space, Time and Gravitation*, 115.

212 "Through cloud. Hopeful": Stanley, "An Expedition to Heal the Wounds of War," 76; *Observatory* (June, 1919), 256.

212 results of twelve plates: Eddington, *Space, Time and Gravitation*, 116.

212 in Sobral, Brazil: Stanley, "An Expedition to Heal the Wounds of War," 77.

213 "Eclipse splendid": *Observatory* (June 1919), 256.

213 "It was found that": Stanley, "An Expedition to Heal the Wounds of War," 77.

213 "showing a very": Eddington, *Space, Time and Gravitation*, 115.

214 The result coming out of the machine: Ibid.; "Joint Eclipse Meeting of the Royal Society and the Royal Astronomical Society," *Observatory*, November 1919, 389–98; Stanley, "An Expedition to Heal the Wounds of War," 77–79.

214 "gave a result": Stanley, "An Expedition to Heal the Wounds of War," 76.

215 "so far nothing": Albert Einstein, letter to Dr. E. Hartmann, September 2, 1919, in Ronald William Clark, *Einstein: The Life and Times* (New York: Avon, 1978), 230.

215 "fully convinced": Chandrasekhar, *Eddington*, 25.

215 "I know of no better": Eddington, *Science and the Unseen World*, 17.

215 Eddington was ever fascinated with large numbers: Chandrasekhar, *Eddington*, 2, 3.

216 "Ah Moon of my Delight": Douglas, *The Life of Arthur Stanley Eddington*, 43, 44.

CHAPTER 20: WHAT HAPPENED ON R STREET

Page

218 the moon: *Washington Post*, June 2, 1919, 14.

218 For the assistant secretary: Roosevelt and Shalett, *Affectionately, F.D.R.*, 59–61.

219 "I'll never forget": Ibid.

219 "Thank thee": Ibid.

219 "I never knew": Ibid.

219 "What a wonderful": Letter, Eleanor Roosevelt to Sara Delano Roosevelt, June 3, 1919, FDR Library, Hyde Park; Blanche Wiesen Cook, *Eleanor Roosevelt: 1884–1933*, Vol. 1 (New York: Viking, 1992), 244.

219 "I had been": *New York Times,* June 3, 1919, 7.

220 "Had I remained": *Washington Post,* June 3, 1919, 1.

220 "The roof of our sun parlor": Letter, Eleanor Roosevelt to Sara Delano Roosevelt, June 3, 1919.

221 "Of the 98-cent variety": *New York Times,* June 3, 1919, 1. Excellent coverage of the bombing appeared in the *Washington Post,* June 3, 1919; *New York Times,* June 3, 1919; Murray, *Red Scare,* 78–80; Talbert, *Negative Intelligence,* 167–70; Powers, *Secrecy and Power,* 63–65.

221 "PLAIN WORDS": *New York Times,* June 3, 1919, 1.

221 "Now that the great war": Ibid.

221 explosions within the same hour: Ibid., 1, 2; Murray, *Red Scare,* 78.

222 "the attempt": *New York Times,* June 3, 1919, 1.

222 "The first sample": *Washington Post,* June 4, 1919, 6.

222 The initial "K.B.": Talbert, *Negative Intelligence,* 169.

222 Union of Russian Workers: *New York Times,* June 5, 1919 1, 4.

223 "a bommerang": Talbert, *Negative Intelligence,* 68, 69 (see note 35 on page 169 for details about the June 12, 1919, report).

223 "interested in terrifying": Ibid., 169.

223 theories of the bombings: Ibid., 168–70; editorials in *The Nation,* July and August, 1919; *The Liberator,* July 1919, 6, 7, and August 1919, 30. For detailed information on the Italian anarchists in relation to the June 2 bombings: William Young and David E. Kaiser, *Post Mortem: New Evidence in the Case of Sacco and Vanzetti* (Amherst: University of Massachusetts Press, 1985), 14–26.

224 "My heartfelt congratulations": *New York Times,* June 5, 1919, 7; Woodrow Wilson Papers, Vol. 60, 114, Manuscript Division, Library of Congress.

224 "apparently being carried": Woodrow Wilson Papers, ibid.; Schmidt, *Red Scare,* 149.

224 a group that was "well known": *New York Times,* June 7, 1919, 7.

225 "known to be sympathetic": Ibid.

225 "Despite strong suspicions": Schmidt, *Red Scare,* 149.

225 "I remember the morning": Coben, *A. Mitchell Palmer,* 206.

CHAPTER 21: WAR OF A DIFFERENT SORT

Page

226 The May Day "riots": *New York Times,* May 4, 1919, 1. (See Stanley A. Coben's excellent discussion of Palmer's initial resistance to zealotry on pages 199–205 in *A. Mitchell Palmer,* and see Joan Jensen's discussion on pages 270–71 in *The Price of Vigilance.*)

226 "entirely at variance": Coben, *A. Mitchell Palmer,* 200.

227 "selective immigration": Hough, *The Web,* 456.

227 "It is time for": Ibid., 471.

227 "all members of": Jensen, *The Price of Vigilance,* 271.

227 "are not wanted": Coben, *A. Mitchell Palmer,* 200.

227 "perhaps a little hasty": Ibid., 201.

227 Palmer indeed appeared to be cautious: Ibid., 200, 201; Jensen, *The Price of Vigilance,* 271.

228 Reexamining the issue of Debs: Coben, *A. Mitchell Palmer,* 201–3.

228 "the wisdom and public effect": Ibid., 202.

228 "imperative": Ibid.

228 "as a means of": Talbert, *Negative Intelligence,* 170.

229 "foremost expert on radicalism": Coben, *A. Mitchell Palmer,* 207; Schmidt, *Red Scare,* 151; *New York Times,* June 4, 1919, 2.

229 This new department: Coben, *A. Mitchell Palmer,* 207.

229 "a combined": Ibid., 211.

229 "We have received": Schmidt, *Red Scare,* 152.

229 "The Russian Bolsheviki": U.S. Congress, Senate, Subcommittee on the Committee on Appropriations, Sundry Civil Appropriation Bill, 1920, Hearing, 66th Cong., 1st Sess., Washington, 1919, 7, 8.

229 "It all depends": Ibid.

230 "Do you think": Ibid.; Schmidt, *Red Scare,* 150.

230 "zone map": Talbert, *Negative Intelligence,* 162.

230 "to assist your": Jensen, *The Price of Vigilance,* 274.

230 The APL did it themselves: Ibid., 274, 275.

231 William McDermid: Ibid., 275.

231 "the traducer of Miss Jane Addams": *The Nation,* June 21, 1919.

231 In the the application for a search warrant: Pfannestiel, *Rethinking the Red Scare,* 64.

231 "be compelled reluctantly": Ibid., 67.

232 "an overwhelming public": Ibid.

232 "the greatest maker": Ibid., 82.

232 "the biggest raid": Ibid.

232 "that people may": Ibid., 83.

232 Flynn devised a cooperative plan: Coben, *A. Mitchell Palmer,* 212.

CHAPTER 22: THRILLING FEATS

This chapter relies on newspaper clippings of the events as they happened and on the book by Sir John Alcock and Sir Arthur Whitten Brown, *Our Transatlantic Flight.*

Page

234 black cat: Alcock and Brown, *Our Transatlantic Flight,* 67.

235 "Vimy Transocean": *New York Times,* June 5, 1919, 4.

235 "keep on flying indefinitely": *New York Times,* June 15, 1919, 1.

237 Cochrane Hotel: Aspi Balsara at the Centre for Newfoundland Studies; Cal Best and Melony Tucker at the Provincial Archive in St. John's, Newfoundland; *Evening Telegram,* St. John's, March 21, 1985, 1.

238 "Sir—As one": *St. John's Daily News,* June 16, 1919, 7.

239 "Being myself a spectator": Alcock and Brown, *Our Transatlantic Flight,* 45.

242 "We had definitely": Ibid., 67.

243 "I can't get": Ibid., 78.

243 "I waited impatiently": Ibid., 84.

243 "For seven long hours": Ibid., 40.

244 "aura of unreality": Ibid., 86.

244 "swung, flew amok": Ibid., 88.

245 "Anybody hurt?": Ibid., 101.

246 "We had finished": Ibid., 105.

246 "Even the worst pessimist": *New York Times*, June 16, 1919, 1.

PART III: SUMMER: PASSION

Page

247 "If we must die": First published in *The Liberator* in July 1919; here taken from Claude McKay, *Selected Poems of Claude McKay* (New York: Harcourt, Brace & World, 1953), 36.

247 "The expedition": Goldhurst, Richard. *The Midnight War: The American Intervention in Russia, 1918–1920.* New York: McGraw Hill, 1978, 21.

CHAPTER 23: MISSICHUSETTS

The title for this chapter was taken from an article about Puffer and Hazzard in *The Guardian*, July 12, 1919, 4. I first discovered the Puffer and Hazzard story in July 1919 issues of both *The Guardian* and the *Chicago Defender*. To flush out the story I relied mostly on newspapers from Concord, New Hampshire, Ayer, Massachusetts, and Boston during the months of June and July 1919, as well as *The Guardian* and *Chicago Defender*. The paper trail through public records for this case is spotty. However, there is an abundance of information, enough surely for a book on the case alone.

Page

249 a man and a woman arrived: *Boston Traveller*, June 19, 1919, 2; *Boston American*, June 19, 1919, 3; *Boston Evening Globe*, June 19, 1919, 1.

249 wait five days: Ibid.

249 Arthur Garfield Hazzard: *Turner's Public Spirit*, June 21, 1919, 5.

250 William H. Hazzard: *Boston Traveller*, June 24, 1919, 7.

250 Happy Hazzards: *Boston Evening Globe*, June, 19, 1919, 1.

250 had not fought: Draft Registration Card, on-line site, Ancestry.com, World War I registration cards, 1917–1918.

251 "the body was": Emerson College of Oratory, a pamphlet without a date of publication, published by Emerson College in the 1890s; "the entire physical person": Ibid.

251 In Puffer's senior year: Puffer's report card listed in the Emerson College records under No. 1139; *Emerson College Magazine*, Vol. 1, No. 5 (1893).

252 After Emerson, Puffer: *Boston Daily Globe*, June 20, 1919, 9.

252 "We used to talk": *Boston Traveller*, July 15, 1919, 4.

253 "In fact I would esteem": *Boston Traveller*, June 19, 1919, 2.

253 twenty-eight lynchings: *Chicago Defender*, July 12, 1919, 1.

254 "shot to pieces" and "was taken from": Ibid., July 5, 1919, 4.

254 area newspapers: *Concord Evening Monitor; Daily Patriot.*

254 "wealthy elocutionist": *Boston Evening Globe,* June 20, 1919, 1, 9 (this quote is from page 9).

254 "Will Marry Negro": *Boston Traveller,* June 19, 1919, 2.

254 "Hope to Prevent": *Boston Evening Globe,* June 20, 1919, 1.

255 "all is spirit": Ibid.

255 "modern Othello and his Desdemona": *Boston American,* June 19, 1919, 3.

255 "I love Mr. Hazzard" through "And I love *you*": *Boston Evening Globe,* June 19, 1919, 1.

255 "I don't see what": *Boston American,* June 19, 1919, 3.

255 "How about that": Ibid.

255 "Now the story is this" through ". . . IS WORTH": *Boston Evening Globe,* June 19, 1919, 1.

256 "aflame with protest": *Boston Evening Globe,* June 20, 1919, 1.

257 "that materialism is": Ibid.

257 "After the conference": *Boston American,* June 21, 1919, 1.

257 "REJECTS APPEAL": *Boston Evening Globe,* June 20, 1919, 1.

257 "passed part of his life": *Concord Evening Monitor,* June 19, 1919, 3.

257 "would have nothing to do": *Daily Patriot,* June 19, 1919, 2.

257 "that the Legislature": Ibid.

257 Maryland: Ibid.

258 "a Negro servant": *Boston Daily Globe,* June 21, 1919, 1.

258 "I glory in your spunk": *Daily Patriot,* June 21, 1919, 1.

259 "lewd and lascivious cohabitation": *Boston Daily Globe,* June 21, 1919, 1.

259 "So tell me how does": *Boston American,* June 21, 1919, 1. (Phrase also used in *Boston American,* June 19, 1919, 3.)

259 "enticement": Ibid.

259 "wrong to do": Ibid.

260 "They'll have to": *Boston Daily Globe,* June 21, 1919, 5.

260 ". . . and Concord gazed": Ibid.

260 "to fight to": *Boston Traveller,* June 21, 1919, 1.

260 "Mr. Hazzard is": *Boston American,* June 22, 1919, 4.

260 "No charge of insanity": Ibid.

260 "Miss Puffer Fights": *Boston Traveller,* June 21, 1919, 1.

260 "Perhaps there is a": *The Guardian,* July 12, 1919, 4.

CHAPTER 24: PARIS

Page

262 William Monroe Trotter was dining: *The Guardian,* July 12, 1919, 1. The exchange of letters between President Wilson and William Monroe Trotter is included in the papers of Woodrow Wilson in the Manuscript Division at the Library of Congress, as well as in the sources indicated below.

262 "Now that the war": *Chicago Defender,* October 9, 1943, 1.

262 Trotter's May 31 letter: *New York Age*, September 16, 1919, 1; *New York Times*, June 2, 1919, 6.

263 had not aroused a response: Fox, *The Guardian of Boston*, 229.

263 "I desire to express": Woodrow Wilson Papers, Manuscript Division, Library of Congress.

263 "In reply to": Ibid.

263 "Give credit to": *New York Age*, September 16, 1919, 1.

263 "Dear Sir: I thank you": Woodrow Wilson Papers, Library of Congress.

264 "Everyone is now asking": Ray Stannard Baker, *American Chronicle*, 432.

264 "If I were a German": Ibid., 419; Robert C. Bannister, Jr., *Ray Stannard Baker: The Mind and Thought of a Progressive* (New Haven: Yale University Press, 1966), 187.

264 "I can see no": Ibid.; Ray Stannard Baker, *American Chronicle*, 419.

265 "The German nation": Ray Stannard Baker, *Woodrow Wilson: Life and Letters* (New York: Doubleday, 1927–1939), Vol. 8, 583.

265 "the electricity of expectation": Ibid., 449.

265 On June 28, at about 2 P.M.: See an excellent description of the signing of the peace treaty in *The Nation*, July 5, 1919, as well as Ray Stannard Baker, *American Chronicle*.

266 "The treaty of peace": *Congressional Record*, vol. 58, 1952, 1953; also Woodrow Wilson Papers, Library of Congress.

266 "It is my desire": Ibid.; Polenberg, *Fighting Faiths*, 325.

266 "such an important issue": Ibid.; letter, A. Mitchell Palmer to President Wilson, June 28, 1919, Woodrow Wilson Papers, Library of Congress.

267 from the palace gates: Ruth Worthy, "A Negro in Our History: William Monroe Trotter, 1872–1934 (MA thesis, Columbia University, 1952).

267 "Despite loyalty": Fox, *The Guardian of Boston*, 230.

267 a black farm laborer in Arkansas: *Chicago Defender*, June 21, 1919, 1.

267 "This is how": Ibid.

267 "partially" confessed and "3,000 Will Burn Negro" and "Negro Jerky": *New Orleans States*, June 26, 1919, 1.

267 "powerless to prevent it" and "John Hartfield Will Be Lynched by Ellisville Mob at 5 o'clock This Afternoon," *Jackson Daily News*, June 26, 1919, 1; Tuttle, *Race Riot*, 23; *New York Times*, June 27, 1919, 1.

268 "The Shame of America": *New York Age*, July 5, 1919, and *The Nation*, July 5, 1919.

268 favorite parks: Worthy, "A Negro in Our History," 131; *Chicago Defender*, July 12, 1919, 4.

268 "In the stern path": Fox, *The Guardian of Boston*, 231.

CHAPTER 25: INDEPENDENCE DAY 1919

Page

269 "Never before was": *New York Times*, July 4, 1919, 1, 4.

269 "reign of terror": Ibid.; *Detroit Free Press*, July 4, 1919, 2; *Washington Post*, July 4, 1919, 1.

269 America was well prepared: *Detroit Free Press*, July 4, 1919, 2.

269 "We have received": U.S. Congress, Senate, Subcommittee on Appropriations Hearing, 66th Cong., 1st Sess., Washington, 1919, 304.

270 William Flynn more than once: *New York Times*, June 7, 1919, 1; *New York Times*, June 13, 1919, 1; Schmidt, *Red Scare*, 150.

270 "might take place": Schmidt, ibid.

270 "handling the possible": *New York Times*, July 4, 1919, 1.

270 "a program": *Christian Science Monitor*, July 4, 1919, 4.

270 "the hands of the government": Ibid.

270 temperatures in New York: *New York Times*, July 5, 1919, 14.

271 "Bomb 'Plot' Is a Fizzle": Ibid., 5.

271 record-high temperatures: Ibid., 14.

271 Jack Dempsey: *Boston Globe*, July 5, 1919, 1; *New York Times*, July 3, 1919, 10; *Charlotte Observer*, July 5, 1919, 1.

271 "Superior punching": *New York Times*, July 3, 1919, 10.

271 "I'll never fight": *Boston Globe*, July 5, 1919, 1. *Charlotte Observer*, July 5, 1919, 1.

272 "187 pounds": *New York Times*, July 2, 1983, 1.

272 "the best of all pugilists": Ibid.

272 "no other unit": *Detroit News*, July 1, 1919, 1.

272 the 339th: *Detroit Free Press*, June 8, 1919, 1; *Detroit News*, June 4, 1919, 1; *Detroit News*, June 17, 1919, 1; *Detroit News*, June 29, 1919, 1.

273 Jay Hayden: *Detroit News*, June 18, 19, 20, 1919, all on page 1.

273 Hoboken: *Detroit Free Press*, July 5, 1919, 1.

273 "Dear Sir: Thinking perhaps": *Detroit Free Press*, June 12, 1919, 1, 2, in the collections at the Bentley Historical Library, University of Michigan, Ann Arbor.

274 Soldiers' uniforms: *Detroit News*, July 2, 1919, 1.

274 "for anything in": Crownover, "Stranded in Russia," 40.

274 "You fought under": *Detroit Free Press*, July 5, 1919, 1.

275 Senator Hiram Johnson: *Detroit Free Press*, July 5, 1919, 1; *Detroit News*, July 5, 1919, 1; *New York Times*, July 5, 1919, 2.

275 "The question of their": *New York Times*, ibid.

275 "the greatest possibility": Ibid.

276 "to be the servants": *Detroit News*, July 5, 1919, 1.

276 The flu epidemic: Crosby, *America's Forgotten Pandemic*, 150–66.

277 "Nothing is too good": *Life*, March 1919, 22.

277 labor strikes: Murray, *Red Scare*, 111.

278 "The citizens of the United States": *New York Times*, May 24, 1919, 4.

CHAPTER 26: THE NARROW PATH

Page

279 "Honor to Woodrow Wilson": Ray Stannard Baker, *American Chronicle*, 457.

279 "At the end of the war": Ibid.

280 "The straight and narrow path": *New York Times*, July 5, 1919, 2.

280 "only hope for mankind": Ray Stannard Baker, *American Chronicle*, 457.

281 "the opportunity to secure": *Chicago Defender,* May 24, 1919, 1.

281 "well-educated": *Shreveport Times,* July 12, 1919, 1; Tuttle, *Race Riot,* 26.

282 "Yes!": Tuttle, *Race Riot,* 27.

282 Longview riot: *Shreveport Times,* July 12, 1919, 12–17, 23, 27; Tuttle, *Race Riot,* 25–29; *Chicago Defender,* July 5, 1919, 2; *The Crisis,* September 1919; *New York Times,* July 12, 14, 1919; Kenneth R. Durham, Jr., "Longview Race Riot of 1919," *East Texas Historical Association Journal,* Vol. 18, No. 2 (1980), 13–24.

283 "in most approved": *The Crisis,* September 1919.

284 "We will not permit": *Shreveport Times,* July 13, 1919, 1.

284 "It may be that a remonstrance": Kornweibel, *Seeing Red,* 41.

284 "decidedly rabid": Ibid.

CHAPTER 27: MISS PUFFER INSANE?

Page

285 "Ayer residents who enjoy": *Boston Traveller,* June 26, 1919, 4.

285 deluge of letters: *Boston Globe,* June 24, 1919, 4; *Boston Globe,* June 25, 1919, 5.

286 "I'd take them": *Boston Traveller,* June 24, 1919, 7.

286 "aided by certain others": *Boston Globe,* June 24, 1919, 4.

286 "Resolved, that marriage": *Boston Traveller,* June 25, 1919, 8.

286 "to give Hazzard": *Boston American,* June 23, 1919, 3; *Boston Globe,* June 24, 1919, 4.

286 "from the Southern regions": Ibid.

287 "Miscegenation": Randall Kennedy, *Interracial Intimacies: Sex, Marriage, Identity, and Adoption* (New York: Vintage, 2004); "Annotated Laws of Massachusetts: containing all the laws of Massachusetts of a general and permanent nature/completely annotated by the editorial staffs of the publishers (Charlottesville, VA: Michie, 1912 to the present), used at the University of Michigan Law Library; Rachel F. Moran, *Interracial Intimacy: The Regulation of Race and Romance* (Chicago: University of Chicago Press, 2001); and Denise Morgan, "Jack Johnson: Reluctant Hero of the Black Community," *Akron Law Review,* Vol. 32 (1999).

287 "No more voracious": Morgan, ibid., 549.

287 "between Negroes or persons": Ibid.

288 "the colored girl": Ibid., 551.

288 "by all means": Ibid., 550.

288 "she loved Johnson": Ibid., 546.

288 "a blot": Ibid., 548.

290 "Miss Puffer wasn't insane": *Boston Sunday Globe,* June 22, 1919, 1.

291 "It seems to me": *Chicago Defender,* July 5, 1919, 4.

291 "ransacked" and "had been removed": *Boston Globe,* June 30, 1919, 1.

291 they found items, between $5,000 and $6,000: *Boston Globe,* July 15, 1919, 1; *Boston Globe,* June 28, 1919, 2.

292 "Very talkative": *Boston Sunday Globe,* June 22, 1919, 1.

293 "She is as sane as we are": *Chicago Defender,* July 5, 1919, 1.

293 "It's too bad": *Chicago Defender,* July 12, 1919, 1.

293 "Anyone who wishes": *The Guardian*, July 12, 1919, 4.

294 "Is McKee white": *Boston Globe*, July 13, 1919, 4.

295 "no good reason": *Boston Globe*, July 15, 1919, 6.

295 "These two people": Ibid.

295 "It was the intention": Ibid.

CHAPTER 28: THAT CERTAIN POINT

The chapter title is from Fox, *The Guardian of Boston*, 232.

Page

298 "But he has reserved": Memo, Major Walter Loving to the director of the MID, "Conditions Among Negroes in New York City and Return of William Monroe Trotter from France" July 16, 1919, and stamped July 19, 1919, Reel 5, File 10218, Negro Subversion microfilm.

298 "Beyond a certain point": Fox, *The Guardian of Boston*, 232.

299 "Calls on Negroes": *Guardian*, July 19, 1919, 1.

299 "radical sentiment": Major Walter Loving's report, Reel 5, File 10218, Negro Subversion microfilm; Talbert, *Negative Intelligence*, 133, 134.

300 "Individual Agitators": Major Loving's report.

300 "set the spark": Ibid.

302 July 19: *Washington Post*, July 20, 1919, 14.

302 "Negroes Attack Girl": *Washington Post*, July 19, 1919, 1.

302 "found in isolated": Arthur I. Waskow, "The 1919 Race Riots: A Study in the Connections Between Conflict" (Ph.D. thesis, University of Wisconsin, 1963), 26.

303 "It was learned that": *Washington Post*, July 21, 1919, 1. (For information on the Washington riot see also Tuttle, *Race Riot*, 29, 30; Waskow, "The 1919 Race Riots," 24–44; and BI Files, RG65, OG369936, National Archives.

303 "mobilization" story: Ibid., 31.

303 That night the rioting resumed: *New York Times*, July 22, 1919, 1.

304 total casualties: Tuttle, *Race Riots*, 30.

304 "small causes": *Washington Post*, July 25, 1919, 1.

304 "There is nothing to be done": *New York Globe*, July 23, 1919, 1.

304 From the white point of view: Waskow, "The 1919 Race Riots," 39–42.

305 "Race War": *Brooklyn Eagle*, July 27, 1919, 1.

305 "the negroes, before": *New York Times*, July 23, 1919, 1.

305 "Bolshevist agitation": Ibid.; Waskow, "The 1919 Race Riots," 37; *The Crisis*, September, 1919.

305 "mutual sharing": Waskow, "The 1919 Race Riots," 38; *Washington Star*, July 27, 1919, 1.

305 "the mobocratic": *Chicago Defender*, August 2, 1919, 1.

306 "the courage to enforce": James Weldon Johnson, "In the Shadow of the Dome of the Capitol," *New York Age*, July 25, 1919, 2.

306 "mobilization notice": Letter, John Shillady to A. Mitchell Palmer, July 25, 1914, in Waskow, "The 1919 Race Riots," 38.

306 "the white men": *New York Times*, July 27, 1919, 4.

306 "assail every form" and "Fiery Orators": *Chicago Defender*, August 2, 1991, 1.

307 "In the same week": Ibid.

307 "representing the voice": Ibid.

307 "Mr. Trotter was": MID records, File 10218, Reel 5, Negro Subversion division microfilm.

CHAPTER 29: WEAPONS IN THEIR HATS

Page

308 "minstrel of our alleys": Niven, *Carl Sandburg*, 335.

308 "NEA Staff Correspondent": Ibid., 327.

308 "Wandering oversea singer": Ibid., 330.

308 "a remarkable man": Letter, Sam Hughes to Carl Sandburg, May 16, 1919, in Mitgang, *The Letters of Carl Sandburg*, 163.

308 "I don't believe": Niven, *Carl Sandburg*, 332.

309 "first hand": Carl Sandburg, *The Chicago Race Riots* (New York: Harcourt, Brace & World, 1969 (first published, 1919), xix.

309 Chicago's Black Belt: Adam Cohen and Elizabeth Taylor, *American Pharaoh: Mayor Richard J. Daley: His Battle for Chicago and the Nation* (Boston: Little, Brown, 2000), 7.

309 The Olivet Baptist Church: Sandburg, *The Chicago Race Riots*, 10.

309 "a menace to health": Ibid., 46

309 "constitutes kindling wood": Ibid., 47.

310 eight such bombs: Ibid., 17.

310 "A colored man": Ibid., 63.

311 Dr. Williams: Ibid., 62.

311 "No city or state": Ibid., 79.

311 "I have fought": Ibid., 80.

312 Rev. W. C. Thompson: Ibid., 71.

312 "New things is comin' ": Ibid., 71, 72.

312 Goodyear dirigible: Ed Schanks, ed., *In Memory of Those Who Died Serving*, special issue publication of the Illinois Trust and Savings Bank, Chicago 1919.

312 one of those sizzling hot Sundays: *New York Times*, July 28, 1919.

312 It began at around 4 P.M.: Tuttle, *Race Riot*, who interviewed Mr. John Turner Harris, who as a boy was with Eugene Williams on the raft in Lake Michigan the day the riots began (Tuttle's source note essays are essential to an understanding of the Chicago race riots); Report of the Chicago Commission, *The Negro in Chicago* (Chicago: University of Chicago Press, 1922); BI files, RG65, OG369914, National Archives; newspapers covering the event, especially the *Chicago Tribune* and *New York Times*, although they must be viewed with some skepticism for obvious reasons; *Chicago Defender*; Waskow, *From Race Riot to Sit In*, Waskow, "The 1919 Race Riots"; Sandburg, *The Chicago Race Riots; The Crisis*, September 1919.

313 "hot and cold": Tuttle, *Race Riot*, 4.

313 "just sort of relaxed": Ibid., 6, 7.

314 Casualties on the first day of the riot: Report of the Chicago Commission, *The Negro in Chicago,* 5.

314 "To me and most": *Chicago Daily News,* July 28, 1919, 1.

314 "It was but": Ibid.

314 "They drew the color line": Ibid.

315 streetcar transit points: Waskow, "The 1919 Race Riots," 41, 42.

315 "I don't see why": *Chicago Daily Tribune,* July 30, 1919, 1.

316 Frank Lowden: Tuttle, *Race Riot,* 50–64.

316 "Brothers we are": *The Crisis,* September 1919, 231.

317 "underway, as soon as": Report of Agent Loula in MID records, File 10218, Reel 5, Negro Subversion division microfilm.

317 "Reds Try to Stir" and "The outbreak of race riots": *New York Times,* July 28, 1919, 1; Waskow, "The 1919 Race Riots," 58.

317 "IWW and other agitators": Kornweibel, *Seeing Red,* 165.

317 "Why should we" and "If there is": *The Crisis,* September 1919, 246–49.

317 "You yourself have": *New York Age,* August 9, 1919, 1.

318 "On the one hand": Sandburg, *The Chicago Race Riots,* 4.

318 "As an example": Major Walter Loving's report, 12.

318 "Defense of himself": Ibid., 14.

319 "segregation of misfits": *Chicago Tribune,* August 6, 1919, 16.

319 "Whereas, the city council": Ibid., 3.

319 "Negro State to be situated": MID weekly summaries, week of September 22, 1919.

319 "changed his viewpoint somewhat" and "agitation and the strongest pressure" and "important" and "one of the best types": Memos written in the War Department, Reel 5, File 10218, Negro Subversion division microfilm.

320 the president had not yet given a public comment: Interview with Professor William Tuttle, University of Kansas.

320 "tolerated": *New York Times,* August 30, 1919, 2.

320 the Negro Subversion division . . . began to fade away: Talbert, *Negative Intelligence,* 134; MID records, Reel 5, File 10218, Negro Subversion division microfilm.

321 "Reds Incite Negro Rioters": *Los Angeles Times,* September 1, 1919, 1.

321 "resort to violence" and "this type of Negro leader" and "We return": Ibid., 1, 2.

321 "sufficiently abusive": Ibid., 2.

CHAPTER 30: KING OF THE INDEX

Page

323 In 1919, those tools were simple: David Lyon, *The Electronic Eye: The Rise of Surveillance Society* (Minneapolis: University of Minnesota Press, 1994), 22–24.

323 Pacific Telephone Company: Jensen, *The Price of Vigilance,* 150.

323 the female undercover agent: Talbert, *Negative Intelligence,* 56–57, 178 (more information on Agent Scully can be found at footnote 62, 168).

324 The American Protective League had enlisted women: Jensen, *The Price of Vigilance,* 142–43.

324 "Thousands of women": Ibid., 143.

324 "It is supposed": Hough, *The Web*, 164.

325 "Triumph of the Index": *New York Times*, May 22, 1919, 14; "Keeper of the" and "mysteries and purposes": *New York Times*, March 2, 1919, 71.

326 "It worked": Ibid, May 22, 1919, 14.

326 "father of Military Intelligence": Talbert, *Negative Intelligence*, 6.

326 Van Deman's budgets: Ibid., 9.

327 "Attached hereto are": Powers, *Secrecy and Power*, 36.

328 "from a more intelligent": U.S. Attorney General's Report, 1919, 15; Schmidt, *Red Scare*, 162.

328 "virtual monopoly over information": Schmidt, *Red Scare*, 164.

328 thirty-five informants: Ibid., 168–70.

329 "At a moment's notice": Polenberg, *Fighting Faiths*, 165.

329 Hoover's staff: Schmidt, *Red Scare*, 159–62.

330 "Red Special": Murray, *Red Scare*, 194, 195.

330 "incommunicado": Ibid.

330 Chemical Foundation: *New York Times*, June 22, 1919, 7.

331 "A. Mitchell Palmer": Ibid.

331 "The Deliberate Destruction": *New York Times*, July 25, 1919, 13.

331 Calder: *New York Times*, August 23, 1919, 6.

331 Palmer fired back: *New York Times*, August 31, 1919, 1, 2.

332 "unconscionable men": Coben, *A. Mitchell Palmer*, 163.

332 was asked to send Hoover its lists: Jensen, *The Price of Vigilance*, 275.

333 high-profile threats: Powers, *Secrecy and Power*, 80–81, 91; Schmidt, *Red Scare*, 246–47.

333 "Agents of the Department of Justice": *New York Times*, August 27, 1919, 11.

CHAPTER 31: "I'LL STAY WITH YOU, MARY"

Page

335 Tanner episode: *Chicago Daily Tribune*, September 2, 1919, 1; September 3, 1919, 5; September 4, 1919, 3.

336 "Chicago's imagination continues": Ibid., September 11, 1919, 16.

336 "The Curse of Capistrano": *All-Story Weekly*, August 9, 16, 23, 30, September 6, 1919.

336 "An Epoch-Making": flyer for the film *Deliverance*, obtained through Helen Keller Archive, American Foundation for the Blind, New York City.

336 Helen Keller: All information in this chapter about Helen Keller was retrieved from files in the Helen Keller Archive, American Foundation for the Blind, New York City.

337 "one of the most powerful minds": review of *Deliverance*, *New York Times*, August 19, 1919, 10.

337 Its many reviewers: File on *Deliverance* at the Helen Keller Archive, American Foundation for the Blind.

338 "We wish every man": A review in a Madison, Wisconsin, newspaper, December 3, 1919, in Helen Keller Archive, American Foundation for the Blind (the name of the newspaper not available).

338 actors strike: *New York Times*, August 1–9, 1919; various files in the Tarmiment Library at New York University.

338 "I can't say anything": Max Eastman, "The Lesson of the Actor's Strike," *The Liberator,* October 1919, 39.

338 "Not More Pay": Ibid.

339 "I began in the chorus": *The Liberator,* October 1919, 40.

339 "one of the most remarkable situations": *New York Times*, August 8, 1919, 1.

339 "I am striking": *The Liberator,* October 1919, 40.

340 "I congratulate you": Helen Keller, "Remarks which I made at a Protest Meeting of the Actors when they went on Strike in the Summer of 1919," Helen Keller Archive, American Foundation for the Blind.

340 *The Grim Game: New York Times*, August 26, 1919, 11; and Dick Brooks, Houdini Museum, Scranton, Pennsylvania.

341 "I was helpless": *New York Times*, August 26, 1919, 11.

341 "We must fight": *New York Call*, August 28, 1919, 1.

342 "No force that": Johnston McCulley, "The Curse of Capistrano," *All-Story Weekly,* August 9, 1919.

PART IV: AUTUMN: STRUGGLE

Page

343 "The Washington riot": *The Crisis*, September 1919, 339.

343 "Intellectual darkness": *New York Call*, September 6, 1919. From Debs's incarceration in April 1919 onward, the *New York Call* published a quote from him each week. Debs first used this sentence in a speech in Indianapolis, Indiana, on September 1, 1904.

CHAPTER 32: "THE RIGHT TO HAPPINESS"

Page

347 "the organization of": Murray, *Red Scare*, 51.

348 "discuss fundamental means": *New York Times*, September 1, 1919, 1; *The Nation*, September 6, 1919.

348 there were sixty-five strikes: Ibid.

348 The steel strike: Murray, *Red Scare*, 135–52; David Brody, *Labor in Crisis: The Steel Strike of 1919* (Urbana: University of Illinois Press, 1987); Interchurch World Movement, Commission of Inquiry, *Report on the Steel Strike of 1919* (New York: Harcourt, Brace & Howe, 1920); *The Nation*, November 15, 1919, 633–35; Samuel Gompers, *Seventy Years of Life and Labor: An Autobiography*, 2 vols. (New York: E. P. Dutton, 1925); Ida Tarbell, *The Life of Elbert H. Gary: A Story of Steel* (New York: D. Appleton, 1925); BI Files, RG65, OG352037, National Archives.

349 "the comfort level" and other details about steel worker conditions: Interchurch World Movement, *Report on the Steel Strike of 1919*, 94–106.

349 the AFL's National Committee sent a letter: Ibid., 13; Brody, *Labor in Crisis*, 98; David Brody, *Steel Workers in America: The Nonunion Era* (Boston: Harvard University Press, 1960), 238.

350 "We do not think" and "You question": Facsimiles of letters at the Chicago Metro History Education Center, Newberry Library, Chicago.

351 "IRON AND STEEL WORKERS!": Brody, *Labor in Crisis*, 111.

351 the Boston police force had walked off the job: *New York Times; Boston Globe;* Murray, *Red Scare*, 122–34; BI files, RG65, OG372926, National Archives.

351 "a crime against civilization": *The Nation*, September 20, 1919.

352 "Lenin and Trotsky": Murray, *Red Scare*, 129.

353 "There is no right": Ibid., 133.

353 "the men will strike": Ibid., 107.

353 "It would be": Brody, *Steel Workers in America*, 239.

CHAPTER 33: TUGS-OF-WAR AND OF THE HEART

Page

356 "I have tried": Ray Stannard Baker, diary entry, September 8, 1919, Baker Papers, in Manuscript Collection, Library of Congress.

356 "It seemed to me": Ray Stannard Baker, *American Chronicle*, 460.

358 "the political independence": Arthur S. Link, *Woodrow Wilson: Revolution, War, and Peace* (Wheeling, IL: Harlan Davidson, 1979), 109.

358 "would be an attempt": Quoted by Elihu Root, Link, *Woodrow Wilson*, 110.

358 "preserve the territorial integrity": Ibid., 112.

359 The reasons he gave publicly: Ibid.; *New York Times*, July 30, 1919.

359 "his life did not matter": Ray Stannard Baker, *American Chronicle*, 460.

360 "The sheer courage": Ibid., 461.

360 Baker began to feel restless: Ibid., 462.

360 "for high crimes": Ibid., 462, 463.

361 "Are they ready?": Ibid., 463.

361 "fed up with": Ibid., 547.

361 "glimpses of the President": Ray Stannard Baker, *What Wilson Did at Paris*, vii, viii.

362 "because by the": Link, *Woodrow Wilson*, 117.

362 "their death warrant": Ibid., 118.

362 Wilson began the tour in a weak and exhausted state: Ray Stannard Baker, *American Chronicle*, 464; Grayson, *Woodrow Wilson*, 96–99.

363 By October 1919: *The Nation*, July 12, 1919, 30. (The July 12 issue of *The Nation* contains an editorial that describes the country's growing indifference to the League.)

CHAPTER 34: AUTUMN LEAFLETS

Page

364 "Awake and change": Leaflets filed in reports of the Bureau of Investigation, RG65, OG362977, National Archives.

364 a small human figure: Details of Mollie Steimer's encounters with the law in September and October 1919 are from numerous reports, fifty pages, in RG65, OG362977, National Archives. These include reports from New York City Bomb Squad detectives Jerome Murphy and Louis Herman, New York detective sergeant James T. Gegan, New York City detective Walter F. Culhane, BI special agent Frank Greene, BI agents Mortimer J. Davis, C. J. Scully, and Frank Faulhaber, among others. Parts of these reports were sent on to Anthony Caminetti, the commissioner-general of immigration in 1919. Many were also sent to Frank Burke, then assistant director of the BI, and some of those were sent to the attention of "Mr. Hoover." (The BI spelled Mollie Steimer's name "Stimer.") The Weinberger Papers, Boxes 2 and 3, at Yale University contain many letters describing the autumn months of activities in the story of Mollie Steimer and her fellow defendants. The finest secondary source on the Steimer story during this period is Polenberg, *Fighting Faiths.*

364 "black-eyed": Polenberg, *Fighting Faiths,* 185; BI Files, RG65, OG362977, National Archives.

365 "I do not desire": Report of Mortimer J. Davis, BI Files, RG65, OG362977; *New York Tribune,* September 19, 1919, 1.

365 "well shadowed upon": Report of Mortimer J. Davis.

365 "anteroom": BI Files, RG65, OG362977, reports of Frank Faulhaber, C. J. Scully, and James Gegan.

366 "would answer questions": Ibid.

366 "This woman is": Ibid.; Polenberg, *Fighting Faiths,* 185, 186.

366 This was a fifty-one-page document: Weinberger Papers, Box 3, Yale University; Polenberg, *Fighting Faiths,* 228, 229.

366 "The right to criticize": Polenberg, ibid.

366 "Absolute freedom of speech": Ibid., 230; (the brief itself) Abrams v. U.S. file, 250U.S.616 (1919) Docket 316, Argued October 21, 1919, Decided November 1919.

367 "It is the consensus": Memo, Frank Burke, BI Files, RG65, OG362977.

367 "With [Wilson's] expressed beliefs": Letter, Harry Weinberger to Ray Stannard Baker, September 20, 1919, Weinberger Papers, Box 2, Yale University.

367 "I do not believe": Letter, Ray Stannard Baker in response to Harry Weinberger, September 23, 1919, Weinberger Papers, Box 2, Yale University.

368 "seems a kind of monstrosity": This letter first came to my attention in Robert Bannister's *Ray Stannard Baker.* Professor Bannister sent excerpts of the letter from R.S.B. to A. M. Palmer, which he had obtained from the Baker Papers at Princeton University. I later found the same letter in the Manuscript Division at the Library of Congress. Professor Bannister said that Palmer sent a "formal" reply, which I later found at the National Archives (RG20) and in Polenberg, *Fighting Faiths,* 231. I

thank both Bannister and Polenberg for the discovery of this letter, which links Baker and Palmer, and Weinberger in an interesting way.

369 "soft on Bolshevism": *Congressional Record,* Senate, 66th Cong. 1st Sess., 6875, 7077, this comment on 7073.

370 BI Report No. 38495: BI Files, RG65, National Archives.

371 On October 10: Polenberg, *Fighting Faiths,* 187; *New York Tribune,* October 11, 1919; *New York World,* October 11, 1919.

371 "as a prisoner": Ibid.

372 two encoded notes: Arthur Wynne, "Mollie Steimer The Little Red," *The World Magazine,* November 30, 1919.

373 "I never saw": Polenberg, *Fighting Faiths,* 189.

373 "My dear Miss Steimer": Weinberger Papers, Box 2, Yale University.

374 "Dear Sir": Ibid.

374 "Miss Steimer weighs": *New York World,* October 29, 1919, 1.

374 "I have just received": Weinberger Papers, Box 2.

CHAPTER 35: NOT EXACTLY PARADISE

Page

376 In 1919, even the weather in America was tumultuous: Front-page *New York Times* stories in April, June, August, September, October 1919.

376 In Omaha: *Chicago Defender,* October 4, 1919, 1; *New York Age,* October 4, 1; *The Crisis,* December 1919, 62; Tuttle, *Race Riot,* 244–45; Waskow, *From Race Riot to Sit-In,* 105–10.

378 "It is said": *The Crisis,* December 1919, 62.

378 "reaching a stage": Ibid.

378 "the Negro in some": *New York Age,* September 20, 1919, 4.

378 "urgently": *The Crisis,* December 1919, 2.

378 "courageous attempt": Ibid.

378 "The new spirit": *New York Age,* October 4, 1919, 2.

379 Progressive Farmers and Household Union of America: Waskow, "The 1919 Race Riots," 152.

379 "The time is at hand": *Arkansas Gazette,* October 10, 1919, 1.

379 The violence in Arkansas began: Grif Stockley, *Blood in Their Eyes* (Fayetteville, AR: University of Arkansas Press, 2001); Tuttle, *Race Riot,* 246–48; Waskow, "The 1919 Race Riots," 152–76.

379 "captured" and "herded": *Chicago Defender,* October 4, 1919, 1, 2.

380 *Searchlight* and its advertisers: Kenneth T. Jackson, *The Ku Klux Klan in the City, 1916–1930* (New York: Oxford University Press, 1967), 33.

380 black strikebreakers: Brody, *Labor in Crisis,* 162.

380 In Donora, Pennsylvania: *New York Times,* October 10, 1919, 4.

381 the MID agents, in their probe: Murray, *Red Scare,* 148.

381 "We're going to take over": Ibid.

381 Coal strike: Ibid., 153–65.

382 "have but one object": Ibid., 154.

382 "a grave moral": Ibid., 156.

382 the Justice Department raid: Ibid., 196; Schmidt, *Red Scare*, 248–49; *New York Times*, November 26, 1919, 1.

383 the World Series: William A. Cook, *The 1919 World Series: What Really Happened?* (New York: McFarland, 2001); Eliot Asinof, *Eight Men Out: The Black Sox and the 1919 World Series* (New York: Henry Holt, 1963). About Babe Ruth: Asinof, *Eight Men Out*, 137.

384 "a profession that": *Chicago Defender*, October 4, 1919, 10.

385 "will have a": Ibid.

385 the nation's first dial telephones: *Virginian-Pilot and the Norfolk Landmark* clips in late October and early November provided by Peggy Haile McPhillips at the Norfolk, Virginia, Public Library.

385 a new writer: Jeffrey Meyers, *F. Scott Fitzgerald: A Biography* (New York: Harper-Collins, 1994).

385 "Beyond a sporting interest": F. Scott Fitzgerald, *This Side of Paradise* (New York: Charles Scribner's Sons, 1920), 57.

CHAPTER 36: ALBERT IN WONDERLAND

Page

386 "We were the chorus": Stanley, "An Expedition to Heal the Wounds of War," 78.

386 "After a careful study": Ibid., 79.

387 "fabric of the universe": "Joint Eclipse Meeting of the Royal Society and the Royal Astronomical Society," *Observatory*, November 1919, 389–98. This quote, p. 393.

387 a very interesting fact: Stanley, "An Expedition to Heal the Wounds of War," 79.

387 "If his theory is right": "Joint Eclipse Meeting," *Observatory*, 394; Clark, *Einstein*, 232; Abraham Pais, *Subtle Is the Lord . . . The Science and the Life of Albert Einstein* (New York: Oxford University Press, 1983), 307.

387 "Eddington found star displacement": Clark, *Einstein*, 227.

387 "Joyous news today": Pais, *Subtle Is the Lord*, 303.

388 "REVOLUTION IN SCIENCE": London *Times*, November 7, 1919, 1.

388 "LIGHTS ALL ASKEW" and other New York headlines: *New York Times*, November 10, 1919, 17; Pais, *Subtle Is the Lord*, 309.

389 "A Book for 12 Wise Men": *New York Times*, November 9, 1919, 1.

389 "So far as we": London *Times*, November 28, 1919, 1; also in *New York Times*, November 29, 1919, 11.

390 "been wandering": *New York Times*, November 16, 1919, 12.

CHAPTER 37: GREATNESS

Page

391 The clerk, Stanley Morrison: Dean Acheson, *Morning and Noon* (Boston: Houghton Mifflin, 1965), 119.

391 "The most stringent": See Chapter 13, "In Like a Lion," for details on the "clear and present danger" clause in the *Schenck* case.

391 "I fear we have" Liva Baker, *The Justice from Beacon Hill*, 537.

392 they visited Holmes in his study: Ibid.; Acheson, *Morning and Noon*, 119.

393 "perfectly unrestrained": Polenberg, *Fighting Faiths*, 230.

393 "I'll go to the stake": G. Edward White, *Justice Oliver Wendell Holmes: Law and the Inner Self* (New York: New York University Press, 1993), 427.

394 "direct and dangerous": Zechariah Chafee, Jr., "Freedom of Speech," *New Republic* (November 16, 1918), 66–69.

394 "the kind of criticism": Ibid.; Liva Baker, *The Justice from Beacon Hill*, 518.

394 "tolerance": Zechariah Chafee, Jr., "Legislation Against Anarchy," *New Republic* (July 23, 1919), 379–85; Polenberg, *Fighting Faiths*, 272.

394 "Never in the history": Zechariah Chafee, Jr., "Freedom of Speech in War Time," *Harvard Law Review* (June 1919), 932–73.

395 In late July Laski invited Holmes: Novick, *Honorable Justice*, 520.

395 "allow a very wide latitude": G. Edward White, *Judge Oliver Wendell Holmes*, 429.

396 "poor and puny anonymities": Liva Baker, *The Justice from Beacon Hill*, 538.

396 "When men have realized": Oliver Wendell Holmes, Jr., his dissent in the *Abrams* case, 250 U.S. 616 (1919), Docket 316, Argued, October 21, 1919, Decided, November 10, 1919.

397 "most-quoted justifications": Liva Baker, *The Justice from Beacon Hill*, 539.

397 "In a few particulars": *New York Times*, November 11, 1919, 2.

397 "Upholds Sentence of Russian": Ibid.

397 "Justice Holmes in his opinion": *New York Tribune*, November 11, 1919, 1.

397 "In making the decision": *New York Call*, November 11, 1919, 1.

397 "Mr. Stone" and "Mr. Green": Polenberg, *Fighting Faiths*, 243.

CHAPTER 38: ARMISTICE DAY 1919

Page

398 Fritz Kreisler: *The Nation*, November 22, 1919, 664.

398 And the most popular book in Norfolk, Virginia: *Virginian-Pilot and the Norfolk Landmark*, November 9, 1919, 1.

398 "that sterling defender": *Wall Street Journal*, November 10, 1919; *New York Call*, November 11, 1919.

399 "There is a real danger": Murray, *Red Scare*, 150.

399 Eugene Steward: William Z. Foster, *The Great Steel Strike and Its Lessons* (New York: B. W. Huebsch, 1920), 207, 208.

399 "We are Americans": Murray, *Red Scare*, 161.

399 The unsettling image: *Los Angeles Times*, November 12, 1919, 11.

400 There were two lynchings: *Chicago Defender*, November 8, 1919, reprinted in *The Crisis*, February 1920.

400 What happened in Centralia: Murray, *Red Scare*, 181–89; Schmidt, *Red Scare*, 106–11.

401 "Shoot me": Ibid.

401 F. W. McIntosh sent a report: BI Files, RG65, OG376413, National Archives.

402 "If the negroes": *New York Times,* December 1, 1919, 16.

402 "Coming from a Southern man": Ibid.

402 "the present attitude": *Congressional Record,* Senate, 66th Cong. 1st Ses., November 15, 1919; Hank Messick, *John Edgar Hoover* (New York: David McKay, 1972), 14.

402 "At this time" and "When it is borne": "Radicalism and Sedition Among the Negroes as Reflected in Their Publications", BI Files, RG65, OG359561, National Archives.

CHAPTER 39: FALLING LADDERS

Page

404 "heart of the Covenant": Link, *The Papers of Woodrow Wilson,* Vol. 27, 121. Link, 121–24, provides a good discussion on those crucial days in October and November, before the Senate vote on the treaty. Also see William C. Widenor, *Henry Cabot Lodge and the Search for an American Foreign Policy.*

405 "A little book of great": *New York Times Book Review,* November 30, 1919, Section 7, 689, 696.

405 "I had tried": Ray Stannard Baker, *American Chronicle,* 475.

405 in the running for a third term: Link, *The Papers of Woodrow Wilson,* Vol. 27, 126.

406 "Your acts will": *The Nation,* November 27, 1919.

406 "Your League of Nations Covenant": Letter, William Monroe Trotter to President Woodrow Wilson, November 25, 1919, Wilson Papers, Manuscript Division, Library of Congress.

406 "The cruelest, most despicable": Ray Stannard Baker, *American Chronicle,* 469.

406 a reel of painful memories: Ibid., 469–71.

406 "It was the most": Ibid., 469.

407 "But [Wilson] did not": Ibid., 471.

407 "It would probably": Ibid., 469.

407 "I can predict": Ibid., 475.

CHAPTER 40: ALL ABOARD

Page

408 "I hope you will": Blossom letters to Harry Weinberger, Weinberger Papers, Box 1, Yale University.

409 round-trip tickets: Polenberg, *Fighting Faiths,* 245.

409 *Report upon the Illegal:* Ibid., 273.

409 "Attorney for Radical Organizations": Ibid., 274.

409 Weinberger's petitions for amnesty: A copy of the petition and signatures, BI Files RG65, OG362977, National Archives.

410 "extremely selfish": Ibid.

410 "taken to the cooler": Polenberg, *Fighting Faiths,* 296.

410 "filthy": letter from Lipman to Weinberger, Weinberger Papers, Box 2, Yale University.

410 "no prisoner is": Handwritten letter from Mollie Steimer to Harry Weinberger, Weinberger Papers, Box 2, Yale University; Polenberg, *Fighting Faiths*, 296.

411 "The United States Supreme Court": BI Files RG65, OG362977, National Archives.

412 "[Bernstein] is 21 years": Letter, Harry Weinberger to A. Mitchell Palmer, December 18, 1919, Weinberger Papers, Box 2, Yale University.

412 "more dangerous Reds": *New York Times*, December 20, 1919, 1.

412 "the brains": Ibid.

412 "the beginning": *New York Herald*, December 21, 1919, 1.

412 The exact day and time of departure: Gentry, *J. Edgar Hoover*, 86.

412 "a Socialistic revolution by force": David Cole, *Enemy Aliens: Double Standards and Constitutional Freedoms in the War on Terrorism* (New York: New Press, 2005), 119.

412 Joseph Polulech: Ibid.

413 For Hoover: Powers, *Secrecy and Power*, 86, 87.

413 "special assistant to Attorney General Palmer": *Washington Post*, December 21, 1919, 1.

413 "The Department of Justice": *New York Tribune*, December 22, 1919, 1.

414 "that slender bundle": Comment by Congressman William Vaile of Colorado, *Congressional Record*, January 5, 1920.

414 "Captain U.S. Transport Buford": BI Files RG65, OG362977, National Archives.

414 "They never had": Polenberg, *Fighting Faiths*, 274.

415 Weinberger now turned his attention: Letter, Harry Weinberger to Mollie Steimer, December 23, 1919, Weinberger Papers, Box 2, Yale University.

415 Weinberger again wrote to Ray Stannard Baker: Letter, Harry Weinberger to Ray Stannard Baker, December 27, 1919, Weinberger Papers, Box 2, Yale University.

416 "Stark poverty and sorrow": *New York Times*, December 25, 1919, 2.

416 "a reminder": *Washington Post*, December 5, 1919, 2.

CHAPTER 41: BOUGHS OF GLORY

Page

417 John D. Rockefeller: *Los Angeles Times*, December 25, 1919, 1.

417 "nation's new high-rollers": *Los Angeles Times*, December 25, 1919, 1.

417 "You have to go back": Ibid.

418 "The whole world" and "spook board": *Los Angeles Times*, December 25, 1919, 1.

418 "to attend any séances": *New York Times*, December 11, 1919, 16.

418 "Even if all claims": Ibid.

419 "Nation's Newly-Rich": *Los Angeles Times*, December 25, 1919, 1.

419 Columbus, Georgia, lynching: *Chicago Defender*, December 27, 1919, 1.

419 North Carolina lynching: *New York Times*, December 28, 1919, 6.

419 "We have entered": *New York Times*, December 26, 1919, 1; *Los Angeles Times*, December 26, 1919, 1.

419 J. Edgar Hoover did not spend his holiday: Powers, *Secrecy and Power*, 88, 89; also see Hoover's scrapbook in the J. Edgar Hoover Memorabilia Collection in the BI Files at the National Archives in College Park, Maryland.

420 "criminals, mistaken idealists": *New York Times*, January 1, 1920, 17.

421 "Red movement": Ibid.

421 On January 2: Murray, *Red Scare*, 213–14.

422 The exact number of arrests: Powers, *Secrecy and Power*, 103.

422 thirty-nine bakers in Lynn, Massachusetts: Murray, *Red Scare*, 214.

422 Or the man in Newark, New Jersey: Ibid., 215.

422 "looked like a radical": Ibid.

422 "ignorant foreigners": Ibid.

422 "All Aboard": Ibid., 218.

422 "There is no time": *Washington Post*, January 4, 1920, 4.

422 "a drive to cut down": *New York Times*, December 22, 1919, 1.

423 "Please convey": London *Times*, December 25, 1919, 1.

424 "I have no criticism": Mitgang, *The Letters of Carl Sandburg*, 328.

EPILOGUE: ENDINGS AND BEGINNINGS

Page

425 "Democracy is the manner of life": Ray Stannard Baker, Diary entry for October 1, 1919, the Papers of Ray Stannard Baker, Manuscript Division of the Library of Congress, Washington, D.C.

427 On Election Day 1920: Ray Stannard Baker, *American Chronicle*, 483.

428 "Freedom has come": *New York Times*, June 5, 1919, 1.

428 "to tear out": A. Mitchell Palmer, "The Case Against the Reds," *Forum* (February 1919), 173–85, quote is on 173.

429 *To the American People*: Murray, *Red Scare*, 255; Polenberg, *Fighting Faiths*, 273.

429 Palmer died: *New York Times*, May 12, 1936, 26.

430 the June 2, 1919, bombing: Young and Kaiser, *Post Mortem*, 124–33.

432 "The A.P.L. had folded": Hough, *The Web*, 14.

432 "I shall be very glad": Letter, Ray Stannard Baker to Harry Weinberger, March 23, 1920, Weinberger Papers, Box 2, Yale University.

432 Weinberger again called upon Baker: Ibid.

432 "would do nothing": Polenberg, *Fighting Faiths*, 332.

433 "If [Wilson] leaves": Letter, Harry Weinberger to Ray Stannard Baker, March 1, 1919, Weinberger Papers, Box 2, Yale University.

433 "I have all along": Letter, Ray Stannard Baker to Harry Weinberger, March 3, 1919, Weinberger Papers, Box 2, Yale University.

433 Still, he was unstoppable: Polenberg, *Fighting Faiths*, 332–42.

434 "laborious and continuous work": Letter, Samuel Lipman to Harry Weinberger, November 23, 1921, Weinberger Papers, Box 2, Yale University.

434 "Is it not strange": Debs speech, February 1925, at the Conference for Progressive Political Action, Lexington Hotel, Chicago, Library of Congress, Microfilm Collection, "Collected Speeches and Writings of Eugene Victor Debs."

435 "fearfully set in her ways": Goldman, *Living My Life*, 702.

435 "A sure sign": *New York Times*, March 6, 1944, 19.

435 "with bare hands": Weinberger, "A Rebel's Interrupted Autobiography," 115.

436 "copyright expert": *New York Times*, March 6, 1944, 19.

436 "I know you": Letter, Jacob Abrams to Harry Weinberger, 1921, Weinberger Papers, Box 2, Yale University.

437 "life, human dignity": *Congressional Record*, Senate. 109th Cong., 1st Sess., February 7, 2005.

437 Sergeant Johnson's later years: Interview with his son, Herman Johnson, in Kansas City in August 2002.

439 "Why, the President is Republican": Fox, *The Guardian of Boston*, 258.

439 "without much assurance": Ibid., 282.

440 "We have come": Ibid., 30.

441 "The anniversary": Wilson Papers, Manuscript Division, Library of Congress.

442 "It was the most notable": Ray Stannard Baker, *American Chronicle*, 506.

442 "The just man": Ibid., 507.

443 "supreme failure": Ray Stannard Baker, *What Wilson Did at Paris*, 112.

443 Baker's opinions on the secret treaties: Bannister, *Ray Stannard Baker*, 215–18.

443 "Men remembered themselves again": Ibid., 215.

444 "Every time you": Ray Stannard Baker, *American Chronicle*, 508.

444 "I have been where": David Grayson, *Under My Elm* (Garden City: Doubleday, Doran, 1942), 15.

445 "Walking out this morning": Bannister, *Ray Stannard Baker*, 311.

445 "Dear Ray died": Ibid.

445 "pre-eminent man that he was": Ray Stannard Baker, *American Chronicle*, 516.

445 "Curious, in time": Ibid.

Selected Bibliography

Abbot, G. G., and A. F. Moore. *Observations of the Total Solar Eclipse of May 29, 1919.* Washington: Smithsonian Institution, 1920.

Acheson, Dean. *Morning and Noon.* Boston: Houghton Mifflin, 1965.

Addams, Jane. *Twenty Years at Hull-House.* Urbana: University of Illinois Press, 1990.

Alcock, Sir John, and Sir Arthur Whitten Brown. *Our Transatlantic Flight.* London: William Kimmer, 1969.

Allen, Frederick Lewis. *Only Yesterday: An Informal History of the 1920's.* New York: Perennial Classics; 1964; originally published 1931.

Alschuler, Albert W. *Law Without Values: The Life, Work, and Legacy of Justice Holmes.* Chicago: University of Chicago Press, 2000.

Anderson, Kristi. *After Suffrage: Women in Partisan and Electoral Politics Before the New Deal.* Chicago: University of Chicago Press, 1996.

Aptheker, Herbert, ed. *A Documentary History of the Negro People in the United States,* Vol. 3. New York: Citadel, 1973.

Asinof, Eliot. *Eight Men Out: The Black Sox and the 1919 World Series.* New York: Henry Holt, 1963.

Avrich, Paul. *Anarchist Portraits.* Princeton: Princeton University Press, 1990.

Baker, Liva. *The Justice from Beacon Hill: The Life and Times of Oliver Wendell Holmes.* New York: HarperCollins, 1991.

Baker, Ray Stannard. *American Chronicle.* New York: Stratford, 1945.

———. *Following the Color Line: An Account of Negro Citizenship in the American Democracy.* Williamstown, MA: Corner House, 1973.

———. "Gathering Clouds Along the Color Line." *World's Work,* Vol. 32 (June 1916).

———, ed. *The Public Papers of Woodrow Wilson.* 6 vols. New York: Harper Bros., 1925–1927.

———. *What Wilson Did at Paris.* New York: Doubleday, Page, 1919.

———. ed., *Woodrow Wilson: Life and Letters,* 8 vols. New York: Doubleday, Doran, 1927–1939.

Bannister, Robert C., Jr. *Ray Stannard Baker: The Mind and Thought of a Progressive.* New Haven: Yale University Press, 1966.

Barnet, Richard J. *The Rockets' Red Glare: When America Goes to War: The Presidents and the People.* New York: Simon & Schuster, 1990.

Barrett, Eileen, and Mary Cullinan, eds. *American Women Writers: Diverse Voices in Prose Since 1845.* New York: St. Martin's, 1993.

Batten, A. H. "A Most Rare Vision: Eddington's Thinking on the Relation Between Science and Religion." *R A S Quarterly Journal,* Vol. 35 (September 1994).

Bidwell, Bruce W. *History of the Military Intelligence Division, Department of the Army General Staff, 1775–1941* (Frederick, MD: University Publications of America, 1986).

Bluestein, Abe, ed. *Fighters for Anarchism: Mollie Steimer and Senya Fleshing.* New York: Libertarian, 1983.

Bontemps, Arna. *The Harlem Renaissance Remembered.* New York: Dodd, Mead, 1972.

Bozich, Stanley J., and Jon R. Bozich. *Detroit's Own Polar Bears: The American North Russian Expeditionary Forces, 1918–1919.* Frankenmuth, MI: Polar Bear Publishing, 1985.

Brands, H. W. *Woodrow Wilson.* New York: Henry Holt, 2003.

Brawley, Benjamin Griffith. *Negro Builders and Heroes.* Chapel Hill: University of North Carolina Press, 1937.

Brecher, Jeremy. *Strike.* San Francisco: Straight Arrow, 1972.

British Astronomical Association. *Journal of the British Astronomical Association,* Vol. 93, pp. 129–30.

Brody, David. *Labor in Crisis: The Steel Strike of 1919.* Urbana: University of Illinois Press, 1987.

———. *Steel Workers in America: The Nonunion Era.* Boston: Harvard University Press, 1960.

Buchwald, Diana Kormos, Robert Schulmann, Josef Illy, Daniel J. Kennefick, and Tilman Sauer, eds. *The Collected Papers of Albert Einstein: The Berlin Years: Correspondence, January 1919–April 1920.* Princeton, Princeton University Press, 2004.

Buckley, Gail. *American Patriots: The Story of Blacks in the Military from the Revolution to Desert Storm.* New York: Random House, 2001.

Bundles, A'Lelia. *On Her Own Ground: The Life and Times of Madam C. J. Walker.* New York: Scribner, 2001.

Carey, Neil G., ed. *Fighting the Bolsheviks: The Russian War Memoir of Private First Class Donald E. Carey, U.S. Army, 1918–1919.* New York: Presidio, 1997.

Chafee, Zechariah, Jr. "Contemporary State Trial—The United States Versus Jacob Abrams et al." *Harvard Law Review,* Vol. 33 (April 1920).

———. "Freedom of Speech in War Time." *Harvard Law Review,* Vol. 32 (June 1919).

———. *Free Speech in the United States.* New York: Atheneum, 1969.

Chandrasekhar, Subrahmanyan. *Eddington: The Most Distinguished Astrophysicist of His Time.* Cambridge: Cambridge University Press, 1983.

Chicago Commission. *The Negro in Chicago.* Chicago: University of Chicago Press, 1922.

Chisholm, George G. *Longmans' Gazetteer of the World.* London: Longmans, Green, 1902.

"Chronicle and Comment: David Grayson." *Bookman,* Vol. 43 (March 1916).

Clark, Ronald William. *Einstein: The Life and Times.* New York: Avon, 1972.

Coben, Stanley. *A. Mitchell Palmer: Politician.* New York: Columbia University Press, 1963.

Colonel Codevelle. *Armistice 1918: The Signing of the Armistice in the Forest Glade of Compiègne.* London: Friends of the Armistice of Compiègne, 1950.

Cohen, Adam, and Elizabeth Taylor. *American Pharaoh: Mayor Richard J. Daley: His Battle for Chicago and the Nation.* Boston: Little, Brown, 2000.

Cole, David. *Enemy Aliens, Double Standards and Constitutional Freedoms in the War on Terrorism.* New York: New Press, 2005.

Coles, Peter. *Einstein and the Total Eclipse.* London: Icon, 1999.

Cook, Blanche Wiesen. *Eleanor Roosevelt: 1884–1933,* Vol. 1. New York: Viking, 1992.

Cook, Raymond Allen. *Fire from the Flint: The Amazing Careers of Thomas Dixon.* New York: John F. Blair, 1968.

Cook, William A. *The 1919 World Series: What Really Happened?* New York: McFarland, 2001.

Cooper, John Milton. *Breaking the Heart of the World.* Cambridge, Eng.: Cambridge Univ. Press, 2001.

———. *The Warrior and the Priest: Woodrow Wilson and Theodore Roosevelt.* Cambridge, Mass.: Belknap Press, 2004.

Costello, Harry J. *Why Did We Go to Russia?* Detroit: H. J. Costello, 1920.

Cottrell, Robert C. *Roger Nash Baldwin and the American Civil Liberties Union.* New York: Columbia University Press, 2000.

Cowan, John F. "The Real Character of David Grayson." *National Magazine,* Vol. 40 (July–August 1932).

Crommelin, A. C. D. "The Eclipse Expedition to Sobral." *Observatory* (October 1919).

Crosby, Alfred W. *America's Forgotten Pandemic: The Influenza of 1918.* Cambridge: Cambridge University Press, 1989.

Crownover, Roger. "Stranded in Russia." *Michigan History Magazine,* Vol. 83, No. 1 (January–February, 1999).

Curtis, S. R. *Zorro Unmasked: The Official History.* New York: Hyperion, 1998.

Cwiklik, Robert. *Albert Einstein and the Theory of Relativity.* Cambridge, Eng.: Barron's Educational Series, 1997.

Daniel, Walter C. *Black Journals of the United States.* New York: Greenwood, 1982.

Daniels, Josephus. *The Life of Woodrow Wilson, 1856–1924.* Philadelphia: John C. Winston, 1924.

Debs, Eugene V. *Walls and Bars: Prisons and Prison Life in the "Land of the Free."* Chicago: Charles H. Kerr, 2000; originally published, 1927.

Dennis, Frank Allen, ed. *Southern Miscellany: Essays in History in Honor of Glover Moore.* Jackson: University Press of Mississippi, 1981.

Diffie, Whitfield, and Susan Landau. *Privacy on the Line: The Politics of Wiretapping and Encryption.* Boston: MIT Press, 1999.

DiSanto, Victor J. "Henry Johnson's Paradox: A Soldier's Story." *Afro-Americans in New York Life and History,* Vol. 21, No. 2 (1997).

Dos Passos, John. *1919,* Vol. 2 of *U.S.A.* (trilogy). New York: Houghton Mifflin, 2000; originally published 1932.

Douglas, Allie Vibert. *The Life of Arthur Stanley Eddington.* London: Thomas Nelson & Sons, 1957.

Drake, Paul Harris. *Democracy Made Safe.* Boston: Four Seas, 1920.

Drake, St. Clair, and Horace A. Cayton. *Black Metropolis: A Study of Negro Life in a Northern City.* Chicago: University of Chicago Press, 1993.

Dray, Philip. *At the Hands of Persons Unknown: The Lynching of Black America.* New York: Random House, 2003.

Du Bois, W. E. B. *Darkwater: Voices from Within the Veil.* New York: Harcourt, Brace, 1921.

———. *Dusk of Dawn: An Essay Toward an Autobiography of a Face Concept.* New York: Schocken, 1968.

Dukas, Helen, and Banesh Hoffmann, eds. *Albert Einstein: The Human Side*. Princeton: Princeton University Press, 1981.

Dulles, Foster Rhea. *America's Rise to World Power*. New York: Harper Torchbooks, 1963.

———. *The Road to Teheran: The Story of Russia and America, 1781–1943*. Princeton: Princeton University Press, 1945.

Durham, Kenneth, Jr. "Longview Race Riot of 1919." *East Texas Historical Association Journal*, Vol. 18, No. 2 (1980).

Dyer, Walter A. *David Grayson: Adventurer*. New York: Doubleday, 1928.

Eddington, Arthur Stanley. *The Nature of the Physical World*. New York: Macmillan, 1933.

———. *Report on the Relativity Theory of Gravitation* (London: Fleetway, 1919).

———. *Science and the Unseen World: Swarthmore Lecture, 1929*. London: George Allen & Unwin, 1930.

———. *Space, Time and Gravitation: An Outline of the General Relativity Theory*. Cambridge: Cambridge University Press, 1920.

———. "The Total Eclipse of 1919 May 29 and the Influence of Gravitation on Light." *Observatory*, Vol. 42, March 1919, 119–22.

Eddington, Arthur Stanley, F. J. M. Stratton, and H. S. Jones, eds. "A Monthly Review of Astronomy, November 14, 1919, Meeting of the Royal Astronomical Society." *Observatory*, Vol. 42, No. 546 (December 1919).

Einstein, Albert. *Relativity: The Special and the General Theory*. Translated by Robert W. Lawson. New York: Bonanza, 1961.

Elshtain, Jean Bethke. *Jane Addams and the Dream of American Democracy*. New York: Basic, 2002.

Evans, David S. *The Eddington Enigma: A Personal Memoir*. London: Xlibris, 1998.

Evans, Martin Marix, ed. *American Voices of World War I: Primary Source Documents, 1917–1920*. Chicago: Fitzroy Dearborn, 2001.

Fabre, Michel. *From Harlem to Paris: Black American Writers in France, 1840–1980*. Urbana: University of Illinois Press, 1993.

Farwell, Byron. *Over There: The United States in the Great War, 1917–1918*. New York: W. W. Norton, 1999.

Filler, Louis. *The Muckrakers*. Palo Alto: Stanford University Press, 1993.

Fitzpatrick, Ellen F., ed. *Muckraking: Three Landmark Articles*. New York: Bedford/St. Martin's, 1994.

Foch, Ferdinand, and Thomas Bentley Mott. *The Memoirs of Marshal Foch*. New York: Doubleday, Doran, 1931.

Foster, William Z. *The Great Steel Strike and Its Lessons*. New York: B. W. Huebsch, 1920.

———. *Pages from a Worker's Life*. New York: International Publishers, 1970.

Fox, Stephen R. *The Guardian of Boston: William Monroe Trotter*. New York: Atheneum, 1971.

Frank, Philipp. *Einstein: His Life and Times*. New York: Alfred A. Knopf, 1947.

Franklin, John Hope, and Isidore Starr, eds. *The Negro in 20th Century America*. New York: Vintage, 1967.

Freund, Ernst. "Debs Case and Freedom of Speech." *New Republic* (May 3, 1919).

Fromkin, David. *A Peace to End All Peace: The Fall of the Ottoman Empire and the Creation of the Modern Middle East*. New York: Henry Holt, 1989.

Gardner, A. E., U.S.N., ed. *Homeward Bound: To Commemorate the Homeward Bound Voyage of the 339th Infantry and Other Units*. Washington, D.C.: John F. Jones, U.S.N. printer, 1919.

Gardner, Martin. *Relativity Simply Explained*. New York: Dover, 1997.

Garraty, John Arthur. *Henry Cabot Lodge: A Biography*. New York: Alfred A. Knopf, 1953.

Gengarelly, W. Anthony. *Distinguished Dissenters and Opposition to the 1919–1920 Red Scare*. Lewiston, ME: E. Mellen, 1996.

Gentry, Curt. *J. Edgar Hoover: The Man and the Secrets*. New York: W. W. Norton, 2001.

George, Henry. *Progress and Poverty*. New York: Robert Schalkenbach Foundation, 1946.

Ginzburg, Ralph. *100 Years of Lynchings: The Shocking Record Behind Today's Black Militancy*. New York: Lancer, 1962.

Goldhurst, Richard. *The Midnight War: The American Intervention in Russia, 1918–1920*. New York: McGraw-Hill, 1978.

Goldman, Emma. *Living My Life*. New York: Dover, 1970, first published by Alfred A. Knopf, 1931.

Gompers, Samuel. *Seventy Years of Life and Labor: An Autobiography*. 2 vols. New York: E. P. Dutton, 1925.

Grant, Robert B. *The Black Man Comes to the City: A Documentary Account from the Great Migration to the Great Depression, 1915 to 1930*. Chicago: Nelson-Hall, 1972.

Grayson, Cary T. *Woodrow Wilson: An Intimate Memoir*. New York: Holt, Rinehart & Winston, 1960.

Grayson, David. *Adventures in Friendship*. New York: Doubleday, Page, 1908.

———. *Adventures in Understanding*. New York: Doubleday, Page, 1925.

———. *Great Possessions*. New York: Doubleday, Page, 1917.

———. *Under My Elm*. Garden City: Doubleday, Doran, 1942.

Grossman, James R. *Land of Hope: Chicago, Black Southerners and the Great Migration*. Chicago: University of Chicago Press, 1991.

Halliday, E. M. *The Ignorant Armies*. New York: Bantam, 1960.

———. *When Hell Froze Over*. New York: Simon & Schuster, 2000.

Harris, Harvey L. *The War as I Saw It: 1918 Letters of a Tank Corps Lieutenant*. St. Paul, Minn: Pogo, 1998.

Harris, Stephen L. "Harlem's Hell Fighters." *The American Legion*, Vol. 158, No. 2 (February 2005).

Heywood, Chester D. *Negro Combat Troops in the World War: The Story of the 371st Infantry*. Worcester, MA: Commonwealth, 1928.

Hinshaw, David. *A Man from Kansas: The Story of William Allen White*. New York: G. P. Putnam's Sons, 1945.

Hofstadter, Richard. *The American Political Tradition and the Men Who Made It*. New York: Alfred A. Knopf, 1968.

Hoover, Herbert, and Hugh Gibson. *The Problems of Lasting Peace*. New York: Doubleday, Doran, 1943.

Hough, Emerson. *The Web: A Revelation of Patriotism: The Story of the American Protective League.* Chicago: Reilly & Lee, 1919.

House, Edward Mandell. *Philip Dru: Administrator.* Appleton, WI: Robert Welch University Press, 1998.

House, Edward M., and Charles Seymour, eds. *What Really Happened at Paris: The Story of the Peace Conference by American Delegates, 1918–1919.* Safety Harbor, Fla.: Simon Publications, 2001.

Hovey, Tamara. *John Reed: Witness to Revolution.* Los Angeles: George Sand, 1975.

"How 'David Grayson' Came into Existence." *New York Sun* (April 15, 1916).

Howe, Frederic C. *The Confessions of a Reformer.* New York: Quadrangle, 1967; originally published, 1925.

Howe, Mark DeWolfe, ed. *Holmes-Laski Letters: The Correspondence of Mr. Justice Holmes and Harold J. Laski, 1916–1935.* Cambridge: Harvard University Press, 1953.

Huggins, Nathan Irvin. *Harlem Renaissance.* New York: Oxford University Press, 1974.

Hunt, Stoker. *Ouija: The Most Dangerous Game.* New York: Harper & Row, 1985.

Interchurch World Movement, Commission of Inquiry. *Report on the Steel Strike of 1919.* New York: Harcourt, Brace & Howe, 1920.

Irwin, Inez Haynes. *Up Hill with Banners Flying: The Story of the Woman's Party.* Penobscot, ME: Traversity Press, 1964.

Izzo, David Garrett, ed. *Advocates and Activists, 1919–1941: Men and Women Who Shaped the Period Between the Wars.* West Cornwall, CT: Locust Hill Press, 2003.

Jackson, Kenneth T. *The Ku Klux Klan in the City, 1916–1930.* New York: Oxford University Press, 1967.

Jeffreys, Harold. "On the Crucial Tests of Einstein's Theory of Gravitation." *Monthly Notices of the Royal Astronomical Society,* Vol. 80 (December 1919).

Jensen, Joan M. *Military Surveillance of Civilians in America.* Morristown, NJ: General Learning Press, 1975.

———. *The Price of Vigilance.* New York: Rand McNally, 1968.

Johnson, Gerald W. *Woodrow Wilson: The Unforgettable Figure Who Has Returned to Haunt Us.* New York: Harper & Brothers, 1944.

Jordan, William G. *Black Newspapers and America's War for Democracy, 1914–1920.* Chapel Hill: University of North Carolina Press, 2001.

Kaku, Michio. *Einstein's Cosmos: How Albert Einstein's Vision Transformed Our Understanding of Space and Time.* New York: W. W. Norton, 2004.

Kaplan, Justin. *Lincoln Steffens: A Biography.* New York: Simon & Schuster, 1974.

Keller, Helen. *The Story of My Life.* Roger Shattuck with Dorothy Herrmann, eds. New York: W. W. Norton, 2003; originally published, 1903.

Kennan, George F. "The Sisson Documents." *Journal of Modern History,* Vol. 28, No. 2, (June 1956).

———. *Soviet-American Relations, 1917–1920,* Vol. 2, *The Decision to Intervene.* Princeton: Princeton University Press, 1958.

Kennedy, David M. *Over Here: The First World War and American Society.* New York: Oxford University Press, 2004.

Kennedy, Randall. *Interracial Intimacies: Sex, Marriage, Identity, and Adoption.* New York: Vintage, 2004.

Keyssar, Alexander. *The Right to Vote: The Contested History of Democracy in the United States.* New York: Basic, 2001.

Knock, Thomas J. *To End All Wars: Woodrow Wilson and the Quest for a New World Order.* New York: Oxford University Press, 1992.

Kolata, Gina. *Flu: The Story of the Great Influenza Pandemic of 1918 and the Search for the Virus That Caused It.* New York: Farrar, Straus & Giroux, 1999.

Kornweibel, Theodore, Jr. *No Crystal Stair: Black Life and the Messenger, 1917–1928.* New York: Greenwood, 1975.

———. *Seeing Red: Federal Campaigns Against Black Militancy, 1919–1925.* Bloomington: Indiana University Press, 1999.

———, ed. *Federal Surveillance of Afro-Americans (1917–1925): The First World War, the Red Scare, and the Garvey Movement.* Frederick, MD: University Publications of America, 1986 (25 reels).

Lansing, Robert. *The Peace Negotiations, A Personal Narrative.* New York: Houghton Mifflin, 1921.

Lehman, Nicholas. *The Promised Land: The Great Black Migration and How It Changed America.* New York: Vintage, 1992.

Leone, Richard C., and Greg Anrig, Jr., eds. *The War on Our Freedoms: Civil Liberties in the Age of Terrorism.* New York: Public Affairs, 2003.

Lessing, Doris. *Under My Skin: My Autobiography to 1949.* New York: HarperPerennial, 1995.

Leuchtenburg, William E. *The Perils of Prosperity, 1914–32.* Chicago: University of Chicago Press, 1958.

Levenson, Thomas. *Einstein in Berlin.* New York: Bantam, 2003.

Levine, Daniel. *Jane Addams and the Liberal Tradition.* Stevens Point, WI: Worzalla Publishing, State Historical Society of Wisconsin, 1971.

Levy, Leonard W., ed. *Report On the Steel Strike of 1919.* New York: Da Capo, 1971.

———. *The Trial of Scott Nearing and the American Socialist Society.* New York: Da Capo, 1970.

Lewis, David Levering. *W. E. B. Du Bois: Biography of a Race.* Markham, Ontario: Fitzhenry, & Whiteside, 1993.

———. *W. E. B. Du Bois: The Fight for Equality and the American Century, 1919–1963.* New York: Henry Holt, 2000.

Link, Arthur S. *Wilson.* 5 vols. Princeton, N.J.: Princeton Univ. Press, 1947–1965.

———. *Woodrow Wilson: Revolution, War, and Peace.* Wheeling, IL: Harlan Davidson, 1979.

Link, Arthur S., et al., eds. *The Papers of* Woodrow Wilson, 69 vols. Princeton: Princeton University Press, 1966–1994.

Little, Arthur W. *From Harlem to the Rhine: The Story of New York's Colored Volunteers.* New York: Covici Friede, 1936.

Locke, Alain, ed. *The New Negro.* New York: Atheneum, 1970.

Lodge, Henry Cabot. *The Senate and the League of Nations.* New York: Charles Scribner's Sons, 1925.

Logan, Rayford W. *The Betrayal of the Negro: From Rutherford B. Hayes to Woodrow Wilson.* New York: Da Capo, 1997.

Lower, Richard Coke. *A Bloc of One: The Political Career of Hiram W. Johnson.* Palo Alto: Stanford University Press, 1993.

Lunardini, Christine A. *From Equal Suffrage to Equal Rights: Alice Paul and the National Woman's Party, 1910–1928.* New York: New York University Press, 1986.

Lusk Committee. *Report: Revolutionary Radicalism: Its History, Purpose and Tactics, with an Exposition and Discussion of the Steps Being Taken and Required to Curb It.* Albany, NY: J. B. Lyon, 1920.

Lynd, Staughton. *Intellectual Origins of American Radicalism.* New York: Pantheon, 1968.

Lyon, David. *The Electronic Eye: The Rise of Surveillance Society.* Minneapolis: University of Minnesota Press, 1994.

Macmillan, Margaret. *Paris, 1919.* New York: Random House, 2002.

Mangum, Charles S., Jr. *The Legal Status of The Negro.* Chapel Hill: University of North Carolina Press, 1940.

Matchette, Robert B., et al. *Guide to Federal Records in the National Archives of the United States: 120.13: Records of the American Expeditionary Forces, North Russia,* Microfilm Publication Record Group M924. Washington: National Archives and Records Administration, 1995.

McKay, Claude. *Selected Poems of Claude McKay.* New York: Harcourt, Brace & World, 1953.

Mecklin, John Moffatt. *The Ku Klux Klan: A Study of the American Mind.* New York: Harcourt, Brace, 1924.

Mee, Charles L., Jr. *The End of Order: Versailles 1919.* New York: E. P. Dutton, 1980.

Meltzer, Milton, ed. *In their Own Words: A History of the American Negro, 1916–1966.* New York: Thomas Y. Crowell, 1967.

Menand, Louis. *The Metaphysical Club.* New York: Farrar, Straus & Giroux, 2001.

Messick, Hank. *John Edgar Hoover.* New York: David McKay, 1972.

Meyers, Jeffrey F. *Scott Fitzgerald: A Biography.* New York: HarperCollins, 1994.

Military Intelligence Division, General Staff, War Department, Washington, D.C. "Weekly Intelligence Summary," 1919.

Miller, Kelly. *The World War for Human Rights.* Washington, D.C.: Austin Jenkins, 1919.

Miller, Nathan. *New World Coming: The 1920's and the Making of Modern America.* New York: Da Capo, 2003.

Miller, William D. *Pretty Bubbles in the Air.* Urbana, Ill.: University of Illinois Press, 1991.

Mitchell, David. *1919 Red Mirage.* New York: Macmillan, 1970.

Mitgang, Herbert. *Dangerous Dossiers: Exposing the Secret War Against America's Greatest Authors.* New York: Primus, 1996.

———, ed. *The Letters of Carl Sandburg.* New York: Harcourt, Brace & World, 1968.

Moran, Rachel F. *Interracial Intimacy: The Regulation of Race and Romance.* Chicago: University of Chicago Press, 2001.

Morley, C. D. "The Graysonians." *Book News Monthly,* Vol. 34 (February 1916).

Murray, Robert K. *Red Scare: A Study in National Hysteria, 1919–1920.* New York: McGraw-Hill, 1964. Originally published by the University of Minnesota Press, 1955.

Nearing, Scott. *The Making of a Radical: A Political Autobiography.* White River Junction, Vt.: Chelsea Green, 2000.

Nevins, Allan. *Henry White: Thirty Years of American Diplomacy.* New York: Harper & Brothers, 1930.

Niven, Penelope. *Carl Sandburg: A Biography.* New York: Charles Scribner's Sons, 1991.

Novick, Sheldon. *Honorable Justice: The Life and Times of Oliver Wendell Holmes.* Boston: Little, Brown, 1989.

O'Leary, Jeremiah A., and Michael A. Kelly. *My Political Trial and Experiences.* New York: Jefferson, 1919.

O'Toole, Patricia. *When Trumpets Call: Theodore Roosevelt After the White House.* New York: Simon & Schuster, 2005.

Pais, Abraham. *Subtle Is the Lord . . . The Science and the Life of Albert Einstein.* New York: Oxford University Press, 1983.

Panunzio, Constantine M. *The Deportation Cases of 1919–1920.* New York: Da Capo, 1970.

Parenti, Christian T. *The Soft Cage: Surveillance in America, from Slavery to the War on Terror.* New York: Basic, 2004.

Patler, Nicholas. *Jim Crow and the Wilson Administration: Protesting Federal Segregation in the Early Twentieth Century.* Boulder: University Press of Colorado, 2004.

Pellegrini, Frank. "Scientists and Thinkers: Albert Einstein." *Time* (March 29, 1999).

Pfannestiel, Todd. *Rethinking the Red Scare: The Lusk Committee and New York's Crusade Against Radicalism, 1919–1923.* New York: Routledge, 2003.

Phillips, John S. "Alias David Grayson—A Tribute." *Bookman,* Vol. 43 (June 1916).

Pietrusza, David. *Rothstein: The Life, Times and Murder of the Criminal Genius Who Fixed the 1919 World Series.* New York: Carroll & Graf, 2003.

Pitkin, Thomas M. *Keepers of the Gate: A History of Ellis Island.* New York: New York University Press, 1975.

Polenberg, Richard. *Fighting Faiths: The Abrams Case, the Supreme Court, and Free Speech.* New York: Penguin, 1989.

Political Prisoners Defense and Relief Committee. *Sentenced to Twenty Years Prison.* New York, 1918.

Posner, Richard A., ed. *The Essential Holmes: Selections from the Letters, Speeches, Judicial Opinions, and Other Writings of Oliver Wendell Holmes, Jr.* Chicago: University of Chicago Press, 1992.

Post, Louis Freeland. *The Deportations Delirium of Nineteen-Twenty: A Personal Narrative of a Historic Official Experience.* Chicago: C. H. Kerr, 1923.

Powell, Corey. *God in the Equation: How Einstein Transformed Religion.* New York: Simon & Schuster, 2002.

Powell, Lyman P. *Mary Baker Eddy: A Life Size Portrait.* New York: Macmillan, 1930.

Powers, Richard Gid. *Not Without Honor: The History of American Anticommunism.* New York: Free Press, 1995.

———. *Secrecy and Power: The Life of J. Edgar Hoover.* New York: Free Press, 1988.

Preston, William, Jr. *Aliens and Dissenters: Federal Suppression of Radicals, 1903–1933.* Urbana: University of Illinois Press, 1963, 2nd ed., 1994.

Pride, Armistead S., and Clinton C. Wilson. *A History of the Black Press.* Washington: Howard University Press, 1997.

Pringle, Henry F. *Theodore Roosevelt: A Biography.* Orlando: Harcourt, Brace, 1984, originally published, 1931.

Puleo, Stephen. *Dark Tide, The Great Boston Molasses Flood of 1919.* Boston Beacon, 2003.

Pyle, Christopher H. *Extradition, Politics, and Human Rights.* Philadelphia: Temple University Press, 2001.

Rabban, David M. *Free Speech in Its Forgotten Years.* Cambridge: Cambridge University Press, 1997.

Rand, Frank Prentice. *The Story of David Grayson.* Amherst, MA: Jones Library, 1963.

Randall, P. J. Clyde. *The Exodus.* Pittsburgh: Peoples Printing Co., 1919.

Reed, John. *Ten Days That Shook the World.* New York: Modern Library, 1935; originally published, 1919.

Resek, Carl, ed. *The Progressives.* Indianapolis: Bobbs-Merrill, 1967.

Rhodes, Benjamin D. *The Anglo-American Winter War with Russia, 1918–1919: A Diplomatic and Military Tragicomedy.* New York: Greenwood, 1988.

Roosevelt, James, and Sidney Shalett. *Affectionately, F.D.R.: A Son's Story of a Lonely Man.* New York: Harcourt, Brace, 1959.

Roosevelt, Theodore, Col. "How Henry Johnson, Colored N.Y. Warrior, Routed Entire Squad of German Raiders." *American Magazine* (August 11, 1927).

Rosenstone, Robert A. *Romantic Revolutionary: A Biography of John Reed.* Cambridge: Harvard University Press, 1990.

Rugg, Winnifred K. "Ray Stannard Baker and David Grayson." *Boston Evening Transcript* (December 31, 1932).

Salvatore, Nick. *Eugene V. Debs: Citizen and Socialist.* Urbana: University of Illinois Press, 1982.

Sandburg, Carl. *The Chicago Race Riots.* New York: Harcourt, Brace & World, 1969, Originally published, 1919.

Schaefer, Eric. *Bold, Daring, Shocking, True: A History of Exploitation Films, 1919–1959.* Durham: Duke University Press, 1999.

Scheiber, Harry N. *The Wilson Administration and Civil Liberties, 1917–1921.* Ithaca: Cornell University Press, 1960.

Schmidt, Regin. *Red Scare, FBI and the Origins of Anticommunism in the United States.* Denmark: Museum Tusculanum Press, University of Copenhagen, 2000.

Seldes, George. *Witness to a Century: Encounters with the Noted, the Notorious and the Three SOBs.* Boston: G. K. Hall, 1988.

Smith, P. D. *Einstein.* London: Haus, 2003.

Sobel, Robert. *RCA.* New York: Stein & Day, 1986.

Spear, Allan H. *Black Chicago: The Making of a Negro Ghetto, 1890–1920.* Chicago: University of Chicago Press, 1967.

Stanley, Matthew. "An Expedition to Heal the Wounds of War: The 1919 Eclipse and Eddington as Quaker Adventurer." *Isis,* Winter 2003.

Steel, Duncan. *Eclipse: The Celestial Phenomenon That Changed the Course of History.* Washington, D.C.: Joseph Henry Press, 1955.

Steel, Ronald. *Walter Lippman and the American Century.* Boston: Little, Brown, 1980.

Steffens, Lincoln. *The Autobiography of Lincoln Steffens,* Vol. 1, *A Boy on Horseback/Seeing New York First.* New York: Harcourt, Brace & World, 1958.

———. *The Autobiography of Lincoln Steffens,* Vol. 2, *Muckraking/Revolution/Seeing America at Last.* New York: Harcourt, Brace & World, 1958.

Stockley, Grif. *Blood in Their Eyes: The Elaine Race Massacres of 1919.* Fayetteville: University of Arkansas Press, 2001.

Stout, Ralph, ed. *Roosevelt in the Kansas City Star: War Time Editorials by Theodore Roosevelt.* Boston: Houghton Mifflin, 1921.

Straubing, Harold Elk. *The Last Magnificent War.* New York: Paragon, 1989.

Strong, Anna Louise. *I Change Worlds: The Remaking of an American.* New York: Garden City Publishing, 1937.

Strong, Tracy B., and Helene Keyssar. *Right in Her Soul: The Life of Anna Louise Strong.* New York: Random House, 1983.

Summers, Anthony. *Official and Confidential: The Secret Life of J. Edgar Hoover.* New York: G. P. Putnam's Sons, 1993.

Talbert, Roy, Jr. *Negative Intelligence: The Army and the American Left, 1917–1941.* Jackson: University Press of Mississippi, 1991.

Tarbell, Ida. *The Life of Elbert H. Gary: A Story of Steel.* New York: D. Appleton, 1925.

Theoharis, Athan G., and John Stuart Cox, eds. *The Boss: J. Edgar Hoover and the Great American Inquisition.* Philadelphia: Temple University Press, 1988.

Thompson, James Westfall. "The Aftermath of the Black Death and the Aftermath of the Great War." *American Journal of Sociology,* vol. 26 (March 1920).

Thompson, John A. *Woodrow Wilson: Profiles in Power.* London: Pearson Education, 2002.

Toomer, Jean. *Cane.* New York: Harper Perennial, 1969.

Tuttle, William M., Jr. *Race Riot: Chicago in the Red Summer of 1919.* New York: Atheneum, 1970.

Twain, Mark. *The Mysterious Stranger and Other Stories.* New York: Dover, 1992; originally published, 1916.

U.S. Congress, Senate Subcommittee of the Committee on the Judiciary, 66th Congress, 1st Sess. *Bolshevik Propaganda.* Report on Hearings, 1919.

U.S. Department of Justice. *Register of the Department of Justice and the Courts of the United States,* 27th edition. Washington: Government Printing Office, 1919.

U.S. Department of Justice, Federal Bureau of Investigation. National Archives, Record Group 65. Investigative Case Files of the Bureau of Investigation, 1908–1922 (955 reels of microfilm at the College Park, Maryland, division of the National Archives).

U.S. Military Intelligence Division. *Correspondence of the Military Intelligence Division Relating to Negro Subversion, 1917–1941.* Washington, D.C.: National Archives, 1986.

U.S. Military Intelligence Division. *United States Military Intelligence (1917–1927),* ed. Richard D. Challenger. New York: Garland, 1978. (Reprint of series of secret documents prepared by the Military Intelligence Division of the U.S. War Department General Staff between 1917 and 1927 and called the *Weekly Intelligence Summary.*)

U.S. Military Intelligence Division. *U.S. Military Intelligence Reports: Surveillance of Radicals in the United States, 1917–1941,* ed. Randolph Boehm. Frederick, MD: University Publications of America, 1984.

U.S. Post Office. National Archives, Record Group 28. College Park, Maryland.

Walker, Samuel. *In Defense of American Liberties: A History of the ACLU.* New York: Oxford University Press, 1990.

Walters, Alexander. *My Life and Work.* New York: Fleming H. Revell, 1917.

Ward, Geoffrey C. *A First-Class Temperament: The Emergence of Franklin Roosevelt.* New York: Harper & Row, 1989.

Waskow, Arthur I. *From Race Riot to Sit In, 1919 and 1960's.* Garden City: Doubleday, 1966.

———. "The 1919 Race Riots: A Study in the Connections Between Conflict." Ph.D. thesis, University of Wisconsin, 1963.

Watson, Steven. *The Harlem Renaissance: Hub of African-American Culture, 1920–1930.* New York: Pantheon, 1995.

Weightman, Gavin. *Signor Marconi's Magic Box.* New York: Da Capo, 2003.

Weinberger, Harry. "A Rebel's Interrupted Autobiography." *American Journal of Economics and Sociology* (October 1942).

Wells, H. G. *The Shape of Things to Come.* London: Corgi, 1933.

Wells, Ida B. *Crusade for Justice: The Autobiography of Ida B. Wells,* ed. Alfreda M. Duster. Chicago: University of Chicago Press, 1970.

White, G. Edward. *Justice Oliver Wendell Holmes: Law and the Inner Self.* New York: New York University Press, 1993.

White, William Allen. *The Autobiography of William Allen White.* New York: Macmillan, 1946.

———. *Woodrow Wilson: The Man, His Times, and His Task.* Boston: Houghton Mifflin 1924.

Whitehead, Alfred North. *Science and the Modern World.* New York: Macmillan, 1947.

Widenor, William C. *Henry Cabot Lodge and the Search for an American Foreign Policy.* Berkeley: University of California Press, 1980.

Williams, Lee E., and Lee E. Williams II. *Anatomy of Four Race Riots: Racial Conflict in Knoxville, Elaine (Arkansas), Tulsa, and Chicago, 1919–1921.* Hattiesburg: University and College Press of Mississippi, 1972.

Wordholt, Jan Willem Schulte, and Herbert H. Rowen, trans. *Woodrow Wilson: A Life for World Peace.* Berkeley: University of California Press, 1991.

Worthy, Ruth. "A Negro in Our History: William Monroe Trotter, 1872–1934." MA thesis, Columbia University, 1952.

Young, Marguerite. *Harp Song for a Radical: The Life and Times of Eugene Victor Debs.* New York: Alfred A. Knopf, 1999.

Young, William, and David E. Kaiser. *Post Mortem: New Evidence in the Case of Sacco and Vanzetti.* Amherst: University of Massachusetts Press, 1985.

Acknowledgments

On May 25, 1921, while Ray Stannard Baker was working on his book *The Public Papers of Woodrow Wilson*, he wrote in his diary, "I am suffocated with paper: I flounder in it, sleep in it, get my nose out two or three times a day for a breath of air and a bit of food. . . . If it had not been for many good friends and much delightful conversation, it often seemed to me that I could not live through it."

When I first read this passage, I identified with Baker immediately. I had not taken a day off from the writing of this book for many months but thanks to exceptionally good friends I was taking breaks during most days, for walks, dinners, or an occasional movie. I have many people to thank for being supportive throughout the years I spent researching and writing *Savage Peace*.

I typically begin my acknowledgments with my editor and my agent. This is not just a matter of professional courtesy, for they are both deserving of such high regard. Throughout the making of *Savage Peace*, Bob Bender, my editor at Simon & Schuster, was always willing to listen to my ideas for structuring the book and my struggles to determine which individuals, stories, and themes on which to focus. From the beginning he and my agent, Alice Martell, saw the magnitude and value of the project. My work on this book was interrupted several times—for the promotion of my third book, for a major move and a renovation of the house to which I moved, and for a serious illness in my family. Yet Alice and Bob were always a support to me, cheering me on, believing in me at times when I was too exhausted to remember how to believe in myself. A special thanks also to Johanna Li at Simon & Schuster and Stephanie Finman at the Martell Agency.

Perhaps, though, the biggest thanks must go to the people who have been supportive on a day-to-day basis. June Zipperian, an avid reader and an exceptionally bright woman, read each chapter as I completed it. Knowing that June was eagerly awaiting the next installment was a great inspiration to me. And her critiques were astute and helpful.

Allen Schwartz, a strong daily booster of the project, carefully read the manuscript before I sent it to Bob, caught a few errors, contributed to the chapter on labor, and brainstormed with me on many occasions. I am especially grateful to him for introducing me to Ray Stannard Baker. Allen is brilliant, generous, and innovative. He's a tough critic and thus keeps me aspiring to higher levels.

Alison Gibson is the head librarian in the town where I live. I referred to her as "a national treasure" in the acknowledgments of my last book; that title still stands despite her humble refusal to accept it. Alison was able to track down crucial primary sources for me and in the middle of her very busy days, she assisted me in often vexing research pursuits.

My research assistants on this book have been exemplary. I extend deep appreciation to Lee Edwards, Sarah Byers, David Fox, and Jess Gugino. Jess, who lives on Sandy Pond near the site of Mabel Puffer's former home, tracked down some problematic details about the Puffer and Hazzard case, and spent some time with me when I ventured to Ayer, Massachusetts, to do research. Among other things, David Fox, who is a professional research librarian, did the very tedious job of finding and copying articles from various newspapers that covered issues of interest to me, especially the Abrams trial and the cat-and-mouse game of Mollie Steimer and the government agents. Sarah Byers, who is my sister and who lives in Ann Arbor, Michigan, spent many hours in Frankenmuth at the Michigan's Own Military and Space Museum, and in Ann Arbor at the University of Michigan's Bentley Historical Library researching the story of the 339th Infantry in northern Russia and the grassroots movement in Michigan to bring the 339th home. I am grateful for her excellent contribution and am pleased that sisters could work so well together.

A special note of gratitude to Lee Edwards, who was truly remarkable on several occasions, especially during the hunt for photos. This was a difficult task, as the photos could not be found in just two or three archives. Indeed, Lee networked worldwide to find the very best depictions available for every item on my list. I may be most grateful to Lee, however, for her suggestion that I dictate the source note citations onto tapes that she then transcribed, putting them into Simon & Schuster's preferred format. This and numerous tools that Lee devised for organizing the vast numbers of files were gifts. Thanks also to Lee as well as Sarah Byers, June Zipperian, Allen Schwartz, and Randy Smith for reading the manuscript. And another thank you to Lee for helping me in the very tedious task of fact checking.

I deeply appreciate Arthur M. Schlesinger, Jr, whose advice on the direction of my research, especially on the topic of civil liberties, was invaluable. Thanks to William Nichols, Robert Bannister, Blanche Wiesen Cook, William Preston, Jr., Jack Kirby, William Tuttle, and Michele Stoddard for listening to my concepts for the book and offering advice on parts of the research. I am grateful, as always, to Clare Coss. I am deeply grateful to Loretta Denner at Simon & Schuster and to Frederick G. Chase for his superb copy editing. And I would like to honor the memory of Arna Bontemps, who advised me, years ago at Yale University, on the Harlem Renaissance for my senior honors thesis—and who inspired me to further explore African-American history and literature.

I dedicated my third book to the people of Ripley, Ohio, where I live. I could have easily done that again. During the last few months of working on the manuscript I would occasionally find a bag of fresh vegetables on my porch with no clues to identify the generous gardener. I thank whoever repeatedly left those wonderful parcels. Also high on the list are: Randy and Diana Smith for their exceptional Wednesday dinners; Roberta Gaudio and her sister Joanne May for their Sunday dinners; June and Don Zipperian for access to their refrigerator and dinners on their porch during summertime; Tara Davis for leaving a large basket of fresh fruit and cheese at my door during the last days of completing the manuscript; and Julie Kline and Debbie Scott, who I know deposited some of those fresh vegetables on my doorstep. Thanks to Linda Ross for spending a day with me working on source notes. And thanks to Oletta Jones, a gift in my life; and to Sandy Bertrum, Sandy Trammel, Kathy Layford, Dorothy Prevost, David and Susan Poole, Terry Neudow, and Wendy Hart Beckman.

I am grateful also to Jim Fletcher, Faye Wells, Robert Q. Millan, Peggy Dobrozsi, Linda Young, Ginny Kuntz, Ann Veith, and Jim Webb for assisting my mother and our family, and equally grateful to my mother for her strength and will power. Thanks also to Rev. Kevin Burney, Scott Byers, Ron Mathis, and Harry Landis. I must also acknowledge the Mercantile Library, Albert Pyle, Buck Niehoff, the Ohio Humanities Council, Gale Peterson, and Pat Williamsen for so kindly giving me a leave of absence from my duties on the boards of directors of both institutions in order to complete this book. My thanks also to Dale Brown, Jenny Clark, Lyn Boone, and Mae Case for being supportive. Thanks to Paul DeMarco for proofreading the legal interpretations in the book. Thanks to Herman Johnson, the son of Sergeant Henry Johnson, and Harry Weinberger's nephew, Warren Weinberger, for their assistance. And thanks to William Tuttle, Theodore Wilson, and Paul Dean for help with my fact checking.

Special thanks to Norm Pearlstine, who continues to be supportive of my writing endeavors. And thanks, as always, to the *Wall Street Journal*, where I learned how to write well. Laura Landro's words "Never fall in love with your own writing" have saved me on more than one occasion from leaving in a paragraph or two that should be cut. I want also to express appreciation to the New York Public Library not only for its superb resources at the main branch and at the Schomburg Library in Harlem, but also for the ever-inspiring atmosphere of the Main Reading Room on 42nd Street. I have a ritual of beginning each book in that room.

I am grateful to the Southeastern Ohio Regional Library, which spent a good deal of time tracking down the information I sought via Interlibrary Loan under the expert guidance of Alison Gibson. I must also extend my deep appreciation for the assistance of the entire staff of the Union Township Library. Thanks too to the helpful scholars, reference librarians, archivists, and curators in all the libraries, archives, historical societies, and universities noted in the Note on Sources. And thanks especially to the following:

Stanley Bozick at Michigan's Own Military and Space Museum in Frankenmuth, Michigan; John Fox, historian at the Federal Bureau of Investigation; Ernie Porter at the FBI; Jim Kelling at the National Archives in College Park, Maryland; Helen Selsdon and Jaclyn Packer at the Helen Keller Archive at the American Foundation for the Blind in New York City; Robert Bannister, Professor Emeritus at Swarthmore College; Erika Gottfried and Peter Falardie at the Tamiment Library, New York University; Elizabeth Bouvier, Massachusetts state archivist; Gregory J. Plunges at the National Archives in New York; Robert Fleming, Emerson College Archives; Sean Noel at Boston University Library; John Aubrey at the Newberry Library in Chicago; Lisa Oppenheim at the Chicago Metro History Education Center, also at the Newberry Library; Mary Caldera and Danelle Moon at Sterling Library, Yale University; Lee Freeman, Sheffield (Alabama) Public Library; Pamela S. Bruner at the Harlan Hatcher Graduate Library, University of Michigan; Julie Herrada, curator of the Labadie Collection in the Special Collections of the University of Michigan Library; Peggy E. Daub, head of Special Collections at the University of Michigan Library; John Howe, historian of the 369th Infantry Veterans Association in Albany, New York; Robert Parks at the Franklin D. Roosevelt Library in Hyde Park, New York; Mark Hammond at Meridian World Data; Zoe Davis at the U.S. Senate Library; Mary Baumann at the U.S. Senate Historical Office; Sandra Davis, librarian at the *Shreveport Times* in Louisiana; William R. Lewis, grandson of William Henry Lewis, who was Arthur Hazzard's attorney; Chalmers Hart Knight, at the University of Michigan; and Crystal Cromarite of the National Archives and Records Administration. A double thanks to Elizabeth Bouvier in Massachusetts, who tried so very hard to find the Puffer and Hazzard trial transcripts, and to Karen L. Jania at the Bentley Historical Library at the University of Michigan. And thanks to Dick Brooks at the Houdini Museum in Scranton, Pennsylvania.

Thanks also to the following individuals who so graciously assisted Lee Edwards in her search for photos: Cynthia Long of Toronto, Canada; Warren Weinberger, Harry's nephew in San Diego; A'Lelia Bundles, Madam Walker's great-great granddaughter in Washington, D.C.; Helen Selsdon, at the Helen Keller Archive in New York City; Lyn White Savage at the Carl Sandburg Home in North Carolina; Erika Gottfried, at the Tamiment Library in New York; Monica Bartoszek at the *Albany Times Union* in New York; Carol Butler at Brown Brothers in Sterling, Pennsylvania; Dr. Barbara Lewis, at the William Monroe Trotter Institute at the University of Massachusetts; Stanley Bozick, at Michigan's Own

Military and Space Museum; Mr. G. D. Bye, at the Cambridge University Library in Cambridge, England.

Lastly, I would like to honor the memory of my two great-uncles, Schenck Simpson, who drove an ambulance in France during the Great War, and Stuart Tattershall, who served in the 331st Infantry; my grandfather Cyrus Null, who died in 1918; and my father, Dwight L. Hagedorn, who fought in World War II and deeply understood the promise and the pain of the aftermath of war.

Index

Abbott, Robert, 103, 104, 200, 281
Abolitionists, 73, 83, 232
Abrams, Jacob, 65–66, 68, 366–68,
    372–73, 391–93, 395, 396, 411,
    414, 415, 436
  amnesty campaign for, 409–10,
    432–33
  arrest of, 66
  bail granted to, 76–77
  deportation of, 433–34
  escape attempt of, 397, 408–9
  at Ferrar Colony, 370
  indictment of, 67
  in Mexico, 435
  trial of, 66–67, 70, 74–75
Acheson, Dean, 391
Actors Equity Association, 338–41
Adams, Edward B., 409
Addams, Jane, 47, 56, 231, 420
Adriatic (ship), 85
Adventures in Solitude (Grayson),
    444
Advocate, The (newspaper), 311
Aero Club of America, 420
Afghanistan, 154
African-Americans, 37–45, 107–11,
    126, 176, 188–202, 346, 354,
    402–4, 406, 419, 439–40
  on Armistice Day, 13–15
  baseball circuit for, 384–85
  censorship of publications of,
    188–93
  government surveillance of, 30, 31,
    38–44, 105–6, 110, 297–301,
    307, 318–21, 323–24, 328, 431

marriages of whites and, *see*
    Interracial marriage
migration to North of, 300–301,
    309–12
and Paris Peace Conference, 13, 14,
    39, 40, 42–43, 104–7, 110–13,
    203–8, 262–64, 267–68
as strikebreakers, 380, 399
in U.S. Army, 13, 37, 44, 91–103,
    111–12, 189–92, 195, 196, 199,
    437–38
violence against, 196–97, 302–6,
    312–19, 343, 376–80 (*see also*
    Lynchings)
African Methodist Episcopal (A.M.E.)
    Church, 298, 306
Agamemnon (ship), 163
Agriculture Department, U.S., 155
Air Mail Service, 4
Aircraft Production Board, 43–44
Airplanes, 234–46, 423
Albany Times Union, 96
Alcock, Captain John, 10, 234–46,
    423
Alien Act (1918), 29, 367, 369
Alien Property Bureau, 229, 330–31
All-Allied Anti-German League, 25
Allied Drug and Chemical Company,
    182
Allied North Russia Expeditionary
    Force, 4; *see also* Russia,
    American military intervention in
All-Story Weekly, 336
Allied American Corporation of
    America, 183